PARTY POLITICS
IN AMERICA

PARTY POLITICS IN AMERICA

SEVENTH EDITION

Paul Allen Beck

The Ohio State University

Frank J. Sorauf

University of Minnesota

HarperCollins*Publishers*

Sponsoring Editor: Catherine Woods
Project Editor: Melonie Parnes
Design Supervisor: Lucy Krikorian
Text Design Adaptation: North 7 Atelier Ltd.
Cover Design: Jan Kessner
Production Manager/Assistant: Willie Lane/Sunaina Sehwani
Compositor: BookMasters, Inc.
Printer and Binder: R. R. Donnelley & Sons Company
Cover Printer: New England Book Components, Inc.

PARTY POLITICS IN AMERICA, Seventh Edition

Library of Congress Cataloging-in-Publication Data

Beck, Paul Allen.
    Party politics in America / Paul Allen Beck, Frank J. Sorauf.—
7th ed.
        p.   cm.
    Sorauf's name appears first on the earlier edition.
    Includes index.
    ISBN 0-06-500076-5
    1. Political parties—United States.   I. Sorauf, Frank J. (Frank
Joseph), 1928–   . II. Title.
JK2265.S65 1992
324.273 dc20   91–25581
                                                            CIP

92 93 94   9 8 7 6 5 4 3 2

Brief Contents

Detailed Contents

Preface

For almost 200 years, political parties have been key actors in the American political process. Both in what they are and what they do, they have contributed significantly to the shape of American politics. At the same time, the nature of American politics and the broader sociocultural environment in which it has operated have placed their indelible stamp upon the political parties. As much as they have been able to influence their world, parties have even more been the products of it. The longevity of the American two-party system and the Democratic and Republican parties within it, in a nation that has experienced enormous changes since its founding, are testimony to their remarkable capacity to adapt to the changing conditions around them. The American parties have indeed shown keen instincts for survival.

Recent decades have posed stern tests to the adaptability of the American parties and the American party system. The quintessential party organization, the political machine, has been driven to the verge of extinction. With the rise of television as the political medium of choice by politicians and voters, the domination of nominations by the direct primary, and the increasing individualism of already-weakly-bridled legislators, American politics, in recent times, became more candidate- and less party-centered than ever before—and candidates always have enjoyed more independence of operation here than in other democracies. Moreover, a citizenry that has characteristically looked askance at parties, even as it has depended upon them, has become less party-oriented.

The parties, as they have done time and time again in American history, have risen to these challenges. They have confronted some of them directly. The demands of the new campaigning in a television-centered world, for example, have been met by the parties' enhanced sophistication in modern-day techniques, especially in the national committees and their congressional counterparts. The U.S. Congress seems to have recoiled from the rampant individualism of a few years ago by giving new authority to the instrumentalities of the party. Local party organizations have been boosted by financial support from higher level committees.

The parties have confronted other challenges indirectly, by adapting what they do and ultimately what they are to the new realities. Their organizations have turned into candidate service centers, for instance, assisting candidates rather than controlling them in the electoral process. These organizations too have become more centralized at the national level, overcoming a long tradition of decentralization and localism in party politics. Pushed to the periphery by

PACs and individual donors as dispensers of campaign capital support, they have responded by performing as "match makers" in bringing donors to the candidates. To counter the centrifugal tendencies of individualism, the legislative parties have invigorated their party caucuses rather than extend powers to party oligarchs.

Since the parties have adapted to the new realities, it is difficult to say whether they now are stronger or weaker than before. They have changed, to be sure. But in the time-honored way of American party politics, whether these adaptations have enhanced or enervated the parties resists a straightforward answer in the short run and requires an evaluation of their roles in a broader political context.

The seventh edition of *Party Politics in America* continues the story told in earlier editions of how the American parties have been both influenced by and responsive to their environment—and what this implies for party politics in America. This is necessarily a story of persistence and of change. Persisting for over 150 years has been a competitive system of two largely decentralized parties straining to comfortably combine organizational, voter, and office-holder sectors. Over most of this period, the system has been dominated by the same two parties, and they dominate today more than ever. Yet American party politics always seems to be in a state of flux. Buffeted by the crises of the American polity, pounded by the powerful tides of political reform and electoral realignment, pushed and pulled by the needs and demands of an everchanging American population, it has hardly stood still for very long.

The revised edition of *Party Politics in America* addresses both this persistence and this change, as any comprehensive treatment of the American parties must. Continuity in essential features of the American parties allows the same theoretical framework that has distinguished past editions to shape this one as well. For all that has changed, the parties remain the tripartite combinations of organizations, public officials, and electorates that they always have been in the American context. Much of party politics also continues to involve the sometimes cooperative, sometimes conflictual interaction among these parts, as well as between them and other intermediaries (especially interest groups) in the electoral process. This tripartite structure and the interaction of parts within it remains the central organizing theme of the seventh edition.

To reflect changes in the American parties and the burgeoning research literature on them since 1987, however, this book has been significantly revised from the sixth edition. The chapters covering the party organizations and the parties in the electoral process have been reordered and reorganized. Throughout the volume, certain topics now receive more extensive treatment: for example, divided government, which has become the central political reality of our time; the effects of the mass media; recent changes in the presidential nomination process; the impact of the Reagan and early Bush years; the techniques and realities of the new campaigning; and the recent renaissance in the party organizations. In a multitude of small yet significant changes, moreover, the seventh edition also incorporates the developments, research findings, and altered conceptualizations of party politics that have emerged in the last four years.

The everchanging nature of the parties is matched by a large and rich research literature on them—to which there have been significant additions since 1987. Capturing both is a challenging task, especially in a way that makes the subject matter accessible to undergraduate students yet not oversimplified in the view of a professional audience. Considerable effort was devoted to making this edition more readable than the last by removing outdated material, recasting difficult passages, and adding new material. It is left for readers to judge the success of these efforts.

Any book is the work of many hands beyond those of the author, and this one is no exception. My greatest debt is to Frank Sorauf, who five years ago generously bequeathed to me the textbook that had been so formative of my own understandings of American political parties. I hope that the sixth edition and this new seventh edition, both of which have been my responsibility, have carried on the fine tradition of *Party Politics in America* that he established.

A substantial debt also is owed to my professional colleagues. My home department has given me "in-house" access to specialists on a variety of the topics embraced by the text. Among these collegial advisors, Larry Baum, Greg Caldeira, Aage Clausen, Richard Gunther, John Kessel, Tony Mughan, Kevin O'Brien, Samuel Patterson, Brad Richardson, Randall Ripley, Elliot Slotnick, and Herb Weisberg were especially helpful. The reviewers of my early plan for revision and then of the final manuscript also contributed in significant ways to the seventh edition. These reviewers include David T. Canon, University of Wisconsin; David J. Hadley, Wabash College; Marjorie R. Hershey, Indiana University; Fred Herzon, Temple University; and James Strandberg, University of Wisconsin. Never before have I received such valuable suggestions about my work, and I am grateful to them for the time they devoted to improving the book. And, of course, the community of political parties scholars provided me with much of the raw material for a book. Without their scholarly contributions, there would be precious little to say about the parties.

No book on political parties could be written without the assistance of the people of the parties themselves. Terry Hitchens, Mike McCurry, and Karla Schurr of the Democratic National Committee and Erich Kimbrough and Jim Nathanson of the Republican National Committee were of great help to me in learning about their respective national committees. Officials at the Federal Election Commission were a useful source as well.

I also am indebted to several graduate students at Ohio State University and to the editorial staff at HarperCollins for their help in preparing the book. At Ohio State, Rodney Anderson served ably as my research assistant in tracking down fugitive information and updating figures and tables from the 1988 NES data. Chuck Smith and Barb Newman provided that one last piece of information needed to complete a chapter. Lynn Maurer and Rosie Clawson aided in finalizing the manuscript. At HarperCollins, Catherine Woods and Melonie Parnes shepherded the book through the review and editorial processes, respectively, with skill and efficiency.

Last but hardly least, I am deeply indebted to my family. Tere, Dan, and David patiently endured my regularly late arrivals for dinner and disappearances at night and on weekends into my study with the understanding that this book in me had to be finished before I could resume a normal life. Finally, I would not be writing on parties but for my parents, my aunts Irene and Lu-allen, my uncle Randy, and my grandmother Lucille, who instilled in me early in life an abiding interest in party politics and in some cases even provided me with valuable political experience in its practice. In its small way, this book is a tribute to their commitment to a democratic party politics.

Paul Allen Beck

PARTIES AND PARTY SYSTEMS

The pervasiveness of politics is a central fact of our times. We have seen in the twentieth century an enormous expansion of governmental activity. The demands of a complex, urban, industrial society, and the dictates of a world beset by international tensions, do not easily permit a return to limited government. For the foreseeable future, a substantial proportion of the important conflicts over the desirable things in American society will be settled within the political system. Indeed, some would argue that intense conflicts can be resolved peacefully only through politics. The really meaningful issues of our time surely will be how influence and power are organized within the political system, who wins the rewards and successes of that political activity, and to whom the people who make the decisions are responsible. The political system still will play a crucial role in deciding, in the candid phrase of Harold Lasswell, "who gets what, when, how."[1]

In the United States, these political contests are directed largely at the regular institutions of government. Few political scientists believe that the real and important political decisions are made clandestinely by murky, semivisible elites and merely ratified by the governmental bodies they control.[2] It may happen, to be sure, that political decisions in a local community are made by a group of influential local citizens rather than by a city council or a mayor or a school board. Nonetheless, one is reasonably safe in looking for the substance of

---

[1]The phrase comes from the title of Harold Lasswell's pioneering book *Politics: Who Gets What, When, How* (New York: McGraw-Hill, 1936).

[2]C. Wright Mills, *The Power Elite* (New York: Oxford University Press, 1956), offers the best-known example of such interpretations of American politics. The alternative "pluralist" perspective adopted by most political scientists is well illustrated in Robert A. Dahl, *Who Governs?* (New Haven: Yale University Press, 1961).

1

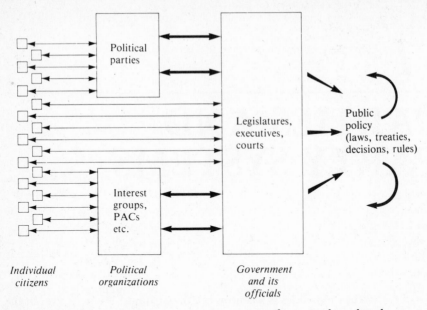

Figure I.1 Political organizations as organizing intermediaries in the political system.

American politics in the legislatures, executives, and courts of the nation, the fifty states, and localities. Considerable activity is directed, therefore, to influence either the making of decisions within these governmental bodies or the selecting of the men and women who will make them.

This struggle for influence is not unorganized, however confusing it may seem to be. Large political organizations attempt to mobilize influence on behalf of aggregates of individuals. In democracies the political party is unquestionably the most important and pervasive of these political organizations. It is not, however, the only one. Interest groups, such as the American Farm Bureau Federation and the AFL-CIO, also mobilize influence. So do smaller factions and cliques, charismatic individuals, and nonparty political organizations such as Americans for Democratic Action and the American Conservative Union. And so in the United States do the political action committees (PACs) that pay a substantial part of the costs of campaigning. Even ostensibly nonpolitical organizations—e.g., churches, civic clubs, ethnic group associations—may from time to time play important roles in the political process.

All these political organizations work as *intermediaries* between the millions of political individuals and the distant policymakers in government (Figure I.1). They build influence into large aggregates in order to have a greater effect on the selection of policymakers and the policies they will make. At the same time, they codify and simplify information about government and politics as it moves back to the individual. In a very real sense, therefore, these political organizers are the informal agents by which individuals are linked to government in the complex democracies of our time. They are both the builders and the agents of majorities.

In any political system, the political intermediary organizations develop an informal division of labor. Political parties concentrate on contesting elections as a way of aggregating influence. Others, especially interest groups, pursue the avenues of direct influence on legislators or administrators in articulating the demands of narrower groups. Still others seek mainly to propagate ideologies or build support on specific issues of foreign or domestic policy. Indeed, the nature of the division of labor among the various political intermediaries says a great deal about any political system and about the general processes of mobilizing influence within it. The division also speaks meaningfully about the political parties. It is a commonplace, for example, that among the parties of the democracies, the American political parties are occupied to an unusual extent with the single activity of contesting elections. The parties of Western Europe, on the other hand, have been more committed to spreading ideologies and disciplining legislators as well. And those of developing countries sometimes play important roles in transmitting political values and information to a citizenry that lacks other avenues of political socialization and communication.

The division of labor among political organizations is, however, neither clear nor permanent. There is always an overlapping—and hence a competition—among political organizations over the performance of their activities. That competition is most obvious when it takes place within the party system, the competition of one party against another. It also takes place between parties and other political intermediaries—for example, in the competition of parties and powerful interest groups for the attention and support of legislators or for the right to name a candidate in a primary election. Furthermore, the extent to which any one kind of political organization controls or participates in any one kind of organizing activity may change radically over time. Certainly, no one would argue that the American political parties today control as much of the business of campaigning as they did a century ago.

All of this competing for a role in American politics implies another kind of competition. The political organizations compete among themselves for political resources: money, skills, expertise, the efforts of men and women. All of these resources are necessary for the fueling of organizational activity, but none of them is in particularly abundant supply in the American society. Then, with those resources at hand, they compete for the support of individual citizens— that is, they seek their support for the goals and leadership of the organization. In sum, the parties and other political organizations compete for scarce resources with which to mobilize the political influence necessary to capture the scarce rewards the political system allocates. They compete first for the capacity to organize influence and then for the influence itself.

Despite these excursions beyond the subject of political parties, however, this *is* a book about political parties. The broader survey of politics and political organizations merely has been background for two themes that will recur throughout the remainder of the book. The first is that the political party is not the unique political organization we have conventionally thought it to be. On the contrary, it is frequently similar to other political organizations, and the difficulty of coming to a clear, agreed-on definition of a political party illustrates that point only too well. When one undertakes any exercise in definition, as we do for the parties in the first chapter, the temptation is always to err on the side of the distinctiveness, even the uniqueness, of the phenomenon one is trying to define. But the distinctions between parties and other political organizations are not so great as one might imagine. Parties do have their distinctive qualities—and it is important to know them—but there is little point in denying their similarity and, in some cases, their functional equivalence to many other political organizations.

Second, a broad perspective is essential in assessing the role and position of political parties in the American democracy. American writers about political parties have not been modest in their claims for them. They have celebrated the parties as agents of democracy and even as the chosen instruments through which a democratic citizenry governs itself. Some have gone a step further to proclaim them the architects of the democratic processes that they now serve. E. E. Schattschneider opened his classic study of the American parties this way in 1942:

> The rise of political parties is indubitably one of the principal distinguishing marks of modern government. The parties, in fact, have played a major role as *makers* of democratic government. It should be stated flatly at the outset that this volume is devoted to the thesis that the political parties created democracy and that modern democracy is unthinkable save in terms of the parties.[3]

Other scholars, and many thoughtful Americans too, agree that American democracy presumes the two-party system of today. Similar paeans to political parties are sounded by some observers of the development of democracy in new nations.[4]

This heroic view of parties stands in stark contrast to recurrent expressions of antiparty sentiment and general ambivalence about the parties in the American political culture. The Republic's Founding Fathers were wary of organized factions in political life, as is exemplified by James Madison's famous peroration against the "mischiefs of faction" in *Federalist* 10. The Progressive reforms a century or so later were directed in large part against the perceived evils of entrenched political parties and their control over the political process. Antiparty sentiment has intensified once again in recent years, providing fertile ground for yet another series of party reforms. Many Americans today, among

---

[3]E. E. Schattschneider, *Party Government* (New York: Rinehart, 1942), p. 1.

[4]Illustrations of this favorable treatment of parties as crucial to the democratization of new nations may be found in David Apter, *The Politics of Modernization* (Chicago: University of Chicago Press, 1965), Chapter 6; and Joseph LaPalombara and Myron Weiner, *Political Parties and Political Development* (Princeton: Princeton University Press, 1966).

them certainly many readers of this book, are skeptical of the value of parties in our politics and may go so far as to view them as the adversaries rather than the guardians of political democracy.[5]

Nor do the immodest claims for political parties give adequate recognition to the fact that the major American parties have changed and continue to change—both in the form of their organization and in the pattern and style of their activities. Political parties as they existed a century ago scarcely exist today, and the political parties we know today may not exist even twenty years from now. In this book, a vigorous case will be made for the proposition that the political parties have lost their preeminent position as political organizations and that competing political organizations and other institutions now perform many of the activities traditionally regarded as the parties' exclusive prerogatives. If this is really the case, we must face the question of whether political parties are indeed indispensable and inevitable shapers of our democratic politics.

These two suspicions—that the parties may be less distinctive and their activities less pervasive than we have thought—add up, perhaps, to no more than a plea for modesty in the study of the American political parties.[6] It is perfectly natural for scholars to identify with the objects of their study and thus to exaggerate their importance. Medievalists often find the late Middle Ages to be the high point of Western civilization, and most scholars of hitherto obscure painters and philosophers find the objects of their study to have been sadly neglected or tragically underestimated. So, too, has it been with students of political parties.

All of this is not to suggest that the American political parties are or have been of little importance. Their long life and their role in the politics of the world's oldest representative democracy scarcely lead to that conclusion. The plea here is merely for a careful assessment of their role. Assertions that political parties are essential to or the keystone of American democracy may or may not be true, but simply as assertions they advance our understanding of politics and parties very little. The same is true of predispositions to the contrary—that political parties are unnecessary or baneful influences upon a democratic politics. To even begin to evaluate such propositions requires a detailed examination of what the political parties are and what they do. That examination is the task of this book.

---

[5]Austin Ranney provides an excellent account of these antiparty attitudes and reforms in *Curing the Mischiefs of Faction* (Berkeley: University of California Press, 1975).

[6]See Anthony King, "Political Parties in Western Democracies," *Polity* 2 (1969): 111–41, for a similar note of caution about the role of parties generally.

Chapter
1

In Search of the
Political Parties

The dramatic explosion of democracy in Eastern Europe at the turn of the decade introduced a multitude of new intermediary groups into a political scene that long had been dominated by one, the Communist party. As these groups quickly prepared to play a role in the first democratic elections their nations had held in over forty years, they wrestled with fundamental questions about their own identities. Could they avoid becoming political parties, with all their negative connotations in these systems, and still effectively compete for power? If they opted for the party route, how could they transform themselves from groupings operating in the shadows of politics or inclusive movements for democracy into electorally distinctive political parties? How much would they have to compromise their principles or broaden their bases to have a reasonable prospect of capturing political office? To Americans, inclined to take for granted their long-established party system, these may seem like trivial and uninteresting questions. But for Eastern Europeans, they lay at the very core of the challenge to establish the new democratic institutions that might fulfill their hopes and dreams.

This recent Eastern European experience raises anew the question of what is a political party. How can party be distinguished from a grouping of like-minded officials, an interest group, or a mass movement? Who is encompassed in the concept of party? Is a party the politicians who share a party label in seeking and filling public offices? Is it the functionaries and activists who staff the offices and work in the campaigns? The ordinary citizens who possess similar political loyalties and who regularly vote alike in elections? A group of people who are like-minded in ideas, values, or stands on issues? Or is a party whatever entity, however organized, that performs a prescribed set of activities, especially centered on the electoral arena? Because political parties can be different things to different people, they may be defined in any or all of these ways (as the sample of alternative definitions in the box on p. 8 illustrates).

What Is a Political Party? Some Alternative Definitions[1]

(A) political party in the modern sense may be thought of as a relatively durable social formation which seeks offices or power in government, exhibits a structure or organization which links leaders at the centers of government to a significant popular following in the political arena and its local enclaves, and generates in-group perspectives or at least symbols of identification or loyalty.

WILLIAM NISBET CHAMBERS (1967)

(W)hat is meant by a political party (is) any group, however loosely organized, seeking to elect governmental office-holders under a given label. Having a label (which may or may not be on the ballot) rather than an organization is the crucial defining element.

LEON EPSTEIN (1979)

A political party is a group organized to gain control of government in the name of the group by winning election to public office.

JOSEPH A. SCHLESINGER (1985)

Party is a body of men united, for promoting by their joint endeavors the national interest, upon some particular principle in which they are all agreed.

EDMUND BURKE (1770)

"Party" or "political party" means any political organization which elects a state committee and officers of a state convention composed of delegates elected from each representative district in which the party has registered members and which nominates candidates for electors of President and Vice President, or nominates candidates for offices to be decided at the general election.

DELAWARE STATUTES (15 DEL. C, SECTION 101)

The political party is a social group, a system of meaningful and patterned activity within the larger society. It consists of a set of individuals populating specific roles and behaving as member-actors of a boundaried and identifiable social unit.

SAMUEL J. ELDERSVELD (1964)

The various conceptions of party reduce to three forms in essence. Those whose approach is ideological (e.g., Edmund Burke) define the parties in terms of commonly held ideas, values, or stands on issues—as a group of like-minded

---

[1]These definitions are taken from: William Nisbet Chambers, "Party Development and the American Mainstream" in William Nisbet Chambers and Walter Dean Burnham, eds., *The American Party Systems* (New York: Oxford University Press, 1967), p. 5; Leon Epstein, *Political Parties in Western Democracies* (New Brunswick, N.J.: Transaction Books, 1980; originally published in 1967),

people. That approach has not enjoyed much favor among students of the American political parties. Ideological homogeneity or purpose has not been a hallmark of the major American parties, even if it may describe those groupings of political leaders that became the first American parties or characterize some European parties, particularly those on the left. While it may be a useful analytic device for some purposes to define the parties as teams of like-minded political actors, that conceptualization does not square very well with political realities in the United States—and it makes it difficult to distinguish parties from factions.

Most of the attempts at definition vacillate between two other options, some even combining them (e.g., Chambers). One views the political party as a hierarchical organization or structure (e.g., Eldersveld, state of Delaware). The other approach sees the parties largely in terms of what they do—their role, function, or activities in the American political systems (e.g., Epstein, Schlesinger). So important have these conceptualizations been to the treatment of the American political parties that we shall dwell on each of them in turn.

THE POLITICAL PARTY AS A SOCIAL STRUCTURE

Large organizations or social structures consist of people in various roles, responsibilities, patterns of activity, and reciprocal relationships. But which people, what activities, and what relationships comprise the two major American parties?

At a minimum, they include current or prospective officeholders who are willing to be identified together under the same party label. Many parties in democratic nations originated in this fashion. So it is understandable that some conceptions of party are content to restrict its meaning to just these leaders and their electoral organizations.

But most structural conceptions see modern parties also as broad-based organizations that transcend office seekers and officeholders. In some localities, the parties have offices and phone listings as political parties—and virtually everywhere they have official standing under state law. It is possible to join them, to work within them, to become officers in them, to participate in setting their goals and strategies—much as one would do within a fraternal organization or union—without ever seeking or holding governmental office, or even directly supporting a particular candidate. Some of their activists even are

---

p. 9; Joseph Schlesinger, "The New American Political Party," *American Political Science Review* 79 (1985): p. 1153; Edmund Burke, "Thoughts on the Cause of the Present Discontents" (1770), in *The Works of Edmund Burke* (Boston: Little, Brown, 1839), vol. I, pp. 425–26; and Samuel Eldersveld, *Political Parties: A Behavioral Analysis* (Chicago: Rand McNally, 1964), p. 1. For an extended discussion of key issues in defining political parties, see Giovanni Sartori, *Parties and Party Systems* (New York: Cambridge University Press, 1976), pp. 3–38; and Leon Epstein, *Political Parties in Western Democracies*.

selected as the official representatives of the party under the statutory authority of the state.

There is a tendency for many scholars, and no doubt most Americans, to close their conceptions of what the political party structures are at this point—to view them as teams of political specialists actively involved in competing for and exercising political power. When held by ordinary citizens, this view enables them to put some distance between themselves and these political entities and to view parties in a dim light. And it has allowed scholars to define parties in a strict, well-structured fashion so as to avoid the messiness in conceptualization that makes inquiry difficult.

Yet, however attractive the simple definition may be, other scholars contend that it ignores a fundamental reality about political parties, especially American parties. As intermediary organizations, political parties reside in citizen *and* elite political circles. Many ordinary voters develop strong and enduring attachments to a particular party—so much so that they can be counted among its members even if they have not taken the steps, such as paying dues, of formal association. Indeed, it is common in discussing the electoral fortunes of the political parties to treat them as coalitions of voters rather than simply groupings of political elites. Recent talk of a realignment in the United States in which the Republicans may become the majority party recognizes the reality of parties as encompassing ordinary voters as well as officeholders and office-seekers, functionaries and activists.

The Progressive tradition, by instituting party registration and nomination through primary elections as regular practices, has made the case for a conceptualization of American parties that includes an even stronger citizen base. Party voters in the United States are directly involved through primary elections in selecting which candidates will run under the party label in elections—a function performed by a thin stratum of party activists and leaders elsewhere in the democratic world. Typically an advance public affirmation of party loyalty is required before voters can participate in a party's nomination process. In a handful of states, though, voters can choose a party in the privacy of the voting booth.

By involving voters directly in the nomination process, the line between elite and mass that demarcates political parties in some political systems is blurred in the American setting, just as the Progressives intended. This creates a situation in which voter/consumers not only choose among competing products in the marketplace but assume the management responsibility to determine just what products will be introduced in the first place—an arrangement that would revolutionize market economies just as it has transformed political parties. Perhaps this makes for a messier concept of political party, but it nonetheless is a more realistic one for the American parties.

The major American political parties are, in truth, best conceptualized as three-headed political giants—tripartite systems of interactions that embrace party leaders and officials and the thousands of anonymous activists who work for candidates and party causes, the people who vote for the party's candidates, and the men and women elected to office on the party's label. As political structures, they may be thought of as the somewhat unwieldy combination of a

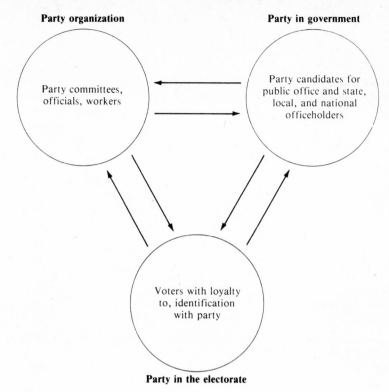

Party organization

Party committees, officials, workers

Party in government

Party candidates for public office and state, local, and national officeholders

Voters with loyalty to, identification with party

Party in the electorate

Figure 1.1 The three-part political party.

party organization, a party in office, and a party in the electorate (see Figure 1.1).[2] Although breaking the parties down into these separate parts may facilitate their examination, it is important not to lose sight of the fact that much of the character of the American parties is defined by how they are combined—by the dynamic interaction among the parts.[3] The reality of this interaction pervades each separate part and is especially pronounced as the parties operate in the electoral process.

The Party Organization

In the party organization, one finds the formally chosen party leaders, the informally anointed ones, the legions of local captains and leaders, the ward and

---

[2]This conception of the political parties is attributed to V. O. Key, Jr., who uses it to organize his classic political parties textbook, *Politics, Parties, and Pressure Groups* (New York: Thomas Crowell, 1964), pp. 163–65.

[3]This point is emphasized by a number of critics of the tripartite approach, especially Denise L. Baer and David A. Bositis, *Elite Cadres and Party Coalitions: Representing the Public in Party Politics* (Westport, Conn.: Greenwood Press, 1988), pp. 21–50.

precinct workers, the members and activists of the party—that is, all those who give their time, money, and skills to the party, whether as leaders or as followers. The organization operates in part through the formal machinery of committees and conventions set by the laws of the fifty states and in part through its own informal apparatus. Here one finds the centers of party authority and bureaucracy, and here one also observes the face-to-face contacts and interactions that characterize an organization of any kind.

The Party in Government

The party in government is made up of those who have captured office under the label of the party and of those who seek to do so. The chief executives and legislative parties of the nation and the states are its major components. Although in many ways they are not subject to the control or discipline of the party organization, they do, in the broadest sense, speak for the party. Their pronouncements are the most audible party statements and carry the greatest weight with the public. A party's president or leader in the Congress claims more attention than its national chairperson. Its governor or state legislative leader usually has more visibility as a party spokesperson than its state chairperson. Even though these two components of the party regularly work together to achieve their many common goals, there sometimes arises a tension between the party organization and the party in government because the goals of holding particular offices and achieving maximal party strength are not always compatible. The existence of such a tension, as the two components compete for scarce resources in pursuit of somewhat different goals, is ample testimony to the need to treat them as separate parts of the party.

The Party in the Electorate

The party in the electorate is the party's least well-defined part. It comprises the men and women who affiliate casually with it, show it some degree of loyalty, participate in the selecting of its candidates for office, and even vote habitually for it, even though they do not participate in the party organization or interact with its leaders and activists. Many of these "partisans" may be registered officially with the party where the state prescribes party registration (and more than half do); but many others are no less a part of the electoral party even though they have not taken the official step of declaring a party for registration purposes. These individuals are not subject to the incentives and disciplines of the party organization and, in the case of party nominations, often vie with the organization for influence. They are, in effect, the regular consumers of the party's candidates and appeals. As such, they make up the coalitions necessary for effective political power in the American political system. Their association with the party is a passive one, however—accepting here, rejecting there, always threatening the party with the fickleness of their affections.

In their three-part structure, therefore, the major American parties include mixed, varied, and even contradictory and conflicting components. Each party, for example, is a political organization with active, even disciplined participants. It is also an aggregate of unorganized partisans who may begrudge the party organization even the merest public gesture of support or loyalty. The party thus embraces the widest range of involvement and commitment. It is a reasonably well-defined, voluntary political organization and, at the same time, an open, public collection of loyalists.

Perhaps the most telling characteristic of the major American parties, therefore, is the relationship that their clientele—the party in the electorate—has to them. The other political organizations, such as interest groups and ad hoc campaign organizations, usually work to attract supporters beyond their members and workers; but this wider clientele remains outside the political organization. This is not so with the political party. The party in the electorate is more than an external group to be wooed and mobilized. State laws usually permit it a voice in the selection of the parties' candidates in the direct primary, and in many states it helps select local party officials such as ward and precinct committeepersons. Consequently, the major American party is an open, inclusive, semipublic political organization. It includes both a tangible political organization and its own political clientele (as well as the party in government, of course). In this combination of exclusive organization and inclusive clientele, of organization and electorate, the political party stands apart from the other political organizations and parties elsewhere.

Finally, each major party differs from state to state in the relationships and interactions among its three sectors. The Republicans and the Democrats are so decentralized and so diverse that virtually every state party has its own distinctive mix of the three. Party organizations, for example, differ in form from state to state; in a few the party organization may dominate the party in government, whereas in others the reverse is the case. Also, party electorates differ in composition and in the bases of their loyalties; in some states the two parties in the electorate divide roughly along social class lines, but in others they do not. The parties also differ from state to state in their inclusivity for the purpose of nominating candidates for office. In some states, a voter can participate in a party's nomination process merely by voting for a candidate of that party on a ballot that includes candidates from both parties. In others, a prior (to election day) act of registering with the party is necessary for a voter to participate in that party's nomination process. Indeed, much of the distinctive quality of a state party is a reflection of the form and composition of each of the party sectors and of their relationships with each other.

THE PARTY AS A CLUSTER OF ACTIVITIES

From a discussion of the political parties as social structures, we move to viewing them in terms of activities—turning from what they are to what they do. In varying degrees, the competitive political parties of every democracy perform three sets of activities: They select candidates and contest elections, they propagandize on behalf of a party ideology or program, and they attempt to guide the elected officeholders of government to provide particular policy or patronage benefits.[4] The degree of emphasis that any particular political party puts on each of these individual activities varies within and between countries, but no party completely escapes the necessity of any of them.

Parties as Electors

It often appears that the American parties are little more than regular attempts to capture public office. Electoral activity so dominates the life of the American party that its metabolism follows almost exactly the cycles of the election calendar. Party activity and vitality reach a peak at the elections; between elections, the parties go into hibernation. Party activity is goal oriented, and in American politics most of the general goals as well as the goals of the individual sectors depend ultimately on electoral victory. It is, in fact, chiefly in the attempt to achieve their often separate goals through winning public office that the three sectors of the party are brought together in unified action.

Parties as Propagandizers

Second, the American parties carry on a series of loosely related activities that perhaps can best be called education or propagandization. There is, of course, a school of thought that argues that the American parties fail almost completely to function on behalf of ideas or ideologies. The Democrats and Republicans, to be sure, do not espouse the all-inclusive ideologies of a European Marxist or proletarian party. They do, however, represent the interests of and the issue stands congenial to the groups that identify with them and support them. In this sense, they become parties of business or labor, of the advantaged or the disadvantaged. Moreover, events since the 1960s suggest that ideology in a purer sense may be coming to the American parties. In presidential politics alone, one merely needs to mention the Goldwater conservatism of 1964, the McGovern liberalism of 1972, and the Reagan conservatism of the 1980s.

Parties as Governors

Virtually all officeholders in American national and state governments were elected as either Democrats or Republicans. Not surprisingly, these partisan perspectives pervade the governmental process. The legislatures of forty-nine states (the exception is nonpartisan Nebraska, but even there clear partisan ties are obvious to close observers and to many voters) and the United States Congress are organized along party lines, and the voting of their members shows

---

[4]The failure to recognize that political parties do not single-mindedly seek only to win office but also are motivated by the benefits that can be derived from control of office has led to some confusion about the electoral goals of parties. For clarification, see Joseph A. Schlesinger, "The Primary Goals of Political Parties: A Clarification of Positive Theory," *American Political Science Review* 69 (1975): 840–49.

noticeable party discipline and cohesion. To be sure, on controversial issues that cohesion is irregular, sporadic, and often unpredictable in most legislatures. Yet, in the aggregate, an important degree of party discipline does exist. In executive branches, presidents and governors depend on their fellow partisans for executive talent and count on their party loyalty to bind them to the executive programs. Even the American judiciary cannot escape the organizing and directing touch of the parties, although the effects of this touch are highly muted.

These, then, are the chief overt activities of democratic political parties generally and of American parties in particular. They are the activities that the parties set out consciously to perform. Large sections of any book on the American parties must be devoted to them.

To list these activities of the parties, however, is not to suggest that the American parties monopolize any or all of them. The parties compete with non-party political organizations over the ability and the right to perform them. The American parties, having organized the legislatures, battle constantly—and often with little success—against interest groups and constituency pressures in order to firm up party lines for votes on major bills. In attempting to nominate candidates for public office, especially at the local level, the party faces often insurmountable competition from interest groups, community elites, and powerful local personalities, each of whom may be sponsoring pet candidates. In stating issues and ideologies, they are often overshadowed by the fervor of the minor (third) parties, the ubiquitous interest groups, the mass media, public figures, and political action groups.

These patterns of party activity also affect the party structure and its three sectors. The emphasis on the electoral activities of American parties, for example, elevates the party in government to a position of unusual power, even dominance. It frequently competes with the party organization for the favor of the party in the electorate. In parties more strongly linked to issues and ideologies—such as those of continental Europe—party organizations, by contrast, often have been able to dictate to legislative parties.

On the other hand, individuals from all three sectors of the party may unite in specific activities. Party organization activists loyal to officeholders may unite with those persons, with other individuals of the party in government, and with individuals in the party electorate to return them to public office. When the election is won or lost, they very likely will drift apart again. Therefore, one finds within the parties certain functional clusters or nuclei, certain groups of individuals, drawn together in a single, concerted action.[5] Small and informal task groups cut across the differences in structure and goals that characterize

---

[5]On the party as a series of task-oriented nuclei see Joseph A. Schlesinger, "Political Party Organization," in James G. March (ed.), *Handbook of Organizations* (Chicago: Rand McNally, 1965), pp. 764–801; and "The New American Political Party." 1152–69.

the three party sectors. In American politics, alliances and coalitions are more common within the parties than between them.

THE INDIRECT CONSEQUENCES OF PARTY ACTIVITY

The goal-seeking behavior of any individual or organization has indirect, sometimes even unintended, consequences. By pursuing its legislating activities, Congress may be said to be either resolving or aggravating great areas of social conflict, depending on the judgment of the observer. Similarly, interest groups, in pursuing their particular goals in the legislative process, are also providing an informal, auxiliary avenue of representation. The same search for the indirect consequences of party activities is an old tradition in the study of the American parties. It produces rich insights into the contributions of the parties to the American political system. Yet it can be frustrating, because it is much easier to prove or establish the activity itself than the results or consequences it brings about.

Some Indirect Consequences

It is not surprising, then, that scholars of the American political parties have seen and recorded differing sets of these indirect consequences or functions, as many refer to them. What follows is a brief list of some of the most readily identifiable—and thus most frequently mentioned—of these consequences of party activity.

1. The parties participate in the *political socialization* of the American electorate by transmitting political values and information to large numbers of current and future voters. They preach the value of political commitment and activity, and they convey information and cues about a confusing political system. By symbolizing and representing a political point of view, they offer uninformed or underinformed citizens a map of the political world. They help them form political judgments and make political choices, and, in both physical and psychological terms, they make it easier to be politically active.

2. The American parties also contribute to the *accumulation of political power*. They aggregate masses of political individuals and groups and thereby organize blocs that are powerful enough to govern or to oppose those who govern. For the confused and confounded citizen, they simplify, and often oversimplify, the political world into more comprehensible choices. By using attachment to the party as a perceptual screen, the voter has a master clue for assessing issues and candidates. Thus, both within the individual and in the external political world, the political party operates to focus political loyalties on a small number of alternatives and then to accumulate support behind them.

3. Because they devote so much effort to contesting elections, the American parties dominate the *recruitment of political leadership*. One needs only to run down a list of the members of the cabinet or even the federal courts to see how many of them entered public service through a political party or through partisan candidacy for office. Because the American parties pervade all governmental levels in the federal system, they may recruit and elevate leadership from one level to another. Furthermore, the orderly contesting of elections enables the parties to routinize political change, especially change of governmental leadership. More than one commentator has noted the disruptive quality of leadership changes in those countries in which no stable political parties compete in regular elections.

4. Finally, the American parties are a *force of unification* in the divided American political system. The fragmentation of government is an incontestably crucial fact of American politics. To the fragmentation of the nation and the fifty states, multiplied by the threefold separation of powers in each, the two great national parties bring a unifying, centripetal force. They unify with an obviously limited efficiency; for example, they often fail to bind the president and the Congress together in causes that can transcend the separation of powers. Their similar symbols and traditions, however, are a force for unity in governmental institutions marked by decentralization and division.

Problems of Definition and Measurement

There are two chief difficulties with this list of party functions. First, scholars are not always in agreement over what the word *function* means. Some use it to denote the obvious activities of the parties (e.g., their contesting of elections), whereas others use it, as we do in this test, to describe the unintended consequences or fortunate by-products of the intended activities of the parties. For yet another group, *function* suggests a contribution the party makes to the operation of the broader political system.[6] Second, there is the problem of formulating the functional categories so that they can be observed and measured. If, as some writers have argued, one function of political parties is to organize social conflict or to articulate important social interests, how do we verify by our own observations whether all parties or some parties do, in fact, perform those functions? For reasons having to do with both of these problems, this book will look largely at the more easily observable, intended activity of the parties rather than its unintended consequences. But it must not be forgotten that political parties have effects that transcend their most immediate activities.

---

[6]Theodore Lowi has brought together a number of descriptions of party functions in his article "Toward Functionalism in Political Science: The Case of Innovation in Party Systems," *American Political Science Review* 57 (1963): 570–83.

THE SPECIAL CHARACTERISTICS
OF POLITICAL PARTIES

Perhaps it is time to end these excursions into related topics and narrow the search for political parties. Our goal is not a memorable, one-sentence definition for no such rendering could hope to capture the fullness of the meaning of *party*. Rather, we seek an understanding of what characterizes the political parties and sets them apart from other political organizations. We need, in other words, a firm grasp of what the political parties are and what they do.

All political organizations exist to organize and mobilize their supporters either to capture public office or to influence the activities of those already in public office. That much, at least, they all have in common. If the term *political party* is to have any meaning at all, however, there must also be differences between parties and other political organizations. Far too much has been made of the differences between the major American parties and other political organizations, especially the large national interest (or pressure) groups. The differences are there, however, even if they are really only differences among species of the same genus.

Commitment to Electoral Activity

Above all, the political party is distinguished from other political organizations by its concentration on the contesting of elections. Although the major American parties do not monopolize the contesting of elections, their preeminence in this activity cannot be questioned. Other political organizations do attempt to influence American electoral politics. Some seem to do little else. In many localities, interest groups encourage or discourage candidates, work for them within parties, contribute to campaign funds, and get their members to the polls to support them. Other nonparty organizations may raise funds, organize endorsements, and recruit workers for some candidate's campaign for public office. The parties, however, are occupied with the contesting of elections in a way and to a degree that the other political organizations are not. Indeed, their names and symbols are the ones the states recognize for inclusion on most ballots, and their presence is felt throughout the nation, intruding even into its remotest corners.

Mobilization of Numbers

Commitment not only to electoral activity but also to its organizational consequences characterizes the political party. Since the party chooses to work toward its goals largely in elections, it must recruit an enormous supportive clientele. Organizations that attempt to influence legislative committees or rule making in administrative agencies may succeed with a few strategists and the support of only a small, well-mobilized clientele. The political parties, in order to win elections, must depend less on the intricate skills and maneuverings of organizational strategists and more on the mobilization of large numbers of citizens. Party appeals must be broad and inclusive; the party cannot afford either exclusivity or a narrow range of concerns. It is at the opposite pole from the "single-issue" group or organization. To put it simply, the major political party has committed itself through its concentration on electoral politics to the mobilization of large numbers of citizens in large numbers of elections, and from that commitment flow many of its other characteristics.

Devotion to Political Activity

The major American political parties and similar parties elsewhere are characterized by a full commitment to political activity. They operate solely as political organizations, solely as instruments of political action. Interest groups and most other political organizations, however, do not. They move freely and frequently from political to nonpolitical activities and back again. The AFL-CIO, for example, seeks many of its goals and interests in nonpolitical ways, especially through collective bargaining. It may, however, turn to political action—to support sympathetic candidates or to lobby before Congress—when political avenues appear to be the best or the only means to achieve its goals. Every organized group in the United States is, as one observer has suggested, a potential political organization.[7] Still, the interest group almost always maintains some sphere of nonpolitical action.

Endurance

Political parties also are marked by an uncommon stability and persistence. The personal clique, the faction, the ad hoc campaign organization, and even many interest groups seem by contrast almost political will-o'-the-wisps, which disappear as suddenly as they appear. The size and the abstractness of the political parties, their relative independence from personalities, and their continuing symbolic strength for thousands of voters assure them of a far greater longevity. Both major American parties can trace their histories well over a century, and the major parties of the other Western democracies have impressive, if shorter, life spans. It is precisely this enduring, ongoing quality that enhances their value as reference symbols. The parties are there as points of reference— year after year, election after election, and candidate after candidate—giving continuity and form to the choices Americans face and the issues they debate.

Political Symbols

Finally, the political parties are distinguished from other political organizations by the extent to which they operate as cues or symbols—or even more vaguely

---

[7]David B. Truman, *The Governmental Process* (New York: Knopf, 1951).

as emotion-laden objects of loyalty. For millions of Americans, the party label is the chief cue for their decisions about candidates or issues. It is the point of reference that allows them to organize and simplify the buzzing confusion and strident rhetoric of American politics. It shapes their perceptions and structures their choices; it relates their political values and goals to the real options of American politics.

Resemblance to Other Organizations

To reemphasize a previous point, however, the differences between parties and other political organizations are often slender. Interest groups certainly contest elections to some degree, and the larger ones have achieved impressive stability and duration and considerable symbolic status. They can recruit candidates and give political clues and cues to their members and fellow travelers. The unique American nomination process enables them to play an important role in selecting party candidates for office. Interest groups also promote interests and issue positions, try to influence and organize officeholders, and (through their political action committees) contribute to their campaigns. They do not, however, and in most localities cannot, offer their names and symbols for candidates to use on the ballot. It is only that difference and the whole question of size and degree that separate their activities and political roles from those of the parties.

So similar are the major parties to some other political organizations that in important respects they resemble them more closely than they do the minor or third parties. The minor political parties are only nominally electoral organizations. Not even the congenital optimism of candidates can lead Socialists or Prohibitionists to expect victories on the ballot. Lacking local organization, as most of them do, they resemble the major parties less than do the complex, nationwide interest groups. Also, their membership base, often dependent upon a single issue, may be just as narrow, just as exclusively recruited, as that of most interest groups. In structure and activities, groups such as the United States Chamber of Commerce and the AFL-CIO resemble the Democrats and Republicans far more than do the Libertarians and the Socialist Workers. Even so, minor parties do appear on the ballot, and their candidates can receive public funding where it is available (assuming they have qualified—typically by attaining a certain number of votes in previous elections). In these respects, they are more like the major parties than are the large interest groups.

THE DEVELOPMENT OF AMERICAN PARTIES

To see the special role and character of political parties, there is no better place to look than at their origins and their rise to importance. In the United States, their history is one of an almost 200-year alliance with an emerging popular democracy. (For a summary of American party history, see the box on p. 35). The American parties grew up in response to the expansion of the adult suffrage and to all the changes it brought to American politics.[8]

In the first years of the Republic, the vote was limited in almost every state to those free men who could meet property-holding or tax-paying requirements. Furthermore, the framers of the new Constitution of 1787 intentionally limited the power of individual voters at elections. The president was to be chosen, not by a direct vote of the electorate, but indirectly by the electoral college. The method of selection of each state's electors was left to the individual state legislatures. Also, although election to the House of Representatives was entrusted to a direct popular vote, that of the Senate was not. Its members were to be chosen by the respective state legislatures. It was, in short, a cautious and limited beginning to democratic self-government.

In their first years, the American parties reflected this politics of a limited suffrage and indirect elections. They began, in fact, largely as caucuses of like-minded members of the Congress. They involved only the men and the issues of politics in the nation's capital. These congressional caucuses nominated presidential candidates and mobilized groups of political figures supportive of or opposed to the administration of the time. Gradually, during the 1790s, these factions began to take on the permanence we associate with political parties. The Federalists, as the dominant group came to be called, were organized around Alexander Hamilton and championed a measure of central direction of the economy. The opposition, rallying around Thomas Jefferson and James Madison, favored the protection of states' rights from national government interference. Party organization at the grass roots initially was restricted to "committees of correspondence," although each side did found a newspaper to propagandize on behalf of its cause. These were the first formal outreaches of the congressional caucuses to the voters "back home," and through them officeholders organized and communicated with the electorate.

One of these incipient parties, the Democratic-Republicans, was transformed into the first semblance of a modern-style party by its organizing efforts in the states and localities in advance of the 1800 presidential elections. On the other hand, the Federalists, their elitism preventing parallel organizational efforts, virtually disappeared in most states shortly after the defeat of their last president, John Adams, in 1800. The pressures for democratization already were powerful enough by the early 1800s to vanquish an infant party that was

---

[8]There are, of course, many histories of the development of American political parties. Most, however, devote virtually all their pages to the candidates and platforms of the parties; few discuss the parties *qua* parties. For three that do, see William N. Chambers, *Political Parties in a New Nation* (New York: Oxford University Press, 1963); Everett C. Ladd, Jr., *American Political Parties* (New York: Norton, 1970); and Chambers and Burnham (eds.), *The American Party Systems*.

unable to adapt to the necessity for organizing a mass electorate, especially in the growing states of the frontier.[9]

The Democratic-Republicans, the new party of agrarian interests and the frontier, quickly established their superiority and enjoyed a twenty-year period of one-party monopoly. So thorough was their domination by the time of James Monroe's presidency that the absence of party and political conflict was dubbed the "Era of Good Feelings." Despite the decline of one party and the rise of another, however, the nature of the parties did not change. It was a time during which government and politics were the business of an elite of well-known, well-established men, and the parties reflected the politics of the time. In both of his successful races for the presidency (1816 and 1820), Monroe was the nominee only of the Democratic-Republican caucus in the Congress. The absence of party competition, moreover, made extensive grass roots organization unnecessary, thus stalling further development of the parties.

The early politics of the country began, however, to undergo sharp changes in the 1820s. The struggle for universal white male suffrage, focused primarily on eliminating real property qualifications for voting, was over in most states by that decade—at least where state and federal elections were concerned. (Property qualifications lingered in local elections, in some places into the twentieth century, where revenues were raised from assessments on property.) The growing tide of democratization also made more public officials subject to popular election.[10]

The most obvious change in the 1820s, occurring so precipitously at the national level that its evolutionary foundation in the states often is obscured, was the emergence of the presidential election process that has endured to this day. The framers of the Constitution had crafted a curious arrangement for the selection of the president, which has come to be known as the electoral college. They prescribed a method of indirect election in which each state, in a manner determined by its legislature, would choose a number of presidential electors equivalent to the size of its congressional delegation; these electors in turn would meet in the state to cast their votes for president, with the winner being the candidate who receive a majority of electoral votes. If no candidate received a majority, the president was to be selected by the House of Representatives, with one vote per state. With the electoral college arrangement, the Constitutional Convention was able to sidestep some difficult and divisive questions regarding selection of the chief executive. Leaving the choice of electors to the state legislatures avoided the setting of uniform election methods and suffrage requirements (involving also the contentious matter of slavery), issues on which

---

[9]See Chambers, *Political Parties in a New Nation;* Joseph Charles, *The Origins of the American Party System* (New York: Harper & Row, 1961); and John F. Hoadley, *Origins of American Political Parties 1789–1803* (Lexington: University of Kentucky Press, 1986).

[10]For a detailed account of the extension of the suffrage, focusing on the separate actions of the states, see Chilton Williamson, *American Suffrage: From Property to Democracy* (Princeton: Princeton University Press, 1960).

the framers themselves were divided and on which federal intervention to dictate state practices where the states had hitherto enjoyed autonomy might have produced state opposition. Requiring electors to meet simultaneously within their respective states also prevented a cabal among electors to put forward their own choice for president.

In the early years state legislatures adopted various methods for selecting presidential electors. From the first, a few states adopted popular elections, albeit typically with electorates restricted to property owners or taxpayers. This number grew during the next three decades, although unevenly as partisan majorities within the state legislatures engaged in the time-honored practice of manipulating election laws to their short-term advantage. Lame-duck Federalist legislatures were especially active around 1800 in turning to popular election to avoid the sure results of a transition in legislative control to the Democratic-Republicans. By the 1820s, though, popular election had come to predominate, and after 1828 only in South Carolina were presidential electors selected by the state legislature.[11]

The move in the states to popular election of presidential electors in the 1820s coincided with and contributed to the demise of the congressional caucus in presidential nominations. With their hegemony in Congress and the country in the two decades after 1800, the Democratic-Republicans were able to select the president through their control of the nomination process. As the tide of democratization strengthened, however, the practice of caucus nominations fell under increasing criticism as the work of a narrow-based and self-perpetuating elite. Quite apart from criticism, however, the caucus system began to decline from its own infirmities. The attempt of the Democratic-Republicans to nominate a presidential candidate in 1824 was a shambles. The chosen candidate of the caucus, William Crawford, ran fourth in the race, and since no candidate won a majority in the electoral college, it was left to the House of Representatives to choose among John Quincy Adams, Henry Clay, and Andrew Jackson. The House chose Adams over Jackson, the popular and electoral vote front runner in the election. Jackson, in turn, defeated Adams in 1828 as the nation teetered on the edge of a new party politics.

The Emergence of a National Two-Party System

The "new" party politics emerged in the 1830s. First, the nonparty politics of the Era of Good Feelings gave way to the two-party system that has prevailed ever since. Andrew Jackson took the frontier and agrarian wing of the Jeffersonians into what we now think of as the Democratic party. The National Republicans, whose candidate in 1832 was Henry Clay, merged with the Whigs, and bipartyism in the United States was born. Second, and just as important, the

---

[11]For a more complete account, see Neal R. Peirce and Lawrence D. Longley, *The People's President* (New Haven: Yale University Press, 1981).

Pressures for Democratization: A Foreign Visitor's View

French nobleman Alexis de Tocqueville is recognized as one of the most astute observers of American democracy. In his travels throughout the country in the early 1830s, he came to appreciate the irresistible force behind the changes in voting rights through the first forty years of the American Republic:

> There is no more invariable rule in the history of society: the further electoral rights are extended, the greater is the need of extending them; for after each concession the strength of the democracy increases, and its demands increase with its strength. The ambition of those who are below the appointed rate is irritated in exact proportion to the great number of those who are above it. The exception at last becomes the rule, concession follows concession, and no stop can be made short of universal suffrage.
>
> ALEXIS DE TOCQUEVILLE
>
> *Democracy in America*
> (New York: Alfred A. Knopf, 1945;
> originally published in French in 1835), p. 57

parties as political institutions began to change. The Jacksonian Democrats held the first national nominating convention in 1832—at which, appropriately, Jackson himself was nominated for a second term. (The Whig and Anti-Masonic parties had both held more limited conventions a year before.) The campaign for the presidency also became more "popular" as new campaign organizations and tactics brought the contest to more and more people. As a consequence, Jackson came to the White House for a second term with a popular mandate as the leader of a national political party. Larger numbers of citizens were voting than had ever voted before as the tide of democratization seemed irresistible (see box).

At the same time, party organization in the states had a new burst of growth, and conventions increasingly replaced caucuses as the means of nominating candidates for state and local office. Before the middle of the century, therefore, party organization was developing throughout the nation, and the party convention—an assemblage of state and local party leaders held both in the states and nationally—became an increasingly common way of picking party candidates. Also, by 1840, the Whigs and the Democrats established themselves as the first truly national party system, one in which both parties were established and competitive in all the states.

Modern political parties—pretty much as we know them today—had thus arrived by the middle of the nineteenth century. They were, in fact, the first modern parties in western history, and their arrival reflected, above all, the early expansion of the electorate in the United States. The comparable development of parties in Great Britain did not occur until the 1870s, after further extension of the adult male electorate in the Reform Acts of 1832 and 1867.

The Dawning of the Golden Age

Just as the parties were reaching their maturity, they and American politics received another massive infusion of voters from a new source: immigration from Europe. Hundreds of thousands of Europeans—the great majority from Ireland and Germany—came to the country before the Civil War. So many immigrated, in fact, that their very coming and their entry into American politics became a political issue. The newcomers found a ready home in the Democratic party; and a nativist third party, the American party (the so-called Know-Nothing party), sprang up in the 1850s. The tide of immigration was only temporarily halted by the Civil War. New nationalities came from 1870 on, in a virtually uninterrupted flow until Congress closed the door to mass immigration in the 1920s. Over five million arrived in the 1880s (they comprised one-tenth of the 1880 resident population), and ten million came between 1905 and 1914 (they comprised one-eighth of the 1900 resident population).

The political parties played an important role in assimilating these huge waves of immigrants. The American cities offered industrial jobs to the newcomers from abroad, and they settled heavily in them. It was there in the cities that a new party organization, the city "machine," developed in response to the immigrants' problems and vulnerabilities. The machines were more than impressively efficient party organizations. They were social service mechanisms that helped the new arrivals cope with a new country and with all the problems of urban, industrial society. They softened the hard edge of poverty, they smoothed the way with government and the law, and they taught the immigrants the ways and customs of their new life. Moreover, they were in many instances indistinguishable from the government of the city; theirs was the classic instance of "party government" in the American experience. They also were the vehicle by which the new urban working class won control of the cities away from the largely Anglo-Saxon, Protestant elites that had prevailed for so long. Thus, the parties again became an instrument of the aspirations of new citizens, just as they had been in the 1830s. In doing so, they achieved the high point of party power and influence in American history.

The American parties—simply as political organizations—thus reached their zenith, something of a "Golden Age" indeed, by the beginning of the twentieth century. Party organization now existed in all the states and localities; it positively flourished in the industrial cities. Parties achieved an all-time high in discipline in the Congress and in most state legislatures. They controlled campaigns for public office—they held rallies, did door-to-door canvassing, and got the voters to the polls. They controlled access to a great deal of public employment. They were an important source of information and guidance for a largely uneducated and often illiterate electorate. Indeed, they rode the crest of an extraordinarily vital American politics; the latter half of the nineteenth century featured the highest voter turnouts in the history of American presidential elections. The parties suited the needs and limitations of the new voters and the problems of mobilizing majorities in the new and raw industrial society. If ever a time and a political organization were well matched, this was it.

Parties after their Golden Age

To be sure, the democratic impetus was not spent by the turn of the century. The electorate continued to expand—with the enfranchisement of women, with the delayed securing of the vote for blacks, and with the lowering of the voting age to eighteen. The move toward direct, popular elections and away from the indirection the Founding Fathers favored also continued its inexorable course with adoption of the Seventeenth Amendment which decreed the direct election of senators. Just as important for the parties, however, were the changes wrought in them in the name of the continuing commitment to egalitarianism and popular democracy. What was a "Golden Age" for parties in terms of their influence over the American political process was seen disparagingly by many as a "Gilded Age," in which party control of politics had bred rampant corruption and inefficiency in government. Fat, powerful, and even arrogant at the end of the nineteenth century, the parties fell under attack by the Progressive reformers and never have regained the exalted position they enjoyed in the three decades after the Civil War. The reformers enacted the direct primary to give the citizenry a voice in party nominations, and large numbers of state legislatures wrote laws to define and limit party organizations. The business of nominating a president was made more popular by the establishment of presidential primaries in the states, and activists within the parties reformed their national conventions. All in all, by the 1990s, Americans had a pair of parties and a party politics born and shaped in the triumph of the democratic ethos and its expectations.[12]

The reforms of the twentieth century were to some extent intended to diminish the power and position the parties had achieved by the end of the 1800s. To that extent, they succeeded. For these and a number of other reasons, the heyday of the American parties passed. The theme of the decline of the parties runs through many commentaries on the American parties these days, and it will certainly run through this one.

Even so, the parties remain to a considerable extent what they were eighty or a hundred years ago: the preeminent political organizations of mass, popular democracy. They developed and grew with the expansion of the suffrage and the popularizing of electoral politics. They were and remain the invention by which large numbers of voters come together to control the selection of their

---

[12]For a spirited account of the development of American political parties from the disapproving normative perspective of a foreign observer, consult Moisei Ostrogorski, *Democracy and the Organization of Political Parties, Volume II: The United States* (Garden City, N.Y.: Anchor Books, Doubleday and Company, 1964; originally published in 1902). On reform of the parties generally, see Austin Ranney, *Curing the Mischiefs of Faction* (Berkeley: University of California Press, 1975).

representatives. They rose to prominence at a time when a new electorate of limited knowledge and limited political sophistication needed the guidance of their symbols. Thus it was that the modern American political party was born and reached its time of glory in the nineteenth century. When one talks today of the decline of the parties, it is the standard of that Golden Age against which the decline is measured.

THE PARTY IN ITS ENVIRONMENT

This brief excursion into the historical development of American parties calls attention to forces in their environment that shape both their form and their activities. There is a temptation in a book on political parties to treat them more or less in isolation. Yet, useful as this isolation is for focusing attention, it may give the false impression that political parties are autonomous structures, moving without constraint within the political system. Once the importance of environmental pressures is recognized, though, one must resist the opposite temptation to imagine a party environment that includes virtually every other structure and process in the political system and a great deal outside it. Some influences on the parties clearly are more powerful and insistent than others. It will suffice to limit a discussion of the parties' environment to these.

Electorates and Elections

As the preceding section indicates, the expansion of the American electorate shaped the very origin and development of the parties as political organizations. Furthermore, each new group of voters that enters the electorate challenges the parties to readjust their appeals. The parties must compete for the votes and support of new voters, and the necessity of doing so forces them to reconsider their strategies for building the coalitions that can win elections.

Similarly, the fortunes of the parties are also bound up with the nature of American elections. The move from indirect toward direct elections transformed both the contesting of elections and the parties that contested them. Should we finally come to direct election of the American president, that change, too, would have its impact on the parties.

The election machinery in a state may indeed be thought of as an extensive regulation of the parties' chief political activity. At least, it is often difficult to determine where the regulation of the party ends and reform of electoral practices begins. Consider, for example, the replacement of nomination by conventions with the direct primary. It is both a significant addition to the machinery of American electoral processes and a sharp regulation of the way a party selects the candidates who bear its label in an election. And it was aimed by its originators, the Progressives, at diminishing party power. Even the relatively minor differences in primary law from one state to another—such as differences in the form of the ballot or the time of the year in which the primary occurs—are not without their impact on the parties. In short, the collective electoral institutions of the nation and of the fifty states set a matrix of rules and boundaries within which the parties compete for public office.

The Political Institutions

Very little in the American political system escapes the influence of the two most prominent American institutional features—federalism and the separation of powers. At the national level and in the states, American legislators and executives are elected independently of one another, and sometimes (frequently in recent years) the legislature and executive have come under the control of opposing parties. Most of the world's democracies, by contrast, have parliamentary systems in which the legislative majority chooses executive officials from among its own members. When that parliamentary majority dissolves, its control of the executive ends, and a new government must be formed. The American legislative parties rarely even approach the degree of party discipline and party cohesion that is common in parliamentary systems, and there is sometimes even conflict between legislators and the executive of the same party. One reason is that the chief executive and cabinet secretaries are not simultaneously legislative party leaders as they are in a parliamentary system. Another is that legislative defiance of the executive on key party issues does not threaten to bring down the entire government and force new elections. Support for and opposition to executive programs often cut sharply across party lines in the American system, to a degree rarely found in the parliamentary democracies.

The decentralization of American federalism, with its islands of state autonomy from national control, also has left its imprint on the American parties. It has instilled in them local political loyalties and generations of local, often provincial, political traditions. It has spawned an awesome range and number of public offices to fill, creating an electoral politics that in size and diversity dwarfs that of all other political systems. By permitting local rewards, local traditions, even local patronage systems, it has sustained a whole set of semi-autonomous local parties within the two parties. The establishment of these local centers of power has worked mightily against the development of strong permanent national party organs.

Statutory Regulation

No other parties among the democracies of the world are so entangled in legal regulations as are the American parties. It was not always this way. Prior to the progressive reforms near the beginning of the twentieth century, American parties essentially were self-governing political organizations, virtually unrestrained by state or federal law in pursuit of their core activities. They nominated candidates for office by their own rules. The arrival of the secret ballot and the direct primary around 1900 and recent reforms of the presidential nomination process at the behest of national party commissions but under the aegis of state laws have severely circumscribed this autonomy. Before the introduction of the secret ballot, the parties printed, distributed, and with a wary eye upon one another often even counted the ballots. The Australian (or secret) ballot reform changed all of this, vesting the responsibility for running elections in government, where it has remained ever since. The parties even played an active role in the distribution of government jobs, a practice that has largely disappeared under successive waves of civil service reform and judicial intervention (some of which has taken place only in the past decade).

Both state and, to a still limited degree, federal laws govern the parties today—producing an almost bewildering fifty-state variety of political parties. The forms of their organization are prescribed by the states in endless, often finicky, detail. The statutes on party organization set up grandiose layers of party committees and often chart the details of who will compose them, when they will meet, and what their agenda will be. State law also defines the parties themselves, often by defining the right to place candidates on the ballot. A number of states also undertake to regulate the activities of parties; many, for example, regulate their finances, and most place at least some limits on their campaign practices. So severe can these regulations be, in fact, that in some states the parties have tried various strategies to evade the worst of the burdens. In recent years, the parties increasingly have been subjected to federal regulation—in campaign practices and finances as well as through federal proscriptions against certain state practices, especially involving primary and general elections.[13]

The Political Culture

It is one thing to specify such tangibles in the parties' environment as regulatory statutes, electoral mechanisms, and even political institutions. It is quite another, however, to pin down so elusive a part of the party environment as the political culture. A nation's political culture is the all-enveloping network of the political norms, values, and expectations of its people. It is, in other words, the people's conglomerate view of what the political system is, what it should be, and what their place is in it.

The feeling that party politics is a compromising, somewhat dirty business has been a major and persistent component of the American political culture. Public opinion polls give evidence of that hostility toward partisan politics in recent years. A number of polls have found, for example, that American parents prefer that their sons and daughters not choose a full-time political career. In their estimation, politics as a vocation compares unfavorably with most occupations. In September of 1988, for example, the Gallup Poll asked a national

---

[13]So extensive is government regulation of political parties that Leon Epstein is moved to regard them as public utilities rather than the private associations they were during the nineteenth century. See his *Political Parties in the American Mold* (Madison: University of Wisconsin Press, 1986), pp. 155–99.

sample to rate the "honesty and ethical standards" of people in a number of vocations. Although a majority rated pharmacists, clergy, college teachers, doctors, and dentists "high" or "very high," political officeholders received ratings no higher than 19 percent. They were ranked in about the same position as lawyers, business executives, union leaders, and insurance salespeople—but somewhat above car salespeople, who are at the bottom of the list.[14]

More systematic review of American attitudes toward the party system points similarly to a low level of popular support for the parties. In 1973, for example, a national sample of adults was asked to pick among four possibilities in identifying which "part of the government" they most often trusted "to do what's right." The Congress and the Supreme Court were each chosen by more than 30 percent of the sample, and almost 24 percent chose the president. Only 1.3 percent chose the political parties.[15] As recently as 1980, moreover, a bare majority of just 52 percent disagreed with the statement "we probably don't need political parties in America anyway."[16]

Suspicion of things partisan is only one element, however, in a multifaceted political culture that shapes the American parties. The views of Americans are relevant on such broad points as representative democracy itself. A Burkean view of representation, which holds that the representative ought to decide public questions on the basis of his or her own information and wisdom, certainly retards the development of party discipline in American legislatures. More detailed public attitudes govern even such matters as the incentives for party activity and the kinds of campaign tactics a party or candidate chooses. Indeed, the whole issue of what we consider fair or ethical campaigning is simply a reflection of the norms and expectations of large numbers of Americans.

The Nonpolitical Environment

Much of the parties' nonpolitical environment works on them through the elements of the political environment. Changes in levels of education, for example, affect the political culture, the skills of the electorate, and the levels of political information. Great jolts in the economy alter the structure of political issues and the goals of the electorate. Educational levels and socioeconomic status also seem related to elements of the political culture. Less-educated Americans seem to accept party loyalty and discipline more easily than the better educated do. Even general social values are quickly translated into political values. Acceptance of a Catholic candidate for the American presidency had to await

---

[14]The Gallup Poll, September 23–26, 1988. Reported in *The Gallup Report* #279, December, 1988, pp. 2–3.

[15]Jack Dennis, "Trends in Public Support for the American Party System," *British Journal of Political Science* 5 (1976): 187–230.

[16]This answer came in response to a question posed to a national sample of Americans in 1980 by the American National Election Study conducted by the Center for Political Studies at the University of Michigan.

changes in social attitudes about religion in general and about Catholicism in particular. A continuing liberalization of social attitudes may extend this acceptance fully to women and blacks as well.

Whether the impact of the nonpolitical environment is direct or indirect, however, may be beside the point. The impact is strong and often disruptive. The advent of a recession, for example, may have important repercussions on the parties. It may make raising money more difficult; it will certainly make patronage positions more attractive and perhaps even shift the incentives for recruiting the workers on whom the party organizations rely. It will also certainly define a very important issue for the electorate. If the crisis is especially severe, as was the Great Depression of the 1930s, it may even fracture and reorganize the pattern of enduring party loyalties.

What began in this chapter as a search for the distinctiveness of the parties has thus concluded by looking at how they became what they are. To be sure, it is important to have a firm grasp of what we mean when we refer to a political party—especially to understand its peculiar three-part nature: the party organization, the party in the electorate, and the party in government. Answers to the questions about party transformation or decline, so prominent in recent years here and in Eastern Europe, depend upon what we mean by *party*. The search for the parties, however, is, paradoxically, a search for more than the parties. It is incomplete without a grasp of the context, the environment, in which they are set and by which they are shaped.

Chapter

2

The American
Two-Party System

The most common party systems are those in which either one political party dominates political life or many parties compete with one another for control of government. One-party systems have appeared in such diverse places as the Soviet Union and Eastern Europe, where only the Communist party could contest elections until recently, and Mexico, where the Partido Revolucionario Institucional (or PRI) has monopolized presidential, gubernatorial, and legislative elections for decades. By contrast, the European democracies typically harbor multiparty systems, in which three, four, or more parties compete with one another without any single party being able to win a majority of the votes.[1]

One-partyism and multipartyism certainly are not alien to the American experience. Some states or cities have had a long tradition of one-party hegemony which, if not as total as that characterizing Eastern Europe and the USSR before 1989 or China today, nonetheless rivals the single-party control enjoyed by Mexico's PRI. In other areas, at certain times multipartyism has flourished. Minor or third parties and independent candidates have played important if transient roles in American politics. These varieties of multipartyism have appeared at the presidential level in recent years. George C. Wallace captured almost 10 million popular votes in 1968 on the American Independent party ticket and came within 32 electoral votes of throwing the entire election into the unpredictable hands of the House of Representatives. In 1980 John Anderson, running without any party label, won almost 6 million popular votes.

However colorful or captivating these incursions into two-party control may have been, we must not let them divert our attention from the routines of American politics. For most of our history in most elections, two parties—not one or many—have fought only one another for victory. Even the rapid rise of

---

[1]See Kenneth Janda, *Political Parties: A Cross-National Survey* (New York: Free Press, 1980), for a comprehensive survey of the world's party systems.

the Republican party from its founding in 1854 to become one of two major parties two years later, displacing the Whig party in the process, is the third party exception that proves the rule. First Democrat versus Whig, and since 1856, Democrat versus Republican, the United States has had a *two-party system*—a duopoly in national party competition.

The conventional terminology we use to describe party systems—one-party, two-party, multiparty—is based on two related major premises: that parties are primarily electoral organizations and that their electoral activities are carried out in direct competition with other electoral parties. The designation of a one-party, two-party, or multiparty system simply indicates the number of political parties able to compete for office with some prospect of success. It depends upon a distinction between the competitive major parties and the noncompetitive minor parties. What we call the party system, therefore, is composed only of the electorally competitive parties.

For all its elegant simplicity (and to some extent because of it), this conventional classification of party systems has a number of significant shortcomings.

- It focuses solely on the electoral dimension of the competition among political organizations. Consequently, it overlooks the possibility that minor parties compete ideologically or programmatically with major parties, even though they do not compete electorally.
- By focusing only on the political parties, it ignores the full range of competition among all kinds of political organizations.
- By classifying parties exclusively by electoral competition, it ignores any differences in organization the parties may have and centers its measurement on the size of the party's electorate.
- Finally, it tends to ignore the implications of the word *system*. It overlooks the relationships and interactions one expects in any system and settles merely for the presence of competitive parties and their presumed competings in elections.

This concept of the party system is deeply ingrained in both everyday use and scholarly literature in spite of its limitations. One has little choice but to work within its terms—while bearing in mind that it may oversimplify, as most classification schemes do, a more complex political reality.[2]

THE NATIONAL PARTY SYSTEM

The American party system is and has been essentially a two-party system for the past 150 years. Beyond all subtle variations in competition, there is the inescapable, crucial fact that almost all partisan political conflict in the United States has been channeled through two major political parties. They rise and

---

[2]For a sophisticated critique of the traditional classification and analysis of party systems, see Giovanni Sartori, *Parties and Party Systems* (New York: Cambridge University Press, 1976).

fall, they establish their seats of strength, they suffer their local weaknesses, but they endure. Perhaps even more remarkable is the fact that one does not easily find another democracy in which two parties have so long and so thoroughly dominated politics.

The Republic, though, has not always had a two-party system (see box). The period before 1836 was one of instability in the party system. The Federalists established a short period of superiority during the presidency of George Washington but faded quickly with the rise and success of the Democratic Republicans. They rode their success to a brief period of dominance that culminated in the one-party (or nonparty) politics of Monroe's two terms. As the caucus method of nominations crumbled in the 1820s, however, new national parties appeared, and by 1836 a stable two-party system had emerged. For the more than 150 years since then, one party—the Democratic party—has sustained a place in the party system. In opposition, the Whigs survived until the 1850s and were replaced almost immediately by the infant Republican party. Both the Democratic and Republican parties were briefly divided by the events of the Civil War, but old party lines and labels survived the war and, indeed, survive to this day.

Thus, the two-party drama is long but its cast of major characters is short. Minor parties have briefly pushed themselves into competitiveness but, significantly, never for two presidential elections in a row. The Democratic and Republican parties have also changed, of course, in their issues and appeals and in the coalitions that are their "parties in the electorate." All of those hedges, however, do not hide the fact that for more than 130 years, the Democratic and Republican parties have together made up the American two-party system.

The longevity of the two major parties, exceptional in itself, is almost overshadowed by the closeness of their competition. Of the thirty-one presidential elections from 1868 through 1988, only six were decided by a spread of more than 20 percent in the popular vote of the two major parties; that is, in twenty-five of the elections, a shift of 10 percent of the vote or less would have given the other party's candidate the lead. Also, only four of the winners of those thirty-one presidential elections received more than 60 percent of the total popular vote: Warren G. Harding in 1920, Franklin Roosevelt in 1936, Lyndon Johnson in 1964, and Richard Nixon in 1972. Thirteen of the thirty-one were decided by a spread of less than 7 percent of the popular vote, and presidential elections have generally been so close that Dwight D. Eisenhower's 57.4 percent of the popular vote in 1956 was widely called a landslide. The shade over 61 percent with which Lyndon Johnson won in 1964 also set a new record for a president's percentage of the popular vote.[3] The 1960s also saw two of the closest presidential elections in American history. In 1960, John F. Kennedy polled only 0.2

[3] The reader may be confused here about political record keeping. Note that this 61.1 percent vote for Lyndon Johnson was his percentage of the total popular vote. Other relevant records in presidential elections are the greatest electoral college vote—Ronald Reagan in 1984, with 525 votes—and the greatest percentage of the two-party popular vote—Calvin Coolidge in 1924, with 65.2 percent.

The American Major Parties

The list of the American major parties is short and select. In almost 200 years of history, only five political parties have achieved a competitive position in American national politics. Three lost it; the Democrats and Republicans maintain it to this day.

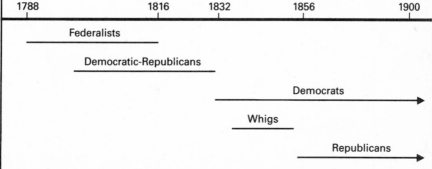

1788   1816   1832   1856   1900

1. *The Federalists.* The party of the new Constitution and strong national government, it was the first American political party. Its strength was rooted in the Northeast and the Atlantic seaboard, where it attracted the support of merchants, landowners, and established families of wealth and status. Limited by its narrow electoral base, it quickly fell before the success of the Democratic-Republicans.
2. *The Democratic-Republicans.* Opposed to the nationalism of the Federalists, it was a party of the small farmers, workers, and less privileged citizens who preferred the authority of the states. Like its founder, Thomas Jefferson, it shared many of the ideals of the French Revolution, especially the extension of the suffrage and the notion of direct popular self-government.
3. *The Democrats.* Growing out of the Jacksonsian wing of the Democratic-Republicans, it was initially Jackson's party and the first really broad-based, popular party in the United States. On behalf of a coalition of less-privileged voters, it opposed such commercial goals as national banking and high tariffs; it also welcomed the new immigrants and opposed nativist opposition to them.
4. *The Whigs.* This party, too, had roots in the old Jeffersonian party—in the Clay-Adams faction and in enmity to the Jacksonians. Opposed in its origins to the strong presidency of Jackson, its greatest leaders, Clay and Webster, were embodiments of legislative supremacy. For its short life, the Whig party was an unstable coalition of many interests, among them nativism, property, and the new business and commerce.
5. *The Republicans.* Born in 1854 as the Civil War approached, it was the party of northern opposition to slavery and its spread to the new territories. Therefore, it was also the party of the Union, the North, Lincoln, the freeing of slaves, victory in the Civil War, and the imposition of Reconstruction. From the Whigs, it also inherited a concern for business, mercantile, and propertied interests.

percent of the popular vote more than Richard Nixon; Mr. Nixon, in turn, led the popular vote by only 0.7 percent in 1968.[4]

As close as the results of the presidential elections have been, the elections to Congress have been even closer. If we move to percentages of the two-party vote for ease of comparison, we quickly note the remarkable balance between the aggregate votes cast for Democratic and Republican candidates for the House of Representatives from all over the United States for over fifty years (Table 2.1). From 1932 through 1990, in none of the biennial elections to the House of Representatives was there a difference greater than seventeen percentage points in the division of the two-party vote. The mean absolute percentage spread between the candidates of the two parties for the House from 1932 through 1990 was 7.5; it was 11.9 for the presidential candidates in the same period. Perhaps even more telling, in every year except 1948, 1960, 1968, 1976, and 1988, the margin between the two parties' Congressional votes was smaller than that between the presidential aspirants.

The closeness and persistence of party competition in national politics is apparent, therefore, in even the quickest survey of recent electoral history. Even more impressive, perhaps, is the resilience of the major parties. Although from time to time the parties have lapsed from closely matched competitiveness, in the long run they have shown a remarkable facility for restoring balance. The Democrats recovered quickly from their failures of the 1920s, and the GOP (a common nickname for the Republican party since the late 1800s) confounded the pessimists by springing back from the Roosevelt victories of the 1930s. Also, despite the catastrophes of Watergate and the Nixon administration, the Republicans came back strongly in the 1980s.

Is this aggregate record of winning and losing in national elections what we mean by a two-party system? Well, yes and no. It does express the vote support for national candidates running on national issues under national party labels. Indeed, the struggle for the presidency every four years is undoubtedly the one occasion on which we actually do have national parties and a national party system. On the other hand, such measures are only aggregates, and they obscure the possibility of other types of party systems at a more localized level. That is, statements about national competitiveness gloss over the issue of how unevenly the competitiveness is spread over the states and localities of the nation.

THE FIFTY AMERICAN PARTY SYSTEMS

Overlooked in the closeness of both presidential elections and the aggregate vote for the House of Representatives is the one-partyism below the national

---

[4]A persuasive case can be made, in fact, that Nixon actually led Kennedy in the popular vote; the different conclusion depends on how one counts the votes cast for the unpledged electors in Alabama. For a statement of the problem, see Lawrence D. Longley and Alan G. Braun, *The Politics of Electoral College Reform*, 2nd ed. (New Haven: Yale University Press, 1975), pp. 5–6.

TABLE 2.1   PERCENTAGE OF TWO-PARTY VOTE WON BY REPUBLICAN CANDIDATES
FOR THE PRESIDENCY AND HOUSE OF REPRESENTATIVES: 1932–90

| | Presidential Election | | House Election | |
Year	Percentage Republican	Percentage Spread Between Republican and Democratic Candidates	Percentage Republican	Percentage Spread Between Republican and Democratic Candidates
1932	40.9	−18.2	43.1	−13.8
1934			43.8	−12.4
1936	37.5	−25.0	41.5	−17.0
1938			49.2	−1.6
1940	45.0	−10.0	47.0	−6.0
1942			52.3	4.6
1944	46.2	−7.6	48.3	−3.4
1946			54.7	9.4
1948	47.7	−4.6	46.8	−6.4
1950			49.9	−0.2
1952	55.4	10.8	50.1	0.2
1954			47.5	−5.0
1956	57.8	15.6	49.0	−2.0
1958			43.9	−12.2
1960	49.9	−0.2	45.0	−10.0
1962			47.4	−5.2
1964	38.7	−22.6	42.5	−15.0
1966			48.7	−2.6
1968	50.4	0.8	49.1	−1.8
1970			45.6	−8.8
1972	61.8	23.6	47.3	−5.4
1974			43.0	−14.0
1976	48.9	−2.2	42.8	−14.4
1978			45.6	−8.8
1980	55.3	10.6	48.7	−2.6
1982			43.8	−12.4
1984	59.2	18.3	47.2	−5.6
1986			44.9	−10.2
1988	53.9	7.8	46.0	−8.0
1990			46.0	−6.8

Sources: Data from 1932 through 1960 from Donald E. Stokes and Gudmund R. Iverson, "On the Existence of Forces Restoring Party Competition," *Public Opinion Quarterly* 26 (Summer 1962): 162. Data for 1962 through 1986 from the *Statistical Abstract of the United States* (1989). Data for 1988 and 1990 from *Congressional Quarterly Weekly Report,* May 6, 1989, p. 1063, and November 10, 1990, pp. 3847–54, respectively.

level. It was not until 1964, for example, that Georgia cast its first electoral votes for a Republican and Vermont voted for a Democrat for the first time since the Civil War. Also, although one may talk of the aggregate closeness of the biennial elections to the House, the aura of competitiveness vanishes if one looks at the individual races. Significant numbers of candidates win election to the House of Representatives with at least 60 percent of the total vote: in 1990, in fact, 73 percent of them did—63 were elected without any opposition whatsoever.

If we are to discuss the varying degrees of competitiveness of the fifty state party systems, however, the practical problem of defining *competitiveness* must be faced. Yet the measurement of competition is hardly straightforward. It requires resolution of several difficult issues. First, which offices should be counted—president, governor, senator, statewide officials, state legislators? Singly or in what combination? A state may show strikingly different competitive patterns between its national and its state and local politics. Second, should we count vote totals and percentages or simply the offices won? Do we regard a party that averages 45 percent of the vote, but never wins office, any differently than one that averages around the 25 percent mark but occasionally is victorious? Third, how can we take into account the relative standings of more than two parties? Measuring two-party competition is easy, because it can be summarized by a single number. Beyond two parties the representation necessarily becomes more complex.

Fortunately, in categorizing the party systems of the American states, one can dismiss the possibility of multiparty systems. To be sure, there are a few examples of them in the American experience. In Minnesota, Wisconsin, and North Dakota in the 1930s and 1940s, remnants of the Progressive movement— the Progressive party in Wisconsin, the Farmer-Labor party in Minnesota, and the Non-Partisan League in North Dakota—competed with some success against the major parties. In these and a few other instances of statewide multipartyism in the recent American past, however, the period of multipartyism was brief and ended with a return to two-partyism.

The Ranney Index

The most familiar approach to measuring interparty competition in the states is the Ranney index.[5] It is an average of three indicators of Democratic strength over a specified time period: the percentage of the popular vote for Democratic

[5]The original measurements were presented for 1946–63 in Austin Ranney, "Parties in State Politics," in Herbert Jacob and Kenneth Vines, eds., *Politics in the American States* (Boston: Little, Brown, 1965), p. 65. Ranney's categories, in turn, were derived from those of Richard Dawson and James Robinson, "Inter-Party Competition, Economic Variables, and Welfare Policies in the American States," *Journal of Politics* 25 (1963): 265–89. For an examination of the properties of the Ranney index, see James D. King, "Interparty Competition in the American States: An Examination of Index Components," *Western Political Quarterly* 42 (1989): 83–92.

TABLE 2.2   THE FIFTY STATES CLASSIFIED ACCORDING TO
DEGREE OF INTERPARTY COMPETITION: 1981–88

One-Party Democratic	Two-Party	Modified One-Party Republican
Mississippi (.86)	Iowa (.64)	Wyoming (.34)
	Minnesota (.64)	New Hampshire (.34)
	Illinois (.64)	Colorado (.33)
Modified One-Party Democratic	Tennessee (.64)	Idaho (.30)
	Missouri (.62)	South Dakota (.26)
	Oregon (.60)	Utah (.25)
Alabama (.84)	Connecticut (.58)	
Louisiana (.81)	Ohio (.54)	**One-Party Republican**
Arkansas (.80)	Vermont (.53)	
South Carolina (.79)	Michigan (.52)	
Kentucky (.77)	Nebraska (.52)	(none)
Hawaii (.77)	Montana (.51)	
West Virginia (.77)	New Jersey (.51)	
Georgia (.76)	North Dakota (.50)	
Maryland (.76)	Delaware (.50)	
Texas (.75)	New York (.49)	
Virginia (.74)	Nevada (.49)	
Massachusetts (.74)	Alaska (.47)	
Florida (.74)	Pennsylvania (.47)	
Oklahoma (.74)	Arizona (.39)	
Rhode Island (.72)	Kansas (.39)	
Maine (.70)	Indiana (.36)	
North Carolina (.70)		
Wisconsin (.68)		
Washington (.67)		
New Mexico (.67)		
California (.66)		

Source: John F. Bibby, Cornelius P. Cotter, James L. Gibson, and Robert J. Huckshorn, "Parties in State Politics," in Virginia Gray, Herbert Jacob, and Robert B. Albritton, eds., *Politics in the American States,* Fifth Edition (Glenview, Ill.: Scott Foresman, 1990). Copyright © 1990 by Virginia Gray, Herbert Jacob, and Robert B. Albitron. Reprinted by permission of HarperCollins Publishers.

gubernatorial candidates, the percentage of seats held by Democrats in the legislature, and the percentage of the time the Democrats held both the governorship and a majority in the state legislature. The resulting scores range from 1.00 (complete Democratic success) through .50 (Democratic and Republican parity) to .00 (complete Republican success).

Like any other summary measure, the Ranney index oversimplifies and sometimes distorts the nature of competition. In particular, it is based wholly on state offices. While this protects the measure from abnormal patterns of national politics that may accompany landslide victories, such as those of Ronald Reagan in 1984, it ignores national electoral patterns that may foreshadow what will occur in voting for state offices. In the South, for example, growing GOP strength has been reflected best in competition for national offices. The result is that a few states have emerged in which one party dominates contests for national offices while the other party dominates in state offices (e.g., Mississippi). A second problem is that the dividing lines between categories are purely arbitrary. There is no magic threshold that separates competitive from one-party. Finally, any index score of course will vary depending upon the years on which it is calculated and the offices it covers, so one must beware of reifying a state's level of competition using its Ranney index number.

Snapshots are of great descriptive value, though, even if they can not capture fully a complex and dynamic reality. Table 2.2 presents the most recent calculations for the Ranney index, covering the elections in the 1980s. It shows only one solidly one-party state—a far cry from the eight states (all southern) that fell into that category during the 1946–63 period. Conversely, the number of modified Democratic states has grown from nine to twenty-one, and there is a slight decline in both two-party and modified Republican states. Compared to the earlier snapshot, then, the states are at once more competitive, because of the decline in one-party states, and somewhat more Democratic.[6]

Variations in two-party competition among the fifty states provide the raw material for explanations of how competition develops and is sustained. For the 1970–80 period, for example, the states exhibiting the greatest degree of competition had several distinctive characteristics, and there is little reason to suppose this has changed in the 1980s. They had a more educated citizenry, stronger local party organizations, larger and more urbanized populations, and more widespread home ownership. That the southern states are less competitive may be attributed in part to their low standing on these characteristics.[7]

Intrastate Competition

Useful as they are for depicting the statewide situation, however, such indices gloss over important differences in competition *within* the states. One rarely finds competitiveness evenly spread through any one state. Party strength typically varies along urban-suburban-rural lines and among sections of the

---

[6]See Harvey J. Tucker, "Interparty Competition in the American States," *American Politics Quarterly* 10 (1982): 93–116; and Patrick J. Kenney and Tom W. Rice, "Party Composition in the American States: Clarifying Concepts and Explaining Changes in Partisanship since the 1950s," *Political Behavior* 7 (1985): 335–51.

[7]These were the results of a study relating the measure in Table 2.2 (but for the 1970–80 period) to various characteristics of the states. See Samuel C. Patterson and Gregory A. Caldeira, "The Etiology of Partisan Competition," *American Political Science Review* 78 (1984): 691–707. Studies of the factors conducive to competition also have been conducted in smaller units. See, for example, Charles M. Bonjean and Robert L. Lineberry, "The Urbanization-Party Competition Hypothesis: A Comparison of All United States Counties," *Journal of Politics* 32 (1970): 305–21.

state on the basis of settlement patterns, dominant economic interests, and life-styles. California, for example, seems to have several different political regions—the Bay Area, Los Angeles County, the southern megalopolis outside of Los Angeles County, the coast between Los Angeles and San Francisco, and the interior. Its two largest metropolitan areas exhibited mirror-image voting patterns in the 1988 presidential elections: The San Francisco media market provided a 393,000-vote advantage to Dukakis, while the Los Angeles media market gave an almost identical 394,000-vote margin to Bush.[8] One result of such checkered patterns of local one-party dominance is that statewide elections generally are more intensely competitive than local contests.

Thus, it is difficult to speak even of a *state* party system. On close inspection, each one is an aggregate of different competitive patterns. It is not at all unusual for a party—even one that wins most statewide elections—to have trouble filling its ticket in some local elections. Also powerful officeholders can use a long term and the advantage of office to build a personal following independent of party strength. For the rest of their careers, they may insulate themselves from the normally competitive politics in their states. In fact, nothing dampens two-party competition more effectively than the power of incumbency exercised in a small and homogeneous constituency.

THE CAUSES AND CONDITIONS OF TWO-PARTYISM

Whereas a two-party system has distinguished American politics for well over 150 years, two-party dominance has been rare in the world's other democracies. The contrast leads to an obvious question: Why should the politics of this one nation among so many others have revolved around only two parties? Scholars have offered several different explanations for this American uniqueness.

Institutional Theories

By far the most widespread explanation of the two-party system, often called Duverger's law, associates it with electoral and governmental institutions.[9] It

---

[8]These totals are cited in Michael Barone and Grant Ujifusa, *The Almanac of American Politics 1990* (Washington, D.C.: National Journal, 1990), p. 72. For an intensive examination of the differences between these two political cultures, see Raymond E. Wolfinger and Fred I. Greenstein, "Comparing Political Regions: The Case of California," *American Political Science Review* 63 (1969): 74–85.

[9]The institutional theorists are best represented by Maurice Duverger, *Political Parties* (New York: Wiley, 1954); and E. E. Schattschneider, *Party Government* (New York: Rinehart, 1942). For more recent evidence of the influence of electoral institutions on the size of the party system, see William Riker, "The Two-Party System and Duverger's Law," *American Political Science Review* 76 (1982):

(*continued*)

argues that single-member districts with plurality electoral systems produce two-party systems. A corollary is multimember constituencies and proportional representation result in multipartyism. Plurality election in a single-member district means simply that one candidate is elected and that the winner is the person who receives the largest number of votes, even if it is not a majority. There are no rewards for parties or candidates that run second, third, or fourth. In a system of proportional representation, on the other hand, legislators are elected on party slates in multimember districts in proportion to the strength of the vote for their parties. Thus, if a district sends five members to the parliament, the breakdown might be:

Party A	39% of vote	2 seats
Party B	36% of vote	2 seats
Party C	20% of vote	1 seat
Party D	5% of vote	—
	100% of vote	5 seats

Parties B and C, by contrast, would win no seats in the American electoral system. The American election system offers no reward of office to any but the single plurality winner and, so the theory goes, thus discourages the minority parties.[10]

Many institutional theorists also argue that the importance of the single executive in the American system strengthens the tendencies toward two-partyism. The American presidency and the governorships—the main prizes of American politics—fall only to parties that can win pluralities. On the contrary, a cabinet in a European nation may be formed by a coalition that includes representatives of minority parties; indeed, even the prize of the premiership may go to a small party. Giovanni Spadolini, the premier of Italy in the early 1980s, came from a party that held less than 3 percent of the parliamentary seats. In countries with a single national executive, the indivisible nature of the office favors the strongest competitors. Beyond the loss of the executive office, moreover, the minor party is denied the national leadership, the focus of the national campaign, and the national spokespersons that increasingly dominate the politics of the democracies. The necessity to contend for a national executive, in other words, works against local or regional parties, even those that may elect candidates in their own bailiwicks.

753–66; and Arend Lijphart, "The Political Consequences of Electoral Laws, 1945–85," *American Political Science Review* 84 (1990): 481–96.

[10]In the past, many states have had multimember districts for one or both houses of the state legislature. As recently as 1955, 58 percent of all state legislative districts were multimember. See Theodore J. Lowi, "Towards a More Responsible Three Party System," *PS* 16 (1983): 699–706. But this number had declined to less than 10 percent by the 1980s. See Samuel C. Patterson, "State Legislators and the Legislatures," in Virginia Gray, Herbert Jacob, and Robert Albritton, eds., *Politics in the American States* (Glenview, Ill.: Scott, Foresman/Little, Brown, 1990), p. 166.

Leon Epstein identifies a third, frequently neglected, institutional factor that has prevented the development of third parties in areas of single-party dominance during the twentieth century—the direct primary. By offering dissident groups an opportunity to compete for nominations within the dominant party, the direct primary keeps them from forming a third party. Thus, in the one-party Democratic South and one-party Republican Wisconsin, where traditional animosities kept most voters from supporting the other major party, factional disputes, that under other conditions would have led to third-party development, were contained within the dominant party by existence of a direct primary.[11]

Dualist Theories

Some theorists maintain that an underlying duality of interest in the American society has sustained the American two-party system. V. O. Key suggested that the initial sectional tension between the eastern financial and commercial interests and the western frontiersmen stamped itself on the parties in their incipient stages and fostered a two-party competition. Later, the dualism shifted to the North-South conflict over the issue of slavery and the Civil War, and then to urban-rural and socioeconomic status divisions. A related line of argument points to a "natural dualism" within democratic institutions: party in power versus party out of power, government versus opposition, pro and anti the status quo, and even the ideological dualism of liberal and conservative. Thus, social and economic interests or the very processes of a democratic politics—or both—reduce the political contestants to two great camps, and that dualism gives rise to two political parties.[12]

Tendencies toward dualism even are apparent in multiparty systems, as the construction of governmental coalitions produces an inevitable dichotomy between government and opposition. In France, for example, the Socialists, Communists, and other parties of the left or the various parties of the right and center often compete against one another initially but then coalesce along largely ideological lines to contest run-off elections or form a government. What distinguishes two-party from multiparty systems, in short, may be where this inherent tendency toward dualism is expressed.

The two major American political parties also play an important role in sustaining this dualism. Their openness to new groups and their adaptability to changing conditions—a permeability rare among democratic parties—undermines the development of strong third parties. Just when a third party rides the crest of a new issue or popular concern to the point where it can challenge the

---

[11]Leon Epstein, *Political Parties in the American Mold* (Madison: University of Wisconsin Press, 1986), pp. 129–32.

[12]See, for example, V. O. Key, Jr., *Politics, Parties and Pressure Groups*, 5th ed. (New York: Crowell, 1964), pp. 229ff.; and Seymour Martin Lipset, Martin A. Trow, and James S. Coleman, *Union Democracy* (New York: Free Press, 1956), especially Part III.

two-party monopoly, one or both of the major parties is likely to absorb the new movement, as the experience of the Populists and the Progressives can attest. Such absorption has become even more likely in the twentieth century as the direct primary has come to be the principal method for selecting party candidates. Disgruntled groups are more likely to pursue opportunities within one of the major parties when those parties offer the possibility of nomination to outsiders.

Cultural Theories

This school of explanation in many ways smacks of the older, largely discredited national character theories. It maintains that the United States and Britain have nurtured two-party systems because of their "political maturity" or their "genius for government." More modestly, it attributes the two-party systems to the development of a political culture that accepts the necessity of compromise, the wisdom of short-term pragmatism, and the avoidance of unyielding dogmatism. Americans and Britons, in other words, are willing to make the kinds of compromises necessary to bring heterogeneous groups of voters into two political parties. Then, as they develop the dual parties, their political cultures also develop the attitudes and norms that endorse the two-party system as a desirable end in itself.[13]

Social Consensus Theories

Finally, the American two-party system has been explained in terms of a wide-sweeping American social consensus. Despite a diverse cultural heritage and society, Americans early achieved a consensus on the fundamentals that divide other societies. Virtually all Americans traditionally have accepted the prevailing social, economic, and political institutions. They accepted the Constitution and its governmental apparatus, a regulated but free-enterprise economy, and (perhaps to a lesser extent) American patterns of social class and status.

In the traditional multiparty countries such as France and Italy, substantial chunks of political opinion have favored radical changes in those and other basic institutions. They have supported programs of fundamental constitutional change, the socialization of the economy, or the disestablishment of the Church. Whether it is because Americans were spared feudalism and its rigid classes, because early widespread enfranchisement obviated the need for American lower classes to organize to gain entry to the system, or because they have had an expanding economic and geographic frontier, they have escaped the division on fundamentals that racks the other democracies and gives rise to large

---

[13]See, for example, James C. Charlesworth, "Is Our Two-Party System Natural?" *Annals of the American Academy of Political and Social Science* 29 (1948): 1–9.

numbers of irreconcilable political divisions. Since the matters that divide Americans are secondary, so the argument goes, the compromises necessary to bring them into one of two major parties are easier to make.[14]

In appraising these explanations of the American two-party system, one has to ask some searching questions. Are the factors proposed in these explanations *causes* of the two-party system, or are they *effects* of it? The chances are that they are, at least in part, effects. Certainly, two competitive parties will choose and perpetuate electoral systems that do not offer entrée to minor parties. Through their control of the legislative process, for example, they have made it difficult for third parties to qualify for the ballot or for third party candidates to receive public funding when it is available. The major parties do what they can to channel opinion into alternatives, reducing and forcing the system's complexities into their dual channels. The two-party system will also create, foster, and perpetuate the political values and attitudes that justify and protect itself. It will even foster some measure of social consensus by denying competitive opportunities to movements that challenge the great consensus of the status quo.

Although these factors may be effects of the two-party system to some degree, they certainly are also causes. The most important cause no doubt is the institutional arrangement of American electoral politics. Without single-member districts, plurality elections, and an indivisible executive, it would have been far easier for third parties to break the virtual electoral monopoly enjoyed by the two major parties. Although third parties play a less subdued role in the other Anglo-American democracies, which share the American institutional arrangements, these systems too tend to be dominated by two parties.

Yet the other forces have contributed to the development of the unique American two-party system as well. The basic, long-run American consensus on fundamental beliefs has prevented the deep cleavages that have marked the politics of many other democracies from developing in the United States. More than one European observer has remarked on the resulting nonideological character of American politics. Consensus has been fostered by American education and social assimilation and has been aided by two major parties inhospitable to challenges to that consensus. If the consensus has eroded to some extent in the last generation, it has done so well after the American two-party system was established and deeply entrenched and seems to pose little threat to the party system.

Lacking cause for deep ideological divisions and disagreeing on few fundamentals, Americans were easily formed into two conglomerate, majority-seeking political parties. The institutions of American electoral politics were free to exert their power to limit the parties to two without having to repulse

---

[14]See Louis Hartz, *The Liberal Tradition in America* (New York: Harcourt, Brace, and World, 1955).

countervailing pressures of social division. So, too, in the absence of deeply felt ideologies, a pragmatic opposition to the party in power was easily able to develop a dualism of the "ins" and the "outs." Moreover, once the two-party system was launched, its very existence fostered the values of moderation, compromise, and political pragmatism that ensured its perpetuation. It also created deep loyalties within the American public to one party or the other and attachments to the two-party system itself.

DEVIATIONS FROM TWO-PARTYISM

That the American party system is essentially a two-party system does not mean that electoral competition is organized around the two parties in every place and at every time. We already have seen that one-partyism is not uncommon within some states and localities. Moreover, some areas have experienced a uniquely American brand of no-party politics, and third parties occasionally have made their presence felt on the political scene. Any exploration of the nature of the American party system, consequently, is incomplete without consideration of these deviations from the predominant two-party mode.

Pockets of One-Party Monopoly

To argue the existence of only two competitive parties is not to argue that their competitiveness is spread evenly over the country. Historically, there have been substantial statewide and local pockets of one-partyism in the United States and signs of these tendencies remain to this day (see Table 2.2). The states of the Deep South have been the country's most celebrated area of one-party domination. Much the same could be said in the past of the rocklike Republicanism of Maine, New Hampshire, and Vermont. Also, scattered throughout the country today are thousands of one-party cities, towns, and counties in which the city hall or county courthouse comes perilously close to being the property of one party. Parallel to the question of the causes of the two-party system, therefore, is the question of the causes of one-partyism within it.

Distribution of the Electorate   One-partyism set within the context of broad, two-party competitiveness often reflects a "fault" in the distribution of the electorates of the competitive parties. Since the 1930s, the major American parties, especially in national elections, have divided the American electorate roughly along lines of socioeconomic status and issues—a point that will be developed later. One-partyism may result from a maldistribution of these characteristics that normally divide the parties. The local constituency may be too small to contain a perfect sample of socioeconomic status (SES) characteristics and thus of competitive politics—hence the noncompetitiveness of the "safe"

Democratic congressional districts of the older, lower-middle-class or black neighborhoods of the cities and the "safe" Republican districts of the more fashionable and spacious suburbs. In other words, the more heterogeneous are its people, the more likely the district is to foster competitiveness.

Regional Loyalties   Alternatively, one-partyism may result from some potent local basis of party loyalty that overrides the SES dualism. In the classic one-partyism of the American South, regional loyalties long overrode the factors that were dividing Americans into two parties in most of the rest of the country. Reaction to the Republican party as the party of abolition, Lincoln, the Civil War, and the hated Reconstruction was so pervasive, even generations after the fact, that the impact of the SES division was greatly diluted. It was thus a one-partyism based on isolation from the factors that normally produced two-party competitiveness and designed to preserve racial segregation. Competitiveness also may reflect the influences of local personages, of powerful officeholders, of local traditions, or of local political conflict, such as that between a dominant industry and its disgruntled employees.

Competitive Disadvantages   That the two parties are not of equal strength in every constituency creates the competitive disadvantages that can enhance one-partyism. These competitive disadvantages begin with stubborn party loyalties. Voters are not easily moved from their attachments to a party, even though the reasons for the original attachment have long passed. Also, a party trying to pull itself into competitiveness may find itself caught in a vicious circle of impotence. Its inability to win elections limits its ability to recruit resources, including manpower, money, and attractive candidates for office, because as a chronic loser it offers so little chance of achieving political goals. It may even find itself without an effective appeal to the electorate. The Republican party in the South, for example, found for many years that the Democrats had pre-empted the salient political issues in that region.

Today, the would-be competitive party finds disadvantage taking another form: the formation of party loyalties along lines determined by national political debate. If the Democratic party is identified nationally with the aspirations of the poor and minority groups, its appeal in a homogeneous, affluent suburb may be limited. Thus, a nationalized politics may increasingly rob the local party organization of the chance to develop strength based on its own issues, personalities, and traditions. To the extent that party loyalties and identifications grow out of national politics, competitiveness (or the lack of it) may be out of the control of the local party organizations.

There are, to be sure, other sources of competitive disadvantage. The dominant party may shore up its supremacy by carefully calculated legislative districting, which is why parties are especially concerned with winning state legislative majorities at the beginning of each decade when district lines are to be redrawn. Another common device for preserving majority party dominance was the malapportionment of legislative districts to overrepresent voters of the party in power, a decades-long practice halted by the Supreme Court in the 1960s. In the past, southern Democrats also stifled competition by maintaining election laws that disenfranchised blacks and poor whites. In addition to these institutional buttresses to one-partyism, of course, the normal processes of socialization and social conformity work to the disadvantage of a local party trying to become competitive. That force of conformity, a number of observers have argued, works especially against competitiveness in closely knit, socially sensitive communities.

The Third Parties

The major party hegemony is occasionally challenged by a new minor party that flashes on to the national scene. But these challenges have been short-lived, and the attention they have received exaggerates their electoral impact. Only seven minor parties in all of American history have carried so much as a single state in a presidential election and only one (the Progressive party) has done so twice (see box). More important, no minor party has come close to winning the presidency. The best minor party records so far were set in 1912 by Teddy Roosevelt and the Progressives, with 17 percent of the electoral vote and 27 percent of the popular vote. That candidacy was, in fact, the only minor party candidacy ever to run ahead of one of the major party candidates in either electoral or popular vote.

Between the peaks of third-party influence are the valleys. In 1964, for example, the leading minor party—the Socialist Labor party—attracted fewer than 46,000 voters, and the minor parties altogether polled only one-sixth of one percent of the popular vote. After the George Wallace phenomenon of 1968—almost 10 million votes for Wallace alone—minor party strength ebbed once again. The total minor party vote for president was only 524,186 in 1984 and 872,638 in 1988 (Table 2.3), or about 0.6 and 1.0 percent, respectively, of the total popular vote for president. More telling, perhaps, was the independent, nonparty campaign of John Anderson in 1980, which drew more than four times the votes of the minor parties combined: 5,720,060.

Third-party successes also can be found below the presidential level, but they are as rare as they are captivating. For every example of third-party success in local elections, such as the 1981–1988 tenure of Socialist Bernard Sanders as mayor of Burlington, Vermont, there are thousands of cases where the major parties have enjoyed unchallenged hegemony. The picture at the state level is even clearer. Of over a thousand governors elected since 1875, only fourteen ran solely on a third-party ticket and another four (all since 1931) were independents. Third-party candidates have been more successful in running for Congress, but the impression gained at high tide when they have won more than ten seats (in 1878, 1880, 1890, 1898, 1912, 1934, and 1936) must be qualified by the low proportion of third-party seats even then and the paucity of third-party representatives in other years. It can be safely said that the Demo-

The Big Little Parties

To put the minor parties in some perspective, we need some point of calibration; that is, we need some measure by which we can compare their electoral strength to that of the major parties and by which we can separate the stronger and weaker minor parties. If we take as a measure the ability to draw at least 10 percent of the popular vote for president, only four parties qualify (numbers 2, 4, 5, and 7 below). If we choose as a more liberal but certainly modest test of strength the ability to carry one state—just one—in a presidential election, only seven minor parties in American history qualify:

1. *Anti-Masonic party.* 1832: 7 electoral votes; 8 percent of the popular vote. A party opposed to the alleged secret political influence of the Masons; later part of an anti-Jackson coalition that formed the Whig party.
2. *American (Know-Nothing) party.* 1856: 8 electoral votes; 22 percent of the popular vote. A nativist party, often in alliance with the fading Whigs, opposed to open immigration and in favor of electing native-born Americans to public office.
3. *People's (Populist) party.* 1892: 22 electoral votes; 8 percent of the popular vote. An outgrowth of a movement of agrarian protest opposed to the economic power of bankers, railroads and fuel industries and in favor of a graduated income tax, government regulation, and currency reform (especially free silver coinage).
4. *Progressive (Bull Moose) party.* 1912: 88 electoral votes; 27 percent of the popular vote. An offshoot of the Republican party, it favored liberal reforms such as expanded suffrage, improved working conditions, conservation of resources, and antimonopoly laws.
5. *Progressive party.* 1924: 13 electoral votes; 17 percent of the popular vote. A continuation of the 1912 Progressive tradition with the candidacy of a man who had been one of its founders and leaders (Robert La Follette).
6. *States Rights Democratic (Dixiecrat) party.* 1948: 39 electoral votes; 2 percent of the popular vote. A southern splinter of the Democratic party, it ran as *the* Democratic party in the South on a conservative, segregationist platform.
7. *American Independent party.* 1968: 46 electoral votes; 14 percent of the popular vote. The party of George Wallace; traditionalist, segregationist, and opposed to the authority of the national government.

cratic and Republican parties have monopolized American electoral politics at all levels of competition.

The very looseness with which we customarily use the term *third party* to designate all minor parties may indicate that third place is as good (or bad) as last place in a two-party system. It would be a serious mistake, however, to treat the minor parties as indistinguishable. They differ in origin, purpose, and

TABLE 2.3   POPULAR VOTES CAST FOR MINOR PARTIES IN 1984 and 1988
            PRESIDENTIAL ELECTIONS

Parties: 1984	Vote: 1984	Parties: 1988	Vote: 1988
Libertarian	228,314	Libertarian	431,616
Citizens	72,200	New Alliance	217,200
Populist	66,336	Populist	46,910
Independent Alliance	46,852	Consumer	30,903
Communist	36,386	American Independent	27,818
Socialist Workers	24,706	Right to Life	20,497
Workers' World	17,985	Workers' League	18,662
American	13,161	Socialist Workers	15,603
Workers' League	10,801	Peace and Freedom	10,370
Others and scattered	7,445	Others and scattered	53,059
Total	524,186		872,638

Note: Lyndon LaRouche ran as an independent in both 1984 and 1988. His totals (78,807 in 1984 and 25,530 in 1988) are not included in this table.

Sources: Guide to U.S. Elections (Washington, D.C.: Congressional Quarterly, Inc., 1986); and 1988 Congressional Quarterly Almanac (Washington, D.C.: Congressional Quarterly, Inc., 1988), p. 7–A.

function, and American political history affords plentiful examples of their activities to illustrate those differences.[15]

Differences in Scope of Ideological Commitment   Although it is true, first of all, that most minor parties are parties of *ideology and issue,* they differ in the scope of that commitment. The narrow, highly specific commitment of such parties as the Prohibition, Vegetarian, and Right to Life parties is apparent in their names. In the 1840s, the Liberty party and its successor, the Free Soil party, campaigned largely on the single issue of the abolition of slavery. At the other extremes are the parties that have the broadest ideological commitments—the Marxist parties and the recent profusion of conservative parties. The Libertarian party, for example—the leading minor party in recent years— advocates a complete withdrawal of government from most of its present programs and responsibilities (see box). In the middle ground between specific issues and total ideologies, the examples are infinitely varied. The farmer-labor parties of economic protest—the Greenback, Populist, and Progressive parties—ran on an extensive program of government regulation of the economy (especially of economic bigness) and social welfare legislation. The Progressive

---

[15]The literature on American third parties is rich and varied. Among the best contributions are John D. Hicks, *The Populist Revolt* (Minneapolis: University of Minnesota Press, 1931); Richard Hofstadter, *The Age of Reform* (New York: Knopf, 1955); David A. Shannon, *The Socialist Party of America* (New York: Macmillan, 1955); George Thayer, *The Farther Shores of Politics* (New York: Simon and Schuster, 1967); Daniel A. Mazmanian, *Third Parties in Presidential Elections* (Washington, D.C.: Brookings, 1974); and Steven J. Rosenstone, Roy L. Behr, and Edward H. Lazarus, *Third Parties in America* (Princeton: Princeton University Press, 1984).

The Libertarian Alternative

Founded in 1972, the Libertarian party grew quickly to become the leading vote-getter among the minor parties in each presidential election from 1976 to 1988. The party received its greatest support in 1980, polling almost a million votes nationwide, including almost 12 percent of the popular vote in Alaska and over 2 percent of the vote in Arizona, Colorado, Montana, Oregon, and Wyoming. Its presidential candidate that year was a California lawyer, Edward E. Clark. Clark had run for governor of California in 1978 and had drawn more than 5 percent of the total vote. His political views, as reported in *The New York Times* account of one of his press conferences in early 1980, provide a good description of what the Libertarian alternative offers:

> "Ultimately," the Libertarian said at a news conference here today, "we believe in the complete privatization of society," with a "vastly restricted" government and a corresponding huge reduction in the taxes that finance the Government.
>
> Mr. Clark told a questioner that eventually he advocated returning highway and street systems to private ownership, "the way they used to be" under Colonial toll-road practices.
>
> In foreign affairs, the Libertarian candidate advocates a "noninterventionist policy," letting other nations defend themselves, reducing defense expenditures substantially and withdrawing from the United Nations and the North Atlantic Treaty Organization, while maintaining extensive social and cultural relations abroad.
>
> WARREN WEAVER, JR.,

---

party of 1948 combined a program of social reform and civil liberties with a foreign policy of friendship with the Soviet Union and reduction of Cold War tensions.

Difference of Origins   The minor parties differ, too, in their *origin*. Some were literally imported into the United States. Much of the early Socialist party strength in the United States came from the freethinkers and radicals who fled Europe after the failures of the revolutions of 1848. Socialist strength in cities such as Milwaukee, New York, and Cincinnati reflected the concentrations of liberal German immigrants there. Other parties—especially the Granger and Populist parties and their successors—were parties of indigenous social protest, born of social inequality and economic hardship in the marginal farmlands of America. Other minor parties began as splinters or factions of one of the major parties. The Gold Democrats of 1896, the Progressives (the Bull Moose party) of 1912, and the Dixiecrats of 1948 come to mind. So great were their objections to the platforms and candidates of their parent parties that the Progressives and Dixiecrats contested the presidential elections with their own slates and programs.

Post-World War II presidential elections have seen the entry of a new variety of minor party in the southern states. These have been dissident movements within the Democratic party, opposed to the civil rights liberalism of the party's presidential nominees, that have refused to run as separate parties on the ballot. Instead, they have exploited two other strategies. In some instances, they have attempted to run their own candidate (rather than the one chosen by the party's national convention) as the official presidential candidate of the Democratic party in the state. The only four states that J. Strom Thurmond carried in 1948 for the Dixiecrats (Alabama, Louisiana, Mississippi, and South Carolina) were those in which he, rather than Harry Truman, was listed on the ballot. George Wallace also captured the Alabama Democratic label in 1968, displacing Hubert Humphrey as the Democratic candidate in that state. In other cases, these party movements have run unpledged slates of presidential electors. In 1960, unpledged slates ran in Louisiana as a States Rights party and in Mississippi as the Democratic party (although there was another Democratic party ticket pledged to Kennedy). In 1964, another unpledged Democratic slate of electors ran in Alabama and prevented the Johnson-Humphrey ticket from appearing on the Alabama ballot.

Differing Tactics   Finally, the third parties differ in their *tactics*. For some, their mere existence is a protest against what they believe is the unqualified support of the status quo by the major parties. Operating as a political party also offers a reasonably effective educational opportunity. The publicity value of the ballot is good, and with it often goes mass media attention the party could not otherwise hope for. Indeed, many of these parties have freely accepted their electoral failures, for they have chosen, by their very nature, not to compromise ideological principles for electoral success. The Prohibition party, for example, has contested presidential elections since 1872 with unflagging devotion to the cause of temperance but equally strong indifference to electoral success (it peaked in 1892 with little more than 2 percent of the popular vote).

Other minor parties, however, do have serious electoral ambitions. Often their goal is local, although today they find it difficult to control an American city as the Socialists did, or an entire state as the Progressives did. More realistically, today they may hope to hold a balance of power between the major parties in the manner of the Dixiecrats of 1948 and Wallace's American Independent party of 1968. Both parties hoped that by carrying a number of states, most likely southern states, they might prevent the major party tickets from winning the necessary majority of votes in the electoral college, thus throwing the stalemated election into the House of Representatives. The Wallace effort of 1968 faltered because Richard Nixon carried an unexpected number of large states.

Independent Presidential Bids   Recent elections have witnessed a significant change in third-party presidential politics: the appearance of independent
presidential candidates, sometimes on third-party tickets created solely as their
personal vehicles but just as often without even a nominal party label. George
Wallace's American Independent party in 1968 was dedicated to his own ambitions and had little more than the degree of organization required by the
states for a place on the ballot. When he backed away from the party's leadership to contest for the Democratic presidential nomination in 1972, the party
slipped into ineffectuality. In a similar vein, Eugene McCarthy, a candidate for
the Democratic nomination in 1968, later flirted with third-party and independent possibilities, eventually running as an independent in 1976. John Anderson unsuccessfully sought the Republican presidential nomination and then ran
as an independent in 1980, but he declined to repeat his independent candidacy
in 1984 in spite of guaranteed federal funding for his campaign. The common
denominator in all these efforts is that they were vehicles for a single presidential candidate and thus were not devoted to fielding a party ticket or building a
third-party organization. In this important respect, they differ from earlier
third-party quests for the presidency, such as the emergence of the Republican
party before the Civil War, the Populists several decades later, and even the
Progressive campaigns of the second and third decades of the twentieth century—all of which were aimed at creating a new major party. These recent independent (rather than truly third-party) presidential bids may signal a
transformation of the very nature of third-partyism in America.

The Question of Impact   Their variety is endless, but what have the minor
parties contributed to American politics? For better or for worse, they have influenced, perhaps even altered, the courses of a few presidential elections. By
threatening—about once a generation—to deadlock the electoral college, they
probably have kept alive movements to reform it. Beyond their role as potential
electoral spoiler, however, can they count any significant accomplishments? The
answer, to be candid, is that they have not assumed the importance that all the
attention lavished on them suggests.

  One line of argument has maintained persistently that the minor parties'
early adoption of unpopular programs ultimately has forced the major parties to
adopt them. Its proponents point to the platforms of the Socialist party in the
years before the 1930s. The issue is whether or not the Socialists' advocacy for
twenty or thirty years of such measures as a minimum wage had anything to do
with their enactment in the 1930s. Unfortunately, there is no way of testing
what might have happened had there been no Socialist party. The evidence suggests, however, that the major parties grasp new programs and proposals in
their "time of ripeness"—when large numbers of Americans have done so and
when such a course is therefore politically useful to the parties. In their earlier,
maturing time, new issues need not depend on minor parties for their advocacy.
Interest groups, the mass media, influential individuals, and factions within the

major parties may perform the propagandizing role, often more effectively than a minor party. More than one commentator has noted that the cause of prohibition in the United States was served far more effectively by interest groups such as the Anti-Saloon League than by the Prohibition party.

In view of their limited impact on American politics, then, why do some voters nonetheless find a third-party alternative attractive? The immediate answer to this question is that few voters have supported third-party candidates under even the most auspicious of circumstances. In only three presidential elections (1856, 1860, and 1912) has the third-party total exceeded 20 percent of the popular vote, and only the first was a situation in which voters were consciously supporting a third party. In most years, third parties have failed to poll more than 5 percent of the popular vote. They labor under a number of constraints on their electoral potential, not the least of which is the self-fulfilling prophecy of many voters that a vote for a third party is wasted.[16]

Yet some voters do end up casting a third-party ballot. A recent investigation of third-party presidential voting from 1840 to 1980 explains their behavior as the result of major party failures "to do what the electorate expects of them—reflect the issue preferences of voters, manage the economy, select attractive and acceptable candidates, and build voter loyalty to the parties and the political system."[17] What this suggests is that the power of the American two-party system embraces its alternatives, permitting their development only when the major parties are failing. The most common niche for third parties, in fact, may be in the period during which the old party alignments are breaking down—but before the party system has been revitalized in a realignment.[18]

Nonpartisan Elections

One of the crowning achievements of the Progressive movement was to restrict the role of parties in elections by removing party labels from many ballots, mostly in local elections. Roughly three-quarters of American towns and cities conduct their local elections on a nonpartisan basis. One state, Nebraska, elects state legislators on a non-partisan ballot, and many states elect judges in this manner. Therefore, the American political system contains many islands of nonpartisanship, which constitute another deviation from the prevailing two-party system.

While this reform certainly has made politics less ostensibly partisan, by itself it probably has not removed partisan influences where parties are already

---

[16]Evidence of the effects of voter skepticism about their chances is the fact that almost all third-party presidential candidates in this century have received less support on election day than they had exhibited in public opinion polls prior to the election. Rosenstone, Behr, and Lazarus, *Third Parties in America*, p. 41.

[17]*Ibid.*, p. 162.

[18]This point is developed more fully in Paul Allen Beck, "The Electoral Cycle and Patterns of American Politics," *British Journal of Political Science* 9 (1979): 129–56.

strong. The nonpartisan ballot did not prevent the development of a powerful political party machine in Chicago or a highly partisan British politics. The resourceful local party organization still can carry out its candidate selection and election functions in the presence of a nonpartisan ballot, even if the task of communicating party endorsements to voters is made more difficult by the absence of a party label on the ballot. But, along with other antiparty measures, nonpartisanship probably has contributed to the erosion of local party strength.

What makes it difficult to assess the effects of nonpartisanship is the tendency for it to have been adopted under conditions that favor nonpartisanship in elections to begin with. This reform took root more commonly in cities and towns with weak parties and for offices in which the traditional American aversion to party practices is most pronounced. Most northeastern cities, where strong party machines were the most visible targets of the progressives, by contrast, were able to resist the reforms and retain partisan local elections to this day.

Beyond the obvious changes in the role of parties, what are the consequences of nonpartisanship? The traditional view among political scientists was that a move to nonpartisan elections shifts the balance of power among contending partisan forces in a pro-Republican direction rather than rendering politics any less partisan or more high-minded. Without party labels on the ballot, the voter is more dependent upon other cues. The greater resources and community visibility typically enjoyed by higher status candidates can fill the void left by the absence of party. In contemporary American politics, these higher status candidates are more likely to be Republicans.[19] A more recent study of council races in cities across the nation, though, challenges the conventional wisdom by showing that the apparent GOP advantage disappears once the partisan nature of the city is taken into account.[20]

WHITHER THE AMERICAN TWO-PARTY SYSTEM?

There are signs that the two-party hegemony is becoming more complete, even as the voter loyalties to the major parties have been weakening. Third-party deviations from the major party duopoly are less common today than ever before. One-partyism in the states and localities is receding with the integration of the South into the mainstream of American politics and the weakening of urban machines. Only the continuation of nonpartisan elections in local politics and the

---

[19]The clearest statements of this view are found in Oliver P. Williams and Charles Adrian, "The Insulation of Local Politics Under the Nonpartisan Ballot," *American Political Science Review* 53 (1959): 1052–63; and Willis D. Hawley, *NonPartisan Elections and the Case for Party Politics* (New York: Wiley, 1973).

[20]See Susan Welch and Timothy Bledsoe, "The Partisan Consequences of Nonpartisan Elections and the Changing Nature of Urban Politics," *American Journal of Political Science* 30 (1986): 128–39.

recent appearance of independent presidential candidates prevent competition between the Democratic and Republican parties from being "the only game in town."

The Demise of Third Parties

It is ironic that third parties are doing less well at a time in which the traditional barriers to their access to the ballot are being challenged. The post-World War II movement toward stiffer state requirements for third parties to qualify for the ballot is being reversed through court action. With Supreme Court intervention, George Wallace gained access to his fiftieth state ballot in the 1968 presidential election and set the legal precedent for subsequent candidates to overcome state attempts to restrict places on the ballot to candidates of the major parties (see box). John Anderson in 1980 spent a good deal of his time and money in assuring that his name would be before the American voters as an independent (see box). These actions may pave the way for a relaxation of the severe restrictions many states have imposed on ballot access for non-major-party candidates, but it could take considerable time and effort before court rulings fully open the electoral process to third parties throughout the nation.[21]

In some ways, the financial barriers to challenges from outside the two major parties are less imposing as well. The Wallace campaign astounded experts by raising and spending some $7 million, by far the largest sum ever spent by a minor party campaign in American history. This achievement demonstrated that a nationwide third-party campaign could attract substantial financial backing. Public funding of presidential campaigns adds another possibility by opening the public treasury to candidates outside the major-party mainstream. John Anderson was the first "outside" candidate to receive federal financing. By polling more than 5 percent of the popular vote as an independent, he qualified for over $4 million in public funds. This money was dispersed to him after the election, but his vote total made him eligible for public funding in the next election—an opportunity he passed up by choosing not to run. A future third-party candidate, or an independent like Anderson, could guarantee a financial base for subsequent campaigns by garnering a similar share of the popular vote. Off-

---

[21]Third parties and independents have compiled a checkered record of success in ballot access cases. State laws requiring filing fees and petitions signed by large numbers of voters before such candidates are allowed on the ballot have been overruled in some cases (see box) but upheld in others. On balance, the courts have made access to the ballot for third parties and independents easier in recent years. But this action has been taken on a piecemeal basis, which requires petitioners to raise the challenge in each state, and has left in place many curbs on access to the ballot as reasonable state efforts to avoid voter confusion and frustration when faced with a long ballot. See Clifton McCleskey, "Parties at the Bar: Equal Protection, Freedom of Association, and the Rights of Political Organization," *Journal of Politics* 46 (1984): 346–68; John Moeller, "The Federal Courts' Involvement in the Reform of Political Parties," *Western Political Quarterly* 40 (1987): 717–34; and Lee Epstein and Charles D. Hadley, "On the Treatment of Political Parties in the U.S. Supreme Court, 1900–1986," *Journal of Politics* 52 (1990): 413–32.

Gaining Access to the Ballot: A Tale of Three Candidates

George Wallace, 1968

George Wallace's lawyers stood before the United States Supreme Court in early October of 1968 to plead that the Court strike down Ohio's election law and permit Wallace's name to be printed on the Ohio ballot as a presidential candidate. To gain a place on the ballot under Ohio law, Wallace would have needed 433,000 signatures very early in his campaign. He sued instead. The Ohio law had been passed, the state argued in its defense, for a legitimate purpose—to preserve the existing two-party system and to make sure small pluralities would not win elections. By a vote of six to three, the Court disagreed. It ruled that the Ohio law violated the equal protection clause of the Fourteenth Amendment in restricting the rights of voting and association of supporters of minor parties.[22]

John Anderson, 1980

A substantial part of John Anderson's independent campaign for the presidency in 1980 involved prodigious efforts to gain a position on each of fifty state ballots. Petitions with large numbers of signatures were required in most states, and formal legal action was necessary in at least ten. The Anderson campaign in many states was built around the drive to gain access to the ballot in the hope that these activities would gain attention and help to create a strong organization. Unfortunately, the ballot access campaign spent $2.5 million and left little money for advertising. Anderson also faced a second hurdle. Some states imposed early filing deadlines on nonparty, independent candidates. Ohio was one of them, and Anderson took the state to court. The issue finally was resolved in Anderson's favor in 1983 when the Supreme Court ruled that Ohio and other states could not discriminate against independent candidates seeking a place on the presidential ballot by imposing early deadlines. [23] Anderson's problems even caught the attention of Doonesbury.

DOONESBURY   by Garry Trudeau

(*continued*)

Adlai Stevenson III, 1986

Six years later, the Democratic nominee for governor in Illinois, Adlai Stevenson, faced a dilemma of a different sort. Nominated in the party primaries as his running mates for lieutenant governor and secretary of state were disciples of Lyndon LaRouche, not regular Democrats. Finding them unacceptable, Stevenson sought to have the party nominations stripped from them. Failing that, he then rejected his party's nomination and ran instead as an independent. However, by an Illinois law designed to prevent "sore losers" in party primaries from competing as independents in the general election, independents have to file before the party primaries, and the courts ruled that Stevenson therefore could not qualify for the ballot as an independent. Ultimately, Stevenson ran unsuccessfully at the head of his own third-party ticket with the two party-endorsed candidates who had been upset in the primaries as his running mates.

setting the advantages of this new campaign finance environment, though, is the enormous cost of modern campaigns, which probably restricts the opportunities to only a few highly visible third-party or independent candidates.

George Wallace also solved—if only in part and for the moment—the problem of a minor party's becoming a national party. Almost all the effective minor party activity of the past century has been intensely local. Each of the minor parties has been concentrated in one state or region or in a city or two. Socialists came from Germany in the middle of the nineteenth century and established Socialist enclaves in cities such as New York, Milwaukee, and Cincinnati. Regional agricultural depressions gave rise to Populism and other similar movements of the plains and prairies. Traditionally, third parties have fed on local loyalties, interests, and troubles, but their appeals increasingly have lost out in a mobile society that receives the same political messages via the same radio and television networks, the same magazines, and the same press services and syndicated columnists. Thus, minor parties have found it hard to become national parties. But, the access to a nationalized media that money can buy, coupled with the 1980 precedent for opening the televised debates to serious candidates beyond the major party nominees, gave minor parties or independent candidates a real opportunity to reach a national audience of voters. Of course only the rare candidate without major party ties will be able to exploit these opportunities.

---

[22]The case was Williams v. Rhodes, 393 U.S. 23 (1968).

[23]This account of Anderson's efforts to gain access to the ballot draws upon Jack W. Germond and Jules Witcover, *Blue Smoke and Mirrors: How Reagan Won and Why Carter Lost the Election of 1980* (New York: Viking, 1981), pp. 236–37. The Supreme Court case was Anderson v. Celebrezze 460 U.S. 780 (1983).

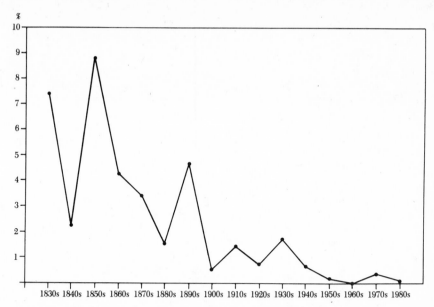

Figure 2.1 Third-Party and independent members of Congress: 1830s–1980s.

Note: Figures are percentages of third party and independent senators and representatives during each decade. 1980s figures are through 1990.

Source: Joseph A. Schlesinger, "On the Theory of Party Organization," *Journal of Politics* 46 (1984): 370. Data for 1980s from the *Statistical Abstract of the United States* (1989).

The proliferation of third party and independent presidential candidates in recent decades is a stark contrast to the demise of third-party candidates in other contests. Third-party and independent members of Congress, quite common in the early years of the two-party system, have been rare throughout the twentieth century, but never so rare as in recent years (Figure 2.1). Since 1952, only two members of Congress have been elected on a third-party ticket. Moreover, during this same period, major-party candidates have completely dominated the state legislatures. Unlike the situation in earlier times, there are presently no local enclaves of considerable minor party strength anywhere in the United States. Independent candidates have been relatively more successful, but their very independence prevents them from presenting any pervasive challenge to the two-party system (see box).

What, then, can we predict for minor parties in American politics? There will continue to be a few local third parties that reflect special local conditions, especially quirks in local election laws. The classic instance, of course, is that of the New York minor parties—the Liberals, the Conservatives, and the Right to Life party. They exist because they can nominate the candidates of a major party to run under their party labels. New York election law thus makes them important brokers in New York elections. For national impact, however, minor parties generally will ride the coattails of a well-known, charismatic candidate.

Successful Third-Party and Independent Candidates in 1990

Two third-party candidates and one independent candidate captured national attention in the 1990 elections with their victories for major offices, marking 1990 as an exceptional year for candidates running outside of the two major parties. Former Republican Congressman Lowell Weicker won the Connecticut gubernatorial race on the ticket of A Connecticut Party, a party he founded solely to advance his candidacy. Former Republican Governor Walter J. Hickel was elected governor of Alaska as an independent. The first successful third-party candidate for the U.S. House of Representatives since 1952 was Bernard Sanders of Vermont, the long-term Socialist mayor of Burlington, elected as a Socialist in 1990.

That an exceptional year for third-party and independent electoral successes was built on only three victories "proves the rule" that the Democratic and Republican parties dominate American electoral politics. Their dominance is further demonstrated in these cases, as only Weicker seems likely to remain aloof from the major parties. Hickel shows every sign that he will govern as a Republican, and Sanders has attempted (unsuccessfully) to join the Democratic congressional caucus.

Increasing Competitiveness

Not only does the two-party system seem to be less threatened by true minor parties, but there are signs of a second general trend in the American party system: the increasing competitiveness between the major parties. No regions of the country, and very few states, can be thought of as wholly one-party areas. In only New Hampshire for example, did one party win all of the contests for senator, governor, and president during the 1980s. The states also are more competitive now than they were in the 1946–79 period in contests for the state legislature and governor (Table 2.2). Leading the way toward a better balance between the major parties are the traditionally one-party southern states, all of which were more competitive than in the earlier period. The GOP has experienced even more success in recent presidential elections in the South. In fact, the region is now more favorable to Republicans than to Democrats at the presidential level.

To take the longer view, presidents increasingly have been winning with popular vote percentages that vary less and less from one state to another. Figure 2.2 indicates that state differences in the presidential vote have progressively narrowed throughout the twentieth century, falling to their lowest point yet in 1988. In other words, presidents are no longer carrying some states by fat margins while losing others in a similarly lopsided way. This trend of increasing uniformity in presidential vote patterns across the country, then, parallels the declining number of states that are one-party bastions in state party com-

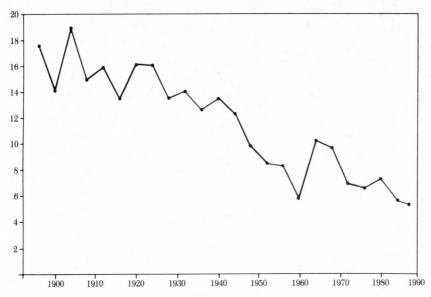

Figure 2.2 The growth of national two-party competitiveness: Interstate differences in the presidential popular vote 1896–1988.

Note: The measure of interstate differences is called the standard deviation. It measures the amount of dispersal of items around the average. It discriminates, therefore, among dispersals in the following three series: 3,6,9; 6,8; and 5,6,7. Even though the means and medians of each series are identical (6), the standard deviations decline in the order in which the three series are listed. The data on which the calculations are based are the percentages of the total vote in each state won by the winning candidate.

petition. The result is a more competitive two-party politics throughout the nation.[24]

The spread of major party competitiveness reflects the same nationalization of life and politics in the United States that threatens local minor parties. It is increasingly difficult for one major party to maintain its dominance on the basis of regional appeals and traditions as the Democrats did in the South from 1875 to 1950. Furthermore, the social and economic conditions that support one-partyism are disappearing. As Americans move about the country, as industry comes to formerly agrarian states, as more and varied people move to the urban centers, each state increasingly becomes a microcosm of the diversity of life

---

[24]The oft-noted decrease in marginal or competitiveness races for Congress at first glance appears to be moving against this trend. Gary C. Jacobson notes, however, that incumbents may have been no safer in the 1970s than in the 1950s. In spite of the increase in the share of votes that incumbents have won, their probability of losing did not decline. The reason is that incumbents who won by large margins in the previous election were more likely to be defeated in the 1970s than earlier. In short, a larger "margin" has been required to secure a safe seat in recent years. For a review of the marginality debate and the evidence for this argument, see Jacobson's "The Marginals Never Vanished: Incumbency and Competition in Elections to the U.S. House of Representatives, 1952–82," *American Journal of Political Science* 31 (1987): 126–141.

and interest that undergirds national party competition. National mass media and national political leaders also bring the conflict between the Democrats and the Republicans to all corners of the country. Thus, the party electorates are increasingly recruited by the appeals of national candidates and issues—regardless of whatever special appeals the local party organization makes. The shifting of important state contests away from presidential election years, now extended to about three-quarters of the states, can mute the influence of national forces to some degree, but it is only a small counterweight to their inexorable power.

State party organizations and leaders cannot hold out against the political issues and images that engulf the rest of the country. They cannot easily set up their own competitive subsystem. As a result, a creeping competitiveness accompanies the end of one-partyism at the state level. First, the states become competitive in national elections; then the old one-party ties and fears slowly break down, and competition seeps down to local elections. Pennsylvania, for example, became competitive in presidential politics in the 1930s after forty years of domination by the GOP; by the 1950s and 1960s, the state was competitive in state and local politics. The same process is under way in a number of southern states.

Ironically, the increasing degree of two-party competition may create a set of vexing problems for the American parties. By reducing pockets of one-party strength, the new competitiveness threatens a source of stability in the party system. When a party holds noncompetitive strongholds of its own, it can survive even a catastrophic national loss through victories and continued office-holding in its own areas of strength. Without those one-party strongholds to fall back on, a losing party in the future may find its loss more sweeping and devastating. Furthermore, the spread of two-party competitiveness expands the scope of party competition and thus makes extra demands on the resources the parties must employ. When one-party areas could be written off in a presidential campaign and election, the area of political combat was reduced. Now the parties must mobilize and organize more resources than ever across more of the states.

Nevertheless, the reign of the existing parties and, more generally, of the American two-party system seems secure. The parties' popularity may not be what it was, but two-party dominance of the electoral systems continues. Talk of the imminent decline of the Republicans after Watergate and the losses of 1974 and 1976 was silenced by the party's resurgence in the 1980s. Similar talk of Democratic decline in the 1980s must be tempered by recognition of the party's continuing strength in Congress and the state houses. Nor has the possibility of sustained third party or independent inroads into the Democratic-Republican duopoly, raised by the Wallace challenge in 1968 or the Anderson campaign in 1980, increased. Events could undo such projections of course, but it seems highly likely that changes in the parties and their appeals will have to take place within the familiar two-party framework.

THE POLITICAL PARTY AS AN ORGANIZATION

It is often easier to see the political activity than the actor. The excitement of a bitterly fought election, the carnival antics and revival meeting fervor of national conventions, the wrangling between partisan blocs in a state legislature—these and the other activities of the political parties could not be more obvious. There is a palpable actor behind the activity, however—a political party with characteristics not unlike those of large national corporations, trade unions, and fraternal societies. The political party is no mere bundle of activities, no disembodied ideology, no unseen hand in the political process. It is a definable, observable social structure that must itself be organized in order to organize political interests.

Within the political party, two of the sectors—the party organization and the party in government—have stable relationships and a rough division of labor and responsibility. In other words, both have the characteristics we associate with an organization of any kind. It is a bit misleading, therefore, to call only one of them the party organization, but such are the semantic vagaries of American politics. In justification of that usage, however, it is true that the party organization alone has the organizational capacity to plan and initiate the major share of party activities. It also has the most systematic network of relationships and roles of all the party sectors. It is the sector that speaks in the name of the party, governs it, and under law is responsible for it. It is the sector in which active partisans work to set the goals of the party and to mobilize and deploy its resources. In that sense, it is the part of the party most concerned with party governance and priorities.

In concrete terms, the party organization is the formal apparatus of the precincts, wards, cities, counties, congressional districts, and state that results from the legislation of the state itself. In addition, each party has set up a national committee, which peaks the pyramid of committees the state has created. The party organization is thus the totality of the machinery operated by party officials, leaders, members, and activists. The three chapters that follow describe it.

The public life of the party organization—its espousal of ideas and recruitment of candidates for public office, for instance—will receive treatment in later chapters. Party organizations have a "private life," however, in addition to their public life. It involves the kinds of internal relationships and behavior one might find in any complex organization. In considering that private life, the three chapters of this part will examine:

- *The formal structure of the organization:* its committees and machinery; the selection of its leadership.
- *The centers of power:* the relative centralization or decentralization of power within the organization; the locus of authority within it.
- *The patterns of decision making:* the processes by which decisions are made, especially the degree of intraorganizational democracy.
- *Cohesion and consent:* the maintenance of unity, discipline, and morale within the organization.
- *The recruitment of resources:* the ability of the organization to attract people, money, and skills and the incentives it uses to do so.
- *The division of labor:* the various roles and relationships among people within the organization.

The private life of the party is far less obvious than its public life. Although we may separate them, however, the two are obviously related. To a considerable extent, the internal, organizational characteristics of the party determine its capacity to carry on its external, public activities.

A comparison with large business organizations is, if not pressed too far, a valid one. The party organization competes with other political organizations for political resources—personnel, knowledge, and money. Its rewards or incentives bring together varied groups of men and women who seek their often differing goals through party action. What are considered rewards and incentives to induce activity from the viewpoint of the party organization are merely the goals for which their activists have come together in the party. Many of the party organization's activities, therefore, may be viewed in terms of its attempts to win those goals and thereby reward the faithful for their investment of resources, loyalties, work, and support.

Ultimately, the most important questions about the party organizations concern their effectiveness, vitality, and capacity. These characteristics can be summed up as *strength*, and the strength of the party organization has two dimensions: its ability to hold its own in its relationships with the two other sectors of the party, and its ability to function efficiently and consistently in mobilizing resources and making decisions. In other words, the party organization must be able to function successfully both within the political party and within the broader political system.

In its relationships with the party in government and the party in the electorate, the party organization rarely achieves any permanent supremacy within the American political party. All three sectors of the party struggle for control of its symbols and its political capabilities. All three have goals—at times, competing goals—and each seeks control of the party as a means to its own particular ends. The states and to a limited degree even the national government, through laws defining and regulating the parties, substantially influence the balance of power in this struggle. Rarely is the party organization able to dictate to the party in government. It is far more common for the organization to be dependent on and even submissive to this other sector—which, after all, writes the laws that regulate the organization. It must also conduct an almost endless wooing of its own party electorate, most of whom are neither formal members nor unfailingly loyal voters.

In addition to these strained and often dependent relationships with the other sectors of the party, the organization confronts formidable problems in maintaining its internal vitality. Contrary to popular impression, which has been shaped by the colorful and rare urban political machines, party organizations are not unified, omnipotent monoliths. They have within them men and women of different values and goals, and they have always been plagued with dissidents and competing factions. They or parts of them often display amazing degrees of organizational disintegration. It is not unusual, for example, to find entire county organizations of the Democratic or Republican party in total dormancy.

Over time and across the many states and localities, there is tremendous variation in the strength and vitality of the American parties' organizations. The next few chapters will illustrate these many varieties, and it is crucial to bear in mind how extensive this variation is in assessing overall party strength—or how it has changed. By the standards of political parties of most Western democracies, though, it is well to remember that the American party organizations are comparatively weak. To a considerable extent, the problem is in the very nature of the animal. The party organization is an expression of some very special qualities of the American political party.

At the risk of considerable oversimplification, one can say that, among democratic political parties, two types of organization appear most frequently: the cadre and the mass membership. In the cadre party, the organizational machinery is run by a relatively small number of leaders and activists. These officials and activists perpetuate the apparatus of the organization, make decisions in its name, and pick the candidates and strategies that will enlist large numbers of voters. In the mass membership party, on the other hand, the party organization grows out of and is more continuously responsible to the party membership. In such parties, substantial portions of the party electorate are involved in the party organization as dues-paying members and even as participants in year-round activities. The party organization therefore has a continuous responsibility to its membership, often providing such nonpolitical benefits as insurance and leisure-time activities. In a mass membership party, the three sectors are drawn together, with the party organization often occupying a central, dominant position. What we think of as the party in the electorate becomes an integral, even guiding, part of the party organization, with the right to pick officers and to vote on policy questions. Because of its great power in the selection of candidates—no primary elections limit it—this organization of the mass membership party exerts far greater control over the party in government. In short, the mass membership party resembles a continuous, participatory organization; the cadre party, on the other hand, is far more a momentary, pragmatic coalition of interests and people brought together in a temporary way to win elections (see Table II.1)[1]

The major American parties usually are cited as prime examples of cadre parties. And in key respects they fit this mold. American parties possess few dues-paying members. Their activities are almost exclusively electoral. Involvement in the organization is rarely a full-time occupation for either leaders or activists. The organization also makes little attempt to influence the party in government. Yet the modern American parties depart from the cadre-party mold in a few important ways. In recent years, they have solicited mass memberships, although more as a means for raising money than as a way to create a party community. Those willing to declare themselves as party members in closed primaries, and they number in the millions, select the party nominees for most offices. The major parties now are affluent enough to maintain a full-time professional staff in their national and state offices, as well as in a few local offices. Even these movements in the direction of mass parties, though, leave them a far cry from an organizational resemblance to the European Socialist or Labor parties of the early 1900s. However, with the dulling of their ideological edge and the massive falloffs in their mass memberships in recent years, even those exemplars of the mass party about which Duverger wrote no longer stand in stark contrast to the American parties.

Still, the major American parties are much more cadre than mass parties, and the American style of party organization is shaped by this reality. It expresses the organizational needs of parties that are preoccupied—indeed, obsessed—with contesting elections. It reflects the organizational needs of parties that must appeal to majorities rather than to 10, 20, or 30 percent of the electorate. It reflects the needs of parties that traditionally have not been concerned with ideology, with vast political causes, or even with taking specific stands on political issues. Finally, it reflects a political system in which the electorate is already organized by a wealth of interest groups and other nonparty political organizations. The party organization of the American parties does *not* reflect the politics of a multiparty system, the politics of a deeply ideological political system, or a political system in which the parties have monopolized the organization of political interests.

There is an insubstantial and even unimpressive quality to the party organizations of the American parties, especially in comparison with their counterparts in other democracies—or, even more, with large business organizations.

---

[1]Maurice Duverger, in *Political Parties* (New York: Wiley, 1954), inaugurated the distinction between cadre and mass membership parties. For an expansion of that analysis and a comparison of the American parties with those of other Western democracies, see Leon D. Epstein, *Political Parties in Western Democracies* (New Brunswick, N.J.: Transaction, 1980).

Table II.1   COMPARISON OF CADRE AND MASS MEMBERSHIP
              PARTY ORGANIZATIONS

Organizational Feature	Cadre Party	Mass Membership Party
Members	Generally few	Many dues-paying members
Activities	Predominantly electoral	Ideological and educational, as well as electoral
Organizational continuity	Active chiefly at elections	Continuously active
Leadership	Few full-time workers or leaders	Permanent bureaucracy and full-time leadership
Position in party	Usually subordinate to party in government	Generally some influence over party in government

In this era of a widely acknowledged decline of parties, their organizations, if anything, perhaps have been spared because they were so weak to begin with. American party organizations were not always so enervated, if the zealous assaults on them by Progressive reformers around the turn of the century are any token of their former strength.[2] Nor has the demise of the powerful urban machine so hated by the reformers been a fatal blow, for recently there are compelling signs of a strengthening of the state and national party organizations, and an unprecedented centralization of party organizational power.

In spite of their comparative weakness and varying health, the American party organizations nonetheless command our attention, for they are at the very center of the political parties. More than the party in government or the party in the electorate, they control the parties' lives, their names, and their symbols. If their organizations are in decline, it may change the nature of the American parties and of American politics. If they are possessed of a new and growing robustness, the consequences may be felt far and wide. Any study of the American political parties must take the measure of the party organizations.

---

[2]These reformers viewed the political party organizations, especially the urban political machines, as powerful (and baneful) entities and were devoted to destroying them. See Moisei Ostrogorski, *Democracy and the Organization of the Political Parties*, Volume II (New York: Anchor, 1964; first published in 1902 and now available in an edition edited and abridged by Seymour Martin Lipset).

3

The State and Local Party Organizations

The popular vocabulary of party organization suggests almost menacing strength. "Machines" headed by "bosses" keep the local "captains" toeing a "party line" and mobilize vast "armies" of workers and seekers of "spoils" to vote the "party slate" at election time. Their power or strength has become their "clout." This vocabulary expresses a pervasive American fear of politics and politicians. In what has become virtually a conspiratorial theory of American politics, the party organization or "machine" is the prime conspirator or corrupter in a wider net of political intrigue.

Even the most cursory experience with American party organizations suggests that behind this extravagant vocabulary lies a vastly less imposing reality. Machine imagery may have aptly characterized the party organizations of some major American cities—and an occasional rural area or town—at the beginning of the twentieth century. Exaggerated claims by machine leaders in boasting of their prowess or by their Progressive opponents in whipping up public indignation against their enemy, though, must be discounted. Even in those times, the machine epitome of party organization hardly characterized the organizations that prevailed in most locales. And today, as the last remnants of machines are disappearing from their once-secure urban outposts, the machine image of the party organization seems ever more anachronistic.

The truth about their party organizations may be difficult for many Americans to accept, for it involves not only a recognition of reality about the parties but also a modification of some dim views of politics in general. Nonetheless, it is necessary to sweep this tenacious myth away in order to gain a clear view of the state and local party organizations. To gain this view requires the blending into focus of three different lenses on reality—the party organizations as they are stipulated in state legislation, the party machines as they have traveled into modern times, and the party organizations as they operate in a wide array of American locales.

THE STATUTORY DEFINITION OF THE PARTY ORGANIZATIONS

A good place to begin to come to grips with the reality of the party organizations is with the constitutions and statutes of the fifty states, which bulge with detailed prescriptions defining the nature of party organizations and the duties they are to perform. The states have, in fact, enacted such a kaleidoscopic variety of legislation on the parties that it defies summary or classification. In scope and extent, the laws range from those of Oregon, which specify party structure in detailed and full-blown provisions of more than 5000 words, to those of states which dispose of the parties in a few sentences or paragraphs. In between are all grades and degrees of statutory specificity.

State Regulations

A study by the Advisory Commission on Intergovernmental Relations (ACIR) provides a good indication of the rich variety to be found in these regulations in the 1980s. (See Table 3.1) Most states attempt to regulate both internal party organization and the party role in the electoral process. (The electoral regulations will be considered later in discussing the electoral process.) The organizational regulations range from specifying the composition of party committees at the local level to stipulating the internal rules under which the parties will operate. Some of the strongest party organizations in the nation are also the most tightly regulated, so state activity here should not be viewed as necessarily weakening the parties.[1]

The variety and detail of state approaches illustrate the cardinal fact that the definition and regulation of political party organization in the United States have been left largely to the states. The United States Constitution makes no mention of parties; it does not have even an oblique reference to them in its elegant paragraphs. Nor has the Congress attempted very often to define or regulate them. Only in the 1970s legislation on campaign finance is there a substantial body of national legislation that affects the parties.

Limitations on State Control

In regulating the parties, though, the states cannot do entirely as they wish. Over the years the federal courts have frequently intervened to protect citizens' voting rights (in cases to be discussed later) and to restrict state laws that limited

---

[1]The results of this study are reported in Timothy Conlan, Ann Martino, and Robert Dilger, "State Parties in the 1980s," *Intergovernmental Perspective* 10 (1984): 6–13, 23; and *The Transformation in American Politics* (Washington, D.C.: Advisory Commission on Intergovernmental Relations, 1986), pp. 95–162.

Deregulating the Party Organizations

The 1980s was a decade of widespread deregulation of private activity. In the *Eu* case, drawing upon precedents in *Tashjian* and earlier cases, Justice Thurgood Marshall applied the logic of deregulation to state governance of the parties. In his opinion for the Court, he concluded:

> . . . a State cannot justify regulating a party's internal affairs without showing that such regulation is necessary to ensure an election that is orderly and fair. Because California has made no such showing here, the challenged laws cannot be upheld. . . . For the reasons stated above, we hold that the challenged California election laws burden the First Amendment rights of political parties and their members without serving a compelling state interest.

Protecting the integrity of the electoral process, therefore, may be a compelling state interest. When the state turns to regulating the structure and rules of the party organization, however, the Court has found the interest far less compelling and has given the parties more freedom to govern themselves as private associations.

---

third parties' and independent candidates' access to the ballot (see Chapter 2). Recently, the courts have even begun to overturn state regulation of party organizational arrangements and practices. In *Tashjian v. Connecticut*, the Supreme Court ruled that the state could not prevent the Republican party from opening up its primary to independents. Most recently, in *Eu v. San Francisco County Democratic Central Committee*, the Court unanimously invalidated California's statutory requirements that the state chair's term be two years, chairs be rotated between southern and northern Californians, and party endorsements be prohibited in primaries. The *Eu* case has far-reaching implications for these non-election-related internal party practices by bringing them under the umbrella of First Amendment protections for free speech and free association against state intrusion (see box). If the parties choose to challenge the state laws that govern them, it now appears that a significant part of the regulatory framework in which parties currently operate could be dismantled.[2]

---

[2]Tashjian v. Republican Party of Connecticut, 479 U.S. 1024 (1986); Eu (Secretary of State of California) v. San Francisco County Democratic Central Committee et al., 103 L. Ed. 2nd 271 (1989). For a review of earlier federal court decisions in this area, see Clifton McCleskey, "Parties at the Bar: Equal Protection, Freedom of Association, and the Rights of Political Organizations," *Journal of Politics* 46 (1984): 346–68. On deregulation of parties in California, see Roy Christman and Barbara Norrander, "A Reflection on Political Party Deregulation Via the Courts: The Case of California," *Journal of Law and Politics* 6 (1990): 723–742.

TABLE 3.1 STATE LAWS REGULATING POLITICAL PARTIES

State	State Comm. Selection[a]	State Comm. Composition[b]	State Comm. Meeting Date[c]	State Comm. Internal Rule[d]	Local Comm. Selection[e]	Local Comm. Composition[f]	Local Comm. Internal Rules or Activities[g]	Cumulative Regulatory Index Score[h]
Light Regulators[i]								
Alaska								0
Delaware								0
Hawaii								0
Kentucky								0
North Carolina								1
Alabama							X	1
Georgia							X	1
Minnesota							X	1
New Mexico							X	1
Oklahoma							X	1
Virginia								1
Connecticut						X	X	3
Maine	X		X		X		X	4
New Hampshire	X				X		X	4
Moderate Regulators								
Arkansas	X				X		X	5
Florida	X	X	X	X		X	X	5
Nebraska	X	X					X	5
Rhode Island		X	X	X	X	X	X	6
Pennsylvania	X	X	X	X	X		X	7
Colorado	X	X				X	X	8
Idaho	X	X			X	X	X	8
Iowa	X	X		X	X	X	X	8
South Carolina	X	X			X	X	X	8
South Dakota	X	X			X	X	X	8
Utah	X	X			X	X	X	8
Mississippi	X	X		X	X	X	X	9
Montana	X	X		X	X	X	X	9
Nevada	X	X	X		X	X	X	9
Vermont	X	X		X		X	X	9
Washington	X	X		X	X	X	X	9
Wisconsin	X	X			X	X	X	9

TABLE 3.1 (continued)

State	State Comm. Selection[a]	State Comm. Composition[b]	State Comm. Meeting Date[c]	State Comm. Internal Rule[d]	Local Comm. Selection[e]	Local Comm. Composition[f]	Local Comm. Internal Rules or Activities[g]	Cumulative Regulatory Index Score[h]
			Heavy Regulators					
Indiana	X	X	X	X	X	X	X	10
Michigan	X	X		X	X	X	X	10
New York	X		X	X	X	X	X	10
North Dakota	X	X	X	X	X	X	X	10
Oregon	X	X	X	X	X	X	X	10
Arizona	X	X		X	X	X	X	11
California	X	X		X	X	X	X	11
Maryland	X	X	X	X	X	X	X	11
Massachusetts	X	X	X	X	X	X	X	11
Missouri	X	X	X	X	X	X	X	11
Tennessee	X	X	X	X	X	X	X	11
West Virginia	X	X	X	X	X	X	X	11
Kansas	X	X	X	X	X	X	X	12
New Jersey	X	X	X	X	X	X	X	12
Texas	X	X	X	X	X	X	X	12
Wyoming	X	X	X	X	X	X	X	12
Illinois	X	X	X	X	X	X	X	13
Ohio	X	X	X	X	X	X	X	13
Louisiana	X	X	X	X	X	X	X	14

[a]Does state allow or require the manner of selecting the parties' state central committees?

[b]Does state law require the composition of the parties' state central committees?

[c]Does state law regulate when the parties' state central committees will meet?

[d]Does state law regulate any of the internal procedures of the parties' state central committees?

[e]Does state law regulate the manner of selecting the parties' local organizations?

[f]Does state law regulate the composition of the parties' local organizations?

[g]Does state law regulate any of the internal rules or activities of the parties' local organizations?

[h]Scores are determined by state regulatory actions in the seven areas examined. Minimum score is 0; maximum score is 14.

"Light" regulators are defined as having an index score of 0-4; "moderate" regulators are those states having index scores of 5-9; and "heavy" regulators are those states having index scores above 10.

Source: Conlan, Martino, and Dilger, "State Parties in the 1980s," p. 12.

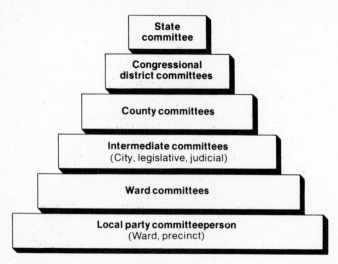

Figure 3.1 A typical pyramid of party organization in a state.

An Organizational Pyramid

Amidst all this variety, the party organizations created by the states have one dominant characteristic in common: They match the voting districts and at least some of the constituencies of the state. They form great step pyramids of the myriad, overlapping constituencies of a democracy committed to the election of vast numbers of officeholders (Figure 3.1). At the bottom, they are usually built on the smallest voting districts of the state. The basic functionary in the party organization is the local committee-person, representing a ward, a precinct, or a township. Then, in a succession of layers, the ward and city committees, county committees, and sometimes even state legislative and congressional districts are piled on top of each other.[3] At the apex of the state pyramid there is invariably a state committee, usually called a state central committee in the idiom of these statutes. The degree to which this entire structure is actually specified by the statutes differs from state to state. State statutes generally ordain the county and the state committees; some then mandate the other levels, whereas others leave the filling out of the organizational hierarchy to the parties themselves.

The Elected Committeeperson   At the base of this pyramid is the local committeeperson (or captain or chairperson) who is chosen from the precinct or whatever is the smallest voting district in the states. Since there are more than

---

[3]Within the same state, the various intermediate committees may cover geographical areas of varying sizes and thus may occupy different positions in the organizational pyramid. Congressional districts, for example, may be smaller than a city or larger than a county, depending on the density of population.

The Occurrence of a Rare Event: Contests for the County Committee

Competition for positions on the county committee is a rare occurrence. Every once in a while, though, an organized attempt to take over the local party organization through penetration of its base reaches public attention. These challenges typically involve battles over the ideological direction of the party, often whether it is to represent a wide-based constituency or be dedicated to a single issue or ideology. The challenges are resolved in favor of the group that most successfully mobilizes its supporters in the low turnout elections in which party officials are selected.

Such an event occurred in Columbus, Ohio, in early 1990, when challenges were mounted for a number of the 133 seats on both the Democratic and Republican county central committees by people identified as Christian conservatives. By seizing these positions, they hoped to be able to move the county parties, in their words, more in the direction of preserving "traditional family values." That the challenges came in the May primaries for statewide offices, in a year when there was no competition within either party for most offices, made the outcome especially dependent upon mobilization efforts on both sides. In the end, the insurgents won only a handful of seats on each committee.

100,000 precincts in the United States, a fully staffed, two-party system would assume the participation of at least some 200,000 men and women. In truth, of course, many of the local committee positions are either vacant or only nominally occupied.

The local committeepersons generally are selected in one of three ways. Most are chosen at local party caucuses or in the primary elections of the party, but in a few instances, higher party authorities appoint them. In states that choose them in the primaries, any voter may place his or her name in nomination for the party position with a petition signed by a handful of local voters. If, as often happens, there are no nominees, the committeeperson may be elected by an even smaller handful of write-in votes. In other states, the statutes direct or permit the party to hold local caucus meetings in the wards and precincts to which any voters of the area who declare themselves attached to the party may come. These party loyalists then elect the committeepersons in the caucuses; they also generally elect delegates to county and/or state conventions. (see box)

The duties of the local party officials are not often fully spelled out in the statutes. In areas where local parties are active, the officials naturally develop organizational responsibilities that the statutes never mention. In the past, the fabled local committeemen or "ward heelers" of the American political machine knew the local voters, catered to their needs and problems, introduced the party candidates to them, and propagandized the parties' issues—all the ultimate purpose of turning out a bloc of votes for the party on election day. In the less active local parties the committeepersons may do little more than occasionally attend meetings and campaign for a party candidate or two.

The Local Committees   A welter of party committees rises above the local committeepersons. Collectively, they often make up the city, town, village, legislative, county, and congressional district committees, or they elect the delegates who do. In a few cases, these committees, or some of them, are chosen at county conventions or by the party's candidates for public office. Regardless of this profusion of committees and the various mechanics of their formation, the chief committee is generally the county committee, although in some states the congressional district committees assume a comparable importance.

Many states regulate the party's activities and its internal processes. They may require that local committees meet within thirty or forty-five days after the primary elections, that they notify the secretary of state or the county clerk of the election of officers within a set time, that they not permit the voting of proxies, that they observe a fixed order of business at their meetings, or that they hold their conventions in certain types of public buildings. Under state law, in short, the political parties are not, in the usual sense, merely private associations. As Leon Epstein has put it, they are public utilities.[4]

The State Central Committees   The state central committees, too, come in fifty state varieties. In some states, the lawmakers have left the composition to the decision of the parties, but in most they have decided the matter themselves. Basically, the differences center on two points: the lower party unit from which the state committee members are chosen and the ways in which they are chosen. The unit represented may be the county, the congressional district, the state legislative district, the state convention, cities, or a mixture of these. The methods of choice include election in the party's primaries, election by a lower committee, ex officio representation, or selection by a party convention. The possible number of combinations of the two factors is considerable, and the states use most of them.

The activities of these state committees often set down in almost painful detail. It is common to assign the committees responsibility for calling and organizing party conventions, for drafting party platforms, for supervising the spending of party campaign funds, and for selecting the party's presidential electors, representatives to the national committee, and national convention delegates and alternates. Regarding the main business of running a party organization and supporting candidates in the primaries and general elections, state statutes are generally silent, except to say, occasionally, that the parties may make whatever rules are necessary for the conduct of party business. Some, however, do forbid or permit the committees to endorse candidates in the primary.

---

[4]Leon Epstein, *Political Parties in the American Mold* (Madison: University of Wisconsin Press, 1986), pp. 155–99.

A number of states assign to statewide conventions many of the powers and responsibilities that other states leave to the state central committees. They may ordain that the state conventions write the platform, select the national committeepersons from the state, nominate presidential electors, and choose delegates and alternates to the party's national convention. Indeed, some states provide that the state convention select the state committee itself. Furthermore, in a small number of states such as Connecticut, the state convention of the party actually nominates candidates for some statewide offices—a reminder of the power of conventions in the days before the direct primary.

Such, then, are the formal organizational structures created for the parties in the states. Three general observations about them are in order. First, the organizational layers relate to voting districts and to the constituencies in which public officials are chosen, and the duties assigned to them are almost exclusively concerned with the contesting of elections. The political party organization—as seen in the statute books of the states—is clearly an auxiliary to the state's regulation of nominations and elections, tasks that before the turn of the century belonged almost exclusively to the parties.

Second, it is clear from the statutes that state legislators have also viewed the parties as skeletal organizations—as cadre parties—run by a small number of party officials. There is little evidence that they have entertained the possibility of mass parties, or even of parties that attract the concerns and labors of many activists. Indeed, they assume the contrary. By opening the election of local committeepersons (and of other party officials) to the electorate in the primary election, they have defined the parties' voters as a quasi-membership group. By legislative fiat, they have tried to democratize the parties, to open them to the ultimate participation and authority of all voters. Thus, the party that results is not a private association whose participating members choose its leaders and chart its affairs; it is the semipublic, easily permeable hybrid of which we have already spoken.

Finally, although the formal organization of the parties appears to be hierarchical, it is not. The state party hierarchies more aptly have been described by V. O. Key as " a system of layers of organization"[5] and by Samuel J. Eldersveld as a "stratarchy."[6] In some states, for example, the state central committee's members are chosen directly by the voters; the committee, therefore, does not grow out of the committees below it. Even when the linkage between the layers of organization is direct, the links move from bottom to top. Such a system hardly would appear to be designed to produce the centralization of power at the apex that the very concept of hierarchy presumes.[7] Basically, the party organization is a system of party committees close to and growing from

[5]V. O. Key, Jr., *Politics, Parties and Pressure Groups* (New York: Crowell, 1964), p. 316.

[6]Samuel J. Eldersveld, *Political Parties: A Behavioral Analysis* (Chicago: Rand McNally, 1964).

[7]The organization of American political parties leads one to question whether Michels' "iron law" of oligarchy that organizations are inevitably controlled from the top is really an iron law after all. See Robert Michels, *Political Parties* (Glencoe, Ill.: Free Press, 1949; originally published in 1915).

the political grass roots. The result is to build into the party organization a great deal of localism and decentralization.

PARTY MACHINES, THEN AND NOW

The best example of the vigorous and disciplined party organization of the sort the most elaborate statutes envision is the classic urban political machine. Its heyday was in the several decades around the turn of the twentieth century, and its habitat was the burgeoning American city. Its characteristics were substantial autonomy in its operations, durability, a hierarchical internal structure, control over nominations, reliance upon material incentives to build loyalty and support among the electorate, and overall control of government in a city or county.[8] Its annals are replete with the colorful histories of Tammany Hall in New York, the knaveries of the Pendergasts in Kansas City and Frank ("I am the law") Hague in Jersey City, the cheeky threats of Chicago's "Big Bill" Thompson to punch the King of England on the nose, and the genial rascality (and mail fraud conviction) of Mayor James Curley of Boston.

The Decay of the Party Machines

In recent years, however, the great urban machines of yore seem to have been disappearing from the political scene. The most recent and most visible symbol of their decay has been the inability of the Chicago machine to hold on to centralized control after the death of Mayor Richard J. Daley in 1976 (see box). All manner of problems have beset other traditional urban machines as well. Some, such as the ones in Pittsburgh and New York, have never recovered after being upset by middle class reformers. Others, such as those in Philadelphia and Gary, Indiana, were displaced by the succession to power of new ethnic groups, especially blacks, who had become the more effective practitioners of the old ethnic politics.

The Foundations of the Party Machines

Urban machines such as Chicago's have depended fundamentally upon their ability to provide tangible material benefits to their clients. The most visible of these benefits have been patronage jobs, which numbered in the thousands in many cities during the heyday of the machine. These appointments won the in-

---

[8]These are the characteristics David Mayhew uses to define *traditional party organizations*, which when they hold overall control of a city or county at the local level are synonymous with machines. See Mayhew's *Placing Parties in American Politics* (Princeton, N.J.: Princeton University Press, 1986), pp. 19–21. This book provides excellent descriptions of traditional party organizations in a variety of states up through the 1960s.

The End of Machine Politics, Chicago Style

The recent difficulties of the fabled Chicago party machine in Chicago may signal the vanishing of that special breed of party organization. In its heyday under the leadership of Mayor Richard J. Daley, the Chicago machine controlled nominations, elections, and the making of public policy in the city. Its dominance was based on control over an estimated 35,000 patronage jobs in government and access to another 10,000 in the private economy. Building from this loyal base by adding their families, friends, and relatives, the organization could deliver 350,000 disciplined votes at election time.

With Daley's death in 1976, the machine lost its already-eroding control over Chicago politics and government. Machine candidates were defeated in two successive Democratic primaries, the second of which saw the party polarize along racial lines. It took black Mayor Harold Washington, the narrow victor of the 1983 primary and general election contests, several years to gain even majority support on the Democratic-dominated Board of Aldermen (Chicago's city council). Washington's re-election in 1987 further consolidated his power—but over a Democratic party riven by racial conflict, a government with declining numbers of patronage jobs, and a city with debilitating economic and social problems. It is doubtful that Washington could have overcome these troubles to reconstruct a Democratic party machine, and his untimely death in 1987 initiated a new round of sharp internecine conflict. When the dust had settled, Chicago had a new mayor, Richard M. Daley, Jr., elected by a substantial majority in 1989 and re-elected without serious opposition in 1991. Only time will tell if he can overcome the same formidable difficulties and resurrect the party machine.

No simple explanation will suffice for the demise of Chicago's heralded machine. Was it the inevitable result of the death of Daley, whose consummate skill had been the only glue binding together antagonistic ethnic, racial, and class groups? Was it just another phase in the inexorable process of ethnic succession, as blacks flexed their muscles in pursuit of their share of political power? Was it the product of a changing political culture in which machine politics was less acceptable? Or was it the simple electoral reaction to a deterioration of city services? As is so often the case, each of these explanations may have some merit.[9]

---

[9]The colorful politics of Chicago has stimulated a rich literature. An early study of the Chicago machine is Harold Foote Gosnell's *Machine Politics: Chicago Style* (Chicago: University of Chicago Press, 1939). Good studies of the Daley years are Edward C. Banfield, *Political Influence* (New York: The Free Press, 1961); Milton Rakove, *Don't Make No Waves, Don't Back No Losers* (Bloomington, Ind.: Indiana University Press, 1975); and Thomas M. Guterbok, *Machine Politics in Transition: Party and Community in Chicago* (Chicago: University of Chicago Press, 1980). On the post-Daley years, see Paul Kleppner, *Chicago Divided: The Making of a Black Mayor* (DeKalb, Ill.: Northern Illinois University Press, 1985).

dispensable loyalty and service of the workers to the machine. Their efforts, in turn, created the vitality that drove the local party organization and produced the party vote—their own votes plus those of their friends, family, and neighbors. Local party workers also won voter loyalties by coping with the problems of their constituencies. Often, those problems were personal—unemployment or a delinquent child—as well as public or governmental. The machine and its workers could earn political gratitude by finding social welfare agencies for the troubled, jobs for the jobless, contracts for local merchants, or even the storied Christmas baskets or deliveries of coal for the needy.

Public jobs and the cadre of loyal party workers they create were only one of the machine's resources. Governments purchase many goods and services from the private sector, which can be exchanged for political support as well. Banks that hold city money, insurance agents who write city policies, lawyers retained to conduct city business, newspapers that print city notices, even suppliers of soap to city washrooms all may be drawn into the web of the political machine. Government also influences economic opportunities in the private sector by zoning and public works decisions. Individuals advantaged by these decisions may be induced to feel a debt of gratitude to political leaders, which will be called in at election time. Finally, city hall regulates a good deal of the economic activity of a city by giving or withholding building permits, health certificates, zoning variances, and so on. Political leadership dedicated to the extraction of political support in exchange for these so-called "preferments" can rather ruthlessly use them to build its political power.

Machines overcame a scarcity of benefits by reducing electoral competition through restricting the electorate, using force and intimidation if necessary, and through manipulation of election rules and (if all else failed) the vote count. Their ability to appeal to ethnic loyalties also should not be discounted. Evidence from studies of the development of machine-like organizations in a variety of nations illustrates this source of support nicely. Political machines are found to develop and flourish where competitive elections with mass suffrage occur in a parochial social context in which loyalties to family, neighborhood, or ethnic group accompany the strong needs for immediate, short-term benefits. Thus, the rise and fall of the American political machine cannot be disassociated from changes in ethnic group loyalties in our cities. The urban machine has been a vehicle for ethnic group integration and succession in American politics, especially for the Irish.[10] It has atrophied where outlooks are more cosmopolitan or where it cannot satisfy the aspirations of competing ethnic groups.[11]

---

[10]Steven P. Erie makes a persuasive argument that the great urban machines were principally organizations of, by, and for the Irish that proved unwilling to accommodate other ethnic groups. See his *Rainbow's End: Irish-Americans and the Dilemmas of Urban Machine Politics, 1840–1985* (Berkeley: University of California Press, 1988).

[11]For an insightful discussion of the conditions for machine politics here and abroad, see James C. Scott, "Corruption, Machine Politics, and Political Change," *American Political Science Review* 63 (1969): 1142–58.

Thus, the classic urban machine has always been part electoral organization, part "informal government," part social service agency, and part ladder for upward social and economic mobility. To a significant degree, it resembles the local organization of a European mass membership party, except that the American machine has no membership base, and it has few, if any, ideological concerns. Its focus on the immediate needs of its constituents has driven it to look almost completely inward and to ignore the issues and ideologies of the political world beyond. It is provincially concerned with the city, and its politics are almost completely divorced from the issues that agitate our national politics.

Even though the most colorful and certainly the most visible American party machines developed in our largest cities, it would be a mistake to view political machines as exclusively urban phenomena. The conditions conducive for the development of machines, especially a large parochially oriented population with short-term material needs, also have existed outside of urban environments, such as in small towns in the South or one-company towns. Even some affluent suburban areas, in defiance of the general rule about the social conditions for machines, have spawned strong machine-style party organizations. In the affluent Long Island suburbs of New York City, for example, lies a Republican Nassau County political machine that controls local government and local politics "with a local party operation that in terms of patronage and party loyalty rivals the machine of the famed Democratic mayor of Chicago, Richard J. Daley."[12]

It is difficult to discern how powerful party machines really were in their heyday. Contemporary evidence from areas of machine strength casts doubt on the vaunted efficiency of the machine. A Chicago study found little evidence that public services were distributed by the party machine to reward political support in either 1967 or 1977. Rather, historical factors and bureaucratic decision rules governed the allocation of services.[13] A New Haven study found that an Italian-led machine distributed summer jobs disproportionately to Italian youths from non-machine wards who rarely engaged in subsequent political work, not to youth from strong machine areas—supporting Steven Erie's observation (see note 10) that ethnic loyalties often overwhelm the machine's devotion to organizational maintenance and expansion.[14]

By the same token, one must not lose sight of the near consensus among scholars that the conditions conducive to the maintenance of political party machines have withered away in recent years. Contemporary evidence, even from the most putatively machine-dominated cities, may not reflect what machines

---

[12]Tom Watson, "All-Powerful Machine of Yore Endures in New York's Nassau," *Congressional Quarterly Weekly Report*, August 17, 1985, p. 1623.

[13]Kenneth R. Mladenka, "The Urban Bureaucracy and the Chicago Political Machine: Who Gets What and the Limits to Political Control," *American Political Science Review* 74 (1980): 991–98.

[14]Michael Johnston, "Patrons and Clients, Jobs and Machines: A Case Study in the Uses of Patronage," *American Political Science Review* 73 (1979): 385–98.

were like in their heyday. It is incontrovertible that the patronage resources now available to local parties cannot match what they once commanded. The extension of civil service protection to municipal employees, through legislation and court decisions as well as the unionization of public employees, has sharply reduced the number of jobs that can be used to reward the party faithful (as will be discussed more fully in Chapter 5). The institutionalization of social services through federal entitlement programs has eroded another important source of machine power. In the post-World War II period, prosperity has raised many Americans to levels of economic security that end their dependence upon government, reduce the attractiveness of public employment, and increase their ability to fend for themselves in a complex bureaucratic society.

A Future for Political Machines?

Nonetheless, we must be careful not to underestimate the persistence of conditions conducive to machine-style party organizations in a few locales. Dependent populations remain in our major cities. Political machines have demonstrated great creativity in subverting civil service regulations to create patronage jobs (e.g., Mayor Daley hired thousands of long-term "temporary" employees) and in brokering federal benefits for the poor (e.g., the summer jobs distributed by the machine in New Haven were provided through the federal CETA program). More fundamentally, because local governments continue to have large budgets, provide a complex array of services, and play an active regulatory role, ample opportunities remain to sustain a patron-client form of politics in a supportive political culture. As government has become more bureaucratized, furthermore, the citizens' needs for intervention have grown rather than declined. While political machines probably have withered tremendously, even after we properly deflate the exaggerated claims made for them in their heyday, it may be premature to announce their death. Indeed, it is possible that their recent demise results from another enervating battle over ethnic succession, this time typically between blacks and white ethnics, and is but a temporary interlude in party organizations' centralization of political authority in American cities.[15]

LOCAL PARTY ORGANIZATION: A MORE REPRESENTATIVE VIEW

Yet the machines of the big cities have never been and are not now typical of party organizations in the United States. They set the standard for effective

---

[15]Raymond Wolfinger stands almost alone among political scientists in resisting the stampede to sound the death knell for political machines. See his "Why Political Machines Have Not Withered Away and Other Revisionist Thoughts," *Journal of Politics* 34 (1972): 365–98.

TABLE 3.2   THE ORGANIZATIONAL STRENGTH OF LOCAL PARTIES, 1979–80

Attribute	Democrats	Republicans
Median number of chairs since 1969	2.5	2.6
Percentage with complete set of officers	90	81
Percentage with year-round office	12	14
Percentage with telephone listing	11	16
Percentage with paid staff		
Full-time	3	4
Part-time	5	6
Percentage with regular annual budget	20	31
Percentage operating a campaign headquarters	55	60
Median number of county committee meetings		
1978	6	6
1977	6	5
Percentage with a constitution, charter, or set of rules	68	68

Note: Based on responses from a total of 2,021 Democratic and 1,980 Republican organizations.

Source: Cotter *et al.*, *Party Organization in American Politics*, p. 43.

party organizations. At the other extreme—essentially unrepresented in the scholarly or popular literature because it offers so little to study—is virtual disorganization. In such cases, most of the party positions are unfilled or are held by completely inactive incumbents. A chairman and a handful of loyal party officials may meet occasionally to carry out the most essential affairs of the party. Their main activity occurs shortly before the primary elections, as they plead with members of the party to become candidates or step in themselves as candidates to "fill the party ticket." They are largely without influence or following, for theirs is often a chronic minority party. They meet infrequently, raise little money for election campaigns, and create little or no public attention. This type of organization is now, and probably always has been more common than the machine. Most American local party organization lies between these two extremes, but probably closer to the pole of disorganization.

A comprehensive picture of these organizations is provided by a national survey of local (principally county) parties, called the Party Transformation Study, conducted in 1979–80.[16] This survey found that most local organizations had formal rules or bylaws and were headed by a chair and executive committee who met regularly and were most active during election campaigns. (See Table 3.2) These local party leaders, plus a few associated activists, made decisions in

---

[16]The results of this survey are reported in James L. Gibson, Cornelius P. Cotter, John F. Bibby, and Robert J. Huckshorn, "Whither the Local Parties?" *American Journal of Political Science* 29 (1985): 139–60 and Cornelius P. Cotter, James L. Gibson, John F. Bibby, and Robert J. Huckshorn, *Party Organization in American Politics* (New York: Praeger, 1984).

the name of the party, raised funds, sought out and screened candidates (or approved candidates who selected themselves), and got involved in election campaigns. Most were volunteers, with meager resources with which to work. Virtually none received salaries for their efforts, and only a few had paid staff to assist them or enjoyed such basic organizational support as a regular budget, a year-round office, or even a telephone listing.

The Party Transformation Study discovered also that the efforts of the typical party organization, where they did anything at all, revolved around the election campaign. Most local organizations campaigned on behalf of the party candidates by performing organizing, fund-raising, and grass-roots voter contact activities. How energetically they devoted themselves to such activities is difficult to gauge from the subjective reports of this study, but it would hardly be surprising to find party performance generally to be lackluster. In many locales, the local party organizations quite likely were only incidental contributors to election campaigns.

When the various indicators of organizational strength at the local level are combined, Democratic and Republican organizations differed little on average. Variation in local organizational strength, though, was found among the states. Some states in the 1979–80 study—most notably New Jersey, New York, Pennsylvania, Indiana, and Ohio—had relatively strong local organizations in both parties, while others—Louisiana, Georgia, Nebraska, Kentucky, Alabama, and, Texas, for example—had relatively weak parties at the local level. In a few states, such as Arizona and Florida, one party was considerably stronger at the local level than the other, but divergence in organizational strength is the exception to a more natural symbiosis: Strong organizations of one party are typically matched with strong organizations in the other party.[17]

An update of the Party Transformation Study in 1984, based on a resurvey of a sample of the local organizations assessed in 1980, showed that virtually no change in organizational strength had taken place in the intervening four years. If anything, the organizations may have become a bit more robust, perhaps as a result of intensive efforts by national and state parties to invigorate local parties. The greatest increases in organizational strength appeared among the southern Democrats, as they struggled to keep up with the growing organizational potency of their GOP counterparts.[18]

While the variation is great, it is accurate to say that few local party organizations enjoy the command of resources and the ranks of party foot soldiers associated with the traditional party machine. The local party organization typ-

---

[17]Cotter *et al.*, *Party Organization in American Politics*, pp. 49–53. The states with strong and weak local organizations, respectively, are virtually the same ones cited in Mayhew's survey of party strength in the late 1960s. See Mayhew, *Placing Parties in American Politics*.

[18]James L. Gibson, John P. Frendreis, and Laura L. Vertz, "Party Dynamics in the 1980s: Change in County Party Organizational Strength, 1980–1984," *American Journal of Political Science* 33 (1989): 67–90.

ically is a weak organizational force in the community, with the real leadership more generally assumed by the party's elected public officials. The organization's leadership must operate not with threats and iron discipline, but with pleading and cajoling. Few incentives and rewards remain with which to recruit all the effort and manpower both the statutory structures and the images of the classic political machine seem to assume.

There also is strong evidence that the average local organization today is increasingly more active in political campaigns than it was over two decades before. By comparing data on the same counties between 1964 and 1979–80, Party Transformation Study researchers assessed changes in organizational activity levels for five important campaign activities—literature distribution, arranging campaign events, fund raising, publicity, and registration drives. In each case, they found that more party organizations were active in the later years; for most activities, the increase was substantial. The 1988 Study of Presidential Campaign Leaders conducted by John Kessel and William Jacoby, permits comparison between the Party Transformation Study and 1988 for a longer list of activities. Here again levels were higher in the later years. Finally, over-time studies of Detroit and Los Angeles contain parallel results.[19]

Thus, the question of whether local party organizations are stronger in the 1980s than before defies a simple answer. Gone are the exemplars of local organization, the party machines, so this extreme end of the organizational strength continuum now is empty.[20] But the party machines never were the typical party organizations. For each one of them, there were surely scores, maybe hundreds, of local parties that were merely skeletal organizations. These ordinary organizations seem stronger and more active, on the average, than they were several decades before. And, with increased competition fostering organization by both parties where previously one would have dominated, minority parties are more robust. Nonetheless, it is questionable whether the **typical** organization is stronger now than it was during the nineteenth century—in that Golden Age of the parties, when they controlled nominations, printed the general election ballot, and mobilized their faithful armies of patronage workers. If the modal organization of the 1990s has gained on its counterpart of the 1890s, it is through the development of a modest organizational presence in previously fallow areas and through professionalism rather than raw strength.

---

[19]See Cotter *et al.*, *Party Organization in American Politics*, p. 54, for the 1964–80 comparison. The 1964 figures come from Paul Allen Beck, "Environment and Party," *American Political Science Review* 68 (1974): 1229–44. The 1988 figures are reported in Charles E. Smith, Jr., "Changes in Party Organizational Strength and Activity 1979–1988," The Ohio State University, unpublished manuscript, 1989. On Detroit and Los Angeles, see Samuel J. Eldersveld, "The Party Activist in Detroit and Los Angeles: A Longitudinal View, 1956–1980," in William J. Crotty, ed., *Political Parties in Local Areas* (Knoxville: University of Tennessee Press, 1986), pp. 89–119.

[20]For excellent descriptions of these traditional organizations before they suffered their recent declines, see Mayhew, *Placing Parties in American Politics*.

STATE PARTY ORGANIZATION

Sitting atop the apex of the pyramid of party organization described in state statutes and conventional depictions of the party hierarchy such as in Figure 3.1 is the state committee and its organizational structure.

Traditional Weakness

The exalted location of the state party organization here, however, is illusory. Most scholars believe that in most states the state committee has not been the major locus of organizational authority.

Instead, many state party organizations are, in fact, federations—and loose ones, at that—of semiautonomous or autonomous local baronies and baronial county chairmen. Added to the fragmentation of this decentralization is the fragmentation of factionalism. Parties divide internally by regions of the state, by rural-urban differences, along ethnic and religious lines, by loyalty to local leaders, and especially by liberal and conservative preferences. Any consolidation of power at the state level seriously threatens the various factions. It is a prize that can be won by only one of them rather than shared. Traditionally it has been avoided through a variety of devices, not the least of which has been to vest few resources in the hands of the state party organization. That, in turn, reinforces their tendencies toward decentralization, which means that power and authority within them resides in the most viable of the local levels—the county organization.

The pervasive localism of American politics has been reinforced by other forces that have weakened the state party organizations. Their roles in the national presidential nominating conventions have been diminished by party reforms, especially since 1968. Convention delegates now are mostly chosen by voters, and almost all come to the convention pledged to a particular candidate for the nomination rather than under the thumb of state party leaders. Continuing extension of civil service protections, the unionization of state employees, and judicial intervention to prevent even the **firing** of patronage workers when the state house changed party hands have all contributed to the erosion of the patronage base for many state parties. Above all, the state parties have lost significant amounts of control over state nomination and election campaigns. Candidates find it increasingly easy to win nominations in primary elections without party organization support; they find it easier than ever to raise money for their own campaigns and thus run them without party help. State legislative leaders raise and dispense campaign money independent of the state party organization. The new importance of the media in politics and the rise of a new breed of campaign experts offer the candidates new ways of reaching voters that have little or nothing to do with the parties.

Strengthening in Recent Years

But in spite of these impediments, state parties seem to have become organizationally stronger in recent years. The Party Transformation Study found that they were healthier in important respects than they had been twenty years before.[21] In 1960–64, only 50 percent of their sample of state organizations had a permanent state headquarters compared with 91 percent in 1979–80. The number with a full-time, salaried chairman or director grew from 63 percent to 90 percent during the same period, and average staff size in the off-election years increased from 3.5 to 5.9. The non-election year budgets of the state parties were higher in absolute dollars as well, although not higher in inflation-adjusted dollars, climbing from an average of $188,125 in 1960–64 to $340,667 in 1979–80.

The increased strength of the state parties allows them to play a more important role in political campaigns. As the authors of the study put it: "The stronger, more virile state parties will be able to use their organizational resources to provide campaign services to state and local candidates (particularly those running for the state legislatures) while supplementing the role of candidate organizations geared to congressional, senatorial, gubernatorial, and presidential elections."[22] The revivified state parties were already moving in that direction. Ninety percent of them, for example, ran campaigning seminars for party candidates, and a great majority of them had mobilization programs through which to identify and turn out their party's likely voters. The state parties, it thus appears, have at last allied themselves with the new campaign skills to recapture a role in the election campaigns.

Most of this activity takes place, of course, not in the unwieldy state central committees, but in the bureaucracies they create. We are therefore seeing the first real signs of the institutionalization of the state parties—their dominance, or at least the dominance of their activity, by full-time, paid, professional staffs (see Table 3.3). From the early 1960s to 1980, for example, the average number of paid staff members in the state parties had doubled. These party bureaucrats cannot easily exert much influence over the party in government; nor do they exert much control over local party units in the state. Theirs is a service organization that brings useful skills and information to party candidates in the election campaigns. Their services will certainly win the appreciation and gratitude of the candidates, which leads one to wonder about the ultimate uses of growing state party organization strength—can the state parties convert the obligation of their successful candidates to support for party positions or programs?

Data from the 1979–80 study and a similar 1984 study[23] also show that, unlike the situation at the county level, Republican state organizations were con-

---

[21]The materials in the text come from Robert J. Huckshorn and John F. Bibby, "State Parties in an Era of Political Change," in Joel L. Fleishman, ed., *The Future of American Political Parties* (Englewood Cliffs, N.J.: Prentice-Hall, 1982), pp. 70–100; and James L. Gibson, Cornelius P. Cotter, John F. Bibby, and Robert J. Huckshorn, "Assessing Party Organization Strength," *American Journal of Political Science* 27 (1983): 193–222.

[22]Huckshorn and Bibby, "State Parties," p. 99.

[23]Advisory Commission on Intergovernmental Relations, *The Transformation in American Politics.*

TABLE 3.3   COMPARISON OF STATE PARTY ORGANIZATIONS: EARLY 1960s AND 1979

Organizational Feature	Percentage of Democratic and Republican State Parties that Have Each Feature	
	1960–64	1979–80
Permanent state headquarters	50	91
Full-time chairman or director	63	90
Voter mobilization programs	39	75

Sources: Data from Huckshorn and Bibby, "State Parties in an Era of Political Change;" and Gibson et al., "Assessing Party Organization Strength."

siderably stronger than their Democratic counterparts. The Republicans had more paid leaders, larger and more specialized staffs, and substantially bigger budgets. This relative advantage in organization strength enabled the GOP to perform more services for the party and its candidates. For example, twice as many Republican as Democratic state organizations provided public opinion polling services. The GOP organizational advantage is not built up on a regional basis but is uniform, reflecting to a considerable degree no doubt the extensive subsidies the national party has been able to provide to all of the state parties. It is an advantage that surely has persisted, and probably even grown, into the 1990s.

To build a powerful state organization is to overcome both the grass-roots localism of American politics and the widespread antipathy to strong party discipline. Understandably, it is not easy. Strong and skillful personal leadership by a governor, a senator, or a state chairman helps. So do political resources— especially money, which is the essential fuel for the modern campaign, and "manpower." It also helps to have a tradition or culture that accepts the notion of a unified and effective party in the state. Similarly, it makes a difference whether or not the state parties are given important political responsibilities. It is no coincidence that central party organization has flourished in the states in which primary elections are least extensive and in which the party organization determines much more directly who the statewide and congressional candidates will be. An environment conducive to strong party organizations is rarely found in the American states. But where it is present (such as in Pennsylvania for both parties; Ohio, Minnesota, and South Dakota for the Republicans; and North Dakota for the Democrats[24]), state organizations have flourished.

---

[24]These were identified as the strongest state organizations in 1979–80 by Cotter *et al.*, *Party Organizations in American Politics*, pp. 28–29.

TRENDS AND CHANGES

Local party organizations are indisputably weaker today than they were a hundred years ago when the parties could be described as:

> . . . armies drawn up for combat (in which) financial and communications "sinews of war" were provided by an elaborate, well-staffed, and strongly motivated organizational structure. In the field of communications, a partisan press was dominant. . . . The "drilling" of voters in this period by their party captains was intense.[25]

While this description surely did not apply uniformly to party organizations throughout the nation, it might be impossible to find a local party organization that would earn this characterization today.

Since their heyday in the latter part of the nineteenth century, the local parties have been buffeted by numerous forces, some explicitly directed at weakening them and others eroding the parties in their wake. Progressive movement reforms adopted around the turn of the century sapped party strength by limiting their control over nominations and general elections as well as over treasured patronage resources. In recent decades, a number of disparate forces—reforms in presidential nominations, bureaucratization of the welfare state, the integration of ethnics into American life, almost total demise of the patronage system, national regulation of previously state-controlled party activities, and greater education of the electorate—have threatened further the viability of the local parties.[26]

Yet local parties have exhibited such great resiliency in adapting to these changes that one must be careful not to exaggerate the extent of their demise. It may even be premature to announce the death of the urban party machines, considering the ample rewards local governments still offer to the resourceful political entrepreneur and the continuing dependency of city residents. The local party organizations, in short, are adapting to meet the new challenges posed by a changing environment, demonstrating once again the resiliency that has enabled them to survive throughout much of the history of the American Republic.

The state party organizations have probably followed a different route to where they are today. Traditionally weak, little more than vessels that could barely contain vibrant and often warring local organizations, the state organizations appear to have achieved an unprecedented robustness in recent years.

---

[25]Walter Dean Burnham, *Critical Elections and the Mainsprings of American Politics* (New York: Norton, 1970), p. 72.

[26]For an intensive examination of how factors such as these undermined Democratic organizations in three different locales, see Alan Ware, *The Breakdown of the Democratic Party Organization 1940–80* (Oxford: Oxford University Press, 1985).

They have located new sources of financial support in mass mailings, contributions from the national parties, and "soft money."[27] This has enabled them to become more professionalized than ever before and to channel their activity into provision of services to the grass-roots local organizations, which in an earlier era rarely looked to their state headquarters for assistance. Recent trends within the states, then, seem to have undermined the long-standing decentralization of the party organizations.

Yet for all of this rejuvenated party power, it is clear that the formal, statutory party organizations at the state and local level affect less of campaign politics than they once did. They have been muscled aside by a motley assortment of new and old actors in the electoral process. Membership clubs, candidates and their organizations, ambitious individuals, campaign technocrats, donors of political money, issue groups and caucuses, and even some traditional interest groups also work the election campaigns. Many of them ally themselves with a party label and, to some extent, with a party organization. Therefore, state and local party organizations are far looser and more flexible today than the words of the statutes would suggest. The state and local party organizations are now generally loose aggregations of:

- The statutory organization (or the active parts of it).
- Elected officials from the party.
- The candidates and their organizations and supporters.
- Related party organizations (the clubs, the caucuses, the factional organizations).
- Active and potentially active individuals (supporters of candidates, issues, and the party itself; would-be candidates and party leaders; important financial contributors).
- Allied nonparty organizations (local interest groups, political action committees, ideological associations).[28]

In other words, the party is a flexible and somewhat undisciplined pool of active groups and individuals. They are recruited to the party for different reasons, and they are activated by different candidates, different issues, and different elections. A hotly contested school board election will activate one cluster of partisans, and a congressional election will activate another. What we have

---

[27] *Soft money* refers to campaign contributions raised by the national parties and presidential candidates that would be illegal under federal law if they remained at the national level but become legal when they are directly funnelled to the state parties for use in nonfederal elections. For more on soft money, see Chapter 12.

[28] This notion of the state and local parties fits Mildred Schwartz's conceptualization of the party as a network of interactions in *The Party Network: The Robust Organization of Illinois Republicans* (Madison: University of Wisconsin Press, 1990). She found that the most central actors within the modern Illinois Republican party were financial contributors, interest groups, advisors, state senators and representatives, county chairs, and the governor—not solely the occupants of the formal party organization.

thought of as the party organization is really a reservoir of organizations and activists from which are drawn the shifting organizational coalitions that speak and act in the name of the party.

In searching for change in American party organization, however, one ought not lose sight of what does not change. The American state and local parties remain largely skeletal, cadre organizations, run by small numbers of activists and involving the great masses of their supporters only at election time. The shift away from the organizational forms inherent in the statutes of the states has largely been a shift from a well-defined cadre organization to a looser, more amorphous cadre organization. Yet, the American parties are still a long way from becoming mass membership parties, and they are still some distance from achieving the continuously active, year-round tempos of parties elsewhere in the world. By the standards of those parties, American party organization continues to be characterized by unusual fluidity and evanescence, by failure to generate activity at nonelection time, and by the ease with which a handful of activists and public officeholders dominate it.

4

National Organizations: A New Presence at the Summit

South of Capitol Hill, a few blocks from the House and Senate offices, stand the national headquarters buildings of the Democratic and Republican parties. These are the offices of the national committees, which occupy the apex of the pyramid of the American party organizations. In important ways, these two buildings symbolize the current standing of the national parties. That each party now owns a modern national headquarters building signifies levels of financial well-being, independence, and permanence unprecedented in the annals of the national parties. Not long ago, the national committees were poor and transient renters (often moving back and forth between New York and Washington), and all but disappeared in the period between presidential campaigns. Location of the offices closer to Congress than to the White House symbolizes movement of the national party beyond its traditional position as handmaiden to the president toward its new role of party-building in the states and localities. The two edifices house professional staffs engaged in a beehive of continuous activity—a far cry from a few years ago when the national committees had few employees, high turnover, and little to do. Finally, the GOP's headquarters was purchased earlier (1970 compared with 1985 for the Democrats) and is larger, which illustrates the great lead the Republicans have enjoyed in the building of an effective national party organization.

All of this supports the realization of most close observers of American political parties that the national committees are stronger today than at any time since their creation by the Democrats in 1848 and by the Republicans in 1856. Stronger, too, in their respective roles are the congressional campaign committees and the national party conventions. Only in the period before 1828 when presidential nominations were made by the congressional caucus were the national parties as important in American politics. Moreover, the national parties seem to be gaining in strength with each passing year and now play ever more vital roles in national, state, and local party politics.

What a contrast the present-day status of the national party committees is to their situation only a few decades ago, which leading students of the national committees could accurately characterize as "politics without power."[1] For most of their history, in fact, the national parties epitomized the summit organizations of a decentralized party system, which was described by one noted scholar of American parties in the following way:

> Decentralization of power is by all odds the most important single characteristic of the American major party; more than anything else this trait distinguishes it from all others. Indeed, once this truth is understood, nearly everything else about American parties is greatly illuminated. . . . The American major party is, to repeat the definition, a loose confederation of state and local bosses for limited purposes.[2]

The bases for decentralization are obvious. State and local party organizations of the major parties pick their own officers, nominate their own candidates, take their own stands on issues, and raise and spend their own funds without much interference from any manifestation of the national party. Often, the national committees have served only as arenas for the bargaining and jockeying among the powerful local and state organizations and presidential candidates within the party. Indeed, it was often said that, in reality, there are no national parties, that what we blithely call the national parties are merely coalitions of jealous, wary, and diverse state and local party organizations.

Since the late 1970s, however, there have been incontestable signs that the national committees are emerging into the light after 150 years of eclipse. Their resources and staffs are growing, and they are undertaking new roles and activities. They have become more active, vital, and influential. There also have been successful attempts to limit the autonomy of state and local organizations in the selection of delegates to the national conventions. These changes have led some to revise the traditional picture of a decentralized party by claiming that the national parties have become "federations" rather than "confederations" of the state and local parties—a shift in terminology that is meant to signify an enhanced potential for national authority that parallels the replacement of the Articles of Confederation by the Constitution in the early days of the American Republic.[3] While the American party system remains decentralized in many significant respects and one must be careful not to exaggerate present

---

[1]Cornelius P. Cotter and Bernard C. Hennessy, *Politics without Power: The National Party Committees* (New York: Atherton, 1964). For a comprehensive history of the national committees, see Ralph M. Goldman, *The National Party Chairmen and Committees* (Armonk, N.Y.: M. E. Sharpe, 1990).

[2]E. E. Schattschneider, *Party Government* (New York: Rinehart, 1942), pp. 129, 132–33.

[3]Leon D. Epstein, *Political Parties in the American Mold* (Madison: University of Wisconsin Press, 1986), pp. 200–238; and Gary D. Wekkin, "National-State Party Relations: The Democrats' New Federal Structure," *Political Science Quarterly* 99 (1984): 45–72.

trends, it is impossible to ignore the signs of unprecedented national vitality in the parties.

But one is compelled to ask what took them so long. Most other aspects of American life have long since been nationalized. The mass media bring the same reporters, TV images, and commentators into homes in all parts of the country. By any other measure, government in the American federal system has been increasingly centered in Washington since the 1930s. Even the other two sectors of the party have been nationalized in the past few decades. The party electorates respond increasingly to national issues, to national candidates, and to national party symbols and positions. Attention now centers as well on the national parties in government; the president and the congressional leadership of the parties are more than ever the prime spokespersons for their parties. The party organization responded belatedly to nationalizing forces for a number of reasons: the state regulation of parties, the thousands of public officials chosen in the states, and the domination of local organization by those officials. All those local pressures still exist, of course, and they will continue to restrain the centralization of authority within the parties.

THE NATIONAL COMMITTEES AND NATIONAL OFFICERS

Before investigating how the national party has changed, though, it is important to establish what it is. Technically speaking, the nominating convention each party holds midway in a presidential election year is the party's supreme national authority. The convention's role, however, rarely goes beyond the selection of presidential and vice-presidential candidates and the formulation of party platforms and party rules. It does specify the structure and powers of the national committee; but since the convention adjourns *sine die* (i.e., without setting a time for a future meeting) until four years later, it can exercise no continuing supervision over the national organizational apparatus of the party.

The Committees

Between conventions, the national committees of the two major parties are the primary governing institutions of the national parties. For years, they were similarly composed. The drastic revision of the Democratic body in 1972 changed that (Table 4.1) The Democratic National Committee (DNC) has now become more than twice the size of its Republican counterpart (the RNC). More important, the Democrats have abandoned the confederational nature of the committee. Traditionally, each state (as well as certain territories) had been represented in both national committees on an approximately equal basis, regardless of the size of its electorate or the extent of its support for the party. The Republicans still do it that way, after a brief flirtation with unequal state representation in the 1950s. Under this arrangement, states, not populations or number of partisans, were represented, much as Alaska and California are rep-

TABLE 4.1   COMPOSITION OF DEMOCRATIC AND REPUBLICAN NATIONAL
COMMITTEES: 1991

	Number of Members
Democratic National Committee	
Chairperson and next highest ranking officer of opposite sex from each state and from D.C., Puerto Rico, American Samoa, Guam, Virgin Islands, Democrats abroad	112
Members apportioned to states, etc., on same basis as delegates to national convention (at least two per state, etc.)	212
Chairperson of Democratic Governors Conference and two additional governors	3
Chairperson of Democratic Mayors Conference and two additional mayors	3
Chairperson of Democratic County Officials Conference and two additional officials	3
Chairperson of Democratic State Legislative Leaders and two additional leaders	3
Chairperson of Democratic Municipal Officials and two additional officials	3
Chairperson of Young Democrats and two additional Young Democrats	3
Chairperson of National Federation of Democratic Women and two additional members	3
Democratic leader and one other member from each house of Congress	4
Officers of National Committee and its auxiliaries	9
Additional members to implement full participation goals (blacks, Hispanics, women, youth, Asians, Native Americans)	45
	403
Republican National Committee	
National committeeman, national committeewoman, and state chairman from each state and from D.C., American Samoa, Guam, Puerto Rico, and Virgin Islands	165
	165

resented equally in the United States Senate. That system overrepresented the state organizations of the smaller states, however, and it also gave roughly equal weight in the national committees to the winning and the losing parts of the party. The practical consequence was a strengthening of the southern and western segments of the parties, which have tended to be more conservative. The newly restructured Democratic National Committee, however, gives weight both to population and to party support. California, for example, has nineteen votes on the committee, and Alaska has four. It also gives representation to a few groups that are not geographically-defined constituencies and to minorities.

National committee members are selected by the states and the other constituencies. The state parties differ from one another in how they make their decisions; and in many states, the two parties choose their national committeemen and committeewomen differently. They use four main methods—selection by state party convention, by the party delegation to the national convention, by the state central committee, and by election in a primary. In this welter of selection processes, one point is worth noting. Although the parties' state organizations usually can control the selection of committee members when they are chosen by the state committee and by the state conventions, they are less effective when the selection is by primaries or by national convention delegates. Especially in states that choose delegates in presidential primaries, the delegation to the national convention may represent voter support of a momentarily popular candidate more than it represents the leadership of the state party. A number of Democratic delegations in 1972, for example, were composed of party newcomers and mavericks who were pledged to George McGovern. The old-line party leaders in those states had supported other contenders and thus were not delegates.

The Officers

The chairpersons and other officers of the national committees do not have to be—and often are not—members of the committees. They are elected and removed by the committees. Immediately after the conventions, however, tradition recognizes the right of the parties' presidential candidates to name the national chairpersons for the course of the presidential campaign in recognition of the important role the national committee once played in the campaign. The committees ratify their choices without question. Moreover, since the party of the president will continue to respect his choice of a national party chairperson after the election, only the committee of the "out" party actually selects its own national chairperson. The committees generally have much greater freedom to select other committee officials—vice-chairpersons, secretaries, and treasurers—many of whom come from the committee itself. In addition, both national committees select executive committees, which include the officers and some other members of the committee.

Within this apparatus—supplemented, of course, by the national committees' permanent staffs—the chairpersons dominate. The full committees meet only two or three times a year, and occasionally even less than that. Cotter and Hennessy's description still applies:

> Collectively the national committee is not much more than a categorical group. . . . The national committee members have very little collective identity, little patterned interaction, and only rudimentary common values and goals.

> Except for occasional meetings—largely for show and newsmaking purposes—the national committees may be thought of not so much as groups, but as lists of people who have obtained their national committee memberships through organizational processes wholly separate in each state.[4]

The other officers of the party are not especially influential, and the executive committees meet only a little more often than the full committees. Like the full committees, the executive committees are composed of men and women whose concern is state (and even local) organizational work rather than the building of a strong national party apparatus. Traditionally, therefore, the national chairperson, with a permanent staff that he or she has chosen, has in effect been the national party organization.

Shifting Roles

In reality, the role of the national committees and chairpersons is flexible. If theirs is the party of the president, they may be little more than managers of the president's campaigns and builders of the president's political support. Presidents came to dominate their national committees early in this century. Their control reached its peak in the 1960s and 1970s.[5] Indeed, during the Nixon years, the president and his staff managed his political matters, and Rogers Morton and Robert Dole, the Republican national chairmen, did little more than serve as liaisons between the president and party leaders around the country. In such a situation, relationships between a chairperson and the political operatives in the White House are often difficult. In the party out of power, the chairperson and committee must often bind up wounds, heal intraparty squabbles, help pay debts from the losing campaign, raise new money, and revivify the party organization around the country. The chairperson of the opposition party may also speak for the party and as an alternative to the president's party.

As the role of the committee and its chairperson shifts, so, too, do the job specifications for a national party chairperson. Within the party of the president, he or she must be congenial to the president, representative of the president's ideological stance, and willing to be loyal primarily to the president. George Bush's selection of Lee Atwater, his 1988 campaign director, for the post in 1989 is not only the most recent bit of evidence to that effect, but it also involved a more important role for the party chairperson in the day-to-day management of the president's political fortunes. Within the opposition party, the chairperson will often be congenial to—or at least trusted by—the various factions or segments of the party. Frequently, he or she is chosen for ideological neutrality or for lack of identification with any of the individuals seeking the

---

[4]Cotter and Hennessy, *Politics without Power*, p. 39.

[5]James W. Ceaser, "Political Parties—Declining, Stabilizing, or Resurging," in Anthony King (ed.), *The New American Political System* (Washington, D.C.: AEI Press, 1990), pp. 87–137 at pp. 114–117.

Lee Atwater and Ron Brown: Alternative Routes to the Top

Lee Atwater and Ron Brown were installed after the 1988 presidential election as chairpersons of the Democratic and Republican national committees. Both had spent most of their adult lives in politics and public affairs. Until assuming their duties as the head of their national parties, though, they had pursued almost diametrically opposed political careers.

Harvey Leroy Atwater began his meteoric rise to national prominence as a college intern in the office of South Carolina Senator Strom Thurmond, and seven years later he became the director of Thurmond's 1978 reelection campaign. In between, he had served as national director of the College Republicans at the same time that George Bush was chairman of the Republican National Committee. By 1988, he was managing the Bush presidential campaign, drawing the barbs of the Democrats for his "hardball" and combative campaign style, and still practicing his populist brand of conservatism and playing blues guitar at every available opportunity. Only his debilitating illness and death in 1991 at age 40 prevented him from leading the RNC well into the 1990s.

Ronald Harmon Brown traveled a different route to the top of his party. His first taste of politics came as a child in a politically-active Harlem family well linked into the black political elite. Educated at prestigious schools, he was the only black in his college class and the first black in his college fraternity. Instead of toiling in the vineyards of grass roots campaign politics like Atwater, Brown enjoyed his early successes as a Washington insider—as chief lobbyist for the National Urban League, counsel for the Senate Judiciary Committee, then the first black partner in a prestigious Washington law firm. His ties to Edward Kennedy (as deputy manager of Kennedy's 1980 presidential campaign) and Jesse Jackson raised suspicions in moderate and conservative Democratic circles. His insider credentials and responsible performance in 1988 as Jackson's convention floor manager, however, were sufficient to blunt worries that he might lead his party to the left and to turn a close early contest for chairperson into a runaway Brown victory.

party's next presidential nomination. Democratic chairperson Paul Kirk's prior association with Edward Kennedy and that of his successor, Ron Brown, with Jesse Jackson, in that regard, were as much problems to overcome as assets in building intraparty support for their candidacies. Experience in the nuts and bolts of party and campaign organization is also desirable. It is hardly coincidental that the 1990 chairpersons in both parties were veteran political operatives. As the job specifications vary, so too do the hunting grounds for prospective chairpersons (see Table 4.2).

Table 4.2 NATIONAL COMMITTEE CHAIRPERSONS OF THE MAJOR PARTIES: 1961–91

Name	Years	Political Position at Appointment
Democrats		
John M. Bailey	1961–68	State party chairman in Connecticut
Lawrence F. O'Brien	1968–69	U.S. postmaster general
Fred R. Harris	1969–70	U.S. senator from Oklahoma
Lawrence F. O'Brien	1970–72	Former national party chairman
Jean Westwood	1972	Active in McGovern preconvention campaign
Robert S. Strauss	1972–77	Democratic national treasurer
Kenneth M. Curtis	1977	Former governor of Maine
John C. White	1977–81	Deputy secretary of agriculture
Charles T. Manatt	1981–85	Finance chairman of Democratic National Committee
Paul G. Kirk, Jr.	1985–89	Former national party treasurer
Ronald H. Brown	1989–	Convention manager for Jesse Jackson's 1988 campaign
Republicans		
William E. Miller	1961–64	U.S. representative from New York
Dean Burch	1964–65	Active in Barry Goldwater campaign
Ray C. Bliss	1965–69	State party chairman in Ohio
Rogers C. Morton	1969–71	U.S. representative from Maryland
Robert J. Dole	1971–73	U.S. senator from Kansas
George H. Bush	1973–74	U.S. ambassador to the United Nations
Mary Louise Smith	1974–77	Cochairperson of Republican National Committee
William E. Brock	1977–81	Former U.S. senator from Tennessee
Richard Richards	1981–83	Regional coordinator for Reagan campaign
Frank J. Fahrenkopf	1983–89	Republican state chairman in Nevada
Harvey Leroy Atwater	1989–91	George Bush's 1988 campaign manager
Clayton Yeutter	1991–	Secretary of agriculture

THE SUPPORTING CAST OF NATIONAL GROUPS

Clustered around the national committees are a set of more or less formal groups that also purport to speak for the national party or for some part of it. Some of them are creatures of the national committees, but some are not. Taken together with the national committee in each party, they come close to constituting that vague entity we call the national party.

Special Constituency Groups

The national party committees occasionally have given formal recognition to certain constituencies, especially supportive groups that might not be well represented otherwise. For a long time, both the Democratic and the Republican national committees have had women's divisions within their structures. In addition, both have had national federations of state and local women's groups: the

National Federation of Democratic Women and the National Federation of Republican Women. Within the past 30 years, however, the importance of these women's divisions and organizations has declined markedly as women increasingly have entered regular leadership positions in the parties and served more frequently as convention delegates. Quite simply, they now want a role in the regular party organizations, or else they prefer to become active in nonparty organizations, such as the National Women's Political Caucus.

The Young Republican National Federation and the Young Democrats of America also have a long history. Both federations traditionally have been represented in their party's national councils, and support for both is provided by the senior party. The organized youth of both parties often have taken stands and have supported candidates in opposition to the senior party organization. The Young Republicans, for instance, had an infatuation with Goldwater conservatism long after the regular leadership of the party had tried to reflect a more centrist position. In the late 1960s and 1970s, their loyalties turned increasingly to the conservatism of Ronald Reagan. The Young Democrats often stood to the left of their senior party organization. In 1969, for instance, their national convention called for repeal of all legal limits on abortion, for liberalization of marijuana laws, for recognition of Cuba and Communist China, and for an "immediate and total withdrawal of all American troops in Vietnam." In recent years, however, the ranks of the Young Democrats have dwindled at the same time as the Young Republicans have attracted unprecedented numbers of members by capitalizing on the popularity of President Reagan and the party's enhanced electoral strength. This illustrates how much the strength of the youth groups depends on the fortunes of the party in general.

The Party's Officeholders in the States

Although they are not part of the official national organizations of their parties, the state governors invariably speak with authority in them. They have the prestige of high office and electoral success. Many lead or command the support of state party organizations, and a few inevitably contend for their party's presidential nominations.

The organization of the gubernatorial presence in the national parties, however, is relatively recent. The Republicans were first. After the Goldwater defeat of 1964, the moderate Republican governors wanted primarily to create a counterweight to the party's conservatives. A few years later, they established a full-time Washington office with financial help from the party's national committee, but their influence waned after the Republican victory of 1968. Like many such groups within the national parties, the governors operate most tellingly in the power vacuums of a party out of power. By the 1970s, the Democratic governors, by then in the party of opposition, began to press for a role in national party affairs. By 1974, they had achieved that voice and had won representation, although in modest numbers, on the national committee. By the late 1970s and early 1980s, therefore, the governors of both parties had Washington offices and staffs. The Democratic Governors Conference even was represented on the national committee. Their organizational influence in the national parties, however, continued to vary inversely with the party's presidential fortunes.

State legislators and local officials in both parties are organized; moreover, they are formally represented on the Democratic National Committee. It would be hard to argue, though, that they greatly influence the national business of either party. A group with perhaps more influence is the Democratic Leadership Council. Founded in 1985, it brings together elected officials, led by influential members of Congress and governors and some prospective candidates for president. The DLC represents the moderate to conservative wing of the party and is attempting to make the party appeal more to southern and western voters.

The Congressional Campaign Committees

The most important of all the supporting cast are each party's House and Senate campaign committees. The Democratic Congressional Campaign Committee (DCCC), the National Republican Congressional Committee (NRCC), the Democratic Senatorial Campaign Committee (DSCC), and the National Republican Senatorial Committee (NRSC) are organized to promote the reelection of their members and the addition of new members to their ranks. They are the campaign organizations of the party in government.

These campaign committees provide party candidates for office with many varieties of campaign assistance, from production facilities for television spots to that most valuable of all resources, money. They also have become increasingly active in channeling contributions from political action committees to the party's candidates for office. While controlled by incumbent officeholders, they have nonetheless been able to resist inevitable pressures to serve only the reelection interests of incumbents and have concentrated considerable resources where they will have the greatest marginal payoff for the congressional party, such as in supporting their party's challengers to incumbents or candidates for open seats.

The new vitality of the congressional campaign committees derives from their increasing ability to raise campaign funds (see Table 4.3). The Republican committees are by far more successful in this endeavor. Together they raised $100 million for the campaigns in 1988 and another $99 million for the 1990 races. Some of those funds went directly to candidates, but the larger part went for candidate recruitment, candidate training, and research on opponents and issues, and for dealing with the media, opinion polling, ads, and other campaign services. The Democrats now function in a similar but much more modest way, raising almost $29 million in 1987–88 and another $27 million in 1989–90. In both parties, the committees of the Hill are vastly more active and effective than they were in the 1970s. In resources and campaigning skills, they have begun to challenge the importance of the national committees of their parties. Their strength also insulates them and the congressional party very well from the national party organization, their sometime competitor.

Table 4.3 POLITICAL PARTY NET RECEIPTS: 1975–76 TO 1989–90 (IN MILLIONS)

	1975–76	1977–78	1979–80	1981–82	1983–84	1985–86	1987–88	1989–90
Democratic Party Committees								
Democratic National Committee	$13.1	$11.3	$ 15.1	$ 16.4	$ 46.6	$ 17.2	$ 52.3	$ 14.5
Democratic Senatorial Campaign Committee	1.0	0.3	1.7	5.6	8.9	13.4	16.3	17.5
Democratic Congressional Campaign Committee	0.9	2.8	2.1	6.5	10.4	12.3	12.5	9.1
Other National Committees	1.1	3.3	1.5	0.2	0.0	0.0	9.7	8.8
State/Local Committees	0.0	8.7	11.7	10.6	24.3	18.8	27.7	36.8
TOTAL	$16.1	$26.4	$ 32.1	$ 39.3	$ 90.2	$ 61.7	$118.5	$ 86.7
Republican Party Committees								
Republican National Committee	$29.1	$34.2	$ 76.2	$ 83.5	$105.9	$ 83.8	$ 91.0	$ 68.7
Republican Senatorial National Committee	12.2	10.9	23.3	48.9	81.7	86.1	65.9	65.1
Republican Congressional National Committee	1.8	14.1	28.6	58.0	58.3	39.8	34.5	33.8
Other National Committees	1.0	4.4	2.2	0.6	0.2	0.1	0.0	0.0
State/Local Committies	—	20.9	33.8	24.0	43.1	42.6	62.2	39.6
TOTAL	$44.1	$84.5	$164.1	$215.0	$289.2	$252.4	$253.6	$207.2

Note: Figures exclude federal funds provided to the parties to run their conventions.

Source: Federal Election Commission.

TWO PATHS TO POWER

These national organizations have been the scene of considerable ferment in recent years, as the hollow organizational shells that once were the national parties have been filled in. The key to the recent development of the national parties has been a growing and independent financial base (Table 4.3), largely achieved through thousands of small contributions solicited by mass mailings to likely party supporters.[6] The Republican committees were the first to experience this new affluence, which grew most dramatically in the 1979–80 electoral cycle. A comparable surge in the income of the Democratic committees followed in the early 1980s, although at first, in spite of stepped-up efforts, they fell further and further behind the GOP. These changes in party income have occurred simultaneously for the Republican's national and congressional campaign committees, but for the Democrats the congressional committees led the way in the mid-term election of 1982. This illustrates the principle for party development that adversity breeds change. The greatest advances in party organizational innovation have come when the party does not hold the presidency.[7]

With this new financing in hand, the Republicans and belatedly the Democrats have developed strong and active national party organizations, which, in turn, have devoted themselves to supporting party candidates and state and local organizations throughout the nation. By the mid-1980s, the national parties had become institutionalized as "service" parties.[8] Simultaneously, through party action often ratified by state law and court decisions, the Democrats vested authority over the presidential nomination process in the national parties. With the legal environment now conducive to procedural nationalization, the GOP too possessed the tools, if not the will, for enforcement of national party rules. Movement along these two separate paths has produced two

---

[6]A financial base on direct contributions has freed the national parties from their previous dependence on assessments upon the state parties, another characteristic of a confederated structure, and from the resultant state party influence. For a description of this earlier system, see Cotter and Hennessy, *Politics without Power*, pp. 180–182. For more on contemporary party finances, see Frank J. Sorauf, *Money in American Elections* (Glenview, Ill.: Scott Foresman/Little, Brown, 1988), Chap. 5.

[7]John H. Kessel, "Organizational Development on National Party Committees: Some Generalizations and Supporting Evidence," *Vox Pop: Newsletter of Political Organizations and Parties*, vol. 7, 1.

[8]F. Christopher Arterton calls them "service vendor" parties, while Paul Herrnson refers to them as "broker" parties. See Arterton's "Political Money and Party Strength," in Joel Fleishman (ed.), *The Future of American Political Parties* (Englewood Cliffs, N.J.: Prentice-Hall, 1982), pp. 101–39; and Herrnson, "National Party Organizations and Congressional Campaigning: National Parties as Brokers," paper presented at the 1986 Annual Meeting of the Midwest Political Science Association, Chicago.

national party organizations that are stronger than ever before—and that in an era that was supposed to have been characterized by the "decline of parties."[9]

The Service Party Path

The service party was born when, at some point in the 1960s, a quiet revolution began in the Republican National Committee. The committee's chairman of those years, Ray Bliss, involved the committee more and more in helping state and local parties with the nuts and bolts of party organizational work. Chairman William Brock carried the work forward in the late 1970s, turning the national party into an extraordinarily effective service organization for the parties of the states and localities. Brock, more than anyone else, revived and strengthened the Republican national party by fashioning a new role for it.

The keys to success in finding the new role or mission were two: new money and mastery of the new campaign technologies. Using direct mail solicitations, which in turn used computer-based mailing lists, the Republicans began to generate ever higher levels of income (see Table 4.3). By the 1983–84 election cycle, the Republican National Committee, along with its subsidiary funds and committees, had raised a record $105.9 million. (Campaign finance is discussed more fully in Chapter 13.) Those resources have enabled the RNC and its affiliates to engage in programs of aid to candidates and local party organizations without parallel in American party history.

As for the Democrats, long mired in debt, they found themselves doing better but still badly overmatched in organizational and service capacity in the 1980s. The good news for the Democrats was that they had dramatically improved their fund-raising capacities (see Table 4.3) and their activities in the states and localities since 1979 or 1980. The bad news was that the Republicans were far ahead of them and that the Republicans, too, were increasing their strength and capacity. Whatever the degree of Democratic success in becoming a service party, there was certainly no doubt that the party, under the national chairmanship of first Charles Manatt and then Paul Kirk had seen that as the only feasible course for party development. Indeed, the national Democrats made no secret of their attempt to mimic the Republican success in fund-raising and in performing the services those funds could buy.

By the mid-1980s both parties were providing unprecedented levels of assistance to state parties and candidates. This assistance included a broad array of services—candidate recruitment and training, research, public opinion polling, data processing, computer networking and software development, production of radio and television commercials, direct mailing, expert consultants, and

---

[9]For illustrations of these antithetical views of party strength, compare David Broder's *The Party's Over*, an early chronicle of the decline of parties thesis, with *The Party Goes On* by Xandra Kayden and Eddie Mahe, Jr. (New York: Basic Books, 1985) or Larry J. Sabato, *The Party's Just Begun* (Glenview, Ill.: Scott Foresman/Little, Brown, 1988).

Table 4.4 THE GROWTH OF NATIONAL PARTY COMMITTEE STAFF, 1972–88

	1972	1976	1980	1984	1988
	Democratic Party Committees				
Democratic National Committee	30	30	40	130	160
Democratic Congressional Campaign Committee	5	6	26	45	80
Democratic Senate Campaign Committee	4	5	20	22	50
	Republican Party Committees				
Republican National Committee	30	200	350	600	425
National Republican Congressional Committee	6	8	40	130	80
National Republican Senatorial Committee	4	6	30	90	88

Source: 1972–84: Paul S. Herrnson, *Party Campaigning in the 1980s* (Cambridge, Mass.: Harvard University Press, 1988), p. 39; 1988: Paul S. Herrnson, "Reemergent National Party Organizations," in L. Sandy Maisel (ed.), *The Parties Respond: Changes in the American Party System* (Boulder, Colo.: Westview Press, 1990), pp. 41–66 at p. 51.

legal services—and millions of dollars to finance campaigns and build party organizations. Concerned with the weakness of party organizations at the grass roots, recent Republican efforts even have turned to party-building there. The Republican National Committee, breaking with its tradition of working only with the state parties, lavished money and assistance in 1984 on 650 key counties containing a majority of the nation's voters. What money made possible, a growing professional staff in the national party headquarters was able to implement (see Table 4.4). Both national parties entered the 1990s as well-staffed, institutionalized political organizations.

The Democrats' Party-Reform Path

That had not, of course, been the path the national Democrats initially pursued. Instead, in the late 1960s and the 1970s, they were concerned with establishing their authority over the selection of delegates to the national nominating conventions. Beginning with efforts in the 1960s to enforce the loyalty of southern delegations to the national party ticket and continuing with the nomination process reforms of the McGovern-Fraser Commission and its successors, the Democrats restricted the autonomy of the state parties and the authority of state law in determining how delegates were to be selected for the presidential nominating conventions. Key court decisions upheld these actions, further solidifying the newfound authority of the national party. The immediate intent of the reformers was to make the nomination process more open and democratic. To achieve that goal, the confederated structure of the party, in which each state was sovereign in internal affairs, had to give way. That the reformers were successful in realizing their goals is testimony to the unusual politics of the period, the inattentiveness of state party leaders to the potential threat posed by the reforms, and the vacuum of power at the national apex of the traditional party organization. (This story is told in more detail in Chapter 11.)[10] Ironically, the GOP, innocent of any strong desire to alter its nomination process rules,[11] was carried along nonetheless by the tide of Democratic party reform because of the bipartisan nature of the state implementing legislation.

By the early 1980s, the national Democratic party had decided to deemphasize organizational reforms and move toward the Republican service model. All of its centralization of national authority on questions of representation and participation, even the overriding of the procedural preferences of state parties and state laws, had done little to win elections. Moreover, it had divided the party and had alienated a good part of the Democratic party in government, much of which was conspicuously absent from party conventions and midyear conferences in the 1970s. Thus, in the early 1980s the Democrats shifted course. The national committee adopted rules for the 1984 national convention that guaranteed a much greater representation of the party's leaders and officeholders. (See Chapter 11 for an extensive discussion of Democratic reforms of the delegate selection process.) The midyear conference was refocused from issues to party building in 1982 and then scrapped in 1986. In addition, in the 1980s, the party rushed to broaden the base of its fund-raising and to provide the means and know-how to recruit candidates and revitalize local party organization. In short, the signs of change were everywhere, authority over party rules had been nationalized, and what had been two models for national party strengthening were rapidly converging into one.[12]

---

[10]On Democratic party reform, see Austin Ranney, *Curing the Mischiefs of Faction: Party Reform in America* (Berkeley: University of California Press, 1975); William J. Crotty, *Decisions for the Democrats: Reforming the Party Structure* (Baltimore: Johns Hopkins University Press, 1978); and Byron E. Shafer, *The Quiet Revolution: The Struggle for the Democratic Party and the Shaping of Post-Reform Politics* (New York: Russell Sage Foundation, 1983).

[11]A reform committee, the Rule 29 Committee, was mandated by the 1972 Republican National Convention, but its recommendations for RNC review of state party "positive action" programs were rejected by the RNC and later by the 1976 convention. The GOP has been far more protective of states' rights for the parties than have the Democrats. See John F. Bibby, "Party Renewal in the Republican National Party," in Gerald M. Pomper (ed.), *Party Renewal in America* (New York: Praeger, 1981), pp. 102–115.

[12]Comprehensive recent accounts of the increased strength of the national parties may be found in A. James Reichley, "The Rise of National Parties," in John E. Chubb and Paul E. Peterson (eds.), *The New Direction in American Politics* (Washington, D.C.: Brookings, 1985), pp. 175–200; Epstein, *Political Parties in the American Mold*, Chap. 7; Herrnson, *Party Campaigning in the 1980s;* Ceaser, "Political Parties—Declining, Stabilizing or Resurging?"; and Herrnson, "Reemergent National Party Organizations," pp. 41–66.

POWER AND AUTHORITY IN THE NATIONAL PARTY

It is clear that there has been a strengthening of the national parties in the last decade and that the most apparent and important strengthening has been in the activities that would regain some of the parties' lost roles in nominating and electing candidates. To an important degree, the parties (especially the Republicans) have begun to "muscle in" on the campaign support functions monopolized just a few years before by PACs and private political consultants, although it is as yet unclear whether parties can displace them. But it is not inconceivable that, when viewed in retrospect, the major significance of these competitors to parties will be found to be their service as temporary bridges between the old party, centered at the grass roots, and the new national service party. The buttressing of the national parties also has the potential to alter the relationships within the parties: between the national party and state-and-local party organizations, the president, and the Congress, as well as among the various representatives of the national parties.

The State and Local Connection

The increased resources and activities of the two national parties, without question, have increased their visibility and presence. The extent to which that kind of nationalization of the parties has also contributed to a centralization of authority within them is not yet clear. The Democrats approach the service party role with far more experience than the Republicans have in drafting and enforcing national rules and a stronger will to assert centralized authority, although the actions have been taken by the convention and its committees rather than the national committee.[13] Moreover, the structure of representation on the DNC can sustain and legitimize more centralized authority. The Republicans, on the other hand, remain a confederation of equal state parties; they are also, by political philosophy, more wary of centralized authority. Due to its vastly superior resources, however, the Republican national party has penetrated more to the state and local level.

Philosophies and organizational formalities aside, it is difficult to imagine that the national subsidization of state and local party organizations and the national intervention into their nominations and elections will not be accompanied by *some* centralization of authority (see box). The temptation to guide and direct from above is strong given the expertise and resources of the national parties. However lightly and informally it is exercised, it is most likely that a notional imprint on issues, on the kinds of candidates recruited, and on the way

---

[13]For a good description of the traditional relationships of state party leadership and the national parties, see Robert J. Huckshorn, *Party Leadership in the States* (Amherst: University of Massachusetts Press, 1976), Chap. 8.

New Tensions between the State and the National Parties: Two Examples

Increased national party activity and authority can produce conflict between traditionally autonomous state parties and assertive national parties. An example from each party illustrates how national party incursions into areas traditionally left to states can offend state party leaders.

RNC FAVORITISM IN CONTESTED PRIMARIES

In its efforts to field the strongest party ticket, the RNC under William Brock adopted a policy of picking one candidate to support in contested state primaries. Occasionally, RNC efforts backfired, such as in 1978 when it supported the primary opponent of the candidate, Lee Dreyfus, who went on to become governor of Wisconsin and no friend of the national party establishment. In response to criticisms from the state party leaders, the party revised this policy in 1980 to require approval by the state party chairperson and the national committeepersons from the state before the RNC could support a candidate for nomination. (This incident and the policy change it induced are discussed in Kayden and Mahe, *The Party Goes On*, pp. 78–79.)

DNC EFFORTS TO REDUCE "PARTY-BASHING"

Recognizing that candidates were undermining their own party by running against the national Democratic party, in 1986 Chairman Paul Kirk asked state Democratic leaders who wished to participate in a DNC-financed program for state party building to sign an agreement that would require them, in the words of the DNC memorandum,

> to insist that Democratic candidates who benefit from this program do not run campaigns against, and instead run with the national Democratic Party. This means exerting all of the state party's influence and bringing to bear all of the pressure it can to ensure that a positive, unified Democratic party campaign develops. It also means that the state party and state committee shall disagree with and disavow any remarks by a candidate or campaign that attack the national party.

Not surprisingly, the Republicans gleefully attacked the Democrats for attempting to impose an undemocratic loyalty oath, and some state Democratic leaders expressed dismay that the national party was over-reacting to what was a minor problem.

For right now, though, such examples are conspicuous exceptions to a much more common rule of cooperation between the state and national parties. Candidates for office, often thankful for assistance of any sort, have welcomed the technical and financial resources offered by the national parties. State and local organizations, recognizing the value of national assistance, usually have been more receptive to than threatened by national intervention in party-building and candidate support.

things are done organizationally will follow. Resistance in the state and local organizations might well be at the price of starvation. Those who pay the pipers more often than not call the tune.[14]

The Presidential Connection

When the party holds the presidency, the president's program and record become the party's. It is the president who interprets the party's platform and the mandate of the voters. His preferences, whether embodied in the formal measures of the State of the Union address or tossed off more casually at a press conference, impose a policy and a record on his party. He may consult the party chairperson or other party notables, but it is his decisions, his successes or failures, that form the party record.

Every president in recent memory has kept his national committee on a short leash, but the White House dominance of the national party reached its zenith in the presidency of Richard M. Nixon. The Watergate tapes reveal that the president's principal assistants, John Erlichman and H. R. Haldeman, were deeply involved in the decisions of the 1972 campaign—a campaign headed, in fact, by another close Nixon associate, former attorney general John Mitchell. So marginal to the 1972 campaign were the Republican party bodies and officials that they remained ignorant and innocent of the wrongdoing and scandals of the campaign. Democratic presidents, too, have wanted the national committee under their control. In 1980 President Jimmy Carter angered party people by diverting crucial DNC personnel and resources for his own reelection campaign.

During the 1980s the national committee of the president's party, here the Republican National Committee, really came into its own as an important independent actor in party politics. Federal funding of presidential campaigns, with its strict limitations on party expenditures for presidential politics, has freed the national committees from their traditional concentration on presidential elections and allowed them to dedicate their now considerable resources to party-building at the state and local level. At the same time, the selection of close advisors to the president as its recent chairs has given the RNC a status it had not enjoyed before, even as presidential influence was being asserted. Designation of Ronald Reagan's longtime friend, Senator Paul Laxalt of Nevada, to the post of general chairman and the appointment of Nevada's party chairman, Frank Fahrenkopf, to the party chairmanship eliminated the tensions between the White House and the national committee that inevitably follow a transition from the leaderless party out of power to a presidential party. This move also brought the party leader into the inner circle of White House advisors. This

---

[14]See Epstein, *Political Parties in the American Mold*, p. 237; and Xandra Kayden, "The Nationalization of the Party System," in Michael J. Malbin (ed.), *Parties, Interest Groups, and the Campaign Finance Laws* (Washington, D.C.: American Enterprise Institute, 1980), pp. 257–82.

relationship continued with the selection of Lee Atwater, George Bush's principal campaign advisor, to the RNC chairmanship in 1989.

By contrast, in those four long years after presidential defeat, a national party suffers an almost incessant jockeying for the right to lead. The defeated presidential candidate, depending on his ties and popularity within the party, may achieve an important voice in the party. Gerald Ford did, but Jimmy Carter, Walter Mondale, and Michael Dukakis did not. A strong and vigorous national chairperson may help to fill the void in national leadership; those with substantial financial and organizational accomplishments are more likely to succeed. Most commonly, however, leadership of the "out" party falls to its leaders in the Congress. The visibility of the party's leadership in Congress is matched by the political support and power of its campaign committees. Above all, the congressional party, simply because its legislative responsibilities force it to take policy stands, formulates the party position and challenges the program of the opposition's president.

It seems safe to predict that strengthened national party committees will assume a more prominent party role in the party out of power. The same is true of their chairpersons. That much seems clear when one considers the Republicans under William Brock in the late 1970s and the Democrats under Charles Manatt, Paul Kirk and Ron Brown since then—but what of a strengthened party and its president? It seems likely that presidents will continue to worry about independent party voices and that they will want the new party power to be at their service. They will certainly want the party committees to mobilize behind their programs all those members of Congress they recruited, trained, financed, and helped elect. Also, if presidents are in their first term, they will very likely want to draw on the assets of the national party for their reelection campaigns as much as the Federal Elections Campaign Act permits. If presidents feared and used the national committees when the committees were weak, they have even more reason to do so when the committees are more formidable. Even as the national parties continue their party-building, it will be in the service of presidential goals.[15]

The Congressional Connection

Nationalizing forces, this time emanating from the congressional party itself rather than the national party committees, have overtaken the Congress as well. Congressional campaign committees elected by the party congressional caucuses have become increasingly active, as we have seen, in recruiting and supporting party candidates for office. This assistance is more valuable to challengers and contenders for open seats than to incumbents, who are easily

---

[15]Party-president relations during the Reagan years are discussed in Reichley, "The Rise of National Parties." The traditional relationship between the president and his party's national committee is discussed in Cotter and Hennessy, *Politics without Power*, pp. 81–94.

able to raise their own campaign resources. The expanded role for the congressional party greatly increases the potential for greater control of the rank-and-file, particularly newly elected members, by the party leadership in each chamber. There is a temptation to attribute the greater intraparty voting cohesion manifested in recent years (see Chapter 14) to the congressional party's financial prowess, but the truth is that the party leadership so far has refrained from allocating campaign funds and services on the basis of support for the party's program. Nevertheless, even though constituency pressures will always be paramount in the Congress, the more senators and representatives can count on campaign support from the congressional party, the more open they will be to party-based appeals.[16] This campaign support also may, to some degree, counterbalance pressures on Congress from PACs and competing centers for party power in Washington—the President and the national party committees.

The Connections Within the National Party

When it comes to election campaigns, each national party has three committees that are of significance—the national committee and the Senate and House campaign committees. As we have seen from Table 4.3, each raises millions of dollars to support its activities. There are, to be sure, many opportunities for cooperation among them, and such cooperation has increased greatly in recent years. All benefit, for example, from voter registration and get-out-the-vote drives, and there often are economies of scale to be realized in a dovetailing of effort in candidate recruitment and campaigns (for example, polling, issues research). In raising and spending their money, however, the committees within each party to some degree are competitors. They seek financial support from the same contributors (and jealously guard their contributor lists), recruit political talent from the same limited pool, and pursue sometimes incompatible goals. Where resources are as scarce as they are in party organizing, it should not be at all surprising that different organizations from the same party will struggle over them.[17]

THE LIMITS OF PARTY ORGANIZATION

Amid all the talk and reports of new strength in the national party organization, it is well to remember that American party organizations remain weak by most standards. They are an anachronism in this era of large-scale organizations. In

---

[16]The national committees may, however, exert considerable influence over the management of a campaign, particularly for non-incumbents, who are most in need of their assistance, through their power to withhold services and funds. See Herrnson, *Party Campaigning in the 1980s*, p. 59.

[17]Herrnson, *Party Campaigning in the 1980s*, pp. 41–42.

business, government, universities, and voluntary organizations, it is a time of complex social structures and of the bureaucrats who have become their symbols. We have every right to include the parties among them, but it is an inescapable fact that the parties, almost alone among our major social institutions, have resisted the development of large, centralized organization.

Even by the standards of the parties of the other democracies, in spite of their greatly improved fund-raising and provision of services, the American party organizations cut an unimpressive figure. They lack the hierarchical control and efficiency, the unified setting of priorities and strategy, and the central responsibility we associate with large contemporary organizations and often find in parties in other nations. Instead of a continuity of relationships and of operations, the American party organizations feature only improvisatory, elusive, and sporadic structure and activities. Also, whereas the party organizations of the other Western democracies have had permanent, highly professional leadership and large party bureaucracies, the American organizations have generally done without a professional bureaucracy or leadership cadre. Except at the national level in recent years, the business of American party organization is still largely in the hands of part-time activists and inexperienced professionals, which is perhaps to say that its business and its organizational relationships require little specialization or high-level professional care. And, even at the national level, as Epstein has observed: "The very word 'committee' suggests limited national structure."[18]

One is compelled to wonder at the reasons for the stunting of American party organization. In part, it results from statutory limits and the federal structure of our polity. Traditional fears of political parties and party strength have certainly contributed as well. (There is little in American political values that would welcome an efficient or "businesslike" operation of the parties.) So has a candidate-centered politics, and the American system of separation of powers. Even recent reforms in campaign financing contribute to the weakness of the party organizations by denying them their traditional position as a major source of campaign funds. By restricting party contributions to $5000 per federal candidate, the statutes now treat parties as just another source of candidate support—along with political action committees, which can also give only $5000, and individuals, who are limited to $1000 per candidate—rather than organizations that are integral to the electoral process.[19] In large part, however, the underorganization of the American parties results from their fundamental character. They have been pragmatic electoral parties, involved chiefly in supporting candidates for public office and active mainly during campaigns. As such, they have long been led and dominated, not by career bureaucrats, but by public office seekers and holders. Perhaps, too, the degree of pragmatic flexibility

---

[18]Epstein, *Political Parties in the American Mold*, p. 200.

[19]This point is made by James Ceaser in "Political Parties—Declining, Stabilizing, or Resurging?" p. 120.

to which Americans have carried their party politics rules out the routine and the fixity of a large organization. Organization is to some extent routine and unchanging, and it is therefore more compatible with the party of unchanging ideology or principle than with one committed to the adjustments necessary for electoral success. Thus, the electoral preoccupations of the American parties have tipped the scales in favor of parties in government and against the party organizations.

The Political Party of the Activists

Behind the imposing facades of the formal, statutory party structures are the living, organizational realities of the political parties. The party is a grouping of people, most of them contributing their time and energy on a purely voluntary basis. Even the paid professional party workers, who increasingly staff the national and state offices, share many of the attributes of volunteers. The statutes ignore these men and women of the party, their goals and motives, their interactions and relationships, the contributions they make to the organizations, and the price they exact for those contributions. Yet the activity and motivations of those men and women are closer to the real world of party politics than all the statutory paragraphs put together.

As an organization, the political party is a mechanism for uniting people in pursuit of goals. It is vastly committed to the winning of elections. In addition, it may seek to spread an ideology, enact a set of public policies, or ease regulations affecting its activities. Goal-seeking also goes on within the party organization on a personal, individual level. Individual party leaders, workers, and members are involved in the party organization for some identifiable, if covert or implicit, set of reasons. They seek some reward or payoff for devoting their time to party activity rather than to the services of their church, their service organization, or even their golf game.

The major task for the party organization is to convert the raw materials of people, resources, and expertise into activity oriented toward fulfilling the party's goals. How it accomplishes this is determined by the private life of the party—its internal division of labor and allocation of authority, its internal system of communication, and the internal decision-making processes through which it chooses how to mobilize its resources, deploy its assets, and set its strategies. To be effective, above all else, the party must be able to fulfill its organizational goals while simultaneously achieving the goals of its individual members. Many are the party organizations that are incapable of meeting the challenge.

INCENTIVES FOR POLITICAL ACTIVITY

The American political parties have never operated primarily in a cash economy. They have rarely bought or hired more than a small proportion of the millions of labor hours they need. Even today, in spite of the increasing professionalization of the national and state party headquarters, paid staffs are small or nonexistent in most local party organizations where most party work is done, and it is a rare local chairman who draws a substantial salary from the party organization.[1] The great number of Americans who are active in the parties receive no cash in return for their considerable time and skills. Even the earthy old customs of paying precinct workers on election day or using government employees as the party's workers at election time are vanishing. What is it, then, that induces party workers to lavish their hours and efforts on the affairs of the parties? If the parties' payments are not made in cash, in which coin are they made?

In their seminal theory of motivations for organizational involvement, Peter B. Clark and James Q. Wilson identified three different types of incentives for activity. *Material* incentives are tangible rewards for activity—if not direct cash payments for work, they often involve implicit understandings that involvement will be rewarded with some kind of material benefits. *Solidary* incentives are the intangible benefits derived from association and fellowship, from being "one of the group." *Purposive* incentives are intangible rewards of a different kind—based on the sense of satisfaction that accompanies involvement in a worthwhile cause or activities that promote some collective principle. This typology of incentives has been widely and fruitfully employed in the study of incentives for party activity.[2]

Material Incentives

Historically, the principal material inducement to party activity has been the opportunity to share in the "spoils" obtained when a party is in control of government. These "spoils" are generally of two types—patronage and preferments. *Patronage* refers to the appointment to governmental positions as a reward for party work. *Preferments* involve, more generally, the discretionary

---

[1]A 1980 national survey of county party chairs found that fewer than 10 percent of the county organizations had paid staff and fewer than 2 percent had paid chairs. Cornelius P. Cotter, James L. Gibson, John F. Bibby, and Robert J. Huckshorn, *Party Organizations in American Politics* (New York: Praeger, 1984), pp. 42–43.

[2]See Peter B. Clark and James Q. Wilson, "Incentive Systems: A Theory of Organizations," *Administrative Science Quarterly* 6 (1961): 129–66, for the original development of this theory; and James Q. Wilson, *The Amateur Democrat* (Chicago: University of Chicago Press, 1960), and *Political Organizations* (New York: Basic Books, 1973), Chap. 6, for the application of this typology to political organizations. Also see M. Margaret Conway and Frank B. Feigert, "Motivation, Incentive Systems and the Political Party Organization," *American Political Science Review* 62 (1968): 1159–73.

granting of the favors of government to party supporters. Both patronage and preferments have played important roles in building and sustaining the American party organizations.[3]

Patronage.   Since the days of Andrew Jackson, Americans have been attracted to party work by the prospect of being rewarded with governmental employment. The use of patronage is hardly unique to American parties, but no other party system has over its history relied so systematically on patronage as the American system. In the heyday of the political machine, for example, city governments were staffed almost entirely by loyalists of the party in power, all of whom faced the prospect of being thrown out of work should their party be turned out of office. Even today, a large number of American ambassadors to foreign nations owe their appointments to their campaign support for the elected president.

As the price to be paid for their "political" jobs, patronage appointees commonly have "volunteered" their time, energy, and often even a part of their salary to the party organization, particularly to help in political campaigns. In many places, the cadres of activists in political campaigns have been filled with public employees. Tales of the entire staff of certain government departments being mobilized in support of their boss's reelection are not uncommon in the annals of American party politics. Money, too, always has been an important resource in campaigns, and patronage workers have been called upon to "invest" in the party through which they received their jobs. (The traditional Indiana practice, discontinued only in the late 1980s, was to have a 2 percent party contribution automatically deducted from the paycheck of each patronage employee.) Even in modern times when such directly partisan practices are increasingly frowned upon, the pressures remain compelling in some places for government employees to work for the party that hired them on a voluntary basis. The line between voluntary and expected, even required, activities, though, is a fine one where employees owe their jobs to the continued success of the party (see box).

Despite the explosive growth of government in this century to almost 17 million public employees today, the amount of patronage available to the parties has declined precipitously. The expansion of civil service and merit systems has been the chief reason. With the establishment of the federal civil service system by the Pendleton Act in 1883, almost 14,000 of the over 131,000 federal employees were removed from patronage appointment.[4] The number of full-time federal positions filled by political appointees has dwindled over the years to 4000–5000 today, plus another 3000 or so part-time and honorific jobs. All

[3]For a lively account of the use of patronage and preferments, see Martin and Susan Tolchin, *To the Victor* (New York: Random House, 1971).

[4]These figures are cited in Stephen Skowronek's study of the reform of the executive branch bureaucracy. See his *Building a New American State* (New York: Cambridge University Press, 1982), p. 69.

The Operation of Patronage Systems in Recent Times

Patronage practices have been deeply embedded in the traditional party politics of many states and localities. A few examples of recent workings of patronage politics illustrate the continuing sway of patronage systems even in an increasingly hostile environment.

ILLINOIS

Besides passing a Civil Service examination, job applicants in Illinois were frequently required to get approval from a precinct captain and the county party chairman. These were often jobs like those of secretaries or prison guards, which did not have any connection to policy making. For higher paying jobs the application often required the approval of an official in the Governor's office.

DIRK JOHNSON

The New York Times, June 23, 1990

NEW YORK CITY

In 1983, (Mayor) Koch set up a City Hall agency called the Talent Bank to recruit minority workers, women and Vietnam veterans. And that it apparently did—sometimes. A former director of the Talent Bank . . . testified that specially coded "hot" and "super priority" resumes had been forwarded to the agency by politicians and by Mr. Koch's longtime advisor, John LoCicero, who is City Hall's liaison to Democratic politicians. She said the applicants with political sponsors were kept on a separate list and were given priority in hiring over other applicants.

FRANK LYNN

The New York Times, January 15, 1989

OHIO

The Grand Old Party is doing what some of its officeholders either can't or won't do to fill the campaign coffers. County employees recently got letters from the Franklin County Republican Party asking them to sign up for a payroll deduction. The GOP wants 1 percent of their salaries. GOP Chairman Mike Colley signed both letters and included checkoff authorization forms. The letters say that contributions are voluntary but some employees think they're being pressured.

JACK WILLEY

Columbus *Dispatch,* July 2, 1987

are listed in a publication, unofficially know as the "Plum Book" (its official title is *U.S. Government Policy and Supporting Positions*), compiled by the House Committee on Post Office and Civil Service. Similar declines have come, albeit more slowly, to the states and localities. Any number of states, counties, and cities—the great majority surely—have virtually abolished patronage, moving to merit systems of some sort. In recent years, even some of the vaunted centers of patronage have seen the merit principle making new and severe inroads. Kentucky in 1960 reduced the number of year-round jobs available for patronage from 16,000 to 4000, about 75 percent of them on the highway maintenance crews. Pennsylvania, which had almost 50,000 patronage positions as late as 1970, lost a sizable number in collective bargaining. In 1971, some 17,500 workers, most of them also with the highway crews, negotiated a contract in which the state agreed not to discriminate against any employee on the basis of political affiliations and forbade state officials from requiring workers to make political contributions or to engage in political activity.

To the spread of civil service reform and public employee unions must be added recent Supreme Court decisions as a powerful force in undermining patronage at the state and local level. The first major judicial blow against patronage was struck by the Court in 1976 when it barred dismissal of Sheriff's office employees in Cook County, Illinois, because of a change of the party in power. Four years later the Court blocked political dismissals of assistant public defenders in Rockland County, New York. Then, in a 1990 case involving the state of Illinois, the Supreme Court moved beyond protecting government employees from political dismissal to rule that politically-based promotion and hiring decisions violated the First Amendment rights to freedom of speech and association. In each of these cases, the Court appreciated that party affiliation might be a relevant condition in filling the top policy-making positions but found such considerations inappropriate for lower-level offices. Barring a sudden reversal in the Court's view (these have been split decisions with 3 or 4 justices strongly dissenting), the use of patronage in filling government positions below the top policymaking levels should become less and less important a weapon in the political parties' arsenal of resources for motivating large numbers of people for political activity (see box).[5]

Even where patronage positions remain, the party often encounters formidable problems in exploiting them as incentives for party activity. Evidence from a variety of locales shows that the parties achieve only a partial return in party work or contributions from their patronage appointees. Also there is frequently a poor fit between the available patronage jobs and the kinds of activists the party wants to recruit. The politics of patronage have always worked best among the depressed and disadvantaged; most patronage positions do not tempt the educated, "respected" middle-class leadership the parties would like to at-

---

[5]The 1976 case is Elrod v. Burns, 427 U.S. 347; the 1980 case is Branti v. Finkel, 445 U.S. 507; and the 1990 case is Rutan v. Republican Party of Illinois, 111 L. Ed. 2d 52.

The Shakman Decrees and the Dismantling of Chicago's Patronage Army

Unable to defeat a candidate of Chicago's Democratic machine in a race for delegate to the state's 1969 constitutional convention, frustrated reformer Michael Shakman sought judicial relief. He challenged the constitutionality of the city's patronage system in the federal courts. His suit triggered a series of court rulings and subsequent consent decrees between 1972 and 1988 through which the city agreed, albeit grudgingly, to eliminate political hiring and firing for all but the top policy-making positions and to protect city employees from being forced to do political work or make political contributions. To implement these agreements, the courts required the city to develop stringent plans for compliance and to submit to yearly external audits of its personnel practices. "While no one would be so naive as to claim that politics has been completely eliminated from the city's personnel operations, the large-scale patronage system of the past seems to be gone."[6]

tract. Furthermore, in an age of candidate-centered politics, elected executives are more interested in using patronage to build their own political followings than to strengthen the party apparatus. And of course as the supply of valuable patronage positions dwindles, the old aphorism that each appointment creates one ingrate who gets the job and many malcontents who do not becomes even more apropos.[7]

Nonetheless, patronage is unlikely to vanish from American political life or as an incentive for political activity. The consequences of antipatronage court rulings will diffuse slowly, case-by-case, through the decentralized political system. Top policy-making positions should continue to be reserved for loyal supporters of a mayor, a governor, a president. Legislative bodies at all levels of government will remain loathe to bring their staff employees under the protection of civil service systems. Honorary positions on government advisory groups will linger on as coveted rewards for loyal party service. Ambassadorial appointments still will be tendered to a few important campaign supporters. Wherever political leaders retain discretion over personnel appointments,

---

[6]For a full account of the Shakman decrees and their effect, see Anne Freedman, "Doing Battle with the Patronage Army: Politics, Courts, and Personnel Administration in Chicago," *Public Administration Review* 48 (1988): 847–59. The quote comes from page 855.

[7]On the problems of using patronage, see Frank J. Sorauf, "State Patronage in a Rural County," *American Political Science Review* 50 (1956): 1046–56; W. Robert Gump, "The Functions of Patronage in American Party Politics: An Empirical Reappraisal," *Midwest Journal of Political Science* 15 (1971): 87–107; and Michael Johnston, "Patrons and Clients, Jobs and Machines: A Case Study of the Uses of Patronage," *American Political Science Review* 73 (1979): 385–98.

understandably they will find a way to award them to their trusted political supporters. The promise of such awards, in turn, will inevitably attract people to political activity—though probably not the large numbers who once served as the "foot soldiers" of the traditional political machines.

Although the decline of patronage surely suits the current norms of the American political culture, some thoughtful observers mourn the passing of a practice that has been central to American political life since early in the nineteenth century. The parties may find it more and more difficult to recruit the labor and talent they need to retain their strength; and those who value strong parties as instruments of democracy will lament this trend. The activists that parties do recruit may demand more ideological pay-offs for their participation—diverting the parties from the pragmatic, inclusive postures they have assumed during most of their histories. By the same token, with the replacement of political appointees by neutral professionals, governmental bureaucracies may become less responsive to elected political leaders and perhaps less sympathetic to their clienteles. And it is virtually impossible in a civil service system for reform-minded leaders to replace a stodgy or ineffective public bureaucracy with more efficient workers. With the stigma attached to patronage in current times, it is easy to forget that patronage practices were first promoted at the federal level by Andrew Jackson to produce a more democratic and less elitist government. Whatever one's normative stance towards patronage, there is widespread agreement that its demise has altered and will continue to alter the nature of the American parties and the American political system.[8]

Elected Office   Patronage jobs in government, though, are not the only employment opportunities a party can offer. In recent years, the party organizations at the state and national levels have become important employers themselves of paid professional campaign workers, and numerous activists are attracted to party work in the hopes of landing these jobs.

The party also offers an efficient—and in a few cases the only—avenue to elective office, so it is inevitable that the possibility of a career in public office should recruit new party activists or sustain activity after other incentives have worn off. About 40 percent of the county chairpersons interviewed in a 1979–80 national survey aspired to hold public office, and an earlier study found that one-third of all state party chairs were candidates for elective office after serving the party.[9] Involvement in the party, like activity in various community organizations, remains an attractive way for aspiring politicians to build a base from which to launch a political career.

A few party organizations enjoy such disciplined control over their primaries that they can and do "give" public office, especially at the state and local

---

[8]The case for patronage has been articulated over the years in *The Washington Monthly* magazine and in the dissenting opinions to the Suprme Court's *Elrod, Branti*, and *Rutan* decisions.

[9]For the 1979–80 results, see Cotter et al, *Party Organizations in American Politics*, p. 42; the figures on state chairs are for 1962-72 and come from Robert J. Huckshorn, *Party Leadership in the States* (Amherst: University of Massachusetts Press, 1976), p. 37.

level, to loyal party workers. That degree of control over nomination and election to office is rare, however. Today, it is far more common for candidates for office to see the party as one of the bases, in some areas the most important one, of support for election or reelection. Candidates need advice, know-how, people (staff and volunteers), and money, and the party remains a likely source of them. Nonetheless, candidates sometimes remain aloof from the party, in part because they may not need the resources it commands and in part because, in an anti-party age, they do not want to be identified too closely with a political party.

Preferments   The tangible, material rewards of politics may take forms other than appointive or elective office. Wherever public officials can exercise discretion in the allocation of government services and the granting of government contracts, and that undoubtedly means everywhere, the potential for political favoritism exists. Many are attracted to party activity and party financial support in search of these favors. The active partisan or the financial "fat cat" may, for example, seek preference in the awarding of public contracts. It is no accident that leaders of the construction industry are so active politically in the states and localities that spend millions every year on roads and public buildings. Preference may take other forms: a tolerant application of regulatory or inspection policies, unusually prompt snow and garbage removal, the fixed traffic ticket, or the granting of admission to crowded mental hospitals or state universities. It may also involve the granting of scarce "opportunities," such as liquor licenses or cable television franchises, or calculated ignoring of prostitution, bookmaking, the numbers game, or traffic in drugs in return for some form of political support. By "preferment," in other words, one means the special treatment or advantage that flows from the party's holding the decision-making positions in government.

Various procedures (such as tight regulations, active oversight, inspectors general, competitive and sealed bidding, conflict of interest statutes, privatization, even affirmative action) have been adopted over the years, often at the behest of "good government" reformers, to constrain the exercise of political discretion in the allocation of government benefits and the procurement of goods and services by government. Nonetheless, where the benefits to be realized are great and the desire to create political support compelling, as is the case in modern day governments, there always seem to be ways to evade even the most stringent controls (see box). There is understandable resistance, in the name of both democracy and efficiency, to sacrificing all discretion to eliminate *political* discretion. The result is that preferments may have taken the place of patronage as the principal material incentive for political activity.

Solidary Incentives

The personal, nonmaterial rewards of party activity are not easy to identify and certainly are not easy to measure. One can sense, however, the social rewards of politics in the camaraderie at party headquarters or the courthouse. Such solidary incentives are evident at a party dinner as the workers press around the

Preferments in Federal Housing Contracts: The HUD Scandals

The scandal that surfaced in 1989 over operations of the federal Department of Housing and Urban Development during the 1980s shows political favoritism at work in rewarding party activists.

> Investigators and Republican consultants agreed, in interviews, on two key points. First, during Secretary Samuel R. Pierce Jr.'s tenure, the agency's (normal) procedure was stood on its head. Instead of applications by local authorities on the basis of need, former H.U.D. employees, many of whom had worked with Mr. Pierce, went to local officials and offered to get them grants for projects that would benefit the local economy and generate profits for the former officials of the housing agencies.
> ... These projects, in turn, generated consultant fees in Washington for Republican political operatives, such as former Interior Secretary James G. Watt, who in some cases know little about housing but were paid to win approval from Mr. Pierce.
>
> RICHARD L. BERKE
>
> *The New York Times,* June 26, 1989
> Copyright © 1989 by The New York Times Company.
> Reprinted by permission.

Consultant fees, totaling hundreds of thousands of dollars in some cases, were legally earned by people whose major credential was their political party connection.

great and near-great of the party, hoping for a word of greeting or a nod of recognition. Even in the amateur political clubs of some large cities, the attractiveness of the social life and friendship circle is important. "Many volunteers are rootless, transient newcomers searching the city for a means of associating with like-minded people." Although the parties' clubs rely on the social incentives, those incentives are probably secondary to the pursuit of political goals.[10] Perhaps one can say more simply that party politics is a splendid vehicle for gregariousness. Almost all reported research on the motivations of party activists has found a substantial number who cite the social life of party politics as a valuable reward.[11]

---

[10]Wilson, *The Amateur Democrat,* p. 165.

[11]A 1980 collaborative study of local parties in five cities, based on interviews with precinct and ward committeepersons, found that social incentives figured prominently among the motivations for activity. See the chapters by Richard W. Murray and Kent L. Tedin on Houston (p. 51), Anne H. Hopkins on Nashville (p. 74), Samuel J. Eldersveld on Detroit and Los Angeles (pp. 104–5), and William Crotty on Chicago (p. 174) in William Crotty, ed., *Political Parties in Local Areas* (Knoxville: University of Tennessee Press, 1986).

Social satisfactions merge almost imperceptibly into the psychological. "Like the theater, politics is a great nourisher of egos," writes one observer. "It attracts men who are hungry for attention, for assurance that somebody loves them, for the soul-stirring music of their own voices."[12] Party work may also offer the individual an enterprise with which to identify, a charismatic leader to follow, a round of activities that can lift him or her above the personally unrewarding tasks of the workaday world. The party may be a small island of excitement in a sea of routine. It may even offer an occasion for the manipulation or domination of others, a chance to decide or command, even an avenue for the projection of aggression and hostilities.

Purposive Incentives

Even the most casual soundings of party rhetoric indicate an increasing identification of partisans as "liberals" or "conservatives." Behind these phrases lies a potent purposive motivation to party activity: a commitment to clusters of related attitudes about government and politics, especially about the proper role of government in contemporary society. On a more modest and limited scale, the spur to activity may be concern for a single issue or interest (tax cuts, the war in Vietnam, abortion, the maintenance of local schools) or a single area of policy concern (foreign policy, civil rights, the environment). The "causes" may, indeed, be the reform or rehabilitation of the political party itself.

Just as the importance of the immediate, material, personal rewards of politics has recently declined, that of issue and ideology has increased. These issue concerns in the local parties have paralleled the ideological triumphs in the national parties: the capture of the Republicans by Goldwater conservatives in 1964, the success of the liberal Democratic ideologues on behalf of Eugene McCarthy (1968) and George McGovern (1972), and the victories of Ronald Reagan in 1980 both within the Republican party and throughout the nation. As these particular movements suggest, the mobilization of issue and ideologically motivated workers into the party often depends upon the drawing power of an attractive leader who champions the cause. We must not underestimate the importance of a Kennedy, a Goldwater, a Reagan in attracting citizens into party politics. Nor can we ignore the importance of ideological motivations when party activists resort to the extreme measure of switching parties in pursuit of greater harmony between their personal views and the positions of their party.[13]

---

[12]John Fischer, "Please Don't Bite the Politicians," *Harper's* (November 1960), 16. The classic treatment of the psychological roots of political behavior is Harold Lasswell's, *Psychopathology and Politics* (Chicago: University of Chicago, 1931).

[13]A 1988 study of county leaders of the Bush campaign organization found that 32 percent of them had switched to the GOP from the Democratic party, typically to align their ideological convictions with their party. John A. Clark, John M. Bruce, John H. Kessel, and William Jacoby, "I'd Rather Switch than Fight: Lifelong Democrats and Converts to Republicanism among Campaign Activists,"

(continued)

Party activists may also be drawn to the party by a more general civic commitment. A sense of obligation and duty as a citizen, a belief in the democratic values of citizen participation, may impel them. Scholars who have questioned party workers about their motives for service in the party know the familiar answers. They were asked to serve, and they assented because it was their civic duty. Often that response, in whatever words it may be couched, merely masks what the respondent feels are less acceptable motives. Often, however, it is an honest reflection of deeply ingrained civic values, developed perhaps from parents who themselves were party activists. Often, too, it may be combined with honest, if vague, commitments to "good government" and political reform.

Mixed Incentives

No party organization depends on a single incentive, and very few partisans labor in the party for only one reason. Most party organizations rely on a variety of incentives. Patronage workers may coexist with workers attracted by policy issues or by a middle-class sense of civic responsibility. Both may gain the satisfactions of social interaction with like-minded people. The mixture of incentives may vary between levels of the party organization, with higher-level activists sustained more by purposive incentives and lower-level activists attracted by material or solidary rewards.[14] Or the mix may differ by political culture, with more traditional cultures conducive to parties built around material motives and reform-oriented cultures attracting purposive activists.

For all the subtleties of the mix and variety of incentives, however, general comments about their overall frequency *are* possible. Scholarly evidence on the point comes from sporadic studies of parties in scattered parts of the country, but what evidence there is points to the dominance of ideological or issue incentives. Put very simply, the desire to use the party as a means to achieve policy goals appears to be the major incentive attracting individuals to party work these days.[15] Although similar data are unavailable for earlier periods, there is

---

American Journal of Political Science 35 (1991): 577–97. Studies of conversions among Democratic and Republican state party convention delegates in 1980 and 1984 corroborate the strong ideological bases of party switching. See Mary Grisez Kweit, "Ideological Congruence of Party Switchers and Nonswitchers: The Case of Party Activists," *American Journal of Political Science* 30 (1986): 184–96; and Dorothy Davidson Nesbit, "Changing Partisanship among Southern Party Activists," *Journal of Politics* 50 (1988): 322–34.

[14]Samuel Eldersveld, *Political Parties: A Behavioral Analysis* (Chicago: Rand McNally, 1964), p. 278 and Chap. 11.

[15]Lewis Bowman, Dennis Ippolito, and William Donaldson, "Incentives for the Maintenance of Grassroots Political Activism," *Midwest Journal of Political Science* 13 (1969): 126–39; Charles W. Wiggins and William L. Turk, "State Party Chairmen: A Profile," *Western Political Quarterly* 23 (1970): 321–32; Conway and Feigert, "Motivation, Incentive Systems and the Political Party Organization"; Dwaine Marvick, "Party Organizational Personnel and Electoral Democracy in Los Angeles, 1963–1972," in William Crotty (ed.), *The Party Symbol: Readings on Political Parties* (San Francisco: Freeman, 1980), pp. 63–86; Barbara C. Burrell, "Local Political Party Committees, Task

reason to believe that this generalization was far less true of party workers a generation or two ago.[16] This is not to say, however, that personal material interests are unimportant as sources of involvement in parties. Parties and political activity continue to offer many attractive material rewards in spite of the declining availability of patronage jobs.

Incentives may change, moreover, for any individual; that is, the incentive that recruits people to party activity may not sustain them in that activity. Several studies suggest that a shift in incentives takes place in those party activists attracted by the purposive incentives—those who seek to achieve issue, ideological, or other impersonal goals through their party activity. To sustain their involvement in party work, they tend to depend more on incentives of social contact, identification with the party itself, and other personal rewards and satisfactions.[17] Perhaps an electorally pragmatic party—one traditionally committed to the flexibilities necessary to win elections—has difficulty providing the ideological successes necessary to sustain workers whose incentives remain ideological for any length of time.

THE PROCESSES OF RECRUITMENT

The mere existence of incentives for work in the party organization will not automatically produce a full roster of active workers. In the political party, as in any other large organization, the organization must recruit actively in order to ensure for itself useful and compatible recruits. Potential activists may lack either the knowledge of the opportunity or the stimulus to act, or both. Therefore, there must be some process of recruitment that will join opportunity and stimulus to incentives in order to attract the activists.

The Difficulties of and Need for Recruiting

Nonetheless, except at the national level, and in some states, where the recent profusion of paid positions and exciting work have transformed dull and inconsequential positions into attractive professional opportunities, the parties do not find it easy to recruit. Frequently, their incentives are not attractive enough to compete even with the modest pleasures of activity in a local service club. They

---

Performance and Organizational Vitality," *Western Political Quarterly* 39 (1986): 48–66; and the various city studies contained in Crotty, *Political Parties in Local Areas.*

[16]The fact that Eldersveld finds little change between 1956 and 1980 in the incentives for party activity (except the expected declines in party loyalty) in Detroit and Los Angeles, though, should rein in sweeping generalizations about motivational change. It is possible that what may distinguish modern from traditional party workers is the direction of their ideology, not its intensity.

[17]Among others, see Conway and Feigert, "Motivation, Incentive Systems, and the Political Organization."

often lack any effective mechanism for recruiting new personnel, and they may even ignore the necessity for self-renewal. Furthermore, state statutes often take at least part of the recruitment process out of their hands; open party caucuses and the election of party officials in primaries tend to encourage self-recruitment at the expense of the party initiatives and control. Above all, the chronic need for personnel of any kind disposes the parties to accept whatever help is available. Even patronage-rich organizations in job-poor communities tend not to be rigorous in recruiting new activists. Friendship and contacts within the party organization may speed the entry of the new activist more effectively than political skills or promise of performance.

The Recruitment System

In the absence of regular and rigorous recruitment by the party, opportunities for party work come in a haphazard way. Initially, a certain degree of awareness of the parties is necessary, as are strong political goals and commitments. Then, at the time of recruitment, there must also be some more immediate occasion or stimulus for the individual to enter party work. Sometimes that stimulus is internal, and the individual in effect recruits himself or herself. In other cases, the stimulus is external, most often the invitation or persuasion of some other individual. Over the years, activists have tended to ascribe their initial recruitment largely to these external stimuli.[18]

Events in the larger political world also play an important role in the recruitment of party activists. Specific candidates for office and political causes often provide the first attraction to party work, which for some is sustained long after the initial reason has disappeared. Just as the Democratic party has been heavily influenced by the influx of liberals activated by the New Deal in the 1930s and the Vietnam war and civil rights movements in modern times, the GOP has been energized by a mobilization of conservatives by Barry Goldwater, Ronald Reagan, and fundamentalist ministers such as Pat Robertson. This process of political recruitment, depending as it does upon the presence of magnetic personalities and powerful issues, is episodic rather than continuous. It produces a generational layering within the party cadres, in which political outlooks may differ considerably by formative experiences and time of initial activation. And it, more than any other single factor, defines the ideological direction of the parties (see box).[19]

---

[18]Phillip Althoff and Samuel C. Patterson, "Political Activism in a Rural County," *Midwest Journal of Political Science* 10 (1966): 39–51; Lewis Bowman and G. R. Boynton, "Recruitment Patterns among Local Party Officials," *American Political Science Review* 60 (1966): 667–76; and Samuel J. Eldersveld, *Political Parties in American Society* (New York: Basic Books, 1982), p. 175.

[19]Paul Allen Beck and M. Kent Jennings found that strong conservatives were the most active participants in the 1956, 1960, and 1964 campaigns but that strong liberals matched their activism in

---

Presidential Campaign Gypsy: A Case Study in Political Recruitment

Modern politics has seen the emergence of a cadre of professional campaign specialists who hone and apply their skills in campaign after campaign. One such "political gypsy," as described by John Homans, is Steve Murphy, who worked for Richard Gephardt's campaign for the Democratic presidential nomination in 1988. His history of political activism typifies a common recruitment pattern in recent decades.

> Steve Murphy, the Gephardt organizer, proudly calls himself a child of the 60's, a member of the generation that was going to change the world. He volunteered for George McGovern's campaign while he was a student at the University of Delaware. After he graduated, he worked as a VISTA volunteer, doing community organizing on New York's Lower East Side. The work satisfied his idealism, but he came to feel that changing Christie Street and changing the world were two different propositions.
>
> "I guess I'm much too impatient," he said. "I figured out that if I wanted to have a real impact, electoral politics was the way to do it."
>
> In 1976, he joined Jimmy Carter's campaign as a paid organizer, corraling votes in the South and the Middle West, sacrificing the minuscule but concrete increments of change that community organizing can produce for the gamble that his man would get to the White House. He loved it. The results were measurable. "Elections have consequences," said Murphy.

JOHN HOMANS

In sum, then, we have an extensive, informal recruitment system—a complex of interrelated factors that selects out of the American population a particular group of men and women. Its chief elements are:

- The motives, goals, and knowledge of the men and women whom the parties want to recruit.
- The incentives to party activity that the party can offer, and the value of those incentives.

1968 and then surpassed it from 1972 through 1980. See their "Political Periods and Political Participation," *American Political Science Review* 73 (1979): 737–50, and "Updating Political Periods and Political Participation," *American Political Science Review* 78 (1984): 198–201. Steven E. Finkel and Gregory Trevor, "Reassessing Ideological Bias in Campaign Participation," *Political Behavior* 8 (1986): 374–90, attribute the hyperactivity of strong liberals in 1984 to the competitiveness of the Democratic primaries that year.

- The role the party is allowed by state statutes to play in recruitment.
- The contacts, opportunities, events, and persuasions that are the immediate, proximate occasions of recruitment.[20]

The components of this system change constantly, and as they do, they affect the supply of personnel entering the organization. Recruitment in any form, however, is a matching of the motives and goals of the individual with the incentives and expectations of the party organization.

Recruitment from Within

An auxiliary recruitment system may work *within* the organization to promote especially successful party workers to positions of greater responsibility. A study of Detroit in the 1950s showed this system at work: Party leaders had risen exclusively through the avenues of party and public office. One group came up through the precinct positions, another came through the auxiliary organizations (e.g., women's groups, youth organizations, political clubs), and a third and smaller group moved from the race for public office to a career within the party.[21] The data we have on the political careers of party activists, however, do not suggest that party activists invariably inch up the career ladder in the party, position by position. Almost half of a national sample of Democratic and Republican county chairs in 1979–80, for example, had held no party office before becoming chair.[22] In general, the most that can be said is that the way stations of a political career vary with the nature of the political organization. In party organizations that have relatively open access and easy mobility, careers in the party are developed easily, almost spontaneously. In disciplined, hierarchical party organizations, party activists must inevitably work up the hierarchy in carefully graded steps and expectations.

THE RECRUITS: AMATEURS AND PROFESSIONALS

The diverse incentives and recruitment processes combine to produce the party cadres, the men and women who do the work of the parties. These activists play a wide variety of roles in party affairs—from campaigning on behalf of party candidates and serving as delegates to party nominating conventions to staffing the party offices.

---

[20]For similar theories of recruitment, see Bowman and Boynton, "Recruitment Patterns"; and C. Richard Hofstetter, "Organizational Activists: The Bases of Participation in Amateur and Professional Groups," *American Politics Quarterly* 1 (1973): 244–76.

[21]Eldersveld, *Political Parties*, pp. 142–43.

[22]Cotter et al., *Party Organizations in American Politics*, p. 42.

Common Characteristics

In spite of their different motivations and activities, American party activists have two characteristics in common that set them apart from the general population of adults. First, they tend, rather uniformly, to come from families with a history of party activity. Study after study indicates that large numbers of party activists had an adult party activist in their immediate family as they were growing up. Second, activists are marked by their relatively high socioeconomic status (SES), whether one measures SES by income, by years of formal education, or by occupation. (Lawyers are especially common among the active partisans.[23]) The parties thus attract men and women with the time and financial resources to afford politics, with the information and knowledge to understand it, and with the skills to be useful in it.[24]

Some local organizations provide exceptions to this general pattern of activists coming from the relatively higher status ranks. The patronage-oriented, favor-dispensing machines in the center cities have drawn party workers and leaders in a more representative fashion from the populations with which they work. For many lower status Americans, the kinds of material incentives the machines could provide probably were the crucial inducements for activism. As patronage and other material incentives have dwindled, the social character of these parties has changed. A comparison of county committee members from both parties in Pittsburgh in 1971, 1976, and 1983 illustrates this transformation of party cadres into a more and more educated group as machine control declined. The mix of incentives parties can provide, in short, has clear implications for the social composition of the activists it can recruit.[25]

The social characteristics of the activist cadres differ between the Democrat and Republican parties as would be expected from the divergent social bases of the parties' electoral coalitions. Democratic activists are more likely than their Republican counterparts to be black, union members, and Catholics. But differences in education, income, and occupation, once perhaps substan-

---

[23]On lawyers in American politics, see Heinz Eulau and John D. Sprague, *Lawyers in Politics* (Indianapolis: Bobbs-Merrill, 1964).

[24]The relatively high status of party activists is documented in Sidney Verba and Norman H. Nie, *Participation in America* (New York: Harper Row, 1972), Chap. 8, for campaign activists; in Crotty, *Political Parties in Local Areas*, pp. 45, 72, 94–95, 162–63, and Cotter et al., *Party Organizations in American Politics*, p. 42, for local leaders; in Wiggins and Turk, "State Party Chairman: A Profile," for state chairmen; in Ronald Rapoport, Alan I. Abramowitz, and John McGlennon, *The Life of the Parties* (Lexington: The University of Kentucky Press, 1986), Chap. 3, for state convention delegates; and in Warren E. Miller and M. Kent Jennings, *Parties in Transition* (New York: Russell Sage Foundation, 1986), pp. 67–85, for national convention delegates. For many years, Republican activists came from higher SES groups than did their Democratic counterparts, reflecting the social class differences between the two party coalitions. These differences have considerably narrowed in recent years.

[25]Michael Margolis and Raymond E. Owen, "From Organization to Personalism: A Note on the Transmogrification of the Local Political Party," *Polity* 18 (1985): 313–28.

Professionals and Amateurs: A Typology

	Professionals	Amateurs
Political style	Pragmatic	Purist
Incentives for activism	Material (patronage, preferments)	Purposive (issues, ideology)
Locus of party loyalty	Party organization	Office-holders, party clubs, other auxiliaries
Desired orientation of party	To candidates, elections	To issues, ideology
Criterion for selecting party candidates	Electability	Principles
Desired process of party governance	Hierarchical	Democratic
Support of party candidates	Automatic	Conditional on issues, principles
Recruitment path	Through party	Through issue, candidate organizations
SES level	Average to above average	Well above average

tial, appear to be negligible in recent years. Although they may come from different backgrounds and certainly possess different political views, the leadership cadres of both parties seem to be drawn from the higher status groups in American society.[26]

Professionals versus Amateurs

Beyond their social characteristics, it also matters what goals, expectations, and skills the activists bring to the party organizations. The goals and activities of the party and the men and women it recruits reflect one another. In fact, observers of the American party organizations have developed a two-part typology of party activists, based not only on their personal characteristics but also on the role they play in the organization and the expectations they have for it. One type of party activist is the professional—the traditional party worker whose prime loyalty is to the party itself and whose operating style is pragmatic. Its antithesis is the amateur—the issue-oriented purist to whom party activity is only one means for realizing important political goals. Professionals and amateurs are

---

[26]These assertions are supported by a potpourri of data. See Martin Plissner and Warren J. Mitofsky, "The Making of the Delegates, 1968–1988," *Public Opinion* 11 (September/October 1988): 45–47, on characteristics of delegates to the national nominating conventions; and Cotter et al., *Party Organizations in American Politics*, p. 42, and the 1988 study of presidential campaign leaders conducted by John Kessel and William Jacoby, on the characteristics of the county chairs.

seen to differ in virtually all of the characteristics important for party activists (see box).

Yet, these polar types are abstractions rather than descriptions of specific individuals. They tend to be purer and more extreme than one finds in reality, and most party workers probably harbor a mixture of professional and amateur orientations. They also have become pejorative labels for the opposition in intraparty factional disputes. Nevertheless, the typology has been usefully employed to distinguish between machine politicians and reformers in city politics, between party regulars and ideological insurgents at the party nominating conventions, and even between "old" and "new" styles of party activity (see box).[27]

The implication of amateurs versus professionals for party organization is clear. A different party is assumed to emerge with one type—or with its predominance—than with the other. Above all, the new or amateur activists are thought to be more issue-oriented and to insist on participation and agenda setting within the organization in order to bring those issue concerns to the party. They are seen as less comfortable with the traditional electoral pragmatism of the parties—that is, with making compromises in their positions in order to win elections. They are drawn into the party, in short, for purposive goals and often disdain material incentives. To the extent that their orientations mold the party organizations, they bring a profound change to the American parties. They also work a change of similar magnitude by bringing to the parties a strong impetus for reform, not only in the internal business of the party but also in its external environment, by favoring, for example, the adoption of presidential primaries and simplified voter registration.

Differences that are clear in theory, however, do not always carry over into practice. Amateurs may be distinguishable from professionals in their incentives for party activity. They may exhibit different attitudes on such key matters as the importance of party loyalty and the use of patronage. But there is persuasive evidence that these differences in motives and attitudes do not necessarily carry over into key realms of behavior. Among delegates to the 1980 state nominating conventions, amateurs were no less likely than professionals to sacrifice ideology for electability in their support of candidates.[28] Among county party chairs in 1972, at the height of the presumed ascendency of the amateurs, the amateurs were no different from professionals in working to communicate within the party, maintain party morale, or run effective campaigns.[29] The contrast

---

[27]This distinction between amateurs and professionals is developed in Clark and Wilson, "Incentive Systems"; Wilson, *The Amateur Democrat*; Aaron Wildavsky, "The Goldwater Phenomenon: Purists, Politicians, and the Two-Party System," *The Review of Politics* 27 (1965): 386–413; and John W. Soule and James W. Clarke, "Amateurs and Professionals: A Study of Delegates to the 1968 Democratic National Convention," *American Political Science Review* 64 (1970): 888–98.

[28]Walter J. Stone and Alan I. Abramowitz, "Winning May Not Be Everything But It's More Than We Thought: Presidential Party Activists in 1980," *American Political Science Review* 77 (1983): 945–56.

[29]Michael A. Maggiotto and Ronald E. Weber, "The Impact of Organizational Incentives on County Party Chairpersons," *American Politics Quarterly* 14 (1986): 201–18.

O'Brien and Lowenstein, Professional and Amateur

Their paths crossed many times in Democratic party politics, especially during the turbulent 1960s, yet they remained fundamentally on opposite paths. Lawrence O'Brien was the party professional extraordinaire. Twice chairman of the Democratic National Committee, top campaign advisor to four presidential candidates (John and Robert Kennedy, Lyndon Johnson, and Hubert Humphrey), O'Brien was

> . . . noted for his savvy, no-nonsense approach to winning elections. (He) disdained "windmill-tilting" amateurs who failed to see that elections were not won by those who insisted on always taking the high road. "The eggheads," he felt . . . "want the candidate to win on his own terms—to defy the party and interest groups. . . . The egghead thinks it's worthwhile to be defeated. I think it's worthwhile to be elected." (Albin Krebs of *The New York Times,* September 29, 1990. Copyright © 1990 by The New York Times Company. Reprinted by permission.)

O'Brien's antithesis and sometime adversary was Allard Lowenstein—who entered politics as an issue-oriented amateur and "tilted" at more than a few windmills in his lifetime. From civil rights activism as a young college student in North Carolina in the 1940s, on behalf of an independent Namibia in the 1950s, and in Mississippi in the early 1960s, Lowenstein turned to the anti-Vietnam movement in the mid-1960s. He spearheaded Eugene McCarthy's challenge to President Lyndon Johnson in the 1988 New Hampshire primary, which was pivotal in Johnson's withdrawal from the presidential race, and was elected as an antiwar candidate to Congress later that year.

These two men epitomized the leadership of the antagonistic sides in the struggles over the direction of the Democratic party in the 1960s, particularly in the tumultuous 1968 nomination contest when they organized the campaigns of competing candidates. Their distinct brands of partisan activism give real-life meaning to the terms professional and amateur.

between professionals and amateurs, and the implications of changes in their relative numbers for the parties, may have been overdrawn.

VITALITY OF THE PARTY ORGANIZATION

Party organizations are apparatuses for assembling political resources and mobilizing them in the pursuit of political goals. Some do it with strength and vitality; others are ineffective. For decades, the American model or ideal in local party organization has been the classic urban machine. Its organizational hierarchy, its full range of year-round services and activities, and its army of eager workers in the wards and precincts have traditionally represented the apex of organizational strength. It is an organizational form in which the personal attention, service, friendship, and persuasiveness of the local party worker are directed at the local electorate. All its activities throughout the year are geared to earning the support of that electorate, thus enabling the activists and office seekers of the party to deliver its vote and achieve their political goals through victory at the polls.

As Chapter 3 suggested, the urban machine ideal has never been the norm for the performance of the party organization. Its chief and indispensable ingredient, the local ward or precinct workers, has too often been inactive or completely absent. Even in American cities two decades or so ago, inactivity at this level of the party organization was common. Many traditional campaign tasks—door-to-door canvassing, telephoning, transporting people to the polls, registration of new voters—were left unperformed.[30] In a more recent study of county organizations in Connecticut and Michigan, no more than 38 percent engaged in all the critical activities of voter registration, canvassing, and getting out the vote; over half of the grass-roots organizations, however, performed canvassing, literature distribution, or fund-raising activities. Indeed, the most common activity of all was fund raising, a task that assumed low priority for the traditional urban machines.[31] By 1980, a comprehensive study of the local parties concluded that they had become more active than ten to fifteen years before. When party activity levels in the same counties were explicitly compared between 1964 and 1980, in fact, the local parties had become more active in distributing literature, arranging campaign events, publicizing their candidates, conducting registration drives, and *fund raising*.[32] Still, by any measure, it must be conceded that party grass-roots activity today falls far short of the storied efficiency of the urban political machine.

The organizational problem extends, however, beyond inert or underactive committeepersons. Parties often cannot maintain the nexus of roles and relationships on which the organizational paragon depends. Communications often are poor within the organization, and leaders at each level operate independently of others.[33] Local workers enter and remain in party service for a splendid variety of motives. They carry out different tasks, have differing political values and differing perceptions of political reality and differ greatly in the way

---

[30]See Robert H. Salisbury, "The Urban Party Organization Member," *Public Opinion Quarterly* 29 (1965–66): 562, 564; Lewis Bowman and G. R. Boynton, "Activities and Role Definitions of Grass Roots Party Officials," *Journal of Politics* 28 (1966): 132–34; and Eldersveld, *Political Parties*, p. 348.

[31]Burrell, "Local Party Committees."

[32]James L. Gibson, Cornelius P. Cotter, John F. Bibby, and Robert J. Huckshorn, "Whither the Local Parties?" *American Journal of Political Science* 29 (1985): 139–160. The 1964 data are reported in Paul Allen Beck, "Environment and Party: The Impact of Political and Demographic County Characteristics on Party Behavior," *American Political Science Review* 68 (1974): 1229–44.

[33]Eldersveld, *Political Parties*, pp. 377, 408.

they perceive their roles as leaders. Many local parties, in short, barely qualify as organizations in the conventional meaning of the term.

If the private life of the party were all that mattered, the vitality of the party organization would be of little concern. But the organization's effectiveness in the political marketplace, measured by the currency of votes, depends crucially on its vitality. Over the years, the evidence has cumulated consistently that a well-organized and active local party can win extra votes for its candidates for office, typically by mobilizing its supporters. The margin is not large; in competitive electoral environments, though, such a small margin may be the critical difference between winning and losing.[34] This net advantage to be gained from a strong and active local organization has even survived the demise of the party machines. A study of the electoral effects of local party organizations in the early 1980s found a similarly small, but significant, impact on the vote. This study also revealed an important role for the local party, especially the minority party in one-party areas, in recruiting candidates for office, a necessary first step in becoming electorally competitive.[35]

It is because organizational effectiveness matters in the quest for electoral victory that the search for the strong, vital party organization goes on. This search, however, is hampered by the lack of agreement on what the ideal ought to be. For many partisans and observers, the ideal remains the classic, turn-of-the-century urban machine. It is an ideal rooted in time, in the methods of campaigning, and in the electorate of a past era. Its operations are not acceptable, however, to the new activists and the reformers; furthermore, voters can be reached by means other than the ubiquitous precinct workers. What we need—but haven't found—is some common conception of strength and effectiveness for the political realities of the late twentieth century.

Accounting for Variations in Organizational Strength

Although the shades of vitality in party organization are not easy to sort out, it is possible to generalize roughly about the conditions under which organizational strength develops. First, because of the density of cities and the special needs of urban populations, it is not surprising that the acmes of party organizations have been reached in the nation's metropolitan centers. Differences in

---

[34]See Phillips Cutright and Peter Rossi, "Grass Roots Politicians and the Vote," *American Sociological Review* 63 (1958): 171–79; Daniel Katz and Samuel J. Eldersveld, "The Impact of Local Party Activity upon the Electorate," *Public Opinion Quarterly* 25 (1961): 1–24; Raymond E. Wolfinger, "The Influence of Precinct Work on Voting Behavior," *Public Opinion Quarterly* 27 (1963): 387–98; Gerald H. Kramer, "The Effects of Precinct-Level Canvassing on Voter Behavior," *Public Opinon Quarterly* 34 (1970–71): 560–72; William J. Crotty, "Party Effort and Its Impact on the Vote," *American Political Science Review* 65 (1971): 439–50; and David E. Price and Michael Lupfer, "Volunteers for Gore: The Impact of a Precinct-Level Canvass in Three Tennessee Cities," *Journal of Politics* 35 (1973): 410–38.

[35]John P. Frendreis, James L. Gibson, and Laura L. Vertz, "The Electoral Relevance of Local Party Organizations," *American Political Science Review* 84 (1990): 225–35.

political culture also affect the development of party organizations. Persistent canvassing by committeepersons and patronage practices are acceptable in some quarters but not in others. Even the mix of amateur and professional orientations within the party organization may vary by political culture. The parties of Berkeley, Manhattan, or suburban Minneapolis may contain more amateurs than those of Columbus, Queens, or Chicago.[36] A third factor is the long-term patterns of party competition. The greatest number of a party's defunct organizations appear where it is an entrenched minority party. One-partyism has the tendency to enervate the majority party as well. Until the 1950s, for example, Republican organizations in the Deep South were largely defunct—and their Democratic counterparts were little stronger. Finally, the statutory forms and regulations of some states are more burdensome than those of others. State laws that make it difficult for the party to remove or replace inactive party officials, to use patronage as an inducement for party work, or to decide which candidates will carry its label hamper the development of strong party organizations.[37]

POWER AND DISCIPLINE IN THE PARTY ORGANIZATION

Organization implies discipline—at least enough discipline to coordinate its parts and to implement its decisions. It also implies some well-established system of authority for making those decisions. Many Americans have gone beyond these implications, however, and have imagined virtually authoritarian control within the party organization. Some leader, generally identified as the boss, has widely been thought to rule the party apparatus by a combination of cunning, toughness, and force of will. The boss, in fact, became something of an American folk hero, feared for his ruthlessness and admired for his rascality and intrepid daring. He has been celebrated in the public arts,[38] and if he had not existed, it might have been necessary to create him, if only to justify the political cynicism of generations of Americans (see box).

Very few organizational leaders ruled absolutely by personal magnetism, tactical adroitness, or the use of sanctions. Even in the era of boss rule, the boss's power was shared with influential underlings, and the terms of that shar-

---

[36]See Daniel Elazar, *American Federalism: A View from the States* (New York: Crowell, 1972), Chap. 4, for the distribution of individualistic, moralistic, and traditionalistic political cultures throughout the nation.

[37]V. O. Key, Jr., *American State Politics* (New York: Knopf, 1956), Chap. 6.

[38]Note, for example, the thinly-disguised fictional accounts of real-life "bosses" in Edwin O'Connor, *The Last Hurrah* (Boston: Little, Brown, 1956); and Robert Penn Warren, *All the King's Men* (New York: Harcourt, Brace, 1946).

The Boss in Cartoon

American artists at the turn of the century caught, for all time, the enduring American view of the urban political boss. Walter Clark's image needs no explanation.

Source: Walter Appleton Clark, "The Boss." From *Collier's Weekly,* November 10, 1906. Reprinted from Ralph F. Shikes, *The Indignant Eye* (Boston: Beacon Press, 1969), p. 321.

ing were deeply rooted in all of the hierarchical traditions of the organization. Much of what centralization there was existed because the foot soldiers in the ranks accepted the hierarchical system of authority. To many, the party's hierarchy may have seemed natural and inevitable. If they sought patronage jobs, they cared little about what else the party did or did not do.

More recently, however, party activists have come to demand a voice in the affairs of the party. A good portion of the ideological fervor of the amateurs has been directed at reforming the party's authoritarianism and bossism, and probably nothing divides amateurs from professionals more than their attitudes toward the political machines and lack of obedience to party authorities. Amateurs are committed to the norms and imperatives of democracy, at least in part because of a higher level of education and political information. Their commitment to intraparty democracy also follows logically from their desire to move the party to ideology, because achievement of their own political goals hinges directly on the party's achievement of congruent goals. Thus, they must reform the American parties if they are to reform American society.[39]

It is not only participation, however, that is cutting into the discipline of the party organization. Discipline depends also on the ability of the organization to withdraw or withhold its incentives. Much of the discipline of the classic machine resulted from the willingness and ability of party leaders to manipulate material rewards. A recalcitrant or inefficient committeeman sacrificed his public job or his hope for it. The newer incentives, however, cannot be given or revoked so easily. The party is only one among many organizations pursuing policy or ideological goals; and given the party's very imperfect control of its legislators, it may not even be the most efficient means to these ends. The ideologically oriented activist may find substitute outlets for his or her activities in interest groups or nonparty political associations, such as neighborhood associations, professional groups, or political action committees of one kind or another.

Other powerful forces in the American polity resisted the creation of centralized, disciplined party organizations even before the changes in their activist cadres took root. Whether or not irresponsible power has been a fact within the party organizations, the American political culture is haunted by fear that a few men, responsible to no one, will control the selection of public officials and set the agendas of policymaking in "smoke-filled rooms." Understandably, the search for mechanisms with which to control that power has been a long and diligent one. The results fall into two broad categories: mechanisms that impose controls from outside the parties and those that look to internal controls.

External Controls

Political laissez-faire suggests that two competitive parties will set limits to each other's exercise of organizational powers by their very competition. This argument directly parallels the argument of the self-regulating effects of economic competition in the free marketplace.[40] If one party offers the electorate a shoddy political product or if it overprices its political goods, it will lose its political consumers to its competitor. One-partyism—monopoly of the political system—negates the automatic corrective action assumed in laissez-faire theory, however, and some of the centers of greater organizational power have been

---

[39]Wilson, *The Amateur Democrat*, Chap. 5. These reform orientations sometimes are rooted as much in the deprivations of being out of power as in principled opposition to the concentration of power in a political machine. For some evidence of this in a Chicago reform club, see David L. Protess and Alan R. Gitelson, "Political Stability, Reform Clubs, and the Amateur Democrat," in William Crotty (ed.), *The Party Symbol* (San Francisco: Freeman, 1980), pp. 87–100.

[40]This theory is elaborated in Anthony Downs, *An Economic Theory of Democracy* (New York: Harper & Row, 1965).

without serious two-party competition. The current spread of two-party competitiveness may expose more party organizations to the discipline of the electoral market.

Anti-organization reformers have generally preferred statutory controls on party power to the unseen hand of competition, but their disappointments have outnumbered their successes. Where voters in the primary pick precinct committeepersons and other party officials, there are rarely contests for offices. Frequently, there is not even a candidate. Attempts to regulate the holding of party caucuses and conventions have not always guaranteed access to all qualified comers. The reformers have not been without their successes, however. Statutorily guaranteed access has opened party organization to competition by other factions and oligarchies or to reinvigoration by new party personnel. Patronage has been massively curtailed. Moreover, in all of the states, the direct primary has at least forced the parties to face the scrutiny of voters on one key decision: the nomination of candidates for office. Some scholars have argued, in fact, that the introduction of the direct primary into American politics in this century is primarily responsible for the atrophy of local party organizations throughout the country.[41]

Internal Controls

In his sweeping "iron law of oligarchy," Robert Michels declared over 75 years ago, without qualification, that organizations are by their nature oligarchic or "minoritarian," for only a few leaders have the experience, interest, and involvement necessary to manage the affairs of complex organizations.

> Organization implies the tendency to oligarchy. In every organization, whether it be a political party, a professional union, or any other association of the kind, the aristocratic tendency manifests itself very clearly. The mechanism of the organization, while conferring a solidity of structure, induces serious changes in the organized mass, completely inverting the respective position of the leaders and the led. As a result of organization, every party or professional union becomes divided into a minority of directors and a majority of directed.[42]

To the extent that we are all believers in the myths of the bosses, the smoke-filled rooms, and the deals between oligarchs, we are all disciples of Michels.

Michels' "iron law" of oligarchy has had little relevance, however, to the organizations of the American major parties. The distribution of power within most American party organizations is best described as a *stratarchy* rather than *hierarchy*. It is "the enlargement of the ruling group of an organization,

---

[41]Key, *American State Politics*; and Walter Dean Burnham, *Critical Elections and the Mainsprings of American Politics* (New York: Norton, 1970), p. 75.

[42]Robert Michels, *Political Parties* (Glencoe, Ill.: Free Press, 1949; originally published in 1915), p. 32.

its power stratification, the involvement of large numbers of people in group decision-making, and, thus, the diffusion and proliferation of control throughout the structure."[43] Various levels of party organization operate at least semi-independently of other levels, even superordinate ones. Precinct committeepersons, district leaders, and even county officials freely define their own political roles and nourish their separate bases of party power. Thus, "although authority to speak for the organization may remain in the hands of the top elite nucleus, there is great autonomy in operations at the lower 'strata' or echelons of the hierarchy, and . . . control from the top is minimal and formal."[44]

What accounts for stratarchy and the failure of top party leaders to centralize organizational power in the hierarchy? Weighing against the pressures of a centralized party oligarchy are these factors:

- *Participatory expectations.* Large percentages of party activists expect to participate in the decision-making processes of their political party. Therefore, the organization may have to tolerate or even create intraparty democracy (or consultation) to maintain vitality, to lift morale, and to achieve cohesion.
- *Controls of lower party levels over higher levels.* The chieftains of the lower-level party organizations typically make up the conventions or consultative bodies that select party officialdom above them. County chairpersons who choose state officers are forces to be reckoned with in the state party organizations. Similarly, precinct workers or delegates often form or choose county committees.
- *Internal competition.* Party organizations rarely are monoliths. They often embrace competing organizations or factions. Differences in goals and political styles produce continuing competition in the selecting of party officials and the mapping of party activities.
- *Independence of officeholders.* Because they do not need to rely upon the party organization for nomination or election, public officials often create their own power bases within the party, which enable them to compete with organizational leaders for control over the party. The most powerful political machines have emerged where the leaders of the party organization were also the top elected officials. In Chicago, for example, Richard Daley was both mayor and chairman of the Cook County Democratic Party.

Diffusion of power marks all but the exceptional party organizations. Top party leaders engage in much mobilizing and placating of support within the organization; their consultations with middle-level leadership are endless. Even the ward or precinct leader with a small electoral following and a single vote at an important convention must be cultivated. Above all, party leaders in modern

---

[43]Eldersveld, *Political Parties*, p. 99.

[44]Eldersveld, *Political Parties*, pp. 99–100.

times rarely command, for their commands no longer carry potent sanctions. They plead, they bargain, they cajole, and they reason—and they even learn to lose gracefully on occasion. They mobilize party power not so much by threats as by the solidarity of common goals and interests.

Recent years, though, have witnessed one development with the potential for counteracting these powerful forces for stratarchy and decentralization. The growth in capabilities of the state and especially the national parties, through their abundant treasuries and their cadres of skilled professional operatives, has converted them into effective organizational forces for the first time in American history. With such resources available at the top of the party hierarchies, there is a temptation for local party organizations to turn away from uncontrollable volunteers and labor-intensive grass roots activity toward a dependence upon professional campaign organizers and capital-intensive campaigning, especially heavy use of television. This greater dependence on the higher organizational levels may bring with it more control and direction from the top. It has not happened yet, and may never happen given the powerful forces preventing centralization of authority in the parties, but it should not come as a complete surprise if these new sources of skilled labor and money were to create new pressures for centralized authority and discipline within the organization.

In a sense, these concerns over power, discipline, and control in American party organization seem misplaced and out of date. Whereas earlier generations may have worried about the excesses of party power, particularly in local party machines, we increasingly worry about the weakness and withering of party organization. Many reformers have turned their energies from curbing the parties to saving them, and there is even an organization called The Committee for Party Renewal, comprised of party activists and scholarly specialists on the parties, dedicated to this end.

American party organizations probably have never commanded incentives and rewards at all equal to their organizational goals and ambitions—or to their reputations. In that sense, they have been chronically "underfinanced." They never have been able to recruit the kinds of resources they would need in order to flesh out the party organization that the state statutes create. The thousands of inactive precinct workers and unfilled precinct positions testify to that poverty of incentive. The parties, therefore, have had no alternative but to tolerate organizational forms that have permitted them to live within their means and to draw upon activists with diverse motives, backgrounds, and styles.

THE POLITICAL PARTY IN THE ELECTORATE

In very few party systems has the separation between the party organization and the party's faithful voters been as great as it is in the American party system. American parties largely have failed to integrate the party's most loyal supporters into the party organization. Even the membership offered for party contributions in recent years is but a nominal reward in that it brings with it little meaningful organizational involvement. Nor have the American parties mounted any substantial program to educate their loyal electorates into the principles and traditions of the party. They view even the most sympathetic voters as a separate clientele to be reinforced anew at each election. Those faithful voters, for all their protestations of loyalty to the party, also stand apart from its organization. They consider their obligation to the party amply fulfilled if they support its candidates in a substantial majority of instances. In these important respects, then, the American parties resemble true cadre parties, top-heavy in leaders and activists without any significant mass membership, not the mass parties that have been such an important part of the European democratic experience.

This "party in the electorate,"[1] unlike the party organization, is largely a categorical group. There is no interaction within it, no structured set of relationships, no organizational or group life. Also, like any categorical group, it is an artifact of the way we choose to define it. There has been widespread scholarly agreement that the party in the electorate is characterized by its feelings of loyalty to or identification with the party.

---

[1]The term was popularized by V. O. Key, Jr., in *Politics, Parties and Pressure Groups*, 5th ed. (New York: Crowell, 1964), p. 164.

In the American political context, partisans are the men and women who consider themselves Democrats and Republicans, just as Presbyterians or Catholics are commonly regarded as those who profess a preference for that religious denomination regardless of whether they attend its services or make any other commitment to the church. Party loyalty may be measured quite simply by asking people with which party, if any, they identify. A variety of different questions have been utilized over the years and, as is typically the case, the answers vary to some degree depending upon the precise question wording that is employed.[2] The two-part question that has dominated research on partisanship, though, comes from surveys conducted by the University of Michigan since 1952, which asks:

> Generally speaking, do you usually think of yourself as a Republican, a Democrat, an independent, or what? [IF REPUBLICAN OR DEMOCRAT] Would you call yourself a strong [Republican or Democrat] or a not very strong [Republican or Democrat]? [IF INDEPENDENT, NO PREFERENCE, OR OTHER PARTY] Do you think of yourself as closer to the Republican party or to the Democratic party?

Answers to this question have allowed researchers to classify people into seven different categories of party identification—strong Democrats, weak Democrats, independent Democrats, independents, independent Republicans, weak Republicans, and strong Republicans—plus, for a handful of people, apolitical or third party groupings.[3]

This measure of the party in the electorate is based upon the psychological identifications of American adults with a party. One can easily imagine other working definitions of partisans. For example, the party in the electorate might be defined as the party's regular voters, regardless of whether they declare any loyalty to the party *per se*. This approach typically has been rejected by analysts of partisanship, however, because it is too much affected by candidate appeal. The loyalties of the party in the electorate are thought to transcend candidate-based deviations; in the American electoral setting with its many elections and strong norm of voting for "the person, rather than the party," someone can remain a committed partisan even while defecting to vote for the opposition party's candidate. An alternative measurement of party affiliation may be sought in the official act of registering with a party. The utility of this approach is com-

---

[2]The different wordings have predictable consequences. Questions that orient people toward expressing their party identification as of "today" yield answers that are more influenced by current voting preferences than is the case when the question is prefaced by "generally speaking" or "regardless of how you have voted." Stephen Borelli, Brad Lockerbie, and Richard G. Niemi, "Why the Democratic-Republican Partisanship Gap Varies from Poll to Poll," *Public Opinion Quarterly* 51 (1987): 115–19.

[3]The concept of party identification and the Michigan measure were first introduced in Angus Campbell, Philip E. Converse, Warren E. Miller, and Donald E. Stokes, *The American Voter* (New York: Wiley, 1960), Chap. 6.

promised, though, by the absence of party registration in almost half of the states (and many of the most populous ones), the instrumental value of registering with the majority party in one-party areas, and the tendency for some voters to retain their original registration long after their party identification has changed.[4]

In addition to the frailties of alternatives, there are good reasons for preferring the concept of party identification. Strong party identifiers do tend to be the party's faithful voters, but they are more than straight-ticket voters. They have a degree of loyalty and emotional attachment to the party that substitutes in some measure for the formal act of membership in a party system in which membership is not common. They are also more apt to be active workers in the party. In short, the party identifiers bring fairly predictable votes to the party, but they also bring it loyalty, activity, and even public support.

Despite their expressions of party loyalty, the members of the parties in the electorate are fickle, and they sometimes waver in their support of the party of their choice. The party organizations and candidates know that even their electoral support cannot be taken for granted; other appeals and loyalties may occasionally override even the staunchest party loyalties. Also, some loyalists—probably a minority—express a loyalty that is little more than an empty formula. They may be Democrats or Republicans in the same sense that many individuals call themselves members of a religious denomination even though they have not stepped inside the church for years. For all of this, however, the members of the party electorates do vote for the candidates of "their" party and do support its public positions with a faithfulness far beyond that of the rest of the electorate. They tend, in other words, to be the party regulars and straight-ticket voters. They are the men and women who, in the argot of Madison Avenue, display the greatest partisan "product loyalty."

For all its uncertainties, the party in the electorate does provide the party organization and candidates with a stable, hard core of electoral support. Its reliability releases the organization and its standard-bearers from the intolerable burden of convincing and mobilizing a full majority of the electorate in every campaign. The party in the electorate also performs additional services for the party. It largely determines who the party's nominees for office will be. It is a reservoir of potential activists for the organization. Its members may also make financial contributions to the party, or they may work in a specific campaign. Those people who attend party rallies, who talk about politics and persuade friends, or who express any form of political enthusiasm in the community very probably come from its ranks. Its members are most active in perpetuating the party by socializing their children into loyalty to the party and possibly activity in it. In sum, party identifiers give the party an image and a presence in the community, and the most involved among them constitute

[4]For an examination of alternatives in identifying party adherents, see Everett C. Ladd and Charles D. Hadley, "Party Definition and Party Differentiation," *Public Opinion Quarterly* 37 (1973): 21–34.

something of an auxiliary semiorganization that supports the work of the loyal party organization.

The party in the electorate is an alarmingly diverse group, largely because the simple gesture of loyalty that defines it—an attitude measured by a word or two in response to a stranger asking questions—means so many different things to different people. Understandably, the boundaries of the party electorate are indistinct. Individuals also move freely in and out of it, either to or from the more active circles of the party organization or the less committed circles of the electorate at large.

A party in the electorate is more, however, than a categorical group or even a quasi organization. It is also an aggregate of cognitive images *within* large numbers of individual voters, a loyalty or identification ordinarily so strong that it structures the individual's cognitive map of politics. In this sense, it is the party *in* the elector. It acts as a reference symbol, a political cue-giver, and a perceptual screen through which the individual sees and evaluates candidates and issues. For voters and citizens, the political party of their cognitions may be far more real and tangible than any overt political activity or any observable political organization, because they react to what they believe and perceive.

Since the American parties are still cadre parties without important membership contingents, the party in the electorate gives the party its mass popular character. It is to the party in the electorate that people generally refer when they speak of Democrats and Republicans. It is certainly to the party in the electorate that the casual observer refers when he says, for example, that the Democratic party is the party of the disadvantaged or that the Republican party is the party of business. Many of the differences in the programs and the public images of the major parties spring from differences in the segments of the American electorate that they are successful in enlisting. In fact, the interplay between the appeals of the party (i.e., its candidates, issues, and traditions) and its loyal electoral clienteles—each one shaping and reinforcing the other—comes very close to determining what the parties are.

All of this is not to suggest that the rest of the American electorate is of less concern to the American party. Rarely can a national party or its candidates find within its party electorate the majorities needed for election to office. Even though the voters outside the loyal party electorates have lighter commitments to party and issues, competition for their support is keen. The two American parties cannot, as can some of the parties of the parliamentary democracies, fall back on a safely committed and heavily ideological 15 or 25 percent of the electorate. They must mobilize majorities partly from a vast pool of fluid, heterogeneous, often disinterested voters beyond the parties in the electorate.

The individuals of the American electorate, therefore, range along a continuum from heavy, almost blind commitment to a political party to total lack of commitment, not only to a political party but to *any* political cause or object. The competitive American parties do not ignore or take for granted any segment of that total electorate. The three chapters in Part III examine the electorate's variety and importance. Chapter 6 deals with the amorphous parties in the electorate, asking who the Democrats are and who the Republicans are. It is concerned, as suggested earlier, with the party electorate as a categorical group. Chapter 7 takes up the party *within* the elector—the party as a set of cognitive images. It deals with the impact of party identification on the political behavior of the individual. Chapter 8 focuses on the differences, large in American elections, between the total eligible electorate and the active electorate. This difference affects the role that party loyalists play in any election and defines the challenges the parties face in mobilizing their faithful and recruiting new supporters.

Chapter
6

The Loyal Electorates

Who are the Democrats? Who are the Republicans? In a political culture which disparages political parties, there is a tendency for some people to view them solely as the candidates and officeholders who carry the party label or as the party organizations—that is, as entities distant from ordinary citizens. But for millions of Americans, the people and groups who loyally support the party and profess identification with it define the political parties as much as do the candidates and the organizations.

In the vernacular, then, the political parties are seen as residing in the electorate. Much of the written history of American parties and politics has reinforced that impression. It has recorded the successes of the parties, not in terms of party organization, strategy, or activity—or even of who holds particular offices—but in terms of the enduring blocs or coalitions of voters that support them. Thus, the parties have been defined at various times as parties of the East or West, the North or South, the city or country, the rich or poor, the white or black, the "Sun Belt" or "Rust Belt."

PARTY REALIGNMENTS AND THE
AMERICAN PARTY SYSTEMS

Throughout the life of the American party system, the coalitions of voters that define the parties in the electorate seem to have been rearranged every generation or so. If we had survey data with which to measure party identifications since about 1800, we could expect to find long periods of stability in the membership of each party coalition punctuated by brief periods of change or what is called "realignment."[1] Unfortunately, survey data were not available until the

---

[1]The most common definition of a realignment, and the one adopted here, involves changes in the party coalitions or their parties in the electorate. See V. O. Key, Jr., "A Theory of Critical Elections," *Journal of Politics* 17 (1955): 3–18; Walter Dean Burnham, *Critical Elections and the Main-*
(continued)

late 1930s. Prior to this time, the composition of the parties in the electorate must be estimated from aggregated voting returns. The changes in both levels and geographical distributions of party support at regular intervals followed by long periods of relative stability that these voting returns show provide the major justification for dividing American electoral politics into a series of electoral eras.[2]

From these patterns of voting stability and change and more recent survey data on partisanship, scholars have concluded that the United States has experienced at least five different periods of partisan politics or, as many call them, party systems.[3] Each party system began with a realignment of the parties in the electorate (or, in the case of the first party system, an initial alignment), followed by a long period of relative stability in voter coalitions. Each party system is distinguished by a unique coalitional structure, even when the parties remain the same and, as circumstances would have it, by a different overall balance of partisan forces. Each party system is also distinctive in its success in controlling the national government and in the substantive directions of government and public policy.[4]

The First Party System

The first party system (1801–28)[5] originated in the conflict between opposing groups within the Washington administration and was ushered in by the hotly

---

springs of American Politics (New York: Norton, 1970); and James L. Sundquist, Dynamics of the Party System (Washington, D.C.: The Brookings Institution, 1973). For an alternative view, see Jerome M. Clubb, William H. Flanigan, and Nancy H. Zingale, Partisan Realignment: Voters, Parties, and Government in American History (Beverly Hills, Calif.: Sage, 1980). They emphasize the importance of control of the national government in defining the realignment and the new party system it created. Each of the party systems we have designated began with over a decade of unbroken unified control of the national government by the new majority party.

[2]Because aggregate election returns (typically reported on county or state units) reflect differential turnout, candidate appeal, and the particular issues of the day as well as party loyalties and portray geographical divisions of the electorate more clearly than coalitions built upon class and other lines, these data do not always sharply define realignment periods and the ensuing party systems and must be interpreted in conjunction with other political patterns.

[3]Attaching the label of party systems to these periods may cause some confusion, because the term "party system" also was used in Chapter 2 to refer to the number of parties—e.g., two-party, multiparty systems. Here it refers to the coalitional structure of the parties in what has almost always been a two-party system nationwide.

[4]For similar periodizations of American political history from the realignment perspective, see Burnham, Critical Elections; William Nisbet Chambers and Walter Dean Burnham (eds.), The American Party Systems (New York: Oxford University Press, 1967); Clubb, Flanigan, and Zingale, Partisan Realignment; Charles Sellers, "The Equilibrium Cycle in Two-Party Politics," Public Opinion Quarterly 30 (1965): 16–38; and Sundquist, Dynamics of the Party System.

[5]The exact beginning and end of a party system can not be reduced to a single year. The realignments that transform one party system into another take place over a period of time rather than occur sharply. For convenience, though, we must locate the beginning of each party system at a

Table 6.1   YEARS OF PARTISAN CONTROL OF CONGRESS AND THE PRESIDENCY: 1801–1968

	House		Senate		President	
	D-R	Opp.	D-R	Opp.	D-R	Opp.
First party system						
(1801–28)	26	2	26	2	28	0
	Dem.	Opp.	Dem.	Opp.	Dem.	Opp.
Second party system						
(1829–60)	24	8	28	4	24	8
	Dem.	Rep.	Dem.	Rep.	Dem.	Rep.
Third party system						
(1861–76)	2	14	0	16	0	16
(1877–96)	14	6	4	16	8	12
Fourth party system						
(1897–1932)	10	26	6	30	8	28
Fifth party system						
(1933–68)	32	4	32	4	28	8

Note: Entries for the first party system are Democratic-Republicans and their opposition, first the Federalists and then the Jacksonians; for the second party system, Democrats and their opposition, first the Whigs and then the Republicans; for subsequent party systems, Democrats and Republicans.

contested 1800 election in which Thomas Jefferson was elected president. For the first time in American history, one of the factions in the nation's capital, under Jefferson's leadership, had organized support for its presidential candidate in the country at large. The partisan balance of each electoral period is signified by party control of the presidency and Congress. Beginning in 1801 the party of Jefferson or the Democratic-Republicans as they came to be called enjoyed over two decades of virtually unchallenged hegemony over American national politics.

The Second Party System

The second party system (1829–60) emerged from the inability of the one-party system that prevailed after the Federalists' demise to contain the issues and conflicts of a rapidly changing nation. The Democratic-Republicans split into an anti-administration populist western faction under Andrew Jackson, which later grew into the Democratic party, and a more elitist and eastern faction represented by John Quincy Adams, which eventually was absorbed by the Whig party. With the controversy over the 1824 presidential election, in which Jackson received the most popular votes in a four-candidate contest but lacked an

---

particular time. We have chosen the year in which the new majority party coalition first *took office* (having been elected at the end of the previous year) to begin the series of years of undisputed control of government that began each of the first five party systems.

electoral college majority and was denied the presidency in the House of Representatives, development of a new party system to reflect the growth and democratization of the nation seemed inevitable. Its first signs appeared in Jackson's election to the presidency four years later—the first time popular voting played the key role in determining the winner. As this party system matured, the nation experienced its first prolonged two-party competition, which the Democrats dominated as the majority party. Their hegemony over the national government was disrupted only twice, both times by the election of Whig war heroes to the presidency. The second party system was a class-based electoral alignment, with the more privileged supporting the Whigs and the less privileged identifying as Democrats.

The Third Party System

The rapid ascendency of the abolitionist Republican party from its birth in 1854 to major party status by 1856, replacing the Whigs in the process, brought about the end of the second party system. The intense conflict of the Civil War ensured that the new third party system (1861–96) would have the most sharply defined coalitional structure of any party system before or since. War and Reconstruction divided the nation roughly along the Mason-Dixon line—the South becoming a Democratic bastion after the return of white southerners to the polls in the 1870s, the North remaining a reliable base for Republicanism. So sharp was the sectional cleavage that northern Democratic strength was restricted to the cities controlled by Democratic machines (e.g., New York City's Tammany Hall) and areas settled by southerners (such as Kentucky, Missouri, and the southern portions of Ohio, Indiana, and Illinois). In the South, only blacks (who were largely disenfranchised as the century drew to a close) and mountain areas originally opposed to secession supported the GOP. By 1876, when southern whites finally were reintegrated into national politics, the Civil War party system had become highly competitive in presidential voting and in the House of Representatives as a product of offsetting sectional monopolies.[6]

The Fourth Party System

While the imprint of the Civil War has shaped southern politics into modern times, the Civil War system moved rapidly toward obsolescence elsewhere. Under the weight of agrarian protest and the economic panic of 1893, the third party system dissolved. Out of its ashes arose a fourth party system (1897–1932) that basically pitted the eastern economic "center" against the western and

---

[6]From the end of the Civil War in 1865 through 1876, Democratic voting strength in the South was held in check by the occupation Union army and various Reconstruction policies and laws. Thus, in presenting party control figures that reflect the true party balance during the third party system, it is necessary to differentiate between 1861–76 and the more representative 1877–96 period.

southern "periphery" and with the South even more Democratic than before, in part reflecting antithetical agrarian and industrial economies and ways of life. With William McKinley's defeat of populist William Jennings Bryan in 1896, the Republican party achieved a hegemony over American national politics, broken only by the intraparty split of 1912 that produced eight years of Democratic rule, that lasted into the 1920s.

Just as earlier party systems began to weaken several decades after their establishment, the fourth party system showed signs of deterioration in the 1920s in the midst of unparalleled Republican successes. The Progressive party made inroads into major party strength early in the decade; and in 1928 the Democratic candidate Al Smith, the first Catholic ever nominated for the presidency, mobilized Catholic voters into Democratic ranks in the North and drove Protestant southerners temporarily into Republican voting.

The Fifth Party System

But it took the Great Depression of 1929 and the subsequent election of Franklin Delano Roosevelt to produce the fifth or New Deal party system. As is evident in the pattern of voting results by 1936 and present-day vestiges of partisan feelings from that time, the new Democratic majority party was a grand coalition of the less privileged minorities—industrial workers (especially union members), poor farmers, Catholics, Jews, blacks—plus the South where the Democratic hegemony established in the aftermath of the Civil War continued to prevail. This New Deal party system has shaped the parties to this day.[7]

Lacking the clarity of hindsight, it is difficult to identify the partisan directions of contemporary politics—even with the abundance of survey evidence on partisan loyalties of the electorate. What can be said for sure is that the coalitional basis of the New Deal party system has eroded in recent decades. Since the mid-1960s, more Americans than before failed to join the electorate of either party—answering "independent" or "no preference" in response to the familiar question eliciting partisan loyalties. The American electorate was clearly less partisan by 1990 than it had been twenty-five years before. After 1964, partisanship declined to its lowest level ever recorded among young adults, who unlike older adults are more likely even now to be nonpartisans than either Democrats or Republicans. These changes first became apparent in 1968, although the seeds for them may have been sown in the 1950s and obscured by the landslide Democratic victory in 1964. They mark an important turning point in the American party system.

---

[7]Comprehensive treatments of the different party systems may be found in Paul Goodman, "The First Party System," in Chambers and Burnham, *The American Party Systems*, pp. 59–89; Richard McCormick, *The Second American Party System: Party Formation in the Jacksonian Era* (Chapel Hill: University of North Carolina Press, 1966); and, for the party systems since the 1850s, Sundquist, *Dynamics of the Party System.*

Dealignment or a New Realignment?

Scholars observing this pervasive decline in the size of the partisan portion of the electorate have used the term "dealignment" to emphasize the contrast to realignment. Some scholars see dealignment (and its corollary characteristics of third party voting and ticket splitting) as a recurrent sign of aging in each American party system, including the most recent one. In their view, dealignment is the final stage of a party system, signaling the obsolescence of the electoral conflicts that established it and paving the way for new party coalitions to emerge. Leading the way in dealignment are the newest members of the electorate. Because they lack the experiences that galvanized the partisanship of the older generations as the party coalitions were being established, they increasingly find the major parties irrelevant to their present needs.[8]

What will follow the dealignment? In each previous party system, the dissolution of the old alignment was finalized by realignment and the emergence of a new party system. Yet, such a change is surely not inevitable. The forces that lead to dealignment (i.e., a withdrawal from party loyalty) are not the same ones that produce realignment (i.e., the development of new party loyalties). Indeed Walter Dean Burnham has argued that the American party system, weakened by the loss of party control over nominations and the insulation of many state and local elections from national forces by scheduling them in off-years, may no longer be capable of realignment.[9] The unparalleled duration of the dealignment that began in the 1960s lends credence to Burnham's view.

The Democratic dominance of the fifth party system and its recent decline are well portrayed in the measurements of the party loyalties of the American electorate taken before each presidential election since 1952 by researchers at the University of Michigan[10] (see Table 6.2). Throughout the entire 1952–64 period, more Americans identified themselves as Democrats than as either Republicans or Independents. This Democratic partisan advantage was perpetuated with an amazing regularity from one presidential election to another. Not even a popular president of the minority party, General Dwight D. Eisenhower, could jar it. The Democratic edge eroded considerably after 1964,

---

[8]See Paul Allen Beck, "The Electoral Cycle and Patterns of American Politics," *British Journal of Political Science* 9 (1979): 129–56. This view of recent nonpartisanship as largely a result of neutrality toward the parties rather than negative rejection of them is developed in Martin P. Wattenberg, *The Decline of American Political Parties, 1952–84* (Cambridge: Harvard University Press, 1986.)

[9]Burnham, *Critical Elections*, Chaps. 4 and 5.

[10]The seminal work on partisanship is based on data from the first two elections in this series. See Angus Campbell, Philip E. Converse, Warren E. Miller, and Donald E. Stokes, *The American Voter* (New York: Wiley, 1960). For a recent report of results from these studies, see Warren E. Miller and Santa A. Traugott, *American National Election Studies Data Sourcebook, 1952–1986* (Cambridge: Harvard University Press, 1989). These figures will be reported throughout this volume as coming from the Center for Political Studies at the University of Michigan, although the Center is only the contemporary name of their source institution.

Table 6.2 MICHIGAN MEASUREMENTS OF PARTY IDENTIFICATION: 1952–88

	1952	1956	1960	1964	1968	1972	1976	1980	1984	1988
Strong Democrats	22%	21%	20%	27%	20%	15%	15%	18%	17%	17%
Weak Democrats	25	23	25	25	25	26	25	23	20	18
Independents closer to Democrats	10	6	6	9	10	11	12	11	11	12
Independents	6	9	10	8	10	13	14	13	11	11
Independents closer to Republicans	7	8	7	6	9	10	10	10	12	13
Weak Republicans	14	14	14	13	14	13	14	14	15	14
Strong Republicans	13	15	15	11	10	10	9	8	12	14
Others	4	4	3	2	2	2	1	3	2	2
	101%	100%	100%	101%	100%	100%	100%	100%	100%	101%
Cases	1793	1762	1928	1571	1556	2707	2864	1614	2236	2040

Note: Based on surveys of the national electorate conducted immediately before each presidential election. Due to rounding, the percentages do not always add up to exactly 100%.

Source: Center for Political Studies, University of Michigan; data made available through the Inter-University Consortium for Political and Social Research.

though, but not to the immediate advantage of the Republicans. Even Richard Nixon's landslide victory in the 1972 presidential contest failed to add party loyalists to GOP ranks. In fact, the Republican party in the electorate did not regain its 1950s levels until the 1980s.

The most recent readings in the series, taken in the 1980s, show the greatest increase in Republican identifiers since 1952; albeit it is a modest 5–6 percent. Perhaps there is to be a new realignment that follows the dealignment? Whereas Eisenhower and Nixon, for all their vote-getting success, did not strengthen the Republican coalition, Ronald Reagan seems to have been able to translate his popularity into growth for his party. The Democrats show a corresponding decline. While it is perilous to infer realignment from such modest changes in partisan standings, these figures raise the possibility that the 1980s may have signaled the long-heralded realignment of the fifth party system—a possibility that receives more careful consideration at the close of this chapter.[11]

Just as important as the question of *how many* Democrats and Republican identifiers there are now or were at earlier times in the New Deal party system, however, are the questions of who they are and why they identify that way. What is the composition of the Democratic or Republican party coalition—its party in the electorate? From what educational backgrounds, what regions, what occupations, what religions, what social groups do they come? On what bases of interest do the parties attract supporters? Why do Americans align themselves with one party rather than the other? Each of America's party systems has had a distinctive coalitional structure as the cleavage lines through the electorate have changed in response to transformations in the dominant issue concerns of the period. To understand contemporary electoral politics and assess the possibilities for realignment, we need to know what these coalitions have been and what they may be becoming, which inevitably leads us to consider how and why people adopt particular party identifications.

THE ACQUISITION OF PARTY LOYALTIES

It is a commonplace among Americans to say that they are Democrats or Republicans because they were brought up that way, just as one was raised as a Methodist, Catholic, or Christian Scientist. The processes of political socialization begin early in life as the child begins to become aware of political parties and absorb judgments about them. He or she soon realizes that one of the parties is the family's party, that it is "good," that it is "our" party.

---

[11]This description of the changes in partisanship since 1952 is justified regardless of whether partisans are defined as strong identifiers, strong plus weak identifiers, or all respondents who indicate some kind of preference for one of the parties.

Childhood Influences

Even though they do not often consciously indoctrinate their children into loyalty to a political party, parents are the primary agents of political socialization in the American culture. Their casual conversations, their references to political events, and the example of their political activity are sufficient to convey their party loyalties to their children. So stable are the results that the intergenerational similarities in party loyalty persist when the children reach adulthood, even during a period when young adults are strongly pulled toward independence (Table 6.3). Furthermore, parents with consistent, reinforcing party loyalties are more likely to produce strong party identifiers among their children. Those without party loyalties or with mixed loyalties produce offspring who are more likely to be independents.[12]

The acquisition of party loyalties normally comes early in childhood. More than 60 percent of the fourth-grade children in a New Haven, Connecticut, study were able to state a party preference. Few of the children, however, supported their identification with much information about party leaders, issues, or traditions. Not until they were eighth-graders did they develop the supportive knowledge that permits party identification to become fully operative in the political world. At that age they began, for example, to associate the parties with general economic interests or groups—with business or labor, with the rich or the poor. The sequence of this learning is critical: First comes party loyalty and afterwards, at least partially filtered through it, is added the content of politics.[13]

Individuals' party loyalties are also supported by a homogeneous environment of family, friends, and secondary groups. Friends, associates, relatives, and spouses typically have the same partisan loyalties that they do. Some offspring, to be sure, do leave the parties of their parents. Those whose initial identification is weak are more likely to change, and when the parents themselves identify with different parties or when their identification is not congruent with their social class—that is, when political signals are mixed—their children are more apt to develop an identification with the other party.[14]

In part, the stability of these party loyalties results from the relative absence in the American political system of other agencies of political socialization that might challenge the early influences of the family. Schools often avoid political studies in the early grades, and if anything probably are more inclined to

---

[12]Paul Allen Beck and M. Kent Jennings, "Family Traditions, Political Periods, and the Development of Partisan Orientations," *Journal of Politics* 53 (1991).

[13]Fred I. Greenstein, *Children and Politics* (New Haven: Yale University Press, 1965). See also Robert D. Hess and Judith V. Torney, *The Development of Political Attitudes in Children* (Chicago: Aldine, 1967), especially pp. 80–81.

[14]Arthur S. Goldberg, "Social Determinism and Rationality As Bases of Party Identification," *American Political Science Review* 63 (1969): 5–25.

Table 6.3   INTERGENERATIONAL SIMILARITIES IN PARTY IDENTIFICATION: 1982

Party of Child as Young Adult	Party of Parent		
	Democrat	Independent	Republican
Democrat	51%	27%	10%
Independent	39	51	46
Republican	10	22	44
	100%	100%	100%
Cases	295	192	211

Note: Democrats and Republicans include strong and weak identifiers. Independents include all respondents answering independent or no preference to the initial party identification question, regardless of whether they later located themselves closer to one of the parties. The young adults had all been high school seniors in 1965 and were aged 34–35 in 1982 when this information was collected.

Source: Three Wave Parent-Child Socialization Study. Provided by its principal investigator, M. Kent Jennings.

inculcate political independence than partisanship. American churches generally have steered clear of partisan commitments in the twentieth century—contrary to the willingness of many European churches, for example, to support the various Christian Democratic parties of Europe—although this nonpartisan stance was deserted by some churches in the 1980s. The American parties themselves engage in very little direct socialization; they do not maintain the youth groups, the flourishing university branches (which may have offices, lounges, and eating facilities), the social or recreational activities, or the occupational organizations that their European counterparts do.

Adult Influences

Carrying a party identification from childhood to adulthood, however, is a complicated process. Initially, the individual acquires it in a process of early socialization dominated by parents. Subsequently, the individual maintains or changes the identification in an increasingly complex set of adult experiences. At this point in the life cycle, adults have tested their party loyalties against political reality. They have evaluated the performance of their favored parties and party leaders, and they also have watched the performance of the "other party." Events and experience may reinforce those loyalties, but they may also undermine them. Thus,

> . . . there is an inertial element in voting behavior that cannot be ignored, but that inertial element has an experiential basis; it is *not* something learned at mommy's knee and never questioned thereafter.[15]

---

[15]Morris P. Fiorina, *Retrospective Voting in American National Elections* (New Haven: Yale University Press, 1981), p. 102. For an analysis of the role contemporary issues may play in disrupting

Beyond the processes of acquiring and maintaining the party identification, there apparently is also a process of strengthening or intensifying existing party attachments for some adults. Party loyalties are most strongly held by older adults, and they are the least likely to change them. That strengthening across the life cycle may reflect an ongoing process of reinforcement in decades of political observation or activity; it may also reflect the usefulness of a party loyalty as a cue that will simplify choice and cut the cost of political decision for older voters.[16]

No period threatens the inherited partisan loyalties of large numbers of voters more than a realignment, when the issue bases of partisanship and with them the party coalitions themselves are altered. Unless the realignment is wholly produced by the mobilization of heretofore nonpartisan groups into partisan politics, at least some voters must desert the partisan tradition of their parents. Evidence from the New Deal realignment of the 1930s as well as from partisan changes in recent years suggests that this desertion may be considerable. Young adults seem to be highly susceptible to the pressures of the period. Childhood socialization alone proves to be a fragile foundation for adult partisanship and often cracks under the intense challenges of adult socialization, especially in response to the powerful forces of electoral realignment. Older adults may be caught up in the momentum of the moment, but their partisanship, typically reinforced by years of consistent partisan behavior, is much more resistant to intense counterpressures (see box). Thus, it is typically young adults who act as the "carriers" of realignment and, consequently, to whom we should look for early signs of partisan change.[17]

The processes of political socialization do not, however, explain the allocations of party loyalties in the United States. They describe *how* an individual may acquire his or her party loyalty but not *why* that loyalty goes to a particular

---

the transmission of partisanship from parents to children, see Robert C. Luskin, John P. McIver, and Edward G. Carmines, "Issues and the Transmission of Partisanship," *American Journal of Political Science* 33 (1989): 440–58. More generally see Beck and Jennings, "Family Traditions . . . "

[16]See William Claggett, "Partisan Acquisition vs. Partisan Intensity: Life-Cycle, Generational, and Period Effects," *American Journal of Political Science* 25 (1981): 193–214. On how much partisanship strengthens as the voter ages, see Philip E. Converse, *The Dynamics of Party Support* (Beverly Hills, Calif.: Sage, 1976); Paul R. Abramson, "Developing Party Identification: A Further Examination of Life-Cycle, Generational, and Period Effects," *American Journal of Political Science* 23 (1979): 78–96; and W. Phillips Shively, "The Development of Party Identification among Adults," *American Political Science Review* 73 (1979): 1039–54.

[17]For the view that realignments are attributable to mobilization of the young and other new voters in realignment, see Andersen, *The Creation of a Democratic Majority 1928–1936* (Chicago: University of Chicago Press, 1979), and Paul Allen Beck, "A Socialization Theory of Partisan Realignment," in Richard G. Niemi (ed.), *The Politics of Future Citizens* (San Francisco: Jossey-Bass, 1974), pp. 199–219. For an alternative view, emphasizing partisan conversions among older voters, see Robert S. Erikson and Kent L. Tedin, "The 1928–1936 Partisan Realignment: The Case for the Conversion Hypothesis," *American Political Science Review* 75 (1981): 951–63. The role of the young in contemporary partisan change is discussed in Helmut Norpoth and Jerrold G. Rusk, "Partisan Dealignment in the American Electorate: Itemizing the Deductions Since 1964," *American Political Science Review* 76 (1982): 522–37.

The Past in the Present

Political events experienced long before, during one's formative years, often powerfully influence contemporary political views. Substituting Franklin Roosevelt or John Kennedy for Grover Cleveland might make the illustration more realistic today—although less humorous.

"Grover Cleveland is dead, sir. Who's your *second* choice for Democratic nominee?"

Source: © 1986; Reprinted courtesy of Hoest and Parade Magazine.

party. For an accounting of why a party attracts some people but repels others, and why each party assumes a distinctive shape, we must turn in another direction—to the role of social groups and issues.

THE SOCIAL BASES OF PARTY IDENTIFICATION

There is a long and hallowed tradition of viewing the political parties as representatives of the various social groups contained in a society. Sectional or regional animosities, ethnic and religious divisions, conflicts between agriculture and industry, and differences in social class and status are common ingredients in the politics of the western democracies. While the United States may have been spared the intensity of some of these conflicts because of its newness and its isolation from the old world, many of them have been important here as well.[18]

Social Status and Class

The search for an explanation of these party loyalties probably should begin with social class. Most of the party systems of the democratic world in modern times contain cleavages along class lines. What is meant by social class, or its common synonym, socioeconomic status? Much of the literature uses the terms almost interchangeably, but the preference here is for the latter term and its conventional abbreviation, SES. Socioeconomic status is simply the relative amount of economic and/or social deference the individual can command based on his or her social and economic characteristics. In the modern industrialized world, it is best measured objectively by a combination of income, education, and occupation. Also individuals identify with different social classes, and this too can be employed to assess their *subjective* socioeconomic status. Regardless of the rubric one chooses, status differences underlie the party electorates of the mature, industrial democracies with which one can most reasonably compare the United States.[19]

The signs and marks of SES conflict are scattered throughout American history, even in the preindustrial decades. James Madison, one of the most knowing observers of human nature among the Founding Fathers, wrote in *The Federalist* that economic differences are the most common source of factions.[20]

---

[18]For a comprehensive treatment of these various cleavages, see Seymour Martin Lipset and Stein Rokkan, "Cleavage Structures, Party Systems, and Voting Alignments," in Seymour Martin Lipset and Stein Rokkan (eds.), *Party Systems and Voter Alignments* (New York: Free Press, 1967), pp. 1–67.

[19]The classic statement of the role of social class in the elections of the western democracies appears in Seymour Martin Lipset, *Political Man* (New York: Doubleday, 1960), especially Chap. 7.

[20]See Madison's *Federalist* 10: "The most common and durable source of factions has been the various and unequal distribution of property."

The early political conflicts in the American polity often lay along sectional lines, but section sometimes denoted status differences as well. Social and economic status differences underlay the battle between the wealthy, aristocratic Federalists and the less privileged Democratic-Republicans and became even sharper between the Jacksonian Democrats and the Whigs a few decades later. In the 1890s, SES conflicts surfaced again in the presidential contest between Republican William McKinley and William Jennings Bryan, who made the Democratic party the vehicle for protests by discontented and disadvantaged farmers. Despite his defeat in the general election of 1896, the Democrats twice (1900 and 1908) returned to him as their presidential candidate for the crusade against corporate wealth, eastern banking interests, and what Bryan liked to call the "plutocracy."

The SES stamp on the parties became more pronounced in the 1930s. Franklin Roosevelt rebuilt the Democratic party more firmly than ever as a party of social and economic reform. His New Deal programs—labor legislation, social security, wage and hours laws—strengthened the Democratic party's image as the party of the relative have-nots. Even groups such as the blacks, long allied with the Republicans as the party of Lincoln, were lured to the Democratic banner; the strength of SES issues even kept them as allies of southern whites in the Roosevelt coalition. In brief, Franklin Roosevelt buttressed the class divisions of industrialism by adding to its conflicts the consequent response of government: the Welfare State. Its programs and expenditures heightened the stakes of socioeconomic status politics.

The relationship between party and SES established in the New Deal party system underlies the partisan preferences of different social groups as recently as the 1988 presidential election (Table 6.4 and Figure 6.1). It is apparent in the data on occupation and income, and the relationship lurks even where it is not obvious. The partisan differences in educational levels, for example, probably have SES roots. There seems little reason to suspect that the intellectually liberating experiences of formal education lead young men and women overwhelmingly to Republicanism. It seems more reasonable to suppose that the higher levels of Republicanism among the better educated result from the meaning of education in SES terms (i.e., a higher percentage of upper SES parents send their sons and daughters to college, and the college degree leads to higher SES). Also, given the somewhat higher SES of Protestants in the United States, their relationship with Republicanism reflects, in part, status differences; and there certainly is no need to elaborate the enormous SES differences between whites and blacks. Furthermore, to the extent that Americans see themselves in different social classes, those differences relate strongly to their party loyalties. Those who see themselves as middle class tend to be Republicans, and Democrats are much more apt to come from those who perceive themselves as working class.

Yet the lines of SES difference between the American parties, even during the heyday of the New Deal party system, have been less distinct than the parties' rhetoric and campaigns might lead one to expect. Socioeconomic status has been less important as a basis for party loyalty in the United States than in most

Table 6.4 SOCIAL CHARACTERISTICS AND PARTY IDENTIFICATION: 1988

	Democrats		Independents			Republicans		Party Difference	Cases
	Strong	Weak	Closer to Demo.	Closer to Neither	Closer to Repub.	Weak	Strong		
Education									
No hi. sch.	26%	19	10	13	11	12	9	24	418
Hi. sch. grad	16%	20	13	13	14	13	11	12	700
College	15%	16	12	8	15	16	19	-4	845
Income									
Lower third	21%	21	14	12	9	14	10	18	584
Middle third	20%	16	11	11	14	14	14	8	650
Upper third	11%	18	12	9	17	15	19	-5	596
Occupation									
Service	21%	19	13	14	13	11	9	20	175
Blue collar	14%	21	12	17	15	11	10	14	334
White collar	16%	16	14	10	15	15	14	3	394
Professional	14%	13	12	9	16	17	19	-9	377
Farm	14%	19	0	11	19	19	19	-5	37
Religion									
Jews	26%	10	19	19	13	10	3	23	31
Catholics	21%	17	13	10	13	14	12	12	483
Protestants	17%	19	11	10	14	15	16	5	1294
Race									
Blacks	40%	24	19	6	5	5	2	57	260
Whites	14%	17	11	12	15	15	16	0	1668
Region									
South	21%	23	14	10	12	10	12	20	629
Non-south	16%	17	11	11	14	16	15	2	1370
Gender									
Female	20%	20	11	10	11	14	13	13	1143
Male	15%	15	13	11	17	14	15	1	856
Subjective Class									
Working	22%	21	13	13	13	11	8	24	1012
Middle	14%	16	11	8	15	17	20	-7	896

Note: Totals add to approximately 100 percent reading across (with slight variations due to rounding). Party difference is calculated by subtracting the percentage of strong and weak Republicans from the percentage of strong and weak Democrats. Negative numbers indicate a Republican advantage in the group.

Source: Center for Political Studies, University of Michigan; data made available by the Inter-University Consortium for Political and Social Research.

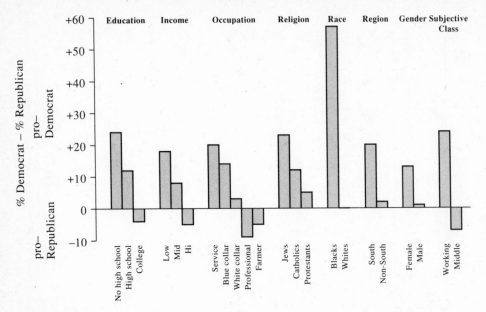

Figure 6.1 Democratic Party Edge among Social Groups.

Note: Entries are party difference scores from Table 6.4.

other western democracies.[21] The electorates of both American parties contain a significant number of people from all status groups. Consequently, the parties find it difficult to formulate overt class appeals or to enunciate ideologies that reflect sharp class differences. The heterogeneity of their loyalists is perfectly consistent with the parties' pragmatic, relatively nonideological tone and with their mission as brokers among diverse social groupings. Thus, the lines of SES division between the major American parties are indistinct and overlapping, and although SES is one explanation of interparty differences, it is by no means the only one.

Sectionalism

Historically, the greatest rival to SES as an explanation for American party differences has been sectionalism. Varying geographic areas or sections of the country sometimes have had separate and deeply felt political interests, which

[21]See Robert A. Alford, *Party and Society* (Chicago: Rand McNally, 1963); and Russell J. Dalton, Scott C. Flanagan, and Paul Allen Beck (eds.), *Electoral Change in Advanced Industrial Democracies* (Princeton, N.J.: Princeton University Press, 1984). For an appraisal of class voting in the western world for the past century from the perspective of working class support for a left-wing party, see Adam Przeworski and John Sprague, *Paper Stones: A History of Electoral Socialism* (Chicago: University of Chicago Press, 1986).

when honored and favored by a political party, united large numbers of otherwise different voters.

The most enduring sectionalism in American party history has been the one-party Democratic control of the South. Even before the Civil War, the interests of the South in slavery and in an agriculture geared to export markets had unified it. The searing experience of that war and the reconstruction that followed made the South into the "Solid South" and delivered it to the Democrats. United by historical experience and by a desperate defense of a way of life against threats from the national government, the eleven states of the Confederacy cast their electoral votes for Democratic presidential candidates in every election from 1880 through 1924, except for Tennessee's defection in 1920. Al Smith's Catholicism frightened four of these states into the Republican column in 1928, but the Roosevelt economic programs reinforced the region's economic interests—and in no way greatly challenged its way of life—and brought the South back to the Democratic party for the four Roosevelt elections. Only with the successes of the Dixiecrat ticket in 1948 and the start of the civil rights movement did the South begin to move away from its traditional party loyalties. Yet, as we saw in Chapter 2, vestiges of this sectional unity have survived into modern times at the state and local level and in partisanship (Table 6.4 and Figure 6.1),[22] if not in presidential voting.

Similarly, strong East-West differences have periodically marked American party conflict, reflecting the competition between the economically dominant East and the economically dependent South and West. In the first years of the Republic, the fading Federalists held to an ever-narrowing base of eastern seaport and financial interests, while the Democratic-Republicans expanded westward with the new settlers. Jackson, too, pointed his party appeals to the men of the frontier, and the protest movements that thrust William Jennings Bryan into the 1896 campaign sprang from the agrarian discontent of the western prairies and the South. Many of the Populists' loudest complaints were directed at eastern capitalism, eastern bankers, and eastern trusts. Indeed, the geographical distribution of the presidential vote of 1896, with the Democrats winning all but three states in the South and West but losing all northern and border states east of the Mississippi River, is striking affirmation of sectional voting.

The pull of sectionalism has declined steadily within the past several generations. The isolation and homogeneity of life in the sections have yielded to a nationalization of life and interests in the nation. Sectional loyalties have not completely disappeared, of course. Southern sectionalism awakened in a new guise in 1964 as five states of the Deep South supported Barry Goldwater, the

---

[22]So powerful have these southern ties to the Democratic party been that some voters, termed "split-level partisans," have retained their Democratic loyalties in state and local politics even after rejecting them for the purpose of national politics. For more on this phenomenon, see Charles D. Hadley, "Dual Partisan Identification in the South," *Journal of Politics* 47 (1985): 254–68; and Richard G. Niemi, Stephen Wright, and Lynda W. Powell, "Multiple Party Identifiers and the Measurement of Party Identification," *Journal of Politics* 49 (1987): 1093–1104.

Republican presidential candidate. Then, in 1968, George Wallace carried five southern states on the American Independent ticket: Alabama, Arkansas, Georgia, Louisiana, and Mississippi. Even in the South, however, sectionalism now appears to have receded into a secondary position in the development of political party loyalties.

In the 1970s and early 1980s, some observers of American politics thought they saw the emergence of a new sectionalism—that of the Sun Belt. Evidence for it is not strong, however. The Republicans have indeed improved their position in a number of the states of the South, Southwest, and West, but the result of that improvement has generally been to increase rather than diminish two-party competition. Moreover, the regional distribution of party loyalties in 1988 offers no support for the emergence of a distinctive Sun Belt section.

In retrospect, it is difficult to say what force sectionalism had even at its zenith. The great difficulty with the sectional explanations is that the term *section* may simply be an obscuring shorthand for a geographic concentration of other identifiable interests—ethnic, economic, or possibly SES. Much sectional voting in the past, for instance, reflected conflicts among crop economies in the various agricultural sections. Thus, the central question is whether the sections themselves are the basic source of sectional interest or whether they are merely categories or concentrations of voters who identify with a party for other reasons. It means little to say that the Midwest supported Franklin Roosevelt in 1936 or that the West backed Reagan in 1980 and 1984. To be sure, the South has been more than a descriptive category; its political behavior has been sectional in the sense of unified interests and an awareness of the region and its distinctiveness. The case for sectional explanations weakens greatly, however, as soon as one looks beyond the South.

Religion

From the beginnings of the American Republic, there always have been religious differences between the party coalitions—just as there are in many other democracies.[23] During the New Deal party system, Catholics and Jews were among the most loyal supporters of the Democratic party (Table 6.4 and Figure 6.1). Some of the relationship between religion and party loyalty is no doubt attributable to the socioeconomic status differences among religious groupings. Yet it does appear that religious conviction and group identification also are involved. A Jewish internationalism and concern for social justice, rooted in the religious and ethnic traditions of Judaism, has disposed many Jews toward the Democratic party as the party of international concern, support for Israel, and

---

[23]Richard Rose and Derek Urwin have shown that religion rivals social class as a basis for partisan loyalties in the western democracies. See their "Social Cohesion, Political Parties and Strains in Regimes," *Comparative Political Studies* 2 (1967): 7–67.

social and economic justice.[24] The traditional ties of Catholics to the Democratic party have been in great part the result of a greater openness within that party to participation by Catholics and their political advancement. Most of the national chairmen of the Democratic party in this century have been Catholics, and the only Catholic presidential nominees of a major party were Democrats.

The sources of white Protestant ties to the Republicans are less obvious, probably in part because of the enormous diversity of sects and orientations that Protestantism embraces. Very possibly, however, the theological individualism of more conservative Protestantism disposes Protestants to Republicanism. In recent years, however, it has been the political conservatism of Protestant fundamentalists, anchored to such non-individualistic issues as abortion and school prayers, that has stimulated a surge in Protestant fervor for the GOP.[25]

Race

Some decades ago, the Republican party—as the party of Lincoln, the Civil War, and Reconstruction—was associated with racial equality in the minds of both black and white Americans. In the generation between 1930 and 1960, however, the wheels of racial politics turned 180 degrees. It is now the Democratic party, the Kennedy and Johnson administrations, the candidacy of Jesse Jackson, and Democratic Congresses that blacks see as advancing racial equality and integration. Blacks identify with the Democratic party in overwhelming numbers and regardless of any other set of social characteristics (Table 6.4 and Figure 6.1).[26] All indications suggest that Hispanics (although not Cuban Americans) also identify heavily with the Democrats.

Gender

In the last decade or so, the votes and stands of adult women diverged from those of men. Women voted about 6 percent more than men did for Jimmy Carter in 1980, and following the 1980 election, the differences between the sexes grew. Women were considerably less approving of President Reagan, and they differed from men on a number of issues beyond the specifically women's

---

[24]Lawrence Fuchs, *The Political Behavior of the American Jews* (Glencoe, Ill.: Free Press, 1956). For a somewhat more recent treatment, see Milton Himmelfarb, "The Case of Jewish Liberalism," in Seymour Martin Lipset, ed., *Emerging Coalitions in American Politics* (San Francisco: Institute for Contemporary Studies, 1978), pp. 297–305.

[25]Kenneth D. Wald, *Religion and Politics in the United States* (New York: St. Martin's, 1987).

[26]On black political behavior, see Patricia Gurin, Shirley Hatchett, and James S. Jackson, *Hope and Independence: Blacks' Response to Electoral and Party Politics* (New York: Russell Sage Foundation, 1989).

issues. Their position on those issues, moreover, was the Democratic (or anti-Reagan) position: supportive of a nuclear freeze and spending for social programs, and critical of increased defense spending. By the mid-1980s, the gender difference had enveloped partisanship, with women more supportive of the Democratic party than men. This partisan gender gap has persisted through the 1988 election (Table 6.4 and Figure 6.1).[27]

The Changing Partisan Complexion of Social Groups

This picture of the social group basis of the American parties reflects the cleavage structure of the New Deal party system. Even as late as 1988, the partisan ties of the various social groups (with the exception of gender) resemble those established in the 1930s when the New Deal system was first established. But these relationships have become increasingly muted in recent years, as the partisan dealignment expressed through weakened partisanship since the early 1960s has embraced waning group ties to the parties as well.

The declining social group bases of the parties is evident when the 1988 figures are compared with those from 1960 (Figure 6.2).[28] Virtually every social group difference in partisanship in that earlier year had narrowed by 1988. Of the groups differentiated in the New Deal system, only blacks and whites diverged more markedly in their partisanship in 1988 than they had in 1960. While these figures contain faint impressions of the social group basis of the New Deal party system, they depict a party system by 1988 that was weakly differentiated along social group lines in comparison with the system from just a few decades before.[29]

This view of parties as coalitions of distinctive groups in the society and the ease with which the partisan loyalties of such groups can be determined, if one is not careful, can lead to a misleading social deterministic view of party identification. Party coalitions cannot be assembled by any simple process of combining group voting blocks. Nor can groups be delivered in block to a party or a candidate. Rather, the group basis of partisan politics is rooted in the common

---

[27]Although a gender gap in partisanship remained through 1988, as our figures show, the gender gap in presidential voting narrowed. See Paul R. Abramson, John H. Aldrich, and David W. Rohde, *Change and Continuity in the 1988 Elections* (Washington, D.C.: Congressional Quarterly Press, 1990), pp. 123–26.

[28]Data from 1960 are more appropriate for this comparison than data from 1964, when the Democratic landslide victory produced a temporary surge in Democratic partisanship across most of the social groups. The 1960 figures are taken from Miller and Traugott, *American National Election Studies Sourcebook, 1952–1986.*

[29]On social group changes in the party coalitions in recent years, see John R. Petrocik, *Party Coalitions* (Chicago: University of Chicago Press, 1981); Robert Axelrod, "Where the Votes Come From: An Analysis of Electoral Coalitions, 1952–1968," *American Political Science Review* 66 (1972): 11–20, and "Presidential Election Coalitions in 1984," *American Political Science Review* 80 (1986): 281–90; and Harold W. Stanley and Richard G. Niemi, "Partisanship and Group Support, 1952–1988," paper delivered at the 1989 Annual Meeting of the American Political Science Association, Atlanta, Ga.

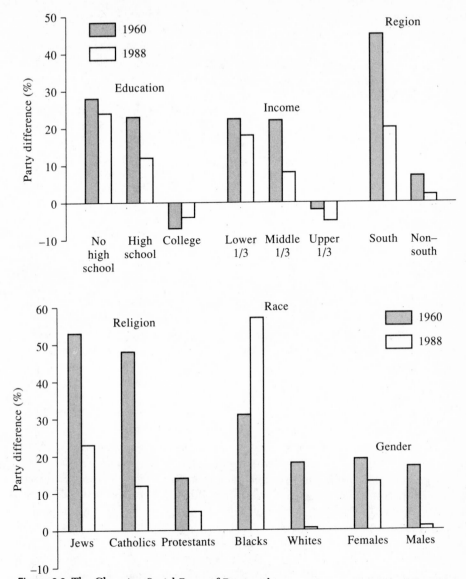

Figure 6.2 The Changing Social Bases of Partisanship.

Source: Center for Political Studies, University of Michigan. Data made available by the Inter-University Consortium for Political and Social Research.

orientations of individuals to the major issues and candidates of the day. These orientations may be shared by members of particular groups, although the pluralism of American society prevents most groups from being very cohesive. It is party differences on political issues and in the representation of aspirations of particular groups, not some sort of unadulterated "group-think," that underlie the partisan distinctiveness of groups in American politics.

Yet there is a strong inertial element to partisan loyalties and therefore to the party coalitions. In ordinary times, the group bases of politics are transmitted, perhaps without much reflection, from parents to children. Moreover, people are slow to reject their inherited party loyalties even when the basis for this loyalty is questioned. Inertia, though, can be overcome. Parties change their postures, especially in realignment periods, and their traditional supporters may forsake them as a result. While party identifications and the coalitional bases of the party system are durable, they are not immutable. In recent years, for example, there is ample evidence that negative party images and votes for opposition candidates have "fed back" upon partisanship and influenced some Americans to change their loyalties. It is these individual decisions, not the lockstep march of groups, that have weakened the New Deal Democratic coalition.[30]

THE ISSUE AND IDEOLOGICAL BASES OF PARTY IDENTIFICATION

These considerations lead us to examine the issue and ideological bases of the different parties in the electorate. The party conflicts that appear among various social groups typically are rooted in differences over what government should do on particular matters and in general what kind of society we should have. Sometimes these attitudinal differences are strongly related to social characteristics, and much political analysis is based on this assumption. But often social characteristics are an imperfect guide to what someone thinks about the issues of the day, especially in modern pluralistic societies. The value of the information on individuals that surveys can supply is that individuals with the same positions on issues and ideology can be identified directly rather than inferred by assuming group homogeneity.

People taking different positions on the major policy issues of the 1988 presidential election campaign also differed in their partisan loyalties (Table 6.5 and Figure 6.3). Party identification seems most closely related to individual stands on the issues of the Welfare State, the ones touching the government's role in spending for services, providing jobs for the unemployed, and helping minority groups. Fundamentally, these issues involve questions of equality and the distribution of wealth. They are SES issues, one might say, because they propose different benefits for people of different economic status.

Clearly, much of the partisan rhetoric and conflict of American politics since the 1930s has run along SES lines—whether it is a debate over jobs, medicaid, how to resolve the budget deficit, or taxes. The American electorate, even

---

[30]For demonstrations of how attitudinal and behavioral deviance from one's partisanship can undermine it, see Fiorina, *Retrospective Voting in American National Elections;* and Benjamin I. Page and Calvin C. Jones, "Reciprocal Effects of Policy Preferences, Party Loyalties and the Vote," *American Political Science Review* 73 (1979): 1071–89.

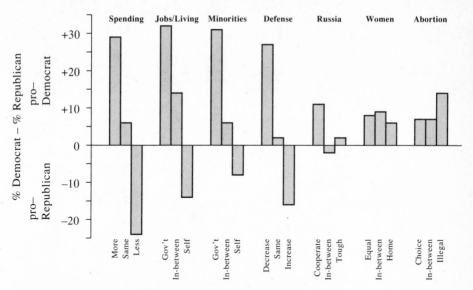

Figure 6.3 Democratic Party Edge among Issue Groups.

Note: Entries are party difference scores from Table 6.5.

in its distribution of partisan loyalties, responds to SES issues. The response comes, however, not as the response of specific social classes or groups, but from individuals who, for one reason or another, have come to hold different attitudes or views about the role of government and its social responsibility for the less advantaged. For many these views have status roots, but others exhibit issue attitudes that are not necessarily congruent with their own socioeconomic status. They may reflect some sympathy for the socioeconomic "underdog," some deference to the socioeconomic "overdog," or some identification with an earlier status of their own. They may even be acting on some personal vision of the good society. Thus, the relationship is not always between socioeconomic characteristics and party identification. It may be between attitudes and party, and socioeconomic status is not always a good guide to attitudes.[31]

The force of issues on party identification is more complex than all of this suggests. For one thing, attitudes on SES-type issues are for many voters absorbed into broader liberal and conservative ideologies. As one might expect, there is a considerable correlation between self-described liberals and Democrats and, conversely, between conservatives and Republicans (Table 6.6). Second, recent elections have seen the rising importance of non-SES issues— issues of American involvement in the world, spending for defense, crime and

---

[31]On this point, see David O. Sears, Richard R. Lau, Tom R. Tyler, and Harris M. Allen, Jr., "Self-Interest vs. Symbolic Politics in Policy Attitudes and Presidential Voting," *American Political Science Review* 74 (1980): 670–84.

Table 6.5 ISSUE POSITIONS AND PARTY IDENTIFICATION: 1988

	Democrats		Independents			Republicans		Party Differences	Cases
	Strong	Weak	Closer to Democrats	Closer to Neither	Closer to Republicans	Weak	Strong		
Government Spending on Services									
More	26%	20	17	10	10	9	8	29	616
Same	15%	19	10	11	18	15	13	6	465
Less	9%	13	9	7	16	20	26	-24	514
Government Role in Providing Jobs and a Good Standard of Living									
Gov't help	31%	18	17	9	8	10	7	32	480
In between	16%	21	13	12	16	14	9	14	361
Help selves	10%	16	10	9	17	18	22	-14	857
Government Role in Improving the Social and Economic Position of Minorities									
Gov't help	26%	21	17	9	10	9	7	31	271
In between	16%	19	15	9	13	18	11	6	211
Help selves	13%	15	8	11	16	16	20	-8	412
Government Spending on Defense									
Decrease	22%	22	18	12	11	10	7	27	578
Same	16%	16	12	10	16	18	12	2	580
Increase	12%	14	8	9	16	17	25	-16	575

Table 6.5 (*continued*)

	Democrats		Independents			Republicans		Party Differences	Cases
	Strong	Weak	Closer to Democrats	Closer to Neither	Closer to Republicans	Weak	Strong		
American Posture toward Russia									
Cooperate more	18%	18	16	10	13	13	12	11	727
In between	17%	15	8	13	15	19	15	-2	416
Get tougher	16%	18	11	8	16	14	18	2	539
Role of Women									
Equal role	17%	18	13	11	14	14	13	8	1289
In between	18%	20	10	10	14	17	12	9	310
Place is in home	23%	16	8	9	12	11	22	6	280
Abortions									
Own choice	17%	17	16	12	12	15	12	7	701
In between	18%	18	10	11	15	14	15	7	1018
Illegal	21%	20	10	9	13	11	16	14	245

Note: Totals add to approximately 100 percent reading across (with slight variations due to rounding). The middle position for the first seven issues is 4 on a 7-point issue scale; for abortions, it includes abortions under conditions of rape, incest, and danger to mother as well as when the need has been clearly established. Party difference is calculated by subtracting the percentage of strong and weak Republicans from the percentage of strong and weak Democrats. Negative numbers indicate a Republican advantage in the group.

Source: Center for Political Studies, University of Michigan; data made available by the Inter-University Consortium for Political and Social Research.

Table 6.6 IDEOLOGICAL SELF-PERCEPTION AND PARTY IDENTIFICATION: 1988

	Democrats		Independents			Republicans		Party Difference	Cases
	Strong	Weak	Closer to Demo.	Closer to Neither	Closer to Repub.	Weak	Strong		
Liberal	27%	23	19	9	8	9	5	36	547
Moderate	14%	22	11	22	15	12	4	20	157
Conservative	12%	15	8	9	17	18	22	-13	1070

Note: Totals add up to 100 percent reading across (with slight variations due to rounding). Party difference is calculated by subtracting the percentage of strong and weak Republicans from the percentage of strong and weak Democrats. Negative numbers indicate a Republican advantage in the group. Individuals who were unable to describe themselves in ideological terms were not included.

Source: Center for Political Studies, University of Michigan; data made available by the Inter-University Consortium for Political and Social Research.

drugs (and thus "law and order"), racial and sexual equality, and moral issues such as abortion. Some of these issues have joined SES issues as sources of party differences. In 1988, for example, defense and foreign policy issues separated Democrats from Republicans more than they had twenty to thirty years before. But other issues, such as abortion or the role of women, cut across party lines, dividing Democrats and Republicans against themselves.[32] They have influenced a good many presidential votes in recent years. Cross-cutting issues such as these, because they do not coincide with existing partisan divisions, moreover, strain the coalitional foundations of a party system and sometimes can even lead to the development of a new party system.

TOWARD A SIXTH PARTY SYSTEM?

The parties in the electorate have changed since the mid-1960s. As we have seen, the Democratic share of the electorate is considerably smaller than before, even if the GOP has not realized comparable gains by capitalizing upon the Democrats' losses (Table 6.2). Among the most recent generations of young adults, the inheritance of partisanship from parents, both Democratic and Republican, seems not nearly as strong as it once was. It is also clear that the social group foundations of the New Deal party system have eroded. Although it is difficult to demonstrate because of alterations in the meaning and measurement of issues over time, it appears that even the traditional issue bases of partisanship have been transformed. Socioeconomic status issues continue to differentiate the party coalitions, but they now must share center stage with powerful social, racial, and international concerns.

That the parties in the electorate have changed significantly since the 1960s there can be no doubt. Just what that change means is more difficult to determine. One interpretation emphasizes the continuing dealignment nature of the change and how it has undermined the foundations of the New Deal party system without building a new party system in its place. A perhaps more common alternative view is that recent changes signify the emergence of a new party system led by an ascendant Republican party. The politics of the 1970s and 1980s lend some credence to each alternative, so scholars remain divided over whether we have witnessed dealignment or realignment in recent years.[33]

---

[32]For a discussion of the cross-cutting nature of some of these new issues, see Warren E. Miller and Teresa E. Levitin, *Leadership and Change: The New Politics and the American Electorate* (Cambridge, Mass.: Winthrop, 1976).

[33]Recent examples of the alternative interpretations of the partisan politics of the post-1964 period may be found in Paul Allen Beck, "Incomplete Realignment: The Reagan Legacy for Parties and Elections," in Charles O. Jones (ed.), *The Reagan Legacy* (Chatham, N.J.: Chatham House, 1988); Walter Dean Burnham, "The Reagan Heritage," in Gerald M. Pomper (ed.), *The Election of 1988* (Chatham, N.J.: Chatham House, 1988); Edward G. Carmines and James A. Stimson, *Issue Evolution* (Princeton, N.J.: Princeton University Press, 1989); Helmut Norpoth and Michael R. Kagay,

(*continued*)

The dealignment scenario emphasizes the erosion of the New Deal party system but the failure of the Republican party to capitalize upon the troubles of that system's majority Democratic party. Despite the decline in Democratic loyalists in the last thirty years, the GOP has been unable to increase its partisan share of the electorate beyond levels achieved before 1964. At the state and local level, a sizable majority of public officials still come from the Democratic party. The clearest evidence of dealignment, though, appears in party representation at the national level. Despite what has been thought to be a Republican "lock" on the presidency, the Democrats' control of the U.S. House of Representatives has remained unbroken for almost forty years and they regained their majority in the Senate after a 1980–86 Republican interlude.

The realignment alternative dwells upon the successes of Republican presidential candidates, the growth of the GOP in the once one-party Democratic South, and the recent upturn in Republican loyalists, especially among the young. Only Jimmy Carter was able to break a Republican string of presidential victories that extends all the way back to 1968—and he just barely did it in the aftermath of the Watergate scandal.[34] Republican growth in the South has been just short of phenomenal—beginning with a beachhead at the presidential level in the 1950s, the party now has become competitive with the Democrats in state-wide gubernatorial and senatorial races.

In the end, though, it is changes in partisan loyalties—the relative sizes of the parties in the electorate—that provide the most suggestive evidence for realignment. No support for realignment could be found in the partisan totals of the 1970s, as both parties lost support (see Table 6.2). The 1980s, however, tell quite a different story. Beginning with Ronald Reagan's upset of Carter and GOP capture of the Senate in 1980, and continuing through the 1984 and 1988 elections into the early 1990s, albeit with temporary reversals in between, the Republican party in the electorate grew while the Democratic share of the electorate continued its decline. The regular readings on partisanship posted by *The New York Times*/CBS News Poll (see Figure 6.4) provide a detailed picture of these changes.[35] Just as significant for a realignment interpre-

---

(*continued*)
"Another Eight Years of Republican Rule and Still No Partisan Realignment?" Paper presented at the 1989 Annual Meeting of the American Political Science Association, Atlanta, Ga.; and Martin P. Wattenberg, *The Decline of American Political Parties*.

[34] The Watergate affair began in 1972 with the arrest of burglars with ties to the Nixon reelection campaign for breaking into the offices of the Democratic National Committee and culminated with the resignation of President Nixon in the face of sure impeachment by the House of Representatives for trying to cover up his role. The unpopularity of the subsequent pardon of Nixon by his former vice-president and successor Gerald Ford played a key role in the 1976 presidential campaign and may have cost Ford the presidency.

[35] The distribution of partisanship is sensitive to political events in the short term, as Dee Allsop and Herbert Weisberg have shown in "Measuring Change in Party Identification in an Election Campaign," *American Journal of Political Science* 32 (1988): 996–1017. Over the long term, however, clear trends are apparent.

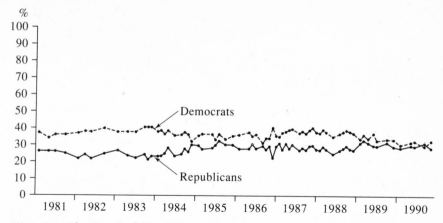

Figure 6.4 *The New York Times*/CBS News Measurements of Party Identification, 1981–1990.

Note: Democrats and Republicans include strong and weak identifiers.

Source: The New York Times/CBS News Poll.

tation is the GOP surge among young voters, who in the 1980s became more Republican than Democratic for the first time in the fifty-year annals of public opinion polling.[36]

The American party system entered the 1990s, then, almost equally balanced among Democratic and Republican loyalists and independents nationwide. (In the immediate aftermath of the Gulf War in 1991, GOP strength surged yet again.) Whether attributable to dealignment (especially of the Democratic New Deal coalition) or a realignment that has not (yet?) established the

Table 6.7   YEARS OF PARTISAN CONTROL OF CONGRESS AND THE PRESIDENCY, 1933–1992

	House		Senate		President	
	Dem.	Rep.	Dem.	Rep.	Dem.	Rep.
Fifth party system						
(1933–68)	32	4	32	4	28	8
Sixth party system?						
(1969–80)	12	0	12	0	4	8
(1981–92)	12	0	6	6	0	12
(1969–92)	24	0	18	6	4	20

[36]On the party loyalties of the young, see Helmut Norpoth, "Under Way and Here to Stay: Party Realignment in the 1980s?" *Public Opinion Quarterly* 51 (1987): 376–91; and Norpoth and Kagay, "Another Eight Years of Republican Rule and Still No Partisan Realignment?"

GOP as the majority party, or some combination of both, contemporary partisan politics has diverged markedly from the patterns of the New Deal party system.

The post-1968 era has been a time of divided control of the national government—to an extent and for a duration unprecedented in American history (Table 6.7). Even the GOP gains of the 1980s have failed to undermine Democratic control of the House of Representatives. With divided control has come a governmental fragmentation conducive to deadlock in policy-making (see Chapter 16), such as those that have characterized the federal budget process into the 1990s. Is this type of government to be the hallmark of the 1990s? Only time, and the outcome of a continuing struggle to build and sustain the parties in the electorate, will tell.

Chapter
7

The Party Within the Voter

The hyperactive world of American politics is difficult to understand, at best. The contest of parties and candidates, the overlapping layers of party organization, the hyperbole of political charge and countercharge may baffle even highly politicized and active party workers. The confusion is inevitably greater among the less experienced and involved members of the party electorate. Their best guide to this trackless political world is their party identification.

For many individuals, therefore, the political party exists in two forms. Obviously, they can see the party of the real world—the party of conventions, candidates, campaigns, and organizations; but they also come to depend on a cognitive party—the party of attitudes, goals, and loyalties, the party within the voter. This party is an organizing point of view, a screen or framework through which individuals see political reality and in terms of which they organize it in their own minds. We all perceive the world about us selectively, and for the committed partisan—the member of the party electorate—party loyalty is the key to this selectivity. Because the party identification will very likely be the individual's most enduring political attachment, it serves as something of a political gyroscope, stabilizing political outlooks against the buffetings of short-term influences.

For all the attention focused on the declines in partisanship since the 1960s, it is easy to lose sight of the fact that these parties in the electorate continue to dominate the electoral landscape. Committed partisans may not be as large a share of the American electorate as they were in the 1950s, but almost a third of the electorate identify themselves as strong Democrats or Republicans, and a roughly equal number profess weak party identifications. Among the remaining independents, a clear majority confess to some partisan leanings. However partisanship is measured (see box), the unmistakable result is that most Americans depend upon party as an important guide to politics. Knowing this one fact about people tells us more about their political perceptions and behavior than any other single piece of information.

The Party Identification Controversies

As we have seen, the Michigan measure of party identification categorizes people into one of seven categories of identification (ranging from strong Democrat through independent to strong Republican)—plus apoliticals, don't knows, and identifiers with minor or third parties who are so few that they may be ignored. Even though widely used by scholars who study elections, this measure has engendered two sorts of controversies.

First, the richness of seven categories makes it difficult to know just where to draw the line between partisans and independents. How this controversy is resolved is consequential; for one thing, it determines our estimate of the number of Democrats and/or Republicans in the electorate. In most of our analysis, therefore, we have presented the full seven categories, allowing readers to draw their own line between partisan and independent.

Second, this dilemma is compounded by a paradox. The party identification index treats weak Democrats and Republicans as more partisan than independents who lean toward a party. Yet the independent leaners often exhibit more partisan behavior than the weak partisans in reality, especially in casting a greater proportion of their votes for their party's candidates in certain elections. This seemingly illogical behavior has led some scholars to conclude that the party identification measure is capturing more than a single attitude toward the parties. One argument is that the illogical partisan behavior of independent leaners is the result of an attempt by researchers to force onto a single continuum running from strong Democrat to strong Republican three different and only partially related orientations to politics—Democratic identifications, Republican identifications, and independence. In particular, independence is not always the opposite of partisanship, as some voters seem attracted both to a party and to an independent posture.

Controversies over the measurement of key concepts in the social sciences, as well as the sciences more generally, are not uncommon. While this controversy over party identification may grip the research community, it is fought out over a relatively narrow ground and is designed to refine, not dismiss, the notion of party loyalties. Moreover, our judgment (reinforced by evidence on the stability of partisanship discussed in footnote 3) is that the traditional measure of party identification emerges from the debate as still a sound indicator of party loyalty.[1]

---

[1]See John R. Petrocik, "An Analysis of the Intransitivities in the Index of Party Identification," *Political Methodology* 1 (1974): 31–47; Ralph W. Bastedo and Milton Lodge, "The Meaning of Party Labels," *Political Behavior* 2 (1980): 287–308; and Herbert F. Weisberg, "A Multidimensional Conceptualization of Party Identification," *Political Behavior* 2 (1980): 33–60.

THE STABILITY OF PARTY IDENTIFICATIONS

For a large number of Americans, partisanship is a stable anchor in an ever-changing political world. By the standards of political attitudes, party identifications do indeed exhibit a remarkable consistency over time. We have seen it suggested already in the durability of the partisan shares of the electorate over an almost forty-year period. Even more impressive is how strongly individuals cling to the same party loyalties over time in the face of powerful challenges. Most Americans, once they have developed such loyalties, retain them without change from election to election. When partisanship does change, moreover, the changes almost always are registered in intensity of partisan feeling (e.g., from strong to weak) rather than in conversions from one party to the other.

It is not often that the opportunity arises to gauge the consistency of party identifications across a fairly lengthy time period. One such opportunity was provided in the early 1970s by the repeated interviewing of the same individuals in three successive University of Michigan surveys—conducted in 1972, 1974, and 1976. Almost two-thirds of the respondents remained in the same broad category of party identification (44 percent were stable Democrats or Republicans, 20 percent stable independents) across all three time points. A third changed from one of the parties to independence. Only three percent actually changed parties.[2]

These results also can be represented in a single number, an index of the degree of which similar positions were taken at two time points called the *coefficient of correlation*. In the language of correlations, where maximum consistency attains a value of 1.00, partisanship is shown to be more stable than evaluations of prominent political figures or policy issues (Figure 7.1). No better testimony could be provided to the stability of partisanship than its consistency during the turbulent period in which the Watergate episode turned a landslide victory for Richard Nixon in 1972 into his ignominious resignation from office two years later and the defeat of the incumbent Republican president in 1976.[3]

---

[2]Paul Allen Beck, "The Dealignment Era in America," in Russell Dalton, Scott Flanagan, and Paul Allen Beck (eds.), *Electoral Change in Advanced Industrial Democracies* (Princeton, N.J.: Princeton University Press, 1964), pp. 244–46.

[3]Philip E. Converse and Gregory B. Markus, *"Plus ca change . . .* : The New CPS Election Study Panel," *American Political Science Review* 73 (1979): 32–49. Even greater stability in partisanship, as expected because of the shorter time period, was found from January to November during the 1980 presidential campaign. See Donald Philip Green and Bradley Palmquist, "Of Artifacts and Partisan Instability," *American Journal of Political Science* 34 (1990): 872–902.

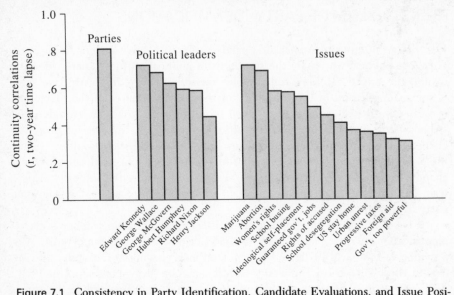

Figure 7.1 Consistency in Party Identification, Candidate Evaluations, and Issue Positions, 1972–1974–1976.

Note: Entries are the average correlations, across a two-year interval. Complete continuity = 1.0; no continuity = 0.0; complete reversal = −1.0.

Source: Converse and Markus, "Plus ca change . . . ," p. 46

THE COGNITIVE SCREENING FUNCTIONS OF PARTY IDENTIFICATIONS

Their early development (discussed in Chapter 6) and their stability from election to election combine to allow partisan loyalties to serve as a filter through which the voter views the political world. Even though voters may form a partisan loyalty in the first place because of a particular issue or candidate, for the most part it is images of the issues and the candidates that are accommodated to the anchor of party. In many instances, of course, these images reflect the realities of the party coalitions. Candidates are drawn to the parties because of what they stand for, and the parties stand for certain things because of what their coalitions have been. Beyond this, though, voters *project* favorable personal characteristics and acceptable issue positions onto the candidates of their party and are *persuaded* to support particular candidates or issues because they are associated with their party.[4]

---

[4]On the political impact of the psychological process of projection and persuasion, see Bernard R. Berelson, Paul F. Lazarsfeld, and William N. McPhee, *Voting* (Chicago: University of Chicago Press, 1954), pp. 215–33; and Benjamin I. Page and Richard A. Brody, "Policy Voting and the Electoral Process: The Vietnam War Issue," *American Political Science Review* 66 (1972): 979–95.

Perceptual Projection

Party identification provides a perceptual predisposition for candidate evaluations. For most members of the parties in the electorate, the knowledge that a candidate for office is a Democrat or a Republican alone induces a positive or negative evaluation. "The stronger the voter's party bias, the more likely he is to see the candidate of his own party as hero, the candidate of the other party as villain."[5] Every once in awhile, for example, a popular entertainment figure or a general like Norman Schwarzkopf becomes the subject of discussion as a possible candidate for office. Evaluations of that person quickly diverge along partisan lines once the name is associated with a party.

There is no better guide than the voters' partisanship to how they view the candidates. Even in the face of strong counter pressures, partisanship proves influential. In the 1960 presidential election, for example, competing perceptual predispositions were at work. Catholics tended to perceive John F. Kennedy more favorably than did Protestants. Nonetheless, party identification kept its organizing power. Among those with similar religious loyalties, party identification still had its effect on the perception of Kennedy. Among those with the same party identification, the religious loyalty had *its* effect. When one says, therefore, that a candidate is attractive or compelling, one says something about the electorate as well as about the candidate. In politics, too, beauty is in the eyes of the beholder.

The control that party identification exercises in the perception of candidates may be somewhat selective, however. Partisan projection appears to extend to the candidate's political traits but not to such purely personal matters as his personality, appearance, or social characteristics (e.g., his religion).[6] The partisan view of candidates is selective in another sense: It is not without limits. Candidates for president who have gone down to defeats of landslide proportions—e.g., Goldwater in 1964, McGovern in 1972, Mondale in 1984—have suffered from low evaluations among their fellow partisans. Yet even here partisanship remains important: however low the candidate's standing may have sunk, he could count on more sympathy from members of his party than from other voters.

The impact of party identification on political issues is not as easy to determine as its impact on the perception of candidates. The candidate is a tangible person, but an issue is an abstraction, with far more subtle components and often a degree of longevity that makes it difficult to discern whether issues or party came first. We have already seen in Chapter 6 that identifiers of the two parties take divergent positions on issues. To a significant degree, of course, these patterns reflect the natural affinity of people to a party that champions

---

[5]Donald E. Stokes, "Some Dynamic Elements of Contests for the Presidency," *American Political Science Review* 60 (1966): 23.

[6]Roberta A. Sigel, "Effects of Partisanship on the Perception of Political Candidates," *Public Opinion Quarterly* 28 (1964): 483–96.

their causes. But they also reflect a tendency for partisans to adopt their party's positions on issues, especially when they involve complicated and remote policy concerns.[7] To a not insignificant degree, then, the electorate's policy positions do follow the partisan flag.

Feedback on Party

The metaphor of party identification as a perceptual screen, however, does not apply to all partisans or at all times. It assumes that a one-way relationship exists between the individual and political reality, that the individual's party loyalty colors his or her perception of that reality. Recent studies have shown, however, that perceptions of candidates and issues can influence party identifications, too. In particular, the evidence is powerful that retrospective evaluations of performance, especially negative assessments of an incumbent president's management of the economy, can feed back on party loyalties and cause them to be weakened or changed.[8] Thus, we confront a complex two-way process, in which loyalty to party affects one's evaluations and yet those evaluations shape the way one views the parties. Even if one concedes that party identification is usually stable and basic enough to withstand a number of conflicting short-term observations and evaluations, it is clear that the inertial force of party loyalty as a perceptual screen can be overcome. An accumulation of perceptions hostile to it can overwhelm its barriers and register on the individual. Under adverse conditions, then, party loyalty within the voter cannot turn unfavorable observations of reality into reinforcements of that very loyalty.

There is good reason to believe that the force of party loyalties as cognitive instruments, as shapers of political reality, has diminished in recent years. With the decline in partisanship that characterized American politics after the mid-1960s, of course, the share of the electorate lacking the partisan lenses through which political reality is colored has increased. Among partisans, moreover, there has been a moderation in the strength of loyalties, which has the effect of reducing the distorting power of the partisan lenses for those who use them. These trends have been paralleled by a diminution of partisan cognitions in recent years *among even the strongest of partisans*. Party remains an important source of political orientations, but it is not as important as it once was.[9]

---

[7]When President Bush pursued a conciliatory policy toward the Communist government of the People's Republic of China in the wake of the Tiananmen Square massacre, for example, many of his fellow partisans concurred while many Democrats opposed. This produced a reversal in the relationship between party and preferred treatment of China: previously hard-line Republicans were now "soft" on China, while Democrats had moved in the reverse direction.

[8]See Morris P. Fiorina, *Retrospective Voting in American National Elections* (New Haven, Conn.: Yale University Press, 1981); and Benjamin I. Page and Calvin C. Jones, "Reciprocal Effects of Policy Preferences, Party Loyalties and the Vote," *American Political Science Review* 73 (1979): 1071–89.

[9]Arthur H. Miller, "Partisan Cognitions in Transition," in Richard R. Lau and David O. Sears (eds.), *Political Cognitions* (Hillsdale, N.J.: Lawrence Erlbaum, 1986), pp. 203–231.

PARTY IDENTIFICATION AND VOTING

The primary significance of the parties in the electorate lies in their patterns of voting. Partisans provide the core support for the candidates of their party. The nature of the American electoral setting—its long ballots and frequent elections, its traditional emphasis on person over party, and even the ambivalence of its partisans about strong parties—discourages absolute party regularity. Nevertheless, partisans support their party with considerable fidelity, which strengthens as the intensity of partisan loyalty grows.

Partisan Loyalty

That certainly has been the case during the entire 1952–1988 period of the Michigan surveys. A majority of partisans have voted for their party's candidate for president in every year except for weak Democrats in 1972 and independent Democrats in 1980 (both GOP landslide years), and strong partisans always have been more faithful than weak or independent partisans (Table 7.1). Even in the Reagan landslide victory of 1984, almost nine out of ten strong Democrats voted for Walter Mondale. Strong Republicans, though, have compiled the more enviable record of party fidelity: only in the Democratic landslide of 1964 did their support for the GOP standard bearer dip as low as 90 percent (see box).

These patterns extend, without exception, to voting for Congress (Table 7.2). A majority within each group of partisans have voted for their party's congressional candidates in each election, with the strong partisans exhibiting the greatest regularity. One key to the Democrats' ability to win congressional majorities in every year since 1954, moreover, may be found in their greater fidelity than their GOP counterparts to their party's congressional candidates.

Similar results appear in voting at the state and local level (Table 7.3). Straight-ticket voting at that level occurs mostly among the partisans. Strong Democrats and strong Republicans have also been more inclined than weaker partisans to vote for only members of their party. For these contests, in fact, rates of party regularity steadily increase with strength of partisanship. The higher level of party voting among independent partisans than among weak partisans, which appeared as a curious anomaly in presidential and congressional voting, is absent at the state and local level.[10]

---

[10]The unexpectedly greater partisan voting of the independent identifiers compared to the weak partisans, and similar "intransitivities" in the relationship between partisanship and political involvement shown in Tables 7.4 and 7.5, are commonly cited as evidence of the weakness of the party identification measure. This anomaly may appear because independents asked to indicate which party is closer will name the one for which they intend to vote that year. A truer indication of their partisan strength, instead, is found in their straight-ticket voting patterns. For a persuasive case that the independent leaners are really partisans, see Bruce E. Keith, David B. Magleby, Candice J. Nelson, Elizabeth Orr, Mark Westlye, and Raymond E. Wolfinger, "The Partisan Affinities of Independent 'Leaners'," *British Journal of Political Science* 16 (1986): 155–84.

The Faithful Republicans

Republicans typically support the candidates of their party more than Democrats do. Popular impressions of their fidelity are nicely captured in this *New Yorker* cartoon.

"Tell me, sir, is there any such thing as just a plain Republican, or are they all staunch?"

Source: Drawing by Stan Hunt; © 1984 *The New Yorker* Magazine, Inc.

Voting patterns such as these are the product of the push of an enduring partisan loyalty and the pull of the candidates and issues particular to each year. Typically this push and pull are reinforcing; they incline the voter in the same direction. On the occasions when they conflict, however, the short-term force of candidates and issues may lead the partisan to defect from his or her party.

Defections

Like reeds in a pond that bend as the wind blows, though, the likelihood that voters will temporarily desert their ordinary partisan location depends upon the strength and direction of that election's "wind" and where their partisan

Table 7.1 VOTING FOR THEIR PARTY'S PRESIDENTIAL CANDIDATES AMONG PARTY IDENTIFIERS: 1952–88

	1952	1956	1960	1964	1968	1972	1976	1980	1984	1988
Strong Democrats	84%	85	90	95	85	73	91	86	87	93
Weak Democrats	62	62	72	82	58	48	74	60	67	70
Independents closer to Democrats	60	68	88	90	52	60	72	45	79	88
Independents	—	—	—	—	—	—	—	—	—	—
Independents closer to Republicans	93	94	87	75	82	86	83	76	92	84
Weak Republicans	94	93	87	56	82	90	77	86	93	83
Strong Republicans	98	100	98	90	96	97	96	92	96	98

Note: The table entries are the percentages of each category of partisans who reported a vote for their party's candidate for president. To find the percentage voting for the opposing party's candidate or some other candidate, subtract the entry from 100 percent. Individuals who did not vote for president are excluded from the table.

Source: Center for Political Studies, University of Michigan; data made available by the Inter-University Consortium for Political and Social Research.

Table 7.2 VOTING FOR THEIR PARTY'S CONGRESSIONAL CANDIDATES AMONG PARTY IDENTIFIERS: 1952-88

	1952	1956	1960	1964	1968	1972	1976	1980	1984	1988
Strong Democrats	89%	94	93	94	88	91	89	85	89	88
Weak Democrats	77	86	86	84	73	80	78	69	70	82
Independents closer to Democrats	64	83	84	79	63	80	76	70	78	87
Independents	—	—	—	—	—	—	—	—	—	—
Independents closer to Republicans	81	83	74	72	81	73	65	68	61	64
Weak Republicans	90	88	84	64	78	75	66	74	66	70
Strong Republicans	95	95	90	92	91	85	83	77	85	77

Note: The table entries are the percentages of each category of partisans who reported a vote for their party's candidate for Congress. To find the percentage voting for the opposing party's candidate or some other candidate, subtract the entry from 100 percent. Individuals who did not vote or did not vote for Congress are excluded from the table.

Source: Center for Political Studies, University of Michigan; data made available by the Inter-University Consortium for Political and Social Research.

Table 7.3 STRAIGHT-TICKET VOTING AMONG PARTY IDENTIFIERS:1952–84

	1952	1956	1960	1964	1968	1972	1976	1980	1984
Strong Democrats	86%	84	87	80	72	66	—	62	69
Weak Democrats	69	72	74	53	43	38	—	39	46
Independents closer to Democrats	56	58	56	37	32	28	—	23	38
Independents	56	43	65	53	24	28	—	21	25
Independents closer to Republicans	65	56	51	33	43	30	—	28	33
Weak Republicans	72	69	68	44	49	40	—	35	41
Strong Republicans	85	83	79	71	74	60	—	61	59

Note: The table entries are the percentages of each category of partisans who reported voting a straight-ticket in state and local elections. To find the percentage splitting their tickets, subtract the entry from 100 percent. Individuals who did not vote or did not vote in state and local elections are excluded from the table. The question was not asked in 1976 and in 1988.

Source: Center for Political Studies, University of Michigan; data made available by the Inter-University Consortium for Political and Social Research.

roots are anchored. In a year during which short-term forces are running in a Republican direction, for example, many Democrats will defect to vote for GOP candidates, but the strong identifiers will remain most steadfast. Of course, the longer these short-term forces continue in the same direction, the greater is the chance that defection may turn into conversion as voters change their partisanship to bring it into line with their vote—just as, to extend the metaphor, reeds may be uprooted by continuously strong winds to be transplanted in a different part of the pond.[11]

These notions underlie the main typology of American Presidential elections which specifies three election types:

1. The *maintaining* election, in which the party attachments of the recent past prevail without any great change or divergence. In these elections, the party with the largest party in the electorate wins.
2. The *deviating* election, in which the basic distribution of party loyalties is not changed, but in which short-term candidate or issue forces cause the defeat of the majority party.
3. The *realigning* election, in which a new coalition of party loyalists emerges and governs the outcome. These elections typically produce a new majority party.

Since 1952 deviating elections have easily outnumbered maintaining elections; in four of them, in fact, the minority party candidate won by the landslide proportions of more than 15 percent of the popular vote. Only in 1960, 1964, and 1976 did the majority Democratic party win the presidency in a maintaining election. In the other years, Republicans were victorious, and they earned their victories by inducing considerable defection among Democrats.

No other period of American history can match the past forty years in terms of the success of the minority party at the presidential level. Whether this era represents a new brand of American politics without strong party alignments (or without party playing much of a role in presidential politics), the prolonged unraveling of the New Deal party system, or the advent of realignment, of course, is the subject of considerable debate. However this debate is resolved, it is unmistakable that in recent American politics party identifications have not played the role in elections traditionally ascribed to them.

One reason for the diminished role of partisanship in voting, of course, is that since the mid-1960s there simply have been fewer partisans—especially fewer strong partisans. But this is not the whole story. Partisan fidelity in voting has also declined within both parties. Republican presidential and congressional voting by Republican partisans has not yet returned to the levels it achieved in the 1950s, even in the 1984 Reagan landslide (Tables 7.1 and 7.2).

---

[11]Philip E. Converse, "The Concept of a Normal Vote," in Angus Campbell, Philip E. Converse, Warren E. Miller, and Donald E. Stokes (eds.), *Elections and the Political Order* (New York: Wiley, 1966), pp. 9–39.

Nor has the level of party voting among Republican loyalists often approached that of 1960, which was not a notable Republican year. Partisan voting among Democrats peaked a decade later, in the 1960 and 1964 elections, and has not attained those levels since.[12]

Party Versus Candidates and Issues

Scholars of voting behavior find it useful to break the influence on the voting decision into party, candidate, and issue components and then to determine the relative influence of each on the vote. Analyses along these lines focused on elections through the 1970s provided evidence that the relative influence of party identifications on the vote indeed had declined, as we know it must have given the decreasing numbers of partisans and their waning party fidelity.[13]

Because the three factors are so strongly interrelated themselves, however, it is difficult to separate their effects.[14] Conclusions about relative importance often depend upon how well each of the factors is measured and what one is willing to assume about the causal priority of one over the other. The classic accounts of the dominant role of party identification in the 1950s assumed that party was causally prior to candidates and issues, influencing them but not in turn influenced by them.[15] Also the early measures of issue positions were not adequate for determining how close the voter felt to the candidates on the issues. With new measures of issue closeness and an allowance for reciprocal influences of issue, candidate, and party orientations upon one another, the role of party identifications was found to be dwarfed by that of short-run issue and candidate evaluations in the 1970s.[16]

This is not to say that party was no longer important. Rather, it had come to be dominated by short-run, election-specific forces—as it quite possibly was in the 1950s as well (which would explain the Eisenhower victories). When a

[12]Split-ticket voting, defined as supporting candidates from different parties on the same ballot, also has been higher since the mid-1960s than it was in the 1950s for both president-House and Senate-House combinations. See Martin P. Wattenberg, *The Decline of American Political Parties: 1952–1988* (Cambridge, Mass.: Harvard University Press, 1990), Chap. 9.

[13]See Norman H. Nie, Sidney Verba, and John R. Petrocik, *The Changing American Voter* (Cambridge: Harvard University Press, 1976), Chaps. 10, 16, and 20 (especially pp. 373–78); Mark A. Schulman and Gerald M. Pomper, "Variability in Electoral Behavior: Longitudinal Perspectives from Causal Modeling," *American Journal of Political Science* 19 (1975): 1–18; and Frederick Hartwig, William R. Jenkins, and Earl M. Temchin, "Variability in Electoral Behavior: The 1960, 1968, and 1976 Elections," *American Journal of Political Science* 24 (1980): 353–58.

[14]The problem is of course that party identifications color views of candidates and issues, but candidates and issues also can influence party identifications.

[15]See Angus Campbell, Philip E. Converse, Warren E. Miller, and Donald E. Stokes, *The American Voter* (New York: Wiley, 1960); and Arthur S. Goldberg, "Discerning a Causal Pattern among Data on Voting Behavior," *American Political Science Review* 60 (1966): 913–22.

[16]Page and Jones, "Reciprocal Effects of Policy Preferences, Party Loyalties and the Vote."

longer-term perspective is adopted by looking at changing orientations across a four-year period among the same voters, however, party identification keeps coming back as a background force of continuing importance in structuring the immediate context of the electoral decision.[17] If it is the general trends of American electoral politics that we want to explain, then, party identification still must play a prominent role.

An Upsurge in Party Fidelity

It is of course always perilous to assume that the most recent event signals some kind of turning point in political trends. With the benefit of hindsight, what at the same time seemed to be major breaks with the past often turned out to be only temporary departures from normality. Nonetheless, there are indications that the last presidential election of the 1980s was different from its predecessors where the behavior of the political party in the electorate is concerned. Obscured in the sizable loss by the Democratic standard bearer, Michael Dukakis, was the return of Democratic identifiers to their party in both presidential and congressional voting. Not since 1964 has party fidelity among Democrats been so high. Not surprisingly, party fidelity in presidential voting (but not congressional voting) was even greater among Republicans, surpassing levels achieved in all elections since 1964 except the GOP landslide victories in 1972 and 1984.

Such enhanced levels of party voting by partisans is what one would expect to find in the early stages of realignment, as the parties in the electorate have re-formed around contemporary causes. Does the 1988 election then mark the end of a dealigning era and the beginning of the long-expected realignment? Perhaps—only time will tell. The stubborn fact that Republican party voting in the 1988 congressional elections continued to tumble, however, is a strong counter sign. The GOP's failure to capture the House of Representatives in recent years begins with its inability to stem defections to Democratic candidates from its own loyalists, which does not augur well for a pro-Republican realignment.

These observations on the impact of party identification on the voter largely reflect decisions in national elections. Party identification may have either more or less impact in state and local elections. Where voters have personal, face-to-face contact with candidates, their evaluation of them may be so strong that it overrides party loyalties. In addition, some voters may find the application of party loyalties inappropriate to the less partisan campaigns for local office, especially when the office appears to have little policymaking responsibility (e.g., the local clerk of the court or the registrar of deeds) or is filled in a nonpartisan election. On the other hand, voters in many state or local elections may have to rely on the guidance of party even more than they do in na-

[17]Gregory B. Markus and Philip E. Converse, "A Dynamic Simultaneous Equation Model of Electoral Choice," *American Political Science Review* 73 (1979): 1055–70.

tional elections. Faced with a long ballot of low-visibility candidates for city, county, state, and other offices, the voter may have no alternative but to rely on the party label.

PARTY IDENTIFICATION AND POLITICAL ACTIVITY

American politics is dominated by the two major parties, so it should hardly be surprising that individuals with attachments to these parties have high rates of involvement in political life. It is the strongest partisans, in fact, who are the members of the electorate most likely to actively follow and participate in politics.

Over the years, strong partisans have consistently exhibited more interest than other citizens in politics in general and in particular election campaigns. The 1988 Michigan survey shows, for example, that strong Democrats and (especially) strong Republicans were more likely than weak identifiers or independents to be attentive to politics and highly interested in the campaign (Table 7.4). Strong partisans also are more inclined than weak partisans or independents to follow reports about politics and the campaign in the mass media. In 1988, they were more likely to have watched television programs about the campaign and to have read about it in the newspapers.

The most partisan members of the parties in the electorate match their greater cognitive involvement with relatively higher levels of political activity. In a year in which the turnout of the adult electorate barely reached 50 percent, a total of 84 percent of the strong partisans voted in 1988. They also were significantly more likely than the remainder of the electorate to try to persuade other people to vote a certain way; to wear campaign buttons, display bumper stickers, or use yard signs; to attend political meetings or rallies; and to contribute money to a candidate or party. The combatants of American electoral politics, in short, come disproportionately from the ranks of the strong Democrats and strong Republicans.

The strong party identifiers also see the parties in sharper terms than do weak identifiers and independents. They are considerably more likely to perceive differences between the Democrats and Republicans in general (Table 7.5) and on specific policy issues. Paralleling this are their more strongly differentiated evaluations of the two parties and their candidates, as well as of the parties' abilities to govern for the benefit of the nation. Strong partisans are even more inclined than weaker partisans and independents to identify the opposition party with extreme ideological views. In the mind of the strong partisan, in sum, the political parties stand in bold relief, sharply polarized along the important dimensions of politics.[18]

---

[18]For further discussion of some of these differences, see Paul R. Abramson, John H. Aldrich, and David W. Rohde, *Change and Continuity in the 1988 Election* (Washington, D.C.: CQ Press, 1990), Chap. 8.

Table 7.4 THE POLITICAL INVOLVEMENT OF PARTISANS AND INDEPENDENTS: 1988

	Democrats		Independents			Republicans	
	Strong	Weak	Closer to Democrats	Closer to neither	Closer to Republicans	Weak	Strong
Very much interested in politics	35%	26	30	17	31	31	49
Follow public affairs most of the time	24%	18	22	16	24	20	35
Great deal of attention to campaign via television	25%	14	10	10	13	9	20
Read about campaign in newspapers	52%	43	52	34	50	52	61
Voted	80%	63	64	50	64	76	89
Tried to persuade people to vote a certain way	35%	26	28	16	28	25	43
Displayed button, bumper sticker, yard sign	13%	7	8	4	5	9	12
Attended rally or meeting	10%	3	12	3	4	7	12
Contributed money to:							
Candidate	5%	5	6	1	6	6	11
Party	6%	3	4	2	4	5	16

Source: Center for Political Studies, University of Michigan: data made available by the Inter-University Consortium for Political and Social Research.

Table 7.5   DIFFERENCES BETWEEN THE PARTIES AS PERCEIVED
BY PARTISANS AND INDEPENDENTS: 1988

	Perceive differences between Democratic and Republican parties
Strong Democrats	74%
Weak Democrats	58
Independents closer to Democrats	64
Independents	33
Independents closer to Republicans	62
Weak Republicans	64
Strong Republicans	81

Source: Center for Political Studies, University of Michigan: data made available by the Inter-University Consortium for Political and Social Research.

Such relationships, by themselves, are no reason to leap to the conclusion that party identification alone produces greater activity or sharper party images. Behavioral and cognitive involvement in political affairs has diverse roots. Higher socioeconomic status, and the greater political sophistication and easier entry into political participation that it often brings, contribute considerably to involvement. The relatively stronger involvement on the Republican side of the party identification continuum, in fact, springs in part from the generally higher socioeconomic status levels of Republicans, as well as their more ideological commitment to politics.[19] Nonetheless, loyal commitment to a party figures prominently in inducing involvement in the world of partisan politics.

THE MYTH OF THE INDEPENDENT

That party loyalties should govern so much political behavior in a culture that so warmly celebrates the independent well-informed voter who is moved by issues and candidates, not parties, is too striking a paradox to ignore. There clearly is a disjuncture between the American myth of the high-minded independent and the reality of widespread partisanship. The problem is with the myth. Before the myth is finally put to rest, however, we ought to be clear about what myth we are burying.

---

[19]On similar Republican hyperactivity in the 1960s, see Verba and Nie, *Participation in America,* (New York: Harper & Row, 1972), Chap. 12. The varying relationships between ideology and campaign activity over a longer period are examined in Paul Allen Beck and M. Kent Jennings, "Political Periods and Political Participation," *American Political Science Review* 73 (1979): 737–50.

Self-Styled Independents

If we mean by the term *independent* those Americans who prefer not to identify with a political party, then the myth *is* a casualty of survey research.[20] Although by definition these independents must vote for candidates and issues (since they do not have a party) and it is true that they split their tickets more frequently and wait longer in the campaign to make their voting decisions, they fall short of the mythical picture of the independent in most other respects. They are less concerned about specific elections than identifiers are, less well informed, and less active politically. Also, they are more likely not to vote at a given election. In 1988, for instance, independents once again had a higher frequency of nonvoting than did party identifiers, and "pure" independents voted less often than independents who leaned toward one party or the other. As a group the pure independents, in fact, are the least involved and least informed of all American citizens (Table 7.4). They look especially pallid in comparison to the strong partisans.

Party Switchers

There is no reason, however, why we cannot define the political independents in terms of their behavior or activity. In his last work, published posthumously, V. O. Key attempted to reclaim the independents from their obloquy by dealing not with the self-styled independents but with voters who switched their party vote in a consecutive pair of presidential elections.[21] The picture of the American voter that emerged from American political folklore and from the electoral studies of the time, Key thought, was not a pretty one; it was one of an electorate whose voting decision was determined by deeply ingrained attitudes, perceptions, and loyalties without its having grasped the major political issues and alternatives.

Key's search for electoral "rationality" centered, therefore, on the switchers—the voters who did *not* keep voting for the same party in consecutive elections. Key's switchers, by the usual criteria, came much closer to the image of the independent than did the self-described independents. He found their levels of political interest no lower than those of the stand-patters, who remained firm in their voting allegiances. By his definition, of course, switchers are not nonvoters. Above all, they are marked by an issue-related rationality that fits well the usual picture of the independent. They agree on policy issues with the stand-patters toward whom they shift and they disagree with the policies of the party from which they defect.[22]

---

[20]The myth of independence as the posture toward politics of the highly informed, sophisticated voter (in contrast to the slavish partisan) is effectively laid to rest in the study of the 1952 and 1956 elections by Campbell, Converse, Miller, and Stokes, published in *The American Voter.*

[21]V. O. Key, Jr. (with the assistance of Milton C. Cummings), *The Responsible Electorate* (Cambridge: Harvard University Press, 1966).

[22]A related concept of the independent as ticket-splitter is developed in Walter DeVries and Lance Tarrance, *The Ticket Splitter* (Grand Rapids, Mich.: Eerdmans, 1972).

A Breakdown of the Self-Styled Independents

It is the self-described independents, however—the ones who voice no party preference or assert their independence—who are the subject of most scholarly inquiry. As their numbers among American voters have increased in recent years (Table 6.2), with the percentage approaching 50 percent among the youngest members of the electorate, more attention has been paid to self-proclaimed independents. The contemporary view is that they are, and always have been, a rather diverse group—containing many of the least involved and least informed voters, but also including some who come close to matching the mythological independent. In fact, when a distinction is made between independents who feel closer to one of the two parties (independent "leaners") and those who do not ("pure" independents), the independent leaners often turn out to be more politically involved (Table 7.4) *and sometimes even more partisan in voting* (especially for president) than weak partisans (Tables 7.1–7.3), in recent years as well as in the 1950s. It is only in comparison to strong partisans that these independents fall short. By contrast, the pure independents typically have the most dismal record, with relatively low levels of political interest and information, turnout, and education.[23]

In recent years, as their number has swollen, a second distinction among independents has become important.[24] Respondents in the Michigan surveys can fall into the independent classification in two different ways—by explicitly choosing the label of "independent" for themselves or by failing to claim any political preference at all. In response to the question "Generally speaking, do you usually consider yourself a Democrat, a Republican, an Independent, or what?" some illustrative "no preference" responses are: "None," "Not anything," "I don't know," "I'm not a Republican, not a Democrat, not an Independent, and not a Communist." In coding these responses into a party identification category, the only thing that distinguishes these "no preference" independents from apoliticals is their level of interest in politics. Those with "no preference" and little interest in or information about politics are classified as apoliticals; those with "no preference" and some interest are treated as independents.

A considerable portion of the growth in independents since 1964 is attributable to this "no preference" group. In spite of the requirement that they exhibit some interest in politics before they can be classified as independent, moreover, the "no preference" independents are much less politically involved

---

[23]The necessity of revisions in the negative portrait of independents is largely obscured when independent leaners and pure independents are combined, as was the case in *The American Voter*. When they are treated as separate categories, the attitudinal and behavioral differences among them—and thereby the distinction between two types of independents—becomes clear. See Petrocik, "An Analysis of Intransitivities in the Index of Party Identification," pp. 31–47; and Keith, Magleby, Nelson, Orr, Westlye, and Wolfinger, "The Partisan Affinities of Independent 'Leaners,'" pp. 155–84.

[24]This discussion is based upon Wattenberg, *The Decline of American Political Parties 1952–1984*, Chap. 3.

than self-styled independents. They vote less frequently, show less interest in the campaign, and have less confidence in their ability to influence politics. By mixing them with self-styled independents (they constituted 39 percent of all pure independents in 1988), the political involvement and sophistication of the independent grouping is diluted. If independents are restricted to only the self-proclaimed, however, their standing is considerably improved. While they do not achieve the exalted position of the mythological independent, they compare more favorably with partisans in political involvement. No doubt the myth of the independent has been debunked by survey research; but it also is survey research that has rescued independence from ignominy.

THE LOYAL ELECTORATES AND THE CHANGING CONDITIONS OF PARTY POLITICS

The leaders of the party organizations scarcely know the men and women of the parties' loyal electorates. They know them largely in the same way that political scientists do—in some abstract, aggregate profile. They know that members of the party in the electorate see the issues and candidates through party-tinted glasses. They know that the party electorate has a somewhat unified and reinforcing view of politics, that it is more likely to vote the party ticket, and that it is easier to recruit into activity for the party or for a candidate. Party strategists know, in other words, that the party electorate is a hard core of party supporters. In a general, if vague, way, they see—as do political scientists—that party identification is a commitment that is often strong enough to affect other commitments and pervasive enough to color and codify perceptions of political reality.

The Nature of the Electorate and Campaign Strategy

Much of the strategy of American political campaigning is based on these assumptions about loyal party electorates. The general strategy is often to stimulate and reinforce the party loyalties of one's own partisans while making candidate and issue appeals to independents and partisans of the other party. The heightened attention to the fair distribution of tax burdens produced by the 1990 federal budget controversy, for example, was seized upon by Democratic candidates in mid-term elections that year to rally the lower and middle socioeconomic status groups that formed their base.

Furthermore, the size and composition of the two party electorates determine the more specific strategies. The pattern of party loyalty after the 1930s required, for example, that the Republicans minimize party-stimulating appeals, party identifications, and SES issues. Their hope lay with attractive candidates and nonclass issues. It is surely not coincidental that both Barry Goldwater in 1964 and Richard Nixon in 1968 and 1972 emphasized a large number of issues that met those specifications: crime and morality, local responsibility for civil rights and racial equality, defense and foreign policy, and the war in Vietnam. In the 1980s, Ronald Reagan and then George Bush did challenge the Democrats on SES issues, especially by appealing to middle-class concerns about inflation and taxation; but cross-cutting issues of defense, foreign policy, and social policy also occupied prominent places on their campaign agenda. By then, though, the SES composition of the electorate was more favorable to the Republicans, and the traditional Democratic edge on economic issues had faded.

So great has been the stabilizing force of these two great party electorates in American politics that a different style of American politics would ensue without them. Because large numbers of people have had party identifications, because they have rarely changed them, and because those identifications have strongly governed their voting decisions, patterns of voting support for the two parties traditionally have been remarkably stable. In election after election, many individual voters have voted straight party tickets. The patterns of party support also have been stable geographically during most of American history. When the votes shifted—enough to tip balances of victory and defeat—they usually shifted so evenly that they did not greatly alter those overall patterns of support. A party's state-to-state profile of support was raised or lowered, but not changed greatly.[25]

Changing Conditions

The events of recent years have jolted this long-term stability. Since 1964, as we saw in Chapter 6, the relative sizes of the parties in the electorate have declined as more Americans rejected partisan loyalties. Stable party voting has broken down everywhere, especially in the South. In the 1980s, this movement toward independence that we have called dealignment has been halted, and some signs are auguring the beginnings of a pro-Republican realignment. These events have affected the parties within the voter as well. Since the mid-sixties, both Democratic and Republican partisans have been less loyal to the candidates of their party for president, congress, and in state and local elections (see Tables 7.1–7.3). This decline in party fidelity is significant for the Democrats because it is measured from a deviating election baseline in the 1950s—and for the Republicans because it has continued into the 1980s.

In terms of both professed identification with a party and loyalty among partisans to the party's candidates, then, political parties are less important to the electorate—possibly less important than they have been since the founding of the American party system. Whether this situation will survive a putative realignment, of course, only time will tell. Perhaps declines in party loyalists

---

[25]V. O. Key and Frank Munger characterized the century-long stable voting patterns of Indiana counties as "standing decisions" to support a particular party. See their "Social Determinism and Electoral Decision," in Eugene Burdick and Arthur J. Brodbeck (eds.), *American Voting Behavior* (Glencoe, Ill.: Free Press, 1959), pp. 281–99.

and in the fidelity of partisans themselves are natural as one party system dies and another takes its place. But, for the moment, political parties play less the leading and more a supporting role in American electoral politics. One important consequence is that elections now turn more on short-run forces—the candidates, the issues, the particular events of the immediate campaign. And this consequence itself has consequences—for the party organizations and their campaign strategies as well as for the role of the parties in government.

Yet, it is important not to go overboard in discounting the importance of party to the electorate. Most Americans—a clear majority using only strong and weak identifiers, almost all if leaners are included as well—profess some degree of loyalty to either the Democratic or the Republican party. And many Americans are faithful to these loyalties in voting for candidates for office—more so in the 1988 contests than in some time. Voters may stray from the party fold here and there, defections which the very abundance of contests for office encourage and thereby mute the impact of in any particular case, but they continue to perceive candidates, issues, and elections in partisan terms and usually to vote accordingly. Although buffeted by strong antiparty forces since the mid-1960s amid the ongoing public ambivalence toward the parties, the party within the voter continues to exert a powerful force on electoral choices and the parties in the electorate remain significant players in American elections.

Chapter
8

The Active Electorate

The political parties in the electorate are defined by those people who profess party attachments, and we have naturally focused our attention upon them. Their composition as well as their place in the party system and American politics more generally, though, depend upon the nature of the electorate itself, in particular what portion of the electorate is actively involved in elections. Both the legally-defined electorate and the active electorate have varied greatly in size and composition over the course of American history, and both still differ considerably across the fifty states. These variations have had a profound effect on party politics.

The nature of the electorate determines what parties enjoy prominence in the party system, which has meant what two parties will dominate in the American two-party system. Much of the early history of political parties can be written in terms of their responses to expansion of the suffrage. Parties first appeared as essentially aristocratic instruments for mobilizing very homogeneous and limited electorates. As electorates were expanded by enfranchising lower status citizens, disadvantaged minorities, and women, the parties were forced to alter their organizations and appeals. Some early parties, like the Federalists, suffered extinction because they were unable to adjust their appeals to accommodate the new electorates. Other parties, largely of the European socialist and labor variety, fought to secure the suffrage for lower status voters and then rode their enfranchisement to prominent positions in the party system. What the parties are, to the degree to which they are defined by their electoral coalitions, depends upon what the electorate is.

But it is the nature of the *active* electorate that has determined the relative standing of the parties and the extent to which the parties in the electorate have dominated the electoral system. If the participating members of the electorate were a representative sample of the adult citizenry, then the issue of their composition would not arise. The effective electorate, however, usually is nothing of the sort. It almost always overrepresents some groups in the society at the expense of others. Because of the preferences of various groups for one party or another, the composition of the active electorate is a matter of differential advantage for the parties.

TURNOUT IN AMERICAN ELECTIONS: THE UNENVIABLE RECORD

In the American system, there is a wide gap between the potential electorate and the active electorate. Barely a majority (50.2 percent to be exact) of the voting age population cast a ballot for president in 1988, continuing the erosion in presidential turnout that began after 1960. The 1988 figure is the lowest in history except for slightly lower turnout levels in the first two elections of the 1920s before many women had become accustomed to their new right to vote (see Fig. 8.1).

These national averages hide considerable state variation. In the 1988 presidential contest, for example, only 39 percent of the voting age population voted in Georgia in comparison to 66 percent in Minnesota. The rate of voting is depressed even further in contests below the presidential level that appear on the same ballot and in nonpresidential years.[1] Participation in contests for local offices and especially in party primaries rarely attains even that modest level.[2]

By whatever standard is employed, turnout in American elections falls short. By the norms of democratic theory, such extensive noninvolvement in elections is a blemish on the American democratic system. Many question the health of a democracy when so few of its citizens participate. In a time when newly-won voting rights have stimulated an explosion of participation in Eastern Europe and the USSR and the quest for democratic rights has attracted worldwide attention in China, many commentators on American civic values find it deplorable that Americans appear so apathetic (see box).

Turnout in the United States compares poorly with real world standards as well. It has declined in the last few decades from its recent peaks for mid-term and presidential elections, respectively, of 53.4 percent in 1958 and 63.7 percent in 1960. Its twentieth century levels have fallen far below those achieved toward the end of the nineteenth century, when involvement in American elec-

---

[1]Preliminary estimates of congressional voting turnout in the 1990 mid-term elections by Curtis Gans' Committee for the Study of the American Electorate put it at 36 percent—among the lowest rates in history.

[2]Official turnout figures deflate the actual rate of electoral participation because they overestimate the number of legally eligible voters and underestimate the number of actual voters. The denominator of the turnout fraction is the total of all residents of voting age as estimated by the United States Bureau of the Census. But not all of the voting age population is legally eligible to vote. Typically excluded by the states are aliens, persons convicted of certain crimes, the institutionalized mentally ill, and those who have just moved to the state. The numerator of the turnout fraction is the number of votes that are counted for each particular office. Not counted are spoiled ballots (more common with voting-machine or punch-card methods) and some write-in votes. Allowing for these corrections boosts turnout considerably (Warren Mitofsky and Martin Plissner in the November 10, 1988, *New York Times* say to about 60 percent in the 1988 presidential election), but it leaves American turnout still at relatively low levels.

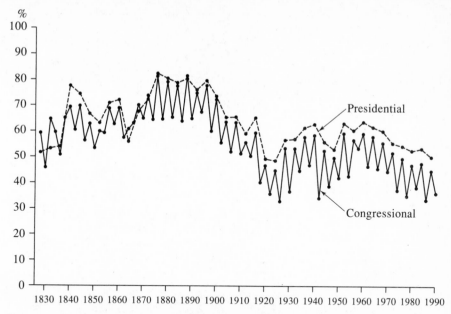

Figure 8.1 Turnout in American Elections: 1828–1990.

Source: 1828–1984: Erik W. Austin, *Political Facts of the United States Since 1789* (New York: Columbia University Press, 1987), Table 3.12. 1986–88: *Statistical Abstract of the United States* (1990) (Washington, D.C.: U.S. Bureau of the Census), p. 265. The 1990 figure is a preliminary estimate from the Committee for the Study of the American Electorate.

toral politics reached an all-time high. In comparison with the other western democracies, in which turnout for the most important elections commonly exceeds 80 percent, today's American turnout levels seem modest indeed. In no other democratic nation does such a small share of the electorate participate in choosing the most important government officials.[3]

The wide gap between the potential electorate and the actual number of voters who cast a ballot in any election is the result of forces both internal and external to the individual. The external influences involve the legal restrictions of the states (including their definitions of the electorate), their application by the administrative machinery of the states, and the informal restrictions of economic and social sanction, as well as the stimulus of politics itself. The internal influences are the values and goals, the motivational levels, the role

---

[3]Data on turnout in other democracies are presented and analyzed in G. Bingham Powell, Jr., "American Voter Turnout in Comparative Perspective," *American Political Science Review* 80 (1986): 17–44; and David Glass, Peverill Squire, and Raymond Wolfinger, "Voter Turnout: An International Comparison," *Public Opinion* 6 (1984): 49–55. Switzerland has lower national turnout levels than the United States, but its national elections are less important than its local contests.

While people in Communist nations fight for the right to vote, Americans exercise their right not to vote.

Source: Reprinted by permission of UFS, Inc.

perceptions, and the sense of civic responsibility within the individual. The external definitions of the American electorate are clearer because they are more tangible, and we turn to them first.

CHANGING LEGAL DEFINITIONS OF THE ELECTORATE

It was undoubtedly the intention of the framers of the Constitution to leave control over the definition of the electorate to states. The only provision for suffrage in the original document is Article I, Section 2, which provides that, for elections to the House of Representatives, "the electors of each state shall have the qualifications requisite for electors of the most numerous branch of the state legislature," and these were left for the states to set. The inevitable result over the years was the absence of a uniform national electorate, even for national elections.

Since the time of the Civil War, though, the national government has been given the authority through constitutional amendments to prevent states from imposing particularly objectionable restrictions on voting. Thus, the definition of the electorate over the past 150 years has expanded and occasionally even contracted through the curiously American interlacing of national and state action.

The enfranchisement of white males was accomplished earlier in the United States than in any other democracy. In the early nineteenth century, the states themselves gradually repealed the property, income, and tax-paying qualification for voting by which they had so severely restricted male suffrage.[4] By 1860 there remained no states that required property holding and only four that required substantial tax paying as a condition for voting. About a century later, the Supreme Court, and then the Twenty-fourth Amendment, finally ended even the small poll tax as a requirement for voting.[5]

Complete women's suffrage did not come until the 20th century, and it required federal action. By the mid-1870s, women had begun to work through the states for their right to vote; in 1890 with its admission to the Union, Wyoming became the first state to grant the full franchise to women. The push for women's suffrage slowly bogged down, especially in the eastern states, and women shifted their hopes to the United States Constitution. The Nineteenth Amendment, forbidding states to deny the vote on grounds of sex, was finally ratified in 1920.

The right to vote for black Americans has a more checkered history. The expansion of black suffrage began by state action in some of the states of New England before the Civil War, but it culminated after the war with the passage of the Fifteenth Amendment, which prohibited abridgements of the right to vote on account of race. As the federal government turned its attention to other matters, however, southern states effectively restricted the franchise for blacks through poll taxes, literacy tests, and outright intimidation. By the early 1900s, black turnout in the south was almost negligible, and it remained that way in most southern states until the 1960s, when the federal government began to enforce the Fifteenth Amendment and new voting rights laws on the reluctant states.

Lowering the voting age to 18 has been the most recent change in the legal definition of the electorate. In the 1960s, only a handful of states allowed young people under the age of twenty-one to vote. Then, in June 1970, the United States Congress passed a law lowering the minimum voting age to eighteen in both state and federal elections. Less than half a year later, the Supreme Court decided by a five to four vote that the act was constitutional as it applied to federal elections but unconstitutional as it applied to state and local elections.[6] Congress then passed and sent to the states for ratification an amendment to the Constitution lowering the age to eighteen for *all* elections. That amendment, the Twenty-sixth Amendment, was ratified by 1971.

---

[4]For background on the early development of the American electorate, see Chilton Williamson, *American Suffrage: From Property to Democracy* (Princeton, N.J.: Princeton University Press, 1960).

[5]The Supreme Court case overturning the poll tax was Harper v. Virginia State Board of Elections, 383 U.S. 633 (1966).

[6]Oregon v. Mitchell, 400 U.S. 112 (1970).

In recent years, the national government, through both the Congress and the Supreme Court, has expanded its role in defining the American electorate. By ordinary statute—rather than by constitutional amendment—the Congress extended the vote to younger voters in federal elections; banned literacy, understanding, and character tests for registration; and waived residence requirements for voting in presidential elections. The newly expanded congressional authority appears to rest on the Supreme Court's interpretation of Article I, Section 4, the section on the control of congressional elections.[7] The Court has enlarged its own powers in the application of constitutional guarantees, that expansion culminating in 1972 in its decision sharply restricting state residence requirements.[8] The Supreme Court also has relied upon the Fourteenth Amendment's equal protection clause ("no state shall make or enforce any law which shall . . . deny to any person within its jurisdiction the equal protection of the laws") to prevent states from discriminating against blacks in defining its electorate. Presumably, this same clause would similarly protect ethnic, religious, occupational, or other social groups.

Between the constitutional territory of the states and that of the nation there is a tiny no-man's-land, the District of Columbia. For almost all of American history, the citizens of the District remained voteless, even in their own local affairs. Since the passage of the Twenty-third Amendment to the Constitution in 1961, however, the voters of the District of Columbia have had three votes in the electoral college. They also elect a nonvoting delegate to Congress and a series of local officials on the authorization of the Congress.

LEGAL-INSTITUTIONAL BARRIERS TO VOTING

Despite their freedom under the Constitution, the states have developed legal definitions of the suffrage that are surprisingly similar. In part, the negative controls of the constitutional amendments have hemmed them in. So, too, have the political pressures for universal adult suffrage, the examples of other states, and increased supervision by the Congress and the Supreme Court. In any event, it is now possible to deal with the state definitions of the suffrage in a small number of categories.

---

[7]Section 4 of Article I is as follows: "The Times, Places, and Manner of holding Elections for Senators and Representatives, shall be prescribed in each State by the Legislature thereof; but the Congress may at any time by Law make or alter such Regulations, except as to the Places of choosing Senators." Every reader can be his or her own constitutional expert in deciding whether questions of suffrage are what the Founding Fathers has in mind in writing this section of Article I.

[8]Dunn v. Blumstein, 405 U.S. 303 (1972). For the legal and constitutional issues involved in defining the electorate, see Richard Claude, *The Supreme Court and the Electoral Process* (Baltimore: The John Hopkins University Press, 1970).

Citizenship

All states now require that voters be citizens of the United States. As surprising as it may now seem, in 1900 eleven states still permitted aliens to vote, although some states required that the individual had begun to seek American citizenship. In 1926, Arkansas, the last state to capitulate, closed off the alien suffrage. Without any doubt, the requirement of citizenship is the major legal barrier to voting for adults now living in the United States. By the most conservative reckoning, there are well over 10 million adults living in the United States who are ineligible to vote until they qualify as citizens. Most of them are concentrated in a handful of states, such as California, Florida, Texas, and New York. Any of these states presumably could enfranchise their resident aliens, but they are not likely to do so.

Residence

For most of the history of the Republic, the states were free to require that citizens live in the state and locality for a certain period of time before they could vote. Indeed, most states devised three-layer residence requirements: a minimum period of time in the state, a shorter time in the county, and an even shorter period in the local voting district. Traditionally, the longest residence requirements were those of the southern states (where migrant and mobile farm labor was disenfranchised), but long waits for eligibility were not uncommon elsewhere. As recently as 1970, the median residence requirement among the fifty states was one year in the state, three months in the county, and one month in the voting district.

Substantial residence requirements began to crumble in the 1950s and 1960s, however, largely in response both to the demands of a physically mobile society and to its rising democratic expectations. States lowered their residence requirements, and many also set up even lower requirements for newcomers wishing to vote in presidential elections. In 1970, Congress settled the latter issue by establishing a national uniform residence requirement of thirty days within a state for voting in a presidential election. Then, in 1972, the Supreme Court struck down Tennessee's one-year residence requirement for voting in state and local elections, indicating a strong preference for a thirty-day limit. The Court later accepted a fifty-day requirement for one state, but in doing so it noted that such a period "approaches the outer constitutional limit."[9] Consequently, almost half of the states have dropped residence requirements

---

[9] The two supreme court cases dealing with residency requirements are Dunn v. Blumstein, 405 U.S. 330 (1972); and Burns v. Fortson, 410 U.S. 686 (1973).

altogether, and most of the rest have fixed them at one month. Only Arizona, with its fifty-day requirements, make new residents wait more than thirty days before they are eligible to vote.[10]

Despite the uniform reduction in the length of residence necessary to qualify for registration, residency requirements still impose a formidable hurdle to voting. The United States is a nation of movers. About 16 percent of the voting age population moved between 1986 and 1987, with about two-thirds of them moving within the same county. Each time they change their address, from one state to another or just from one street to the next, reregistration is required. One recent study shows that those who have recently moved are far less likely than nonmovers to vote in elections, even if they are identical on other characteristics related to turnout. With the depressing effects of mobility removed, this study estimates that turnout would be about 9 percent higher.[11]

Disqualifications

Virtually all the states restrict the suffrage for reasons of crime or mental incompetence. Institutionalization for insanity or severe mental illness temporarily removes an individual from the suffrage in all states; and in the great majority of states, so does conviction for certain categories of crimes, the most common being felonies and electoral corruption. The disqualification for mental illness is generally limited to the time of illness or incapacity. The disqualification for felonies, however, lasts indefinitely in some states, even after release from prison. Only gubernatorial pardon or some formal administrative or legislative action will restore the franchise.

Registration

One of the most effective external barriers to voting is the requirement in most states that voters *themselves* must take the initiative to register in order to participate in an election. Placing the responsibility for registration on the shoulders of the individual was a reform of the Progressive movement, designed to limit illegal voting in the teeming cities. It was implemented in most states toward the end of the nineteenth century. Before then, voters only had to show up on election day or to be listed on an electoral roll compiled by the government, which is the practice in most European democracies, to be able to cast a ballot. The adoption of registration requirements, largely in the 1890s, is widely credited with reducing the high turnout levels of the late nineteenth century—

---

[10]State residence requirements are reported in *The Book of the States* (Lexington, Ky.: The Council of State Governments). For the 1990 requirements, see the 1990 edition, p. 208.

[11]Peverill Squire, Raymond E. Wolfinger, and David P. Glass, "Residential Mobility and Voter Turnout," *American Political Science Review* 81 (1987): 45–65.

because it both increased the motivation necessary to vote and reduced the fraudulent padding of voter rolls.[12]

At present, only North Dakota does not require voter registration. But different provisions for registration among the remaining states produce considerable variation in how much of a burden registration places on the individual. Half of the states permit mail registration by any voter; and all of the states (except North Dakota, of course) allow some voters, usually in specified classes, to register absentee. Other provisions affecting the ease of registration are the closing date for registration before the election, how frequently the registration rolls are purged of nonvoters, and the accessibility of registrars. The closing date is election day in three states, but it ranges from five to fifty days before the election in the others. Most states also cancel the registration of citizens who have not voted for a few years. About a dozen purge voters from the registration rolls if they have not voted in at least two years. New Hampshire and Michigan, at the other extreme, are the most lenient, allowing voters to cast a ballot once every ten years without being removed from the rolls. Finally, some states make it easy to register by establishing regular hours, keeping registration offices open on evenings and weekends, and allowing registration at many different places.

Restricting the right to vote only to those who have registered under the myriad provisions of the various states imposes additional burdens or "costs" on the exercise of the franchise. The higher these costs, the more citizens will choose not to participate in elections. While registration requirements have been liberalized in recent years, they still pose a formidable obstacle to higher turnout. One study estimated that turnout in presidential elections could be raised by approximately 9 percent if all states eliminated a closing date for registration, opened registration offices for forty hours during the week and in the evenings and/or on Saturday, and permitted absentee registration for the sick, disabled, or absent. The greatest gains, about 6 percent, would be realized by elimination of the closing date, because this would enable previous nonvoters, who were stimulated by the election campaign, to vote.[13]

Registration laws, however, are not the insurmountable barriers to the vote that most of the other provisions defining the electorate are. Rather, they make voting only more difficult by increasing its "costs"—the amount of time, effort, and even knowledge required to gain access to the polls. Like voting, then, registration is a matter of individual choice. Because of this, in calculating turnout rates we should not restrict the definition of the potential electorate only to

[12]See Philip E. Converse, "Change in the American Electorate," in Angus Campbell and Philip E. Converse (eds.), *The Human Meaning of Social Change* (New York: Russell Sage Foundation, 1972), pp. 263–337; and Frances Fox Piven and Richard A. Cloward, *Why Americans Don't Vote* (New York: Pantheon Books, 1988).

[13]Raymond E. Wolfinger and Steven J. Rosenstone, *Who Votes?* (New Haven, Conn.: Yale University Press, 1982)., pp. 61–78.

those who are registered, as some have suggested, however much that might improve American turnout levels relative to other democracies.

THE SPECIAL CASE OF VOTING RIGHTS FOR AMERICAN BLACKS

Throughout much of American history, black people have been the target of a variety of practices designed to restrict their right to vote. Before slavery was abolished at the end of the Civil War, most blacks of course could not vote; only a few free blacks in a handful of northern states enjoyed that privilege. With the defeat of the Confederacy and the passage of the Reconstruction Amendments to extend to blacks the rights of citizenship, black males were enfranchised nationwide. Once Union occupation troops withdrew from the South as the Reconstruction came to an end, however, southern states set about to systematically remove blacks from the active electorate. They had succeeded by the beginning of the twentieth century.

Systematic Disenfranchisement

The story of the disenfranchisement of the southern black electorate is a tale of blatant manipulation of the electoral system to control political outcomes. Legal restrictions on voting, capricious administration of the laws, and outright intimidation and violence when these "nicer" methods were not effective combined to reverse the tide of democratization for blacks—and often for poor whites as well—in the former Confederacy and some neighboring states. Only in contemporary times have southern blacks regained this essential right of democratic citizenship.

Southern states employed an arsenal of weapons to restrict the black vote. Residence requirements were most stringent in the South. Most states in that region required payment of a poll tax as a qualification for voting. Only one or two dollars a year, its disenfranchising effect was often increased by a stipulation that it be cumulative, that it be paid well in advance of the election, or that the taxpayer keep a receipt and present it at the voting booth. Many states also required passage of a literacy test, often of both reading ability and understanding (as graded by a hostile registrar) as a condition for voting. These laws were intentionally directed at the poor, uneducated, and often itinerant black population. They created huge barriers to voting.

If the law did not prove sufficient to discourage black participation, other devises were available. Faced with the threat of black voting in the Democratic party's primary elections, some states declared the party a private club open only to whites. Blacks who were able to negotiate the legal maize traditionally found themselves blocked by the administration of registration and election laws. Endless delay, unavailable or antagonistic registrars, niggling technicalities, and double standards were formidable barriers (see box). To those who

---

Administrative Barriers to Black Registration in the South

In their account of the civil rights movement in the South, Pat Watters and Reese Cleghorn describe how blacks were prevented from registering by administrative practices:

> Slowdowns were common. Separate tables would be assigned whites and Negroes. If a line of Negroes were waiting for the Negro table, a white might go ahead of them, use the empty white table, and leave. In Anniston, Alabama, a report said the white table was larger, and Negroes were not allowed in the room when a white was using it. Another variation was to seat four Negroes at a table, and make three wait until the slowest had finished, while others waited outside in line. These methods were particularly effective when coupled with the one or two day a month registration periods. . . . In one north Florida county, the registrar didn't bother with any of these refinements, and didn't close his office when Negro applicants appeared. He simply sat with his legs stretched out across the doorway. Negroes didn't break through them.

Excerpt from *Climbing Jacob's Ladder* by Pat Watters and Reese Cleghorn, copyright © 1967 by Southern Regional Council, Inc., reprinted by permission of Harcourt Brace Jovanovich, Inc.

---

nonetheless persevered, the threat—and all too often the reality—of economic reprisal (the loss of a job or a home) and physical violence proved a powerful deterrent. Left alone to pursue their constitutionally-given voting rights in an unremittingly hostile and threatening environment, it is little wonder that only five percent of voting-age blacks were registered in the eleven southern states as recently as 1940.[14]

A Long Struggle for Voting Rights

The struggle for the black franchise began in the classic American way as a constitutional issue. For years after the end of Reconstruction, in fact, the states and the United States Supreme Court played a grim game of constitutional "hide and seek." The states would devise a scheme of disenfranchisement, the Court would strike it down, and the states would find another—ad infinitum. The states sometimes were careful not to disenfranchise poorer whites along with blacks—hence their devising of grandfather clauses, which automatically registered all persons whose ancestors had been eligible to vote before the Civil

---

[14]The story of black disenfranchisement in the South is well told by V. O. Key, Jr., in *Southern Politics in State and Nation* (New York: Knopf, 1949). See also J. Morgan Kousser, *The Shaping of Southern Politics* (New Haven: Yale University Press, 1974); and Donald R. Matthews and James W. Prothro, *Negroes and the New Southern Politics* (New York: Harcourt, Brace and World, 1966).

War. The manic quality of this constitutional chase is perhaps best illustrated by the white primary cases. The white primary was simply a party primary in which blacks were forbidden to vote; it arose at a time in which the candidate who won the Democratic primary in southern states was assured of victory in the general election against an enfeebled Republican party. It finally expired, but only after twenty-one years of litigation and five cases before the United States Supreme Court.[15]

Court action is not nearly so well adapted, however, to dealing with informal administrative evasions. Increasingly, the most useful remedies were legislative and administrative—a fighting of fire with fire. The federal civil rights acts of 1957, 1960, 1964, 1965, 1970 and 1982 all made this kind of attack on discrimination against black would-be voters. The 1965 Voting Rights Act and its 1982 extension involved the national government directly in local registration practices:

- The *attorney general* was authorized to seek injunctions against individuals who prevented blacks from voting in primaries or general elections. When he could convince a federal court that a "pattern or practice" of discrimination existed in a district, the court could order registration and send federal registrars and observers to the area.
- The *Justice Department* acquired authority to supervise voting procedures in states and counties in which less than 50 percent of potential voters had voted in the most recent presidential election. Any changes in voting procedures had to be approved by the attorney general or by the United States District Court in the District of Columbia. The attorney general could also send registrars and observers there.
- *Local registrars* were brought under greater regulation and control. They were required to keep voting and registration records for twenty-two months and prohibited from applying voting requirements unequally. Nor were they permitted to seize on immaterial errors or omissions in the application process as a reason for refusing registration.[16]

Results

As a result of this extensive federal government intervention in electoral practices and the unrelenting activities of the civil rights movement in mobilizing black voters, the black electorate has grown enormously in the South. Black registration increased from 5 percent of the black voting age population in 1940

---

[15]The end of the white primary is recorded in Smith v. Allwright, 321 U.S. 649 (1944).

[16]For a review of the consequences of the Voting Rights Act of 1965, see the report of the U.S. Civil Rights Commission, *The Voting Rights Act: Ten Years After* (1975); Steven F. Lawson, *In Pursuit of Power: Southern Blacks and Electoral Politics, 1965–1982* (New York: Columbia University, 1985); and the entire issue of *Publius* 16 (1987). On black turnout in the South generally, see Harold W. Stanley, *Voter Mobilization and the Politics of Race* (New York: Praeger, 1987).

Table 8.1   BLACK AND WHITE VOTER REGISTRATION IN THE SOUTH: 1960 AND 1986

State	1960			1986		
	Whites	Blacks	Diff.	Whites	Blacks	Diff.
Alabama	63.6%	13.7%	+ 49.9	77.5%	68.9%	+ 8.6
Arkansas	60.9	38.0	+ 22.9	67.2	57.9	+ 9.3
Florida	69.3	39.4	+ 29.9	66.9	58.2	+ 8.7
Georgia	56.8	29.3	+ 27.5	62.3	52.8	+ 9.5
Louisiana	76.9	31.1	+ 45.8	67.8	60.6	+ 7.2
Mississippi	63.9	5.2	+ 58.7	91.6	70.8	+ 20.8
North Carolina	92.1	39.1	+ 53.0	67.4	58.4	+ 9.0
South Carolina	57.1	13.7	+ 43.4	53.4	52.5	+ 0.9
Tennessee	73.0	59.1	+ 13.9	70.0	65.3	+ 4.7
Texas	42.5	35.5	+ 7.0	79.0	68.0	+ 11.0
Virginia	46.1	23.1	+ 23.0	60.3	56.2	+ 4.1
Total	61.1	29.1	+ 32.0	69.9	60.8	+ 9.1

Note: Table entries are the percentage of each group in that year who are registered to vote. No explanations for the improbably high percentage of registered white adults in North Carolina in 1960 or in Mississippi in 1984 accompanies the data.

Source: For 1960 figures, *Statistical Abstract of the United States (1980)*, p. 514; for 1986 figures, *Statistical Abstract of the United States* (1990), p. 264. All data come from the Voter Education Project, Atlanta, Georgia.

to 29 percent in 1960 on the eve of the massive efforts to protect black voting rights, then surged dramatically to 61 percent in the mid-term elections of 1986—levels that approach those achieved by white southerners. Considerable variation in black registration levels remains among the southern states, however, reflecting their differences in the size and socioeconomic characteristics of their black population, in their political traditions and in the legal and extralegal barriers they raise to black participation (Table 8.1).[17]

A Shifting Frontier

Virtually erased by now is the systematic exclusion of blacks from the electorate by legislation or administrative delay. Significantly, the frontier of discrimination has shifted from preventing black voting to limiting the impact of black votes.

---

[17]See Matthews and Prothro, *Negroes and the New Southern Politics*; H. Douglas Price, *The Negro and Southern Politics* (New York: New York University Press, 1957); David Campbell and Joe R. Feagin, "Black Politics in the South: A Descriptive Analysis," *Journal of Politics* 37 (1975): 129–62 and Lester M. Salamon and Stephen Van Evera, "Fear, Apathy, and Participation," *American Political Science Review* 67 (1973): 1288–1306.

In fact, in the debate over the extension of the 1965 Voting Rights Act in 1981 and 1982, the major issue was the inclination of governmental bodies to dilute black voting power or limit the opportunities for blacks to choose black officeholders by such changes as shifts to at-large local elections, legislative redistricting to divide black voters among a number of districts, or annexation of white suburbs to offset black majorities in the cities or towns. Any such change now must be approved ahead of time, and the Justice Department's basis for rejecting a change was broadened somewhat in 1982.

POLITICAL INFLUENCES ON TURNOUT

Often ignored among external influences on turnout, so manifest are the legal-institutional barriers to voting, is politics itself. Through such features as the level of competition between the parties, the attractiveness of the specific candidates for office, the importance and salience of the electoral contest, and even the organizational abilities of the political parties themselves, voters can be attracted to the polls or repelled by politics. A logical explanation for the considerable variation in turnout levels across constituencies and across years may be found in the variability of our politics.

Inherent Differences in Interest among Elections

The attention and interest of American voters flag as they face the four-year cycle of American politics, and many of them respond only to the elections of greatest prominence. Probably no electorate in the democratic world is more frequently called to the polls than the American electorate. Within four years, it confronts national, state, and local elections for legislative and executive offices (and for the judiciary in a majority of the states), not to mention elections for school boards and assorted other local authorities. Most of these elections are preceded by primaries; and initiatives, referenda, and even an occasional recall election further complicate the calendar. Thus, whereas British voters may go to the polls only twice in a four- or five-year cycle—once for a parliamentary election and once for the election of local officials—civic obligation may call their beleaguered American counterparts to the polls for as many as ten or more primaries and general elections in four years.

Voter participation varies substantially across these different elections. It is generally greatest in presidential elections and smallest in local elections. For each office level, moreover, general elections normally attract far more voters than primaries. The reason for these variations in turnout are not hard to imagine. The more intense general election campaigns for the presidency and the governorships unquestionably spark greater voter interest and involvement. The personalities are well known, and the issues seem more momentous. Furthermore, party fortunes are involved and party loyalties are inflamed—contrary to the case in many nonpartisan local and judicial elections. To put it very simply, one should hardly be surprised that a presidential election in which two national political figures and two national parties engage in a three-month mass-media campaign draws three or four times more voters to the polls than does a nonpartisan judicial campaign in which the candidates talk discreetly and a bit dully of the efficient administration of the courts or a primary for local offices. The wonder perhaps is that it is not eight or ten times the number.[18]

Initiatives and referenda, the Progressives' devices for allowing voters to decide issues and constitutional questions directly, typically elicit much lower levels of participation than ordinary elections. Even when these issues are on the ballot of a regular election, fewer voters choose to vote on them than for the candidates at the top of the ballot. Very possibly, the absence of a personal clash in these questions reduces their interest and immediacy. Perhaps, too, their frequent complexity confuses many would-be voters. Having made these general statements about issue elections, however, we should note that voter turnout for referenda fluctuates greatly. Emotionally charged and relatively clear issues—such as referenda on property taxes, equal rights for homosexuals, or the sale of alcoholic beverages—attract far more voters than esoteric questions of bonding authority or reorganization of state administrative agencies.[19]

Interparty Competition

It should not be surprising that competition in elections heightens voter participation. Turnout is higher in areas where the two parties regularly compete on a fairly even basis—for example, in the states in Table 2.2 that fall into the two-party range.[20] Turnout also tends to be higher in elections that have hotly contested races.[21] This relationship between competition, in its various forms, and turnout appears in contests for a variety of different offices and holds up even when difference in SES characteristics of the electorate and all historical voting trends in the district are held constant. Understandably, voters seem to be stimulated politically by the excitement of closely contested elections and by

[18]For systematic explanations of variations in turnout across the election calendar and for different combinations of contests, see Richard W. Boyd, "Election Calendars and Voter Turnout," *American Politics Quarterly* 14 (1986): 89–104; and "The Effects of Primaries and Statewide Races on Voter Turnout," *Journal of Politics* 51:730–39.

[19]The fall-off in voting for issues is especially pronounced among lower socioeconomic status voters. For an extensive review of voting on ballot propositions, see David B. Magleby, *Direct Legislation: Voting on Ballot Propositions in the United States* (Baltimore: The Johns Hopkins University Press, 1984); and Thomas E. Cronin, *Direct Democracy* (Cambridge: Harvard University Press, 1989).

[20]Jae-On Kim, John R. Petrocik, and Stephen N. Enokson, "Voter Turnout among the American States: Systemic and Individual Components," *American Political Science Review* 69 (1975): 107–23.

[21]Gregory A. Caldeira and Samuel C. Patterson, "Contextual Influences on Participation in U.S. State Legislative Contests," *Legislative Studies Quarterly* 3 (1982): 359–81; Samuel C. Patterson and Gregory A. Caldeira, "Getting Out the Vote: Participation in Gubernatorial Elections," *American Political Science Review* 77 (1983): 675–89; and Gregory A. Caldeira, Samuel C. Patterson, and Gregory A. Markko, "The Mobilization of Voters in Congressional Elections," *Journal of Politics* 47 (1985): 490–509.

the fact that their votes may well affect the outcomes. Conversely, there is little appeal in trying to undo a foregone conclusion.

Historical changes in electoral turnout also have been linked to interparty competition. After the realignment of 1896, participation in presidential elections declined precipitously—from almost 80 percent of the voting age population in prior elections to about 65 percent in the early 1900s. Some scholars have attributed this substantial demise in electoral participation to the effects of the realignment of 1896 on interparty competition. Electoral politics in the two decades before 1900 was fiercely competitive—at the national level where control of government turned on razor thin margins of victory, and in many states and localities as well. The realignment of 1896, these scholars contend, brought an abrupt end to all of this. In the South, the absorption of the Populist movement into the Democratic party in the absence of an effective Republican opposition destroyed every semblance of interparty electoral competition—a result that was reinforced by restrictions on the electorate, black and white, through poll taxes, literacy tests, heightened residency requirements, and various other devices. Outside of the South, the identification of the Democratic party with agrarian populism weakened its appeal, in industrialized areas especially, and turned many areas into GOP monopolies. Even the realignment of the 1930s, while it produced some increases in turnout, was unsuccessful in restoring the highly competitive and participative politics of that earlier era.[22]

Other scholars, though, have challenged this explanation of the turnout declines registered after 1896. They counter that this also was a time of significant changes in the legal definition of the electorate. Not only was the electorate constricted in the South as detailed above, but the introduction of the secret ballot and the tightening of registration requirements throughout the nation, as a part of the Progressive reforms, had the dual effects of reducing election fraud and increasing the effort required to cast a ballot.[23] Reconciling these divergent accounts of the turn-of-the-century turnout declines requires careful detective work with largely circumstantial evidence. The facts are indisputable—electoral competition declined, restrictions on voting increased, and turnout fell. The mystery lies in what the causal relationships were among these events. Even though it may be impossible to reconstruct the causal sequence of events in full, it seems undeniable that the decline in competition produced by the realignment of 1896 reduced turnout to some degree.

---

[22]This thesis is expounded in the work of Walter Dean Burnham. See particularly his "The Changing Shape of the American Political Universe" and "Theory and Voting Research: Some Reflections on Converse's 'Change in the American Electorate,' " *American Political Science Review* 68 (1974): 1002–23. Also see Paul Kleppner, *Who Voted?* (New York: Praeger, 1982).

[23]The challenge to Burnham is raised primarily by Converse, "Change in the American Electorate;" and Jerrold G. Rusk, "The American Electoral Universe: Speculation and Evidence," *American Political Science Review* 68 (1974): 1028–49. The colloquy between Burnham and his critics is continued in this 1974 issue of the *American Political Science Review*; see also later works by Burnham, especially *The Current Crisis in American Politics* (New York: Oxford University Press, 1982), pp. 121–65.

The Representativeness of the Party System

More generally, how effectively the party system gives voice to citizen interests and needs seems to be related to turnout. In European multiparty systems, where each sizable group in the society often is represented by its own party, turnout tends to be much higher than it is in two-party systems where so-called "catch-all" parties contain broad electoral coalitions. One price the United States may pay for its two-party system, then, is lower turnout.[24] Which of the various possible social, economic, and religious conflicts are represented by the dominant party cleavages also affects citizen participation. It should hardly be surprising that those citizens who perceive they have no stake in the prevailing political game refrain from voting.[25]

TURNOUT: THE PERSONAL EQUATION

Turnout can also be explained from the point of view of the individual citizen. He or she bears the burdens and the costs of voting—costs not in cash, but in energy, attention, time, and self-esteem. Indeed, when viewed as the result of a strictly rational calculation of costs and benefits, it is surprising that so many people make the effort to vote when the impact of their single vote seems so small.[26] More generally, it seems that the willingness to bear these burdens and costs is a function of the individual's own motivations—his or her personal political goals, values of civic responsibility (the "good citizen" factor), awareness of political alternatives, and feelings of political effectiveness.

Personal Aversions to Voting

For the nonvoter, the many and varied costs of voting very likely outweigh any total of satisfactions or achievements that the act of voting brings. For some non-voters, the act of voting is often a threatening act. For adults whose political cues are mixed—those, for example, who were raised as Democrats but had

---

[24]At least this is the conclusion reached by scholars who have attempted to explain why American turnout levels are so much lower than those in other democratic nations. See Sidney Verba, Norman H. Nie, and Jae-On Kim, *Participation and Political Equality* (Cambridge: Cambridge University Press, 1978) and Powell, "American Voter Turnout in Comparative Perspective."

[25]Of course, this is why turnout may change as the result of a realignment. For an insightful discussion of how the nature of political conflict affects participation, see E. E. Schattschneider, *The Semi-Sovereign People* (New York: Holt, Rinehart, and Winston, 1960).

[26]From the perspective of strict rationality, some theorists have argued, it is paradoxical that people do vote in a large electorate. On why it may be rational to vote under these conditions, nonetheless, see John A. Ferejohn and Morris P. Fiorina, "The Paradox of Not Voting: A Decision Theoretic Analysis," *American Political Science Review* 68 (1974): 525–36; Carroll B. Foster, "The Performance of Rational Choice Models in Recent Presidential Elections," *American Political Science Review* 78 (1984): 678–90; and Carole J. Uhlaner, "Rational Turnout: The Neglected Role of Groups," *American Journal of Political Science* 33 (1989): 390–422.

Republicanism urged on them by persuasive spouses—the necessity of voting threatens a personal turmoil. Similarly, the uneducated and unsophisticated voter may very well find the imposing facade of the voting machine more than a little intimidating. Some people even refuse to register because the registration rolls are used to choose citizens for duties they want to avoid, such as serving on a jury. And, of course, some nonvoting can be accounted for by unanticipated election day problems such as illness or bad weather (see box).

SES

Explanations for nonvoting due to personal factors begin with an identification of the differences between voters and nonvoters. The principal contrast between them involves socioeconomic status.[27] Lower status Americans are considerably less likely to vote, even more so in recent years. Interestingly, the strong relationship between status and voting participation that occurs in the United States is muted in many other democracies. Outside of the United States it appears that the initial disadvantages of low status can be overcome through a lowering of the costs of voting and a mobilization of lower status citizens by political parties and other electoral organizations.[28]

The most careful study of voting attributes the relationship between status and turnout almost solely to education level, finding that the effects of income and occupation are meager once education is taken into account. According to this study:

> Education . . . does three things. First, it increases cognitive skills, which facilitates learning about politics. Schooling increases one's capacity for understanding and working with complex, abstract, and intangible subjects such as politics. This heightens one's ability to pay attention to politics, to understand politics, and to gather the information necessary for making political choices. . . . Second, better educated people are likely to get more gratification from political participation. They are more likely to have a strong sense of citizen duty, to feel moral pressure to participate, and to receive expressive benefits from voting. Finally, schooling imparts experience with a variety of bureaucratic relationships: learning requirements, filling out forms, and meeting deadlines. This experience helps one overcome the procedural hurdles required first to register and then to vote.[29]

Youth

After SES explanations, the next most powerful personal factor in accounting for differences between voters and nonvoters is youth. For a long time, younger

[27]Sidney Verba and Norman H. Nie, *Participation in America* (New York: Harper and Row, 1972), pp. 125–37.

[28]Verba, Nie, and Kim, *Participation and Political Equality.*

[29]Wolfinger and Rosenstone, *Who Votes?* pp. 35–36.

Excuses for Nonvoting

The advertisement below appeared as a full page in *The New York Times* the day before the 1977 local elections in that city (Monday, November 7, 1977). It carried no title or heading and indeed, it hardly needed one. Barney's is a clothing store in New York City.

THE NEW YORK TIMES, MONDAY NOVEMBER 7, 1977

I only vote for President.
The polls are too far away.
I don't want to be called for jury duty.
I had to work late.
I was too tired when I got home.
It's raining.
I didn't know I had to register.
I have a headache.
I hate making decisions.
Whenever I vote, they lose.
I forgot.
Tuesday's my bowling night.
I hate waiting on lines.
The voting booth gives me claustrophobia.
I didn't know where to vote.
My company doesn't give me off.
I was out of town.
There's no one to watch the kids.
I broke my glasses.
The polls were closed when I got there.
I hate crowds.
The Knicks were playing.
I'm moving anyway.
My car broke down.
Everyone knows who's gonna win.
I had a doctor's appointment.
When was the election?
I already voted in the primaries.
I had to study for a test.
It was my vacation day.
My vote won't make the difference.

A collection of the classics from Barney's.

Polls will be open tomorrow from 6:00 AM to 9:00 PM

Courtesy of Barney's, New York.

Table 8.2   PERSONAL CHARACTERISTICS AND VOTER TURN-
OUT: 1988

	Percentage Voting	
	Michigan	US Census
Education		
No high school degree	50%	39%
High school graduate	62	55
Attended college	85	71
Gender		
Females	68	58
Males	72	56
Race		
Blacks	60	52
Whites	72	59
Years of age		
Under 35	56	40
35 or more	76	66
Party identification		
Strong Democrats	80	N.A.
Weak Democrats	63	N.A.
Independents closer to Democrats	64	N.A.
Independents	50	N.A.
Independents closer to Republicans	64	N.A.
Weak Republicans	76	N.A.
Strong Republicans	89	N.A.
Interest in politics		
Very Much	89	N.A.
Somewhat	72	N.A.
Not much	36	N.A.

Note: Table entries in the Michigan column are the percentage of each group
from the Michigan sample who were recorded as having voted in the 1988 presidential election in the official records. Table entries in the U.S. Census column
are the self-reported turnout for each group in the 1988 Current Population Survey conducted by the U.S. Census Bureau. N.A. means not ascertained.

Source: Center for Political Studies, University of Michigan; data made avail-
able through the Inter-University Consortium for Political and Social Research.
The census study data are derived from the *Statistical Abstract of the United
States: 1990* (Washington, D.C., 1990).

Americans have voted at rates well below the average. This tendency is largely
attributable to the high "start up" costs the young must pay—the difficulties of
settling into a community, registering for the first time, and establishing the
habit of voting, all at a time when other, more personal interests dominate their
lives.[30] The lowering of the national voting age to eighteen in 1971 and the entry

---

[30]Verba and Nie, *Participation in America*, pp. 145–47.

of the unusually large "baby boom" generation into the electorate magnified the impact of youthful nonvoting well into the 1980s.

Other Factors

Education and age have not been the only important difference between voters and nonvoters (Table 8.2). For many decades after their enfranchisement in 1920, women voted less frequently than men. With the changes of recent decades in the role of women in society and their growing education levels, especially among the youngest generations, though, that difference has disappeared. Traditionally, too, blacks have been less likely to vote than whites, a gap that has narrowed but still persists into the most recent elections. But whites on the average have considerably more education and higher status than blacks, and differences in turnout between the races vanish if status differences are taken into account.[31] Voters and nonvoters also are clearly differentiated, quite unsurprisingly, by basic interest in politics.

THE PUZZLE OF DECLINING VOTER TURNOUT

Since 1960, turnout in presidential elections has fallen off considerably—and, after 1966, so did turnout in congressional elections. In some respects, this has been a puzzling change because it occurred in the face of powerful forces working in the opposite direction—to increase turnout levels. Southern blacks won much greater access to the ballot and voted in increasing numbers after 1960. Southern whites, stimulated in part by the presence of blacks at the polls, increased their turnout levels as well. Throughout the nation, restrictive residency and registration requirements were lifted, vastly reducing the costs of voting. The generation of women who had come of voting age in an earlier era, when women did not vote, shrank in size and was replaced by a new generation for whom voting was unquestionably consistent with their expected role. Finally, the educational levels of the electorate rose enormously, as the percentage of the population continuing on to college doubled in a generation. Yet, in spite of all of these boons for turnout, it declined overall—although, significantly, only outside of the South![32]

Some of this change may be attributed to such personal factors as the greater percentage of young adults in the electorate and increases in residential mobility. Declining turnout also is heavily concentrated among the least educated groups in the American electorate. But the largest role in the change is played by two political attitudes—party loyalties and beliefs that government is

---

[31]Lawrence Bobo and Franklin D. Gilliam, Jr., "Race, Sociopolitical Participation, and Black Empowerment," *American Political Science Review* 84 (1990): 377–94.

[32]See Richard A. Brody, "The Puzzle of Participation in America," in Anthony King (ed.), *The New American Political System* (Washington, D.C.: American Enterprise Institute, 1978), pp. 287–324.

Table 8.3   VOTING PARTICIPATION AMONG CATEGORIES OF PARTISAN
STRENGTH AND EXTERNAL POLITICAL EFFICACY: 1988

External Political Efficacy	Strong Partisans	Weak Partisans	Independents Closer to Party	Independents
High	81%	67	64	66
Medium	72	63	63	37
Low	60	48	44	29

Note: Table entries are the percentage of each combined efficacy-partisan group from the Michigan surveys who were recorded in the official records as having voted in the presidential election.

Source: Paul R. Abramson, John H. Aldrich, and David W. Rohde, *Change and Continuity in the 1988 Elections* (Washington, D.C.: CQ Press, 1990), p. 105; Data from Center for Political Studies, University of Michigan.

responsive to its citizens, or what is called external (because its source is external to the individual) political efficacy. Both partisanship and efficacy decreased substantially after 1960, especially through 1980. Because turnout falls off with each step decrease in partisanship and efficacy, as the levels of partisanship and efficacy in the electorate decrease, turnout decreases. Each contributed separately to the turnout declines from 1960 through 1988, with efficacy accounting for more than three times as much of the change as partisanship among whites. Their combined effects were even stronger (Table 8.3).[33]

Many thoughtful Americans are troubled by these low levels of voting participation and have proposed various measures to stimulate higher turnouts. Their focus typically has been placed on eliminating the legal and administrative barriers to voting—in other words, on reducing its cost. After all, these restrictions are easier to reform than the psyches and attitudes of individuals or the nature of politics.

Nonetheless, it is important not to overlook the remedies for nonvoting that can be used by the parties and other political organizations. Individuals otherwise not inclined to vote can be mobilized into voting. When political party organizations flowered in the wards and precincts of America, one of their major activities was the registering of new voters and the turning out of all voters on election day. Organized labor has spent millions of dollars in the past forty or fifty years doing the same thing. In recent years, several groups have conducted registration drives that have added large numbers of previous non-voters to the rolls. Efforts by the Voter Education Project and other civil rights organizations have registered millions of southern blacks since the 1960s. Similar efforts have

[33]This discussion is based upon Paul R. Abramson and John H. Aldrich, "The Decline of Electoral Participation in America," *American Political Science Review* 76 (1982): 502–21; and Paul R. Abramson, John H. Aldrich, and David W. Rohde, *Change and Continuity in the 1988 Election* (Washington, D.C.: CQ Press, 1990), pp. 103–107. See also Ruy A. Teixeira, *Why Americans Don't Vote: Turnout Decline in the United States, 1960–1984* (New York: Greenwood Press, 1987).

A NEW FOCUS OF REFORM: ATTEMPTS TO INCREASE VOTER TURNOUT

A century ago, political reformers (mostly Progressives) who were concerned with eliminating electoral fraud and dishonesty instituted personal registration requirements that had the effect of making it more difficult for people to register and vote. Today, driven by concern over sinking turnout levels, reformers are taking the opposite tack.

Proposals to require the states to provide voter registration forms as a part of the application for drivers' licenses (the so-called "motor voter" bill), to permit mail registration, and to have the filing of post office change-of-address cards also initiate reregistration at the new address have received serious consideration in Congress. Moreover, some states have adopted innovative techniques to make voting easier. In Texas, people now can vote at special sites up to twenty days before election day. In Ohio, those who have recently moved can vote at the board of elections offices in each county. In California and several other states, absentee ballots now are distributed without question to anyone who requests one. (Previously, people had to justify why they could not go to the polls on election day before being allowed to vote absentee.) The city of San Diego even conducted a referendum by mail. Whether these various provisions have added many new voters to the rolls or merely made it easier for habitual voters, however, is uncertain.

---

been made with Hispanics by the Southwest Voter Registration and Education Project. In the 1980s, fundamentalist organizations enrolled many conservative Christians who had not participated before. With the flow of political party money to grass roots organizing in recent years, the political parties have stepped up the pace of their mobilizing efforts. Existing evidence suggests that those enrolled through registration drives are less likely to vote in both the immediate and future elections than are the self-registered, but organized attempts to stimulate voting have succeeded in overcoming the margins of citizen apathy, especially for voters new to the political system.[34]

CONSEQUENCES FOR THE POLITICAL PARTIES

The American parties must operate, therefore, within an American electorate that is never a sample either of the full American adult population or of that

---

[34]On the effectiveness of registration drives, see Bruce E. Cain and Ken McCue, "The Efficacy of Registration Drives," *Journal of Politics* 47 (1985): 1221–30; Arnold Vedlitz, "Voter Registration Drives and Black Voting in the South," *Journal of Politics* 47 (1985): 643–51; and Piven and Cloward, *Why Americans Don't Vote*, Chap. 6.

segment of it eligible to vote and one that constantly shifts in size and composition. Much of the strategy of the parties in pursuing their goals, especially the contesting of elections, must take account of those facts.

Long-Range Consequences

The long-run consequences for the parties of changes in the electorate spring from basic changes in its legal definitions. Since electorates in democracies usually expand rather than contract, the changes most often result from the addition of new groups to the eligible electorate. Most recently, the American parties have absorbed two major groups: previously disenfranchised American blacks and young citizens between eighteen and twenty-one. With the flood of Hispanic immigrants in recent years and the amnesty for illegal aliens in the 1986 immigration reform law, the need to absorb a third major group less than a third of which voted in 1988 clearly is on the horizon.

The effects of these newly enfranchised groups on the parties have been substantial. Blacks have flowed into the Democratic party: three-quarters of them identify as Democrats, and in each presidential election since 1964 more than 80 percent have given their vote to the Democratic candidate. The mobilization of blacks has been a mixed blessing for the party, though, because it seems to have triggered a countermovement of whites, particularly in the South, away from the Democrats.[35] The impact of young voters entering the electorate in recent years is more complex. In the first few years after the voting age was reduced to eighteen, the newly-of-age voters exhibited more pro-Democratic than pro-Republican dispositions. By 1984 and 1988, however, the youngest voters had become more favorable toward the Republicans. These youth seem to have been more responsive to the short-term forces of a particular election setting than to any fundamental appeals of the parties.[36]

Long-range consequences for the parties also stem from changes in the composition and distribution, rather than the size, of the American electorate. Population growth and migration are a case in point. The parties of ten states— Alaska, Arizona, California, Florida, Georgia, New Hampshire, New Mexico, Nevada, Texas, and Utah—have faced increases in state populations in excess of 20 percent between the 1980 and 1990 censuses. Similarly, the aging of the American population has enlarged the group of over-sixty-five voters in each successive presidential election. These shifts and growths are differential: the groups (and their goals) added in each case are not a representative sample of

---

[35]On this point, see Edward G. Carmines and James A. Stimson, *Issue Evolution* (Princeton, N.J.: Princeton University Press, 1989).

[36]The partisan behavior of young voters is tracked through ten years of CBS News/*New York Times* polls by Helmut Norpoth and Michael R. Kagay, "Another Eight Years of Republican Rule and Still No Partisan Realignment?" Paper delivered at the 1989 Annual Meeting of the American Political Science Association, Atlanta.

the entire American electorate. Change in the electorate of any magnitude necessitates a party response if the parties are to preserve, much less enhance, their standing.

The long-term standing of the parties also is affected by the difference between the potential and actual electorates. There were about 60 million adults of voting age in 1988 who were not registered to vote—whether for reasons of disqualification or their own unconcern. Those adults are widely considered more likely recruits for the Democratic party than for the Republicans because of their lower SES characteristics. Therefore, legislation that would expand the electorate—by permitting registration at the polls, for instance, or by making illegal aliens eligible for citizenship and thus for the suffrage—probably would benefit the Democrats, although perhaps not the Democratic party as it is presently constituted. The addition of large numbers of new Democrats—who are likely to be poorer and less educated, and maybe even from different ethnic backgrounds, than current Democratic voters—would alter the nature of that party's electoral base.

The most basic of all the consequences of voting and nonvoting concerns the distribution of political influence in the American political system. Citizens who fail to register or vote deny themselves a potent voice in American politics, and the implications of that loss are all the more serious when the nonvoters differ markedly from the voters. Reduced levels of turnout among low status Americans likely limit the attention elected officials will pay to their needs and concerns. To some degree, then, increases in the marginalization of the disadvantaged in American society may be attributable to their failure to participate in the electoral process.[37]

Yet this observation must be tempered by the finding of Wolfinger and Rosenstone that nonvoters, despite their social backgrounds, tend not to have very different views on the issues from those of voters.[38] What their political views and goals might be if they were mobilized into the American electorate is the fundamental question, however, and on that point scholars are of necessity reduced to speculation.

Short-Range Consequences

In addition to the long-range consequences of changes in the basic structure of the eligible electorate, the political parties must react to the short-range consequences of changes in turnout from election to election. Since increases or decreases in turnout are unlikely to benefit all parties and candidates equally—

[37]On this point, see Verba and Nie, *Participation in America*, Part III; and Stephen Earl Bennett and David Resnick, "The Implications of Nonvoting for Democracy in the United States," *American Journal of Political Science* 34 (1990): 771–802.

[38]Wolfinger and Rosenstone, *Who Votes?*, Chap. 6.

because nonvoters as a group have different political characteristics from voters—these changes too, have potent political consequences. The increasing or decreasing of voter turnout and the exploiting of variations in turnout between various elections frequently become focal points in party strategy.

The conventional wisdom has it that big turnouts favor the Democrats. There is little room to quarrel with the underlying logic of that maxim. The greatest percentage of nonvoters in the United States comes from groups ordinarily disposed to the Democratic party. It is for this reason that effective registration or get-out-the-vote campaigns are thought to help the Democrats more often than not. The maxim explains the money and manpower that organized labor spends in registration campaigns. It explains the ancillary maxim that rainy weather is Republican weather. It also suggests why, in some states Republicans prefer an electoral calendar in which the gubernatorial elections are held in the nonpresidential years and therefore in a smaller electorate that is a bit more favorable to Republican candidates.

Despite the general appeal of the maxim linking big turnouts with the Democrats, the relationship is more subtle and complicated than that—particularly because it fails to take the one-sided nature of defections from party among peripherally-involved voters into account. Three of the last five presidential elections with turnouts exceeding 60 percent—in 1952, 1956, and 1968—were won by the Republican, and in recent years Republicans have fared better in presidential election years than in mid-term elections. Especially since nonvoters are less partisan, they also may be more responsive to the momentary, dramatic appeal of issue or candidate. Since 1952, in fact, Republican candidates have been favored among nonvoters in four of the ten presidential contests, including those in 1984 and 1988 (Table 8.4)[39]

Party strategists cannot fail to consider the likely voting electorate as they prepare their campaigns. They nourish the often fragile hope that turnouts can be affected selectively and differentially, and they attempt, therefore, to mold the size and makeup of the participating electorate itself in the campaign. When they must contest a primary election, they may hope by discreet and selective campaigning to minimize the turnout—for (generally) the smaller the turnout, the larger will be the proportion of it accounted for by the party's most loyal electorate. In general elections, the strategists may try to concentrate campaigns in areas of known party strength, thus maximizing that turnout. Individuals planning a congressional career always confront the fact that they will seek reelection by different electorates in alternate elections—the large turnout of the presidential election followed by the smaller turnout of the mid-term elections two years later—as well as in their party's primary and general election.

---

[39]For a similar analysis, see James DeNardo, "Turnout and the Vote: The Joke's on the Democrats," *American Political Science Review* 74 (1980): 406–20; and the exchange between DeNardo and Harvey J. Tucker and Arnold Vedlitz, "Does Heavy Turnout Help Democrats in Presidential Elections?" *American Political Science Review* 80 (1986): 1291–1304.

Table 8.4   PRESIDENTIAL CANDIDATE PREFERENCES OF NONVOTERS: 1952–88

	1952	1956	1960	1964	1968	1972	1976	1980	1984	1988
Would have voted Democratic	52%	28%	51%	80%	45%	35%	57%	47%	39%	45%
Would have voted Republican	48	72	49	20	41	65	43	45	61	55
	100%	100%	100%	100%	86%	100%	100%	92%	100%	100%

Note: The figures in 1968 and 1980 add to less than 100 percent because some nonvoters preferred the third-party candidate Wallace in 1968 and the independent Anderson in 1980.

Source: Angus Campbell *et al., The American Voter* (New York: Wiley, 1960), p. 111, and, since 1960, Campbell's table has been updated by survey data from the University of Michigan's Center for Political Studies made available by the Inter-University Consortium in Political and Social Research.

THE BROADER ISSUES

The democratic ethos assumes the desirability of full popular participation in the affairs of democratic self-government. The case for democracy itself rests on the wisdom of the widest possible sharing of political power and political decision making within the society. It is precisely this ethos that is offended by the relatively low voting percentages of American adults. The affront to the democratic ethos seems all the greater in view of the fact that voting percentages are higher in most other democracies and in countries that Americans would like to think have less stable and responsive democracies.

Widespread nonvoting also casts some doubt on the effectiveness with which the political parties—the political organizations primarily concerned with contesting elections—manage to involve the total eligible electorate. Presumably, the parties, heralded so often as the instruments of democratic politics, should maximize political participation in the American society. The political parties themselves are, after all, the political organizations that developed to mobilize the new democratic masses. All of their capabilities are directed to recruiting large political aggregates, and much of the case for their superiority as political organizations rests on that ability.

Clearly, the record of the parties in mobilizing and involving the American electorate is mixed. We can cite examples of effective competition for the support of new groups entering the electorate. Even so, the hands of the parties are not completely clean. They often appear not to relish the challenges of new voters, especially those of low status. The experience of political power has made them (especially their parties in government) sympathetic to the comfortable status quo of two-party competition. They do not welcome the uncertainties that a radical alteration in the electorate would bring. The party in government, which will have to make the changes in the formal definition of the electorate, has won office with the support of the electorate as it now exists, and it is understandably not anxious to alter it greatly.

All in all, the American parties work within a somewhat homogeneous active electorate. That electorate reduces the totality of political conflict and the range of political interests to which the parties must respond. The parties find it easier to be moderate and pragmatic because the electorate to which they respond is largely settled in and committed to the present basic social arrangements. Compromise and tactical movement come more easily when the effective electorate is homogeneous and agrees on fundamentals. In brief, although it has been fashionable to say that the moderate, pragmatic, nondoctrinaire American parties are the result of an electorate that agrees on the fundamental questions, it is probably also true that the pragmatic, majoritarian parties in a two-party system do not easily draw into their ambit the low-status, alienated, dissident individuals who are not a part of that moderate consensus. In a predominantly middle-class society, that may be the price of a two-party system.

Of course some devotees of political democracy may be comfortable about paying that price. They fear the dilution in the quality of voting that might come from the sudden influx of an army of uninformed new voters into the active electorate. The annals of history also contain sobering examples of extremist movements such as the German Nazi's in the 1920s and 1930s, which have rejected the norms of civility and tolerance for minority opinion on which democracy rests, that were fueled by the fears and resentments of the previously uninvolved. Thus, democracy itself is seen to be threatened by the mobilization of large numbers of new voters. Even though other western democracies with fuller electorates seem to have avoided such problems in modern times, the possibility that an enlargement of the American electorate might erode the very foundations of political democracy can not be entirely dismissed. How this concern can be reconciled with the primacy of participation in the democratic ethos is one of the perplexing normative issues of our time.

THE POLITICAL PARTIES IN THE ELECTORAL PROCESS

Separate treatment of the party organization, the party in the electorate, and the party in government obscures the very real and important interactions among these different parts of the party at key moments of American party politics. At no time is this interaction more visible than in the role the parties play in the electoral process.

The party organization, the party electorate, and the elected officials and candidates wearing the party label all contribute to the selection of the candidates for office—to an extent unrivaled in the other democracies. Both the struggles among the various parts of the party to secure their preferences and the momentary reconciliation of these differences in uniting around the party nominees are contained within the American candidate selection process. Once a candidate is chosen, the various parts of the party also combine, albeit not always smoothly or wholeheartedly, their efforts in the ensuing campaign. American political campaigns always have been more candidate-centered than most, but the party organizations play important roles in mobilizing support across the party ticket.

The contesting of elections unites the American parties in yet another crucial way. However briefly, it overcomes their decentralized and fragmented character. The choice of a presidential candidate and the following campaign bind the state and local parties into a fleeting coalition with the national party. A statewide election similarly focuses the activities and energies of local organizations and leaders within the state. It is these joint ventures that introduce the primary centripetal tendencies into an otherwise decentralized party system.

The pursuit of victory in elections unites the party for a number of reasons. The election is the event that elevates the business of politics to a visibility that stimulates even the less concerned members of the electorate. The candidates personify and simplify the difficult choices of American politics. Furthermore, the recruitment of resources for the party organization depends on the party's establishment of the likelihood, or at least the possibility, of electoral victory. In the long run, the incentives that lure resources to the party flow only to those parties that win. Electoral victory is a critical condition for the patronage, the triumph of an interest or an ideology, and the social and psychological rewards that motivate involvement.

Since the American parties are parties that must win elections, they must mobilize majorities in the electorate. The conventional references to the American parties as electoral parties are, however, a little too glib and hackneyed. For one thing, these references imply that the parties carry out their electoral activities with ease. To the contrary, the party organizations find it difficult to control the selection of candidates, to take stands on issues, to fix campaign strategies, even to raise money. Those aspects of election politics are controlled, in the name of the whole party, by its candidates—its party in government and the candidates hoping to join it—and the candidates themselves are not always the choices of the organization.[1] Increasingly, it is these party candidates who have organized their own campaigns, recruited their own workers, hired their own campaign advice, and raised their own campaign funds. If it is true that the party in government controls the central, most visible activities of the party (at the expense of a frustrated party organization), can the party organizations reasonably achieve the goals set by their activists?

At the same time that the party stages an internal competition over the control of its electoral strategies, it also faces the competition of other political organizations. They increasingly seek their political goals in the electoral process. Over the past twenty years, the nonparty political organizations have played aggressive, overt roles in the nomination and election of candidates. It is not uncommon now to see accounts of the electoral activities of trade unions, candidate organizations, public relations firms, reform groups, and political action committees.

The continuing contest for influence in American electoral politics raises questions about the very role and viability of the parties. The outcomes of the competition for the election role within the parties and between parties and other political organizations determine, in great measure, what the parties are and what they do in the political system.

---

[1]In recent years, Louisiana has broken the tradition of separate nomination and election steps. For races other than those for the presidency, it now holds a single election. All candidates of all parties run in it and are designated by party on the ballot. If one candidate wins a majority of the vote, he or she is elected to the office. If not, the top two candidates, regardless of their party, face each other in a runoff election.

Throughout the coming chapters there also runs a related theme: the impact of political institutions on the nature of the parties. Nowhere are the effects of political institutions on the parties clearer than in the electoral process. The direct primary, for example, touches every attempt the parties make to control the nomination of candidates. In fact, it is the primary that so often turns the control of nominations from the party organization to the candidates themselves or to other political organizations. In so doing, it has changed the very nature of American electoral and party politics.

The chapters of this section, therefore, take a temporary detour from our focus on the separate parts of the party to deal with the interrelationship among these parts as the parties participate in the electoral process. This is the process that produces the government, so full treatment of the party in government naturally is reserved for the following section. But members of the party in government of course are deeply involved in the electoral process and will appear as prime players in the next several chapters.

The parties are involved at two points in the electoral process. First, the parties nominate the candidates for office who will carry the party label. The process of nomination will constitute a major focus of this section in terms of both its general nature and the fascinating and peculiar practices through which the parties select their presidential candidates. So complex and controversial, and so obviously important for American politics, is the presidential nomination process that we will devote two full chapters to its consideration. The second point of party involvement in the electoral process comes in the contesting of the general election. The electoral campaign and the party's multifaceted role within it, therefore, will be the topic of another chapter.

The final chapter of Part IV discusses the key resource for the contesting of elections at all levels—money. Campaign money has come to pay an increasingly important and controversial role in the American electoral process. Amidst extensive efforts to reform campaign financing practices, the inexorable quest for dollars to run campaigns continues. A focus on the role of money highlights what the parties do and what they do not do in electoral campaigns—and how this affects the place of parties in the electoral process.

Chapter
9

The Naming of the
Party Candidates

Few Americans realize that the American system of nominating candidates for office, with its dependence upon primary elections in which ordinary citizens rather than party leaders select the party's candidates, is unique. Having devised the direct primary and adopted it almost universally for the nomination of candidates, they seem unaware that the rest of the democratic world uses a very different method—placing the choice of the party's candidates in the hands of party activists or the party's elected officials. No other single factor goes so far to explain the differences between American party politics and those of the other Western nations as their contrasting methods for nomination. The direct primary has forced upon the American parties a different set of strategies in making nominations, in contesting elections, and in attempting eventually to maintain responsibility over their successful candidates in office.

In the irresistible advance of the direct primary in the twentieth century, no state has been untouched. The great majority of states employ it in all nominations, and the rest use it in most. It has even now been adopted by most states in the presidential nomination process (see Chapter 10). For the present, it suffices to say that by the direct primary (or, more simply, the primary), we mean a special election in which the party electorate, variously defined, chooses candidates to run for public office under the party label. At a subsequent general election, the total electorate then makes the final choice from among the nominees of the parties.

Even though the nomination does not formally settle the electoral outcome, its importance is great. The major screening of candidates takes place at the nomination; the choice is reduced to two in most constituencies. Especially in areas of one-party domination, the real choice is made at the primary. Moreover, the nominees of the party bring their images and visibility, their priorities and positions on issues, to the party. In the eyes of many voters, they *are* the party. Their quality and ability also determine, to a considerable extent, the party's chance for victory in the general election.

ADVENT OF THE DIRECT PRIMARY

The almost universal reliance upon the direct primary for the selection of party candidates in the United States is an achievement of the twentieth century. For the first 110 years of the Republic, first the party caucus and then the party convention dominated the nomination of candidates for public office. Each gave way successively under the criticism that it permitted, if not encouraged, the making of nominations by self-chosen and often irresponsible party elites. Finally, early in the twentieth century, the primary triumphed on the belief that the greatest possible number of party members ought to take part in the nomination of the party's candidates. This triumph became complete only in the 1970s, when a majority of states turned to primaries in the selection of party candidates for president.

The Caucus Method

Formal systems of nomination developed in the United States along with and as a part of the development of the party system. In fact, parties as parties (rather than as legislative associations) developed and evolved largely as nominators of candidates for public office. In the early years of the Republic, local caucuses met to select candidates; and frequently, caucuses of like-minded partisans in legislatures met to nominate candidates for governorships and other statewide offices. Similar congressional caucuses met to nominate presidential and vice-presidential candidates. Whatever their form, the caucuses were self-selected. There was no machinery, no procedure for ensuring even the participation of all the major figures in the party.

The Convention System

The caucus method of nomination could not withstand the spread of the democratic ethos. "King Caucus" was an inviting target for the Jacksonians, who attacked it as an aristocratic device that thwarted popular wishes. In 1832, the Jacksonian Democrats met in a national convention for the first time and, appropriately, nominated Andrew Jackson for the presidency. From then on, the convention system quickly triumphed along with Jacksonian popular democracy, whose values it shared. It dominated the making of nominations for the rest of the nineteenth century. Broadly representative at its best, the nominating convention was composed of delegates chosen by state and especially local party leaders. Even though they were representative in form, however, the large and chaotic conventions were scarcely that in reality. Both in the picking of delegates and in the management of the conventions, the fine, guiding hands of party leaders were too obvious and oppressive. Party insurgents, unhappy with bossism at the conventions and with the alliance of the bosses and "the interests," belabored the convention system with considerable fervor and cun-

---

La Follette and the Primary

No one has captured the rhetoric and fervor of the movement for the direct primary as well as its leader, Robert M. La Follette, governor and then United States senator from Wisconsin. Writing in his autobiography, in the chapter "Struggle with the Bosses," La Follette reports a speech of his in February 1897 at the University of Chicago. Here are some excerpts from its conclusion:

> Put aside the caucus and convention. They have been and will continue to be prostituted to the service of corrupt organizations. They answer no purpose further than to give respectable form to political robbery. Abolish the caucus and the convention. Go back to the first principles of democracy; go back to the people. Substitute for both the caucus and the convention a primary election . . . where the citizen may cast his vote directly to nominate the candidate of the party with which he affiliates. . . . The nomination of the party will not be the result of "compromise" or impulse, or evil design—the "barrel" and the machine—but the candidates of the majority, honestly and fairly nominated.

> ROBERT M. LA FOLLETTE,
> *La Follette's Autobiography*
> (Madison: R. M. La Follette,
> 1913), pp. 197–98.

---

ning. The Progressives led the anti-convention movement, and their journalistic allies, the muckrakers, furnished the often shocking, often piquant, corroborative details.[1]

The Direct Primary

The cure offered by the Progressives—the direct primary—comported easily with their democratic norms. It was an article of faith among them that to cure the ills of democracy, one needed only to prescribe larger doses of democracy. Appropriately, it was one of progressivism's high priests, Robert M. La Follette, who authored the country's first statewide primary law in Wisconsin in 1902 (see box). Some southern states had adopted primaries at the local level in the years after the Civil War, but in the first two decades of the twentieth century, all but four states turned to them statewide for at least some of their nominations.

---

[1] For the story of the convention system and the early years of the direct primary, see Charles E. Merriam and Louise Overacker, *Primary Elections* (Chicago: University of Chicago Press, 1928). For a discussion of the spread of the direct primary at the local level in the South, see V. O. Key, Jr., *American State Politics: An Introduction* (New York: Knopf, 1956), pp. 87–97.

Although the primary was designed to reform the nominating processes by "democratization," many of its supporters saw in it an instrument for crippling the political party itself. For them, the primary was an attempt to cut back the power of the parties by striking at their chief activity as a party organization: the nomination of candidates. Party leaders had done the nominating under the caucus and convention systems, but primaries took from them the control of who would run under the party name and symbols by vesting the power to nominate in a broad party electorate. Extending this principle to its logical extreme, some states such as Wisconsin adopted so permissive a definition of the party electorate that it included any voters who chose to vote in the party's primary on election day. Regardless of the motives of the enactors of the primary laws, there is little doubt that the laws badly hurt the power of party organizations. Not only did they greatly circumscribe the influence of party leaders on nominations, but they also opened up the party to possible penetration of its top leadership echelons by officeholders without any loyalty to the party organization or party principles. Largely because of the existence of primaries, party leaders have less control over who will receive the party nomination in the United States than in other democratic political systems.

The quick success of the direct primary happened during the years of the greatest one-partyism in American history immediately following the realignment of 1896. In the early years of the twentieth century, sectionalism was pervasive, and one party or the other dominated the politics of many states. One-partyism made the nomination of the dominant party crucial. Although the failings of the conventions might be tolerated when a real choice remained in the general election, they were more difficult to bear when the nomination of one party was equivalent to election. The convention could choose the weariest party hack without fear of challenge from the other party. Thus, the Progressives, who fought economic monopoly with antitrust legislation, fought political monopoly with the direct primary.

THE PRESENT MIX OF PRIMARY AND CONVENTION

The convention as a device for nominating candidates has faded in the face of the democratic appeal of the direct primary. Decline has not meant death, however, and the convention as a nominating device lingers in a few states, most conspicuously in the contest for the presidency.[2] Because the legal authority for devising nomination practices resides with the states, the result is a mosaic of primary and convention methods for choosing candidates for state offices.

All fifty states now provide for the nomination of statewide officials through the direct primary, and thirty-eight of them (and the District of Columbia) use

---

[2]The methods for selecting delegates to the national nominating conventions (hence, of nominating the presidential candidates) also vary across the states, but, as we shall see, they are not always the same as the methods employed for choosing party nominees for statewide office.

this method exclusively. Two more require its use for major party nominations but mandate conventions for minor parties. In another two states, the state party committees may choose to hold a convention instead of a primary.

Some combination of convention and primary is employed in the remaining eight states. Iowa provides for a convention when no candidate in the primary has won at least 35 percent of the vote. Three additional states (Illinois, Indiana, and Michigan) use alternative methods for different offices. Finally, four states use the convention to screen candidates for the primary ballot. Connecticut employs a challenge primary in which the convention's choice may be challenged in the primary by candidates who received at least 20 percent of the convention vote. Colorado and Massachusetts restrict access to the primary ballot to those candidates who polled 20 and 15 percent, respectively, of convention votes. Utah slots the top two convention vote-getters in its primary, with the provision that a candidate winning 70 percent of the convention vote is automatically the party nominee.[3]

VARIETIES OF THE DIRECT PRIMARY

Even though there are multiple varieties in the criteria for eligibility to participate in state primary elections, the basic distinctions boil down to three. In the states with so-called "closed" primaries, only voters who have publicly expressed party allegiance are able to participate. In states with "open" primaries, public expression of party allegiance is not a requirement for participation. Voters can decide in which party's primary to participate in the privacy of the voting booth. Finally, a few states with "blanket" primaries allow voters to choose from among all the candidates for office, Democratic and Republican— in effect not restricting voters to the nomination contests of a single party.[4]

The Closed Primary

The closed primary—found in thirty-eight states and the District of Columbia—requires voters to publicly declare their party affiliation before they can vote in that party's primary. In most of these states, voters specify their party affiliation when they register in advance of the election. Then, at the primary election, they are given only the primary ballot of their party so that they may choose among their fellow partisans who seek nomination. They may always

[3]*The Book of the States 1990–91* (Lexington, Ky.: The Council of State Governments, 1990), pp. 234–35; and Malcolm E. Jewell and David M. Olson, *Political Parties and Elections in American States* (Chicago: Dorsey, 1988), pp. 94–97.

[4]For an account of variations within these broad categories, see Craig L. Carr and Gary L. Scott, "The Logic of State Primary Classification Schemes," *American Politics Quarterly* 12 (1984): 465–76; and Steven E. Finkel and Howard A. Scarrow, "Party Identification and Party Enrollment: The Difference and the Consequence," *Journal of Politics* 47 (1985): 620–52.

change their party affiliation on the registration rolls, but most states require that this be done sometime ahead of the date of the primary. A few states permit a change of party registration at the polls.

In the other closed primary states, voters simply declare their party "membership"—or, more accurately, their party attachments or preferences—when they go to the polling place. They are then given the primary ballot of their party. In some states, their declarations can be challenged by one of the party observers at the polls; they may then be required to take an oath of party loyalty. Some states require voters to affirm that they have voted for the candidates of the party in the past; some demand that they declare themselves sympathetic at the moment to the candidates and principles of the party; and others ask nothing at all. These latter provisions make it possible for independents to participate in party primaries.

The Open Primary

In the nine states of the open primary—Hawaii, Idaho, Michigan, Minnesota, Montana, North Dakota, Utah, Vermont, and Wisconsin—the voter votes in the primary without disclosing any party affiliation or preference.[5] On entering the polling booth, voters are given either ballots for every party (one of which is selected in the privacy of the booth) or a consolidated ballot on which the part with the party of the voter's choice is selected. A voter may not, however, participate in the primary of more than one party.

The Blanket Primary

The blanket primary—found in Alaska, Louisiana, and Washington—goes one step in freedom beyond the open primary. Not only do the voters not need to disclose any party affiliation, but they are free to vote in the primary of more than one party; that is, they may choose a Democrat for one office and a Republican for another. Louisiana's version of the blanket primary, called by some the unitary primary, goes beyond this in two respects. Any candidate who wins a majority of votes in the primary is elected to the office. If no candidate wins an outright majority, then the general election serves as a runoff between the top two vote-getters regardless of party (see box).

Among these forms of primaries, the party organizations clearly prefer the closed primary with party registration prior to the primary. It pays greater respect to the right of the party itself to make nominations by limiting the party's primary electorate to voters willing to make a public declaration of party loyalty

---

[5]The Republican party's challenge primary in Connecticut also can be opened to independents as the result of a 1986 Supreme Court decision (Tashjian v. Republican Party of Connecticut, 106 S.Ct. 783 and 1257) which upheld the party's attempts to override the state's closed primary law. This decision affirms the authority of the party, rather than the state, to control its own nomination process and clears the way for other state parties to turn to open primaries if they wish.

David Duke and the Louisiana Blanket Primary

The operations of the Louisiana blanket primary system—as well as the dilemma posed to a party when it can not control its own nominations—can be illustrated by the state's 1990 U.S. Senate election. This contest received national attention because one of the contestants was former Ku Klux Klan leader and American Nazi party member David Duke, who had been spurned by Republican leaders in his successful campaign for a state legislative seat in 1989.

The five major-party candidates who vied for votes in the October Senate primary included incumbent Democrat J. Bennett Johnston, Republican state senator Ben Bagert, and Duke. Bagert carried the endorsement of prominent Republican party leaders, including President George Bush, and had received considerable financial support from the party. On the eve of the election, however, public opinion polls showed that Duke was running second to Johnston and might even receive enough votes to deny Johnston the majority required to win the election outright, thus necessitating a run-off between Democrat Johnston and Republican Duke and further embarrassing the GOP. At the last moment, though, Bagert withdrew and (along with major GOP leaders) reluctantly threw his support to Johnston, who won the resulting four-way contest but with only 54 percent of the vote. Duke received 44 percent of the total and more than half of the white vote.

---

in advance of any particular election. Prior registration of party affiliation also gives the parties an added bonus: published lists of their partisans. It is not quite that simple, however. Party registration is, at best, an approximation of party loyalties at the moment. People are slow to change their party affiliations, and the party totals lag behind the pattern of voting. Furthermore, the registration figures of the majority or leading party tend to be swollen by conformists and by a few "political strategists," who register in a party solely to vote in its crucial primary.

The parties would gladly accept these uncertainties, however, in preference to what they regard as the more serious perils of the open primary, and the blanket primary enjoys even less favor. Party leaders level two charges against the open primary: crossing over and raiding. The terms are sometimes used synonymously, but a distinction can be made between them. Crossing over is the participation by voters in the primary of the party they do not generally support or feel a loyalty to. It is a drifting across party lines in search of the excitement of a primary battle. Raiding is an organized attempt on the part of one party to send its partisans into the primary of the other party in order to foist the least attractive candidates on it.

That crossing over happens in open primary states is beyond doubt. Consider the case of primary contests in Wisconsin, cradle of the open primary and home of an especially rambunctious political tradition. Austin Ranney's study of two gubernatorial primaries in the 1960s put the crossover vote at between 6 and 8 percent of the primary voters. Crossing over was doubtless kept to a minimum in the gubernatorial primaries by the need to stay in one's party's primary to decide other party contests. Since the presidential primaries involve only one contest, they impose no such constraints on crossover voting and consequently it often is higher. During the 1968 to 1984 period in Wisconsin, Ronald Hedland and Meredith Watts found that from 8 to 11 percent of primary voters were loyalists of one party who voted in the opposing party's primary and 28 to 45 percent were independents. In 1972 for the Democrats and 1980 for the Republicans, these independent and partisan crossover voters comprised a *majority* of the primary electorate. Moreover, David Adamany has shown that the candidate preferences of crossover voters may differ substantially from those of regular party voters. In 1964, for example, crossover voters favored George Wallace by a two-to-one margin; regular voters, by contrast, opposed Wallace by a margin of over nine-to-one.[6]

As for organized raiding, there is little evidence to suggest that it is more than a worrisome myth. Every party fears that voters drifting to the other party's primary will develop bad voting habits. Furthermore, the party must also be watchful lest the migration from its primary permit its contests to be settled by unrepresentative minorities. In other words, a party has every reason to encourage its loyalists to remain and vote in its primary. Two recent studies explored the possibility that individual voters may engage in such strategic voting, but no substantial evidence of it turned up.[7]

PRIMARIES: RULES OF THE GAME

The states also vary in candidate access to the primary ballot and in the support required to win the nomination.

Candidate Access to the Primary Ballot

First of all, the states must deal with the problem of how a candidate gets on the primary ballot. Most states permit access to the ballot by petition (called nomination papers in some states). State election laws vary considerably in what is

---

[6]Austin Ranney, "Turnout and Representation in Presidential Primary Elections," *American Political Science Review* 66 (1972): 21–37; Ronald D. Hedland and Meredith W. Watts, "The Wisconsin Open Primary: 1968 to 1984," *American Politics Quarterly* 14 (1986): 55–74; and David Adamany, "Cross-over Voting and the Democratic Party's Reform Rules," *American Political Science Review* 70 (1976): 536–41. See also Gary D. Wekkin, "The Conceptualization and Measurement of Cross-over Voting," *Western Political Quarterly* 41 (1988): 105–14.

[7]Alan Abramowitz, John McGlennon, and Ronald Rapoport, "A Note on Strategic Voting in a Primary Election," *Journal of Politics* 43 (1981): 899–904; and Gary D. Wekkin, "Why Crossover Voters Are Not 'Mischievous' Voters," *American Politics Quarterly* 19 (1991): 229–47.

The Formidable Barriers to Ballot Access in New York

The difficulties in gaining a place on the New York primary ballot are well illustrated in an October 18, 1990, *New York Times* article by Martin Gottlieb with Dean Baquet on Agustin Alamo's attempts to run for the state legislature from the Bronx.

> . . . Seven times he has entered Democratic primaries for the State Senate and Assembly. . . . And seven times he has failed, defeated not only by his opponents . . . but by an election process that many consider the worst in the nation. . . . In his ten years as a candidate, Mr. Alamo has been thrown off the ballot for omitting five words from the cover sheet of his nominating petitions. Yet, when he discovered two missing words on the cover sheets of his Bronx Democratic organization opponent, the Board of Elections and the courts let the petitions stand. . . . He has had to engage in costly and wearying challenges to his nomination petitions. Withstanding these, he has rarely bothered to press flesh on street corners and outside subway stations because most of the people he would meet are not registered and legal restrictions make it next to senseless to sign them up. He has visited numerous polling places where the inspectors hired to preside over the balloting are political allies of his opponents. And in election districts where he has tallied well, the Board of Elections has moved polling places to less convenient locations. . . . All of which may explain why other candidates describe their efforts as a cause or a passion but Mr. Alamo forlornly and accurately calls his "an addiction."

New York City politics is unusual in the protection afforded its parties from insurgent candidates in primary elections. But it is not unusual for the parties to employ devices such as these to cope with the challenges to their control over nominations posed by the direct primary.

---

required for nomination by petition. State statutes fix the number of required signatures—generally, either a specific number or a percentage of the vote for the office in the last election. New York, with its complicated 369-page law that favors party insiders, has the most stringent requirements for filing (see box). At the other extreme, in some states it is sufficient for the would-be candidates to present themselves to the clerk of elections and pay a usually modest fee. Finally, a few states put candidates on the ballot if they have formal party support as demonstrated in party conventions.

Even such mundane matters as access to the primary ballot have consequences for the parties. The easier access is, the easier it is for crank or dissident candidates to engage the party organization's candidates in costly primary battles. Sometimes such candidates even win. For example, ease of access to the Illinois primary ballot permitted the stunning nomination of followers of Lyndon LaRouche as Democratic candidates for lieutenant governor and secretary of state in 1986 (see box on p. 241).[8]

Runoff Primaries

At the other end of the nomination process, some states have tried to cope with primaries that are settled by less than a majority of the voters. In cases in which candidates win only a 35, 40, or 45 percent plurality, most states simply hope that the general election will produce a majority winner. Nine states, all from the South and its borders, have runoff primaries, however, if the winner in the regular primary wins less than 50 percent. In these second primaries, the two candidates with the highest vote totals face each other. This southern institution, first adopted in Mississippi in 1902, reflects the period of Republican impotence in which the Democratic nomination was, in effect, election and in which intense Democratic factionalism often produced three, four, or five serious candidates for a single office. Two northern states provide for runoffs if no candidate receives at least 35 percent of the vote. Iowa conducts its runoff through a party convention; South Dakota uses a second primary.

In recent years, the southern runoff primary has been the subject of considerable controversy. Citing instances in which black winners of the first primary in the South have lost to whites in the subsequent primary, some have charged that runoffs discriminate against minority groups in violation of the Constitution and the Federal Voting Rights Act. In striking down the New York runoff primary in 1985, a federal district court used this rationale and set the stage for lawsuits against these second primaries in other states. Defenders of this form of primary have countered that the runoff is not the source of minority disadvantage in electoral politics and, furthermore, that its presence is valuable in forcing southern parties, especially the Democrats, to build biracial coalitions.[9]

---

[8]Access to the ballot has become easier as a result of court action in recent years. The United States Supreme Court, for example, has invalidated a Texas law requiring candidates to pay both a flat fee for candidacy and a share of the cost of the election. The total charges had run as high as $9,000 for a candidate. Bullock v. Carter, 405 U.S. 134 (1972). The Court also overturned the California scale of filing fees. It did not prohibit filing fees per se, but the justices ruled that states using them must provide an alternative means of access to the ballot (such as a petition) for candidates unable to pay the fee. Lubin v. Panish, 415 U.S. 709 (1974).

[9]That blacks are necessarily disadvantaged by runoff primaries is challenged by Charles S. Bullock, III, and A. Brock Smith in "Black Success in Local Runoff Elections," *Journal of Politics* 52 (1990): 1205–20. They found that in Georgia black candidates fared more poorly than white candidates in runoffs until 1977 but black-white differences virtually vanished after 1977. For more on the discriminatory impact of runoff primaries, see Harold Stanley, "The Runoff: The Case for Retention," *PS* 18 (1985): 231–36; and Charles S. Bullock, III, and Loch K. Johnson, *Runoff Elections in the United States* (Knoxville: University of Tennessee Press, 1991).

A Party's Worst Fears Realized: Illinois, 1986

In the 1986 Democratic primary in Illinois, two followers of Lyndon H. LaRouche, Mark J. Fairchild and Janice Hart, upset the party-endorsed candidates to win nominations for lieutenant governor and secretary of state. These two political unknowns, running on a far-right platform, had spent a total of $200 on their campaigns. Cited as reasons for the surprising outcome were the LaRouchites' "all-American" names (their Anglo-Saxon flavor was seen as more attractive than Pucinski and Sangmeister, the endorsed candidates), a media that ignored them and their extremist political philosophies, a Democratic party organization in Chicago that was so distracted by internal squabbles that it failed to list the regular candidates on its slate card and took the contests for granted, and general voter inattention. This electoral outcome began the ill-fated odyssey of Democratic gubernatorial nominee and former U.S. Senator, Adlai Stevenson III, who refused to run on the same ticket with the LaRouchites. First he sought to purge his unwanted running mates from the party ballot; failing that, he renounced his party's nomination and attempted to gain a ballot position as an independent. Failing in these efforts too, he finally ran unsuccessfully as a third-party candidate, managing to win only 43 percent of the vote.

THE THREAT OF THE DIRECT PRIMARY

The parties' worst fear about a direct primary is that a candidate will win the nomination who, because of poor qualifications or repugnant issue stands, has no chance of gaining much party support in the general election. Every election year seems to bring forth a few nominees, usually for low-level offices, whose only electoral advantage is that they possess a famous name. Every once in a while also a candidate can ride strong feelings on a controversial issue to the nomination in spite of the more sober judgments of party leaders or the electorate in the general election. Imagine the discomfort of party leaders in 1990, for instance, when conservative Reagan-supporter John Silber upset the party's endorsed candidate to win the Democratic nomination for Governor in Massachusetts or former Ku Klux Klan leader David Duke emerged as the leading Republican candidate for the U.S. Senate in Louisiana (see earlier box). Without enthusiastic party backing in the general election, though, both Silber and Duke lost in the general election. The classic example of the damage a direct primary can do is the nomination of two followers of Lyndon LaRouche for top state offices in the 1986 Illinois Democratic primary (see box).

Although such a disaster befalls a party only rarely, the primary often causes it many lesser inconveniences, disruptions, and problems. Consider the threats the primary makes to the well-being of a political party organization:

Pandora's Box
By Ariail, For the State, Columbia, S.C.

- For the party that wants to influence nominations, the primary greatly escalates the costs of politics. Supporting candidates in a contested primary is almost always more expensive than holding a convention.
- By curbing party control over nominations, the primary denies the party a powerful lever for ensuring the loyalty of its officeholders to the party. If the party cannot control or prevent the reelection of a maverick officeholder, it really has no effective sanction for enforcing loyalty.
- The primary permits the nomination of a candidate (1) hostile to the party organization and leadership, (2) opposed to the party's platforms or programs, or (3) out of step with the public image party leaders want to project—or all of the above! At worst, it may permit the nomination of an individual who will be a severe embarrassment to the party (see box).
- The primary creates the distinct possibility that the party will find itself saddled with an unbalanced ticket for the general election if voters at the primary select all or most of the candidates from a particular group or region.
- Party activists also fear that the primary may produce a losing candidate for the party. The nominee may have appealed to only a shade more than half of the dedicated 20 or 30 percent of the electorate that votes in the

party's primary. Such a candidate may be poorly equipped to make the broader appeal necessary in the general election.

In addition, there is a general impression that the primary exacerbates party rifts. It often pits party worker against party worker, party group against party group.

> A genuine primary is a fight within the family of the party—and, like any family fight, is apt to be more bitter and leave more enduring wounds than battles with the November enemy. In primaries, ambitions spur from no-where; unknown men carve their mark; old men are sent relentlessly to their political graves; bosses and leaders may be humiliated or unseated. At ward, county, or state level, all primaries are fought with spurious family folksiness—and sharp knives.[10]

The resulting wounds are often deep and slow to heal. The cost to the health and strength of the party is considerable.

The effects of primary divisiveness on the party are easier to gauge in the short-term, at the subsequent general election, than over the long haul. First, party activists who have campaigned for the losing candidate in the primaries are unlikely to work for their party's nominees in the fall. The damage is miti-gated to some extent, however, because a contested primary recruits new ac-tivists into party politics.[11] Second, victors in a contested primary can not always count on the voters of their party opponent to support them in the gen-eral election.[12] It is natural perhaps for those committed to a losing candidate to be so disgruntled that they may withdraw from political activity or even vote for the other party's candidate. What is not entirely clear, though, is how much more a divisive primary may arouse these feelings than does the normal con-tention among possible candidates for a party nomination.

---

[10]Theodore H. White, *The Making of the President 1960* (New York: Atheneum, 1961), p. 78.

[11]Among the numerous scholarly studies of the effects of divisive primaries on activists, see Donald B. Johnson and James L. Gibson, "The Divisive Primary Revisited: Party Activists in Iowa," *American Political Science Review* 68 (1974): 67–77; and Emmett H. Buehl, Jr., "Divisive Primaries and Participation in Fall Presidential Campaigns," *American Politics Quarterly* 14 (1986): 376–90. The presence of this phenomenon in caucus states suggests, though, that the effect of divisiveness tran-scends primaries. See Walter J. Stone, "The Carryover Effect in Presidential Elections," *American Political Science Review* 80 (1986): 271–80.

[12]On the effects of divisive primaries on voters, the scholarly literature is substantial but the evi-dence is mixed. The most recent and comprehensive studies have found that divisiveness affects presidential, gubernatorial, and (for the Democrats) senatorial voting, but not voting for the House. See Patrick J. Kenney and Tom W. Rice, "The Effect of Primary Divisiveness in Gubernatorial and Senatorial Elections," *Journal of Politics* 46 (1984): 904–15; Patrick J. Kenney and Tom W. Rice, "The Relationship between Divisive Primaries and General Election Outcomes," *American Journal of Political Science* 31 (1987): 31–44; Patrick J. Kenney, "Sorting Out the Effects of Primary Divi-siveness in Congressional and Senatorial Elections," *Western Political Quarterly* 41 (1988): 765–77; and Patrick J. Kenney and Tom W. Rice, "Presidential Prenomination Preferences and Candidate Evaluations," *American Political Science Review* 82 (1988): 1309–19.

Not even the gloomiest Cassandra expects all these misfortunes to result from any given primary or even from a series of them. They are distinct possibilities for any party, however; especially a relatively weak and passive one. The parties recognize the danger, but they recognize, too, the futility of a direct assault on the primary. Thus, in the best American tradition of "joining 'em if you can't beat 'em," some parties have set out to control the primary. Others have lacked the will or the strength to do so. Still others have lost ground to local political cultures that disapprove of a party role in the primary. The result is a range of party responses to the primary that extends from no response at all to complete party domination.

THE PARTY ORGANIZATION FIGHTS BACK

One axiom and a corollary deriving from it govern party strategy in the primary. The axiom is simple to the point of truism: The surest way to control the primary is to prevent competition with the party's choice. The corollary is equally clear: The party must act as early as possible in the preprimary jockeying of would-be candidates if it is to choke off unwanted competition.

Party Control of Candidate Entry

Within some party organizations, a powerful party leader or a few party oligarchs make the preprimary decisions for the party organization—or it may be a party executive committee or a candidate selection committee. If their sources of information are good, they will know who intends to run and who is merely considering the race. They may arbitrate among them, or they may coax an unwilling candidate into the primary. If they command a strong and winning organization, their inducements to the nonfavored candidates to withdraw may be considerable. They may be able to offer a patronage position or a chance to run in the future. On the negative side, they may threaten to block a candidate's access to funds for the campaign (see box). Such control of nominations by the party organization and its leadership—a control not at all easy to achieve under the American primary election—is the norm in most of the parliamentary democracies of the world.

This informal and often covert selection of candidates—communicated to the party faithful by the "nod" or by the "word"—has been replaced within more and more parties by representative, publicized party conventions. Eight states have formalized them; but in those cases, state law usually prevents an unqualified endorsement. Colorado laws provide that all candidates who poll more than 30 percent of a convention endorsement vote shall go on the primary ballot in the order of their vote percentage. Utah directs the parties to nominate two candidates for each office. Conversely a few states have attempted by law to minimize the possibility or the power of endorsing conventions. In 1963, California prohibited party organizations from "officially" endorsing candidates for office but the state supreme court overturned this ban in 1984.

Creating the Strongest Party Ticket

In early 1990, the Ohio Republican party faced a dilemma. Its two best-known candidates for statewide office that year—former Cleveland Mayor George Voinovich and Hamilton County (Cincinnati) Commissioner Bob Taft, scion of Ohio's most famous political family—had both announced for governor. The Republican candidates for the other state government positions, on the other hand, seemed relatively weak.

The Republicans resolved their dilemma in the time-honored fashion of pressuring Taft, who was at the time running behind Voinovich in the polls, out of the governor's race and into the contest for secretary of state. The party's state central committee unanimously passed a resolution asking the state chair to meet with both Voinovich and Taft to persuade one of them to run for another office. This action was aimed at Taft, target of a less conciliatory resolution passed a day earlier by the party's finance and policy committees naming him as the party's choice for secretary of state. At the request of state party leaders, Republican National Chairman Lee Atwater also intervened by trying to persuade Taft to shift to secretary of state. But the most effective pressures were financial. Following the state party's threat that it would not provide him with financial support if he persisted in his campaign for governor, Taft's financial supporters announced they would not bankroll his campaign.

These efforts paid handsome dividends for the GOP. Voinovich and Taft easily won the party's nominations for governor and secretary of state, respectively, in the primary and went on to be elected to those positions in November. Coupled with their control of the state senate, the gain of these two offices gave the Republicans a majority of seats on the state apportionment board that determines the congressional districts for the next ten years.

In some states party endorsing bodies act informally and extralegally—that is, without the laws of the state taking notice of them. This form of endorsement has proved less effective, however, because it is not communicated by the ballot.[13] In the 1990 Massachusetts gubernatorial primaries, for instance, Boston University President John Silber won the Democratic nomination over the endorsed candidate in spite of receiving only the bare minimum of convention votes necessary to qualify for the primary ballot.

Party Support for Preferred Candidates

The most effective party control over the nomination process is attained by preventing viable challenges to the party's preferred candidates from emerging in

---

[13]Jewell and Olson, *Political Parties and Elections in American States*, p. 96.

the first place. But if a primary contest does develop despite all plans and strategies, the party then falls back on its resources in conventional ways. It may urge party committeepersons to help the anointed candidates circulate nominating petitions and leave the other candidates to their own devices. It may make available to the chosen ticket money, know-how, party workers, and the party bureaucracy. It may print advertisements announcing the party endorsees or may issue handy reference cards that the forgetful voter can take right into the polling booth. On the day of the primary, the party organization may help get the party's voters to the polls. Whether the party organization acts overtly or covertly in the primary campaign depends both on the local political culture and on the candidates' own appraisals of it. The party and/or the candidates may feel that voter sensitivity to party intervention (i.e., bossism) may dictate that the candidates appear untouched by party hands.

It is impossible to write authoritatively of the frequency of party attempts to manage or influence American primaries. Practices vary, not only from state to state but within states, and descriptions of local party practice are hard to come by. One is probably safe in generalizing that the most common nominating activity is the recruiting of candidates to seek the nomination. Surely less common are attempts to dissuade would-be nominees. Moreover, in most parts of the country, the political party is only one of a number of agencies seeking out and supporting men and women to run for office. It shares their recruitment with local business, professional, farm, and labor groups, with civic and community associations, with ethnic, racial, and religious organizations, with interest groups, and with officeholders. There are some party organizations, however, that *do* control the recruitment of candidates and the other preprimary processes. Generally, they are the parties that also intervene in the primary itself.

CANDIDATES AND VOTERS IN THE PRIMARIES

What the parties can accomplish in the primaries depends to a considerable extent on the candidates and on the electorate, who both are often the parties' unwitting allies. To put it simply, the primaries are more "manageable" because serious candidates do not often contest them and because the vast majority of voters do not vote in them. Very possibly, one or both of these conditions is of the party's making; the absence of candidates, for example, may reflect the skill of the party's preprimary persuading and dissuading. Regardless of cause, however, the result tends to be a nomination politics of a limited scope more easily controlled by aggressive party organization.

The Candidates

Simple countings will confirm that, in every part of the United States, large numbers of primary candidates win nomination without a contest. A study of state legislative primaries in fourteen states from 1972 to 1978 found that a median of 53 percent of the Democratic primaries and 83 percent of the Republican primaries had no contests.[14] Competition appears to be much more plentiful, however, for the more prestigious statewide offices. In a survey of gubernatorial primaries in forty-nine states from 1960 to 1986, Malcolm Jewell and David Olson found that the major parties had contests for the gubernatorial nominations 74 percent of the time overall, but that competition fell off in races with an incumbent and where there were party endorsements.[15]

Generally speaking, competition in American primaries is enhanced by certain rather predictable circumstances. The chief factor is probably the party's prospects for victory in the general election; candidates are not inclined to fight for the right to go down to almost certain defeat. The attractiveness of the office and the ease of getting on the ballot also affect competition. Finally, competition seems to thrive in primaries in which no incumbent officeholder is seeking nomination and in the absence of effective party control or endorsement.[16]

The power of incumbency in discouraging competition is one of the ironies of the primary. By placing a premium on popular appeal and exposure that often only the well-known incumbent can muster, the primary fosters the conditions that diminish its own effectiveness. By weakening party control of nominations through the direct primary, therefore, reformers may have achieved the unanticipated (and surely to them undesirable) consequence of strengthening the hold of incumbents on their positions. Where the hold of incumbents on their party's renomination is broken, though, one typically finds it to be the work of challengers who are able to spend large sums of money, often their own. This too would surely be a disappointment to the Progressive reformers.

The Voters

If competition is scarce at the primaries, so are voters. All evidence points overwhelmingly to one cardinal fact about the participation of the American electorate in primaries: Most do not vote. Even the study of gubernatorial primaries (1960–86) that identified a relatively high incidence of contested races found modest turnout levels. In all of the contested races in that period, only 30 percent of voting age adults voted.[17]

---

[14]Craig H. Grau, "Competition in State Legislative Primaries," *Legislative Studies Quarterly* 6 (1981): 35–54.

[15]Jewell and Olson, *Political Parties and Elections in American States*, pp. 104–6.

[16]On the factors that promote or suppress competition in the primaries, see Tom W. Rice, "Gubernatorial and Senatorial Primary Elections: Determinants of Competition," *American Politics Quarterly* 13 (1985): 427–46; Harvey L. Schantz, "Contested and Uncontested Primaries for the U.S. House," *Legislative Studies Quarterly* 4 (1980): 545–62; and Jewell and Olson, *Political Parties and Elections in American States*, pp. 104–6.

[17]Jewell and Olson, *Political Parties and Elections in American States*, p. 129.

How is this low turnout to be explained? In large part, it reflects the lower interest in intraparty contests for nomination, which lack the inherent drama of a general election. Turnout also is dampened by the absence of a real primary contest (a lack of competition within the majority party or in contests dominated by an incumbent), by the relative unimportance of the minority party primary in states with low levels of interparty competition or of primaries held separately from the presidential primaries, and by closing primaries to independents and members of the other party.[18]

The primary electorate possesses some special characteristics. A substantial sector of it generally comes from party loyalists and activists. Primary voters, as one might expect, have higher levels of political interest and higher educational attainments. Conventional political wisdom has also held that primary voters represent more extreme ideological positions than those of the party's full electorate. While early studies of Wisconsin's open primary found little support for that assumption, more recent research (coming largely from presidential primaries, which will be considered later) suggests otherwise.[19] Even if the ideological positions of primary voters turn out not to be distinctive, the intensity of their ideological commitment may be.

Even this generally interested electorate often lapses into unpredictable voting behavior. For large numbers of voters in the primary, the choice is more difficult than the one at the general election. Since all the candidates come from the same party, party loyalties cannot guide the voters' decisions. The primary campaign is brief, the candidates are often not well known, and the issues, if any, are unclear. Therefore, the voter's choice is not so well structured or predictable; the presence of an incumbent in the race may be the only continuing, stabilizing element. Consequently, many voter decisions are made right in the polling booth; the effect of the ballot position and the success of candidates with famous names indicate that. Small wonder, then, that parties are never confident in primaries and that public opinion pollsters prefer not to predict primary outcomes.

There has been one great exception to all the generalizations on competition and voter turnout in American primaries: the South. From the end of Re-

---

[18]Malcolm E. Jewell, "Northern State Gubernatorial Primary Elections: Explaining Voting Turnout," *American Politics Quarterly* 12 (1984): 101–16; and Patrick J. Kenney, "Explaining Turnout in Gubernatorial Primaries," *American Politics Quarterly* 11 (1983): 315–26.

[19]Austin Ranney and Leon D. Epstein, "The Two Electorates: Voters and Non-Voters in a Wisconsin Primary," *Journal of Politics* 28 (1966): 598–616; and Austin Ranney, "The Representativeness of Primary Electorates," *Midwest Journal of Political Science* 12 (1968): 224–38. Similar results appear for turnout in Senate primaries, especially in the effects of competition, of the simultaneous existence of a presidential primary, and of an open primary without party endorsements. See Patrick J. Kenney, "Explaining Primary Turnout: The Senatorial Case," *Legislative Studies Quarterly* 11 (1986): 65–74. For the most recent results on presidential primaries, see John G. Geer, "Assessing the Representativeness of Electorates in Presidential Primaries," *American Journal of Political Science* 32 (1988): 929–45.

construction to the years right after World War II, the South was securely and overwhelmingly a one-party Democratic area. For most offices, therefore, winning the Democratic nomination was tantamount to winning the office itself. The effective competitive politics of the southern states thus centered in the Democratic primary and produced relatively high turnout levels—sometimes even higher than in the general elections.

As the Republican party has built strength and competitiveness, however, the Democratic primaries in the South are gradually losing their special standing. The result has been a downturn of participation in them, even at a time when blacks have been mobilized into Democratic party politics. In spite of the greater prospects for Republican candidates, however, the GOP primaries have not attracted a compensating increase in participation, although participation certainly has risen. Overall turnout in southern primaries, then, is lower than it once was.[20]

THE DIRECT PRIMARY IN RETROSPECT

American experience with the statewide direct primary is approaching a century. What difference has it all made? Has the primary democratized the nomination process by taking it out of the hands of party oligarchs? Has it materially increased popular participation in the selection of candidates for public office? These, after all, were the principal intentions of its architects, the Progressives, and it seems reasonable to inquire whether they have been realized.

The Impact on Democratization

Basically, the democratic hopes behind the direct primary are threatened by the lack of competition and low voter turnout. There must be participation—both by candidates and by voters—if there are to be meaningful choices based on meaningful alternatives. The primary, however—by its nature—tends to diminish such participation. The need for broad public appeal, the cost of a contest, and the sheer difficulty of getting on the primary ballot discourage candidacies. In addition, the multiplicity of primaries, with their unstructured, confusing, and unclear choices, probably reduces both the quantity and the quality of voter participation. Clearly, if widespread mass participation in the nominating processes was a goal of the reformers who initiated the primary, their hopes have not been realized.

Second, if one purpose of the primary was to replace the caucuses and conventions of the party organizations as nominators, the primary fails when it falls under the sway of those organizations. Even if the party organization cannot

---

[20]Jewell and Olson, *Political Parties and Elections in American States,* pp. 112–13.

eliminate primary competition, it can sometimes defeat it. It may command the money, symbols, and organization essential for primary victory. The party organization also often commands the chief political loyalty of a significant share of those who vote in the primary. If only 30 or 40 percent of registered voters vote in the primary, some 15 or 20 percent will be sufficient to nominate a candidate. Parties count on the fact that a substantial part of that group is likely to be loyalists who respond to the cues of party leaders or endorsements. Thus, strong party organizations able to mobilize voters, money, and manpower are still very effective determiners of primary outcomes.

For a variety of reasons, however, the parties control the primaries only imperfectly. The sheer size of the task deters some of them. The Jacksonian tradition of electing every public official down to the local coroner has confronted them with numerous contests. The expense of supporting a number of candidates—not to mention the expenditures of organizational energy—forces many organizations to be selective in their primary interventions. In other instances, parties stand aside because a role in the primary would threaten their internal harmony and cohesion. They may be paralyzed by the fear that their activity in the primary will open new wounds or heat up old resentments—or run the risk of offending the possible victor. Still others are stymied by their own weakness or by local political cultures that resist party activity as a violation of the spirit of the primary.

Yet to argue that the primary has not fulfilled the most optimistic hopes is not to argue that it has had no effect. In competitive districts—especially when an incumbent has stepped down—voters often do play the kind of role the reformers envisioned. Also, even for a strong party organization, the primaries set tangible limits. Many no longer find it possible to whisk just any "warm body" through the nomination process. The direct primary perhaps can best be thought of both as creating a veto body that passes on the work of party nominators and as affording an opportunity for intraparty dissidents to take their case to the party's electorate.

The Impact on the Parties

What has been the more general impact of the primary on the political parties? V. O. Key argued that the primary leads to one-partyism by increasingly drawing both the voter and the attractive, prestigious candidates to the primary of the dominant party. Little by little, the majority party becomes the only viable instrument of political influence and the minority party atrophies, a victim of "the more general proposition that institutional decay follows deprivation of function."[21] The burden of opposition is then shifted to contests within the primary of the majority party. However persuasive this argument may be, it is of questionable validity today. One-partyism has receded in recent years, bringing

---

[21]V. O. Key, Jr., *American State Politics*, Chap. 6.

with it a demise in a single party's monopoly on political talent. The success of candidates who run without party support, moreover, signals that opportunities exist outside of the normal party channels.

It is more likely that the direct primary has been a prime contributor to a general atrophy in party organization—in dominant as well as minority parties. The stronger and more centralized party organizations appear in those states in which conventions either nominate candidates or the parties make preprimary endorsements.[22] Even in these states, though, the inability of parties to effectively control who carries the party label into the general election contest has deprived the party organization of one of its key resources.

Furthermore, the direct primary unquestionably has altered the distribution of power within the party. When one speaks of party control of nominations, one means control by the party organization, and any weakening of that control obviously weakens the organization and enhances the power of the party candidates and the party in government. Their ability, especially as incumbents, to defy the organization and to win primary battles frees them from its discipline and, indeed, often opens up to them positions of party leadership. In fact, the inability of the party organization in the United States to control the party in government (as it does in so many other democracies) begins with its failure to control its nominations. The direct primary undercuts the ability of the party organization to recruit to public office those partisans who share its goals and accept its discipline.

The goal of the Progressives and the other proponents of the primary was to substitute the party electorate for the party organization as the nominator. With the primary, they thwarted the organization's quest for its own goals. Instead of achieving any genuine mass control of party nominations, however, they shifted the control from the elites of the organization to the elites of the party in government. They succeeded in multiplying the party oligarchies rather than in democratizing them.

Recent trends in American politics have added a new dimension to the Progressives' achievement. Incumbents are not the only ones to benefit from restricted party organization control over primaries. With the increased role of television, especially as a substitute for the kind of labor-intensive door-to-door campaigning that strong party organizations traditionally supplied, television image-building and the need for funds to pay for it have come to dominate campaigns—particularly primary campaigns where party labels do not function to guide voter choice. It would be the supreme irony if, in their quest to free the electoral process of control by party bosses, the Progressives were to vest that control in the hands of an even more invisible and unresponsive (to the public) group of "bosses"—media consultants and the special interests who are the

---

[22]On the relationships among party, mechanism of nomination, and primary competition, see Andrew D. McNitt, "The Effect of Preprimary Endorsement on Competition for Nominations: An Examination of Different Nominating Systems," *Journal of Politics* (1980): 257–66.

most likely to finance political campaigns—or to restrict primary elections to contests between incumbents and wealthy or special-interest challengers.[23]

A Force for Decentralization

Finally, the direct primary has buttressed the prevailing decentralization of power in the American parties. So long as the candidates or incumbents can appeal to a majority of local primary voters, they are free from the control and discipline of a state or national party. Even so powerful a president as Franklin Roosevelt in 1938 met his greatest political defeat in trying to purge a number of Democratic senators and representatives in their local Democratic primaries; only one of his conservative targets was defeated. The primary plays on local loyalties and appeals to the local electorate, and its localism puts it beyond the control of a central party organization.

If the advocates of the direct primary wanted to aim beyond the nomination process and strike the parties themselves, they found their target. In many instances, the direct primary has weakened the control of nominations by the party organizations—even robbing them of an important raison d'etre and liberating their officeholders. In many important ways, it has made the American political parties what they are today.

Who Should Select the Party Candidates?

How party candidates should be nominated has been a controversial matter since political parties first appeared in the United States in the early 1800s. At base, the question of who should make party nominations raises the question of what a political party is. Is it merely an alliance of officeholders, the party in government, as reflected by the early system of caucus nominations? Or does it also embrace the activists and party officials, the party organization, who played their greatest role in the convention system? Or should the party mantle be extended, well beyond the limits of most other democracies, to include the great mass of party voters? And, if so, which ones—only the ones willing to officially register a party loyalty or anyone who decides to vote for a party candidate in a primary election? Even though political scientists continue to debate this question, the American answer to it has evolved over the years toward the most inclusive definition of party. In the states with an open or blanket primary, the party indeed has become so permeable that no one can be excluded—raising the possibility that a party could become coterminous with the entire electorate.

---

[23]A study of gubernatorial nominations in 1982 suggests this by showing that more money was spent on campaigns and the spending was more related to the outcome of the contests in states where party organizations did not make preprimary endorsements. Sarah M. Morehouse, "Money versus Party Effort: Nominating for Governor," *American Journal of Political Science* 34 (1990): 706–24.

Behind the scenes, of course, what we have here is no less than simply another venue for the eternal struggle over the distribution of power—within the parties and, more generally, within the American political system. The Progressives and their modern-day counterparts, however high-minded their idealism, also have used party reform as a weapon with which to wrest control of the party, and ultimately of government, from party regulars. To the degree to which the nomination process defines voter choices in American elections, those who control this process have substantial influence over the agenda of politics and consequently over who gets what in the political system. The stakes of the controversies over party nominations, then, are considerable.

Chapter
10

Choosing the Presidential Nominees: Primaries and Caucuses

In the naming of their candidates for president, the American parties stand at the crossroads between the old and the new. The Democrats and Republicans, as they have done for well over a century, choose their nominees in quadrennial national party conventions. This makes the presidential nomination process the last redoubt of the old convention system. Yet this continuity in structure masks a transformation in function. Now that most delegates to the conventions are allocated to the presidential candidates well before the conventions, even if the actual delegates are chosen by more traditional methods, the national conventions in recent years have merely confirmed a predetermined result.

The transformation of the traditional system for presidential nominations has been intermittent and, in the last analysis, incomplete.[1] Under the lead of its Progressive Governor Robert LaFollette, Wisconsin adopted the first presidential primary in 1905, and by 1916 a total of twenty-five states had followed suit. This early enthusiasm for primaries, however, soon waned. Advocates may have lost faith in them because they did not prove to be decisive in the nomination contests. Opponents may have redoubled their efforts to get rid of them because they nonetheless made party control of nominations more difficult. Whatever the cause, by 1936 only fourteen states had retained primaries for

---

[1]With the movement to direct primaries for nominations of state officials beginning in 1902, it seemed only natural to involve voters in the selection of presidential candidates as well. But the national conventions remained in place, as meetings to which *state* parties sent their representatives, and in some primary states these delegates (who ended up voting on the presidential nominees) were themselves selected by the old methods. Thus, primaries only supplemented rather than displaced the traditional convention system for selecting party candidates for America's one national office. The idea of a national primary, as a national parallel to the contests for statewide offices, did not take root until many years later.

selecting national convention delegates—the same number (and virtually the same states) that used them as recently as 1968. In the furor over the 1968 Democratic nomination, the direct primary movement was reborn. By the 1980s, most of the states had adopted presidential primaries and, more significantly, a decisive majority of the delegates were selected by this method.

Even though it can be said that primaries now dominate the presidential nomination process, their domination is far from complete. In most of the states, delegates to the national conventions are *allocated* on the basis of popular support for presidential candidates in primaries. Yet most state parties *select* the actual delegates through a caucus/convention system. In some states delegate allocation too is determined by the old system, although reforms since 1968 have made it more open and democratic as well. Moreover, the ultimate nomination decision remains in the hands of the convention rather than being subject to direct popular determination. Compared to how candidates for virtually every other major office are selected, then, the presidential nomination process deserves special treatment. Considering the attention it commands in the press and the public at large, a comprehensive treatment is in order.

FIRST STEPS TOWARD THE NOMINATIONS

The national conventions of the two major parties conclude the complicated process of nomination. It is very difficult to say, however, just when that nominating process begins. For some especially ambitious and far-sighted politicians, it may have begun in their own career planning some six or eight years before. Within the party defeated in a presidential election, jockeying for the next nomination begins the morning after that defeat. Legally speaking, the campaigns of candidates for president begin when they form a campaign committee to raise private money after January 1 of the year preceding election year in order to meet Federal Election Commission requirements for public financing. In a more traditional sense, the nomination process begins as the advance men and women for would-be candidates straggle into New Hampshire and Iowa to enter their candidates in the earliest of the processes in which convention delegates are chosen. The 1992 nomination process, however, has defied traditional patterns, as the first announced candidate did not emerge until spring of 1991 and other candidates delayed their entry even longer.

Delegate Selection Procedures in the States

For years, the national parties, in preparing for the conventions, had stipulated only the number of delegates the states would have. It was left to the states or their parties to decide how the delegates would be chosen. Beginning in 1972, the Democrats ended that tradition. They began to control a number of the other aspects of delegate selection.

The means through which the national Democratic party took control of the delegate selection process from the states is a fascinating tale of political reform.

After their tumultuous 1968 convention, in which insurgent forces within the party protested that the nomination of Hubert Humphrey betrayed the wishes of Democratic voters in the primaries, the national party attempted to mollify its internal critics by altering the methods of delegate selection. A commission chaired by Senator George McGovern of South Dakota and Representative Donald Fraser of Minnesota recommended and the Democratic National Committee subsequently approved numerous changes for the 1972 nominating process. In attempting to comply with the complex new rules, many states substituted primary elections for their caucus/convention systems. In the process, not only were the delegate selection rules radically transformed, but the principle was established that the national parties (acting through their national committees and presidential nominating conventions) rather than the state parties or even the states themselves determine the rules of presidential nomination.[2] What is remarkable about these reforms is how readily party leaders acceded to rules changes that significantly reduced their influence in awarding the party's greatest prize, the presidential nomination.[3]

Once the reform genie was let out of the bottle, it proved difficult to contain. The Democrats have reformed their presidential nomination process, to a greater or lesser degree, in each election since 1968. Initially they attempted to use national party leverage to make the process more open and more representative of the various party constituencies—although sometimes the means, such as delegate quotas for women, young people, and blacks, occasioned bitter debate. Recently, however, the Democrats have focused their attention on alleviating the most controversial consequences of the reforms. States have been prevented from leapfrogging one another in a stampede to hold the earliest primary or caucus by limiting these contests mostly to the months of March through June. But states have been allowed somewhat more leeway in preserving their own traditions in scheduling the contests (e.g., Iowa and New Hampshire have been allowed to continue to begin before March) and in defining who can participate. (Wisconsin has been allowed by the party to retain its open primary). The party also has tried to increase the influence of the party regulars by making certain that a large number of elected public and party officials are automatically included in the national conventions as so-called superdelegates. The most recent Democratic reforms have addressed the controversy over winner-take-all elections (see box).

---

[2]In a case involving the Wisconsin open primary, the Supreme Court has upheld the power of the national party to refuse to seat delegates chosen under a state law of which it disapproves. See Democratic Party of the United States v. La Follette, 450 U.S. 107 (1981).

[3]For an excellent account of this episode, a rare event of political leaders willingly giving up power, see Byron E. Shafer, *Quiet Revolution* (New York: Russell Sage Foundation, 1983). Other useful sources on the reform of the presidential nomination process are James W. Ceaser, *Presidential Selection* (Princeton, N.J.: Princeton University Press, 1979); William J. Crotty, *Party Reform* (New York: Longman, 1983); Nelson W. Polsby, *The Consequences of Party Reform* (Oxford: Oxford University Press, 1983); and Austin Ranney, *Curing the Mischiefs of Faction: Party Reform in America* (Berkeley, Calif.: University of California Press, 1975).

Reforming the Delegate Selection Process Once Again: The Democrats' Rules for 1992

For the first time in two decades, the Democrats did not create a special commission after the 1988 national convention to review the nomination process. Nevertheless, the Democratic National Committee's Rules and Bylaws Committee could not refrain from making some important changes for the 1992 nominations. One of these changes, moving the opening of the primary season "window" from the second to the first Tuesday in March (with an exemption still for New Hampshire) was intended to encourage California to reschedule its primary from June to the beginning of March, but the California legislature so far has been reluctant to make the change.

The most important change involved ratification of the move to proportional representation that was negotiated between Dukakis and Jackson forces at the 1988 convention. Prior to the reforms of the 1970s and 1980s, many states awarded all of their delegates to the state-wide winner in the primaries. Early Democratic reform efforts eliminated state-wide *winner-take-all* primaries and moved toward a *proportional representation* system whereby delegates were apportioned in proportion to the number of votes each candidate attained above a certain minimum (e.g., 20 percent in 1984, 15 percent in 1988). In 1988, though, fifteen states retained some vestige of the winner-take-all system. Ten states awarded a bonus delegate to the winner of each congressional district. The other five used winner-take-all rules at the congressional district level.[4] In 1992, neither of these winner-take-all systems will be permitted. Candidates who win at least 15 percent of the vote will be awarded a share of the state's delegates proportionate to their popular vote total. This reform could make it more difficult for one candidate to dominate the nominations process and increase the (still small) likelihood that no candidate will command a majority of the delegates before the convention.

Also significant was the Democratic National Committee's refusal to go along with another concession made by the Dukakis camp to gain Jesse Jackson's support in 1988. The Dukakis-Jackson agreement called for a reduction in the number of delegates who were not elected in the primaries or caucuses, called superdelegates, by eliminating the automatic slots for members of the Democratic National Committee. With the support of new DNC Chairman Ron Brown, who had been Jackson's convention manager in 1988, the DNC slots were restored. The Democrats remain committed to guaranteeing that party leaders and top elected officials will serve as delegates to the national convention even if they are not popularly elected.

---

[4]Because of these so-called "loophole" primaries, caucus results in the past have tended to represent popular votes more proportionally than primary results, and, as he charged, Jesse Jackson in 1988 did receive fewer delegates than he would have earned under a strict proportional representation system. See Stephen Ansolabehere and Gary King, "Measuring the Consequences of Delegate Selection Rules in Presidential Nominations," *Journal of Politics* 52 (1990): 609–21.

The legacy of this reform era is nothing short of a stunning transformation in how Americans, especially Democrats, select their nominees for president. The traditional caucus/convention method favored by most states in 1968, and often tightly controlled by a small group of party leaders, is now governed by party rules requiring selection of delegates in timely, open, and well-publicized meetings and proscribing the techniques (e.g., unannounced meetings, proxy votes, slate making) traditionally employed by party organizations to control delegates selection. Even more important, the predominance of the caucus method has ended, as most states have come to utilize primaries to allocate delegates among the presidential contenders. The traditional practice of allocating all the state's delegates to the winner also has been a casualty of the reform efforts. In Democratic caucuses and primaries, the states now must apportion delegates to the presidential candidates in proportion to their voting strength and must ensure representation of women and minorities.

The Presidential Primaries

Since 1968, presidential primaries have come to dominate the presidential selection process. They are now utilized in well over half of the states, including most of the largest. As the easiest way for states to comply with the new Democratic reforms, primaries were increasingly popular from 1968 through 1980. Their attractiveness ebbed in 1984, especially for the Democrats who automatically awarded about 15 percent of the delegate slots to ex officio "superdelegates," but it rose again in 1988 as more states moved to primaries (Table 10.1). The proportion of delegates from primary states seems to be stabilizing at about three quarters for the Republicans and two thirds for the Democrats, who are unique in setting aside spots for elected and party officials. Because the decisions to use primaries or caucuses are made by the states, though, it is possible that their relative numbers may continue to fluctuate.

Table 10.1   THE USE OF PRESIDENTIAL PRIMARIES: 1968–88

	Democrats		Republicans	
Year	No. of States	Percent of delegate votes	No. of states	Percent of delegate votes
1968	17	37.5%	16	34.3%
1972	23	60.5	22	52.7
1976	29	72.6	28	67.9
1980	35	71.8	34	76.0
1984	25	62.1	30	71.0
1988	34	66.6	35	76.9

Note: Includes all convention constituencies (50 states plus D.C. and other areas). Excludes states with non-binding preference primaries in which delegates were chosen by caucus/convention methods.

Source: William Crotty and John S. Jackson III, *Presidential Primaries and Nominations* (Washington, D.C.: CQ Press, 1985), p. 63, for 1968–84; *Congressional Quarterly Weekly Report* (Washington, D.C.: Congressional Quarterly, Inc., 1988), 532, for 1988.

Continuing reform efforts by the Democrats after 1968, implemented by fifty different state legislatures that occasionally have allowed each party to set its own rules, have produced an almost bewildering variety of presidential primary practices. States face two different tasks in the presidential election process. First, they need to formulate some method for allocating delegates to the party's national convention among the various contenders for the presidency. Second, they must select the actual delegates who are to attend the conventions. The caucus/convention system provides a simple solution to these two tasks: It selects delegates, sometimes already committed to candidates, who in turn decide whom to support at the conventions.

By injecting the principle that ordinary voters ought to have a direct influence on whom their state delegation supports at the convention, the primary has complicated the performance of these tasks. In the spirit of American federalism, the 34-35 primary states combined these allocation and selection tasks in a variety of ways in 1988. In essential respects, though, this variety reduces to just three different practices, which together with the caucus system produce a fourfold typology of state nomination methods (Table 10.2).

Mixed Systems: Allocation by Primaries/Selection by Caucuses   A majority of the states using primaries in 1988 employed the primaries to allocate delegate slots among the candidates but chose the delegates themselves through the caucus/convention method. The states varied, however, in whether delegates were selected before or after the primary. Four states (e.g., California and Ohio for the Democrats; Connecticut and South Carolina for the Republicans) held caucuses to select delegates first, then the results from the subsequent preferential primary determined which candidates those delegates should support. The other states held the caucus after the preferential primary to select delegates to reflect the popular results.

Mixed Systems: Allocation by Primaries/Selection by Candidates   In three states delegates were allocated automatically among the candidates on the basis of the primary vote, with the California Republicans using a winner-take-all system (banned from Democratic contests), in which the candidate with the most votes received all of the delegates. The delegates came from hand-picked slates assembled by the candidate(s).

Pure Primary Systems   In a number of states, voters directly elected delegates to the national convention (or sometimes to an intervening state convention, which in turn selected the national convention delegates). The candidate preference of each delegate usually was listed on the ballot, or they were listed as uncommitted. (An exception was the Pennsylvania Republican primary in which delegate names were not accompanied by any information about whom they supported.)

In a number of these pure primary states, the delegate primary was accompanied by a presidential preference primary in which voters could independently choose a presidential candidate. In Indiana, Rhode Island, and New

Table 10.2   STATE PRESIDENTIAL NOMINATION METHODS, 1988

Caucus systems

Alaska	Idaho, D	Minnesota	Texas, D
Arizona	Iowa	Montana, R	Utah
Colorado	Kansas	Nevada	Virginia, R
Delaware	Maine	North Dakota, D	Wyoming
Hawaii	Michigan	South Carolina, D	

Mixed systems: Allocation by primaries/Selection by caucuses

Arkansas	Louisiana	New Mexico	South Carolina, R
California, D	Massachusetts	North Carolina	South Dakota
Connecticut	Mississippi	North Dakota, R	Tennessee, D
Florida	Missouri	Ohio, D	Texas
Georgia	Montana, D	Oklahoma	Virginia, D
Kentucky	Nebraska, D	Oregon	Wisconsin

Mixed systems: Allocation by primaries/Selection by candidates

California, R	New Hampshire	Ohio, R

Pure primary systems

Alabama	Indiana	New Jersey	Rhode Island
Idaho, R	Maryland	New York	Tennessee, R
Illinois	Nebraska, R	Pennsylvania	West Virginia

Note: In a number of states, the parties used different methods. Where this occurred a *D* or *R* indicates which party is involved. In Texas, the Democrats used both the caucus and a mixed caucus/primary system, with some delegates selected in each.

Source: Based on materials contained in the *Congressional Quarterly Weekly Report,* August 29, 1987.

York, the result of this preference primary actually determined the allocation of delegates among the candidates.

In Illinois, New Jersey, Pennsylvania, and West Virginia, by contrast, the presidential preference primary, appropriately called a "beauty contest," had no effect on delegate selection. All that counted in these elections was how people had voted for delegates. Because separate decisions are required, the results of these two decisions can diverge—as they did in the 1984 Florida Democratic primary in which Gary Hart won the popularity contest but took home only about half as many delegates as Walter Mondale. Unless "beauty contest" preferences help to build a candidate's momentum for subsequent elections, the presidential preference results are irrelevant to the nomination process.

These various methods of allocating and selecting delegates in the primaries represent the different accommodations in 1988 to the uneasy relationship between the interests of the party organizations and the spirit of direct primary reforms. Most methods allow the parties to retain an element of control over the nomination process, which could prove especially important if the nominating conventions ever deadlocked on the first ballot. When a party caucus or convention chooses them, the delegates are more likely to be party loyalists regardless of their commitment to a particular candidate. When voters directly choose the delegates, on the other hand, the parties can only hope that the more familiar party and elected officials will be favored in spite of their presidential preference—an outcome that is encouraged in some states by failing to list delegates' preferences on the ballot. The party organizations' interests are threatened most when the winning candidates can designate their own delegate slates. In this situation, candidate loyalty usually is at a premium and party loyalty is secondary. Even here, though, the parties are not inevitably without influence; where candidates need party support, they often will place party stalwarts on their slates.

Beyond these basic forms, there remain other important differences among the states' presidential primaries. First, in some states, the convention delegates are elected from the state at large; in others, they are chosen from the individual congressional districts; and in still others, they are elected from both. Such a seemingly minor variation, however, can have major political consequences. The chances of a divided state delegation (and its attendant intraparty squabbles), for example, are much greater when delegates are chosen by congressional district. Nonetheless, the rules of the Democratic party that forbid statewide winner-take-all elections have fostered greater selection of delegates by district.

Second, some states elect in their primaries all the delegates the parties will send to the conventions, and some elect only some of them. In Pennsylvania, for example, over a third of the delegates in 1988 were chosen by the parties' state central committees. Such provisions have helped meet one of the parties' major objections to the presidential primary by permitting them to make sure that the important leaders of the state organizations go as delegates to the national convention and also have been useful in balancing state delegations to represent women and minorities.

Third, the states vary on the issue of whether a presidential hopeful must consent to being involved in the state's primary. Most states, but not all, require the candidate's approval (or permit his or her disapproval) before his or her name may be entered in a presidential preference poll or before delegates run as pledged to that candidate. In Oregon, the primary law entrusts to the Secretary of State the delicate decision of putting on the preference poll the names of *all* candidates "generally recognized in the national news media" to be candidates for the presidential nomination. A similar decision in Wisconsin is entrusted to an eleven-person committee made up largely of the leadership of the two major parties, although overlooked candidates may earn a ballot spot through petitions. The purpose clearly is to make it less possible for potential candidates to avoid some of the primaries and thus diminish competition and interest in them.

Fourth, the presidential primaries differ in the nature of the candidate commitment of the delegates. In many cases, the pledge of a delegate to support a certain candidate for the nomination is buttressed only by enthusiasm for the candidate, by a personal code of honor, or by a sense of the political value of integrity. In other states, delegates are required by law to take a pledge of loyalty to the candidate. Wisconsin, for instance, specifies by law the content of the pledge:

> I will, unless prevented by the death of the candidate, vote for his candidacy on the first ballot; and vote for his candidacy on any additional ballot, unless released by said candidate, until said candidate fails to receive at least one-third of the vote authorized to be cast; and that, thereafter, I shall have the right to cast my convention vote according to my own judgment.[5]

Recent Democratic party reforms addressed this issue first by binding delegates to a first-ballot vote for the candidate to whom they were pledged and then from 1984 and 1988 by requiring only that delegates make a good conscience attempt to reflect the sentiments of those electing them. National party action on the issue, however, probably overrides enforcement of tougher state requirements.[6]

Finally, although most primary states use one form or another of the closed primary, the open primary has survived vigorous assaults by successive Democratic party reform commissions, which were determined to ban open primaries because they permit participation by voters who lack party loyalties—members of the other party and independents. After succeeding in 1984 in shutting down Wisconsin's open primary as a means for selecting convention delegates (Wisconsin held its open primary as a presidential preference contest, but chose delegates by the caucus method that year), the national party relented in adopting its rules for the 1988 convention. Wisconsin was able to return to its cherished practice, and the handful of other states that hold open primaries need no longer fear reproach by the national party.[7]

The GOP has been carried along by the Democratic reform efforts because in many states the response to new Democratic party requirements was to change state election practices for both parties. For example, the increase in the use of primaries was largely a bipartisan matter. On their own, however, the Republicans have made only minor changes in their rules since 1968. They continue to give state parties wide latitude in developing their own rules, which prevents issues of rules reform from regularly coming before the national party. They have retained statewide winner-take-all elections and given little encouragement to proportional representation, adopting it only where state law required. Nor have the Republicans formally set aside seats for party and public officials or maintained affirmative action programs for women or minorities. Re-

---

[5]*Wisconsin Statutes*, Chap. 8.12.

[6]A careful treatment of this issue may be found in David E. Price, *Bringing Back the Parties* (Washington, D.C.: CQ Press, 1984), pp. 174–76.

[7]On the struggle between the Wisconsin Democratic party and the national party over this matter, see Gary D. Wekkin, *Democrats versus Democrats* (Columbia: University of Missouri Press, 1983).

form of the nomination process did not become a central issue of internal party conflict for the Republicans as it did for the Democrats, perhaps because traditional party machines and their devices for controlling nominations have not been as prevalent in Republican politics.[8]

The Party Caucuses

The presidential primaries are dramatic and are reported every four years in the most intricate detail. Nonetheless, the parties of a significant number of the states allocate and choose delegates by assorted internal party processes. Those processes usually begin with local caucuses. Unlike primaries, these meetings typically require face-to-face interaction among participants, can take a considerable amount of time to conclude their business (often several hours), and usually conduct their balloting in the open. As a result of these features, the caucuses and primaries also differ in levels of participation and, often, in outcome (see box).

Caucuses usually are held within each precinct or voting district to enable ordinary party voters (variously defined across the states) to choose delegates to regional or state conventions. Generally, the regional conventions choose a fixed and equal number of delegates, and the state convention selects the remainder from the state at large. In a few states, some or all of the delegates are chosen by the state central committee of the party.[9]

For years, the selection of delegates in the caucus states was relatively invisible. The events of 1976, however, changed all that. A virtually unknown seeker after the Democratic nomination, Jimmy Carter, vaulted himself into serious candidacy by a strenuous campaign in Iowa that netted him both media attention and about 30 percent of the state's Democratic delegates. Within the Republican party in that year, Gerald Ford and Ronald Reagan emerged from the primaries almost deadlocked in the delegate count, and they consequently turned all of their considerable persuasive efforts toward the remaining state conventions and uncommitted delegates.

As a result, the caucus states probably will never be invisible again, and party officials in them will find it harder to control their outcomes or keep their delegations uncommitted. Michigan GOP leaders, for example, scheduled the precinct contests that began their nomination process in 1986, two years before the state convention, in order to boost the influence of their brand of moderate Republicanism in national nomination politics. Their efforts backfired, however, when supporters of Pat Robertson flooded the local caucuses and threw the entire process into turmoil for the next two years. (Michigan Republicans

---

[8]Robert J. Huckshorn and John F. Bibby, "National Party Rules and Delegate Selection in the Republican Party," *PS* 16 (1983): 656–66.

[9]For a study of the politics of electing convention delegates in a state convention, see Richard G. Niemi and M. Kent Jennings, "Intraparty Communications and the Selection of Delegates to a National Convention," *Western Political Quarterly* 22 (1969): 29–46.

The Rules Matter: Contrasts Between Primaries and Caucuses in 1988

Because they are different types of political events, primaries and caucuses can produce divergent results. This point is illustrated by a comparison of participation in and outcomes of the two different methods in three states that held both as a part of the 1988 Democratic nomination process. In Idaho and Vermont, the primary was a nonbinding "beauty contest" and delegates were apportioned and selected in accordance with caucus results. In Texas, delegate selection was based on both primary and caucus results.

	Primary		Caucus	
	Turnout	Vote result	Turnout	Vote result
Idaho	(May 24)		(March 8)	
	51,242	Dukakis 73%	4,633	Dukakis 38%
		Jackson 16%		Uncommitted 29%
Texas	(March 8)		(March 8)	
	1,766,904	Dukakis 33%	100,000	Jackson 40%
		Jackson 25%		Dukakis 38%
		Gore 20%		Uncommitted 10%
Vermont	(March 1)		(April 19)	
	50,791	Dukakis 56%	6,000	Jackson 46%
		Jackson 26%		Dukakis 45%

Note: Caucus turnout figures for Texas and Vermont are estimates.

Source: Congressional Quarterly Weekly Report (Washington, D.C.: Congressional Quarterly, Inc., 1988), p. 1527.

changed to primaries for 1992.) Caucuses will remain a focus of attention, in particular, because the "great delegate hunt" begins with the Iowa caucus. In spite of the inconsequential nature of its results in 1988, with Republican Robert Dole and Democratic Richard Gephardt as the leading vote-getters, it should continue to receive early and intense scrutiny.

THE POLITICS OF SELECTING DELEGATES

The politics of winning a presidential nomination obviously depends on enlisting the support of a majority of the delegates at the national convention. While the possibility still exists of a deadlocked convention turning to a newcomer for the nomination, it now seems inconceivable that any candidate could come to the convention with significant delegate support who had not actively con-

tested the primaries and caucuses. Every presidential nomination in both parties since 1956 has been won on the first ballot of the convention. Not since 1968
has the party nominee been someone other than the leader in delegates gained
through the primaries and caucuses. Since 1976, in fact, the party nominee has
led the field in primary election votes. Indeed, so much has the politics of
nomination shifted to the preconvention phase, and within it to the struggle to
win delegates in the states, that many observers feel the convention no longer
plays an important role in presidential selection. In its place is a dynamic process of primaries and caucuses with even more surprising vicissitudes. About
the only certainty in the new nomination process is the unpredictability of its
results (see box).

Candidate Strategies

In their competition to "sew up" the nomination before the convention meets,
the candidates face a number of strategic choices in their campaigns for delegates. They have to decide when to begin the planning for their campaign and
when to officially enter the fray. The foundation for many campaigns is laid as
early as the presidential election four years before, and virtually all serious candidates now enter the race a year before the presidential election year. Candidates need to decide from what political position their campaign should be
launched. Gone are the days when a big-state governorship or some other
prominent public office is seen as a necessary launching pad for the presidency.
Since Jimmy Carter's "dark horse" victory in 1976, some candidates have found
an advantage in being out of public office in the years before the election. Candidates also must choose which states to contest and what pace or timing to
adopt for their campaign, although the importance of the early caucuses and
primaries in recent races suggests that candidates must focus their attention on
the front end of the nomination calendar.

In making their many strategic choices, potential contenders for the party
nominations for president must weigh a number of factors, among the most important of which are:

- *The presence or absence of an incumbent.* When presidents are eligible
  for another term, they usually can arrange their own renomination. Their
  popular standing also affects the other party's nomination. Perceived
  chances of victory in the general election by the opposition party influence the strength of the field of candidates who vie for its nomination.
- *The nature of the opposition.* A leading candidate has no alternative but
  to go all out in the preconvention campaign; if he (or she) does not, risks
  an erosion of confidence among the supporters, and an early upset that
  can completely derail the campaign. A candidate with less support in a
  crowded field, on the other hand, can improve his or her chances for the
  nomination simply by exceeding expectations. Yet, in the new nomination
  politics of the 1970s and 1980s, only candidates who were already active
  campaigners have been able to capitalize on the failures of the front-
  runners.

1988's "Dark Horse" Candidate?

The contemporary nomination process, with its sequence of primary and caucus electoral tests, creates its own dynamic—which, as the following cartoon illustrates in humorists' hyperbole, can produce unexpected results. While the Republican nomination of Mick Jagger certainly would be even more of a shock than the Democrats' selection of Jimmy Carter was in 1976, it is hard to predict victors or even front-runners in advance. The wide-open contest of 1988, for example, produced more than the usual share of surprises.

BLOOM COUNTY  by Berke Breathed

© 1986 Washington Writer's Group, reprinted with permission.

- *The resources of the candidates.* Candidates must build nationwide campaign organizations to take the seemingly necessary step of qualifying for public funding. Then they must decide on which contests to allocate their resources in personnel and money. The early state contests typically receive the greatest investments, but because public funding is inadequate for full-blown campaigns in every state, candidates must decide which of the remaining ones are their priorities. Last-minute campaigns may be a relic of the past because of legal restrictions on campaign financial contributions. Moreover, the mere existence of federal financing for primary campaigns may have placed an insurmountable burden of public disapproval on the candidate who finances a campaign privately. The last candidate to fund his campaign entirely from private sources was John Connally, who mounted a futile effort against the Reagan tide of 1980.
- *The electoral and party strength of the candidate.* Candidates obviously prefer not to enter races in the states in which they are weak; if they must, they will likely concede defeat and then minimize its impact by doing little campaigning in the state and telling the press that they will regard anything more than 20 percent of the vote as a "moral victory."

All these decisions are made, of course, in the context of the rules set down by the two national parties and the various states. Thus, more resources will be needed, for example, to organize and contest a state primary that chooses delegates by congressional district than one that elects at large in the state. Moreover, these rules of the game differ from party to party. Since Democrats require a "fair reflection" of candidate strength in the selection of delegates, no front-running candidate risks a total shutout in any state any more. In the California Republican primary, however, it is still possible for a candidate to get 49 percent of the votes and still come away without a single delegate.[10]

The Importance of Timing

Of all the strategic imperatives, none is stronger than the need to win early. The strategy of staying back in the pack and making a run in the final stretch is less and less feasible. Victories in the early primaries and caucuses get attention in the mass media and name recognition in the wider public. They create credibility for the campaign and make it easier to raise money; and, above all, they create that mysterious psychological advantage, momentum. Early victories, in short, bring the support and resources that increase the likelihood of later victories. Victors in the early stages thus become increasingly difficult to overtake, and so the pressure increases to spend much, work hard, and do well in the early stages of the delegate hunt. Front-runners must do so to keep the support of their voters and financial backers; other candidates must do so to keep the front-runners from opening insuperable leads. Thus, in the contested Democratic race of 1984, the field of eight recognized contenders was winnowed to Walter Mondale, Gary Hart, and Jesse Jackson after the March 13 primaries. By the time the dust had settled after the March 8 contests in 1988, only Dukakis and Jackson remained as viable contenders from the seven serious aspirants who began the race.

These considerations of timing have not been lost on other participants in presidential politics. Some states, not wanting the selection of their delegates to come in the less influential later stages of the process, have moved their caucuses and primaries forward to the early weeks of the campaign. They increasingly have bunched them in the weeks immediately following the New Hampshire primary. In 1988, in fact, many southern states moved up their contests to March 8—so-called super Tuesday (see box)—to increase southern influence on the nomination.[11] For 1992, California has toyed with the idea of changing its primary from early June to early March so that it could play a "kingmaker" role, but its state legislature has so far been unwilling to make such a bold move in 1990 because of the complications an early date posed for nominations for state offices. If California were to move its primary to a point near

---

[10]On all these strategic considerations, see John H. Aldrich, *Before the Convention* (Chicago: University of Chicago Press, 1980).

[11]For a good account of the movement to the super Tuesday primaries by southern states in 1988, see Harold W. Stanley and Charles D. Hadley, "The Southern Regional Primary: Regional Intentions with National Implications," *Publius* 17 (1987): 83–100.

Super Tuesday in the South, 1988

The movement toward concentrating state delegate selection contests near the beginning of the primary and caucus season, so-called front-loading, turned into a stampede in advance of the 1988 presidential elections. In 1984, only five states held their primaries on the second Tuesday in March, and four other states began their caucus/convention process at about the same time. This number increased to twenty-one in 1988. In particular, ten of eleven southern and four of five border states scheduled their primaries on March 8 to create what many thought would be tantamount to a southern regional primary. The rationale behind the synchronization of the southern states' primaries and caucuses was to increase the influence of the South on the Democratic nomination process and thereby improve the prospects for the kind of candidate, presumably with moderate or conservative ideological leanings, who could win that region in the general election.

The outcome of the super Tuesday contests, though, dashed the fond hopes of their architects. The big winners in the South that day were Michael Dukakis and Jesse Jackson, hardly the kind of candidates moderate-to-conservative southern leaders expected to boost by concentrating their states' elections early in the process. Dukakis received the most delegates in the region's two largest states, Florida and Texas, while Albert Gore and Jackson split the remaining five states. By not seriously contesting earlier primaries and caucuses and then failing to garner stronger support in his home region, Gore's super Tuesday victories proved insufficient to sustain his candidacy. The best he could do in subsequent contests was to win 17 percent of the Wisconsin primary vote, good enough only for a distant third-place finish, a month later. By April 21, out of money and of hopes for victory, he had suspended his campaign.

The unexpected outcome of the super Tuesday contests understandably has dampened the enthusiasm of state party leaders everywhere for moving up their primaries or trying to create a regional primary. In the debate over the rescheduling of the California primary to the first Tuesday in March for 1992, for instance, some party strategists worried that selecting such a large delegation so early might create an irreversible bandwagon for the New Hampshire or Iowa winner or, under proportional representation rules, so fragment the field that no clear winner would emerge before the convention itself. Given their experience in 1988, even many white southern Democratic leaders are reconsidering their move to the early March date.

the beginning of the nomination process, it would significantly alter the strategies of the contenders.

Party Interests

The state party organizations and leaders also have interests at stake in the selection of delegates, and their interests often run counter to those of the aspiring presidential nominees. For the local and state parties, a hotly contested selection of delegates is often an occasion for intraparty conflict. Moreover, a state party organization (or one of its leaders) may want to preserve its bargaining power to affect the platform, to win a cabinet seat for a notable of the state party, to affect the vice-presidential choice, or just to enhance its value in the presidential nomination process. It may also fear that a weak presidential candidate will hurt the party's ticket for statewide office.

Historically, the state parties protected their interests by selecting delegates uncommitted to any candidate. The bargaining power of such a delegation enhanced the power of the state party at the convention. The ability of the parties to engineer the selection of an uncommitted delegation has been greatly eroded by the new system, however. As the nationally prominent candidates intensify the preconvention campaign, delegates committed to them simply have a greater appeal to the voters and party activists. Moreover, for delegates to remain uncommitted while one of the contenders for the nomination is locking up a majority of the convention votes is to squander all influence over the nomination and perhaps also some influence over the business of the convention. In a process dominated by the candidates, refusing to take sides carries considerable risk.

CITIZEN PARTICIPATION AND CHOICE IN PRESIDENTIAL NOMINATIONS

With the reforms of the presidential selection process in recent years has come increased attention to citizen participation and, for those who participate, the bases of voting choice in the contests for nomination. The parties' moves to primaries have increased citizen participation in presidential nominations to unprecedented levels. Many more people vote in primaries than in the caucuses, although turnout in the primaries still falls far short of levels attained in the presidential elections. In 1988, for example, the primary electorate was well less than half the size of the November electorate and less than a quarter of the voting age population.[12] Caucus turnout, by contrast, was only 7 percent of

---

[12]Turnout rates in nomination contests are not easy to calculate because of the difficulties in determining their denominator, the number of voters eligible to vote in that primary or caucus. The states use various methods for determining eligibility. Moreover, where primaries or caucuses are

(*continued*)

Table 10.3　TURNOUT IN THE PRESIDENTIAL THE PRIMARIES AND CAUCUSES, 1988

	Primaries		Caucuses	
	As % of general election vote	As % of voting age population	As % of general election vote	As % of voting age population
Highest state	62%	34%	19%	11%
	(New Hampshire)		(Iowa)	
Lowest state	16%	8%	2%	1%
	(Rhode Island)		(Wyoming)	
Average	44%	24%	7%	4%
	(34 states)		(9 states)	

Note: Only states in which both parties had primaries or both parties had caucuses are included. Meaningful turnout rates can not be calculated for the other states.

Source: Constructed from raw figures provided in *Congressional Quarterly Weekly Report* (1988), pp. 1894, 1897, 1950, and 2254; and (1989), p. 139.

general election turnout and about 4 percent of the voting age population (Table 10.3). Even considering that some regular voters are not eligible to vote in closed primaries or caucuses, participation in primaries is indeed light. Nonetheless, it is much higher than caucus turnout and represents far greater voter involvement in the nomination process than occurred in the decades before the recent upsurge in primaries.

Variations in Turnout

There is a considerable variation of course in primary turnout levels among the different states in any one year and across different years in any one state. Not unsurprisingly, the first caucus (Iowa) and the first primary (New Hampshire) led the way in their respective categories in 1988. In general, turnout tends to be higher year in and year out in those states with a better educated citizenry, higher percentages of registered voters, and a tradition of two-party competition—the same states that enjoy higher general election turnout. But voters also are differentially mobilized by the nature of the contest. The hotly contested primaries, where candidates spend more money and there is the excite-

(continued)

open, an exciting race in one party also may attract crossover voters, thus increasing both numerator and denominator for it while depressing them both for the other party. To avoid these problems, we calculate primary and caucus turnout only for states in which both parties had a contest and then only for both parties together.

ment of competition, and the key early contests attract many more voters.[13] When the focus turns from state participation levels to individual decisions to participate, similar factors are involved: In general, participation is a function of the closeness of the primary contest and voter interest in the race.[14]

Representativeness

In spite of the lower turnout in primaries than in general elections, there is little evidence to support the common charge that primary electorates are unrepresentative. Primary voters are better educated, better off, and older than nonvoters, but so are general election voters. The more appropriate comparison is between primary voters and political party followers, however, because primaries are devices through which the party in the electorate is to choose its nominees. When this comparison is made, few important differences emerge. Primary voters are only slightly older, better educated, more affluent, better integrated into their communities, less black or Hispanic, or attentive to politics. But their ideological positions seem little different from party followers.[15] On empirical grounds, then, it is difficult to sustain the argument that primary electorates are less representative than those who chose party nominees several decades ago.

Quality of Choice

Another serious criticism of the primaries is that voter choices, rather than being unrepresentative, are uninformed. Primary electorates have been found to have only superficial knowledge about the candidates. Candidate momentum plays an important role in the formation of voter preferences, as bandwagons form for candidates who have demonstrated their viability and electability by winning, or merely exceeding expectations in, the immediately preceding

---

[13]See Jack Moran and Mark Fenster, "Voter Turnout in Presidential Primaries: A Diachronic Analysis," *American Politics Quarterly* 10 (1982): 453–76; Patrick J. Kenney and Tom W. Rice, "Voter Turnout in Presidential Primaries: A Cross-Sectional Examination," *Political Behavior* 7 (1985): 101–12; and Barbara Norrander and Gregg W. Smith, "Type of Contest, Candidate Strategy, and Turnout in Presidential Primaries," *American Politics Quarterly* 13 (1985): 28–50.

[14]See Barbara Norrander, "Selective Participation: Presidential Voters as a Subset of General Election Voters," *American Politics Quarterly* 14 (1986): 35–54; and Patrick J. Kenney, "Explaining Turnout in Presidential Primaries," 1990, unpublished manuscript.

[15]Recent evidence on the representatives of primary electorates may be found in Larry M. Bartels, *Presidential Primaries and the Dynamics of Public Choice* (Princeton, N.J.: Princeton University Press, 1988), pp. 140–48; John G. Geer, "The Representativeness of Presidential Primary Electorates," *American Journal of Political Science* 32 (1988): 929–45; and Barbara Norrander, "Ideological Representativeness of Primary Voters," *American Journal of Political Science* 33 (1989): 570–87. The classic case for the unrepresentativeness of primaries is made by V. O. Key, Jr., *American State Politics: An Introduction* (New York: Knopf, 1967), pp. 133–68.

contests. Especially in the early contests, voters are heavily influenced by media interpretations of results in "horse race" terms. Of demonstrated importance, too, in the voter's calculus are candidates' personal characteristics, defined in large part by the themes stressed in the candidates' own campaigns. Ideology, issues, and of course (since the primaries are within-party contests) party attachments may play only minor roles in primary-election voting behavior. The result, so this argument goes, is a series of electoral contests decided principally on the basis of short-run—and inherently more fickle—considerations.[16]

Many scholars, however, believe that this indictment of the primaries goes too far. Larry Bartels' sophisticated modeling of primary voting emphasizes that candidate momentum, developed through performance that exceeds expectations in previous primaries, is a rational basis for supporting one of a pack of low visibility candidates, especially among those voters who are searching for an alternative to the front-runner. Candidates favored by momentum, though, are quickly subjected to more searching evaluations. The dynamics of the campaign, he goes on to show, matter most where there are no well-known front-runners (e.g., the Democratic contests in 1976 or perhaps 1988). Where there is at least one well-known candidate in the contest, by contrast, voters' decisions are more likely to be based on matters of substance.[17]

Even though primary contests demand much more information than the general election, then, there is an emerging view that voter choices are not uninformed. In intraparty contests, issue, ideological, and, of course, party differences among candidates are necessarily muted. It should not be at all surprising that, in their place, candidate characteristics would loom large and issue priorities rather than positions might become important. Moreover, taking candidate viability (i.e., chances of winning the nomination) and even electability (i.e., chances of winning the presidency) into account is a rational act of the strategic voter, not an indication of irrationality or ignorance. Primaries provide a different institutional context for voting behavior, but beyond that the bases for voter decision-making in primaries may differ little from those in a general election.[18]

---

[16]The most severe indictment of the primaries on these grounds appears in Scott Keeter and Cliff Zukin, *Uninformed Choice* (New York: Praeger, 1983). The classic treatment of the role of expectations and momentum in primaries is Bartels, *Presidential Primaries and the Dynamics of Public Choice*. On the restricted influence of ideology and issues, see John G. Geer, *Nominating Presidents: An Evaluation of Voters and Primaries* (New York: Greenwood Press, 1989) and Barbara Norrander, "Correlates of Vote Choice in the 1980 Presidential Primaries," *Journal of Politics* 48 (1986): 156–66. Also see J. David Gopoian, "Issue Preferences and Candidate Choice in the 1980 Presidential Primaries," *American Journal of Political Science* 26 (1982): 523–46.

[17]Bartels, *Presidential Primaries and the Dynamics of Public Choice*.

[18]This is the conclusion reached in a recent unpublished paper by John H. Aldrich and R. Michael Alvarez, "Voting in the 1988 Presidential Primaries," Duke University, 1991. Aldrich and Alvarez also can be credited for showing that, in primaries, issue priorities tend to take the place of issue

That the nomination process imposes greater information costs on voters, though, is undeniable. Whether these costs are unrealistically high is quite another matter. Thus, the debate over the quality of electoral decision making in primaries will doubtlessly continue as long as unexpected nominees emerge and one's own favorite is defeated. Of course, these conditions are hardly unique to primaries, and the same questions could be raised about the quality of judgment of party leaders in making nominations under the earlier caucus-convention system.

PRIMARY VERSUS PARTY SELECTION

Apart from the interests of parties and candidates, however, has it really made any difference whether delegates to the national conventions have been chosen by primaries or by party processes? Do the delegates chosen by a primary behave any differently from those chosen through party bodies? Do the presidential primaries have an impact on the nominations commensurate with the time and money spent in them?

Not too long ago in American politics, the processes of delegate selection were sharply bifurcated. In the states of the presidential primaries, a more open, popular candidate-centered politics worked to the advantage of well-known personalities and generally helped insurgents in the party. In the other states, the party organization controlled delegate selection and could apply, with few exceptions, tests of party acceptability both to delegates and ultimately to the seekers after the party's nomination. Estes Kefauver in 1952 and 1956 and Eugene McCarthy in 1968 used the primaries to challenge the party apparatus for the nominations. They failed, as did all other challengers with little support outside the primary states. They failed if for no other reason than that there were not enough primaries; the delegates selected in the primaries were 40 percent or less of the total. Before the 1970s, the party nominees invariably fell into two categories: those, such as John Kennedy in 1960, who mixed victories in primary and nonprimary states, and those, such as Wendell Willkie in 1940 and Adlai Stevenson in 1952, who entered no primaries and who won nomination in brokered conventions.

As the differences between the primary and nonprimary processes have diminished since the 1970s, however, the situation has changed. On the one hand, it now seems necessary for a successful candidate to win many primary victories, and it is even possible to succeed by winning largely primary victories. That is so if for no other reason than that a majority of the convention delegates

---

positions. For a persuasive analysis of strategic voting in primaries, in which voters temper their "sincere" preferences with calculations of their candidate's viability, see Paul R. Abramson, John H. Aldrich, Phil Paolino, and David W. Rohde, " 'Sophisticated' Voting in the 1988 Presidential Primaries," paper presented at the 1990 Annual Meeting of the American Political Science Association, August 30–September 2, San Francisco.

are now chosen in primaries. On the other hand, the comparison between primary and nonprimary selection is losing its importance simply because the politics of choosing delegates is now more similar in all states, primary and nonprimary alike. National candidates, media coverage, and more open and better publicized processes make for one long but continuous and homogeneous preconvention politics. As a consequence, the results of the primaries and the caucuses do not greatly diverge. The shift to a more open, mass politics has touched the traditional presidential preliminaries as well.[19]

Still, the primaries maintain their special role and appeal. Because of their openness to the voters, their results confer great legitimacy on the winners. Victories acquired in primaries may still be as important for these symbolic purposes as for the number of delegates required. The primaries also provide an opportunity for candidates to show their appeal and to build a following, and to show their stamina and adaptability under various pressures. Cruelly, too, they help weed out the nonviable candidates. As Lyndon Johnson discovered in 1968, disappointing results in the primaries may even help drive an incumbent president from office.

A SYSTEM IN NEED OF REFORM?

It has been over two decades since the recent wave of reform of the presidential nomination process got underway. Nonetheless, the debate continues about the wisdom of the old system versus the new.

The briefs against both the presidential primaries and party selection of delegates are long and weighty. In fact, they seem to outweigh the briefs in favor of each process to the extent that the observer might easily conclude that, once again in American politics, one must choose between the lesser of two evils.

The Case Against the Presidential Primaries

The broader question of reform of the delegate-selection process inevitably begins with a hard look at the presidential primaries. The case against them is impressive:

- They consume an enormous amount of time, energy, and money before the presidential campaign has even begun. Leading contenders can arrive at the party convention personally and financially exhausted.
- They put a premium on campaign strategy and candidate image-making rather than the kinds of leadership abilities required in the presidency.

---

[19]The creation of a group of unpledged ex officio superdelegates by the Democrats in 1984, though, interjects the possibility of a divergence in final results from the popular processes. See Priscilla L. Southwell, "The 1984 Democratic Nomination Process: The Significance of Unpledged Superdelegates," *American Politics Quarterly* 14 (1986): 75–88.

- The importance of any one of them may easily be distorted out of all perspective. In the mass of publicity surrounding the primaries, candidates and voters alike often fail to assess them soberly. The nation's first and most influential primary, in fact, is held in a state (New Hampshire) that has less that one-half of one percent of the nation's population.[20]
- The presidential primaries frequently result in internal divisions in state party organizations, in warring delegations to the national conventions, and in delegates not representative of the party organization and leadership in the state. Like any other primary, they take an important party process out of the control of the party organizations and thus weaken them.
- The serial nature of the nomination process creates its own dynamic in which minor campaign events and the unexpected replace the deliberative decision making of a national convention and raise the risk that a party will select a nominee who is doomed to failure in the fall election.

The Case Against Party Selection of Delegates

On the other hand, the charges against party selection of a state's delegates rest on the traditional complaint about party processes—that they are too easily controlled and manipulated by a handful of party oligarchs. In any event, that has been the charge of the reformers in the Democratic party since 1968. Furthermore, in the nonprimary states, the party electorates and even some of the party activists are excluded from the crucial first step in picking a president. Also, it is undoubtedly true that, in these states, the would-be presidential nominees have had to fight for the access and visibility they enjoy in the presidential primaries. A number of state parties would still prefer to send uncommitted delegations to their national conventions.[21]

Debating points aside, however, recent years have been a time of a great revival of interest in the primaries. After a period of disenchantment, the states have returned to them with the enthusiasm they first had. Increasing media coverage has spotlighted the role of the primaries in the nomination process; and their basic rationale—the twin democratic norms of mass popular partici-

---

[20]One study found that New Hampshire received 19.2 percent of all the media coverage given the 1984 nomination contests by ABC, CBS, NBC, and *The New York Times*. Iowa, the first traditional caucus state, received another 12.8 percent of the coverage that year. The fact that these two unrepresentative states containing a mere 2.9 percent of the U.S. population garnered a third of the media coverage in 1984 is a tribute to the disproportionate role a few contests can play in the nomination process. See William C. Adams, "As New Hampshire Goes . . . ," in Gary R. Orren and Nelson W. Polsby (eds.), *Media and Momentum* (Chatham, N.J.: Chatham House, 1987), pp. 42–59.

[21]A good statement of the case against recent party reforms may be found in Polsby, *Consequences of Party Reform*. The case for party reforms is covered in William J. Crotty, *Decision for the Democrats* (Baltimore: The Johns Hopkins University Press, 1978).

The Public Views the Nomination Process

In spite of the continuing debate among political activists and scholars over recent reforms of the nominating process, especially the greater reliance on primaries, the American public seems to be quite satisfied with the primary process. This at least was the result of a national survey conducted by the Gallup Organization for The Times Mirror Company in January 1988 and analyzed in Michael W. Traugott and Margaret Petrella, "Public Evaluations of the Presidential Nomination Process," *Political Behavior* 11 (1989): 335–52.

In answer to the question "Thinking about the presidential primaries, generally do you think they are a good way of determining who the best qualified nominees are, or not?", 61 percent of those interviewed responded affirmatively. Political activists, partisans, the college educated, and likely primary voters were even more satisfied than that. When asked about their dissatisfaction with various aspects of the process, the worry that high campaign costs discouraged good candidates led the way: 64 percent voiced this concern.

---

pation and fear of party oligarchies—seems more powerful than ever. Some states have ventured into the primaries for the first time to increase their own political leverage. No reform movement can ignore, therefore, the presently secure place of the primaries.

Possible Reforms

If we cannot live without the primaries, is it possible that we might learn to live more comfortably with them? The most drastic reform proposal of recent years was to do away with the national nominating conventions altogether and to choose the presidential nominees in a single national primary. Another possibility is the scheduling of primaries on the same day in each region, with a few weeks separating the different regional election days. The disappointing (to their organizers at least, if not to Michael Dukakis or Jesse Jackson) results of the southern super Tuesday primaries, though, seem to have dampened enthusiasm for this reform. If one assumes the survival of the nominating conventions, however, is no change possible in the way we select delegates to them? By designating ex officio superdelegates in 1984 and again in 1988, in an attempt to leaven the popular contest for the nomination with the perspectives of party leaders and elected officials, the Democrats already have made a change that recaptures some of the lost elements of the old system.

Even at these early stages of presidential politics, one sees the beginning of the repetition of an old theme in American politics. It is difficult for the party organizers to control the presidential nomination, just as it is difficult for them to control other party nominations. In part, the presidential primary weakens organizational control and shifts it to the candidates. In part, too, the organizations are weak because they have no means of uniting or coordinating their own preferences prior to the nominating conventions. Thus, candidates with comparatively rational and unified national strategies increasingly find it easy to take the initiative from individual state party organizations in this phase of presidential politics. To the extent that they are able to win the commitments of enough delegates to capture the nominations, they and the party in government capture the nomination before the party organizations ever gather themselves together to act as a national party at the convention.

Chapter
11

The Changing Role
of the National
Party Conventions

That cynical observer of American politics, H. L. Mencken, especially loved the challenge of reporting a national nominating convention. After ruminating on the Democrats convention of 1924 and the 103 ballots it took to nominate John W. Davis, the Sage of Baltimore wrote:

> There is something about a national convention that makes it as fascinating as a revival or a hanging. It is vulgar, it is ugly, it is stupid, it is tedious, it is hard upon both the higher cerebral centers and the *gluteus maximus*, and yet it is somehow charming. One sits through long sessions wishing heartily that all the delegates and alternates were dead and in hell—and then suddenly there comes a show so gaudy and hilarious, so melodramatic and obscene, so unimaginably exhilarating and preposterous that one lives a gorgeous year in an hour.[1]

Former President Dwight D. Eisenhower felt the irritation without experiencing the exhilaration. The conventions, he said, were "a picture of confusion, noise, impossible deportment, and indifference to what is being discussed on the platform." He dismissed the banner-waving demonstrations that typify the carnival gaiety of the conventions as "spurious demonstration(s) of unwarranted enthusiasm."[2]

---

[1]Malcolm Moos (ed.), *H. L. Mencken on Politics* (New York: Vintage, 1960), p. 83.

[2]*The New York Times*, June 29, 1965.

In spite of the tongue-clicking appraisals of their critics and the increasing domination of the presidential nominations by the direct primary, though, the national party conventions live on. For several days every four years, they alone enable the Democrats and Republicans to assemble as *national* parties, like their counterparts in other democracies, engaged in decision making on a national scale. They provide a forum in which the different parts of the party— the party organization, the party in the electorate, and even the party in government—are drawn together for collective action. They serve as a primary reference for millions of Americans when they think of the political parties. Thus, beneath the curious combination of somber ceremony and exuberant carnival lies an important institution for party politics in America.

THE ORIGINS AND DEVELOPMENT OF THE PARTY CONVENTIONS

By the standards of American political life, the national party conventions are venerable institutions. They first emerged as vehicles for the decentralization and, hence, the democratization of the party system—as the means through which the state parties and their leaders could wrest control of the presidential selection process from congressional leaders. Credit for the national party convention idea can be claimed by a long-forgotten minor party, the Anti-Masons, who brought together their supporters in a Baltimore meeting in 1831 to nominate a candidate for president. But it is the major parties who have made the convention a familiar institution of American politics.

In 1832, the Democratic-Republican party, soon to be transformed into the Democratic party, became the first major party to hold a convention. Because the nomination of Andrew Jackson was a foregone conclusion, the principal purpose for meeting in convention was to enable state political leaders to secure the vice-presidential nomination for Martin Van Buren over Henry Clay, the favorite of the congressional caucus. By the time the Republican party emerged in 1854, the convention had become institutionalized as the means through which a major party's candidates for president and vice-president were to be selected. The Republicans held their first national convention for this purpose in 1856.

Since their origins, then, America's two major parties have held quadrennial national party conventions. For their entire lives, they have used these conventions to nominate their candidates for president. Even though this core function has been undermined with the emergence of the direct primary, especially in recent decades, the conventions remain key party institutions.[3]

---

[3]This brief historical account relies on Byron E. Shafer, *Bifurcated Politics: Evolution and Reform in the National Party Convention* (Cambridge, Mass.: Harvard University Press, 1988), Chapter 1; and *Guide to U.S. Elections* (Washington, D.C.: Congressional Quarterly, Inc., 1985), pp. 31–159.

THE STRUCTURE OF THE CONVENTION

The conventions are the creatures of the parties themselves. They are subject to no congressional or state regulation, and even the federal courts have been reluctant to intervene in their operation. Responsibility for them falls to the national party committees and their staffs, although an incumbent president inevitably influences the planning for his party's convention.

The Committees

Months before the convention, its major committees begin their work. Like all other major American institutions, both political and nonpolitical, the conventions function, in part, through committees. Generally, there have been four important ones:

- *Credentials*. The credentials committee considers the qualifications of delegates and alternates and makes up the official delegate list of the convention. Its prickliest duty is deciding contests (between two delegates or slates vying for the same seats) and challenges (of the qualifications of any delegate or alternate, or indeed, of any delegation).
- *Permanent organization*. This committee selects the permanent officials of the convention—the chairperson, secretary, and sergeant at arms, for example. Generally, its work provokes little controversy.
- *Rules*. This committee sets the rules of the convention, particularly the specific procedures for selecting the presidential nominee. The main procedures have been fixed for some time, but the committee struggles at every convention with rules such as those governing the length and number of nomination speeches, the number of nondelegate demonstrators that will be permitted on the convention floor, and the method of polling delegations should controversy arise within them.
- *Platform (or Resolutions.)* This committee's chief responsibility is to draft the party's platform for action by the convention. It holds open hearings to receive the ideas of citizens, party activists, and the potential presidential nominees.

Early appointment of these committees is necessary if only because they begin to function before the convention convenes. Platform committees, especially, begin to scour the party and the nation for ideas months before the convention opens.

The Input of the Committees

The first three of these committees—credentials, permanent organization, and rules—make decisions that define the structure and procedures of the convention. What these committees decide often has enormous impact on the important decisions the convention makes on the nominees or the platform. The committee decisions, though, can be reversed by the convention itself, which acts as the ultimate arbiter of its own structure and procedures.

Some of the most famous battles on the floor of the convention have involved disputes over committee recommendations on how the convention should be organized rather than candidates or issues, although they often also serve as initial tests of strength for the contending forces. In 1980, for example, the supporters of Senator Edward Kennedy sought to repeal the rule forcing delegates to support the candidate to whom they were pledged in hopes of picking up some wavering Carter delegates at the convention. The Carter forces beat back the challenge, and the president won renomination on the first ballot. It is precisely because procedural decisions such as these so affect the distribution of power at the conventions that state parties, the candidates, and the ideological camps within the parties work so hard to win representation on the committees that initially make them.

In the last thirty to forty years, the decisions of the credentials committees have had the greatest repercussions. The 1952 contest for the Republican nomination between Senator Robert Taft and General Dwight Eisenhower hinged in great part on the battle over delegates from Georgia, Louisiana, and Texas. The credentials committee voted to seat the pro-Taft delegates from the three states, but the convention as a whole seated the pro-Eisenhower claimants. With the votes of those contested delegates, Taft would have led Eisenhower on the convention's first ballot. In 1972, George McGovern's quest for the Democratic nomination was aided by the convention's decisions to seat the California delegates loyal to him and not to seat the Illinois delegation loyal to Mayor Daley. In fact, in that convention, a modern record of more than a dozen credential disputes received full floor debate.

A more serious problem plagued the Democratic conventions after World War II: the unwillingness of some southern state delegations to take a pledge to support the candidates and platform of the convention. In 1948, delegates from Mississippi and Alabama marched out of an evening session of the convention after northern liberals, led by Mayor Hubert Humphrey of Minneapolis, nailed a strong civil rights plank onto the platform. Many of those delegates and their state parties later supported the Dixiecrat party ticket or, worse from the standpoint of the Democrats, put the Dixiecrat slate on their state presidential ballot as the ticket of the Democratic party. The loyalty issue in the Democratic party was supplemented in the 1960s by the failure of the delegate-selection processes in some southern states to be open to blacks. In 1968 and 1972, the regular Mississippi delegation (and half of the Georgia regulars in 1968) was replaced by challengers loyal to the national ticket.

The Keynote Address

Finally, to complete the organization of the convention, the national committee selects the temporary chairperson, who usually delivers an extravagantly partisan keynote address. His or her qualifications are only two—an aloofness from the major contestants for the nomination and a telegenic oratorical style—but the candidates are many. They may remember that Alben Barkley's oratorical flights in praise of the Democratic party won him the vice-presidential nomination in 1948.[4] Even at lower levels of ambition, however, the assignment is an ideal showcase, one that does no politician's future any harm. Ann Richard's stridently partisan keynote address at the 1988 Democratic convention, for example, earned her considerable national attention and helped to propel her into the governorship of Texas two years later.

The description of the formal structure of the convention fails to convey anything of its ambience, however. Born of a rough-and-tumble political tradition and related to the institution of the boisterous convention in other areas of American life, the national party conventions have been part carnival, part "fling at the big city," and part (a large part, actually) serious party conclave. At one and the same time, they mix well-rehearsed demonstrations of enthusiasm with serious thought about presidential stature, the military precision of floor managers with the aimless amblings of ordinary delegates, perfunctory afternoon oratorical fillers with the often eloquent messages of the party worthies. If television has now made them somewhat more sedate, they can still offer moments of raw political excitement unmatched in the rest of American politics.

THE DELEGATES

For the many Americans who are watching these quadrennial spectacles on television, it is the people who have assembled in the convention hall that provide their image of the party. After all, the conventions are designed to represent their respective parties—even if, in recent years, this representation is strongly linked to the relative standings of the various party candidates for president. Thus, who the delegates are says a great deal about what the parties are.

Apportionment of Convention Delegates Among the States

The first step in determining the delegates for the national conventions is taken by the parties themselves. Operating through their national committees and conventions, they determine how many delegates will be apportioned to each state and territory or other constituency.

For many years both parties awarded equal numbers of delegates to each state, regardless of its population size, with some additional bonus delegates assigned to states in accordance with how much they had supported the party's candidates. In recent years, the apportionment formulas each has adopted have given more weight to the state's population and its support for the party's can-

---

[4]For a contrary case, they may remember that General of the Army Douglas MacArthur disappointed his supporters by failing to light any fires with his keynote speech before the Republicans in 1952.

didates. Nonetheless, the Republicans have continued to allocate delegates more equally among the states, thereby overrepresenting the less populous states; while the Democrats have tended to represent population size and strength of Democratic voting more heavily (see box).

Nothing seems more boring than the intricacies of delegate apportionment formulas. Yet they are subjects of regular intraparty struggle because they play a critical role in determining the strength of the various groups within the party coalitions. The GOP's decision to give more equal representation to the states in allocating convention delegates has given the smaller, less industrialized, states more influence in Republican nomination politics than their population would warrant. One political consequence is that conservative Republicans have been advantaged—an advantage that is then compounded when states more supportive of Republican candidates are allocated bonus delegates. By giving relatively more weight to the larger states with stronger Democratic voting traditions, by contrast, the Democrats have favored the more liberal interests in their party. Different delegate allocation formulas, within the range of reason at last, may have only marginal effects on the balance of forces within the parties, but many a nomination has been won—and lost—at the margin.

The combination of large numbers of delegates and equally large numbers of alternate delegates produces gargantuan conventions. There were 4,162 delegates at the Democratic convention in 1988, and to that total must be added 1,170 alternates. The Republicans had a total of 2,277 delegates and an equal number of alternates at their 1988 meetings. The national committees are under tremendous pressure from the state party organizations to increase the number of delegates. Party people in the states cherish the prestige of attending a convention, and the experience of being a delegate is also likely to stimulate them to work in the campaign that follows. Large convention size is also increasingly the price of representing the large, populous states in some reasonable ratio to the representation of the small ones. Finally, big conventions create a mass rally atmosphere for television coverage. Especially when the convention is certain to renominate a popular incumbent president—as the Democrats did in 1964 and the Republicans did in 1972 and 1984—the rally aspects of the convention replace its nominating duties.

Who Are the Convention Delegates?

The delegates to the Democratic and Republican conventions have never been a cross section of American citizens. Whites, males, the well-educated, and upper income groups traditionally have been overrepresented. There have also been differences between the two parties, which reflect their different coalitional bases. Democratic delegations have had more Catholics, Jews, and trade unionists; the Republicans more Protestants and businessmen. Recently, however, both parties have attempted to broaden the representativeness of their delegations, with the Democrats making by far the greater change through the use of affirmative action plans adopted after 1968 to increase the representation of women, blacks, and for a time, young people. These plans were successful in

Apportioning Power to the States: The Democratic and Republican Delegate Allocation Formulas

For their 1988 presidential nominating conventions, the Democrats and Republicans used different formulas for apportioning delegates. These formulas are complicated, but in them one can see the different ways (indicated in brackets on the right) in which the two parties represent the states (we ignore provisions for territories and other entities, and some minor provisions of each set of rules):

REPUBLICAN ALLOCATION FORMULA, 1988

Number of delegates
given to each state   =   6   [Equality]
             + 3 for each U.S.
                Representative   [Population]
             + 1 each for: [Republican
                                       strength]

- each Republican U.S. Senator
- a Republican governor
- when state's U.S. House delegation is at least ½ Republican
- a Republican majority in one state legislative chamber or an increase of 25% or more in Republicans in a state legislative chamber

DEMOCRATIC ALLOCATION FORMULA, 1988

Number of delegates
given to each state   =   1500 × a state's
                 proportion of   [Population]
                 the congressional
                 membership
          +   1500 × (average
                 % Democratic   [Democratic
                 in past 3 presi-   strength]
                 tial elections)

(continued)

+	15% of preceding total to represent certain party and elected officials	[Population/ Democratic strength]
+	2 Democratic National Committee members	[Equality]
+	former national leaders	
+	Democratic governor	[Democratic strength]
+	U.S. Senators and Representative chosen by their party caucuses	[Democratic strength]

increasing the percentage of black and female delegates in attendance at Democratic conventions; and their attendance at the Republican conclaves has increased as well, although not as sharply (see Table 11.1).

Representation of Women, Blacks, and Young People How these changes have affected the *representation* of each group is a more complicated question, because it involves comparison to some baseline. Using the percentages of each group identifying with the party as his baseline, Howard Reiter found that women were much better represented in both parties after 1968, and blacks were much better represented in the Democratic party. Except for the almost unavoidable overrepresentation by a handful of blacks in GOP delegations of the negligible number of black Republicans, however, these groups remained underrepresented in the delegations to the national party conventions through 1984.[5] While this situation has improved for women and blacks, the representation of young people in both parties has worsened since 1972, although a plausible case can be made that the underrepresentation of any particular generation in its early years is a less serious problem because it inevitably will be corrected with age.

Income The focus of concern over representation inevitably shifts with the times. In 1982, the Democratic National Committee recognized that delegates to its convention were atypically high in status and income, regardless of their other demographic characteristics, and urged its state party organizations to recruit more delegates of "low and moderate income." This admonition has had little lasting effect, however, for in 1988 only 6 percent of the Democratic dele-

---

[5]Reiter, *Selecting the President*, pp. 59–63.

Table 11.1   PERCENTAGE OF BLACKS, WOMEN, AND YOUNG PEOPLE SERVING AS
DELEGATES TO DEMOCRATIC AND REPUBLICAN CONVENTIONS: 1968–88.

	Blacks		Women		Under 30	
Year	Dem.	Repub.	Dem.	Repub.	Dem.	Repub.
1968	5%	2%	13%	16%	3%	4%
1972	15	4	40	29	22	8
1976	11	3	33	31	15	7
1980	15	3	49	29	11	5
1984	18	4	50	44	8	4
1988	21	3	52	37	4	4

Source: Figures for 1968–84 are adapted from Howard L. Reiter, Selecting the President (Philadelphia: University of Pennsylvania Press, 1985), pp. 61–63; figures for 1988 come from The New York Times, August 14, 1988, p. 14.

gates had incomes under $25,000 compared with 43 percent of all Democrats. Moreover, 59 percent of the Democratic delegates earned over $50,000, and 74% of the Republican delegates had attained that income level.[6] Convention delegates remain a highly affluent elite.

Turnover   Several additional characteristics of delegates are politically relevant to the convention's business and, therefore, have been a focus of party reform efforts. Some critics have felt that the conventions had become the conclaves of a self-perpetuating set of party elites. Careful attention to turnover in convention delegates, however, makes this charge hard to sustain. Well before the reforms of the post-1968 era, a majority of the delegates were attending a party convention for the first time (see Figure 11.1) This number has been affected by party reforms and the nature of intraparty competition: It increased after 1968 to peaks of well over 80 percent for both parties in 1980 and then fell to pre-1972 levels in 1988.

The Party Elite   Even if there is considerable turnover among delegates in general, elite control of the conventions can be accomplished by the continuing dominance of a few top party leaders over their state delegations. For the better part of this century, governors and senators have been well represented at the Democratic conventions, although the proportions of U.S. Representatives in attendance have been much lower (Figure 11.2) Lore has it that these top state Democratic leaders and some big city mayors were commanding presences in-

---

[6]These figures on delegate income result from surveys of convention delegates conducted by The New York Times in the weeks before the conventions were held in 1988 and reported in The New York Times, August 14, 1988, p. 14.

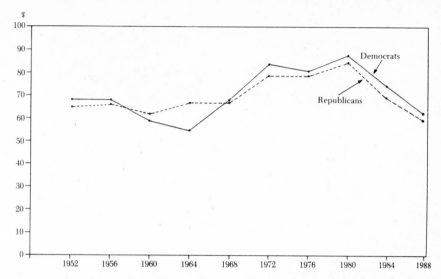

Figure 11.1 Percentage of Delegates Attending Their First Convention: 1952–88.

Source: The 1952–1984 figures are adapted from Table 4.4 in Reiter, *Selecting the President,* p. 64. The figures for 1988 come from *The New York Times* poll, as reported in *The New York Times,* August 14, 1988 p. 14.

deed for many years, and there is ample anecdotal evidence to back this up. Comparable Republican leaders have been much less represented in the convention hall and, correspondingly, less visible as power brokers.

Recent changes, though, have brought an end to the possibility of conventions under the control of a few powerful state leaders. First, by opening up the delegate selection process, the Democrats made it difficult for elected leaders to win delegate seats. Their relative numbers declined rather dramatically until Democratic reforms in 1984 guaranteed most of them spots as "superdelegates." Indeed Democratic governors, senators, and representatives were better represented in 1988 than they had been at any time in the last sixty years; oddly enough (since they have no guaranteed seats), so too were their Republican counterparts.[7] Second, even with their greater presence, the role of these party leaders is necessarily restricted because, in both parties, delegates come to the conventions today already committed to candidates and unavailable for "delivery" by state leaders to the candidates of their choice.

Even though the argument that a few elites control the conventions now seems misplaced, however accurate it may once have been, it is undeniable that the party conclaves are populated by political elites. In 1988, about 43 percent of the Democratic delegates and 60 percent of the Republican delegates currently held some kind of party position at the local, state, or national level. A

---

[7]See Reiter, *Selecting the President,* pp. 63–71.

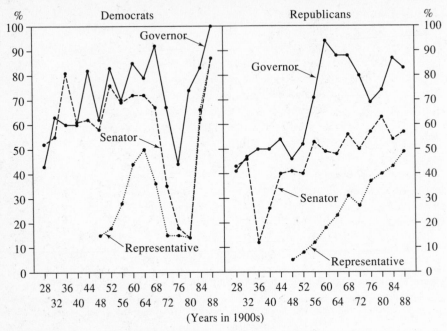

Figure 11.2 Percentage of Officeholders as Delegates: 1928–88.

Source: The 1928–84 figures are adapted from Tables 4.5 and 4.6 in Reiter, *Selecting the President*, pp. 66 and 68. The 1988 figures were calculated from convention records. Data were not available for Representatives before 1948.

total of 26 and 28 percent, respectively, were elected officials.[8] For all the reforms, the national party conventions still draw heavily from the parties' leadership cadres.

Political Views and Preferences   But a focus on the demographic characteristics and party positions of the delegates overlooks the most important meaning of representativeness. The political views and preferences of the delegates are certainly more important than who they are. Convention delegates are more committed, more aware of issues and issue positions, than the ordinary voters of their party. They also tend more to the ideological poles than do the electorates of their parties—with, as expected, Democratic delegates clustering toward the liberal end and Republic delegates toward the conservative end of the liberal-conservative ideological continuum.

In 1988, for example, 39 percent of the Democratic delegates described themselves as liberals, but only 25 percent of the registered Democratic voters

---

[8]These are the percentages reporting party and elected office among the respondents to *The New York Times* 1988 preconvention surveys. Because some delegates may hold multiple offices, these figures probably exaggerate the numbers of party or elected officials at the conventions.

adopted this ideological self-description. Some 60 percent of the Republican delegates identified themselves as conservatives, compared to 43 percent among registered Republicans. This ideological polarization of the parties' delegates relative to ordinary party supporters continued across a wide range of political issues in 1988. For each major campaign issue, the percentage taking the liberal position steadily declined from Democratic delegates to Democratic voters to Republican voters and then on to Republican delegates.[9]

Comparison of the ideological tendencies of a party's convention delegates with those of its rank and file members addresses a central issue in the debate over reforms in the presidential nomination process. Democratic reformers attacked the old caucus-convention system as *unrepresentative* of the view of regular party supporters. Their critics, in turn, have charged that the reformed system has produced a set of convention delegates who are ideologically out of step with the party rank and file.

The reality is that reforming the party conventions has not necessarily made them more representative of the views and values of the parties in the electorate. Prior to 1972, it was the Republican conventions whose delegates appeared to be more ideologically out of step with party voters—and even more so with the general voting public.[10] The first postreform conventions in 1972 reversed that pattern. Democratic delegates in that year were found to be more ideologically distant from their party electorate than were Republican delegates from their rank and file—and even farther away from the public in general. This result led to an initial conclusion that the Democratic reforms had made Democratic conventions less rather than more representative.[11]

Comparisons of delegates with party supporters in subsequent conventions have shown, though, that the 1972 Democratic convention was an anomaly in the extent to which liberals were over-represented. Later Democratic delegations were more in line, ideologically-speaking, with Democratic party identifiers. The infusion of superdelegates in 1984 and 1988 seems to have reduced the ideological gap between Democratic party delegates and party voters even more. The 1988 Democratic and Republican conventions, in fact, were about equally representative of their respective parties in the electorate.[12]

---

[9]Data from *The New York Times* delegate survey and *The New York Times*/CBS News national survey, reported in *The New York Times*, August 14, 1988, p. 14.

[10]The classic account of this relationship, comparing delegates to the 1956 conventions with Democratic and Republican identifiers from a national survey, is found in Herbert McClosky, Paul Hoffman, and Rosemary O'Hara, "Issue Conflict and Consensus among Party Leaders and Followers," *American Political Science Review* 54 (1960): 406–27.

[11]These were the findings and the conclusion of Jeane Kirkpatrick, *The New Presidential Elite* (New York: Russell Sage Foundation and Twentieth Century Fund, 1976).

[12]For comparisons of post-1972 convention delegates with their respective party rank and files, see John S. Jackson III, Barbara L. Brown, and David Bositis, "Herbert McClosky and Friends Revisited: 1980 Democratic and Republican Party Elites Compared to the Mass Public," *American Politics Quarterly* 10 (1982): 158–80; Warren E. Miller and M. Kent Jennings, *Parties in Transition*

(*continued*)

The post-1968 reforms, most plausibly, increased the *probability* that any particular convention could be unrepresentative of the party rank and file rather than rendering either of the party delegations naturally more ideological. By linking the selection of delegates more tightly to candidate preferences, the new nomination system opened the convention doors to more members of the ideologically committed cadre of the parties when the more ideologically extreme candidates received substantial voter support. Thus, 1972 was a high point in the representation of liberals at the Democratic conclave, just as the Republican zenith in the attendance of conservatives at the GOP convention was probably attained in 1980. Without the leavening of substantial party organization representatives, especially for the Democrats, more ideological front-runners will probably produce more ideological convention delegates—and, in that respect, conventions that are less representative of the party in the electorate. But not every nomination contest will find ideologically-extreme candidates in the lead, as the example of both Bush and Dukakis in 1988 demonstrates.

Actually, the differences among the delegates at any single convention may be as significant as the differences between any two party conventions. In an age where many delegates are chosen because of their commitments to a particular candidate, the delegates will be divided among the leading candidates for the nomination, often in such a fashion as to reflect the various factions within the party. In the 1988 Democratic convention, for example, Jackson delegates were considerably more liberal than Dukakis delegates, just as Reagan delegates were more conservative than Ford delegates in 1976 or Bush delegates in 1980.[13]

Amateurs or Professionals   These differences may extend to style and approach to politics as well. The McCarthy delegates to the 1968 Democratic convention tended to be "amateurs" in the typology discussed in Chapter 5. They were more attracted by programs and issues, more insistent on intraparty democracy, less willing to compromise, and less committed to the prime importance of winning elections. The Humphrey delegates, on the other hand, were more likely to be "professionals." The division between amateurs (purists) and professionals in any particular delegation has continued to interest scholars because of the presumption that a changing mix of professionals and amateurs affects the continuing vitality of the party. The most recent study of these differences, focused on the 1980 and 1984 conventions, though, concludes

---

(continued)

(New York: Russell Sage Foundation, 1986), Chaps. 7–9; Denise L. Baer and David A. Bositis, *Elite Cadres and Party Coalitions* (New York: Greenwood Press, 1988), Chap. 8; and Shafer, *Bifurcated Politics*, (1988), pp. 100–107. The comparisons of delegates and party identifiers for 1988 are taken from *The New York Times* Delegate Surveys and *The New York Times*/CBS News national survey as reported in *The New York Times*, August 14, 1988, p. 14.

[13]Results of *The New York Times* Delegate Survey reported in *The New York Times*, August 14, 1988, p. 14.

that the supposed threat to the parties posed by an infusion of amateurs is greatly exaggerated. Even after the reforms, convention delegates remain strongly committed to their parties and to enduring party goals.[14]

Who the delegates are to their national nominating conventions, then, tells us a great deal about the Democratic and Republican parties. The conventions bring together all three parts of the party—the party organization, the party in the electorate, and the party in government—to take action in the name of the national party. The ideological currents coursing through the parties, the motivations that underlie commitments to party politics, the backgrounds that bring people into party activity, the factional discords that threaten party harmony are all reflected in the turmoil and the drama that characterize these quadrennial political events. It is little wonder that the party conventions have attracted so much attention, from political observers and citizens alike, even if their roles in the nomination process seem to have atrophied.

THE BUSINESS OF THE CONVENTION

The convention begins in low key, with stiff formalities and the business of organizations. It warms up with the keynote address, tries to maintain momentum and expectation through consideration of the platform, and reaches a dramatic peak in the nomination of the presidential and vice-presidential candidates. This general format remains basically the same convention after convention. Television coverage has necessitated some rearrangement into a more compact convention, with the events of major interest reserved for prime evening transmission time, but the tempo of the convention is still governed by the pace of business more than any dramatic considerations.

Aside from the rites of nomination, the approval of the platform is the convention's chief business. The platform committees begin hearings long before the convention opens, so that the platform will be in draft form for convention hearings. The finished platform is then presented to the convention for its approval. That approval is not always pro forma; the platform has occasioned some spirited convention battles. In 1968, the forces supporting Hubert H. Humphrey engaged the McCarthy delegates in a three-hour floor debate over what the platform would say about the war in Vietnam while police battled antiwar protestors on the streets outside. The Democrats' discussion of the 1972 plat-

---

[14]On the distinction between amateurs and professionals among convention delegates, see John W. Soule and James W. Clarke, "Amateurs and Professionals: A Study of Delegates to the 1968 Democratic National Convention," *American Political Science Review* 64 (1970): 888–98; Dennis G. Sullivan, Jeffrey L. Pressman, Benjamin I. Page, and John J. Lyons, *The Politics of Representation: The Democratic Convention 1972* (New York: St. Martin's, 1974); Kirkpatrick, *The New Presidential Elite*; and Thomas H. Roback, "Motivations for Activism among Republican National Convention Delegates," *Journal of Politics* 42 (1980); 181–201. The 1980 and 1984 study is Baer and Bositis, *Elite Cadres and Party Coalitions*, Chap. 7.

form touched on the controversial subjects of abortion and gay rights and set a record for the longest discussion of a platform in American convention history.

Few aspects of American politics so openly invite skepticism, even cynicism, as do the party platforms. They are long and prolix. Furthermore, they are not often read; the congressional party generally ignores them, and even presidential standard-bearers reserve the right to disagree with them. Basically, the problem is that platforms are the instruments of ideology, and the two major American parties really have no total political philosophy that unites their followers and a long tradition of avoiding attempts to impose philosophical positions upon their members. The American party platform, rather than being a statement of the party, is much more likely to be a string of pragmatic stands on quite separate issues, one not necessarily related to another.

Rather than a statement of continuing party philosophy, the platform is really a manifesto of the majority that happens to control the convention in that year. Thus, the conservative wing of the Republican party that supported Ronald Reagan in the Republican convention of 1980 was strong enough to drop the party's historic commitment to the Equal Rights Amendment from the 1980 platform. Since the party's presidential nominee generally controls the convention, the platform ordinarily has also been a reflection of his views. When it has not been, nominees have either changed the platform or have gone their own way. In 1960, Richard Nixon, clearly about to receive the Republican nomination, bowed to the criticisms of the draft platform by the party moderates, rushed to New York to confer with their spokesman, Governor Nelson Rockefeller, and then hurried back to Chicago to force revisions on an unhappy committee. In 1980, a Democratic convention somewhat unenthusiastic about the man it was about to nominate forced the contenders for the nomination to state in writing any objections they had to the platform. President Carter noted reservations about clauses on the public funding of abortions and about the denial of party support to candidates not supporting the ERA. Some feminist delegates were unhappy, but the event did not seriously threaten his renomination.

Part of the cynicism about the platforms grows from the impression that they are exercises in semantic virtuosity. The words and phrases used are sometimes intended to obfuscate rather than clarify, for phrases that mean all things to all people achieve compromises of a sort. Vague or artful as the platforms may be, however, they do take stands on some issues, and they are not identical. In recent years, the parties' platforms have differed over social security, labor-management relations, farm price supports, medicare, racial integration, deficit spending, war and peace in Vietnam and Nicaragua, abortion, women's rights, and taxes. Above all, the platforms are campaign documents in which the parties pick their issues and positions selectively to promote the assembling of a majority coalition. The party platform is important, its leading scholar says,

> but not as an inspired goal to which politicians resort for policy guidance. It is important because it summarizes, crystallizes, and presents to the voters the character of the party coalition. Platform pledges are not simply good ideas, or even original ones. In their programs, Democrats and Republicans are not typ-

ically breaking new paths; they are promising to proceed along one or another path which has already become involved in political controversy. The stands taken in the platform clarify the parties' positions on these controversies and reveal the nature of their support and appeals.[15]

Finally, the platforms are what they are largely because they are drafted and approved in conventions mainly concerned with picking a presidential candidate. Every convention vote tends to become a test of the strength of the various candidates, and votes on the platform are no exception.[16]

FINDING A PRESIDENTIAL CANDIDATE

The pièce de résistance of the convention—the selection of a presidential candidate—begins with the nominations from the floor, as the secretary calls the roll of the states: Alabama, Alaska, Arkansas . . . As the secretary progresses through the states, the contenders for the nominations are entered, each one by a formal speech of nomination and shorter seconding speeches. It is at this point that, traditionally, the conventions reached back to a nineteenth-century political style. The speeches of nomination rolled out in great rhetorical flourishes, often seeming to be parodies; seconding speeches, carefully chosen to provide a cross section of the party, were frequently vest-pocket versions of the main speech. After each set of nomination speeches, the supporters of the nominee, usually augmented by young, tireless nondelegates, snaked their way through the crowded aisles of the hall, singing, chanting, and waving banners and signs for almost an hour.

The first modifications of those hoary traditions began with the advent of television, for the endless hijinks often pushed the most dramatic portions of the convention out of prime evening time. What had seemed colorfully old-fashioned in the hall looked grotesque or vulgar on the TV screen. The Democrats, spurred again by the reform impulses springing from their ill-fated 1968 convention, made further inroads in 1972. They banned all floor demonstrations, shortened nomination speeches drastically, and made the nomination of favorite-son candidates—noncontenders with support in only one state delegation—vastly more difficult.

The Casting of the Votes

Once all the names have been presented to the convention, the task of settling on a single presidential nominee begins in earnest. The secretary of the

---

[15]Gerald Pomper, *Elections in America* (New York: Dodd, Mead, 1968), p. 201.

[16]All the party platforms through 1976 are available in one volume: Donald B. Johnson, *National Party Platforms, 1840–1976* (Urbana: University of Illinois Press, 1978). For summaries of all platforms through 1984, see the *Guide to U.S. Elections*.

Table 11.2   NUMBER OF BALLOTS REQUIRED TO NOMINATE AND NUMBER OF
CANDIDATES POLLING 10 PERCENT OF VOTES IN DEMOCRATIC AND
REPUBLICAN CONVENTIONS: 1948–88

| | Democratic conventions | | Republican conventions | |
Year	Candidates Polling over 10%	Number of Ballots	Candidates Polling over 10%	Number of Ballots
1948	2	1	3	3
1952	4	3	2	1
1956	2	1	1	1
1960	2	1	1	1
1964	1	1	2	1
1968	2	1	3	1
1972	3	1	1	1
1976	2	1	2	1
1980	2	1	1	1
1984	3	1	1	1
1988	2	1	1	1

Source: Data from *Guide to U.S. Elections* and the 1988 *Congressional Quarterly Almanac* (Washington, D.C.: Congressional Quarterly, Inc., 1989), pp. 38-A and 82-A.

convention starts again through the states (and the other voting units), asking each delegation to report its vote. If no candidate wins the necessary majority of votes, the convention presses on to a second ballot. A number of nominations have been settled on the first ballot, but in 1924 the Democrats plodded through 103 ballots in sultry New York's Madison Square Garden before nominating John W. Davis. (That record number of ballots resulted, at least in part, from the Democratic rule, abandoned in 1936, that required that the nominee be supported by two-thirds of the delegates.) Since 1952, no nomination contest in either party has consumed more than one ballot. Furthermore, since 1948, the conventions have averaged only two candidates who polled more than 10 percent of the convention votes on any ballot (Table 11.2)

The casting of the votes takes place in a context of some of the most compressed political activity in all of American politics. Even before the opening of the convention, representatives of the various contenders have stalked uncommitted or wavering delegates across the country by mail, phone, and personal visit. Once the convention opens, the process is stepped up. Front-runners generally know they must win quickly. The only strategy the other candidates can employ is to join in a coalition to prevent a first-ballot victory. That imperative can unite—however temporarily—men of such divergent views as Nelson Rockefeller and Ronald Reagan, who tried unsuccessfully in 1968 to prevent the first-ballot nomination of Richard Nixon. It also explains many of the early skirmishes over delegate credentials and convention rules, such as the unsuccessful attempt by Senator Edward Kennedy's forces at the 1980 Democratic convention to block a Carter first-ballot victory by changing the rules to release delegates from their binding commitments to a particular candidate on the first ballot.

Even though no major party convention has gone beyond the first ballot to select its nominee since 1952, a multiballot convention remains possible—and perhaps now is even more likely because of the increasing use of proportional representation. While experience may not completely portend the politics of a divided convention under reform rules, the past does contain useful lessons for a multiballot convention.

If the convention has passed through an inconclusive ballot, negotiations renew with even greater intensity. The leading candidates must take care to prevent a chipping away of their supporters—a genuine danger if they fail to increase their votes on a second or third ballot. New support comes most easily from the delegates preferring minor candidates or uncommitted delegates, since most delegates of the major candidates are too loyal to those commitments to be lured away. Because modern delegates are tied more tightly to candidates than to state party leaders or party organizations, however, it is uncertain who would play the traditional role of broker for today's divided convention. One possibility is that the various candidates for the nomination would play a leading role in the negotiations.[17]

Selecting a Vice-Presidential Nominee

Following the naming of the presidential nominee, the secretary begins the roll call ritual again—usually on the next day—to select a vice-presidential nominee. Conventions uniformly ratify the choice of the presidential candidate. Rebellions flash occasionally but always fail; in the Democratic meetings of 1944, for instance, the supporters of Vice-President Henry Wallace tried futilely to resist the decision of President Roosevelt to replace him with Harry S. Truman. Once in recent years, the presidential candidate did not indicate his preference. Adlai Stevenson convulsed the 1956 Democratic convention by opening the vice-presidential choice to the convention; Senator Estes Kefauver was selected on the second ballot.

The method of selecting vice-presidential candidates has drawn some criticism. It is not so much that they are hand-picked by the presidential candidate but that the decision is made by a tired candidate and tired advisors in so short a span of time. The withdrawal of the initial Democratic vice-presidential nominee in 1972 (Thomas Eagleton) and the eventual resignation of Vice-President Spiro Agnew in the following year illustrate the problems of a hurried and superficial screening of vice-presidential possibilities. But no new procedure is waiting to replace it. Even when the controversy over the financial affairs of Geraldine Ferraro's husband tarnished the unprecedented nomination of a woman for the post in 1984 or the flap over Dan Quayle's military record seized

---

[17]For a study of traditional convention politics, see Paul T. David, Ralph M. Goldman, and Richard C. Bain, *The Politics of National Party Conventions* (Washington, D.C.: Brookings, 1960), p. 379.

the headlines in 1988, there were few cries of reform. The choice of vice-presidential nominee, and the responsibility for a poor selection, seems destined to remain in the hands of the party's presidential nominee, or whomever he (or she) delegates to make it.

THE "AVAILABILITY" OF PRESIDENTIAL NOMINEES

There is a bland and misleading term in American politics that describes the personal, social, and political characteristics the parties seek in their presidential nominees. An individual who possesses the right attributes is said to be *available*. Contrary to its popular use, the word in this idiomatic sense has nothing to do with a person's willingness to be a candidate; one can assume, in that sense, that almost every native-born American adult is available for the presidency (see box).

Size of Home State

The concept of availability sums up the qualities the parties believe make a politically appealing and acceptable candidate. In part, the canons of availability reflect the distribution of political power in presidential politics. It is said, for instance, that the presidential candidate must come from a large state—that is, a state with a large electoral vote that he or she can be presumed to carry. From 1896 to the present, only five of the twenty-nine men originally nominated for the presidency by a convention came from the smaller states. Twenty-two came from eight large states: seven from New York, four from Ohio, three from California, three from Massachusetts, two from Texas, and one each from Illinois, Michigan, and New Jersey. Two came from Minnesota and one from Georgia, states that would appear to be "in between." None of the five from the smaller states—Landon of Kansas, Davis of West Virginia, Bryan of Nebraska, Goldwater of Arizona, and McGovern of South Dakota—won the presidency.[18]

Personal Characteristics

In part, too, the concept of availability is a codification of widely held expectations in the American electorate of what a president should be. It is an aggregate of the characteristics the parties think the American electorate would vote for in a presidential candidate. Some years ago, it was commonly said that for a person to be considered seriously for the office, he had to be a personal success in business or public life; married (only once) and blessed with an attractive family; a reasonably observant Protestant; a white male under sixty-five; of

---

[18]If one uses the 1988 electoral vote as a measure, none of the seven large states referred to here had an electoral vote smaller than thirteen, and none of the small states had one greater than seven. Minnesota had ten, and Georgia had twelve.

The "Shermanesque" Standard of Availability

Not everyone aspires to the presidency, although denials of interest often are coy responses of those who wish to be courted. In reference to his candidacy for president, Civil War hero General William Tecumseh Sherman told the 1884 Republican convention: "I will not accept if nominated, and will not serve if elected." Since then, denials of interest in the presidency by potential candidates have been measured against Sherman's to gauge availability. In 1948, for instance, Dwight Eisenhower phrased his "Shermanesque" denials as "No matter under what terms, conditions, or premises a proposal might be couched, I would refuse to accept the nomination" and "I cannot conceive of any circumstance that could draw out of me permission to consider me for any political post from dogcatcher to Grand High Supreme King of the Universe." Four years later, Eisenhower won the Republican nomination and was elected president.[19]

Anglo-Saxon or north-northwestern European ethnic background; and the product of small city or rural life.

Recent years have witnessed a chipping away at this list of traditional qualifications. Adlai Stevenson and Ronald Reagan, both divorced, were nominated twice; an urban Catholic, John F. Kennedy, was nominated in 1960; Michael Dukakis, of Greek Orthodox faith, won his party's nomination in 1988; Ronald Reagan, at sixty-nine, was nominated in 1980. Those nominations probably indicate, at least in part, the declining social stigma attached to divorce, old age, the life of the big city, and Catholicism in contemporary America. In coming decades, changing attitudes about women and blacks in public life will probably also strike the white male qualification from the formula of availability.

Career Experience

Related to the issue of availability is the question of career pattern. Although not all presidential candidates have had prior governmental or officeholding experience, most have. Thus, the question arises of what positions provide the better jumping-off points and training for the presidency. The general answer is that the most serious contenders for the presidency have come from three offices—vice president, governor, or senator. These offices, increasingly in modern times with the growth of the mass media, have given their occupants the necessary national visibility to be viable candidates.[20]

---

[19]The quotations are taken from William Safire, *Safire's Political Dictionary* (New York: Random House, 1978), pp. 643–44.

[20]See John H. Aldrich, *Before the Convention* (Chicago: University of Chicago Press, 1980).

For the first half of this century, the position of governor seemed the best launching pad for a presidential candidacy, whereas the Senate was seen as the graveyard of presidential ambitions. Senators, it was said, were forced to cast too many politically sensitive votes and risk too many political enemies. Between 1900 and 1956, eleven of the nineteen different men running for president on the Democratic and Republican tickets had served as governors; only two had been senators.

Since 1956, this situation has changed. The Senate too has become a prime breeding ground for presidential contenders. From 1960 through 1972, all of the parties' nominees were former senators; none had gubernatorial experience. Beginning in 1976, though, governors returned to prominence: Jimmy Carter, Ronald Reagan, and Michael Dukakis all rose from that office to the presidential nomination. Only Walter Mondale in 1984 came from a Senate career, although many prominent candidates for the nominations in recent years have been senators (e.g., Robert Dole, Gary Hart, Ted Kennedy). The House of Representatives also has become a bountiful source of presidential aspirants in recent years. Presidents George Bush and Gerald Ford had roots there, as did a number of other serious contenders for the office.

Abilities

Finally, convention delegates consider the personal qualities of the contenders and their abilities to meet the demands of the presidency. They do so, however, in the context of loyalties to specific candidates and often, too, to specific ideologies. In other words, the standards for presidential timber are not universally agreed on. Furthermore, delegates may face a dilemma in the fact that the qualities that ensure effective performance in office are not necessarily those that win it in the first place. Difficult as such evaluations of presidential candidates are, however, they are far less likely to be made in the speed and confusion with which vice-presidential candidates are found.

CONVENTIONS: YESTERDAY AND TODAY

It is unlikely that small bands of national kingmakers bargaining in smoke-filled rooms ever did control the national conventions to the extent that popular myth has it. Even the celebrated negotiations at the Republican convention of 1920— in the course of which Warren G. Harding emerged as the party's nominee— took place in a convention deadlocked by other candidates with large popular and delegate followings. Whatever power the kingmakers may have had in the past, however, is declining rapidly. In that and in a number of other important ways, the national nominating conventions are not what they were a generation or two ago.

New Preconvention Politics

All nominations have been decided on the first convention ballot in recent years, and the chances of the convention's picking a "dark horse" have diminished. This is all the result of a new style of campaigning for delegates, which was ushered in, perhaps, by the 1960 preconvention campaign of John F. Kennedy. More effective organization, greater resources, jet planes, polls, and expanded media exposure all permit it. The press services keep count of the number of delegates committed to various candidates, and the pollsters periodically report the state of public enthusiasm for them. Both candidates and delegates have fuller information about the entire nomination politics before they get to the convention than they ever did before. Delegates are more likely to be committed to a contender before the convention opens. Consequently, the crucial bargaining and trading of support, the committing of delegates, and the weeding out of candidates take place increasingly at the preconvention stages. As Byron E. Shafer has chronicled more fully than anyone else, in short, the heart of presidential nomination politics now precedes the conventions.[21]

New Centers of Power

To an important extent, political power has shifted away from the state and local party leaders, who at one time came as ambassadors to the convention with control of blocs of votes for the purpose of negotiating within a fragmented, decentralized party. Power in the parties in the late twentieth century is less decentralized as national issues, national candidates, presidents, and congresses dominate the political loyalties and perceptions of voters. National party figures and national concerns—and party identifications shaped by national politics—have cut into the autonomy of state parties and leaders. So, too, has the increased power of potential candidates in the convention, power that is largely a product of their preconvention successes in rounding up delegates, who in the reformed primaries and caucuses typically were elected as committed to a particular candidate. Therefore, we find in many recent nominating conventions a tension among the old and new centers of power. In 1968, both Richard Nixon and Hubert Humphrey were supported by the leaders of the states and localities; their major challengers, Nelson Rockefeller and Eugene McCarthy, staked their campaigns on national issues and sought their support in a broader national public. Even though these challenges failed, the 1968 contests represent the "last hurrah" of the old centers of power around state and local leaders.

As ideologies and issues become more important in the parties generally, they structure more and more of the choices in the conventions. Ideological factions or tendencies and their associated interests thus become new centers of power. The battle for the Democratic nomination in 1972 clearly was a battle between the liberal and moderate centers of gravity within the party. In the Republican party, those ideological clusters were evident in the 1976 contest, and they persisted, though less dramatically, in the 1980 contest between George Bush and Ronald Reagan. The post-1968 reforms have made issue and ideological differences even more likely and predictable within the Democratic

---

[21]Shafer, *Bifurcated Politics*, especially Chap. 5.

party. In response, the party's national committee seated many Democratic party and public officials as superdelegates to the 1984 and 1988 party conventions in the hope of restoring some of the lost power of the party's traditional leaders. Ironically, most of them were national leaders (U.S. Representatives and Senators) rather than the traditional state and local leaders, and they made commitments to candidates (primarily, Walter Mondale in 1984 and Michael Dukakis in 1988) well in advance of the convention.

News Media Coverage

The mass media have increasingly turned the conventions into national political spectaculars, intended as much for the national audience as for the delegates in attendance. Party officials have given key roles to telegenic partisans, have speeded up the pace of business, and have virtually eliminated serious business from daytime hours. The strategic moves of major candidates, the arrival of powerful figures in the party, and the defection of individual delegates are reported fully. Even the formerly secret hagglings of platform and credentials committees are done in the public eye. For the party, then, television coverage offers a priceless opportunity to reach voters and party workers and to launch its presidential campaign with maximum impact. Thus, the media spotlight shifts the role of the convention—not completely but perceptibly—from the conduct of party business to the stimulation of wider political audiences.

Yet there is a problem with the modern convention. As media attention to it has increased, the convention has lost its excitement and suspense; we increasingly know who will win the presidential nomination before the proceedings begin. It is little wonder, then, that media reporters, straining for excitement, have been transformed from observers into participants and are more than willing to blow out of proportion whatever conflict or rumors they can find (see box). Nor should it be surprising that network coverage of convention proceedings, in response to declining audiences, was reduced considerably in the 1980s and will be streamlined even further in 1992.[22]

Media coverage is thus a two-edged sword, and its results are not always the ones the parties want. Television's capacity to relay so dramatically the scenes of violence in Chicago's streets and parks during the Democratic convention of 1968 provided an embarrassing counterpoint to the deliberations of the party within the convention hall. Media exposure is also problematic in other ways. It encourages some participants to use the convention as a podium to advance their own causes, even if they may undermine the candidacy of the party nominee. The public visibility gained by Jesse Jackson at both the 1984 and 1988 Democratic conventions, for example, surely exceeded that of losing candidates in previous years and was thought by some to have threatened the subsequent general election campaigns of Mondale and Dukakis. The availability of prime

---

[22]See the figures cited in Shafer, *Bifurcated Politics*, Chap. 8, especially p. 280.

The Convention: A Made-for-TV Event?

The tailoring of the conventions in recent years to meet the needs of the television networks is troublesome to many observers and practitioners of party politics. The following excerpts from a speech at a National Press Foundation dinner by Don Hewitt, at the time executive producer of CBS' "60 Minutes," show that it also has become a cause of concern within the television news industry itself.

There is no doubt whose convention this really is. The politicians meeting there are now extras in our television show. My job for more years than I want to remember was to oversee the CBS floor reporters. In truth, my job was not all that different from a circus ringmaster. I was given the responsibility of seeing that my ring was more exciting than NBC or ABC's ring. And if Ed Bradley had to get into a contretemps with the Mayor of Chicago to keep my show moving, so be it.

When I first went to political conventions, we were observers and reporters. Now we're participants. And there's something a lot wrong with that.

In the old days, before the primaries took the steam out of political conventions, you could watch a good credentials fight or a good platform fight—even though a week later no one could remember what they were fighting about. Today, if you want to see a good fight at a political convention, if you want to see a real fight at a political convention, let CBS News's sign be an inch bigger than NBC's. Now you'll see a fight at a convention. All hell breaks loose.

It's time we gave the politicians back their convention. Tell them it's nothing but a big commercial and that it's not Rather, Brokaw, or Jennings's job to be the emcee of their commercial.

Reprinted in *The New York Times,* February 28, 1986.

evening time encouraged issue enthusiasts in the 1972 Democratic convention to debate the platform far longer than the media-oriented schedule provided. As a result, George McGovern began his acceptance speech at 2:48 A.M. before a TV audience reduced to one-fifth of what it had been earlier in the evening. Occasionally, the media even manage to participate directly in party decisions. While Ronald Reagan was trying to persuade former President Gerald Ford to be his vice-presidential candidate at the 1980 Republican convention, CBS anchorman Walter Cronkite's use of the phrase "co-presidency" in a live interview with Ford came to characterize the commitments Ford was seeking from Reagan and probably made the reaching of an agreement between them more difficult, perhaps even impossible.

The conventions have therefore lost some of their deliberative character and independence. Genuinely brokered conventions and last-minute compromise candidates seem now to belong to the past. The unlikelihood of lightning striking the unknown statesmen does not, of course, signal the end of the convention. If no candidate has won a majority prior to the convention, delegates still may have to choose from among a small number of candidates who have established themselves in the preconvention stages. When the choice must be made among these well-known hopefuls, it will be made by a freer, more open bargaining that involves the majority of delegates as well as the prominent party leaders.

The conventions simply reflect, as never before, a heterogeneous mix of political roles and expectations. There are the traditional state and local leaders, representing the interests of their party organizations, and now there are also new national party leaders, national officeholders, and powerful candidates with blocks of loyal delegates. Old organizational styles also mix incongruously with new styles of media-based politics; professional party leadership rubs elbows with volunteer, amateur party activists. The old electoral pragmatism—the traditional convention emphasis on picking the winning candidate—can sometimes clash with the unwillingness of the ideologues to compromise. In reflecting all these conflicts, the conventions only mirror the broader conflicts and divisions of American party politics. Nonetheless, the stresses and strains that result can be debilitating.

Taking a broader overview, one may put the matter of change another way. Aided by media-reported campaigning and by the results of periodic polling, the entire process of nominating a president has fallen under the spell of a national, popular democracy. More and more people are becoming aware of the candidates and the choices before the party, and more and more of them are formulating views about those choices. Therefore, nominating an unknown candidate today is doubly dangerous—first, for the seeming affront to the popularly supported contestants and, second, for the handicap of running an unknown candidate against the well-known candidate of the other party. Even the style, manners, and seriousness of the convention are under a new mass popular scrutiny. To the extent that secretive or apparently manipulated party conventions are incompatible with the democratization of the presidential nominating process, they have had to change.

Although change and declining power may beset the conventions, the parties are not likely to abandon them. Even in its altered condition the national convention of the 1980s and likely the 1990s is too precious an institution to surrender. It is the only real, palpable existence of a national political party. It is the only occasion for rediscovery of common traditions and common interests, the only time for common decision making and a coming together to celebrate old glories and achievements. It stimulates the workers and contributors to party labors, and it encourages party candidates in the states and localities. Its rites may not mean a great deal to the majority of Americans passively peering at the TV screen (and a bit sullen about missing the summer reruns), much less to those who have tuned to other programming, but they do mean something to the men and women of the party organization. The conventions are, in short, a vital integrative force in the life of the American national parties.

Parties and the Campaign for Election

The formidable Democratic party organization of Pennsylvania had long had a reputation for winning primaries and general elections. At the outset of the campaign in the gubernatorial primary of 1966, few observers gave any chance to Milton Shapp, a Philadelphia industrialist who was challenging the organization's candidate, a thirty-four-year-old lawyer and state legislative leader, Robert B. Casey. In what was billed as a battle of "exposure versus organization," however, the Shapp campaign employed some 7,000 spot radio commercials, thirty-four half-hour television shows in prime time, an assortment of thirty or so pamphlets and leaflets, more than sixty campaign headquarters across the state, and a mailing of one large brochure to a million and a half voters. The total cost of the primary campaign, financed in large part from Shapp's personal fortune, ran over a million dollars. Shapp won the primary. After it was all over, a reflective Robert Casey observed about the campaign he had lost:

> Politics is changing tremendously. The old ways no longer work. From that election, I learned that these days you need a combination of two things. First, the traditional grass-roots effort, the telephoning and the door-knocking. But more than that, you have to use the new sophisticated techniques, the polling, the television, the heavy staffing, and the direct mail. You can't rely any more on political organizations. They don't work any more. These days, who wants a job in the courthouse or with the highway department? Why, the sons of courthouse janitors are probably doctors or professional men. You can't give those jobs away any more. We're at the tag end of an era in Pennsylvania.[1]

The final chapter in this story was written sixteen years later. In 1986, this time using an effective media campaign, Robert Casey upset William Scranton III to win the Pennsylvania governorship. He had adapted to the new media era.

---

[1]*National Observer*, September 26, 1966.

Stories such as this one—typifying the clash of old and new campaigning—were news in the 1960s and 1970s. They heralded a great change, a watershed, in the contesting of American elections that we increasingly take for granted by now. It is clear to us now that the professional managers, media specialists, pollsters, and advertising and public relations people have become a powerful and regular force in American political campaigning. They have replaced the state and local party organizations as the major planners and executors of campaigns.

It is easy to understand, then, why many have come to the conclusion that the traditional grass-roots party organization has become technologically obsolete—that it has been superseded by newer, more efficient, and more timely avenues and techniques of campaigning. Therefore, the argument continues, the old-style party organization has lost an important measure of control over the contesting of American elections and, ultimately, over its candidates elected to public office. But this conclusion overlooks the great adaptability of the party organizations. Throughout their history, the Democratic and Republican parties have a record of being responsive to new realities, which in part accounts for their longevity. Before relegating the parties to the sidelines, then, we need to carefully examine their current role in political campaigns.

The impact of changing technologies also illustrates a fundamental fact of political campaigning: A campaign for election operates within a much broader context, a context determined by a variety of forces beyond the immediate control of the campaigners themselves. Before we can understand the nature of campaigning and the changes in it, the full extent of this context must be considered. Previous chapters have examined the nature of the party system; the organizational strength of the local, state, and even national parties; the motivations and skills of political activists; the party loyalties and participation of the electorate; and the rules governing selection of party candidates—and weighed the impact of each of these forces, and changes in them, on the candidates and their campaigns. Other contextual forces, especially the role of the party in government, will be dealt with in later chapters. For right now, however, we turn to the legal context of campaigns—the regulation and definition of the electoral process itself. The strategies of the electoral game make sense only if one first understands its rules.

THE ELECTORAL INSTITUTIONS

Each part of the legal framework, each rule of the electoral game, places a strategic limit on the campaign. Each adjustment in any one rule may affect one party or candidate more than another. Thus, the framework, however much it is taken for granted, is much more than a neutral presence in the campaign and election.

Political parties around the world have been quick to realize the possible advantages to be gained by selective tinkering with election law. The major American parties are no exception. Americans, however, have generally tinkered more with the size and shape of the electoral districts; gerrymandering is a peculiarly American art form. The rest of the American electoral rules have remained surprisingly stable in this century. The kinds of repeated electoral tinkerings common in Europe—the shifts to systems of proportional representation and back again, for instance—have not been common here.

The Secret Ballot

The American ballot is now uniformly secret, but it was not always so. Until the late nineteenth century, the oral vote was common in many states and jurisdictions. The voter simply stated to the electoral officials which candidates he preferred. During the nineteenth century, the oral vote was gradually replaced by ballots printed by the parties or candidates. The voter brought the ballot of his candidate or party to the polling place and deposited it in the box. Since the ballots were by no means identical, the vote was often apparent to observers. Moreover, this type of ballot discouraged ticket-splitting.

The secret ballot was introduced as a way of curbing election corruption, especially vote buying; with a secret ballot, the corrupter could never be sure the "bought" vote would be delivered. Called the Australian ballot after the country of its origin, the secret ballot quickly swept the nation in the 1890s. By the beginning of the twentieth century, its success was complete, and it remains the practice today. The ballot is prepared at public expense by public authorities, and it lists all candidates for office on its single, consolidated form. It is made available at the polling places only to bona fide voters, who then indicate their choices in the seclusion of a voting booth.[2]

Forms of Ballots

Now that voting is done uniformly through secret ballot, it is the format of the ballot itself that has the greatest impact on the campaign, especially in how it affects the connection between candidates and their parties in the voter's mind. Two basic types of ballots are in use in the United States. In many states, the *party-column* ballot prevails. The grouping of all the candidates from each party together, so that voters can perceive them as a party ticket, is the distinguishing feature of the party-column form (see Michigan column in Figure 12.1). A number of other states have adopted an alternative form—the *office-block* ballot, which groups the candidates according to the offices they seek (see Nebraska column in Figure 12.1). By their very nature, of course, nonpartisan elections employ the office-block ballot.

---

[2]Jerrold G. Rusk found that the introduction of the Australian ballot was accompanied by an increase in split-ticket voting. See his article, "The Effect of the Australian Ballot Reform on Split Ticket Voting: 1876–1908," *American Political Science Review* 64 (1970): 1220–38.

Michigan party–column ballot

Form No. P-881

NAMES OF OFFICES VOTED FOR:	DEMOCRATIC PARTY	REPUBLICAN
STATE GOVERNOR AND LIEUTENANT GOVERNOR VOTE FOR NOT MORE THAN ONE	Governor and Lieutenant Governor JAMES J. BLANCHARD MARTHA W. GRIFFITHS	Governor and Lieutenant Governor RICHARD H. HEADLEE THOMAS E. BRENNAN
SECRETARY OF STATE VOTE FOR NOT MORE THAN ONE	Secretary of State RICHARD H. AUSTIN	Secretary of State ELIZABETH A. ANDRUS
ATTORNEY GENERAL VOTE FOR NOT MORE THAN ONE	Attorney General FRANK J. KELLEY	Attorney General L. BROOKS PATTERSON
CONGRESSIONAL UNITED STATES SENATOR VOTE FOR NOT MORE THAN ONE	United States Senator DONALD W. RIEGLE, JR.	United States Senator PHILIP E. RUPPE
REPRESENTATIVE IN CONGRESS, ___ DISTRICT VOTE FOR NOT MORE THAN ONE	Representative in Congress	Representative in Congress
LEGISLATIVE STATE SENATOR, ___ DISTRICT VOTE FOR NOT MORE THAN ONE	State Senator	State Senator
REPRESENTATIVE IN STATE LEGISLATURE, ___ DIST. VOTE FOR NOT MORE THAN ONE	Representative in State Legislature	Representative in State Legislature
STATE BOARDS MEMBERS OF THE STATE BOARD OF EDUCATION VOTE FOR NOT MORE THAN TWO	Member of the State Board of Education CARROLL HUTTON BARBARA ROBERTS MASON	Member of the State Board of Education RONALD G. ERICKSON JACQUELINE McGREGOR
MEMBERS OF THE BOARD OF REGENTS OF UNIVERSITY OF MICHIGAN VOTE FOR NOT MORE THAN TWO	Board of Regents, University of Michigan SARAH GODDARD POWER THOMAS A. ROACH	Board of Regents, University of Michigan ROCKWELL T. GUST, JR. ELLEN M. TEMPLIN
MEMBERS OF THE BOARD OF TRUSTEES OF MICHIGAN STATE UNIVERSITY VOTE FOR NOT MORE THAN TWO	Trustee of Michigan State University JOHN B. BRUFF BOBBY D. CRIM	Trustee of Michigan State University LAURA HRUSER GEORGE A. McMANUS, JR.
MEMBERS OF THE BOARD OF GOVERNORS OF WAYNE STATE UNIVERSITY VOTE FOR NOT MORE THAN TWO	Board of Governors, Wayne State University MICHAEL EINHEUSER MILDRED JEFFREY	Board of Governors, Wayne State University NANCY BOYKIN SAM TRENTACOSTA

Nebraska office–bloc ballot

Senatorial Ticket

FOR UNITED STATES SENATOR
Vote for ONE

- Jim Keck .... Republican
- Edward Zorinsky .... Democrat
- Virginia Walsh .... By Petition

Congressional Ticket

FOR REPRESENTATIVE IN CONGRESS FIRST DISTRICT
Vote for ONE

- Doug Bereuter .... Republican
- Curt Donaldson .... Democrat

FOR REPRESENTATIVE IN CONGRESS SECOND DISTRICT
Vote for ONE

- Hal Daub .... Republican
- Richard M. Fellman .... Democrat

FOR REPRESENTATIVE IN CONGRESS THIRD DISTRICT
Vote for ONE

- Virginia Smith .... Republican

State Ticket

FOR GOVERNOR
Vote in ONE Square Only

- Charles Thone — Governor
Roland A. Luedtke — Lieutenant Governor } Republican
- Bob Kerrey — Governor
Don McGinley — Lieutenant Governor } Democrat
- Governor
Lieutenant Governor }

FOR MEMBER OF THE STATE BOARD OF EDUCATION SEVENTH DISTRICT
Vote for ONE

- Daniel G. Urwiller
- Gerald L. Clausen

FOR MEMBER OF THE STATE BOARD OF EDUCATION EIGHTH DISTRICT
Vote for ONE

- William C. Ramsey
- Eileen Dietz

FOR MEMBER OF THE LEGISLATURE SECOND DISTRICT
Vote for ONE

- Calvin F. Carsten
- Boyd Linder

FOR MEMBER OF THE LEGISLATURE FOURTH DISTRICT
Vote for ONE

- Gary E. Hannibal
- Bev Laing

FOR MEMBER OF THE LEGISLATURE SIXTH DISTRICT
Vote for ONE

- Gayle L. Stock
- Peter Hoogland

FOR MEMBER OF THE LEGISLATURE EIGHTH DISTRICT
Vote for ONE

- Wayne Hohndorf
- Vard Johnson

FOR MEMBER OF THE LEGISLATURE TENTH DISTRICT
Vote for ONE

- Carol McBride Pirsch
- James S. Beutel

Figure 12.1 The Party-Column and Office-Bloc Ballots: Selected Portions of the Michigan and Nebraska General Election Ballots, 1982.

All evidence indicates that the parties are correct in their belief that the party-column ballot encourages straight-ticket voting (i.e., voting for all of a party's candidates for all the offices being filled at the election). The amount of straight-ticket voting also hinges, however, on the presence or absence on the ballot of a single square or circle (or a single lever on machines) by which the voter can, in one action, cast a vote for the entire party ticket. These squares or circles appear on most of the party-column ballots, in a total of 21 states at last count, but rarely are they found on the office-block ballot. Thus, the format of the ballot can affect the way the voter sees the electoral contest and the nature of the choices in it.[3]

Three other aspects of ballot forms deserve mention. First, almost every ballot makes some provision for voters to write in the names of persons not listed on the ballot. The success of write-in candidates is so rare, however, that it is hardly a real question in American politics.[4]

Second, the order in which candidates' names appear may affect the outcome of the election. American voters have shown a notorious disposition to vote for the first name on a list of candidates.[5] Ballot position probably confers the greatest advantages in primaries and other nonpartisan contests in which no information about the candidates is included on the ballot. Recognizing the value of being listed first on a ballot, some states randomly select the candidates' placements while others rotate positions throughout all the ballots so that each candidate is first on an equal number. But the prize of appearing first on the ballot sometimes is awarded to the incumbents, further heightening their electoral chances. In the general election, at issue is *party* position. The states frequently give the preferred position to the majority party in the state. Even where assignment is *officially* randomized to offer an equal chance of selection to each party, outcomes that almost always favor the majority party seem to give new meaning to the word "random." In Essex County, New Jersey, for example, the Democratic County Clerk (the so-called man with the golden arm) over the years "randomly" drew the capsule giving the Democrats the top ballot line in 40 out of 41 drawings.

---

[3]The best account of the effects of ballot form on voting remains Angus Campbell, Philip E. Converse, Warren E. Miller, and Donald E. Stokes, *The American Voter* (New York: Wiley, 1960), Chap. 11. For a recent inventory of ballot provisions in the various states, see *The Transformation in American Politics: Implications for American Federalism* (Washington, D.C.: Advisory Commission on Intergovernmental Affairs, 1986).

[4]Provisions for write-ins allow access to the ballot by candidates who have not been nominated by any of the parties. As was shown in Chapter 2, the states typically have protected the parties by making it difficult for such candidates to earn a position on the ballot. Moreover, a majority of states have so-called sore loser laws which prevent candidates who have lost in the contest for their party's nomination from qualifying for the general election ballot as an independent.

[5]Delbert A. Taebel, "The Effect of Ballot Position on Electoral Success," *American Journal of Political Science* 19 (1975): 519–26.

Finally, the American ballot is and has always been a long ballot. It reflects the American tradition of electing, rather than appointing, a great number of state and local officials. The major observable effect of the long ballot is voter fatigue. With so many contests on the ballot at the same time, voters must gather a considerable amount of information about the candidates to cast a meaningful vote. In 1990, for example, San Francisco voters faced a ballot containing 17 initiatives and constitutional amendments, 11 bond measures, 11 local propositions, plus an array of statewide elected offices. The ballot guide provided voters by the California Secretary of State was more than 200 pages in length. In such an election, it is hardly surprising that many voters find that the price of acquiring the requisite amount of information exceeds their sense of the worth of some offices and selectively abstain from voting. Such partial voting (or roll-off) is most common for minor offices (and referendum issues) and can be practiced by as many as 20 or 30 percent of the voters at a given election.[6]

Structure and Rules of the Choice

Overwhelmingly, American elections are governed by the twin principles of single-member constituencies and plurality election. In other words, we typically elect only one person per constituency to a city council, to the House or Senate, to the local mayoralty. The candidate who gets the most votes (i.e., the plurality), even if it is not the majority of 50 percent plus one, is elected. Even in cases of multimember districts the principle often is not altered.[7] The voter casts the same number of votes as there are officials to be elected from the district, and the plurality principle still governs. In a two-member state legislative district, for example, each voter casts two votes; and the two candidates with the greatest number of votes are the winners.

The American states have experimented very little with the systems of *proportional representation* (PR) that so often enchant the other democracies of the world. In these systems, which are of necessity based on multimember constituencies, the voter casts his or her vote for a party slate of candidates. The parties then share the seats according to the percentage of the votes they polled.[8]

---

[6]The introduction of the secret ballot at the end of the nineteenth century increased roll-off. See Walter Dean Burnham, "The Changing Shape of the American Political Universe," *American Political Science Review* 59 (1965): 7–28. The effects of the secret ballot on roll-off, though, are reduced by ballot forms that encourage straight-ticket voting. See Rusk, "The Effect of the Australian Ballot Reform on Split Ticket Voting," p. 1237; and Jack L. Walker, "Ballot Forms and Voter Fatigue: An Analysis of the Office Block and Party Column Ballots," *Midwest Journal of Political Science* 10 (1966): 448–63.

[7]For a good survey of the effects of various types of districts, see Howard D. Hamilton, "Legislative Constituencies: Single-Member Districts, Multi-Member Districts, and Floterial Districts," *Western Political Quarterly* 20 (1967): 321–40.

[8]For an excursion into some of the complexities of proportional representation, see Douglas W. Rae, *The Political Consequences of Electoral Law* (New Haven: Yale University Press, 1967).

Whether elections are conducted under proportional representation or plurality rules has several important implications for the political parties. First, proportional representation encourages minor political parties (and candidates) by giving them a share of the elective offices. Receiving 10 or 20 percent of the vote will rarely win any public offices in the plurality elections of American politics; but in several European countries, it wins parliamentary seats and cabinet positions for a number of parties. Second, by giving parties that cannot hope to capture a plurality victory some share of political representation, proportional representation affects all of the parties. It decreases both the electoral risk of being ideologically distinctive and the need to broaden the party's appeal in quest of a plurality victory; thus, it is more conductive to programmatic (or ideological) parties. Third, proportional representation strengthens the hand of the party vis-à-vis its candidates. In many elections in multimember districts operating under proportional representation rules, the voters cast a ballot for a party list of candidates rather than individual candidates. In drawing up their list and determining what position on it each candidate will have, the parties directly affect the chances of election for each of their candidates. The prevailing single-member, plurality structure of American elections, on the contrary, reinforces both the two-party system of broadly-based parties and the independence of candidates and officeholders.

A few American states and localities have experimented with proportional representation. New York City adopted a variety of proportional representation from 1938 to 1947, with a resulting growth and representation of minor political parties. In modern times, proportional representation has played an important role in presidential nomination politics. Since the 1970s, in many states the Democratic party and, to a lesser degree, the GOP has followed this principle in the election of delegates to the presidential nominating conventions (see Chapter 10). Understanding the complexities and the strategic options of proportional representation has not come easy to many American voters, however, unaccustomed as they are to anything other than "first past the post" or plurality elections.

Election Calendars

In 1845, the Congress took up its constitutional power to determine the dates of presidential and congressional elections (Article I, Section 4; Article II, Section 1). It provided that all states would select their presidential electors on the first Tuesday after the first Monday of November and that the same date would be used for electing members of Congress unless a state's constitution provided otherwise. All fifty states now use the November date. Since considerations of economy dictate that the states hold statewide elections at the same time, they have accepted the same date. No such uniformity on primary dates exists, however. Some come in April and May, some not until September. Consequently, a general election campaign may be six months or more in some states and two or less in others.

Furthermore, in an attempt to insulate elections at one level of government from the influence of contests at other levels (especially the presidential election), federal, state, and local elections typically have been given separate places on the electoral calendar. Most states now hold their elections for governor and other top state officials on the second November after the presidential election in conjunction with the midterm congressional contests, and a few have chosen years when no federal contests are on the ballot. Most local elections are scheduled at some other time. This practice of insulating elected officials from one another limits the possibilities for so-called coattail effects—the ability of a candidate at the top of the ticket (especially the president) to carry into office "on his coattails" his party's candidates on the same ticket—and has the intended effect of reducing the cohesiveness of the party in government.[9]

The Electoral Districts

The size and composition of the districts from which officials are elected also affects campaign strategies. Small, compact districts encourage a kind of face-to-face campaigning that simply is not possible in a large, sprawling constituency; voters in the latter may be reachable only through the mass media. The partisan composition of a district influences what the parties and candidates do in a different way. By setting the initial odds of victory or defeat, it determines the quality of the candidates who are attracted to the race and, quite often, the level of effort that will be expended by candidates and parties in the quest for victory. Districts with lopsided majorities in favor of one party discourage minority party activity, just as districts that are well-balanced between the parties can be scenes of spirited campaigns by both candidates and parties.

The peculiar American institution of the electoral college produces another kind of electoral district effect. Since the 1830s, American presidents have been chosen by a faceless group of electors in each state, who in turn are selected in accordance with which presidential candidate wins the most popular votes in that state. Victory comes from winning a majority of the state electoral votes rather than compiling the highest national vote total, and the strategies of presidential candidates are adjusted accordingly. Candidates tend to concentrate their attention on the states with the largest number of electoral votes and the highest degree of interparty competition—which generally turn out to be the largest and most diverse states. They typically write off the less populous states or states in which the result is predictable regardless of their efforts.[10]

---

[9]Walter Dean Burnham, *Critical Elections and the Mainsprings of American Politics* (New York: Norton, 1970), p. 94; and V. O. Key, Jr., *American State Politics: An Introduction*, (New York: Knopf, 1967), pp. 41–49 and 52–84.

[10]For an analysis of the relative importance of states in presidential elections due to the electoral college, see George Rabinowitz and Stuart Elaine MacDonald, "The Power of the States in U.S. Presidential Elections," *American Political Science Review* 80 (1986): 65–87. Several studies have shown that presidential candidates concentrate their campaign resources on the most populous and

POLITICAL CONSEQUENCES OF ELECTORAL LAW

Perhaps the chief impact of American political institutions on the politics of campaigning has been to focus attention on the candidates rather than on the parties. The American electoral process is relatively free from such institutions as parliamentary-cabinet government or proportional representation, which encourage the voter to see electoral contests in terms of the greater fortunes and future of political parties. On the contrary, such details of electoral law as the office-block ballot tend to structure the electoral choice as a series of contests between individual candidates and not as a single, multifaceted campaign between two great parties. Nonpartisan elections for lower-level office have even further reduced the visibility of the party in elections, and the separate scheduling of contests at different levels of government makes it difficult for the parties to coordinate their programmatic activities.

Who Benefits?

The details of American electoral law often do not touch the parties or candidates equally. If voting machines confuse less well educated, lower SES voters, and if office-block ballots encourage greater voter fatigue (roll-off) among less-educated voters,[11] then the disadvantages may accrue more to the Democratic party. If the state refuses absentee ballots to travelers, whether on business or pleasure, the disadvantages may strike mainly the upper-status Republicans. If the state encourages and facilitates absentee voting as some have recently done, by contrast, it can redound to the benefit of the Republicans or any well organized local party. Any ballot form that facilitates party-ticket voting works to the advantage of the majority party in the constituency. Prime ballot position helps the incumbent and the majority party; so do designations of incumbency printed on the ballot. Even the hours and places for polling may have some marginal benefits for one party or the other.

Just how aware the parties and state legislators are of the possible advantages in refining electoral law is not easy to say. It is always difficult to establish the motives of legislators, especially when those motives may not be of the highest type. Occasionally, however, an attempt is just too persistent, too transparent, not to reveal the motives of party or political advantage. For example:

> In the state of Ohio the ballot has been changed six times during the twentieth century, and in each case the Republican majority tried to gain an advantage for itself by tampering with the election machinery. In 1940 Governor

---

most competitive states, which are often the same. See especially Claude S. Colantoni, Terrence J. Levesque, and Peter C. Ordeshook, "Campaign Resource Allocation under the Electoral College," *American Political Science Review* 69 (1975): 141–54; and Larry M. Bartels, "Resource Allocation in Presidential Campaigns," *Journal of Politics* 47 (1985): 928–36.

[11]Walker, "Ballot Forms and Voter Fatigue," makes the latter point.

Bricker tried to avoid the influences of F.D.R.'s "coattails" by calling a special session of the legislature which approved a separation of the ballot carrying national races from the one on which state and local races appeared. Bricker reasoned that if a normally Republican voter who was determined to vote for Roosevelt had to use a second ballot in state races he would be less likely to vote a straight Democratic ticket (the ballots were later consolidated once again to capitalize on Eisenhower's coattails). In 1949 over $85,000 was spent in a campaign to substitute the Office Block ballot for the Party Column ballot in an effort to save Senator Robert Taft from defeat in the bitter 1950 election. . . . The Taft forces thought that by eliminating the party lever they would substantially reduce the number of straight Democratic votes and thus increase the Senator's chances among normally Democratic, working class voters. Key quotes Taft as claiming that the change "was responsible 'for something between 100,000 and 200,000' of his total majority of 430,000."[12]

The Drawing of Constituency Lines

Finally, in one way above all—the drawing of constituency lines—the American parties have tried repeatedly to steal an advantage in electoral politics. Traditionally, there have been two general tactics: constituencies of unequal populations and gerrymandered districts. The first and more obvious of the two—districts of unequal populations or malapportionment—simply involved stretching the popular vote of the majority party by putting fewer people in districts in its strongholds than in districts located in the other party's areas of strength. In the past, when the heavily populated districts were usually in urban areas, malapportionment worked to the disadvantage of Republicans in the South and Democrats elsewhere. In 1962, however, the Supreme Court put an end to these inequities. As the courts have applied the "one man, one vote" rule to constituencies of all varieties, they have closed off a classically American way of exploiting the rules of the electoral game.[13]

The Gerrymander   More subtle and less easy to detect, the gerrymander survives. It consists of one party's drawing district lines in such a way as to use its own popular vote most efficiently while forcing the other party to use its vote inefficiently. That goal can be achieved either by dividing and diluting pockets of the other party's strength to prevent it from winning office, or (if the other party's strength is too great for dilution) by bunching its strength into a few districts and forcing it to win elections by large, wasteful majorities. Sometimes, the resulting constituencies, instead of being compact and contiguous, have bizarre and fanciful shapes (see box). Which party reaps the advantage of the

---

[12]Ibid., pp. 448–49.

[13]For the political ramifications of apportionment, see Robert S. Erikson, "The Partisan Impact of State Legislative Reapportionment," *Midwest Journal of Political Science* 15 (1971): 57–71; and Timothy G. O'Rourke, *The Impact of Reapportionment* (New Brunswick, N.J.: Transaction, 1980).

The Gerrymander

This is the nickname given to the artful drawing of legislative district lines by the party in power so as to give it a greater share of legislative seats than its share of votes. As is reported by Charles Ledyard Norton in his 1890 book, *Political Americanisms:*

> The term is derived from the name of Governor Gerry, of Massachu-setts, who, in 1811, signed a bill readjusting the representative dis-tricts so as to favor the Democrats and weaken the Federalists, although the last named party polled nearly two-thirds of the votes cast. A fancied resemblance of a map of the districts thus treated led [Gilbert] Stuart, the painter, to add a few lines with his pencil, and say to Mr. Russell, editor of the Boston *Centinel,* "That will do for a salamander." Russell glanced at it: "Salamander?" said he, "Call it a Gerrymander!" The epithet took at once and became a Federalist warcry, the map caricature being published as a campaign document.
>
> Quoted in William Safire, *Safire's*
> *Political Dictionary* (New York:
> Random House, 1978), pp. 254–55

The term reappears in common use about every ten years when the states set about to redraw their legislative district lines to take into ac-count the new distribution of population as determined by the decennial census.

gerrymander traditionally has depended on which party controls the legislature or other body that draws the district lines.

Involvement of the Courts   Lately, however, state legislatures have lost some control over the redrawing of those district lines. Federal courts have taken an increasingly active role in the task, in response to suits charging leg-islatures with evading constitutional standards of equality. Approximately a dozen states were redistricted by court-adopted plans after the 1980 census. At the same time, the Justice Department rejected the reapportionment plans of nine states under the authority conferred by the Voting Rights Act to screen proposed electoral changes in certain states to protect the voting rights of mi-norities. Under the 1982 Voting Rights Act, the states are required to go one step further in their reapportionment efforts for the 1990s. They are to create congressional districts that maximize the opportunities for black and Hispanic candidates.

The political consequences of these shifts of control over redistricting are predictable. In some states, the voting power of racial and ethnic minorities has been enhanced; in others, the weaker of the two major parties has been strengthened. Furthermore, the courts and the Justice Department are far less inclined than state legislative majorities to gerrymander for party advantage and to protect the districts of incumbents. Nonetheless, legal requirements can have partisan effects. In redistricting for the 1990s, for example, Republicans in many states (especially in the South and Southwest) have found common cause with minority groups, even to the point of lending them their redistricting computer programs, on the assumption that the creation of black and Hispanic districts will concentrate Democratic voters and open up more districts to Republican control.[14] Legal authorities are also more willing, in many instances, to draw district lines across the lines of civil subdivisions (e.g., counties) and thus across the lines of local party organization. The result is to make it harder in yet another way for party organizations to maintain a role in electoral politics.

The involvement of the courts and other legal authorities has significantly reduced the partisan advantages of party control over redistricting by forcing districts to be of equal population size.[15] While examples of blatantly partisan gerrymanders remain (e.g., the California and Indiana plans after the 1980 census), they appear to be less common than before. This makes party control of the post-decennial-census state legislatures less critical for party fortunes during the remainder of the decade than the conventional wisdom has held—at the same time, ironically, that the use of computers has turned the drawing of district lines from an art into a science.

Empirical studies of the effects of redistricting in recent decades show that, with the exception of a few blatantly partisan gerrymanders perhaps, they typically advantage the party in charge only marginally and do not systematically favor incumbent officeholders. In examining legislative elections in six states in the 1970s, Gary King found modest but short-lived advantages for the party drawing the new lines, especially through the removal of opposition party incumbents. Congressional redistricting in the 1970s, moreover, was shown to preserve the status quo rather than favor either a particular party or incumbents in general. A study of congressional redistricting from 1952–82 also found few significant party gains, especially after the court intervention in redistricting began in 1964.[16] In spite of the spirited interparty battles in 1990 to gain

---

[14]Analysis of various plans for redistricting in South Carolina after the 1980 census showed that those advantaging blacks also helped Republicans. Kimball Brace, Bernard Grofman, and Lisa Handley, "Does Redistricting Aimed to Help Blacks Necessarily Help Republicans," *Journal of Politics* 49 (1987): 169–85.

[15]In Karcher v. Daggett (462 U.S. 725 [1983]), the Supreme Court struck down a New Jersey plan because, by creating districts that differed in population size by seven-tenths of one percent from the average, it violated the constitutional requirements of "precise mathematical equality." While ruling that partisan gerrymanders may be challenged in the courts, however, the Supreme Court has refrained from invalidating even the notorious Indiana (Davis v. Bandamer, 478 U.S. 109 [1986]) and California redistricting plans (Badham v. Eu, 488 U.S. 1024 [1989]).

[16]See Gary King, "Representation through Legislative Redistricting: A Stochastic Model," *American Journal of Political Science* 33 (1989): 787–824. On how redistricting preserves the status quo, see Amihai Glazer, Bernard Grofman, and Marc Robbins, "Partisan and Incumbency Effects of

control over the redistricting process in several states, then, there is good reason to believe that most redistricting plans will effect little change in the fortunes of either the parties or incumbents. But the California example shows that skillful and determined gerrymandering, however rarely it may be practiced, can greatly benefit a political party.

CAMPAIGN STRATEGY

The folk wisdom about all aspects of American politics is more than ample, but on the subject of campaign tactics it is overwhelming. Much of it has been brought together into little books on campaigning that read like modern how-to-do-it manuals. Since many of the recent books have been written by advertising and public relations specialists, much of the wisdom has a modern tone. Candidates are advised on dress and makeup for TV, and there is a good deal of emphasis on catchy phrases and slogans.[17]

There is much of value in the received wisdom about American campaigning. Generally, it represents the distillation of concrete experience. Yet it suffers from two deficiencies that themselves are generally warnings about the crafts of political campaigning. The conventional wisdom seems to suggest, first of all, that most political campaigns are run on a master battle plan adhered to

---

1970s Congressional Redistricting," *American Journal of Political Science* 31 (1987): 680–707. The 1952–1982 congressional study is Richard Born, "Partisan Intentions and Election Day Realities in the Congressional Redistricting Process," *American Political Science Review* 79 (1985): 305–19. The two notorious congressional gerrymanders of the 1980s, however, seem to stand as important exceptions to the minimal effects rule. The California plan clearly advantaged the Democrats; while the GOP's effort in Indiana seemed to benefit the Republicans, although not nearly as decisively or longlastingly (the state's congressional delegation, 6–5 Democratic in 1981, was 8–2 Democratic 10 years later!). On California, see Bruce E. Cain, "Assessing the Partisan Effects of Redistricting," *American Political Science Review* 79 (1985): 320–34. On Indiana, see John D. Cranor, Gary L. Crawley, and Raymond H. Scheele, "The Anatomy of a Gerrymander," *American Journal of Political Science* 33 (1989): 222–39.

[17]An example of the how-to-do-it genre is Joe Napolitan, *The Election Game and How to Win It* (Garden City, N.Y.: Doubleday, 1972). Also the magazine, *Election Politics,* published by the Free Congress Foundation's Institute for Government and Politics contains articles on the art and practice of campaigning. More scholarly analyses of campaigns may be found in Stephen Hess, *The Presidential Campaign* (Washington, D.C.: Brookings, 1978); Edie N. Goldenberg and Michael W. Traugott, *Campaigning for Congress* (Washington, D.C.: CQ Press, 1984); and John H. Kessel, *Presidential Campaign Politics* (Chicago: Dorsey, 1988). A third genre of works, case studies of particular campaigns, rounds out the literature on campaigning. Notable recent examples are Lucius J. Barker and Ronald W. Walters, *Jesse Jackson's 1984 Presidential Campaign: Challenge and Change in American Politics* (Champaign: University of Illinois Press, 1979); Sidney Blumenthal, *Pledging Allegiance: The Last Campaign of the Cold War* (New York: HarperCollins, 1990); Marjorie Randon Hershey, *Running for Office: The Political Education of Campaigners* (Chatham, N.J.: Chatham House, 1984); L. Sandy Maisel, *From Obscurity to Oblivion: Running in the Congressional Primary* (Knoxville: University of Tennessee Press, 1986); and David R. Runkel, *Campaign for President: The Managers Look at '88* (Dover, Mass.: Auburn House, 1989).

with almost military discipline and precision. In reality, most American political campaigns lurch along from one improvisation to another, from one immediate crisis to another. They are frequently underorganized, underplanned, underfinanced, and understaffed; consequently, they often play by ear with a surprising lack of information.

The folk wisdom also suggests that there are principles of good campaigning that have an almost universal applicability. In truth, however, optimum campaign strategy depends on a great number of variables, and the only general rule is that there is no general rule. Strategy will vary with:

- *The skills of the candidate:* Does he or she project well on television, at a press conference, or at an informal coffee hour?
- *The nature of the constituency:* Is it several square miles of urban slum, 30,000 square miles of prairie, or the entire nation?
- *The office being sought:* Is it a city councillorship, or perhaps a judgeship that will call for a more restrained campaign?
- *The nature of the electoral system:* Is the ballot partisan or nonpartisan? Is the general election two or six months after the primary?
- *The party organizations in the constituency:* To what extent can their organized resources be counted on? What can they do?
- *The availability of political resources:* What manpower, skills, and money will be available, and when?
- *The nature of the electorate:* What are the voters' political norms, party loyalties, perceptions of issues and candidates? What political styles and tactics do they approve? What turnout and voting record do they have?

There are other factors, of course. The chief early task of campaign strategists is the sober evaluation of all the factors and of the consequent demands and limits they place on the campaign.

The nub of the strategic task in a campaign is selectivity in the expenditures of scarce time, energy, and resources in order to achieve the maximum effect on the electorate. The candidate and his or her managers must decide how to spend each unit of campaign resources so that it will return the maximum number of votes. Will they work on areas normally loyal to the other party in hopes of cutting losses there, or will they hammer at their own party strongholds? They must also decide how to tailor their appeals to different parts of the electorate. For some of the voters, there must be stimuli to party loyalty; for others, appeals of issue or personality are necessary. The problem is to know the variety and diversity of the voters, the likely bases of their decisions, and the ways of reaching and stimulating them differentially.[18]

All these decisions must be made within the context of political reality, and the political characteristics of the election race probably set the chief limits of

---

[18]For an examination of how presidential candidates allocated one scarce resource, campaign visits, among various constituency groups, see Darrell M. West, "Constituencies and Travel Allocations in the 1980 Presidential Campaign," *American Journal of Political Science* 27 (1983): 515–29.

campaign strategy. The presence or absence of an incumbent in the race and the competitiveness of the constituency exceed all other considerations in significance. Those two factors, perhaps, determine whether there is a possibility of victory. They affect the ability of the candidate to recruit workers and resources, to line up the support of groups to attract the attention of voters. The fact that a candidate is an incumbent running for reelection in a competitive district or a nonincumbent of the losing party in a noncompetitive district, for example, sets some major limits on campaign strategy before the imaginations of the candidate and his or her advisors even begin to work.

Finally, the very nature of the office being sought places important constraints on the nature of the campaign and its strategies. The most visible campaigns are those for the most visible and important offices—for governorships, major city offices, for president of course, as well as Congress. Candidates for them tend to have name recognition already, and the attention given to the campaign increases it. They can raise large sums of money for splashy media campaigns aimed at reaching the mass of voters. The great majority of campaigns in the United States, however, are far less visible. Candidates whose names are hardly household words and whose campaign resources are modest must run far less ambitious campaigns. They must seek different ways to reach the voter, in fact. One study finds, for example, that such candidates tend to campaign indirectly—that is, to rely on the building of voter support through intermediary devices, such as the endorsement of better known political figures or the support of organized groups, whether of the party or not.[19]

THE NEW CAMPAIGNING

Within less than a generation, changes amounting to a revolution have altered much of American political campaigning. The skills of the mass media specialists have brought new persuasive techniques to bear on the American electorate—with attendant fears that presidents and lesser officials are now sold to the electorate much as Madison Avenue sells a new mouthwash or toothpaste. With the new techniques have also come the new technicians—the campaign management specialists, a new breed of sophisticated, hard-headed advisors who, as political mercenaries, deploy their troops and artillery for a suitable fee.

The New Campaign Professionals

Professional campaign consultants have been drawn from the worlds of advertising and public relations, as well as from political work of one kind or another. Not only have they prospered in American politics, they have also begun to

---

[19]Susan E. Howell, "Local Election Campaigns: The Effects of Office Level on Campaign Style," *Journal of Politics* 42 (1980): 1135–45.

export American campaign expertise to the rest of the democratic world.[20] Campaign firms and specialists come in all sizes and shapes. Some are experts in the use of the mass media. Some can provide organizational skills, sometimes even lists of local party people and possible volunteer workers; they can organize rallies, coffee parties, phone banks, and hand-shaking tours of shopping centers. Some provide lawyers and accountants to steer the campaign away from legal shoals and to speed the reporting of campaign finances to the appropriate regulatory bodies. Some are publicists who write speeches and press releases; some sample public opinion; and some are very skilled in raising money. Some can offer virtually all of those services. It is a profession of both specialists and generalists, of both contractors and subcontractors. In it there is a scope and a skill for every candidate's need. There is no better testimony to the takeover of modern campaigns by "hired-gun" specialists, displacing the candidate loyalist of previous times, than the fact that these campaign professionals—e.g., Roger Ailes, Charles Black, Patrick Caddell, David Garth, Peter Hart, Matt Reese, Robert Squier, Lance Tarrance, Richard Viguerie—have become as familiar as some of the candidates for office and sometimes even become issues in the campaign.[21]

The existence of this new breed of campaign professionals signifies a major departure from past practices, at least in contests for major offices, when campaign expertise was drawn from a candidate's loyal staff or from political party workers. Instead, these professional campaign consultants work as independent political entrepreneurs in the service of different candidates, often several in the same year. Their skills are available to candidates who can pay their fees, although they almost always restrict themselves to clients from only one of the parties and some may impose an ideological criterion as well. Even though the parties in recent years have built impressive in-house campaign expertise, campaigns for the most visible offices still are dominated by these independent consultants. Neither from the party in government nor from the party organization, the new professionals occupy a political niche on the periphery of the political parties.

The New Sources of Information

The development of modern social science has opened up new sources of information and knowledge to the political campaigner. Computers and data-processing systems permit a party to keep records about constituencies and to process that information rapidly. Carefully kept records usually yield a faster

---

[20]For a colorful account of American campaign professionals in other foreign nations, see John M. Russonello, "The Making of the President . . . in the Philippines, Venezuela, France . . . ," *Public Opinion* 9 (1986): 10–12.

[21]Among the many recent books on the subject, see Sidney Blumenthal, *The Permanent Campaign* (New York: Simon and Schuster, 1980); and Larry J. Sabato, *The Rise of Political Consultants* (New York: Basic, 1981).

and more accurate answer to how the twenty-first ward went four years ago, for example, than even the most experienced party workers can. Wily parties and candidates have similarly used the scholarly data and findings on the demographic bases of Republican and Democratic strength. Perhaps the first sophisticated use of computers in campaigns occurred when the managers of John F. Kennedy's presidential campaign commissioned a simulation of the 1960 electorate as an aid to campaign planning. The simulation attempted to coordinate and correlate knowledge about the American electorate and to project the effects that various events of the campaign might have on it.[22] Other candidates have computerized records of canvassing so that they can quickly compile lists of voters to contact on election day. Computers also have been used to great advantage to produce lists of potential contributors, and these lists themselves have proven to be an invaluable campaign resource.

No new avenue to political knowledge has been more fully exploited than the public opinion poll. It may be employed at the beginning of a campaign to assess the political issues uppermost in the minds of voters. Early polls can also develop candidate profiles—information about how the voting public views the two opponents. If it is found that voters think a candidate too bookish or intellectual, he or she may be sent to plowing contests, athletic events, or on a weekend fishing trip. Candidates viewed as weak-kneed can compensate by demonstrations of toughness during their campaign. Polls can also indicate whether the campaign ought to capitalize on party loyalties or whether the candidate would be better advised to ignore an unpopular party or candidate at the top of the ticket. During the campaign, a poll or two can chart its progress and indicate where time and resources ought to be concentrated in its waning days (see box).

Parties and candidates have not been uniformly willing or able to avail themselves of such new techniques. Much of the knowledge thus far accumulated, especially about voting behavior, derives chiefly from presidential campaigns and elections and has only limited applicability. Also, many of the techniques are beyond the resources of local campaigns, although recent technical support efforts by the parties' national committees and congressional campaign committees (reviewed in Chapter 4) have made these new tools of campaigning available to even the campaigns with the slimmest budgets. The difficulty runs deeper, however. American political campaigns, despite popular impressions to the contrary, have rarely been run on a solid base of information. Thousands of party organizations around the country never have kept even basic voting data by precincts, wards, townships, cities, and counties. Thus, such a shift to the "new knowledge" involves a basic commitment to knowledge itself, as well as a willingness to bear the costs of acquiring it.

---

[22]Described in Ithiel de Sola Pool, Robert P. Abelson, and Samuel Popkin, *Candidates, Issues, and Strategies* (Cambridge, Mass.: MIT Press, 1964). A fictionalized version can be found in Eugene Burdick, *The 480* (New York: McGraw-Hill, 1964).

Daily Readings of Public Opinion: The Wirthlin Tracking Polls

The most recent innovation in gathering information about the electorate is the so-called "tracking poll" based on the daily monitoring of opinion. The most extensive usage of tracking polls yet has been by campaign consultant Richard Wirthlin's firm Decision/Making/Information for Ronald Reagan's reelection campaign in 1984. D/M/I conducted 250 telephone interviews nationwide per night beginning June 1, 1984. They increased the number to 500 per night on October 5 and then to 1000 per night on November 1. These daily samples were large enough to be able to detect immediate public reactions to particular campaign events and apparently played an important role in the strategic planning of the Reagan campaign.

The New Techniques of Persuasion

Campaigns are basically exercises in mass persuasion, and the commercial arts of persuasion have increasingly been applied to them. There was a time when strong party organizations were the great persuaders in American campaigns. Changes in the organizations and in American politics, however, have diminished that role. Party organizations do not control votes and turn them out as they once did. It is left increasingly to candidates to do their own persuading of voters.

Predominant among the new persuasive techniques is the use of the mass communications media. Frequently, now, a candidate takes the time and effort to address a rally or meeting largely in the hope that it will produce a news report or a brief film clip on the local TV news. (Of course, the question of whether it produces a news report is not left to chance; the staff prepares news releases and copies of the speech for the local media.) Early in the campaign, candidates may vie to commit choice TV time and billboard space for the concluding weeks of the campaign. As the campaign progresses, the candidates' faces, names, and slogans blossom on billboards, newspaper ads, radio and TV spot announcements—even on lawn signs, automobile bumpers, and construction fences.

For the offices for which the new campaigning is most appropriate, television has become the major medium of persuasion. Time on TV may consume the majority of the campaign's funds. In the early and inexpensive days of television, candidates bought large chunks of time for entire speeches that were carried nationwide, but this is no longer done. Increasingly, the political message is compressed into the thirty- or sixty-*second* spot advertisement that can be run everywhere or targeted to particular areas of the country. The writing, the filming, and the placing of those messages (after the pro football game? before the evening news?) become a major part of the campaign and, except in the case of the publicly-financed presidential campaign, so does the ability to raise

The Made-for-Television Candidate

the necessary money for it. Thus, what was a long, stem-winding speech by the candidate in a sweaty hall fifty or sixty years ago is now a few carefully crafted visual images and a very simple text put together by professionals. More people depend upon television for their political news than upon any other medium, and the intermediary role between candidates and voters once dominated by local group and party leaders seems to have eroded as well (see box).

At the same time, high-speed computers have brought the postal service back to the center of the campaign. Computers can produce personalized, targeted letters by the millions. They are effective both for campaigning and for fund raising; the well-written letter seeking money is indeed also an appeal for the candidate seeking the funds.

Long gone, of course, are the days when a direct mailer began a form letter with an awkward "Dear Mr. Smith," printed in different type, usually above or below the line. Now, the "computer" types each letter individually, using the receiver's name throughout the text, in exactly the type of the letter body. If a letter to a Congressman is suggested, the computer knows the name of that representative by the person's zip code. The one thing direct mail letters are not is dispassionate. "You've got to have a devil," said Mr. (Roger) Craver. "If you don't have a devil, you're in trouble." . . . "You need a letter filled with ideas and passion. . . . It does not beat around the bush, it is not academic, it is not objective."[23]

Gradually building a list of contributors and supporters—a list that can be returned to with good results—is also building for the political future. It is one of the many advantages an experienced and veteran campaigner enjoys.

All of this is not to argue that the traditional campaign techniques are obsolete. Handshaking on the streets and in the stores, speeches before anyone who will listen, endorsements by local groups and party organizations—all the old ways are very much alive. The new campaigning is too expensive for many candidates, particularly at the local level. Also, these techniques are inefficient for candidates in small constituencies, because the radio, television, billboard, and newspaper space they purchase is wasted in great part on readers, viewers, and listeners who cannot vote for them.[24]

THE NEW CAMPAIGNING FOR THE PRESIDENCY

Nowhere are the techniques and technicians of the new campaigning more visible than in the presidential election campaigns. The campaign for the presidency is in many ways the generic American political campaign "writ large." Its main problems and tasks are different in degree but similar in kind. Yet many of the usual campaign problems are heightened by the nature of the presidential office and constituency. Keeping posted on how the campaign is going is a tremendous problem for the candidate. The vast expanse of the country, the variety of local conditions, and the candidate's isolation from the grass roots make any kind of assessment difficult. To solve this problem, modern presidential candidates have relied on professional pollsters to supplement and, increasingly, replace the reports of local politicians. Campaigning across a huge country also places heavy demands on the candidates. Their packed schedules and their need to address the concerns of varied audiences (all within the clear view of a press corps that follows them almost continuously) put exceptional physical and mental strains on a candidate.

Given these difficulties, it is little wonder that presidential candidates find it hard to resist channeling much of their campaign through the mass media, especially television. A media-based campaign possesses a number of advantages for presidential aspirants. Through it, they can communicate efficiently

---

[23]E. J. Dionne, Jr., in *The New York Times*, September 7, 1980. Copyright © 1980 by The New York Times Company. Reprinted by permission.

[24]Herbert Alexander estimates that television accounted for about 8 percent of the $2.7 billion spent in campaigns for 1988. Television consumed, by contrast, 57 percent ($52.5 million) of the money spent by the Bush and Dukakis general election campaigns. See Herbert E. Alexander and Monica Bauer, *Financing the 1988 Election*, (Boulder, Colo.: Westview Press, 1991) Chap. 1.

with a national audience, reaching more potential voters than they ever could hope for with any series of local campaign appearances. Nonetheless, these local appearances remain important for the free media coverage they generate. This very fact has fostered a proliferation of campaign activities that are staged mostly, sometimes even wholly, for the media coverage they attract. Presidential candidates also transmit their message through paid media advertising, especially on television.[25] Of course, such extensive usage of the media by presidential candidates is made possible by sums of money that few other candidates can command; but, ironically, it is made all the more necessary by the limits on campaign expenditures that go along with public funding of the presidential campaigns.

TO WHAT EFFECT THE CAMPAIGN?

Many candidates—whether their campaigns are old or new style—have wondered about the impact of a campaign's sound and fury. The barrage of words and pictures is staggering, but is anyone listening or watching? Has the apparent upsurge in negative political advertising turned voters away? Do the spot commercials, the literature, even the canvassing make any difference in the ultimate voting decision? No one really knows for sure.

Selective Exposure

Logical deduction leads to some plausible and probably reliable answers. We know that American voters expose themselves to a campaign with great selectivity. First of all, they tend to surround themselves with friends, literature, and even personal experiences (such as rallies and meetings) that support their perceptions and loyalties. Furthermore, they tend to perceive what they are exposed to through a filter of stable, long-term loyalties, the most stable of which is their loyalty to a political party. What we think of as a campaign may to some extent be two campaigns—one party and its candidates shouting at their supporters and the other party and its candidates doing the same. Thus, a good deal of American campaigning has the effect of stimulating, activating, and reinforcing given political predispositions, as it always has. Much of the campaigning, too, is directed as much at getting people out to vote as at influencing their voting decision.[26]

---

[25]A recent audit by the Federal Communications Commission (reported in the *New York Times*, September 8, 1990) has found that television and radio stations often charge candidates higher rates than other advertisers for the same times—in violation of federal law.

[26]The classic studies of the mobilizing effects of a political campaign were conducted in the 1940s before the appearance of television. See Paul Lazarsfeld, Bernard Berelson, and Hazel Gaudet, *The People's Choice* (New York: Columbia University Press, 1948); and Bernard Berelson, Paul

(*continued*)

The Dominance of Short-Term Impressions

Yet in the contemporary environment of weakened partisan loyalties and large numbers of independents, the potential of the campaign for shaping voter perceptions of the candidates may be higher than it has ever been. As long-term voter commitments to party become less important, short-term impressions come to predominate, especially where there is no incumbent candidate in the race. Recent campaigns have witnessed tremendous swings in public support for candidates right up to election day and an increase in the effectiveness of personal attacks by opponents and single-issue groups through negative television advertising (see box),[27] both signs of an electorate that lacks deep-seated commitments to candidates or to parties.

The Impact of Television

Now that the traditional intermediaries (local party and group leaders) seem to play a reduced role as cue-givers for voters, television has become the primary medium for winning their support. The importance of television for their campaigns is a fact that few modern-day politicians have failed to appreciate. As Austin Ranney has observed, they

> recognize that in the 1980s' world of mass constituencies and of voters who would rather stay home and watch television than attend a political rally in some auditorium, appearing on television is the closest candidates can get to all but a handful of their constituents and provides by far the most cost-effective campaigning device they have. Moreover, . . . while eye-to-eye contact and a warm handshake between politician and voter may be best, having the politician's voice and face appear in living color on the tube a few feet away from the constituent in his own living room is surely second best.[28]

The importance of television is suggested by data from a national sample of Americans. A minority of the adult public is contacted by a party worker in

---

(*continued*)
Lazarsfeld, and William McPhee, *Voting* (Chicago: University of Chicago Press, 1954). Evidence that most voters continue to be found in highly homogeneous political environments, and consequently are more likely to be mobilized than persuaded, may be found in Robert Huckfeldt and John Sprague, "Networks in Context: The Social Flow of Political Information," *American Political Science Review* 81 (1987): 1197–1216; and Paul Allen Beck, "Voters' Intermediation Environments in the 1988 Presidential Context," *Public Opinion Quarterly* 55 (1991).

[27]For an illuminating examination of campaigns filled with negative advertising by single-issue groups, see Marjorie Hershey's study of six Senate races in 1980 in which the incumbents had been targeted for attack by prolife groups and four were ultimately defeated. Hershey, *Running for Office.*

[28]Austin Ranney, *Channels of Power: The Impact of Television on American Politics* (New York: Basic Books, 1983), p. 90.

A Case Study in Negative Advertising: The Willie Horton Commercial

American political campaigns traditionally have been filled with partisan "mudslinging," as some candidates have found it hard to refrain from attacking their opponents in ways that cross the bounds of civility. These practices appear to many observers to have become more frequent in recent campaigns, as negative or "attack" advertisements have become especially common.

The most infamous in these negative ads is the "Willie Horton" commercial aired nationally for 28 days on cable television during the 1988 presidential race. It was described by a November 3, 1988, article in *The New York Times* in the following terms:

> "Weekend Passes" is the title of the 30-second advertisement about Willie Horton. As side-by-side photographs of . . . Bush and . . . Dukakis flash on the screen, an announcer says, 'Bush and Dukakis on crime . . . Bush supports the death penalty for first-degree murderers. . . . Dukakis not only opposes the death penalty, he allowed first-degree murderers to have weekend passes from prison.' Flash to a mugshot of a glaring Willie Horton. 'One was Willie Horton, who murdered a boy in a robbery, stabbing him 19 times. . . . Despite a life sentence, Horton received 10 weekend passes from prison. (He) fled, kidnapped a young couple, stabbing the man and repeatedly raping his girlfriend.' As the announcer gives those details, the words 'kidnapping,' 'stabbing' and 'raping' flash on the screen. The last photo is of Mr. Dukakis. The announcer says: "Weekend prison passes. Dukakis on crime."

The Willie Horton commercial, denounced by Democrats as racist because Willie Horton was black, was devastatingly effective. It was, however, not directly linked to the Bush campaign, even though they had researched the Willie Horton case and had tested its effect on voters. Bush denounced the ad after it had been run and Lee Atwater, his campaign manager, apologized for it two years later as he lay dying from a brain tumor. The ad was produced, though, by advertising consultants long associated with the Republican party and paid for by an independent conservative political action committee, which claimed that they had the tacit approval of the Bush campaign organization and had offered Bush campaign leaders the opportunity to veto the ad.

Source: Stephen Engelberg, *The New York Times*, November 3, 1988. Copyright © 1988 by The New York Times Company. Reprinted by permission.

presidential election campaigns. Only 24 percent, for example, reported being approached by one of the parties in the 1988 campaign, and only 8 percent went to a political meeting, rally, or dinner. Media exposure, on the other hand, reaches the great majority of the electorate. In 1988, 70 percent of the respondents paid at least some attention to television news about the presidential campaign.[29] Among likely voters, another study found that 89 percent had seen Dukakis ads and 90 percent had seen Bush ads in the week before the election.[30]

In spite of their importance as a source of information about politics, the actual impact of the media on political attitudes and behavior is unclear. There is ample evidence that the media do not directly determine political preferences, in large part because the modern media provides fairly balanced coverage of political candidates and issues.[31] Rather, media influence is more subtle. By the kinds of issues and events it emphasizes, the media affect what people see as important in a political campaign (the process is called *agenda-setting*), and this "agenda" in turn becomes the basis for candidate evaluation (the process is called *priming*).[32] By its more or less balanced treatment of the candidates, however, the media does break the cocoon of homogeneous political views in which many voters otherwise would find themselves—and, in that way, it may undermine their traditional political viewpoints.

---

[29]These figures come from the 1988 National Election Study conducted by the Center for Political Studies of the University of Michigan; they were made available through the Inter-University Consortium for Political and Social Research.

[30]The estimates on attention to candidate advertising come from *Adweek*, November 7, p. 38, as reported in Harold W. Stanley and Richard G. Niemi, *Vital Statistics on American Politics* (Washington, D.C.: CQ Press, 1990), p. 66. For more on presidential campaign advertising, see Kathleen Hall Jamieson, *Packaging the Presidency: A History and Criticism of Presidential Campaign Advertising* (New York: Oxford University Press, 1984).

[31]Various studies of media content have demonstrated that the media do not systematically favor either candidate in presidential elections, except for newspaper editorial page endorsements. A content analysis of ABC, CBS, and NBC evening news by the Center for Media and Public Affairs during the 1988 presidential campaign found that Bush and Dukakis received about an equal percentage of positive assessments. See Stanley and Niemi, *Vital Statistics on American Politics*, p. 65. Similar findings for earlier years are reported in Doris A. Graber, *Mass Media and American Politics* (Washington, D.C.: CQ Press, 1989); C. Richard Hofstetter, *Bias in the News* (Columbus: Ohio State University Press, 1976); Thomas Patterson, *The Mass Media Election* (New York: Praeger, 1980); and Michael J. Robinson and Margaret A. Sheehan, *Over the Wire and On TV: CBS and UPI in Campaign '80* (New York: Russell Sage Foundation, 1983).

[32]For evidence on the agenda-setting effects of the media, see Donald Shaw and Maxwell E. McCombs, *The Emergence of American Political Issues: The Agenda-Setting Function of the Press* (St. Paul, Minn.: West, 1977); Lutz Erbring, Edie Goldenberg, and Arthur Miller, "Front-Page News and Real-World Cues: A New Look at Agenda-Setting by the Media," *American Journal of Political Science* 24 (1980): 16–49; and Shanto Iyengar and Donald Kinder, *News That Matters* (Chicago: University of Chicago Press, 1987). For evidence on priming, also see Iyengar and Kinder, *News That Matters*.

The Impact of the Campaign

Documenting the impact of the campaign itself is extremely difficult. For one thing, there are all manner of methodological difficulties. What we call the campaign is a congeries of events and activities; some of them are the activities of the parties and the candidates, and some are not. Consequently, it is difficult to say what part of the total impact can be attributed to any part of the campaign or its context. It is also difficult to determine what part of the campaign the individual voter has been aware of and how he or she has perceived it.

In spite of these difficulties, some empirical knowledge of the effects of the campaign is available although most of it dates from the period before the new technologies and television were widely used. Two early studies of local elections indicated that personal contacts activate politically apathetic voters more often than mailed propaganda does, and that door-to-door canvassing is more successful in affecting voting decisions than telephone calls are.[33] Other early research showed, in varying degrees of conclusiveness, that traditional precinct work by party committeepersons produces a 5 to 10 percent boost in the expected or usual party vote. The research suggests, further, that the effect of precinct work may well be greater in local elections than in media-centered presidential elections because there are apt to be fewer alternative cues and sources of information.[34] Those conclusions are buttressed by another set of findings—that precinct canvassing in a presidential campaign increases turnout but has little effect on voter choice and that active local party organization (before, during, and after the campaign) is associated with a vote increase over the expected norm.[35]

Recent trends suggest that the campaign should play a more important role now than ever before in influencing vote preferences. Furthermore, while face-to-face personal contact seems to be the most efficacious kind of campaigning, candidates increasingly are relying upon techniques of personalized indirect contact—the personally targeted letter or phone call—and, above all, television. Even though scholars know less about the effectiveness of the new techniques, rapid growth in their utilization in political campaigns suggests at the

---

[33]Samuel J. Eldersveld, "Experimental Propaganda Techniques and Voting Behavior," *American Political Science Review* 50 (1956): 154–65; and John C. Blydenburg, "A Controlled Experiment to Measure the Effects of Personal Contact Campaigning," *Midwest Journal of Political Science* 15 (1971): 365–81.

[34]Phillips Cutright and Peter H. Rossi, "Grass Roots Politicians and the Vote," *American Sociological Review* 23 (1958): 171–79; Daniel Katz and Samuel J. Eldersveld, "The Impact of Local Party Activity upon the Electorate," *Public Opinion Quarterly* 25 (1961): 1–24; and Raymond E. Wolfinger, "The Influence of Precinct Work on Voting Behavior," *Public Opinion Quarterly* 27 (1963): 387–98.

[35]Gerald H. Kramer, "The Effects of Precinct-Level Canvassing on Voter Behavior," *Public Opinion Quarterly* 34 (1970): 560–72; and William J. Crotty, "Party Effort and Its Impact on the Vote," *American Political Science Review* 65 (1971): 439–50.

very least that the candidates think they are effective. In the competitive world of politics, candidates cannot wait until the carefully analyzed empirical evidence is in before judging the various campaign techniques. Instead, they operate with a cruder, but perhaps more useful, measure: What have past winners done? What are their opponents likely to do?

THE PARTY ORGANIZATION'S ROLE IN MODERN CAMPAIGNING

Nothing assures the party organizations a place in the American campaign. They must compete constantly for a role in it, just as they fought without much success to control the nominations after introduction of the direct primary. Their adversaries in this struggle are the candidates, the personal campaign organizations they create, the new professional managers of campaigns, and the new financiers of election campaigns. Although the realities of American politics usually force candidates to run under party symbols that will help them attract the votes of a party electorate, nothing forces them to let the party organization control or even participate in their campaigns.

In a few places, however, the party organization still retains assets that make it indispensable to the campaign. If it can command armies of local workers, it can provide the candidate with a campaign vehicle that ensures success but costs very little. These organizational campaigns occur chiefly in a declining number of one-party urban areas, in which parties control primaries and voters habitually vote the party ticket in the general election. Canvassing and turning out the vote are still relevant there. Furthermore, the urban candidate is much more likely to have been nominated by the party organization through its control of the primary and thus to be its creature in the general election campaign.

The Resurgent Parties

The most recent study of the effects of party organization on campaign activity, though, demonstrates that many local parties have adapted to the new realities sufficiently well to play a continuing role in campaigns. Nationwide, as of the mid-1980s, the activity levels of the county parties were *increasing* not decreasing. Where the parties were active, the vote share for that party was enhanced by 2–3 percent—a modest amount perhaps in absolute terms but a critical margin in competitive areas. Moreover, because of the campaign support they presumably offer, active local parties were found to be better able to recruit candidates for lower offices, and this too is relevant for the party's electoral fortunes.[36]

---

[36]John P. Frendreis, James L. Gibson, and Laura L. Vertz, "The Electoral Relevance of Local Party Organizations," *American Political Science Review* 84 (1990): 225–35. Data from the 1988 Study of Presidential Campaign Leaders directed by William Jacoby and John Kessel show that the campaign activities of a national sample of county party organizations continued to increase through 1988.

Indeed, the 1980s may well have seen an enduring resurgence in the role of the party organizations in electoral campaigns. The large sums of money that have flowed to the national parties have enabled them, through selective investments of money and expertise, to stimulate greater activity in the state and local parties as well as to directly assist candidates in their own campaigns.[37] Moreover, the recent transfusion of millions of dollars in so-called soft money into the coffers of the state and local parties to promote activities on behalf of the party ticket and the increased fund-raising capabilities of the subnational party organizations themselves have enabled the parties at the grass roots to expand their campaign roles even more.[38] With these new financial resources dedicated to their traditional activities in mobilizing the vote, the state and local parties no longer seem to be relics of a bygone era. With their new-found wealth and the services it can buy, of course, the national parties have become significant players in political campaigns at all levels as well.

Candidate Control

In most races for public office, of course, neither party organizations nor the new campaign professionals reign—the candidate is in control. Some candidates, indeed, are as suspicious of the new practitioners as they are of the party organization. These candidate-run campaigns tend to rely on a campaign organization composed of friends, followers, and nonparty groups. They often involve people who are chary of party ties or who think of themselves as of the other party. Such campaigns enable the candidate to draw support by personality and charisma. They are also appropriate in scale and skills to the less visible, less publicized races for local office. For these campaigns, however, there is no reason why the candidates or their managers cannot decide to make limited use of some of the new campaign crafts.

The Continuing Struggle for Control

Behind the struggle of the candidate and the party organization for control of the campaign there is a basic truth: Their interests never completely converge. The candidate, unless he or she has been dragooned to fill a ticket in a lost cause, takes the candidacy seriously. Even the longest shot among candidates expects to win; the degree of ego involvement in the campaign almost demands it. The party, on the other hand, wants to be selective in its use of campaign

---

[37]An excellent account of these developments is provided by Paul S. Herrnson, *Party Campaigning in the 1980s* (Cambridge, Mass.: Harvard University Press, 1988).

[38]*Soft money* refers to contributions to the national parties that would be illegal under federal law if they stayed at the national level. Acting under the aegis of a 1979 amendment to the federal campaign finance laws, the parties have been able to make these contributions legal by passing them on to the states for party-building and voter mobilization activities. See Frank J. Sorauf, *Money in American Elections* (Glenview, Ill.: Scott Foresman/Little, Brown, 1988), pp. 320–23.

resources. It may see some races as lost and thus may be glad to turn these candidates loose for their own independent campaigns. Party organizations want to set overall priorities and allocations of scarce resources; they want to eliminate the inefficient and uneconomical parts of the campaign. Furthermore, the party organization wants to activate party loyalty, and candidates may not care to do so. The organization may also want to protect a platform and a program, help a presidential or gubernatorial candidate, or win control of a legislature, but these may not be the goals and interests of individual candidates.

To be sure, there are potent advantages to a party-led series of campaigns on behalf of an entire ticket. Such planning can eliminate the embarrassment and futility of two candidates competing for audiences in the same small town. The party organization can distribute campaign literature for a number of candidates at the same time and mount voter registration drives. Also, it alone can conduct the major election-day activities: setting up operation headquarters, providing cars and babysitters, checking voter lists to alert nonvoters late in the day, and providing poll watchers to oversee the balloting and counting. Efficiency and integration of the campaign, however, often threaten the interests of specific candidates. Although the party organization may prefer to raise money and prevent unseemly competition for the political dollar, a candidate may well believe he or she can raise more individually. Although the party may prefer billboard posters that celebrate the full party ticket of candidates, some among them may prefer to go it alone.

In this battle for control of campaigning, the party organizations have historically been disadvantaged by the very nature of American elections. The sheer number of offices to be contested has forced the parties to surrender control by default. Electoral institutions, from the direct primary to the office-block ballot, have been on the side of the candidates. Now, recent revolutions in the ways of campaigning threaten to set the parties aside further. New sources of political information, political expertise, and political communication are available to the candidate, and so, too, are the sources of money to pay for them. They enable candidates to run campaigns and to communicate with voters without the mediation of the party. Even if the parties have more to offer to candidates for office than they did just a few years ago, many candidates can do quite well on their own.

The battle between the party organizations and the parties in government thus intensifies over the control of nominations and election campaigns. If the American parties are indeed electoral parties, then whoever controls the picking of candidates and the staging of campaigns controls the parties. At stake here is not only pride, but the fruits of victory. In the old days, the activists of the party organization were satisfied with electoral victory by itself, for their goals were largely satisfied by public office per se and by the patronage and preferments that flowed from it. The new activists, however, seek much more than mere victory; they seek candidates and officials who will pursue specific issues and policy options after victory. Thus, to achieve their goals, the workers of the party organization need to assert greater control over the party's candidates and officeholders at the very time when it seems harder to do so.

The new campaigning works against the party and the party organization in another way. It reinforces the development of personalism in politics. It is the candidate, not the party, who is "sold." The image transmitted by TV and the other media is of a person, not of the abstraction known as a political party. The campaign techniques, therefore, foster a tie between candidate and voter in which the role of party loyalty is less important. The new campaign techniques thus threaten to displace the party *within* the voter as well as the party organization in the campaign.

By controlling their own nominations and elections, candidates are free of party organizational dominance and free to pursue their own relationships with their constituencies and their alliances with nonparty organizations. The failures of the party organizations also enhance the competitive positions of other groups that want to play electoral politics and influence public policy. At stake in the battle, therefore, are the control and health of the political parties and the very nature of representative government in the United States.

Chapter
13

Financing the Campaigns

To the old adage "money isn't everything," people of practical bent often are inclined to add the coda "but it sure helps in getting what you want." Money has been an important ingredient in successful political campaigns since the beginnings of American politics.

> When [George Washington] ran for the Virginia House of Burgesses from Fairfax County in 1757, he provided his friends with the 'customary means of winning votes': namely 28 gallons of rum, 50 gallons of rum punch, 34 gallons of wine, 46 gallons of beer, and 2 gallons of cider royal. Even in those days this was considered a large campaign expenditure, because there were only 391 voters in his district for an average outlay of more than a quart and a half per person.[1]

But money probably has never been more important to electoral politics than it is today. As the volunteer manpower traditionally supplied by the party organizations has diminished and campaigns have come to depend more on television for getting their messages across, money has become increasingly crucial in marshalling the resources necessary for serious campaigns. At all levels of government, but especially for the top state and national offices, candidates cannot compete without a substantial campaign bankroll. This chapter is primarily concerned with that money.

Traditionally, manpower was the principal contribution of the party organization to a campaign, and the principal contribution of the candidates was the money they could raise. This division of labor has eroded in recent years. Without vast armies of patronage employees and other dedicated party workers, the party organizations have had less manpower to supply. Furthermore, the rise of issue and ideologically oriented activists, wedded to candidates and causes rather than party, has given the candidates greater access to volunteer workers. Access to money also has broadened. As we saw in Chapter 4, the national party

---

[1]George Thayer, *Who Shakes the Money Tree?* (New York: Simon and Schuster, 1973), p. 25.

organizations now are able to raise and invest considerable financial resources in political campaigns, and many state organizations have stepped up their campaign funding efforts as well. Nonetheless, the prime responsibility for financing the campaign still falls upon the candidate. This fact helps to account for the separation of the party organization from the party in government that continues to characterize the American political system.

Until very recent times, a forbidding secrecy veiled the budgets of parties and candidates. Contributors were hesitant to be identified publicly, and candidates feared public disapproval of even the most modest expenditures. This veil of secrecy has been lifted by campaign finance reform in the last two decades. At the federal level, earlier reforms had banned contributions from corporate treasuries, required public disclosure of receipts and expenditures, and limited the amounts that could be spent by House and Senate candidates. Yet these regulations, full of loopholes, were easily avoided. In the case of presidential elections, for example, no centralized accounting was required of spending by the myriad campaign and party committees until the 1970s. Also vast sums of money could be raised and spent for many state and local contests without any public accounting of either contributions or expenditures. Reform efforts at the state and national level during the 1970s, powerfully fueled by the Watergate scandal, have changed all of that. A wealth of campaign finance data are now publicly available through the Federal Election Commission in Washington and in most of the individual states. Where once the problem was secrecy, it is now a flood of data.[2]

The mind-boggling complexity of the world of campaign finance, though, makes it difficult to explore even after extensive data on contributions and expenditures have become available. Its practices are governed by the laws of the United States and the fifty states, where there is any regulation at all, and these laws have been in considerable flux during the last two decades. Moreover, even where campaign finance reports are dutifully filed, they lie in raw form in the files of many a state, and extensive effort is required to convert them into comprehensive accounts of campaign contributions and expenditures. There is no state counterpart to the Federal Election Commission in providing citizens, reporters, and scholars with good summaries of campaign finance data for any particular candidate or year. Finally, as is often the case when human activity is regulated by new and changing rules, candidates and contributors are adept at finding loopholes through which they can pursue their objectives. Amid all this complexity, the only realistic approach is to seek answers to some basic questions: How much money is spent on election campaigns and by whom? From where does the money come? How have recent reforms changed the practices

---

[2]The standard historical accounts of campaign financing are Louise Overacker, *Money in Elections* (New York: Macmillan, 1932) and *Presidential Campaign Funds* (Boston: Boston University Press, 1944); and Alexander Heard, *The Costs of Democracy* (Chapel Hill: The University of North Carolina Press, 1960).

of campaign contributions and expenditures? Answers to these questions will illuminate the party role in financing.

HOW BIG IS THE MONEY?

Alexander Heard and Herbert Alexander, the most authoritative sources on the sums of money spent on campaigns in the last generation or so, have estimated total campaign expenditures in every presidential year from 1952 through 1988 (see Table 13.1). By their calculations, expenditures for all offices at all electoral levels, including both nominations and general elections, have increased twenty-fold between 1952 and 1988. Growth in actual expenditures was especially explosive after 1964, and just from 1976 to 1980 they doubled.

Because inflation reduces the purchasing power of the dollar, though, strict dollar comparisons can be misleading. Campaign expenditures have increased in inflation-adjusted constant dollars (see the adjusted column of Table 13.1) by only about fivefold from 1952 to 1988. As the temporary result of major campaign financing reforms, they even decreased from 1972 to 1976, although they have since experienced their greatest surges.[3]

Presidential Campaigns

The most expensive campaign for public office in the United States is that for the presidency. Just winning the party nomination—that is, the right to run—in 1988 cost Michael Dukakis $28.2 million and George Bush $30.6 million, including $9 million and $8.4 million, respectively, in federal matching funds. Unsuccessful GOP candidate Pat Robertson spent a total of $30.9 million, $9.7 million of it in public funds, to finish first in only three caucuses and no primaries. Democratic candidate Jesse Jackson spent $19.4 million and Republican Robert Dole $26.5 million in futile quests for the nomination.

The general election campaign raises the ante conspicuously (Table 13.2). Before the advent of public financing in 1974, Richard Nixon set records in his

---

[3]The data from 1952 and 1956 come from Heard, *The Costs of Democracy*. Those for 1960 through 1984 are from Herbert E. Alexander's studies: *Financing the 1960 Election* (Princeton: Citizens' Research Foundation, 1962); *Financing the 1964 Election* (Princeton: Citizens' Research Foundation, 1966); *Financing the 1968 Election* (Lexington, Mass.: Heath, 1971); *Financing the 1972 Election* (Lexington, Mass.: Heath, 1976); *Financing the 1976 Election* (Washington, D.C.: Congressional Quarterly, Inc., 1979); *Financing the 1980 Election* (Lexington, Mass.: Heath, 1983); Herbert E. Alexander and Brian A. Haggerty, *Financing the 1984 Election* (Lexington, Mass.: Heath, 1987); and Herbert E. Alexander and Monica Bauer, *Financing the 1988 Election* (Boulder, Colo.: Westview Press, 1991). Estimates of the costs of presidential campaigns from 1860 through 1984 are provided in Erik W. Austin, *Political Facts of the United States since 1789* (New York: Columbia University Press, 1987), Table 3.9. Since 1976, the Federal Election Commission has served as the primary souce of campaign financing data for federal office, which are reported in occasional press releases and more fully in the FEC *Reports on Financial Activity* for each two-year federal election cycle.

Table 13.1   TOTAL CAMPAIGN EXPENDITURES FOR ALL OFFICES IN PRESIDENTIAL
YEARS: 1952–88

	Expenditures (in millions)		Percentage change since previous election	
Year	Actual	Adjusted	Actual	Adjusted
1952	$ 140	$140	—	—
1956	155	151	+ 10.7	+ 7.9
1960	175	157	+ 12.9	+ 4.0
1964	200	171	+ 14.3	+ 8.9
1968	300	229	+ 50.0	+ 33.9
1972	425	270	+ 41.7	+ 17.9
1976	540	252	+ 27.1	− 6.7
1980	1203	388	+ 122.8	+ 54.0
1984	1840	470	+ 53.3	+ 18.9
1988	2728	666	+ 48.3	+ 41.7

Note: Estimates are for two-year cycles ending in the presidential election years. Adjusted figures are computed by deflating the actual expenditures by changes in the price level as measured by the Consumer Price Index using a 1952 base.

Source: Studies by Alexander Heard and Herbert Alexander; see text of footnote 3.

Table 13.2   TOTAL SPENDING BY CANDIDATES, PARTIES, AND GROUPS IN
PRESIDENTIAL GENERAL ELECTIONS: 1960–88

	Expenditures (in millions)		Percentage change since previous election	
Year	Actual	Adjusted	Actual	Adjusted
1960	$ 19.9	$17.8	—	—
1964	24.8	21.2	+ 24.6	+ 19.1
1968	44.2	33.7	+ 78.2	+ 59.0
1972	103.7	65.8	+ 134.6	+ 95.3
1976	88.7	41.4	− 14.5	− 62.9
1980	142.9	46.0	+ 61.1	+ 11.1
1984	159.3	40.7	+ 11.5	− 11.5
1988	208.3	51.5	+ 30.8	+ 26.6

Note: Estimates are for two-year cycle ending in the presidential election years. Adjusted figures are computed by deflating the actual expenditures by changes in the price level as measured by the Consumer Price Index using a 1952 base.

Source: Alexander, *Financing the 1980 Election,* Table 4-6; and Alexander and Haggerty, *Financing the 1984 Election,* Table 3-3; Alexander and Bauer, *Financing the 1988 Election,* Table 2.1.

successful campaign in 1972 by spending about $62 million. Because all major party candidates since public funding for presidential campaigns became available in 1976 have accepted the federal funds, they have also accepted the condition that they spend only the public contributions. Thus, in 1984 Reagan and Mondale spent $40.4 million apiece in public funds, and in 1988 Bush and Dukakis each spent $46.1 million. John Anderson was free to spend $14.4 million in 1980 because he had not yet qualified for public funding. (He did so by getting more than 5 percent of the popular vote, and he thus received $4.2 million in public monies after the election.) Since the public funding limits are indexed to the cost of living, the expenditure levels in 1988 were considerably higher than they were in earlier years. In inflation-adjusted dollars, however, the 1972 spending levels may never be topped, unless current public financing formulas are increased or some candidate does not accept public money and manages to raise a lot of private money. The reforms stimulated by improprieties in 1972 campaign financing managed to reduce spending from 1972 to 1976 *even in actual dollars* and to slow the previously explosive growth in the costs of competing for the presidency. The one-sided 1984 presidential race, in fact, cost less in constant dollars than the more competitive 1980 contest.

Congressional Campaigns

It is difficult to generalize about the cost of races for the House and Senate because of the enormous disparities among constituencies and races in the amount of money needed to run a competitive campaign. By now it has become commonplace for a Senate candidate to spend several million dollars, and the days of serious Senate campaigns for under a million dollars even in small states seem to have ended except perhaps for an incumbent without viable opposition. The spending record was set in the 1984 Senate contest between Republican Senator Jesse Helms and Democratic Governor James Hunt in North Carolina, hardly a state previously known for costly political campaigns. In winning re-election, Helms spent about $16.5 million ($14 per vote) to Hunt's $9.5 million. In the most expensive 1990 contest, Helms spent $13.4 million ($13 per vote) to defeat Democrat Harvey Gantt, whose spending reached $7.9 million. The least costly 1990 Senate contest occurred in Kansas, where Republican Nancy Kassebaum spent $407,000 (70 cents per vote) to only $16,600 by her unsuccessful Democratic challenger. Even without adjusting for inflation, the Helms-Hunt record should stand for some years.

The average 1988 House contest cost nearly $70,000, with the greatest expenditures being concentrated on contests involving open seats. In recent years, spending for House candidates often has broken the million dollar mark. A total of 33 House candidates spent over one million dollars in the 1988 and 1990 contests. Leading the way were two *unsuccessful* candidates for the Democratic nomination in an early 1988 special election to fill an open seat in Tennessee's fifth district (Nashville), who spent $2.6 and $1.9 million respectively. The winner of that election spent $0.9 million, hardly an immodest sum but small in comparison to the amounts spent by his opponents. This congressional race probably holds the record for priming the local economy with campaign money.[4]

State and Local Campaigns

Beyond these quests for national office are the thousands of campaigns for state and local offices. Hard information is rare, and generalizations are questionable. Many of these campaigns involve almost unbelievably small sums. Each year, hundreds of candidates win office in the United States in campaigns that involve cash outlays of a few hundred dollars; on the other hand, the mayoralty campaign in a large American city may cost a candidate and his or her supporters hundreds of thousands of dollars. Edward Koch spent almost $6 million in 1985 in his successful reelection bid for mayor of New York City; one mayoralty candidate in Dallas spent over $1 million for that $50 per week part-time job. Campaigns for governor of the larger states typically spend in the millions as well. In the spirited 1990 contest for governor of California, for example, preliminary estimates had Pete Wilson, the ultimate victor, spending about $18 million, and Diane Feinstein's total reaching over $12 million. Successful contests for the state legislature in large states now sometimes require more than $100,000, and spending in these contests seems to be growing more rapidly than for any other office. As usual, the record for campaign spending in these races seems to be set by California. As long ago as 1982–84, the *average* expenditure per seat in the lower house of the California legislature had reached almost $400,000.[5]

These, then, are preliminary answers to the question of how big the political money is. They show a level of campaign expenditures that has grown enormously in recent years, far outstripping the costs of most other items in the American economy. The numbers alone leave unanswered, though, the question of how big campaign spending **really** is—that is, how it measures up to the needs for communication in a democracy and the relative values and utilities of Americans (see box).

---

[4]These figures on Senate and House spending for the 1988 and 1990 races come from the Federal Election Commission's February 24, 1989, and February 22, 1991, press releases.

[5]The figure for Koch are reported in *The New York Times*, March 21, 1988; on the Dallas race, in *The New York Times*, April 4, 1987; for the 1990 California gubernatorial race, in *The New York Times*, October 14, 1990; and for the California house races, in Frank J. Sorauf, *Money in American Elections* (Glenview, Ill.: Scott Foresman/Little, Brown, 1988), p. 264.

Campaign Spending: Too Much or Too Little?

The expenditure of $2,728,000,000 on political campaigns in 1988 is a tremendous sum of money by anyone's reckoning. Yet it is only 2.3 percent of the $118 billion that was spent on all product advertising in 1988 and just slightly more than the combined cost of advertising for automobiles, beer and wine, and toiletries on *network television* in the same year. Moreover, it represents only .06 percent of the $4,880.6 *billion* gross national product in 1988.

To many Americans, distressed at what they see as the low quality of political candidates and political campaigns, these expenditures are surely not worthwhile. Considering the large number of candidates running for office in the United States and the role that advertising plays in the American culture in providing citizens with information that they need to make important decisions about goods or candidates, however, a persuasive case can be made that this key cost of democracy is not at all excessive and may even be insufficient.

WHO SPENDS THE CAMPAIGN MONEY?

The money consumed by American campaigning is spent by a variety of different individuals and groups. Most attention of course focuses on the candidates for office and their committees. Yet party committees and nonparty groups, especially political action committees, also invest considerable funds in elections beyond what they may contribute directly to candidates. To understand the flow of money in American campaign politics, it is first necessary to disentangle the various actors who employ it.

Presidential Campaigns

Alexander and Bauer's figures for the presidential election of 1988 are a good place to begin (Table 13.3). The major party candidates spent almost two-thirds ($313.3 million of the $500 million total) of the expenditures in the 1988 race for the presidency. There were numerous serious candidates in the prenomination phase of the campaign, especially because no incumbent president had preempted the field, so it is not surprising that spending in this phase surpassed the levels of the general election.

The other categories of expenditure are less obvious and bear some explanation. The major party organizations and their committees spent substantial sums on their national conventions and directly in the general election. Individuals and nonparty groups also made substantial independent expenditures—expenditures on behalf of or in opposition to a candidate that are supposed to be made without the knowledge or cooperation of any candidate or party. Most of these independent expenditures, as in previous years, were made in support of the Republican candidate or in opposition to the

Table 13.3   COSTS OF NOMINATION AND ELECTING A PRESIDENT: 1988

	Amount ($000,000)	
I. Prenomination		
Spending by candidates for major party nomination	$199.6	
Compliance costs	12.4	
Independent expenditures	4.1	
Communication costs	0.2	
Labor spending	15.0	
Spending by minor party candidates	2.1	
Delegate candidate expenditures	0.1	
		$233.5
II. Conventions		
Republicans' expenditures	$ 18.0	
Democrats' expenditures	22.4	
		$ 40.4
III. General Election		
Spending by major party candidates	$ 92.2	
Spending by minor party candidates	3.0	
Compliance costs	6.1	
Party committee spending	61.6	
Republican National Committee media	5.8	
Expenditures by labor, corporations, associations	27.5	
Independent expenditures	10.1	
Communication costs	2.0	
		$208.3
Miscellaneous expenses	17.8	
		$500.0

Source: Alexander and Bauer, *Financing the 1988 Election,* Table 2-1, (1991), Westview Press, Boulder, Colo. Reprinted by permission of Westview Press from *Financing the 1988 Election,* by Herbert E. Alexander and Monica Bauer. Published by Westview Press, 1991. Boulder, Colorado

Democrat.[6] The communication costs noted in Table 13.3 refer to expenditures made by organizations to urge their workers or members to vote for a particular candidate; labor unions account for most of the expenditures reported. The general expenditures of labor unions, corporations, and membership associations in "nonpartisan" voter mobilization—largely in voter registration and get-out-the-vote programs—are put at $27.5 million for the election. Again, labor accounts for the largest part of the expenditure. Finally, compliance costs are expenses (lawyers' and accountants' fees, for example) incurred

---

[6]The costs of the Willie Horton commercial discussed in Chapter 12 are included in this independent expenditure category. They were paid for by a political action committee that was, technically speaking, independent from the Bush campaign or the Republican party—and did not count against the Bush campaign expenditure limit.

by the candidates in preparing reports required under the law. Even though they do not count against the spending limits for the presidential candidates, they were counted above as candidate expenditures.

Congressional Campaigns

Similar analyses of congressional campaigns are possible with the data of the Federal Election Commission (Table 13.4). Campaigns for nomination and election to the two houses of the Congress went on simultaneously with the 1988 presidential election. Candidates for Congress spent a total of $459 million in the primaries and general elections, with Democrats outspending their Republican rivals overall. Candidate spending dwarfs spending by any other campaign actor, underscoring the extent to which the candidates run their congressional campaigns.

The parties and independent groups also invest money in the congressional campaigns beyond what they contribute directly to the candidates. The parties' House and Senate campaign committees, national committees, and state and local committees spent a total of $24 million "on behalf of" candidates of their parties. The Republican party outdid the Democrats in both coordinated expenditures and direct contributions (see Table 13.5 on p. 342) to the candidates in 1988—by a total of $15.1 million to $9.8 million. Over $7 million was spent by independent groups, both individuals (e.g., Thomas Foley of New York spent $210,445) and political action committees (e.g., the National Security PAC spent the most) usually in support of congressional candidates. Unlimited independent expenditures were protected by the Supreme Court as expressions of free speech in *Buckley v. Valeo*. They must be made independently from the candidate's campaign or they count as campaign contributions subject to the FEC limits.

Finally, over $2 million was expended by corporations, labor unions, and other organizations to oppose or to advocate to members of their organization the election of a particular candidate. Of these independent expenditures most went for a Republican or against a Democratic candidate. On the matter of expenditures for voter registration and get-out-the-vote campaigns, there are no estimates. In any event, those activities are rarely focused on congressional elections; efforts to "get out" a vote usually are geared to a full party ticket or a presidential candidate.

Although individuals and groups do spend directly in presidential and congressional campaigns, most of their political resources go in contributions to candidates. Only the party organization and their finance committees maintain a major financial role in campaigns in addition to their contributions to candidates. Of them, the Republican party committees are now raising and spending much more than the Democrats are. In the 1987–88 electoral cycle, for example, national, state, and local Republican party committees spent $257 million, while their Democratic counterparts spent only $122 million. This two-to-one GOP advantage, though, is less than GOP edges of three-to-one in 1984 and five-to-one in 1980. While the Republican party remains way ahead in the

Table 13.4 SOURCES OF SPENDING IN CONGRESSIONAL CAMPAIGNS, 1987–88 (IN MILLIONS)

	Democrats			Republicans			Total		
	House	Senate	Total	House	Senate	Total	House	Senate	Total
Candidate net disbursements	$145.6	$107.9	$253.5	$111.0	$93.1	$204.2	$257.6	$201.4	$459.0
Coordinated expenditures by party committees	2.8	6.5	9.3	4.2	10.3	14.4	7.0	16.8	23.8
Nonparty and independent expenditures									
For candidate	1.5	0.8	2.4	0.9	2.7	3.6	2.3	3.6	5.9
Against candidate	0.3	0.6	0.9	0.2	0.0	0.2	0.4	0.7	1.1
Communication expenditures									
For candidate	0.9	0.9	1.8	0.3	0.2	0.6	1.2	1.2	2.4
Against candidate	0.0	0.0	0.0	0.0	0.0	0.0	0.0	0.0	0.0

Note: The figures are for the two-year cycles ending in the presidential election year. Totals may differ slightly from sum of entries due to rounding.

Source: FEC Reports on Financial Activity 1987–88, Final Report, U.S. Senate and House Campaigns (Washington, D.C.: Federal Election Commission, September, 1989), pp. 94–99.

Table 13.5 SOURCES OF CAMPAIGN FUNDS FOR PRESIDENTIAL AND CONGRESSIONAL CANDIDATES: 1987–88 (IN MILLIONS)

Presidential

	Democrats		Republicans		Total	
	Nomination	General	Nomination	General	Nomination	General
Individuals	$ 63.1	—	$ 76.8	—	$139.9	—
Candidates	—	—	—	—	—	—
PACs	2.0	—	3.4	—	5.3	—
Party	—	—	—	—	—	—
Public Funding	30.1	$ 46.1	34.7	$46.1	64.7	$ 92.2
Other	0.4	—	1.1	—	1.8	—
Total	$ 95.6	$ 46.1	$116.0	$46.1	$211.6	$ 92.2

Congressional

	Democrats		Republicans		Total		
	House	Senate	House	Senate	House	Senate	Total
Individuals	$ 65.3	$ 67.3	$ 63.9	$60.7	$129.9	$128.1	$258.0
Candidates	11.0	9.2	8.1	3.4	19.2	12.7	31.9
PACs	67.4	24.2	34.8	24.2	102.2	45.7	147.9
Party	1.3	0.5	2.6	0.7	3.9	1.2	5.1
Public Funding	—	—	—	—	—	—	—
Other	15.3	6.5	7.6	2.3	23.1	11.6	34.7
Total	$160.3	$107.7	$117.0	$91.3	$278.3	$199.3	$477.6

Note: The figures are for the two-year cycles ending in the presidential election year. The total column for congressional funds includes Democratic, Republican, and other candidates. The row category labeled "other" includes transfers from other candidates, loans from non-candidate sources, refunds, and interest earned on campaign fund investments.

Source: For Congress, *FEC Reports on Financial Activity 1987–88*, Final Report, U.S. Senate and House Campaigns (Washington, D.C.: Federal Election Commission, September, 1989), pp. 94–99. For President, Federal Election Commission press release of April 9, 1989.

amounts of money it can invest in political campaigns, the Democrats have steadily narrowed the gap.

TO WHAT EFFECT IS CAMPAIGN SPENDING?

Victory is not automatically awarded to the side with the most money; money is only one of the ingredients for a successful campaign. How much it contributes to winning votes is not clear. In presidential contests, where both candidates have enough money to reach voters with their messages, the candidate with the largest war chest probably gains no significant advantage. In seeking the presidential nomination, money is undoubtedly more important, especially in buying crucial early visibility for the underdogs. Yet having a large campaign war chest did not seem to help Pat Robertson in the 1988 GOP nomination contests, and similar examples can be found from earlier years. Once the candidate has qualified for federal matching funds, though, the advantage money can confer narrows considerably.

The most systematic studies of the importance of campaign spending have focused on congressional races, where the large number of contests at any one time enables the analyst to control other possible influences on the outcome. It should come as no surprise that these studies conclude that money is important in running for congress. There is no doubt that the more challengers spend in races against incumbents, the more votes they win and the better their chances of victory become.

The effects of campaign spending, however, are not so clear cut for incumbents. Based on a careful examination of the relationship between spending levels and votes that takes into account other influences on votes, Gary C. Jacobson has concluded that the more incumbents spend, the worse they do. The reason is that high levels of incumbent spending typically come in response to a spirited election challenge. Donald Philip Green and Jonathan S. Krasno, however, have challenged Jacobson's assertion. If the quality of the challenger is taken into account, their analysis finds that increased incumbent spending yields more electoral support for the incumbent. Even though this dispute is mired in thorny questions about the proper way to estimate the impact of spending, two things about the efficacy of incumbent spending seem clear. First, strong challenges to incumbents are infrequent occurrences. Second, when they do occur, representatives may not be able to survive the challenge by pouring more money into their reelection effort.[7]

---

[7]The divergent conclusions reached from analysis of spending levels and outcomes for congressional races are well represented in a recent exchange in the *American Journal of Political Science*. See Donald Philip Green and Jonathan S. Krasno, "Salvation for the Spendthrift Incumbent: Re-estimating the Effects of Campaign Spending in House Elections," 32 (1988): 884–907; Gary C. Jacobson, "The Effects of Campaign Spending in House Elections: New Evidence for Old Arguments," 34 (1990): 334–62; and Donald Philip Green and Jonathan S. Krasno, "Rebuttal to Jacobson's 'New Evidence for Old Arguments'," 34 (1990): 363–72.

As these scholars point out, how spending levels affect votes has important implications for current reform efforts to limit campaign spending. If the chances of incumbents and challengers improve equally with spending increases, then spending caps do not particularly benefit either of them. If the chances of challengers increase as they spend more, while those of incumbents decline, then any reasonable ceiling on campaign spending benefits incumbents. In this situation, campaign finance reform becomes a form of incumbent protection and, because it has more incumbents in Congress, benefits the Democratic party. As we shall see, in recent attempts to reform campaign finance laws, congressional Democrats and Republicans have assumed, following Jacobson and most scholars, that spending limitations do favor incumbents and have divided their votes on that issue accordingly.

It even is questionable that independent expenditures always benefit the candidates they support. This spending favored the Republicans, in both presidential and congressional races, in the 1980s. Made independently of Republican candidates and committees and of their campaign plans and strategies, however, it may have achieved Republican goals very imperfectly. Sometimes independent expenditures even backfire, as some observers think happened when the National Conservative Political Action Committee (NCPAC) defeated only one of the thirteen Democratic Senators it had targeted for defeat in 1982 as NCPAC support itself became a campaign issue.

Estimating the partisan advantage of other forms of non-candidate spending faces similar problems. The communications costs incurred by organized labor overwhelmingly support Democrats, yet their effectiveness is unclear. When it is seized upon as a campaign issue, in fact, labor support can even be counterproductive in certain locales. Nor is it clear how the effects of "nonpartisan" voter registration and voter activation campaigns should be calculated. They are nonpartisan on the surface, but the unions, corporations, and associations that mount them usually do so in the confidence that they are mobilizing voters strongly in favor of one party or ideological preference.

SOURCES OF THE FUNDS

Candidates raise their campaign money from five basic sources: individual contributors, political action committees, political parties, the candidates' own resources, and public funds. Aside from a few incidental sources of revenue, there are no possibilities beyond those five. All candidates are limited to them. Anyone who proposes reform in the American system of campaign finance, unless they desire a return to direct contributions from corporations and labor unions, must prescribe a changing role for them (Table 13.5).

Individual Contributors

It is one of the best kept secrets in American politics that the individual contributor still dominates campaign finance. While public funding of presidential general elections has greatly reduced the role of the individual contributor (who still can support his or her candidate by contributing to the party or by making independent expenditures), individual contributions dominate the prenomination contests both directly and through the federal matching funds they generate. Almost all money spent in the 1988 primaries came from individuals or the federal treasury in matching individual contributions. Even though PACs have come to play important roles in the funding of House and Senate races, individual donors still provide most of the congressional candidates' campaign funds as well. Individuals accounted for 54 percent of the contributions to House candidates in 1987–88 and 64 percent of all of the money given to Senate candidates. Although the precise numbers are difficult to come by, it is clear that individual contributors also provide the majority of funds for state campaigns.[8]

The reforms of 1974, by limiting individuals to $1,000 donations, also changed the nature of the individual contributor in federal races. They ended the era of the genuinely big contributors to political campaigns. Now congressional campaigns are financed by large numbers of people making small contributions rather than a handful of "fat cats." Small contributors also dominate in the nomination phase of the presidential campaigns, the only time when individual contributions can be made directly to presidential candidates. Even these small contributors, though, comprise a very unrepresentative slice of the American electorate. Generally speaking, they are older, more involved in politics, more conservative, and more affluent than the average American.[9] Still, they resemble the typical American voter far more closely than did the storied "fat cats" of a generation ago.

Amendments to the Federal Election Campaign Act in 1979, however, have opened up a window through which large contributors have been able to re-enter federal political campaigns, although not to play their traditionally dominant role. To strengthen parties at the state and local level, the new law exempted from federal regulation money spent by the state/local parties for volunteer, voter registration, and get-out-the-vote activities even if they were conducted in support of the presidential or congressional campaigns. This law was interpreted to allow unlimited and undisclosed soft money contributions to pass through the national party and presidential campaign committees on their way to the state parties. Direct corporate and labor contributions for this purpose also are permissible in states that do not restrict them as a matter of state law.

Tremendous sums of money have flowed through the soft money conduit in recent years. In 1988, for example, Bush and Dukakis campaign fund-raisers

[8]For a discussion of campaign spending in the states, see Ruth S. Jones, "State Election Campaign Financing: 1980," in Michael J. Malbin (ed.), *Money and Politics in the United States* (Chatham, N.J.: Chatham House, 1984), pp. 172–213; and Sorauf, *Money in American Elections*, Chap. 9.

[9]Ruth S. Jones and Warren E. Miller, "Financing Campaigns: Macro Level Information and Micro Level Response," *Western Political Quarterly* 38 (June, 1985), 187–210.

Frederick Bush and Robert Farmer raised millions of dollars (perhaps as much as $40–50 million each) in soft money for the state parties. Much of it came from individuals contributing at least $100,000 apiece (see box, p. 347).

Over the years, the parties and the candidates have devised all manner of ways to entice the political contributions of individuals (see box, pp. 348–9). Personal visits, phone calls, and conversations with the candidate or the candidate's workers raise substantial sums and are the preferred form of soliciting large contributions. Aided by computerized mailing lists and printers and the ability of the machines to "personalize" letters, though, the parties, PACs, and candidates increasingly raise funds by mail. It is a method of solicitation well adapted to the important search for small contributors. Computer-generated mail can be routinely sent to a large list of contributors at minimal expense. Even though the yield from each mailing is typically small, the sheer volume and repetition of the effort often produces substantial quantities of money. Lists of dependable donors, in fact, have become one of the most valuable resources in modern campaign politics.

Group events also are important means for reaching individual donors. Part of the structure of American campaign finance rests on a foundation of banquet chicken, mashed potatoes, and half-warm peas. For a ticket price of between twenty and several thousand dollars, a contributor has dinner in a large hall, listens to endless political exhortations, rubs elbows with the party elite, and— if the price warrants it—observes a "name" guest, who gives the major speech. Taking their cue from the success of dinners, money raisers have begun to rely on cocktail parties, receptions, theater parties, even rock concerts and art shows as well. We tend to raise political money in many of the same ways we raise money for the arts and charities in American society.

Although patronage is passing from national politics, the holder of a public job in some states still is expected to make a political contribution at campaign time. In Indiana, the state's patronage holders long were called the "Two Percent Club," because the size of their contributions was not left to their discretion. Indiana no longer requires such contributions and prohibits government employees from soliciting or receiving contributions. As recently as 1988, however, a "baker's dozen" states had no restrictions on the solicitation of campaign contributions from government employees. Many other states permitted such solicitations on the (not always enforced) condition that employees not be required to contribute.

Political Action Committees

Political action committees (PACs) are political committees that are connected with neither parties nor (officially declared) candidates but which raise and spend money to influence election outcomes. The great majority of PACs are the creature of a sponsoring parent organization; that is, they are PACs of corporations, labor unions, and membership associations. Some, however, have no sponsoring organization; these are most likely to be ideological PACs of

The New "Fat Cats": Soft Money Contributors in 1988

In response to considerable public and press pressure, the Democratic and Republican parties released the names and amounts of their large soft money donors to the 1988 campaigns. The following small selection of names and amounts given from their lists (as reported in the *Washington Post* National Weekly Edition, November 28–December 4, 1988) provides a nice perspective on who is likely to make large political contributions through this legal "loophole" in federal campaign finance laws.

REPUBLICAN CONTRIBUTORS

Edward J. DeBartolo Jr., Youngstown, OH ($100,000)

Henry and Elsie Hillman, Pittsburgh ($101,600)

Marriott Corp., Richard E. Marriott, and J. W. Marriott, Washington D.C. ($95,000)

David Murdoch, Los Angeles ($121,000)

Occidental Petroleum Corp., Los Angeles ($100,000)

Paine Webber Group, Inc., New York ($100,000)

R. J. Reynolds, Winston-Salem, NC ($120,000)

Revlon, New York ($110,000)

Lawrence S. Rockefeller ($50,000)

Donald Trump, New York ($100,000)

DEMOCRATIC CONTRIBUTORS

Thomas J. Watson, IBM, Armonk, NY ($50,000)

Robert Bass, Ft. Worth, TX ($100,000)

Ann Cox Chambers, Atlanta ($100,000)

Marvin Davis, Los Angeles ($100,000)

Mark B. Dayton, Minneapolis ($100,000)

Philip M. Klutznick, Chicago ($100,000)

Carl Lindner, Cincinnati ($100,000)

Joseph Robbie, Miami ($50,000)

John D. Rockefeller IV, Washington, D.C. ($100,000)

An Wang, Lowell, MA ($90,000)

Legendary Figures in Political Fund-Raising

Perhaps America's most prodigious presidential fund-raiser was Ohio industrialist Marcus Alonzo Hanna, who personally financed the nomination campaign of William McKinley in 1896 and then raised most of the reputed $6–7 million (the equivalent of almost $80 million in 1988 dollars) spent in McKinley's successful general election campaign. Hanna raised to a new level the art of extracting campaign contributions from American corporations. "Assessments were apportioned according to each company's 'stake in the general prosperity'. . . . Banks, for instance, were assessed one quarter of one percent of their capital; Standard Oil contributed about a quarter of a million dollars, and the large insurance companies slightly less. If a company sent in a check Hanna believed to be too small, it was returned; if a company paid too much, a refund was sent out." Hanna's accomplishments fanned the reform flame that led to federal prohibition of corporate contributions in 1907 and a federal campaign fund disclosure law in 1910.

In the 1940 elections, a young congressman from Texas named Lyndon B. Johnson wrote a new chapter in the annals of campaign finance by raising, through the Democratic Congressional Campaign Committee, huge sums of Texas oil and construction money to support Democratic congressional candidates. "Lyndon Johnson's work with Democratic congressional candidates . . . added a new factor to the equation of American politics. The concept of financing congressional races across the country from a single central source was not new, but the Democrats had seldom if ever implemented the concept on the necessary scale or with the necessary energy." This accomplishment catapulted Johnson onto the national political stage, foreshadowed the importance of congressional campaign committees in modern times, and initiated the vital role Texas money was to play in Democratic, and later Republican, politics for many years.

The era of big contributors ended with the greatest feat of fund-raising in this century—the collection of well over $60 million in support of the reelection campaign of President Richard M. Nixon in 1972. Under the leadership of Maurice Stans and Herbert Kalmbach, much of this sum was raised from a few large contributors before tough campaign financing laws went into effect on April 7 of the election year. Chicago insurance magnate W. Clement Stone alone contributed $2 million to the Nixon cause, and Mellon-heir Richard Mellon Scaife donated another $1 million. Some of this largesse was illegally diverted to finance the Watergate break-in and related activities, and Stans subsequently was convicted for his role in funding them. The massive size and illegalities of this 1972 effort stimulated reforms of campaign fund-raising practices that ended over a century's reliance upon large contributors.

The master of modern campaign fund-raising techniques is Richard Viguerie, whose direct-mail methods for raising political money first attracted widespread attention after 1972 in the ill-fated presidential

(continued)

campaign of George Wallace. From a base of Goldwater and Wallace contributors, Viguerie built a computerized list of millions of donors to conservative causes and candidates. For a fee (averaging 50 percent of the proceeds) and access to his client's own list of contributors for the purpose of enlarging his master file, Viguerie put his fund-raising prowess in the service of conservative candidates and causes. The cost of raising money in small amounts from tens and hundreds of thousands of contributors is high, but in the post-reform era computerized direct mail has become the principal means of raising campaign funds.[10]

the right or the left. The PACs spend their money in three different ways: They transfer it to parties or to other PACs, they spend it independently to support or oppose candidates, and they give it directly to candidates. Since the first route (transfers) is negligible, and since we have already discussed independent expenditures, the concern here is with the PACs as contributors to the candidates.

On the last day of 1974, there were only 608 PACs operating in national elections, but by the very end of 1990 that number had climbed to 4,172. The greatest growth in the intervening years came in the number of corporate and independent (typically ideological and issue-oriented) PACs. Corporate PACs climbed from 15 percent of the 1974 total to 43 percent by 1990, and independent PACs grew from 0 to 25 percent. During this same period, labor and association PACs increased as well but at far smaller rates.[11]

A number of factors account for that growth. The decline of the parties and the advent of a more fragmented, issue-centered politics helped to foster it. Most important of all was the reform legislation of the post-Watergate years. The Federal Election Campaign Act of 1974, for example, in its zeal to limit the big individual spenders of American politics, put the limit on individual contributions far below that for the PACs (see the discussion of contribution limits later in this chapter). The new law also explicitly permitted corporations doing business with government to have PACs, which clarified a previous law that had barred direct *or indirect* contributions to federal election campaigns by govern-

---

[10]On Hanna, see Thayer, *Who Shakes the Money Tree?*, pp. 48–52; the quotation is taken from pp. 49–50. On Johnson, see Robert A. Caro, *The Years of Lyndon Johnson: The Path to Power* (New York: Alfred A. Knopf, 1982), pp. 606–64; the quote is from p. 662. For a discussion of campaign financing in the 1972 election, see Thayer, *Who Shakes the Money Tree?*, pp. 108–16; and Michael J. Malbin, "Looking Back at the Future of Campaign Finance Reform," in Michael J. Malbin (ed.), *Money and Politics in the United States*, Chatham, N.J.: Chatham House, 1984, pp. 245–47. The discussion of Richard Viguerie is based on Nick Kotz, "King Midas of 'The New Right,' " *The Atlantic* 242 (1978): 52–61.

[11]FEC press release, January 11, 1991.

ment contractors. Furthermore, decisions of the federal courts and the Federal Election Commission made clear the legality of PACs and confirmed the right of sponsoring organizations to pay their administrative and overhead expenses. (Their political funds, though, must be collected and kept separately in what federal statutes call a "separate segregated fund"; under federal law, the sponsoring corporation or labor union may not use its regular assets and revenues for political expenditures.)

For all of the bad press PACs have received recently, it may come as a surprise to learn that they do not dominate American campaign finance. Because of public funding, PACs are not direct contributors to presidential general election campaigns, although they contribute to candidates for the presidential nominations (over $5 million in 1988, with more going to Republicans than to Democrats) and can make sizable independent expenditures for or against presidential candidates. Their independent expenditures totaled $13.3 million in the 1987–88 electoral cycle.

Most PAC contributions instead go to congressional candidates (see box). PACs contributed almost $150 million directly to such candidates in 1988. Of this total, corporate PACs accounted for 34 percent, associational PACs (a catchall category containing trade, health, and membership associations) 26 percent, labor PACs 24 percent, and non-connected PACs (mostly ideological and issue organizations) 13 percent. Despite all this largesse, political action committees do not dominate congressional fund raising. They accounted for less than a third of all the money received by congressional candidates in 1987–88. The PACs also make independent expenditures for or against particular candidates to influence the congressional races. This spending reached almost $7 million in 1987–88—only about 5 percent of their direct candidate contributions.

It is important to realize, finally, that these various figures represent the *sum* of contributions from several thousand different PACs, representing a similar number of diverse and sometimes even competing interests. There is no monolithic PAC "interest." Nor are PACs solely the representatives of business or disproportionately supporters of Republican candidates and causes. Corporate PACs contributed the most to congressional candidates in 1988, with slightly more money going to Republicans than to Democrats. Labor PACs invested less money in the congressional races, but by concentrating almost all of it on Democratic candidates (92 percent), they more than compensated for the Republican edge in corporate contributions. Associational and unconnected PACs also skewed their money in a Democratic direction—55 and 64 percent of their totals, respectively.

The objective of most PAC campaign giving is not partisan or ideological, but rather is an underwriting of the status quo. Most PAC contributions go to incumbents; and, because there have been more Democratic than Republican incumbents in recent years, Democratic House and Senate candidates have received more PAC money.

Candidates pursue the PACs just as sedulously as they pursue individual contributors. Both parties' congressional and senatorial campaign committees put their candidates in touch with PACs likely to be sympathetic to their causes,

Would Restrictions on PACs Violate the Principles of American Democracy? Obviously PACs—and Many of Their Beneficiaries—Think So.

Copyright 1986 The Boston Globe. Distributed by Los Angeles Times Syndicate.

and the parties are increasingly active in channeling PAC money directly to candidates. Candidates and their campaign managers also track the PACs at first hand, assisted by the directories and information services that list PACs by their issue positions, the size of their resources, and their previous contributions. Incumbent members of Congress also invite the PACs or lobbyists of their parent organizations to fund-raising parties in Washington, at which a check gets the PAC people hors d'oeuvres, drinks, and legislative gratitude. On the other hand, the PACs also take the contributing initiative. Unlike most individual contributors, they are in the business of making political contributions, and they don't necessarily wait to be asked.[12]

---

[12]For a more extensive discussion of the role of PACs in campaign financing, see Sorauf, *Money in American Elections*, Chap. 4. See also Larry J. Sabato, *PAC Power: Inside the World of Political Action Committees* (New York: Norton, 1984).

What do PACs buy with their extensive spending on congressional campaigns? It is unquestionable that their campaign contributions gain them access to lawmakers. What political officials will fail to listen to representatives of interests that have provided financial support for their political campaigns? How hard they listen and how much what they hear changes their legislative behavior, however, are more difficult to determine. Research on the relationship between PAC contributions and subsequent roll call votes has not produced much evidence that contributions influence votes.[13] PAC money does, however, seem to produce greater access to members of Congress and more committee activity by recipients on behalf of issues of PAC concern.[14]

There are ample reasons why the straightforward exchange of votes for PAC money rarely occurs. A single PAC is limited to a contribution of $5,000 per member of Congress in each election, which makes it only one of many contributors and thus may dilute its influence. The concentration of PAC money on incumbents, who have the easiest time of raising campaign funds, may also limit its effectiveness. Another factor is that contributions often flow mostly to well-known friends, whose support does not need to be won, rather than to those whose support has to be wooed. There even is evidence that PACs are constrained from pursuing the most effective strategies for influence by their need to decentralize efforts in response to the local orientations of their members.[15] Finally, PACs often face formidable competition from party leaders and constituents for the ear and the vote of a legislator. They are most successful in this competition, no doubt, when they represent powerful constituency interests and do not encounter party opposition or when the issue is of little concern to anyone else.

Political Parties

Amidst such a heavy flow of political money it is easy to lose sight of the party role in campaign financing. In addition to all of their spending on party business, on running party conventions and other party processes, and for the general party ticket in campaigns, however, the parties contribute to candidates directly and make considerable expenditures (for polling, advertising, etc.) on their behalf. For some years, the Republican party has enjoyed a huge edge over the Democrats in the amount of money it was able to use in support of

---

[13]The conclusion that PAC contributions do not influence voting is reached by, among others, Janet M. Grenzke, "Shopping in the Congressional Supermarket: The Currency is Complex," *American Journal of Political Science* 33 (1989): 1–24; and John R. Wright, "PACs, Contributions, and Roll Calls: An Organizational Perspective," *American Political Science Review* 79 (1985): 400–14.

[14]On access, see Laura I. Langbein, "Money and Access: Some Empirical Evidence," *Journal of Politics* 48 (1986): 1052–64. On committee involvement, see Richard L. Hall and Frank W. Wayman, "Buying Time: Moneyed Interests and the Mobilization of Bias in Congressional Committees," *American Political Science Review* 84 (1990): 797–820.

[15]Wright, "PACs, Contributions, and Roll Calls."

congressional campaigns. In 1988, the parties (through national and congressional campaign committees, as well as state and local committees) invested $5.1 million in direct contributions to candidates and another $23.8 million in coordinated expenditures (i.e., money spent directly *by the party* to support a candidate) on their behalf. In total, however, the parties contributed only about 1 percent of the money spent by the congressional campaigns and nothing to presidential candidates. That almost insignificant figure suggests how much more money the parties will have to raise and spend before they can reestablish a major role for themselves in American electoral politics. This contrasts sharply with the substantial role of parties in financing and running campaigns in the other democracies of the world. Finally, modest though those sums are, they come predominantly from the party committees in the Congress. The congressional party in government, at least, relies heavily on its own financial instruments rather than on those of the party organizations.

The Candidates Themselves

No government agency, either national or local, easily makes available any data on the candidates' use of their own fortunes and those of their immediate families. In 1988, the congressional candidates ended up bankrolling their campaigns to the tune of $32 million, but this represented only 7 percent of all contributions (Table 13.5). Of all the sources of campaign funds, this one is the most unevenly distributed. The average figure is greatly inflated by the self-financing of a few relatively wealthy candidates. In 1982, a Democrat from Minnesota, Mark Dayton, spent $7.1 million in an unsuccessful bid for a seat in the Senate; $6.8 million of it came from the candidate and his family. (Dayton is the scion of a large mercantile family; his wife is a direct descendant of John D. Rockefeller.) In 1986, for example, John S. Dyson spent almost $6 million of his own money in an unsuccessful attempt to gain the Democratic nomination for a New York Senate seat. The greatest personal contribution in 1988, over $6 million, was made by Democrat Senate candidate and Milwaukee Bucks owner Herbert Kohl in Wisconsin. Kohl accepted no PAC contributions, stressed that his wealth enabled him to be "nobody's Senator but yours," and won.

Public Funding

Finally, for some campaigns, public funding is available if the candidate wishes to claim it. Claiming it, of course, often means accepting spending limitations as a condition of receiving the money. Public monies are most conspicuously available for the presidential campaigns (see box). In 1988, public matching funds for the many preconvention contenders in the most wide-open contests since public funding was adopted, subsidies for the national conventions, and grants to Bush and Dukakis for the general election campaign totaled $304 million, or 61 percent of the total costs in the nomination contest and general election. The full costs of the general election were covered out of the federal treasury. By contrast, there is no public funding of congressional elections. Public funding,

If Public Funding Goes Dry

In late 1990 the Federal Election Commission estimated that the public funds available to finance presidential election campaigns would be insufficient by 1992. Public funds are generated by a checkoff on yearly income tax returns that can channel, if the taxpayer desires, $1 of taxes paid to the presidential election fund. Since 1980, there has been a drop-off from 29 percent to 20 percent in the taxpayers who have checked this box. Moreover, while the $1 earmarked for the fund has been the same since the inception of public funding, pay-outs from the fund have grown with inflation—and, though less steadily, with the number of qualified candidates for each party's nomination.

If public money for the campaigns runs out, payments to candidates for the party nominations would have to be rationed somehow to preserve money for the party conventions and the general election campaign, as the law requires. This would pose new difficulties for the primary candidates who accepted public funding. They would be legally bound by artifically low spending restrictions without being able to realize full public funding benefits. This might shift the advantage to candidates for the presidential nomination who chose not to accept public funding, ironically penalizing the very candidates who cooperated with the spirit of campaign finance reform.

however, is available to defray some of the costs of political campaigns in a minority of states, but it more often goes to the parties than to the candidates and in amounts that are far less generous than at the presidential level.[16]

The preceding paragraphs have focused largely on the national funding experience. The picture in the fifty states is, as usual, both confusing and unclear. All evidence suggests that national patterns generally prevail in state and local election campaigns. Individual contributors are the most important source of campaign funds, followed by PAC contributions and then, at greater distance, by party and personal funds. Several modifications to that pattern should be noted, however. First, individual contributions become relatively more important in local campaigns, since the interest of parties and PACs in those campaigns is less lively. Candidates in the localities are also more limited in the ways in which they raise money; fund-raising experts are usually beyond their means, for example, and the practicalities rule out such techniques as telethons

---

[16]On the state experience with public funding, see Ruth S. Jones, "State Public Campaign Finance: Implications for Partisan Politics," *American Journal of Political Science* 25 (1981): 342–61; and Jack L. Noragon, "Political Finance and Political Reform: The Experience with State Income Tax Check-offs," *American Political Science Review* 75 (1981): 667–87.

and mass mail solicitation. Second, because campaign finance regulations vary considerably across fifty different states, there always will be exceptions to the general patterns. For example, in California, PACs provide a majority of the campaign funds for legislative candidates. Third, legislative leaders and legislative caucuses in an increasing number of states are supplying campaign funds to their party's legislative candidates. Because many states do not impose low ceilings, or in some cases any limits at all, on campaign contributions in state legislative contests, such donations can play a significant role in a candidate's campaign.[17]

Ultimately, all campaign funds in American politics come from individuals. They pay the taxes (or divert the tax payments) that provide public funding, contribute the dollars that parties and PACs have available for their contributions, and provide enormous sums directly to candidates. Of the Americans sampled in the National Election Studies 1988 postelection survey, 6 percent reported having given money to a candidate, 6 percent reported having contributed to a party, and 4 percent said they had donated to a political group that supported candidates. Even if there is no overlap among these various kinds of contributors, this adds up to only a small minority who spend their money on political campaigns. In the same study, 27 percent of the sample reported diverting a dollar of their tax liability ($2 for married persons filing jointly) to the federal fund from which the presidential campaigns were financed.

Such levels of participation indicate a funding base broader than that of the rest of the world's democracies. The special American tradition of voluntarism extends to our politics. Even so, the low figures, on the tax checkoff especially, suggest a widespread refusal by many Americans to accept the current options in the funding of campaigns. Large numbers of Americans will not contribute voluntarily, and they accuse the wealthy candidate who finances his or her own campaign of buying the office. They are inclined to accuse candidates who rely on large contributions from PACs of selling out to special interests, yet they do not find public funding as an acceptable alternative either. These critics provide little solace in solving the vexing problem of how candidates can provide voters with the information they need to make intelligent voting decisions.

REFORM AND REGULATION

For a long time, the regulation of campaign finance in the United States was a jerry-built structure of assorted and not very well integrated federal and state

---

[17]For a general review of state campaign financing, see Malcolm E. Jewell and David M. Olson, *Political Parties and Elections in American States* (Chicago: Dorsey, 1988), pp. 154–73. On the regulation of PAC contributions in the states, see Arnold Fleischmann and David C. Nice, "States and PACs: The Legacy of Established Decision Rules," *Political Behavior* 10 (1988): 349–63. On legislative caucus and leadership funds in the states, see Anthony Gierzynski and Malcolm E. Jewell, "Legislative Party Campaign Committee Activity: A Comparative State Analysis," paper presented at the Annual Meeting of the Midwest Political Science Association, Chicago, 1989.

statutes. Periodically, reformers attempted to bring order out of that legislation and at the same time to strengthen legal controls over the raising and spending of campaign money. A new episode of reform was under way in the early 1970s when the Watergate scandals broke over the country. The result in 1974 was the most extensive federal legislation on the subject in the history of the Republic.

The 1974 law, as many laws are, was set down on an already existing web of legislation, superseding some of it and supplementing some of it. Some of the 1974 law, in turn, was invalidated by the United States Supreme Court in late January 1976. It was then supplemented by amendments passed in the late 1970s. The resulting structure of federal legislation falls into two main categories: the limitations on campaign contributions and spending and the provisions for setting up a system of public funding of national politics.[18]

Limitations on Contributions and Expenditures

The chief provisions of existing federal law, which apply only to candidates for president and Congress, are these (see Table 13.6 for a summary):

1. Restrictions on sources of money:

Each individual is limited to a contribution of $1,000 per candidate in primary elections, $1,000 per candidate in the ensuing general election, $5,000 to a political action committee, and $20,000 to a national party committee. The contributor is also limited to a total of $25,000 in all such contributions in any one calendar year.

Political action committees are limited to contributions of $5,000 to any candidate in any election if they qualify as "multicandidate committees" by making contributions to at least five candidates.

Corporations and labor unions themselves may not contribute. (They may, however, set up political action committees and pay their overhead and administrative costs.)

Federal employees may not solicit funds from other federal employees on the job. The same limitation also applies to state or local employees whose activities are financed by federal loans or grants.

The new limits on the size of contributions in the 1974 legislation have already curbed the role of the very large contributor. Even with the loopholes (and the possiblity that all adults in a family can contribute within the ceiling), under these laws, the large contributors will be unlimited only in their per-

---

[18]Good accounts of federal campaign finance reform legislation may be found in Sorauf, *Money in American Elections*, Chaps. 2, 8, and 12; and Robert E. Mutch, *Campaigns, Congress, and the Courts* (New York: Praeger, 1988).

Table 13.6   LIMITS ON CAMPAIGN CONTRIBUTIONS UNDER FEDERAL LAW

	Limit on Contributions			
	To candidate or candidate committee (per election)	To national party committee (per year)	To any nonparty committee (PAC) (per year)	Total contributions (per year)
Individual	$1,000	$20,000	$5,000	$25,000
Political action committee	$5,000[a]	$15,000	$5,000	no limit
Party committee	$5,000[a]	no limit	$5,000	no limit

[a]If the political action committee or the party committee qualifies as a "multicandidate committee" under federal law by making contributions to five or more federal candidates, the limit is $5,000. Otherwise, it is $1,000. Party committees can contribute up to $17,500 to Senate candidates.

Source: Adapted from Federal Election Commission Campaign Guide (June, 1985).

sonal, independent efforts on behalf of candidates (or their soft money contributions to state parties).

2. Restrictions on expenditures:

If presidential candidates accept federal subsidies for the prenomination and general election campaigns (see following discussion for details), they must agree to spend no more than the law permits. They are therefore limited to $10 million before the convention and $20 million after it in 1974 dollars—or $27.7 million to gain the nomination (including a 20 percent allowance of $4.6 million for the costs of fund raising) and $46.1 million in the 1988 elections. Moreover, they must abide by prenomination spending limits in each of the 50 states based on their voting age populations that ranged from $7.9 million in California to $461,000 in the 16 smallest states in 1988.

If presidential and vice-presidential candidates accept the public subsidies, they are also limited to expenditures of no more than $50,000 of their own or their family's money on the campaigns.

The 1974 law's limits on spending in House and Senate campaigns were the chief casualties of a Supreme Court decision in 1976.[19] The challengers to the statutes—an unlikely coalition extending from Senator James Buckley and the conservative Human Events magazine to Eugene McCarthy and the New York Civil Liberties Union—had argued that restrictions on campaign expenditures

[19]Buckley v. Valeo, 424 U.S. 1 (1976).

infringed the rights of free speech and political activity. The Supreme Court agreed. Expenditure limits, therefore, are permissible only when they are a condition of the voluntary acceptance of public subsidies. Congress could thus reinstate the expenditure limits on its own campaigns only as part of a plan for subsidizing them. Candidates, of course, would have to be free to reject the subsidies, as the presidential candidates are. (The restrictions on contributions make rejecting subsidies a hazardous option, however, for the presidential contestants.)

3. Requirements for accounting and reporting:

> All contributions to a federal candidate must go through and be accounted for by a single campaign committee.

> Each candidate must file quarterly reports on his or her finances and then supplement them with reports ten days before the election and thirty days after it.

> All contributors of $200 or more must be identified by name, address, occupation, and name of employer.

The publicity provisions of earlier legislation had not been notably effective. Reports were sketchy at best and missing at worst. The new legislation has improved the quality of reporting, however, by centralizing candidate responsibility in a single committee, by creating a new public interest in reporting, and by setting up an agency (the Federal Election Commission) to collect the data and make them available.

Public Funding of Presidential Campaigns

Although the Congress has not yet been willing to fund its own challengers from the public treasury, it has embarked on a program of public support for presidential candidates. The 1976 elections marked the inauguration of this program.

Candidates seeking their party nominations were aided only if they first passed a private funding test. They had to raise $5,000 in contributions of $250 or less in each of twenty states. If they so established their eligibility, public funds matched every contribution up to $250, to a total of $11.6 million in 1988. In addition, each of the major parties received $9.22 million to offset the costs of its national nominating convention.

Provisions for funding the general election campaign are somewhat simpler. Candidates may draw on a public fund for some or all of their expenses up to the $20 million ceiling. (That $20 million figure is in 1974 dollars; it is recalculated for each presidential year according to rises in the consumer price index.) Minor parties fare less well. They receive only a fraction of the $20 million maximum, and then only *after* the election if they have received at least 5 percent of the vote. (If they drew at least 5 percent of the vote in the previous election, they can receive their payment before the election. Thus, John Anderson received $4.2 million after the 1980 election and was entitled to a comparable sum before the 1984 election, but he chose not to run.) The section dealing with minor parties has received a major part of the criticism directed at the 1974 statute. Critics charge that it will enfeeble minor parties, certainly making it hard for them to reach major party status and, in view of the need to pay cash for many campaign expenses, making it hard for them to finance even a modest campaign.

Results of Campaign Finance Reform

The new structure of federal regulation and subsidy worked a number of changes in the campaign finance system and the nature of campaign politics. Because the reforms were finalized (at least for the present) only in 1979 and campaign actors have been learning in the interim how to both live with them and get around them, their impact is only now becoming clear.

To a considerable degree, the reforms have achieved their paramount purpose. They have lowered the scale of presidential campaign expenditures. They have not been entirely successful, however, in realizing their other paramount goal—ending the role of the giant contributors to both presidential and congressional campaigns. In presidential nominations, the day of the big contributors (when a candidate could raise hundreds of thousands of dollars in one Manhattan or Hollywood visit) has ended. Similar activity has been restricted in congressional campaigns as well, although determined donors still can find ways to channel large amounts of money to receptive candidates. The possibility of unlimited contributions to the state parties for "party" activities, however, has opened a window through which "fat cats" have been able to reenter presidential election politics (see box).

In achieving these purposes, however, the campaign finance reforms of the 1970s have altered the nature of federal campaigning in important and not always desirable ways. First, as large individual donors have become less important in congressional campaigns, alternative sources of money—PACs, wealthy candidates, and small contributors—have become more valuable and plentiful. No one decries the growing importance of the small contributors, although reliance upon them does enhance the influence of the direct mail fund-raising specialists—a prospect some thoughtful observers of politics find disturbing. On the other hand, that PACs and wealthy candidates now play more of a role in congressional campaigns has obviously raised a new set of concerns.

Second, as expenditure ceilings were lowered for the 1976 presidential campaign, the patterns of spending changed. Candidates cut down less on media advertising and more on other advertisements (e.g., billboards), organizers and professional staff, and the traditional paraphernalia of campaigns—buttons, leaflets, and bumper stickers, for example. Amendments to the Federal Election Campaign Act in 1979 were designed to restore some of these traditional activities by permitting state and local parties to spend unlimited amounts for campaign materials. Tighter planning and setting of priorities has become the

The Continuing Role of Large Contributions: The Case of the "Keating Five"

In 1990 and early 1991, the Ethics Committee of the United States Senate investigated the role of five Senators in interventions on behalf of Charles Keating with the Federal Home Loan Bank Board, which was attempting to tighten regulations on Keating's California-based Lincoln Savings and Loan Association. Lincoln was the most conspicuous of the S and L's in the late 1980s that sank under the weight of unprofitable high-risk loans and ultimately were seized by federal regulators. The government may end up covering $2 billion of Lincoln's losses.

Keating attempted to mobilize a variety of political leaders to protect Lincoln from its federal regulators. It is how his campaign contributions to five Senators were linked to the Senators' subsequent activities with the regulators that came under the scrutiny of the Senate Ethics Committee. The Keating five either directly or indirectly received $1.5 million in legal contributions from Charles Keating in the following ways as noted by the *Congressional Quarterly Weekly Report* (Washington, D.C.: Congressional Quarterly, Inc.), March 2, 1991, p. 526:

Alan Cranston (Democrat, California): $49,000 for presidential and reelection campaigns; $85,000 for the California Democratic party; $850,000 for three nonpartisan voter education projects with which Cranston was associated; a $300,000 unused line of credit for his reelection campaign; $10,000 to Cranston-affiliated PAC.

Dennis DeConcini (Democrat, Arizona): $85,000 for two reelection campaigns (returned in 1989).

John Glenn (Democrat, Ohio): $42,000 for presidential and reelection campaigns; $200,000 for his nonfederal PAC.

John McCain (Republican, Arizona): $110,000 for two House and one Senate campaigns.

Donald W. Riegle Jr. (Democrat, Michigan): $78,250 for a reelection campaign (returned in 1988).

The Senators contended that the contributions did not lead them to do things for Keating that they would not have done for any other constituent (Keating had major business interests in all four of the states involved). In a February 27, 1991 finding, the Senate Ethics Committee determined that all but Cranston were guilty only of poor judgment (though DeConcini and Riegle had acted improperly) and recommended no punishment for them. The committee ordered a formal investigation of Cranston and left the impression that it would ultimately recommend punishment for him.

order of the day in presidential camps; by general agreement, there was less activity in the smaller states, for instance.

Third, the new limits on spending in the presidential nominations process may be too low. Low state spending ceilings in the early primary and caucus states may provide insufficient money for the intense campaigning there. Moreover, by spending up to the federal levels in the early states, candidates often reach their overall spending ceiling before the last primaries and caucuses occur. If future nomination contests go down to the last few states in June, it is quite possible that they will be waged without candidates being able to spend any money on television and the other usual forms of campaign advertising.

Fourth, regulation and the 1976 Supreme Court decision have clearly stimulated the growth of independent expenditures—initially by individuals and ideological PACs (the most famous of which is the National Conservative Political Action Committee, which played a prominent role in the upsets of a number of liberal Democratic Senators in 1980) and more recently by business and trade association committees. Moreover, the clear favoring of Republican causes in those expenditures has introduced a new source of inequality into campaign finance.

Finally, strict regulations and extensive reporting requirements have increased centralized control of campaigns and have made lawyers and accountants indispensable members of the modern campaign staff. Campaigns rely much less on the loosely coordinated efforts of local campaign organizations and volunteers and much more upon paid professionals than was the case prior to the reforms.

Nor have the reforms been politically neutral. Most observers thought that the new subsidies and expenditure limits helped Jimmy Carter to the White House and Gary Hart's challenge to frontrunner Walter Mondale in 1984. The preconvention grants obviously benefit the less well-known candidates for the presidential nomination, especially the ones with a limited financial base. The grants and limits in the presidential campaign also have erased the usual GOP advantage in spending and have prevented affluent campaigns from developing a late media blitz that conceivably could carry a close election. On the other hand, contribution limits and the entry of PACs may have redounded to the benefit of the already-advantaged incumbents in congressional races.

More generally, as perhaps the recent avalanche of soft money contributions or the independent expenditures exemplify, we are learning that in a capitalistic society where freedom of speech is constitutionally protected, money always is going to play an important role in the selection of government officials. Campaign finance reforms may erect dikes to contain it, but the dikes may channel the money in other, sometimes equally undesirable, directions. The dikes also inevitably develop leaks that may take some time to close. The lesson is that the role of money can be altered, although not always in predictable ways given human resourcefulness and the necessary incompleteness of laws, but it cannot be eliminated.

In one important way, however, the experience did *not* have the result many expected. It has not yet led to public subsidies for elections to Congress.

The main issues here were two. First, there was a good deal of concern about voter reaction—a concern that voters would view subsidies as an improper use of tax monies or as a congressional raid on the treasury for its own advantage. (The lack of public support was evident in the polls.) The second issue concerned a possible incumbent and partisan bias in public funding. A few members of Congress grumbled that they would be encouraging their own opponents, but the Republicans and many observers thought the plan would further entrench the incumbent Democrats. What scholarly evidence there is on the point suggests a significant relationship between a challenger's level of expenditures and his or her ability to give an incumbent a close race.

It is as of yet unclear what effect these reforms have had upon the role of political parties in the electoral process. Two broad questions are involved. Have the reforms strengthened or weakened today's parties in comparison to yesterday's? How have they affected parties in comparison to their competitors—especially the candidates, individual contributors, and organized groups—in influencing the party in government? At first glance, the parties seem to have been victims of the reforms, especially in their role as contributors to federal campaigns. They have been limited in the cash contributions they can make to presidential and congressional candidates. Moreover, direct public funding of presidential candidates, rather than parties (which is the common practice in other democracies and some states), enhances the traditional separation between the presidential campaign and the party organization. More important, the absence of limits on independent expenditures by individuals or PACs has given the advantage to the parties' major competitors for influence over candidates.

But this first glance is deceiving. Higher ceilings on contributions to parties than to PACs or candidates give the parties a valuable edge in fund-raising, and both national parties are now more successful fundraisers than they have ever been. Contribution limits on individuals make party funds more attractive to the congressional candidates. The parties also have been able to circumvent the $5,000 limit on their contributions to candidates by providing valuable services, acting as conduits for individual contributions to candidates (so-called bundling), channeling soft money to the state parties, making coordinated expenditures for the party ticket as a whole, and investing in long-term state and local party building.

Thus, the national party committees (especially of the GOP) now play a much more important role in political campaigns than ever before, which increases the potential of some centralized direction for the American parties and their candidates. There are signs too that the state and local parties, energized by the new funding directed their way from the national parties and by their own successes in fund-raising, are becoming more actively involved in campaigns—especially in the labor-intensive grass roots work that was the staple of party organizations in an earlier era. Amid this continuing transformation in campaign practices and traditional party roles, it is difficult to come to any final conclusion about the impact of campaign finance reform on the parties except to predict that the parties' role in campaigns ultimately may depend more upon their own initiative than present financing laws.[20]

State Regulation and Financing

To the maze of federal legislation must be added the even more complicated fabric of fifty different state regulations. The states have long set at least some limits to campaign activity. Most states, for example, have some law prohibiting certain election-day expenditures; all states prohibit bribery and vote buying; and some prohibit such practices as buying a voter a drink on election day. Most states also require reporting of campaign contributions and expenditures. In general, however, state regulations have never achieved the effectiveness of the federal legislation.

The Watergate scandals spurred a new round of campaign finance legislation in the states after 1972, and the states have continued to be active in this area. The most popular measure is a requirement that campaign contributions be publicly disclosed. Many states also have acted to restrict campaign contributions. By 1988, a total of thirty-four states limited the contributions of individuals in some respect, and forty-four states restricted contributions from organizations such as corporations, labor unions, PACs, or political parties. Only one state (Nevada) has imposed no limitations whatsoever on individuals or organizational contributions. In many of the states with limitations on campaign contributors, however, the hand of regulation is lighter than at the federal level. For example, six states ban only cash contributions from individuals, and some impose very high limits on the total amount of spending.

A minority of states have ventured into public funding for state elections. A total of twenty-one states have some kind of arrangement for allocating money from their treasuries to political campaigns. In twelve states the payments go to the political parties; in seven states they go directly to the candidates; and in two states public funding is provided for both the parties and the candidates. The level of state support for campaigns, though, falls far short of being proportionate to the full funding that is provided by the federal treasury to the presidential general election campaigns.[21]

The burst of post-Watergate legislative activity in the Congress and the states has not put the question of reform to rest. Pressures for new regulations follow changes in the patterns of campaign finance. The growth of the PAC role has spawned a new set of proposed remedies: reduced limits on PAC contribu-

---

[20]The preceding discussion of the effects of campaign finance reforms on the parties draws upon F. Christopher Arterton, "Political Money and Party Strength," in Joel L. Fleishman (ed.), *The Future of American Political Parties* (Englewood Cliffs, N.J.: Prentice-Hall, 1982), pp. 101–39.

[21]The data on the states are drawn from *The Book of the States: 1990–91* (Lexington, Ky.: Council of State Governments, 1990), pp. 246–60.

tions to candidates or their elimination altogether, a new limit on the total dollar amount congressional candidates could accept from PACs, restrictions on the amount a candidate can raise out of state, and, ultimately, public finance, with its condition of limits on how much the candidate can raise and spend. Similarly, the growth of independent expenditures, especially in national politics, has spurred the search for limitations on them. At a minimum, the reformers would like to tighten the statutory definition of independence to eliminate the possibility of coordination between candidate or party and the independent spender.

At least three considerations now slow the course of additional reform. First, unless the Supreme Court retreats from its position in *Buckley* and subsequent cases, the reform options are sharply limited. By holding limits on expenditures unconstitutional for independent groups or individuals and for candidates without public funding, for example, the Court sharply curtails the feasible ways for capping the costs of campaigning or independent spending. Second, campaign finance has increasingly become a partisan and ideological issue, with liberals and Democrats favoring one set of restrictions and conservatives and Republicans another. It would thus appear that substantial reform at the national level would be difficult or unlikely unless one party controlled both the Congress and the presidency. Third, even one-party control of all branches of government would not necessarily favor reform. Incumbent legislators are leery about changing the rules under which they have been elected, especially in ways that might give an advantage to challengers. Unless powerful popular pressures for reform return or incumbents feel that certain rules disadvantage them, the chances for major changes in current campaign financing laws seem slim (see box).[22]

MONEY, POWER, AND PARTY IN AMERICAN POLITICS

The status quo in American campaign finance raises a series of questions about power and influence in the American democracy. The first is the basic question of influence in the parties and electoral processes. Political contributors have political goals and incentives, just as do activists who contribute their skills and labor to the party organization or to a candidate's campaign. Large numbers of Americans wonder what kinds of demands or expectations accompany their financial contributions. Money is obviously a major resource of American politics, and its contributors clearly acquire some form of political influence. What is not yet clear is the nature of the influence and the differences, both quantitative

---

[22]Some of the most interesting new proposals for campaign finance reform include reduced broadcast and postal rates for candidates, free broadcast time for parties to be used by their candidates, and exemptions from spending limits for some part of the contributions from the candidate's home state. They were key recommendations in a 1990 report of the Campaign Finance Reform Panel established by the Democratic and Republican party leaders of the U.S. Senate.

The 1990 Congress Fails to Enact Campaign Finance Reform

The most serious efforts at campaign finance reform since the 1970s occurred in the 1990 Congress. In the end, however, partisan wrangling, the threat of a presidential veto, and differences between Senate and House reform packages doomed those efforts to failure.

The 1990 experience provides some insight into the issues of campaign finance and the political realities that influence their settlement. Both the House and Senate bills contained a voluntary spending limit coupled with incentives such as lower costs of mailing and television time for those who accepted limits, designed to satisfy Supreme Court requirements as articulated in *Buckley v. Valeo.* Both houses also proposed restrictions on bundling, a practice through which party committees served as intermediaries in collecting donations from multiple contributors and then passing along the money to candidates, and on soft money transfers to the state parties. But where the House limited the PAC money a candidate could receive, the Senate banned PACs altogether. Another difference was that the Senate provided, on a limited basis, for some public funding of congressional campaigns.

Even if the House and Senate had been able to agree on a bill, it would have faced Republican opposition and a likely presidential veto. Most Republicans strenuously opposed spending limits and public funding, fearing that, in a race in which opposing candidates spend equally, Democrats (more of whom are incumbents) have the advantage. Democrats have tended to favor limits and public funding, in part because they fear the great fund-raising potential of the GOP and its candidates. The GOP has countered with proposals to eliminate PACs, which give more to incumbents, and to restrict the amount of money candidates can receive from out of state sources.

and qualitative, between it and the influence that results from nonmoney contributions to the parties and candidates.

It is not easy to specify with certainty the goals or incentives that motivate the financial contributor. Very likely they come from the same range of incentives that stir the activist to contribute his or her time to the party organization: patronage, preferment, a political career; personal, social, or psychological satisfactions; and interest, issue, and ideology. Unquestionably, the chief incentive is the combination of interest, issue, and ideology—the desire, that is, to influence the establishment or administration of some kind of public policy. The concentration of PAC contributions on incumbent members of Congress is a case in point. The contributor's desire may be for direct access or for the ear of the powerful. More commonly, it is only a desire to elect public officials with values and preferences that promise a sympathy for the goals of the contributor.

Thus, the demands of the contributor are largely indirect; certainly, very few contributors seek a direct quid pro quo.

Second, in addition to the issue of influence on policy, there is the question of power within the party. The status quo in American political finance supports current officeholders, the parties in government, and helps them maintain their independence from the party organizations. So long as candidates and officeholders continue to finance their own primary and general election campaigns, they block the organizations' control of access to public office. Unquestionably, the reluctance of Congress and state legislatures to disturb the present patterns of political finance grows, in large part, from their satisfaction with the political independence these patterns ensure them. Despite the spate of reforms of recent years, candidate spending—as opposed to party organization spending—remains entrenched. The candidate, rather than the party, raises and spends large sums of money. Even in the sorties into public financing of campaigns, in contrast to the practice in many other democracies, the funds go to candidates (not to party organizations) in presidential elections and in a majority of states with public funding. To be sure, there has been some indirect support of a party role—the federal legislation permitting party committees to spend beyond candidate expenditure ceilings and the allowance for unrestricted "soft money" donations to state parties, for example—but it is far less than would be necessary to establish strong and disciplined parties with sanctions over their candidates and officeholders.

Third, reform in campaign finance, like all other party reform, never affects all individuals and parties alike. It works to some people's advantage and to others' disadvantage. The cumulative effect of the reforms of the 1970s will surely be to diminish the influence of wealthy contributors and to make the "little" contributor more valuable than ever. (In that respect, one ought to note, however, that it is hardly certain that one contributor of $10,000 actually made more effective demands on the recipient than 10 contributors of $1,000 will.) New influence and access also accrue to the technicians who can raise small gifts as well as to group contributors and incumbents. Also, some advantages clearly accrue to candidates who can raise substantially greater sums than their opponents can. Concern over the effect of unequal cash resources cuts two ways, however. Some of the support for public funding comes from those who see it as a way of equalizing resources and thus eliminating unfair advantages; but cash is not the only resource a candidate needs. Incumbent officeholders have all manner of other advantages over challengers—staffs, media access, and name recognition, for example—and challengers may well need to have a cash advantage if they are to have a chance of winning and if elections are to remain competitive.

Campaign Finance—A Reflection of the American Way

The American way of campaign finance reflects the American way of politics. Campaign costs reflect the vastness of the country, the many elective offices on many levels of government, the localism of American politics, and the unbridled length of our campaigns for office. The domination of spending by candidates reflects our candidate-dominated campaigns and, more generally, the dominance within American parties of the party in government. The importance of the mass media in major American campaigns speaks volumes about the media themselves, while it also reflects the sheer size of our constituencies. By contrast, campaign finance in Great Britain involves far smaller sums more firmly in the control of the party organizations. In Britain, however, there is free time on the government-run BBC and a long-standing tradition of the "soft sell" rather than the American-style "hard sell" in all forms of public persuasion. Moreover, the British election campaign runs for only about three weeks, during which paid radio and television political advertising is banned, and the average constituency in the House of Commons has less than one-fifth as many people as the average American congressional district. Most significantly, there is no larger constituency, no office with a constituency as vast as most American states, not to mention the American presidency's national constituency.

Aided by institutions such as the direct primary and the office-block ballot and supported by their ability to recruit the campaign resources they need, the American parties in government thus largely escape the control of party organizations. Even two of each party's national organizations, the congressional campaign committees, are under the thumb of elected officeholders rather than *party* professionals. In many states and localities, the officeholders also dominate. But what price does the American political system pay for this? Certainly, there is the price of a loss of cohesion as a party in government—for example, in the loss of a unified presence as party representatives in American legislatures. Certainly, too, there is the price of a weakening of party organization, not only vis-à-vis the party in government, but also internally, in terms of its ability to achieve the goals of its activists. Finally, nowhere in the life of the parties is the competition between party in government and party organization any clearer than in the competition for campaign funds and campaign control. As the costs of campaigning rise and as all participants are forced to shift to a cash economy of enormous magnitude, the future is with the sector of the party with access to those cash resources. So far, the advantage is clearly with the candidates and officeholders.

THE PARTY IN GOVERNMENT

America's first political parties, and the first parties in most other democracies as well, were built around opposing factions in the government.[1] Later developing parties here and elsewhere were erected on a broader foundation, in keeping with the more democratic system in which they emerged, but typically at their core also were identifiable factions within the government. With such ancestry, it is little wonder that the party in government so dominates the political party, so structures partisan political conflict, and so profoundly shapes our images of the party.

Yet, unlike their counterparts in parliamentary systems, the American parties in government are notoriously loose coalitions, sometimes exhibiting little more cohesiveness than a "pick-up" team of playground basketball players. Each party member represents a different constituency and heeds his or her constituency more than the party leaders. Furthermore, the structural separation of legislature from executive denies to the American parties in government the prime unifying activity of governing—the creation and maintenance of the *government*. Few scholars have made this point as pungently as E. E. Schattschneider:

> Yet, when all is said, it remains true that . . . the parties are unable to hold their lines on a controversial public issue when the pressure is on. . . . (This) constitutes the most important single fact concerning the American parties. He

---

[1]See John F. Hoadley, "The Emergence of Political Parties in Congress, 1789–1803," *American Political Science Review* 74 (1980): 757–79.

who knows this fact, and knows nothing else, knows more about American parties than he who knows everything except this fact. What kind of party is it that, having won control of government, is unable to govern.[2]

Nonetheless, in the face of evidence that the American parties do not and cannot control government, it remains true that party lines, however loosely drawn, are the chief lines in American legislative voting behavior. There is a degree of intraparty cohesion and interparty division in the roll calls of Congress and the states that cannot be lightly dismissed. The party winning the presidency even succeeds in carrying out a good portion of its party platform.[3] Furthermore, partisan considerations apply in the staffing of the top, appointive levels of national, state, and local executive offices and in the appointment of judges to the bench. Public-policymaking in the United States does vary significantly with the composition of the party in government, however faint its imprint sometimes may be.

Some distinctions are important here. When public officials are elected on a partisan basis, as they are almost always in most democratic systems, including the American, whichever party or coalition of parties can command a majority determines which one is nominally in charge of each governmental institution. Constitutional separation of powers throughout the various levels of the American system complicates this situation by permitting split control of the different governmental institutions. Since 1969, in fact split party control of the national government has been the norm, not the exception. But nominal control is only the first step in party control over policymaking, the initial point on a continuum measuring the extent of *party government*—the ability of public officials of the same party to enact the programs of their party. Political systems can be located at various points along this continuum of party government, and where they are at any one time depends upon the cohesiveness of the party in government as well as whether control of the different institutions is divided.

Furthermore, since it is *party* government about which we speak, which parts of the party do we expect to set the policy by which the party will govern—all three sectors, the party organization, or just the party in government? If the latter, would it be the entire party in government, or is it possible that the executive party has propensities and abilities to govern different from those of the legislative party? It is well to remember that although the three sectors of the party are brought together in the search for power at elections, each has its own goals and motives. The activists of the party organization may seek to translate a program or ideology into policy, but they may also seek patronage jobs, other forms of reward or preference, the sensations of victory, or the defeat of a hated opposition. The party's voters may be stimulated by an issue, a program, or an ideology, but they also respond to personalities, to incumbency, to

---

[2]E. E. Schattschneider, *Party Government* (New York: Rinehart, 1942), pp. 131–32.

[3]Gerald M. Pomper, *Elections in America* (New York: Dodd, Mead, 1968), Chap. 8.

abstract and traditional loyalties to a candidate or party, or to the urging of friends and family. The candidates and officeholders seek the office, its tangible rewards, its intangible satisfactions, and its opportunities to make public decisions. The important point is that none of the three sectors is committed wholly—or possibly even predominantly—to the capture of public office for the purpose of enacting party policies into law.

The classic American statement on party government (or party responsibility) was made in the late 1940s by a committee of the American Political Science Association in a report entitled *Toward a More Responsible Two-Party System.*[4] The report argued that the American parties ought to articulate more specific and comprehensive policy programs, nominate candidates pledged to those programs, and then see to it that their successful candidates enact the programs while they are in office. In other words, the major parties ought to serve as the mechanisms through which American voters can choose between competing programs, and through which the winning majority of voters can be assured of the enactment of its choice.

Put in such terms, the question of party government (or responsibility) concerns not just the nature of the parties but the nature of American democracy itself. If the parties were to become policy initiators, they would assume a central representative role in the American democracy. They would bring great, amorphous majorities in the American electorate into alliance with groups of officeholders by means of some kind of party program or platform. They would forge a new representative link between the mass democratic electorate and the powerful few in government. To put the issue another way, responsible parties would bring electorates closer to the choices of government by giving them a way to register choices on policy alternatives. Those choices might be partly before the fact (in the mobilization of grass-roots support behind proposed programs) and partly retrospective judgments on the stewardship of two different, distinguishable parties in government. In both cases, the proposal is an attempt to restore initiative and significant choice to the great number of voters.

The critics of such proposals for party government have concentrated on one insistent theme: the nonideological, heterogeneous, and pragmatic nature of the American parties. They argue that agreement on and enforcement of a coherent policy program is very difficult, if not impossible in the American setting. Recently, of course, the party organizations are more oriented toward programs and ideology—and thus toward the uses of governmental authority for specific policy goals. There was a time when the activists of the party organization contested elections largely for the spoils at stake: jobs, contracts, honors, access, and other forms of special consideration. It made little difference to them what uses public officeholders made of the governmental power in their hands. That time is passing. As more and more citizens are attracted to the

---

[4]The report was published in New York by Rinehart in 1950. It also appears as a supplement to the September 1950 issue of the *American Political Science Review.*

party organizations and electorates for reasons of policy, important intraparty pressure builds for some degree of party responsibility.

Discussion of more programmatic and disciplined political parties leads always to the European parties, especially those of England. Parliamentary institutions foster the kind of legislative cohesion and discipline—the sharply drawn party lines—that the advocates of responsible parties have in mind. Giving the House of Commons the power to select the chief executive of the government, the Prime Minister, from its own ranks and making the Prime Minister dependent upon command of a legislative majority to continue in office creates powerful incentives for party government. Party organizations in parliamentary systems, especially those of the parties of the left, seek to enforce the party's program on its legislators. In some cases, they have succeeded—in many of the socialist and communist parties, among others. In others, they have not, but even in these cases the national party leaders speak powerfully for the party's program. One often sees a concerted effort on the part of the party in government (all of which sits in parliament) and the party organization to carry out a program that was adopted with the help of the party members at an earlier party conference. Indeed, so strong has been party discipline in the legislative process in some European countries that scholars complained about the decline of parliaments and journalists wrote darkly of "partyocracy." Ironically, in these circles, it is not uncommon to hear envious talk of the flexible, nondogmatic American parties and the uncontrolled and deliberative American legislatures.

The European experience is important for perspective and comparison. It is also important because the European variety of party government, with its focus on parliamentary discipline, has dominated the thinking of many Americans about party government. Any change in the American parties toward greater responsibility, however, will probably follow no European route. The role the parties now have in American politics and the roles toward which they move will be as uniquely American as the institutional complex of American federalism, separation of powers, and electoral processes that influence them. Given the power of the executive in American government, its ability to convert party goals or platforms into public policy may be as important as the legislature's.

Beyond this question of the party's contribution to the making of public policy—to the organizing of majority decisions in a democracy—there is another one: the question of the impact of winning office and making policy on the political party. The achievement of party goals (the goals of all three sectors) depends directly on the holding of governmental power—but in what way? To put it bluntly, what does governmental power do for the parties? What kinds of rewards does it generate for the men and women who have invested so much in politics and the party? How does it contribute to the health and vitality of the party and its various sectors?

The first two chapters in this part examine the present role of the political party in the organization and operation of the three branches of government. They are primarily concerned with the degrees of party direction or party cohesion in legislative and executive policymaking. In short, they deal with the impact of internalized party loyalties and external party influences on public officials. The third chapter in this part faces the general question of party government—its desirability and its possibility in the American political setting. It also addresses the question of whether the new programmatic orientations within the parties create conditions hospitable to the development of party government.

Chapter
14

Party and Partisans in the Legislature

The political party assumes an obvious, very public form—yet a very shadowy role—in American legislatures. The parties organize majority and minority power in the legislatures, and the legislative leaders and committee chairpersons are usually party oligarchs. Yet, despite the appearance and panoply of party power, voting on crucial issues often crosses party lines and violates party pledges and platforms. The party in many forms dominates the American legislatures; yet the effect of party effort and loyalty is often negligible. On this paradox turns much of the scholarly concern and reformist zeal expended on American legislatures.

The character of the American legislative party has been deeply affected by the American separation of powers. In a parliamentary regime, such as that of Great Britain, a majority party or a multiparty coalition in the legislature must cohere in support of the cabinet (and its government), thus creating a constitutional presumption and pressure on behalf of unity within the legislative party. When the parliamentary majority no longer supports the cabinet, a political adjustment follows. Either reorganization of the cabinet or a reshuffling of the legislative coalition supporting it ensues, or else the legislature is dissolved and sent home to face a new election.

No such institutional and constitutional pressures weigh on American legislators. They suffer no great penalty for voting in opposition to their party's legislative leaders. They may divide on, dispute with, or reject executive programs, even if the executive is of their own party, without dire consequences. In American legislatures, the party role is not institutionalized as it is in parliaments. The American legislature may not run so smoothly without party cohesion and discipline, but it can run, and executives survive its faithlessness.

PARTY ORGANIZATIONS IN LEGISLATURES

In forty-nine of the state legislatures and the Congress, almost all members come to their legislative tasks as elected candidates of a political party.[1] The ways in which they form and behave as a legislative party, however, differ enormously. In some states, the legislative party scarcely can be said to exist; in others, it dominates the legislative process through an almost daily regimen of party caucuses. Parties in most of the state legislatures and in the Congress, however, fall comfortably in the territory between these two poles.

Parties in the Congress

Party organization in the United States Congress stands as something of a benchmark for observations of the American legislatures because it is the best known of the legislatures. Both parties in both houses of Congress meet at the beginning of each congressional session to select the party leadership. In addition, the party meetings (called caucuses by the Democrats or conferences by the Republicans) nominate candidates for the position of Speaker of the House or president pro tempore of the Senate, and they set up procedures for the appointment of party members to the regular committees of the chamber. In selecting the leadership for the entire House or Senate, of course, the unified majority party is in control. In effect, then, the basic unit of party organization conducts the initial business of organizing the chamber. From its decisions rises the machinery of the party as a party (the leaders, whips, policy committees) and the organization of the chamber itself (the presiding officer and the committees).

In this fashion, the organization of the two parties and the organization of the House and Senate are woven into what appears to be a single fabric (see Figure 14.1). This organizational system is dominated by the majority party, which, except for a 1981–86 interlude in the Senate, since 1955 has been the Democratic party. The party with a voting majority has control of the committees and of the floor. It chooses the presiding officer or Speaker of the House of Representatives and the chairs of all the standing committees in both houses. The presiding officer of the Senate is the Vice President of the United States, but it is the majority party that manages floor action to the degree that it is managed in that highly democratic institution. A majority of the membership of each committee also comes from the majority party, and by a margin that reflects the majority's margin in the entire house.

Each party fills out its own internal organizational structure as well (see Figure 14.1), which is elected by the entire party membership of the chamber. At the top of the party hierarchy is the party leader (called the majority or mi-

---

[1]The Nebraska legislature is chosen in nonpartisan elections, although the partisan affiliation of its members is no secret.

HOUSE OF REPRESENTATIVES

Democrats	Republicans

Speaker
Thomas Foley, Wash.

Majority Leader
Richard Gephardt, Mo.

Minority Leader
Robert Michel, Ill.

Majority Whip
David Bonior, Mich.

Minority Whip
Newt Gingrich, Ga.

Caucus Chairman
Steny Hoyer, Md.

Conference Chairman
Jerry Lewis, Calif.

Campaign Committee Chairman
Vic Fazio, Calif.

Campaign Committee Chairman
Guy Vander Jagt, Mich.

SENATE

Democrats	Republicans

Majority Leader
George Mitchell, Maine

Minority Leader
Robert Dole, Kans.

Majority Whip
Wendell Ford, Ky.

Assistant Minority Leader
Alan Simpson, Wyo.

Deputy Whip
Alan Dixon, Ill.

Conference Chairman
Thad Cochran, Miss.

Conference Secretary
David Pryor, Ark.

Conference Secretary
Bob Kasten, Wis.

Campaign Committee Chairman
Charles Robb, Va.

Campaign Committee Chairman
Phil Gramm, Tex.

Policy Committee Co-Chairman
Tom Daschle, S. Dak.

Policy Committee Chairman
Don Nickles, Okla.

Steering Committee Chairman
Daniel Inouye, Hawaii

Figure 14.1 Top Party Leaders in the U.S. Congress: 1991–92

Note: The leader's state follows his name.

nority leader, depending on whether the party controls the chamber). In the House of Representatives, though, it is the Speaker who serves as the true leader of the majority party. Beneath these leaders in the party hierarchy come the assistant party leader or "whip" and a panoply of assistant whips, so-called because of their traditional role in mobilizing the party members to vote the way the party leadership wants. Each congressional party also fills some specialized positions—for example, chairs of its caucus or conference (i.e., the meeting of all members), its steering or policy committee, its campaign committee.

These are all positions of considerable power and authority within the party. That their occupants are chosen by the vote of all party members, though, makes their relationship with rank-and-file members more reciprocal than hierarchical. The leaders serve subject to the approval of their party—an approval the perquisites of leadership give them great advantage in, but no guarantee of, securing. Some top party leaders, even in the more democratic Congresses of modern times, have wielded more power and authority than others—due no doubt to both their personal characteristics and the willingness of the party rank and file to accept strong leadership.[2]

These party structures often have difficulty, however, in moving beyond organizing the two chambers to mobilize the party members for coordinated action in public policymaking. The policy committees do not function as broadly-based instruments of party policymaking or strategy setting even though they were created for that purpose. Instead of being a collective party leadership, they tend to represent the assorted blocs and wings of the party, which themselves often play the important role of uniting their members on behalf of some policy goal.[3]

Nor have the party caucuses or conferences typically served to consolidate the party in common cause. When they do meet on important issues during the session, only rarely do they undertake to bind their members to vote the same way.

Yet some movement toward greater party coordination in the House of Representatives in recent years is reflected in the reactivation of the party caucuses. The Republicans enhanced the role of the caucus in the late 1960s, giving rank-and-file party members more opportunity to influence party policy, but the most dramatic moves in this direction were made by the Democrats in the 1970s. The Democratic caucus was given the power to challenge incumbent committee chairs by secret ballot at the beginning of each new Congress. While most incumbent chairs have been reelected easily, the occasional denial of reappointment and the continuing threat thereof (acting to topple an incumbent committee chair for the first time since 1985, for instance, the Democratic caucus in the House of Representatives stripped Public Works Chairman Glenn M. Anderson and Administrative Chairman Frank Annunzio of their positions in the 1991–92 Congress) makes committee chairs more responsive to the views and needs of fellow party members, particularly on their committee.[4]

This form of enhanced caucus coordination, though, is not necessarily a tool of party centralization or policy coordination, but rather a sign of greater intra-

---

[2]See John G. Stewart, "Two Strategies of Leadership: Johnson and Mansfield," in Nelson W. Polsby (ed.), *Congressional Behavior* (New York: Random House, 1971), pp. 61–92.

[3]On how one such ideological group has functioned, see Arthur G. Stevens, Arthur H. Miller, and Thomas E. Mann, "Mobilization of Liberal Strength in the House, 1955–1970: The Democratic Study Group," *American Political Science Review* 68 (1974): 667–81.

[4]One study suggests that this reform seems to have induced greater party loyalty in roll call voting among House Democrats who chair committees or sub-committees—or who are next in line to be a chair. Sara Brandes Crook and John R. Hibbing, "Congressional Reform and Party Discipline: The Effects of Changes in the Seniority System on Party Loyalty in the U.S. House of Representatives," *British Journal of Political Science* 15 (1985): 207–26.

party collegiality and egalitarianism.[5] As the parties become more ideologically cohesive, though, the caucus can operate to articulate a party position on substantive legislation and to persuade straggling party members to come into line. This seems to have happened to some degree within the Democratic caucus in the House in recent years. As southern conservative Democrats have become less numerous and have held fewer powerful committee positions, the Democrats have increased their ideological cohesiveness. While this has led to more attempts to work out party policy positions in the caucus, however, the caucus has as of yet refrained from trying to force those positions upon its members.

To the extent that there is party policy in the houses of Congress, though, it is largely set by the party leadership, although more so in the large and unwieldy House than in the smaller, less centralized upper chamber. The floor leaders and the powerful figures of the party consult widely throughout the party, but the final codification of party policy, the sensing of a will or consensus, rests primarily on their judgment. If they are of the president's party, their actions and decisions are limited by his legislative program and his influence within the Congress. Within the nonpresidential party, the leadership in the House and Senate may act not only without a continuing check by the legislative party but also without a continuing check by any party organ or spokesperson. Senate party leaders such as Lyndon Johnson and Everett Dirksen, and Speaker of the House Tip O'Neill, in fact, established themselves as spokesmen for both the legislative and the national parties.[6]

What emerge as the decisions and priorities of the party leadership, however, are not really "party policy"—except in the sense that they are voiced by leaders of the legislative party. They are, rather, an amalgam of or a negotiated compromise among the goals of the party members who hold committee power, the party leaders themselves, the rank and file of the legislative party, and (in one party) the president. They rarely flow from any national party program or platform. They speak, instead, of the powers and perquisites of the legislature, the need to support or oppose a president, and the demands of the legislative constituencies. The party leaders, in other words, do not enforce a prior party policy. They make policy for and with their fellow legislators in an ad hoc way. Their party policy is purely that of the legislative party and is developed as

---

[5]On this point, see Steven S. Smith, "New Patterns of Decisionmaking in Congress," in John E. Chubb and Paul E. Peterson (eds.), *The New Direction in American Politics* (Washington, D.C.: The Brookings Institution, 1985), pp. 203–33.

[6]More generally, on party leadership in the Congress, see Ralph K. Huitt, "Democratic Party Leadership in the Senate," *American Political Science Review* 55 (1961): 333–44; Charles O. Jones, *The Minority Party in Congress* (Boston: Little, Brown, 1970); Robert L. Peabody, *Leadership in Congress* (Boston: Little, Brown, 1976); Randall B. Ripley, *Party Leaders in the House of Representatives* (Washington, D.C.: The Brookings Institution, 1967); Sidney Waldman, "Majority Leadership in the House of Representatives," *Political Science Quarterly* 95 (1980): 373–94; and Barbara Sinclair, *Majority Leadership in the U.S. House* (Baltimore: John Hopkins University Press, 1983).

much to serve the individual reelection needs of each party member as to implement any coherent party philosophy or program (see box).[7]

Party leadership in the Congress has not always been so limited. Before House members revolted against Speaker ("Czar") Joe Cannon in 1911, power in the House of Representatives was highly centralized in the hands of the speaker. Cannon chaired the Rules Committee, through which he could control the flow of legislation to the floor; appointed committees and committee chairs, putting his lieutenants in the key positions; and generally possessed the resources and sanctions necessary for enforcing party discipline. Speakers since Cannon have not commanded such a powerful institutional position. Instead, they have had to operate in a far more decentralized House, in which party discipline could only be maintained through skillful bargaining and strong personal loyalties. Successful Speakers since Cannon, such as Sam Rayburn and Tip O'Neill, have been consummate brokers rather than czars.[8]

By the late 1980s, however, it was clear that the seeds had been sown for a resurgence in party leadership power within the House of Representatives. First, Democratic party reforms in the House in the early 1970s provided the levers for a more forceful Democratic leadership. The power to assign members to committees was vested in the new Steering and Policy Committee chaired by the Speaker. The Speaker also was allowed to choose, subject to caucus ratification, the chair and other Democratic members of the Rules Committee, which serves as the "traffic cop" for legislation on the floor. The whip system was made more responsive to party leaders as well. Second, by 1987 the political context had changed to produce a Democratic majority that, because of its greater ideological cohesiveness and the opportunities provided by the party's recapture of the Senate, was ready for stronger leadership. During his brief tenure as Speaker, Jim Wright took advantage of these opportunities to become one of the most assertive Democratic leaders in decades.[9]

Parties in the State Legislatures

Among the state legislatures are those in which daily caucuses, binding party discipline, and autocratic party leadership make for a party far more potent than exists in the two houses of Congress. There are also state legislatures, however—especially those of the traditional one-party states—in which party organization is perceptibly weaker than it is in the Congress. Even in states

---

[7]That the activity of Congress is organized around the election needs of its members is a view powerfully articulated in David R. Mayhew, *Congress: The Electoral Connection* (New Haven, Conn.: Yale University Press, 1974).

[8]See Joseph Cooper and David W. Brady, "Institutional Context and Leadership Style: The House from Cannon to Rayburn," *American Political Science Review* 75 (1981): 411–25.

[9]See Barbara Sinclair, "The Changing Role of Party and Party Leadership in the U.S. House," paper delivered at the 1989 Annual Meeting of the American Political Science Association, Atlanta. On the reforms, see Leroy Reiselbach, *Congressional Reform* (Washington: CQ Press, 1986).

The Problems of Party Leadership:
The Budget Compromise of 1990

The difficulties party leaders experience in unifying their party is well illustrated by the House response to the compromise Fiscal Year 1991 budget package. The deal was negotiated among Democratic and Republican congressional leaders and White House representatives in an extraordinary series of budget summit meetings in 1990. Faced with the perceived need to reduce the budget deficit amidst deep partisan disagreement over spending priorities, these leaders labored hard to produce a compromise that they could live with.

Working out an agreement among a few congressional and White House leaders at the budget summit was one thing. Getting members of each legislative party to enact the agreement into law was quite another. The compromise package created a firestorm of opposition within the President's party, led by conservative minority party whip Newt Gingrich who felt that the President had abandoned his party's most powerful campaign issue of "no new taxes" and who urged Republican candidates to oppose the President's position. The package also upset many Democrats, who saw in it undesirable cuts in Medicare and increased burdens on low- and middle-income Americans.

"WE'RE ALL ON BOARD"
—Sen. Dole, after White House unity meeting

COPYRIGHT 1990 BY HERBLOCK IN THE WASHINGTON POST.

(continued)

The House vote on the budget compromise in early October, in the first few days of the new budget year, produced a stinging rebuke to both Democratic and Republican party leaders and the President. Preferring a possible shutdown of the government or the automatic Gramm-Rudman spending cuts to the compromise package, a majority of both Democrats (149–108) and Republicans (105–71) voted *against* it, with conservative Republicans and liberal Democrats leading the way. Two weeks later, a more partisan budget package revised to satisfy the Democratic rank-and-file passed in the House 227–203, with Democrats voting 217–40 in favor and Republicans 163–10 in opposition.

This highly-publicized affair exemplifies the limits of congressional party loyalty to their leaders, and provides ample material for the political cartoonist's pen as demonstrated above.

that have a complete apparatus of party organization, the parties fail more frequently than the congressional parties to make the apparatus operate effectively.

The party caucuses in Congress at least maintain cohesion in their initial organizational tasks; they always agree on candidates for the presiding officers. State legislative parties periodically find themselves too divided by factionalism or ambition even to organize the legislature. In some states with comparatively weak legislative parties, such as California, coalitions across party lines to elect legislative leaders have not been rare. Party discipline in selecting the legislative leaders also often breaks down under the pressure of electoral change. In Florida, for example, conservative Democrats joined with a growing minority of Republicans to choose the leadership of the state senate in 1987. Legislative leaders in Illinois, North Carolina, and Oklahoma were similarly elected by a bipartisan coalition rather than a strict party vote in 1988.

In one-party states, of course, the party caucus has had little excuse for existing. Disagreement over organization, leadership positions, and policy issues in these states usually has fallen along factional lines within the party or along the lines of followings of powerful personages. In the heyday of the Long dynasty in Louisiana, one Democratic faction adhered to the Longs and others supported their opponents. In this particular case and in others, factional lines built on personal and family followings coincide with differing regional loyalties. Alternatively, the legislative caucuses in one-party states may reflect ideological differences; from 1910 to the 1930s in Wisconsin, for example, the La Follette Progressive Republicans organized one legislative caucus, the conservative Republicans another, and the very feeble Democrats a third.

Party leadership in the state legislatures also assumes a number of forms. The traditional floor leaders and whips exist in most. In others, the Speaker of the House or a spokesperson for the governor may mobilize the party's legislators. State party officials, unlike national party officials, may have a powerful voice in the legislative party. Whatever their relationship with state party leaders may be, however, the state legislative leaders often enjoy enormous power in the day-to-day workings of the legislature. Their influence on party caucuses is great, and they do not often have to defer to steering or policy committees. In most states, especially in the lower houses, they appoint the committees and their chairs.

The modern-day Czar Cannon's then are found, if anywhere, in some of the state houses rather than in the U.S. House of Representatives. They may be throwbacks to an earlier era, however, before state legislatures had achieved a significant degree of professionalization. As this professionalization, along with two-party competition, spreads across the states, legislative practices may become more similar, more homogeneous—and less subject to a high degree of centralized control.

Yet there remains, and probably will remain, wide variation in party legislative organization across the states. Their structure is fairly uniform with the familiar panoply of party offices, the appointment to positions of legislative power by the party leaders, and the existence of party caucuses. What differs is their practice. State party leaders vary enormously in power across the ninety-nine state legislative chambers, even between two houses in the same state. There is also a wide range of practice in the importance of the party caucus. Malcolm Jewell and David Olson report that the caucus is active beyond selecting the leaders in all but seven states. In two states the majority caucus actually binds its members on budget bills, while twenty-eight have caucuses in one or both parties that play a role in policymaking by frequently meeting to discuss legislation, take straw votes of their members, and determine what bills should be pushed on the floor. At the other end of the continuum are party caucuses in eleven states whose major purpose is informational and where no attempt is made to either guage party opinion or build party consensus.[10]

THE EFFECTS AND INFLUENCE OF PARTY

The shape of party power is clearly evident in American legislatures—but power for what? Is it power for organizing party support for a set of party programs or merely for parceling out the perquisites of legislative office? Or does the legislative party seek both policy and perquisites? How the legislative parties, typically through their party leadership but also as caucuses, use power is clearly important to understanding the role of party in government.

Effects in the Congress

The parties in the United States Congress have amply illustrated over the last century that they can impose party sanctions on only one issue: the failure of a

---

[10]Malcolm E. Jewell and David M. Olson, *Political Parties and Elections in American States* (Chicago: Dorsey, 1988), pp. 235–44.

member of the legislative party to support its presidential candidate in the general election. Representatives or senators can freely vote against the party's platform, majority, or leadership—or against the program of their party's president. They risk punishment, however, if they undercut their party's presidential candidate. In 1925, the Republican caucus in the Senate expelled Senators La Follette, Ladd, Frazier, and Brookhart after they had supported La Follette and the Progressive ticket in the 1924 elections. That decision also robbed the four senators of their Republican committee assignments and the seniority they had accumulated through their years of service on the committees.

Expulsion from the party is very rare, however. Even the greatest displeasure in legislative parties rarely leads to more than a stripping of seniority or committee assignments. In 1965, the Democratic caucus in the House took all committee seniority from two southern Democrats who had supported the Republican presidential candidate, Barry Goldwater, the year before. In 1968, the same fate befell Representative John Rarick, a Democrat from Louisiana, for supporting George Wallace. In early 1983, the Democratic caucus removed Representative Phil Gramm from his seat on the House Budget Committee; in view of his Democratic colleagues, Gramm, a conservative Democrat from Texas, had betrayed his party by divulging to the Republicans the proceedings of secret Democratic party meetings on the Reagan budget. (Gramm resigned his seat shortly thereafter and was reelected to it as a Republican in a special election some weeks later. In 1984, he was elected as a Republican U.S. Senator from Texas.) It is no accident, of course, that all of these instances of discipline occurred in the Democratic caucus of the House. The House Democrats, largely because of greater divisions and greater power in the hands of the caucus itself, have sought a far greater degree of discipline than have any of the other three legislative parties in the Congress.

Beyond these relatively infrequent disciplinary actions, the party organizations in Congress rely on informal pressure of one sort or another to increase party cohesiveness. If they are of the president's party, they convey the president's wishes and with them the president's influence and sanctions. In other instances—not frequently, indeed—legislative leaders report and transmit the feelings of party leaders outside the Congress. Chiefly, however, they depend on their own legislative leverage. They may, for example, give the choicest committee assignments to the most loyal supporters of the party leadership. The favors they give—the help in passing favorite bills or the additional office space, for example—can cultivate a measure of party support. So, too, can their political help to their fellow legislators; party leaders give political speeches and raise campaign funds at least in part for that purpose.[11] When party leaders fail in their attempts to maintain party unity in the legislature, it is not so much for lack of leverage as for the strength of the pressures from the local congressional

---

[11]See Barbara Sinclair, "Majority Party Leadership Strategies for Coping with the New U.S. House," *Legislative Studies Quarterly* 6 (1981): 391–414.

constituencies. The chief limit to their success is always the need of the individual member of Congress to satisfy this constituency in order to win reelection. When party and constituency conflict, responsiveness to the folks back home usually outweighs the calls for party unity in Congress.

Attempts to build party discipline in Congress also were undercut in the past by the power of the committees and by a tradition of seniority that automatically awarded committee chairmanships to the majority party members with the longest continuous service on the committee. The independence of the committees places them, as a system of influence, squarely in opposition to any influences that the parties might exert. Seniority as a key to power in the committees puts a premium on getting reelected rather than on party loyalty or regularity within the Congress. Thus, attempts by a legislative party to reform seniority and the committee system—such as those of the House Democrats in the 1970s—are nothing less than struggles for control of the business of the Congress. The Democrats of the House have succeeded in their reform efforts by modifying the power of committee chairpersons and establishing the principle that the party caucuses vote every two years to approve the continuance in power of every committee chairperson—and by occasionally unseating a chair. As a committee chair's power was diminished, one barrier to the influence of party organization was lowered.

Effects in the State Legislatures

In some state legislatures, party leadership and organization operate far more effectively than they do in the Congress. Positions of party leadership and committee power much more frequently go to legislators loyal to the party and to its programs. Furthermore, either the party leaders, the party speaking through a periodic caucus decision, or the party's governor or state committee may expect the legislators to support the party program or stand on a particular issue. It is not surprising that state legislators have looked to party leaders for cues and direction much more frequently than have the members of Congress.[12] For excessive lapses of party loyalty, legislators in these states may suffer sanctions that would be inconceivable in the United States Congress. Their influence may wane in the legislature, and they may ultimately lose positions of power. In a state that has numerous patronage jobs, they may find that the applicants they sponsor fare less well than formerly. They may also find in the next election campaign that they no longer receive campaign funds from the state or local party or, worse yet, that the party is supporting competitiors in the primaries.

Clearly, the parties in some of the competitive, two-party state legislatures have advanced the art of discipline far beyond its state in the Congress. The reasons for their success tell us a good deal about the building of party power in legislatures.

---

[12]Eric M. Uslaner and Ronald E. Weber, *Patterns of Decision Making in State Legislatures* (New York: Praeger, 1977).

Absence of Competing Centers of Power   In the Congress, the committees traditionally have been the centers of legislative power, centrifugal forces countering the centripetal tendencies of party. A vast amount of the real business of Congress goes on in them. They are the screens that sift through the great mass of legislative proposals for those relatively few nuggets of legislative metal. The result has been the creation of important centers of power in the Congress. The more these committees become autonomous units in which influence derives from seniority, the less they owe to the parties and reflect the party organization or aims. (In fact, one can argue that since seniority and its power accrue most to members of Congress from noncompetitive, one-party areas, committee power can be definitely unrepresentative of the party in the country at large.) In the states, on the other hand, because the legislature is less attractive as a career (although this is changing) legislators accumulate less seniority, and deference to seniority in allocating positions of power is far less common. The parties in the states are freer to appoint their loyalists to positions of legislative power; the committees and other legislative agencies of the states generally operate as instruments of party power in a way unknown in the Congress.[13]

Patronage and Preferences   Patronage and other forms of governmental preference still exist in some states to a far greater extent than they do in the national government. Especially in the hands of a vigorous and determined governor, these rewards may be potent inducements to party discipline in state legislatures. Legislators who ignore their party, if it is the party of the governor, may not be able to secure the political appointments that their constituents and local party workers have been waiting for. Conversely, the loyal and faithful party legislator is amply rewarded. In the Congress, little such patronage remains with which to induce party discipline.

Influence of the Party Organization   State and local party organizations exert greater influence on state legislators than does the national committee of the party over the members of Congress. In the states, the party organization and the legislative party are far more likely to be allies. State party leaders may inhibit the political ambitions of party mavericks or deny them advancement within the party, especially in states in which they can influence the nomination processes. They may prevail on local parties to oppose renomination for those who are disloyal, although the spread of nominations through primaries has deprived the party of the control over nominations it once enjoyed. Moreover, it

---

[13]The rise of seniority as a principle for allocating committee positions in the House of Representatives can be traced to the institutionalization of the Congress in the early 1900s and especially the weakening of the Speaker after 1911. See Nelson W. Polsby, Miriam Gallaher, and Barry Spencer Rundquist, "The Growth of the Seniority System in the U.S. House of Representatives," *American Political Science Review* 68 (1969): 787–807.

is not rare in the states—as it is in Washington, where serving in Congress is a full-time job—for state and local party leaders also to be legislative leaders.

The state and local parties figure more prominently in the lives of state legislative candidates in yet another way—the provision of campaign money. State legislative campaigns are more likely to depend upon the party organization for financial support than are congressional campaigns for several reasons. First, states that provide public funding for campaigns sometimes channel that money through the parties rather than give it directly to candidates. Second, many states also impose no ceilings on party contributions to campaigns, unlike the situation at the congressional level, and consequently the parties can make substantial investments if they wish. Third, the division of labor between the national party committees and the congressional campaign committees is not paralleled at the state level. Even though more states now have significant legislative campaign committees, many candidates still are forced to look beyond them to the party for campaign funds and services—and the state parties are better prepared to respond than they have been in past years.

Greater Political Homogeneity Greater party cohesion in some state legislatures also reflects the greater homogeneity of state parties. While a legislative party in Congress reflects the full range of differences within the nation, that same party in any given state embraces a narrower spectrum of interests and ideologies. This greater political homogeneity of the states produces legislative parties in which the ranges of differences and disagreements are smaller and in which there are fewer sources of internal conflict. The political culture of the state also is more homogeneous and, in some cases, more tolerant of party discipline over legislators than the national constituency is. Legislative party strength has traditionally flourished, for example, in the northeastern part of the country (such as in Rhode Island, Connecticut, Pennsylvania, New Jersey), the states of party organizational strength, patronage, weak primaries, and, one infers, a political culture tolerant of centralized political control.

Lesser Legislative Professionalism in the States Over the years, the Congress has evolved into a highly professionalized legislative body. Each member controls a sizable and well-paid personal staff and a considerable budget, which are employed to meet *personal* legislative tasks and reelection needs. Congress now meets almost continuously and the office has become a full-time job with high pay and benefits. The state legislatures have become much more professional in recent years, but very few provide ordinary members with levels of support that even approach those in the Congress. State legislators are fortunate to have as much as a private office and personal secretary. Staff and budget resources typically are minimal (only a minority of the legislatures provide any personal staff at all), and sometimes they are under the control of the party leadership rather than the individual member. Many state legislatures also have retained their traditional part-time orientation, meeting for only a part of the year and providing such low levels of compensation that most members must hold other jobs. As a result of these restrictions, state legislators in most of the states are much less able to operate independently of their party leaders than are members of Congress.[14]

PARTY COHESION IN LEGISLATIVE VOTING

Party organization in Congress and the state legislatures—with caucuses, leaders, whips, and policy committees—is only the most apparent, overt manifestation of the party in the legislature. Its efforts on behalf of party unity and discipline among its legislators are tangible, if difficult to document. Party influence in legislatures, however, is broader and more pervasive than the enforcing activities of the organized legislative party. Party in a broader, more figurative sense may also operate "within" the legislator as a series of internalized loyalties and frameworks for organizing his or her legislative decisions. To speak of party only in the organizational sense of leaders and caucuses, therefore, is to miss the richness and complexity of party influence on the legislative process.

The political party is only one of a number of claimants for the vote of a legislator on any given issue. The voters of the home constituency make their demands, too, and so do the more ideological and militant workers of the party back home. Nor can the wishes of the president or a governor be easily dismissed. To all of these pressures one must also add those of interest groups, financial contributors, friends and associates in the legislature, and the legislator's own system of beliefs. Happily, all or most of these pressures point in the same direction on many issues. When they do not, party loyalty understandably gives way.

The cumulative consequences of party influence amid the many other sources of voting cues can be gauged by looking at how legislators behave, in particular how they vote on legislation. Their formal, recorded roll call votes on bills, amendments, and resolutions of course are not the only important dimensions of legislative behavior. Yet the public nature of the roll call vote makes it a good test of the ability of the party to maintain discipline among its members.

---

[14]The influence of party in the states, though, must not be exaggerated. In one survey, state legislators were asked who made the most significant legislative decisions. A majority cited the party leadership in sixty-seven of ninety-nine legislative chambers and the party caucus was important in fifty chambers, but committees were significant in eighty-seven. The party leadership dominated only five chambers. The party leaders and party caucus shared dominance in twelve more. But, in most state legislatures, committee and party shared the stage as important centers of decision making. Of course, committee power is allocated by the party leadership, rather than by strict seniority rules, in many states, so party power may have an indirect influence as well. See Wayne L. Francis, "Leadership, Party Caucuses, and Committees in the U.S. State Legislatures," *Legislative Studies Quarterly* 10 (1985): 243–57.

Incidence of Party Cohesion

Answers always depend on the questions. So it is with the question of the cohesion or discipline the American parties generate in legislatures. The answer depends to a considerable extent on the definition of the term *cohesion*.

One classic measure of party cohesion in legislatures has been the party vote—any nonunamimous legislative roll call in which 90 percent or more of the members of one party vote yes and 90 percent or more of the other party vote no. By such a stringent test, party discipline appears regularly in the British House of Commons but rarely in American legislatures. Julius Turner found that from 1921 through 1948, only 17 percent of the role calls in the House of Representatives met such a criterion of party discipline. In the 1950s and 1960s, the number of party division roll calls dropped steadily to about 2 or 3 percent.[15] During approximately the same period, in the British House of Commons, the percentage of party votes averaged very close to 100 percent.[16]

Although the "90 percent versus 90 percent" standard discriminates between British and American party cohesion—indeed, between parliamentary and other systems—it is too stringent a standard for comparisons within the American experience. Scholars of the American legislatures have opted for less demanding criteria. Whatever criterion one accepts, it may be used to describe both the overall incidence of cohesion in the legislatures and the party loyalty of individual legislators. For example, one can make statements about the percentage of instances in which the majority of one party opposed a majority of the other—what are called "party votes." One can also figure the percentage of times that an individual legislator votes with his or her party when party opposes party, which is referred to as "party cohesion."

By these measures, recent years have produced the highest levels of congressional party voting in years (Figure 14.2). A majority of Democrats opposed a majority of Republicans in 54 percent of all contested votes in the Senate—the highest level of party voting since 1961. Party voting has been even more prevalent in the House. In each year since 1983, it has attained levels higher than at any time since 1965. House party voting dropped off somewhat in 1990, as it usually does in an election year,[17] but it still reached an impressive (by American standards at least!) 49 percent.

---

[15]The corresponding number of uncontested or "universalistic" votes, in which 90 percent of Congress votes the same way, conversely, has increased steadily from the late 1940s into modern times. See Melissa P. Collie, "Universalism and the Parties in the U.S. House of Representatives," *American Journal of Political Science* 32 (1988): 865–83.

[16]Julius Turner, *Party and Constituency: Pressures on Congress*, rev. ed. by Edward V. Schneier (Baltimore: The Johns Hopkins University Press, 1970), pp. 16–17.

[17]To even out this "session effect," the data in Figure 14.2 are averaged across the two sessions of each Congress. The downturn in party voting in the even years, when House members stand for election, goes back as far as the 1830s. See Duncan MacRae, Jr., *Issues and Parties in Legislative Voting: Methods of Statistical Analysis* (New York: Harper & Row, 1970), pp. 200–07.

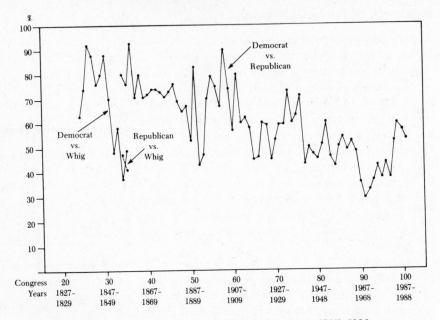

Figure 14.2 Party Voting in the House of Representatives: 1835–1990.

Note: Entries are the percentage of roll call votes on which a majority of one party opposed a majority of the other party for both sessions combined.

Source: For 24th through 36th congresses, Thomas B. Alexander, *Sectional Stress and Party Strength* (Nashville, Tennessee: Vanderbilt University Press, 1967). For 37th through 93rd congresses, Jerome B. Chubb and Santa A. Traugott, "Partisan Cleavage and Cohesion in the House of Representatives, 1861–1974," *Journal of Interdisciplinary History* 7 (1977), 382–383. For the 94th through 101st (1989–90) congresses, *Congressional Quarterly Weekly Report,* December 22, 1990, 4188–91.

David Rohde has attributed this increased party voting to two factors within the majority Democratic party. First, changes in the composition of the southern congressional delegation, wrought by the Voting Rights Act and growing two-party competition, have narrowed the policy differences between northern and southern Democrats and sharpened those between the Democrats and the Republicans in Congress. The old "conservative coalition" of northern Republicans and southern Democrats has weakened, leaving the Democratic party more cohesive than it has been in years.[18] Second, organizational reforms (mainly reducing the power of committee chairs and strengthening the powers

---

[18]David W. Rohde, " 'The Reports of My Death Are Greatly Exaggerated': Parties and Party Voting in the House of Representatives," in Glenn R. Parker (ed.), *Changing Perspectives on Congress* (Knoxville: University of Tennessee Press, 1990). Also see Franklin D. Gilliam, Jr., and Kenny Whitby, "A Longitudinal Analysis of Competing Explanations for the Transformation of Southern Politics," *Journal of Politics* 53 (1991), 504–18.

of party leaders) have made it easier for the Democratic leadership to unify its party and to fend off Republican appeals to more conservative Democrats.[19]

In voting on issues where majorities of the parties disagreed, the Democrats were indeed more cohesive than the Republicans from 1982 through 1990, with the gap between them widening after 1985. In 1990, for example, 81 percent of the Democrats voted with their party when its majority opposed a Republican majority compared to a 74-percent rate for the Republicans. This reverses the pattern from the 1960s and 1970s when, with conservative Democrats from the South often crossing the aisle to vote with Republicans under a more decentralized party leadership, Democratic cohesion usually was weaker than Republican cohesion.[20]

Levels of party voting in the Congress, though, have varied enormously since the beginning of regular two-party competition in the 1830s (see Figure 14.2) In the nineteenth century—when interparty competition was high in most congressional districts, party leaders exercised considerable legislative authority, and Congress was far less professional—party voting attained levels comparable to those of the most partisan state legislatures, although still far below those of the British parliament. After 1900, following what Nelson W. Polsby has termed the "institutionalization" of Congress and what Walter Dean Burnham has seen as a "disaggregation" of party,[21] party voting fell precipitously. Although the New Deal realignment of the 1930s boosted legislative party cohesiveness, it did not recapture its nineteenth century levels or approach that of the most party-oriented of the states.

Beyond these variations from one party system to another, levels of party voting also have varied considerably within party systems. Samuel Patterson and Gregory Caldeira have examined the period from 1949 through 1984 to determine what accounts for the ebbs and flows of party voting in both the Senate and the House of Representatives. The political and electoral context of Congress proved to be the most significant factor. Party voting peaked when Democrats controlled the White House and Congress— conditions under which the polarization inherent in party government flourished—and when the parties exhibited the greatest differences in their platforms. Large and homogeneous

---

[19]David W. Rohde, "Democratic Party Leadership, Agenda Control and the Resurgence of Partisanship in the House," paper delivered at the 1989 Annual Meeting of the American Political Science Association, Atlanta.

[20]These figures on party voting and party cohesion come from the *Congressional Quarterly Weekly Report*, December 22, 1990.

[21]Institutionalization is the term Polsby uses to characterize the development of a professionalized Congress, with greater specialization of party and committee roles, established norms, deference to congressional experience, and greater longevity in office. Nelson W. Polsby, "The Institutionalization of the United States House of Representatives," *American Political Science Review* 62 (1968): 144–68. By disaggregation, Burnham means a decline in the party-based linkage among candidates for various offices. Walter Dean Burnham, *Critical Elections and the Mainsprings of American Politics* (New York: Norton, 1970) pp. 91–134.

majorities in the House also enhanced party voting, while the Senate was found to respond mainly, pro and con, to presidential leadership.[22]

Information on the levels of party voting across the American state legislatures is not available for recent years, as there is no equivalent to the *Congressional Quarterly Weekly Report* at the state level. Studies of selected states in the 1950s and 1960s, supplemented by occasional measurements since, however, suggest great variation in the extent to which their legislatures divide along party lines and their legislative parties exhibit voting cohesiveness. In some states, especially those with strong party organizations, competitive politics, and ideological divisions between the parties, party is the dominant force in legislative voting—attaining a significance that was attained in Congress only in the previous century. In others, probably most, party voting may be no more, and possibly much less, prominent than in the modern Congress.[23]

Party voting, by the measure we have employed, occurs when a majority of one party opposes a majority of the opposing party. But the extent of party voting says little about how united the two party majorities are. This facet of legislative voting too has varied over time, and an examination of this variation tells us a great deal about the nature of the legislative parties.

Occasions for Cohesion

Cohesive voting among members of the same legislative party is greater on some issues and questions than on others. Studies in the Congress and in the state legislatures find that three kinds of legislative concerns are most likely to stimulate high levels of party discipline: those touching the interests of the legislative party as a group, those involving support of or opposition to an executive program, and those concerning the socioeconomic issues and interests that tend to divide the party electorates.

Party-Oriented Cohesion   The interests of the legislative parties as parties—as interest groups, one might say—often spur the greatest party unity in legislatures. The range of such issues is broad. It includes, especially in two-party legislatures, the basic votes to organize the legislative chamber. In the Congress, for example, one can safely predict 100 percent party cohesion on the early-session votes to elect a Speaker of the House. Cohesion also tends to be extremely high on issues affecting party strength. In a 1985 vote on whether to award the congressional seat to Democrat Frank McCloskey or Republican Richard McIntyre after a disputed Indiana election, for example, the House of

[22]Samuel C. Patterson and Gregory A. Caldeira, "Party Voting in the United States Congress," *British Journal of Political Science* 18 (1988): 111–31.

[23]On party voting in state legislatures, see Jewell and Olson, *Political Parties and Elections*, pp. 246–49. Data on party voting and cohesion in selected state legislatures from 1959 to 1974 are provided by Malcom E. Jewell and Samuel C. Patterson, *The Legislative Process in the United States* (New York: Random House, 1977), pp. 384–85.

Representatives divided along partisan lines, with Democrats voting 236–10 to seat McCloskey and Republicans voting 180–0 in opposition.

Discipline runs high in the state legislatures over issues such as patronage (and merit system reform), the laws regulating parties and campaigning, the seating of challenged members of the legislature, election and registration laws, or the creation or alteration of legislative districts. Whatever form these issues take, they all touch the basic interests of the party as a political organization. They threaten some aspects of the party status quo: the party's activists, its internal organizational structure, its system of rewards, its electorate, or its electoral competitiveness.

Executive-Oriented Cohesion   Legislators of a party may also rally around the party's executive or unite against the executive of the other party. Perhaps the reaction to an executive program is not so predictable as it is in a parliamentary system, for American presidents freely court the support of the other party. Nonetheless, it is a significant partisan issue even in the American context. The *Congressional Quarterly* regularly measures the support that each legislative party gives to the president on issues that he has clearly designated a part of his program (Table 14.1). In the 1980s, almost 70 percent of the Republicans on average supported the programs of Presidents Reagan and Bush. By contrast, only slightly more than a third of the Democrats did the same.

This executive-oriented cohesion in the Congress, which appears in the state legislatures as well, reflects a number of realities of American politics. It may result from the executive's control of political sanctions—patronage in some states, personal support in fund raising and campaigning, or support of programs for the legislator's constituency. It also results from the fact that the executive increasingly symbolizes the party and its performance. Legislators of the president's party or the governor's party know that they threaten their party and their own political future if they make the party's executive appear ineffective. And of course it may result from the coincidence of preferences and constituencies between the congressional party and its president.

Nonetheless, there are occasions when loyalty to the chief executive of a legislator's party can not withstand other pressures and demands. Although legislative party disloyalty to its president can be particularly embarrassing to the president and a source of tension between the White House and Capitol Hill, it does not carry with it the threat of a new election or a new leader (see box, p. 394) as it does in a parliamentary system, where major opposition to a prime minister's legislation from within his or her party can bring down the government.

Issue-Oriented Cohesion   Finally, legislative cohesion remains firm on those issues that involve the welfare state, the whole complex debate over government responsibilities that can be summed up as the liberal-conservative dualism which has dominated party conflict since the 1930s. In the states, such issues include labor-management relations, aid to agriculture or other sectors of

Table 14.1   PERCENTAGE OF TIMES THAT MEMBERS OF CONGRESS SUPPORTED
BILLS FROM THE PRESIDENT'S PROGRAMS: 1966–1990

Party of the President	Year	Senate Democrats	Senate Republicans	House Democrats	House Republicans
Democrat	1966	57%	43%	63%	37%
Democrat	1967	61	53	69	46
Democrat	1968	48	47	64	51
Republican	1969	47	66	48	57
Republican	1970	45	60	53	66
Republican	1971	40	64	47	72
Republican	1972	44	66	47	64
Republican	1973	37	61	35	62
Republican	1974	39	56	44	58
Republican	1975	47	68	38	63
Republican	1976	39	62	32	63
Democrat	1977	70	52	63	42
Democrat	1978	66	41	60	36
Democrat	1979	68	47	64	34
Democrat	1980	62	45	63	40
Republican	1981	49	80	42	68
Republican	1982	43	74	39	64
Republican	1983	42	73	28	70
Republican	1984	41	76	34	60
Republican	1985	35	75	30	67
Republican	1986	38	79	25	66
Republican	1987	36	64	24	62
Republican	1988	47	68	25	57
Republican	1989	55	82	36	69
Republican	1990	38	70	25	63

Source Data from *Congressional Quarterly Almanacs* for each year through 1989; 1990 data from *Congressional Quarterly Weekly Report,* December 23, 1990, p. 408.

the economy, programs of social security and insurance, wages and hours legislation, unemployment compensation, and relief and welfare programs. In Congress, a similar set of issues—government management of the economy, agricultural assistance, and social welfare—has stimulated the most partisan voting over the years.[24]

The Constituency Basis of Cohesion

The cohesiveness of the legislative parties primarily depends upon how well those parties represent the fundamental differences in interests and values

---

[24]See Aage Clausen, *How Congressmen Decide* (New York: St. Martin's, 1973).

Contrasting Cases of Republicans' Loyalty to Their President

Two congressional votes just several months apart, involving the two most important policy actions of the early Bush presidency, illustrate how different circumstances can induce divergent levels of loyalty to a president by the members of his party.

On issues involving the president's authority in foreign affairs, the congressional party is usually united in support of its president, especially when his actions are in line with their ideological convictions. Such loyalty was manifested in the January 12, 1991, vote to authorize the president to use military force if Iraq had not withdrawn by Kuwait by January 15. This resolution was supported 164–3 by House Republicans and 42–2 by Senate Republicans (but by House Democrats 86–179 and Senate Democrats 10–45).

The October 1990, votes on the Fiscal Year 1991 budget discussed earlier in this chapter, however, stand in sharp contrast to the use of force resolution. They involved a domestic policy matter in which the president had deviated from party policy and his campaign promises in order to attract the Democratic votes he needed to fulfill his legislative objective of whittling down the size of the budget deficit. On this matter, a majority of Republicans deserted the president to vote against the compromise package he had negotiated with Democratic leaders.

within the electorate. Party cohesion is greatest where politics is most competitive along party lines—along two-party lines in the United States, of course. One-partyism in a legislature invites the disintegrating squabbles of factions and regional or personal cliques within the dominant party. The South, therefore, has been the region of the least cohesive legislative parties. Representatives from the one-party South also were the ones most responsible for undermining the cohesion of the Democratic majority in Congress during much of the post-World War II period.

Party cohesion, furthermore, typically has reached its maximum in the legislatures of urban, industrialized states. The key here—and perhaps the key to the entire riddle of legislative party cohesion—is in the types of constituencies the different parties represent. In these urban, industrial states, the parties tend to divide the constituencies along the urban-rural and SES lines that have most differentiated the parties during the New Deal party system, and they develop an issue-oriented politics that reflects those lines. Party cohesion in the legislature, therefore, reflects the relative homogeneity of the interests and constituencies the party represents. Moreover, the legislators of one party usually have different backgrounds and life-styles from those of the legislators of the other party; that is, differences in their own values and experiences reinforce the party differences in constituencies. Thus, in such state legislatures, an attempt to change eligibility for an unemployment compensation program will put two cohesive parties in sharp opposition, with the prolabor and pro-management sides each reinforced by their roots in their home districts and by their own lives and values.

In the broader historical perspective, the constituency bases of party cohesion have been found to vary with changes in the cleavages underlying the party system described in Chapter 6. As realignments of partisan forces have transformed the party systems over the course of American history, the issues that dominate interparty conflict and consequently form the bases of legislative party cohesion have changed. Slavery and Reconstruction may have generated the greatest interparty conflict and intraparty cohesion around the time of the Civil War, but they were displaced by issues centered around agrarian-industrial conflicts by the realignment of 1896. If issues of social welfare and government management of the economy have come to produce the greatest party voting since the 1930s, it is because they capture best the differences between the Democratic and Republican parties during the New Deal party system. These issues in turn may give way to a new set of issues (e.g., affirmative action, abortion, America's role in the world) to define interparty conflict if a new party system emerges. The parties, in short, should not be expected to divide sharply on all issues that come before the legislature, but rather they will be most distinctive on those policy matters closest to the electoral cleavage underlying the current party system.[25]

It also is notable that the party voting in the House described in Figure 14.2 generally has peaked during partisan realignments. By focusing attention on national rather than local issues and thereby overcoming the inherent localism of Congress, as well as inducing membership turnover and a larger majority party, realignments promote party unity on the issues most central to the new party cleavage and thereby permit a degree of party responsibilitiy that is rare in the American political systems. This newly "responsible" majority party is then in a position to enact the major policy changes that we have come to associate with realignments.[26]

Corresponding declines in party voting and party cohesion are associated with the aging of the prevailing party system and partisan dealignment.[27] Low

[25]This theme underlies such diverse historical studies of party voting in the House of Representatives as Jerome M. Clubb and Santa A. Traugott, "Partisan Cleavage and Cohesion in the House of Representatives, 1861–1974," *Journal of Interdisciplinary History* 7 (1977): 374–401; David W. Brady and Philip Althoff, "Party Voting in the U.S. House of Representatives, 1890–1910: Elements of a Responsible Party System," *Journal of Politics* 36 (1974): 752–75; and Barbara Sinclair, "Party Realignment and the Transformation of the Political Agenda: The House of Representatives, 1925–1938," *American Political Science Review* 71 (1977): 940–53.

[26]David W. Brady, "A Reevaluation of Realignments in American Politics: Evidence from the House of Representatives," *American Political Science Review* 79 (1985): 28–49; and *Critical Elections and Congressional Policy Making* (Stanford, Cal.: Stanford University Press, 1988).

[27]See Paul Allen Beck, "The Electoral Cycle and Patterns of American Politics," *British Journal of Political Science* 9 (1979): 129–56.

levels of party voting through the 1970s, therefore, may be attributable to the obsolescence of the New Deal party system and, as a consequence of electoral dealignment, the increasing insulation of incumbents from partisan tides. The enhanced levels of party voting in the early 1980s, then, may be yet another sign that the long-awaited realignment has finally arrived.

While they are the principal basis of party cohesion in the states and Congress, it must be acknowledged that constituency pressures also can form a stubborn barrier to cohesion. On some legislative issues, the representative must bend to constituency wishes in opposition to the party position, acting more or less as an instructed *delegate*, if he or she wishes to be reelected. Party leaders rarely demand the member's loyalty in this situation. A study of the congruence between constituency opinion and the representative's vote in the 1958 U.S. House of Representatives found delegate-like behavior on civil rights issues, for example, especially in the South where constituency pressures were intense. So powerful were constituency pressures on that issue in Arkansas that an incumbent U.S. Representative, who defied anti-integration constituency sentiment by attempting to mediate the tense confrontation over desegregation of the Little Rock schools, was unseated by a *write-in* segregationist candidate in the general elections.[28] As long as the party can not protect legislators from such constituency pressures, it stands to reason that party cohesion will suffer.

The Other Bases of Cohesion

Clear and unmistakable though the constituency bases of party regularity may be, they do not explain all party cohesion in American legislatures. The parties as operating political organizations account for some. Centralization of the party leadership in Congress has been linked to high levels of party voting during the 1881 and 1911 period, and the weakening of the party leadership since then surely is in part responsible for the lower levels of party voting in the twentieth century.[29] Daily caucuses, party representatives roaming the legislative corridors, and the party pressures of a vigorous governor or powerful party leader enhance cohesion in some of the states today. These party leaders often control resources of considerable value to the individual legislator, which can serve as a carrot or stick to secure compliance with the leader's wishes. Assignment as the chair or member of a key committee, campaign contributions at the critical point of a close reelection contest, and endorsements from prominent party leaders are particularly effective at the state level where legislators are less able to go it alone in election campaigns. Whatever actual organizational pressure the legislator feels, however, rarely comes from the local party, which, if it makes any demands at all, generally makes them on purely local, service issues.

---

[28]Warren E. Miller and Donald E. Stokes, "Constituency Influence in Congress," *American Political Science Review* 57 (1963): 45–57.

[29]Brady and Althoff, "Party Voting in the U.S. House of Representatives," 752–75.

The local party is much more concerned with matters of local interest and its own perquisities than it is with questions of state or national policy.[30]

Party regularity may also be related to the political competitiveness of the legislator's constituency. Legislators from the unsafe, marginal districts with finely balanced parties are more likely to defect from their fellow partisans in the legislature than are those from the safer districts. To be sure, it is likely that many of these marginal districts are the districts with SES characteristics atypical of the parties' usual constituencies. Marginality may also be a product, however, of the organizational strength of the opposing party or the appeal of its candidates, which in turn forces the legislator to be more than usually sensitive to the constituency.

Since the 1950s, there has been a considerable decline in competition for congressional seats—in, that is, the number of marginal districts. House incumbents have become more secure in their seats than probably ever before, with their reelection defeats largely attributable to redistricting or personal scandal. This phenomenon may contribute to the increased party voting and party cohesion found in the recent House. It also has implications for democratic accountability, of individual representatives as well as the House of Representatives as a whole.[31]

Finally, as obvious and even banal as it may seem, parties must cohere in order to get the business of the legislature conducted. If bills are to be passed and the public's business done, majorities must be put together. Putting together those majorities is the prime task of the leadership of the majority party. In truth, that leadership is far more likely to be concerned with the smooth operation of the legislative body than with the enactment of some stated party policy, which often leads it to settle for compromise solutions rather than complete policy victories. The leadership is also persuasive and influential at least in part because it dominates the group life of the legislative party and controls access to its esteem and camaraderie.

LEGISLATIVE PARTIES AND PARTY GOVERNMENT

Even though party cohesion in American legislatures falls far short of the standards of some parliamentary parties, it remains the most powerful determinant

---

[30]David M. Olson, "U.S. Congressmen and Their Diverse Congressional District Parties," *Legislative Studies Quarterly* 3 (1978): 239–64.

[31]See, *inter alia*, David R. Mayhew, "Congressional Elections: The Case of the Vanishing Marginals," *Polity* 6 (1974): 295–17; and Monica Bauer and John R. Hibbing, "Which Incumbents Lose in House Elections: A Response to Jacobson's 'The Marginals Never Vanished,'" *American Journal of Political Science* 33 (1989): 262–71. For evidence that incumbent House members may not have become so safe after all, at least during the most of the 1970s, however, see Gary Jacobson, "The Marginals Never Vanished: Incumbency and Competition in Elections to the U.S. House of Representatives," *American Journal of Political Science* 31 (1987): 126–41.

of roll call voting within them. Party affiliation goes further to explain the legislative behavior of American legislators than any other single factor in the legislator's environment. Legislators' normal dispositions seem to be to support the leadership of their party unless some particularly pressing consideration intervenes. All other things being equal (i.e., being quiescent and not demanding), party loyalty usually gets their votes.[32]

Yet, despite the relative importance of party cohesion, the fact remains that most American legislative parties achieve only modest levels of cohesion. Party lines are often obliterated in the coalitions that enact important legislation. Interest groups, powerful governors, local political leaders, influential legislative leaders—all contend with the legislative party for the ability to organize legislative majorities. In this system of fragmented legislative power, the legislative party governs only occasionally. It often finds itself in conflict with other party voices in the struggle to mobilize majorities in the legislatures. Governors or presidents, as party leaders and expounders of the party platform, may find themselves repeatedly at odds with legislators of their party whose roots are deeply implanted in local, virtually autonomous electorates.

Thus, the fragmenting institutions of American government once again have their impact. With the separation of powers, there is no institutionalized need for party cohesion, as there is in the parliamentary systems.[33] It is possible for government in the United States to act, even to govern, without disciplined party support in the legislature. In fact, at those times when one party controls both houses of Congress and the other controls the presidency—or one controls both houses of the state legislature and the other the governorship—it would be difficult to govern if high levels of cohesion behind an a priori program *did* prevail in each party.

Even when one finds party cohesion or discipline in an American legislature, however, party government or party responsibility need not result. Cohesion is a necessary but not sufficient condition of responsibility—and there's the rub. The American legislative party tends to have only the most tenuous

---

[32]Political ideology of course provides a powerful explanation of legislators' votes, and some scholars have even argued that it can account for most voting behavior in the Congress. But ideology is not an *external* referent that guides roll call voting but rather a reflection of the legislator's *personal* belief system. Therefore, it influences party loyalties and party voting, so we leave it for treatment in Chapter 16. On the importance of ideological voting in the Congress, see Keith T. Poole, "Recent Developments in Analytical Models of Voting in the U.S. Congress," *Legislative Studies Quarterly* 13 (1988): 117–33; and Jerrold Schneider, *Ideological Coalitions in Congress* (Westport, Conn.: Greenwood Press, 1979).

[33]Studies of legislative party voting in Britain and Canada suggest that it is the parliamentary form more than anything else that accounts for greater party cohesion there than in the United States. On Britain, see Austin Ranney, "Candidate Selection and Party Cohesion in Britain and the U.S.," in William J. Crotty (ed.), *Approaches to the Study of Party Organization* (Boston: Allyn and Bacon, 1968), pp. 139–68. On Canada, see Leon D. Epstein, "A Comparative Study of Canadian Parties," *American Political Science Review* 58 (1964): 46–59; and Allan Kornberg, "Caucus and Cohesion in Canadian Parliamentary Parties," *American Political Science Review* 60 (1966): 83–92.

ties to the various units of the party organization. The legislative parties of Congress do not recognize the equality—much less the superiority—of the party's national committee. Many state legislative parties similarly escape any effective control, or even any persistent influence, by their state party committees. Nor do the legislative parties have a great deal of contact with local party organizations. Many legislators depend on personal organizations for reelection help, and even those who rely on the party at election time receive no advice from the party back home during the legislative session. Local party organizations do not often sustain enough activity between elections to keep even the most fleeting supervisory watch over their legislators.

The American legislative party, therefore, has often found it easy to remain aloof from and independent of the party organization and its platforms and program commitments. The legislative party creates the major part of its own cohesion, employing its own persuasions, sanctions, and rewards. What discipline it commands generally serves a program or a set of proposals that originates in the executive or within the legislative party itself. Only rarely is the legislative party in any sense redeeming earlier programmatic commitments or accepting the overriding discipline of the party organization. As a legislative party, it is politically self-sufficient; it controls its own rewards to a considerable extent. In some cases, it also attempts to control its own political future; the party campaign committees of both houses of Congress are good examples. So long as the members of the legislative party can protect their own renomination and reelection, they can keep the rest of the party at arm's length.

This freedom—or irresponsibility, if one prefers—of the American legislative party grows in large part from its unity and homogeneity of interests in a total party structure where disorder and disunity prevail. Even if local party organizations were to establish supervisory relationships with their legislators, no party responsibility would result unless those relationships were unified and integrated within the state as a whole. In other words, there exists no unified political party that could establish some control over and responsibility for the actions of its legislative party. There is only a party divided geographically along the lines of American federalism, functionally along the dimensions of the separation of powers, and politically by the differing goals and commitments its various participants bring to it.

At the most, therefore, the American legislative parties are tied to the rest of their parties by some agreement on an inarticulate ideology of common interests, attitudes, and loyalties. In many state legislatures and in the United States Congress, the mute ideology of one party and its majority districts differs enough (even though roughly) from that of the other party to promote the tensions of interparty disagreement and intraparty cohesion. These modal sets of interests and attitudes—we most often give them the imprecise labels "liberal" and "conservative"—may or may not find expression in platforms, and they may or may not be articulated or supported by the party organizations. Legislative parties may even ignore them in the short run. Nonetheless, they are there, and they are the chief centripetal force in a political party that has difficulty articulating a central set of goals for all its activists and adherents. Whether this inarticulate ideology can produce a measure of party responsibility is another question, however, and it will wait until the considerations of Chapter 16.

Chapter

15

The Party in the Executive and Judiciary

The American involvement of the executive and the courts in party politics stems in considerable part from the traditions of nineteenth-century popular democracy. The framers of the American Constitution saw to it that the president would be independent from the legislative branch of government to a degree that is unparalleled in a modern-day democratic world dominated by parliamentary governments. But it was not until the emergence of the presidency as a popularly elected office in the early 1800s that it became possible for the president to be a party leader at the national level as many governors had long been in their states.

These forces for popular democracy have enabled party politics to penetrate even more deeply into the executive and to extend to the judiciary as well. The belief that democratic control can best be guaranteed through the ballot box led to the long ballot, on which judges and all manner of administrative officials (from local coroners to state auditors) were elected. Popular election led easily to party influences in those elections. At the same time, the tenets of Jacksonian democracy supported the spoils system and the value of turnover in office, justifying the use of party influence in appointments to administrative office. Thus, in the name of popular democracy, the access of parties to the executive and judicial branches was established to an extent quite unknown in the other Western democracies.

It is one thing for the political party to influence—or even control—the recruitment or selection of officeholders. It is quite another, however, for it to mobilize them in the exercise of their powers of office. The parties have had success in mobilizing American legislatures. The pertinent question here is whether they have had equal success with the executive and judicial branches. In other words, in the decisions that affect us all, has it made any difference that the men and women making them have been selected by a party? Does the pursuit of public office by the political parties serve only their internal organizational needs for rewards and incentives, or does it also promote party positions and programs?

THE EXECUTIVE AS A PARTY LEADER

The twentieth century has been a century of political leadership of mass publics, both in the democracies and in the dictatorships of the world. In the democracies, electorates have expanded to include virtually all adults. At the same time, the revolutions in mass media and communications have brought political leaders closer than ever to the electorates. In the United States, these changes have culminated in the personal leadership of the presidency in the twentieth century—a trend summed up by merely listing such names as Wilson, Roosevelt, Eisenhower, Kennedy, and Reagan, names that signify both executive power and a personal tie to millions of American citizens. The post-Watergate reaction against the "imperial presidency" only temporarily stalled the trend. Even the parliamentary systems and their prime ministers have been energized by the growth of personal leadership, and their election campaigns increasingly center on the potential prime ministers.[1]

Unquestionably, one major ingredient of executive leadership in the United States has been leadership of a mass political party. When Andrew Jackson combined the contest for executive office with leadership of a popular political party, he began a revolution in both the American presidency and the American political party. The presidency ceased to be the repository of elitist good sense and conservatism that Hamilton hoped it would be and became, slowly and fitfully, an agency of mass political leadership. Ultimately, it was the president rather than the Congress who became the tribune of the people in the American political system. Popular democracy found its two chief agents—a popularly elected leader and a mass political party—merged in the American chief executive, the power of the office reinforced by the power of the party.

It is easy to speak glibly of the American chief executive as the leader of a party. The specific components of leadership are more elusive, however, for the president and governors rarely are formal party leaders. National and state party chairpersons hold that responsibility. The chief executive's role as party leader is really a subtle, complex combination of a number of overlapping partisan roles. Among them, certainly, are the roles discussed below.

Party Leader as Representative of the Whole Constituency

One of the unique features of the American system is that the president and the Congress represent different constituencies. The national constituency the president represents differs from the sum total of the congressional constituencies. Whereas the congressional constituencies are local and particularistic ones that (especially in the Senate) collectively overrepresent the rural areas of the country, the president's constituency overrepresents the large, urban, industrial

---

[1]See Clive Bean and Anthony Mughan, "Leadership Effects in Parliamentary Elections in Australia and Britain," *American Political Science Review* 83 (1989): 1165–80.

states on which the electoral college places such a premium. It is a constituency that often makes its incumbent more committed to government responsibility for solutions to national problems than the congressional party is. Furthermore, since his is the only truly national constituency—especially in contrast to the localism of the congressional party—the president or the presidential candidate is the only candidate of the national party. Apart from the party's national convention, he is its only manifestation.

Many of the same observations may be made of the American governors. They, too, represent the entire state in contrast to the local ties of the state legislators. Other public officials may also have statewide constituencies (the constitution writers of many states have seen fit to elect such officials as treasurers, attorneys general, and state insurance commissioners), but unlike these less known fellow executives, the governor embodies the party on the statewide level. He or she is the political executive and is so recognized by the voters of the states. Like the president, most governors must make political and policy records appealing to the voters of the entire state, and like him, they embody concern for the problems of the whole constituency.

Party Leader as Organizational Leader

At the same time, the American executive may choose to be concerned with the organizational affairs of his political party. Some, like President Eisenhower in the 1950s, may consciously cultivate an image of being above partisan politics.[2] But far more common is the president who recognizes that for millions of Americans he symbolizes his party and who takes seriously his partisan leadership role. Ronald Reagan, for example, championed his party's cause more actively than perhaps any president since Franklin Roosevelt. Lyndon Johnson drew on years of experience in American politics to involve himself in the Democratic National Committee and, through it, in state and local party politics.

The president's greatest influence in the business of the party organization rests in his control of the national party committee. Its chairperson must be acceptable to him, and in many instances is actually selected by him (see box). The president also is free to shape the committee's role, even if only to turn it into his personal campaign organization. Presidents' relationships with state and local party organizations, however, have become increasingly attenuated. Presidents are less and less willing to put their executive appointments to the political uses of those party organizations. They are now virtually unwilling to do the kind of "party building"—strengthening of state parties and their leadership—that presidents routinely did early in the century. While President Reagan campaigned unusually hard for Republican candidates, particularly in

---

[2]Fred Greenstein finds persuasive evidence that Eisenhower's public avoidance of partisan politics masked, in his characteristic "hidden hand" fashion, an abiding sense of partisanship and a commitment to strengthening the Republican party. See his "Eisenhower As an Activist President: A Look at New Evidence," *Political Science Quarterly* 94 (1979–80): 575–99.

The President Chooses the RNC Chair

In principle, national committee chairs are selected by the vote of the national party committee. In practice, when a party controls the presidency, it is the White House that chooses the chair, and the national committee merely ratifies that choice. There is no better illustration of this practice than the selection of a Republican National Committee Chairman to replace Lee Atwater in 1990–91 by President Bush. On November 30, 1990, ignoring any pretense that this was an RNC decision, President Bush announced his choice of William J. Bennett for the position at a news conference. Bennett was to be confirmed by the RNC at its January meeting. Soon thereafter, Bennett announced that he did not want the job after all. By early January, the White House had settled on Clayton Yeutter as Bennett's replacement. He was confirmed by the RNC, without dissent, at its January 25, 1991 meeting. Throughout this entire period, there was never any suggestion that anyone but President Bush should be choosing the national committee chair, and all of the activity concerning the appointment emanated from the White House.

---

the midterm congressional elections, the extensive "party building" efforts of the Republican National Committee have been largely independent of the White House. Moreover, the national committee and state party organizations of the president have lost virtually all of their role in making executive appointments to the president's immediate White House staff.[3] Presidents now use their appointments for governing and for protecting their own political positions—rather than for rewarding various party factions.

To find a way through all the thickets of party politics, presidents do not usually rely on the national committee or its officers. Earlier in this century, presidents used the cabinet position of postmaster general as the post for an advisor knowledgeable in the intricacies of the party's many organizations. Franklin Roosevelt relied on James Farley, and Dwight Eisenhower chose Arthur Summerfield; each had extensive party organizational experience, and each served simultaneously as the national party chairman. This was the tradition that Lyndon Johnson honored in 1965 by appointing Lawrence O'Brien, his predecessor's shrewdest political counselor, as his postmaster general. Now that the postal service is reorganized and the postmaster general no longer sits in the cabinet, political advisors hold positions on the White House staff. The exception was Lee Atwater, who initially served as President Bush's top political advisor from his position as chairman of the Republican National Committee. After health problems prevented Atwater from continuing in that role, the

---

[3]Roger G. Brown, "Party and Bureaucracy: From Kennedy to Reagan," *Political Science Quarterly* 97 (1982): 279–94.

President returned to the practice of depending upon his immediate staff for political advice.

Party Leader as Electoral Leader

The common sense of the executive's role as electoral leader is that executives, by their successes or failures and by their popularity or lack of it, affect the electoral fortunes of other office-seekers of their party. One sees, for example, a strong correspondence between the fortunes of presidents and their parties. Lyndon Johnson's landslide victory over Barry Goldwater in 1964 was accompanied by a sharp upturn in Democratic fortunes in congressional elections. That landslide also swept Democratic parties to power in the states. The presence of Ronald Reagan on the ticket in both 1980 and 1984 similarly was associated with higher than normal levels of support for other Republican candidates. The Republicans captured control of the Senate in the 1980 election for the first time since the election of 1952. Republican House candidates also received a higher percentage of the votes cast in the two presidential election years than in the preceding and following midterm elections, when Reagan was not a candidate.

Coattail Effects The traditional explanation for the relationship between presidential fortunes and party success has employed the old metaphor of presidential coattails. Presidents ran "at the top of the ticket," the explanation goes, and the rest of the party ticket came into office clutching and clinging to their sturdy coattails. (Nineteenth-century dress coats did have tails.) Coattail effects seemed especially prominent in the nineteenth century when, in a time when the parties printed their own ballots, it was difficult to split the ticket in voting for candidates from different parties.

Recent research has found that coattail effects in congressional elections remain significant, even though they have declined since World War II.[4] The decline appears to be related to decreased competitiveness, a result, in turn, of the increased ability of incumbent representatives to insulate themselves from external electoral forces through increased attentiveness to their districts and through their significant advantage in campaign resources over the challengers. The importance of presidential coattails also is demonstrated in the familiar phenomenon of the president's party losing seats in the U.S. House of Representatives in mid-term elections when the president is not at the top of the

[4]On presidential coattails in U.S. House elections, see Randall L. Calvert and John A. Ferejohn, "Coattail Voting in Recent Presidential Elections," *American Political Science Review* 77 (1983): 407–19; John A. Ferejohn and Randall L. Calvert, "Presidential Coattails in Historical Perspective," *American Journal of Political Science* 28 (1984): 127–46; Richard Born, "Reassessing the Decline of Presidential Coattails: U.S. House Elections from 1952–80," *Journal of Politics* 46 (1984): 60–79; and James E. Campbell, "Predicting Seat Gains from Presidential Coattails," *American Journal of Political Science* 30 (1986): 164–83.

ticket. In the 1990 elections, for example, the GOP lost eight House seats and one Senate seat even though George Bush's coattails seemed unusually weak two years before.

Both the significance of coattail effects and their limits can be seen in election outcomes in the 1980s for the House of Representatives. Sizable Reagan presidential victories in 1980 and 1984 were accompanied by GOP gains in votes for and ultimately seats in the House, but these gains were modest and left the party far short of achieving majority status. In 1980, an increase from 45 to 48 percent in the vote for House GOP candidates gave them thirty-five more seats, bringing the Republicans to 44 percent of the total. In 1984, in spite of a larger Reagan presidential victory, his party picked up only seventeen more House seats, leaving them ten short of the total they had won four years before. And in 1988, even though George Bush defeated Michael Dukakis 54 to 46 percent in the popular vote, the Republicans actually *lost* two seats in the House of Representatives.

Presidential coattails appear to extend beyond House elections to contests for the state legislature and for the U.S. Senate.[5] From 1944 through 1984, when a president ran strongly in a state, the president's party typically did better in state legislative contests on the same ballot. The presidential effect on state legislative races, however, was somewhat less than on congressional contests. That presidential coattails seemed significant in many Senate elections from 1972 to 1988 may be even more surprising, considering the high visibility of contestants for this office. This demonstrates the pervasiveness of presidential coattails.

The president's influence on election results for other contests may not be restricted solely to when he is on the ballot. In the years of the mid-term congressional elections, the intention of voters to vote for candidates of the president's party fluctuates during the campaign with the level of their approval of how the president is managing the presidency as measured by questions such as the Gallup organization's familiar "Do you approve or disapprove of the way George Bush is handling his job as president?" There has been a substantial relationship between presidential approval and midterm seat gains (or losses) since the late 1930s and early 1940s.[6] This relationship, though, seems to have

---

[5]See James E. Campbell, "Presidential Coattails and Midterm Losses in State Legislative Elections," *American Political Science Review* 80 (1986): 45–63; and James E. Campbell and Joe A. Sumners, "Presidential Coattails in Senate Elections," *American Political Science Review* 84 (1990): 512–24. The first Campbell study finds evidence of gubernatorial coattails as well.

[6]This view that midterm congressional contests are in part a referendum on presidential performance was initially offered by Edward R. Tufte, "Determinants of the Outcomes of Midterm Congressional Elections," *American Political Science Review* 69 (1975): 812–26; and *Political Control of the Economy* (Princeton, N.J.: Princeton University Press, 1978), Chap. 5. Even more persuasive evidence of the relationship between presidential approval and mid-term congressional outcomes may be found in Robin F. Marra and Charles W. Ostrom, Jr., "Explaining Seat Change in the U.S. House of Representatives, 1950–86," *American Journal of Political Science* 33 (1989): 541–69.

been attenuated in at least one recent mid-term election. In 1986, President Reagan's popularity had soared to unprecedented heights (before postelection revelations about the Iran-contra affair brought it back down), yet the Republicans lost eight Senate seats (and their majority) and five seats in the House of Representatives.

Where does all of this leave the American president as electoral leader of his party? First of all, presidential coattails extend to a variety of legislative contests on the same ticket, and the popularity of the president even influences congressional election outcomes when he is not on the ballot. An important component of the president's electoral leadership, then, is the tendency for voters to be influenced by his standing in casting ballots for other offices—and, of course, the knowledge that his partisan running mates and their potential challengers have of the significance of the relationship.[7]

Second, the impact of his popularity and his coattails seems not to be what it once was. That fact reduces both an important aspect of his party leadership and an important source of his influence over the Congress. Even if presidential influence accounts for only small percentage shifts in the total vote, however, small shifts can have a significant impact on party strength in the Congress. From 1952 to 1970, each shift of 1 percent in the popular vote added or subtracted about eight seats in the House of Representatives.[8] Even though House seats may have become less responsive to popular vote changes since, the balance in Congress between conservative and liberal forces and the less than perfect levels of party cohesion allow even a small shift in seats to have an important bearing on policymaking.

Also, voters do continue to evaluate presidential performance. This popular support is a valuable resource for the chief executive in getting Congress to go along with his programs. In the first year of the Reagan administration, for example, President Reagan's popularity in the country could be credited in part for his considerable success on the Hill. There also is some suggestion that voters who disapprove of presidential performance vote in larger numbers in mid-term elections than those who approve, and that their negativism leads them to

---

[7]An attractive "strategic politicians" explanation for this relationship has been offered by Gary Jacobsen. Rather than voters explicitly linking presidents to legislators, the Jacobsen thesis is that presidential popularity and other factors impinging upon the standing of the party determine the quality of candidates (especially challengers) in the president's party which, in turn, affects outcomes in the fall election. See his "Strategic Politicians and the Dynamics of U.S. House Elections, 1946–86," *American Political Science Review* 83 (1989): 773–93.

[8]This translation of votes into seats is based on the swing ratio calculated by Edward R. Tufte in "The Relationship between Seats and Votes in Two-Party Systems," *American Political Science Review* 67 (1973): 540–54. The swing ratio declined sharply to a low of 0.71 in 1966–70 and may have stayed at that level since, which means that only 0.71 percent of 435 seats (or 3 seats) changed hands for each 1 percent vote change.

prefer the other party and its candidates.[9] It is also very likely that perceptions and evaluations of the president (and governor) affect the way individuals view the parties. Executive programs are party programs, and the successes and failures of executives are party successes and failures. For a public that views politics chiefly in personal terms, a president or a governor is the personification of the party. Finally, the fund-raising capabilities of a popular president confer considerable advantages on his party's candidates, especially the ones he favors. This gives the president important leverage over party office seekers.

Limits on Electoral Leadership   Imposing as these ties between the chief executive and the party may be, they are not without real and tangible limits. First of all, the executive may be limited by his own political experience and taste for political leadership. Some presidents and governors do not want to lead a party, or they do not think it proper for an executive to do so. They find it politically advantageous to remain "above" party politics. Even those who do want to be party leaders may find that the representational demands of the office—the pressures to be a president or governor of "all of the people"—limit their partisan work and identification.

Presidents and governors also may lead only part of a party. Governors from one-party states, for example, often lead only a party faction. Executives also may share leadership of the party with other partisans. Presidents who are not especially secure in national party affairs may find the more experienced leaders of the congressional party asserting major leadership in the national party. Governors may find senators, who represent as broad a constituency, and representatives of their party pressing parallel leadership claims over the state party. These legislators and state party leaders may fear that the governor will use party control for his or her own political ambitions.

The Executive-Centered Party   Nonetheless, the president heads, and occasionally even unifies, the national party. He dominates the national committee and the rest of the national organization, and, through a combination of his powers of office and his party leverage, he often exerts enough mastery of the legislative party to speak for the party in government. Most important, per-

---

[9]Samuel Kernell, "Presidential Popularity and Negative Voting: An Alternative Explanation of the Midterm Congressional Decline of the President's Party," *American Political Science Review* 71 (1977): 44–66. The negative voting thesis, though, has been challenged by Richard Born, who concludes that it is the return of presidential defectors to their home party and not negative voting that accounts for the presidential party's loss of seats at mid-term. See his "Surge and Decline, Negative Voting, and the Midterm Loss Phenomenon: A Simultaneous Choice Analysis," *American Journal of Political Science* 34 (1990): 615–45. An alternative surge and decline explanation, based on the withdrawal of nonpartisans from the mid-term election, is found in Angus Campbell, "Surge and Decline: A Study of Electoral Change," in Angus Campbell, Philip E. Converse, Warren E. Miller, and Donald E. Stokes (eds.), *Elections and the Political Order* (New York: Wiley, 1966), pp. 40–62.

haps, for millions of American voters he is the symbol of the party, its programs, and its performance. The national constituency is his, and his nomination and campaign are the chief activities of the national party. They are the only activities with any visibility in this age of media politics. Within the state parties, the governors have the same unifying, symbolizing role, and they, too, have their leverage on legislative parties and state organizations.[10]

Therefore, it is no exaggeration to speak of the American parties as executive-centered coalitions. No alternative leader can compete with the executive in representing the party to the public, in commanding a broad array of tools of influence, or in enjoying as much legitimacy as the center of party leadership. Even in the party out of power, the executive office and its opportunities dominate. Opposition to the other party's executive and his coalition, as well as planning for the next election's assault on the office, provide the chief unifying focus. Moreover, it is the headless quality of the party out of power that most typifies its melancholy condition.

To some extent, the executive-centered party is a coalition of the executive-dominated party in government with the party in the electorate. That alliance, of necessity, bypasses the party organization. The identifications and loyalties of voters are not to the party organization but to the party symbols, the meaning for which comes largely from executives and their programs. The men and women of the party in government often build their own supporting organizations and thus bypass the party organizations in their quest for office. Even in the use of patronage, executives maximize support for their programs and their own political futures rather than maintain or rebuild the strength of the party organization.

Once in office, executives generally put the leverage they derive from their position as party leaders into the business of governing, rather than into any concern for the party as an organization. The president, for example, finds himself without sufficient constitutional powers to hold his own in the struggles of the American separation of powers. Indeed, if the proverbial man from Mars should obtain a copy of the United States Constitution, he could not imagine from its niggardly grants of power to the president what the office has come to be. American presidents, faced with that shortage of formal powers, have had to rely heavily on their extraconstitutional powers. They derive an important portion of those powers from party leadership.

PARTY LEADERSHIP AND LEGISLATIVE RELATIONS

The American chief executive does not possess a large area of policymaking autonomy. Aside from the president's primacy in the fields of defense and international relations, little major policymaking power is reserved solely

---

[10]On the role of the governor in party leadership, see Lynn Muchmore, "The Governor as Party Leader," *State Government* 53 (1980), 121–24.

for the American executive. What impact the executive is to have on the making of policy or on the enacting of a party program largely must come about through the formal actions of the legislature. In this pursuit of policy by influencing a legislature, the president and the governors turn repeatedly to the ties of party.

The coordination of legislative and executive decision making under the aegis of a political party is not easily accomplished, however. The possibility of divided control of government in the American system is a formidable obstacle to legislative-executive cooperation. Between 1968 and 1992, for example, the president's party controlled Congress for only four years, and all but three states plus nonpartisan Nebraska experienced divided party control of the legislature and the governorship. At such times, the executives often have no choice but to minimize partisan appeals. In view of the closeness of the party division in many legislatures and the unreliability of some legislators of their own party, they must also curry the favor of some legislators of the opposing party. Thus, the president and the governors follow a mixed strategy: partisan appeals and sanctions for their own party and nonpartisan or bipartisan politics for those of the opposition.

The role of the president vis-à-vis the Congress is too well known to require a great deal of repetition here. Presidents rely on their nonparty sources of leadership, of course—their prestige and persuasiveness, their command of the communications media, their own attention and favors. Overtly or not, they also use their identification with the party, the lingering patronage, their ability to influence coming elections. Members of the president's party know that if they make him look bad, to some extent they also make themselves and their party look bad. That awareness surely accounts for their tendency to rally around a presidential veto despite their own legislative preferences (Table 15.1). Nor can they escape the fact that the president heads the party ticket when he runs and that his performance becomes the party's record when he does not. In fact, members of Congress who benefited in the past from presidential coattails are more likely to support the president's program than those who did not. Legislators thus appear both to anticipate and to react to presidential leadership at the polls. The president figures even more prominently in legislators' hopes and fears of a change in the competitive position of their party and, by extension, themselves. Only he has sufficient political visibility to seize the opportunities to move party supporters or opponents into a partisan realignment, or by incautious misstep to turn the mood of the moment against the party as happened with the Watergate affair.

Even so, Congress is often stubbornly resistant to presidential leadership, and recent presidents have been successful only about half of the time in securing congressional approval of measures they endorse. There are signs, moreover, that the president's party leverage in the Congress is less than it once was. On the whole, presidential success rates in winning support for their programs in the House of Representatives were slightly lower in the 1970s and 1980s than in earlier years, largely because recent presidents have more often faced a Congress controlled by the opposition party (Figure 15.1). When the difference in

Table 15.1   PRE- AND POST-VETO SUPPORT OF PRESIDENT BY HIS PARTY, 1973–90,
             SELECTED VOTES

	Percent of president's party supporting president's position	
	Original passage	Vote on veto override
President Nixon		
Vocational Rehabilitation, Senate, 1973	5	76
Water-Sewer Program, House, 1973	31	87
OMB Confirmation, Senate, 1973	52	61
OMB Confirmation, House, 1973	89	90
Cambodia Bombing Halt, House, 1973	66	72
President Ford		
Public Works Employment, House, 1976	53	59
Public Works Employment, Senate, 1976	44	68
Aid to Day Care Centers, Senate, 1976	47	70
Hatch Act Revisions, House, 1976	65	84
President Carter		
Weapons Procurement Authorization, House, 1978	26	69
Public Works Appropriations, House, 1978	18	48
Oil Import Fee Abolition, House, 1980	17	15
Oil Import Fee Abolition, Senate, 1980	12	22
President Reagan		
Standby Petroleum Allocation Act, Senate, 1982	13	62
Supplemental Appropriations, House, 1982	50	79
Supplemental Appropriations, House, 1982	27	56
Resolution against Saudi Arms Sales, Senate, 1986	41	55
South African Sanctions, House, 1986	45	49
South African Sanctions, Senate, 1986	27	40
President Bush		
FS-X Development Restrictions, Senate, 1989	56	73
Chinese Student Visa Extension, House, 1989–90	0	15
Hatch Act Revision, House, 1990	48	52
Hatch Act Revision, Senate, 1990	70	78

Source: For presidents Nixon through Reagan: Reprinted from CONGRESS, Process and Policy, Fourth Edition, by Randall B. Ripley, by permission of W. W. Norton & Company, Inc. Copyright © 1988, 1983, 1978, 1975 by W. W. Norton & Company, Inc. For President Bush, various issues of *Congressional Quarterly Weekly Report.*

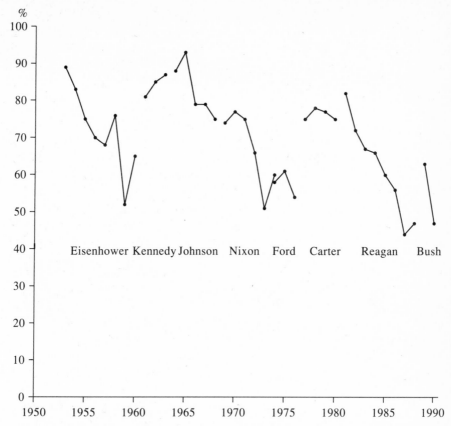

Figure 15.1 Presidential Success in the U.S. House of Representatives, 1953–90.

Source: Congressional Quarterly Weekly Report, December 22, 1990, 4208.

party between the President and the House majority is taken into account, though, presidential success still is lower than in the 1950s and 1960s.[11]

Important reasons for diminished presidential influence lie in new electoral realities for members of Congress. The impact of presidential coattails and presidential influence on congressional elections is somewhat lower than before. Incumbent members of Congress are increasingly secure in their constituencies. The quantity and the closeness of the competition they face are not as great as they were a few decades ago. A congressional politics of cultivating the constituency by greater attention to its interests and increased services to individual constituents secures these legislators' political futures and insulates them from

[11]In addition to the figures in Table 14.2, see George C. Edwards III, "Measuring Presidential Success in Congress: Alternative Approaches," *Journal of Politics* 47 (1985): 667–85.

the electoral influences of the presidency.[12] As they lose party leverage, then, presidents are forced back on the nonparty components of their influence. Inevitably, their role as party leaders seems less important to them.

Governors, on the other hand, are frequently in a position to exercise far greater and more direct party organizational power over the legislators of their own party. In many states, their legislatures are unbound by the traditions of seniority, and a few governors may even take an active part in selecting committee chairpersons and influential party floor leaders at the beginning of the session. They may view the party's legislative leaders as "their" leaders, chosen to steer their programs through legislative waters. They may also lead powerful, ongoing state party organizations. To cross them may be to run the risk of falling from party favor; a legislator's career in the legislature, not to mention his future ambition, may be at the mercy of a determined, politically skillful governor. In short, the average governor has far greater control over party rewards and incentives than a president does. On the other hand, in the symbolic aspects of party leadership a governor probably exerts less influence than a president. Since governors are less visible and salient than presidents, their coattails and prestige are likely to be less potent than those of presidents.

PARTY POWER AND ADMINISTRATIVE POLICY

The very size and complexity of modern government and modern society necessitates broad exercises of discretion in the administration of the laws. In spite of a burst of deregulation in the 1980s, agencies still regulate vast areas of the economy—nuclear energy, radio and TV, the banking system, for example—under only the vaguest legislative mandates. Obviously, then, any concept of party responsibility or party government cannot be restricted to legislatures. The administration clearly shapes policy in its applications, and, to be effective, party programs require sympathetic administrative leadership.

There are substantial limits, many of them resulting from Progressive reforms enacted decades ago, however, on the executive's ability to unify an administration and hold it responsible to a party program:

- The legislature may place administrative positions outside executive control by stipulating terms of appointment that last beyond a president's or governor's term, by limiting the executive's power of removal, or by placing policymakers under a merit system and tenure.
- Special precautions may also be taken to thwart partisan control of an administrative agency. Some federal agencies, especially regulatory commissions, are headed by five-person commissions or boards, but not more than three of the members of each board may be of the same political party.

---

[12]See Bruce Cain, John Ferejohn, and Morris Fiorina, *The Personal Vote: Constituency Service and Electoral Independence* (Cambridge: Harvard University Press, 1987).

- In a number of states, top administrative positions, in addition to the gubernatorial office, are filled by election. At worst, that places members of both parties—a Republican governor and a Democratic state treasurer, for example—in an uncomfortable alliance. Even if the offices are filled by candidates of the same party, they are often politically and constitutionally independent. In many ways, this plural executive system diminishes the authority of the governor.
- Furthermore, American executives suffer some diminution of political power as their terms approach a predetermined end. The Twenty-second Amendment to the United States Constitution limits the presidential term to between eight and ten years, and a majority of the states limit the gubernatorial time in office to one or two consecutive terms.
- Finally, political realities may force executives to share the instruments of party leadership with others. Senatorial courtesy and other political considerations guarantee that the Senate's confirmation of presidential appointments will be more than pro forma. Also, in forming a cabinet, the president cannot ignore the feelings and aspirations of groups within the party that contributed to his victory.

Establishing control of the executive branch, however, is far more complex than simply putting fellow partisans into positions of power. The chief executive faces essentially the same problem in enforcing party discipline on administrative subordinates that a party leader in the legislative faces. In both cases, the problem is loyalty to and the power of a constituency. Just as the legislators identify with the problems and outlooks of the citizens they know and represent, so administrators often identify with the problems and outlooks of the groups and individuals with which their agencies deal. Also, just as legislators must depend on the folks back home to protect their political careers, top-level administrators know that the support of client groups is their best personal political protection and the only protection for an agency, its mission, and its budget. In this way, the Department of Veterans Affairs enjoys the protection of the American Legion and the Veterans of Foreign Wars, and the Environmental Protection Agency depends on the support of organized naturalists and environmentalists as well as the industries it regulates. Only with the greatest difficulty does the pressure of party loyalties and party sanctions overcome the power of these administrative constituencies. In the executive as well as the legislative branch, the party has less to give and less to take away than the constituency does.

In that part of the administrative establishment closest to the chief executive lies the greatest chance of party responsibility. At these top administrative levels, the appointee often has been politically active and has associated actively with a political party. He or she has very likely come to recognize the claims of the party organization and has developed a commitment to party goals and programs. The cabinet of a president such as George Bush (see box) suggests the extent to which the political party remains a reservoir of talent, even a recruiter of talent, for modern administrations. It is undoubtedly true that

Partisan Republican Backgrounds of the Bush Cabinet

All but two of the members of President George Bush's cabinet in Summer 1991 had been active in Republican party politics as elected office-holders and candidates for office, appointees to political positions in previous Republican administrations, or campaign managers. What follows is a short sketch of the partisan political positions of each.

Lamar Alexander (Education): Republican governor of Tennessee, 1979–86.

James A. Baker III (State): Under secretary of Commerce in Ford administration; campaign manager for George Bush's Senate campaign in 1970, Gerald Ford's presidential campaign in 1976, George Bush's presidential nomination campaign in 1980, and Ronald Reagan's presidential general election campaign in 1980; White House chief of staff and treasury secretary in Reagan administration.

Nicholas F. Brady (Treasury): Appointed to fill a vacancy as Republican U.S. Senator from New Jersey, 1982; treasury secretary in Reagan administration.

Richard B. Cheney (Defense): White house chief of staff in Ford administration; Republican congressman from Wyoming, 1978–89; House minority whip.

Edward J. Derwinski (Veterans Affairs): Republican congressman from Illinois, 1959–83; under secretary of State in Reagan administration; former member of the National Republican Heritage Groups Council.

Jack F. Kemp (Housing and Urban Development): Republican congressman from New York, 1971–88; chair of Republican Congressional Conference; Republican candidate for President, 1988.

Manuel Lujan, Jr. (Interior): Republican congressman from New Mexico, 1969–89.

Edward Madigan (Agriculture): Republican congressman from Illinois, 1972–91.

Lynn Martin (Labor): Republican congresswoman from Illinois, 1981–89.

Robert Mosbacher (Commerce): Chief fund-raiser for presidential campaigns of Gerald Ford in 1976 and George Bush in 1980 and 1988.

Samuel K. Skinner (Transportation): Illinois cochair of George Bush's 1980 and 1988 presidential campaigns.

(continued)

Louis W. Sullivan (Health and Human Services): No previous partisan political activity.

Dick Thornburgh (Justice): Republican governor of Pennsylvania, 1979–1986; attorney general in Reagan administration.

James D. Watkins (Energy): No previous partisan political activity.

presidents no longer are as explicitly partisan as they once were in their cabinet appointments, that they no longer use them as rewards for party service or as symbolic rewards to some part of the party. Presidents increasingly draw on individuals with experience in the areas of policy they will administer.[13] At the same time, however, presidents largely find their appointees among those who have earlier held public office as members of the party or who have experience in the affairs of the party itself. Their political careers and their values and commitments have in some significant degree been shaped by their political party.

When one looks a step below in the administrative structure to the assistant secretary level, however, party and governmental experience may dwindle. In many administrations these individuals are most often chosen for their skills and experience in administration and only secondarily for their political credentials. In the selection of many of them, the role of the party organization may not have extended beyond determining whether they were politically acceptable (i.e., inoffensive) in their home states. Yet they continue to come largely from the party of the president. Although these positions no longer serve so frequently as party patronage, the party link is still there to guarantee a commitment to a common outlook.[14] Some administrations—the Reagan administration is a good example—have taken great pains to ensure this common political outlook. They recruit ideological sympathizers rather than just fellow partisans into executive positions, with the inevitable result that a certain tension develops between party loyalists and the ideologues in the top leadership circles of the administration. While appointing ideological sympathizers produces an even more cohesive administration in terms of policy viewpoints, it can weaken the party link and undermine the president's influence with fellow partisans in the Congress.

All things considered, the problem of political control over the executive bureaucracy is formidable, especially at the national level. Modern presidents are limited to only about 3,000 political appointees, fewer appointive positions than are available to some governors, with which to try to gain control of a federal executive branch containing almost 3 million civilian employees. Many of

---

[13]Hugh Heclo, "Issue Networks and the Executive Establishment," in Anthony King (ed.), *The New American Political System* (Washington, D.C.: American Enterprise Institute, 1979), pp. 87–124.

[14]Dean E. Mann, *The Assistant Secretaries* (Washington, D.C.: The Brookings Institution, 1965); and Brown, "Party and Bureaucracy."

the president's men and women are novices, who have little time to "learn the ropes" and little prospect of gaining the necessary support of career bureaucrats without compromising their commitment to presidential designs. Furthermore, as Hugh Heclo has so convincingly shown, together they comprise "a government of strangers"—a set of executives whose limited familiarity and interaction with one another prevent them from constituting an effective team—which is often overwhelmed by a huge, fragmented, and more or less permanent bureaucracy.[15]

It is little wonder that recent presidents have relied more and more on their immediate White House staff and the Office of Management and Budget in trying to mobilize the executive branch on behalf of their policy goals.[16] Therefore, even though party is an important instrument for presidential or gubernatorial control of the administrative bureaucracy, serving as both a recruitment channel for scarce executive talent and a common bond linking the interests of the chief executive and the top bureaucrats, it is inadequate for accomplishing the difficult task of executive leadership.

Yet, in its own way, the federal bureaucracy (and many of the state bureaucracies as well) is responsive to partisan political forces. With the expansion of the federal government in the 1930s, President Franklin Roosevelt was able to draw into the career service bureaucracy, especially to agencies handling New Deal programs, personnel committed to his programs and dedicated to implementing them through government service. They constituted a powerful bulwark against subsequent diminution of these programmatic commitments, especially as they were promoted over the years to more and more senior positions in their agencies.

Thus, it should come as no surprise that when Richard Nixon became president in 1969, he perceived that he faced a federal bureaucracy that was unsympathetic, perhaps even hostile, to his more conservative political agenda. Interviews with top career officials in domestic agencies by Joel Aberbach and Bert Rockman in 1970 showed that Nixon's perceptions were to a considerable degree anchored in reality. Just short of a majority of these career bureaucrats proclaimed that they normally voted Democratic, and only 17 percent normally voted Republican. Moreover, in the social service agencies especially, even those officials who were not Democrats tended to favor liberal policy postures. It is little wonder that the Nixon Administration devoted considerable energy to trying to control a bureaucracy with "clashing beliefs" to its own.[17]

---

[15]Hugh Heclo, *A Government of Strangers: Executive Politics in Washington* (Washington, D.C.: The Brookings Institution, 1977).

[16]See Terry M. Moe, "The Politicized Presidency," in John E. Chubb and Paul E. Peterson (eds.), *The New Direction in American Politics* (Washington, D.C.: The Brookings Institution, 1985), pp. 235–71.

[17]Joel Aberbach and Bert A. Rockman, "Clashing Beliefs Within the Executive Branch: The Nixon Administration Bureaucracy," *American Political Science Review* 70 (1976): 456–68.

By 1986–87, after the battles of the Nixon years and five full years of the Reagan presidency, the bureaucratic environment had changed. When Aberbach and Rockman returned to interview career administrators in comparable positions to those they talked to in 1970, they found a Republican plurality and many fewer liberals, although the career executives still were considerably more Democratic and liberal than the Reagan political appointees. Among the forces to which they attribute change in the partisan tenor of the bureaucracy are the turnover of civil servants through retirement and departure for other jobs (perhaps brought on by despair over the long-term Republican control of the presidency) and changes in civil service laws that allowed positions formerly reserved for career employees to be filled by political appointees, who were carefully screened by the White House. Whatever the cause, what had been "Nixon's problem" now could be credited as "Reagan's achievement," however much the inherent difficulties of controlling even a generally sympathetic bureaucracy remained.[18]

For what purposes, then, do executives use the executive party and their leadership role in it? Their power and influence go chiefly for the tasks of governing, of meeting their executive decision-making responsibilities. Only secondarily can they attend to the goals and interests of the party organization. Many governors use some chunk of their patronage purely for party goals, and presidents may use cabinet appointments to assuage and satisfy the need for recognition of various groups or factions within the party. Such concessions may satisfy the political demands of the party and build party cohesion, but they may also thwart the executive or administrative goals of the president. Ultimately, chief executives need whatever party loyalty and cohesion they can build for their own programs and, if they are in their first term, for their own reelection. It is the goals of the office, not of the party, that they pursue.

THE MYSTERIOUS CASE OF THE JUDICIAL PARTY

While custom and the privacy of decision making have subdued their visibility, political party considerations are hardly absent from the judiciary. Many American judges are political men and women, who are often drawn to the bench after careers that involved them in some aspect of partisan politics. Moreover, as much as judicial reformers have attempted to insulate the bench from politics, especially party politics, the selection of judges in many locales and states and at the federal level continues to be strongly shaped by partisanship through both elections and appointment. The very nature of the judiciary, though, makes demonstrating the influence of party on it no easy task.

---

[18]Joel Aberbach and Bert A. Rockman with Robert M. Copland, "From Nixon's Problem to Reagan's Achievement—The Federal Executive Reexamined," in Larry Berman (ed.), *Looking Back on the Reagan Presidency* (Baltimore: Johns Hopkins University Press, 1990), pp. 175–94.

Judicial Voting Along Party Lines

Nothing illustrates the difficulties of evaluating the party in office quite so clearly as the examples of cohesive party voting in American appellate courts. Several studies pointed to the presence of party-rooted blocs in state appellate courts a few decades ago in cases such as those involving workers' compensation, and there is no reason to believe that those partisan blocs have not endured into modern times. Another study, cutting across a number of states, found that Democratic and Republican judges differ significantly in the ways they decide certain types of cases. Democrats on the bench, for example, tend to decide more frequently for the defendant in criminal cases, for the government in taxation cases, for the regulatory agency in cases involving the regulation of business, and for the claimants in workers' compensation, unemployment compensation, and auto accident cases.[19] To be sure, no one suggests that the incidence of party cohesion in judicial decision making approaches that in legislatures. It appears only in certain types of cases; and the amount of disagreement within an appellate court that can be explained by party division falls far below the amount of legislative division that can be explained by partisanship. Yet there *is* party cohesion in the American judiciary.

It may infrequently happen that an American judge is swayed by some subtle persuasion of his or her political party. If it does happen, though, it doesn't happen frequently enough to explain party cohesion in the courts. The explanation rests in the different sets of values, even the different ideologies, that the major parties reflect. Quite simply, judges of the same party vote together on cases for the same reasons of values and outlook that led them to join the same political party. In other words, two judges will vote together on the issue of administrative regulation of utilities because of deep-seated values they share about the relationship of government and the economy. Those same values or perceptions led them some years earlier to join the same party, or they were developed out of experience in the same political party.

Partisan Considerations in Judicial Selection

The impact of the party on the decision-making processes of the judiciary, therefore, is indirect. It stems largely from the role of the party as symbol of its members' commitments. This should not surprise anyone, for the appointment

---

[19]See Sidney Ulmer, "The Political Party Variable on the Michigan Supreme Court," *Journal of Public Law* 11 (1962): 352–62; Stuart Nagel, "Political Party Affiliation and Judges' Decisions," *American Political Science Review* 55 (1961): 843–50; Glendon A. Schubert, *Quantitative Analysis of Judicial Behavior* (Glencoe, Ill.: Free Press, 1959), pp. 129–42; and David W. Adamany, "The Party Variable in Judges' Voting: Conceptual Notes and a Case Study," *American Political Science Review* 63 (1969): 57–73. For a review of party influence in the federal courts, see Robert A. Carp and Ronald Stidham, *The Federal Courts* (Washington, D.C.: CQ Press, 1985), 142–48.

of judges in the United States traditionally has taken the values and attitudes of judges into account. Although we have only recently accepted in any overt way the notion of judicial policymaking—the notion that, in some instances, judges have options and that in making these choices they may reflect, in part, their own prior experiences, perceptions, and values—we have acknowledged it implicitly for some time. President Theodore Roosevelt, considering a replacement for Justice Horace Gray on the Supreme Court, wrote Senator Henry Lodge to inquire about a certain Judge Oliver Wendell Holmes of the Massachusetts Supreme Court:

> In the ordinary and low sense which we attach to the words "partisan" and "politician," a judge of the Supreme Court should be neither. But in the higher sense, in the proper sense, he is not in my judgment fitted for the position unless he is a party man, a constructive statesman, constantly keeping in mind his adherence to the principles and policies under which this nation has been built up and in accordance with which it must go on.
>
> Now I should like to know that Judge Holmes was in entire sympathy with our views, that is, with your views and mine and Judge Gray's, just as we know that ex-Attorney General Knowlton is, before I would feel justified in appointing him. Judge Gray has been one of the most valuable members of the Court. I should hold myself as guilty of an irreparable wrong to the nation if I should put in his place any man who was not absolutely sane and sound on the great national policies for which we stand in public life.[20]

Congress, too, has often examined such issues in reviewing presidential nominations to the federal judiciary. In 1969 and 1970, the Senate rejected two Nixon appointees to the Supreme Court (Clement Haynesworth and G. Harold Carswell) at least partly because of the general conservatism of their views on race and labor. The major judicial confirmation battles in the Reagan years were over his nominations of outspoken conservatives Robert H. Bork to the Supreme Court and Daniel A. Manion and Jefferson B. Sessions III to lower courts. Even party platforms occasionally have stipulated criteria for judicial appointments, as the 1980 Republican platform did in calling for judges who valued the sanctity of human life.

Whether or not it should be within the province of a president or a governor to consider such matters in proposing judicial appointments, the appointee's political party and ideological loyalties serve as some indication of his or her values and attitudes. Indeed, it is one of the reasons that, in the last century, American presidents have appointed judges largely from their own parties. They have generally chosen more than 90 percent of their appointees from their own partisans, and in every case, from Cleveland through the early Bush years, the percentage has been above 80 percent (Table 15.2). The Reagan and

---

[20]The Roosevelt letter is quoted more fully in Walter F. Murphy and C. Herman Pritchett, *Courts, Judges, and Politics* (New York: Random House, 1961), pp. 82–83.

Table 15.2 PERCENTAGES OF JUDICIAL APPOINTMENTS TO FEDERAL DISTRICT AND APPEALS COURTS FROM THE PARTY OF THE PRESIDENT: GROVER CLEVELAND THROUGH GEORGE BUSH'S FIRST TWO YEARS

Cleveland	97.3	F. Roosevelt	96.4
Harrison	87.9	Truman	90.1
McKinley	95.7	Eisenhower	94.1
T. Roosevelt	95.8	Kennedy	90.1
Taft	82.2	Johnson	94.4
Wilson	98.6	Nixon	92.9
Harding	97.7	Ford	81.2
Coolidge	94.1	Carter	90.3
Hoover	85.7	Reagan	93.1
		Bush (first 2 years)	93.9

Source: Data from Evan A. Evans, "Political Influence in the Selection of Federal Judges," *Wisconsin Law Review* (May 1948), pp. 300–51; Harold W. Chase, *Federal Judges: The Appointing Process* (Minneapolis: University of Minnesota Press, 1972); and Goldman, "The Bush Imprint on the Judiciary."

early Bush appointees to the federal courts have been more partisan than the average among recent presidents, and they also stand out in the extent to which they have been active in partisan politics over the course of their lives.[21]

The Reagan and Bush administrations have taken special care to screen candidates for the desired judicial philosophy through personal interviews and evaluations of their judicial records (if they have served as judges before) and through weekly meetings of White House and Justice Department representatives to the President's Committee on Judicial Selection. The old tradition of allowing candidates for district and appellate courts to be identified by the party's Senators was modified to give the administration more influence on the final choices by asking Senators to submit three names for consideration. This overturned the Carter administration innovation of relying upon nonpartisan judicial selection committees for recommending appellate and district court candidates.[22]

There are substantial differences between the federal courts and the state courts in how judges are selected. First, four different selection methods are employed by the states—appointment (usually by the governor), partisan election, nonpartisan election, and the "Missouri plan" in which judges are selected (again, usually by the governor) from a list compiled by a nonpartisan screening committee and then must run in a retention election within several years of their appointment. Second, many states rely upon different methods of judicial selection for different courts. Third, lawyers play a more decisive role

---

[21]Sheldon Goldman, "The Bush Imprint on the Judiciary: Carrying on a Tradition," *Judicature* 74 (1991), 294–306.

[22]On the Reagan and Bush practices, see Goldman, "The Bush Imprint on the Judiciary."

in screening candidates in the states, particularly in states using the Missouri plan, where they often are the dominant influence on the ultimate choices.

By 1990, taking into account multiple methods used in many states, the states were divided fairly evenly among the four different selection methods. Appointment of judges was used by more states (twenty-seven of the fifty) than any other single method; in about half of these, however, only lower level judges were chosen in this way. Partisanship intrudes directly into the selection process in seventeen states: candidates for at least some of their judgeships must run for office in partisan elections. This partisanship is sometimes illusory, however, as both parties will endorse the same candidate, who often is the choice of the state bar association.

In most states, extensive attempts have been made to take the partisanship of appointment by a party leader or of partisan elections out of judicial selection. Nineteen states, following the Progressive tradition, elect judges on a nonpartisan ballot. But in some of these, like Ohio, it is common practice for each party to publicly endorse its own slate of candidates, so nonpartisanship is a facade. Merit selection by the Missouri plan is an increasingly popular alternative for taking partisan politics out of the judicial selection process. Not only did seventeen states employ this method in 1990, but all but one relied upon it to select the judges for their highest courts.[23]

Regardless of the selection process, partisanship is unmistakably present in most of the state judiciaries. Indeed, in a nation where the judiciary plays such an important policymaking role, it may be naive to think that the bench can be—or should be—purged of partisan influences. Many a judge selected on a nonpartisan ballot or through the Missouri plan comes to the bench with the values represented by a particular party, and party lines are often apparent in the divisions on multijudge panels no matter what selection procedure is used.

Judicial terms also tend to be so long that many elective judgeships become appointive. Death or retirement often takes a nonpartisan judge from the bench in midterm, and the vacancy is filled before the next election by a gubernatorial appointment. The political considerations attending such appointments may then prevail, and with the advantage of even a brief period of incumbency, the appointee usually wins a full, regular term at the next election. Only the low probabilities of defeat in retention elections may free appointed judges from partisan pressures, but they are so often already internalized in the judge's values and preferences that a long-term judgeship merely allows them to flourish.[24]

---

[23]These data on judicial selection in the states come from *The Book of the States: 1990–91* (Lexington, Ky.: Council of State Governments, 1990), pp. 210–12.

[24]On the political effects of different state selection systems, see Henry R. Glick and Craig F. Emmert, "Selection Systems and Judicial Characteristics: The Recruitment of State Supreme Court Judges," *Judicature* 70 (Dec/Jan, 1987), 228–35.

The point, then, comes down to this. There is no way to eliminate the important political frames of reference that judges bring to their work. Judges have been men and women of the world; they know the issues of their times and the ways the parties relate to them. Furthermore, given the tradition of political activity of the American lawyer, there is a good chance that the judge has had some active, political party experience. Beyond this, the political party has an opportunity for active and overt influence in the selection process through the initiatives of governors or the president or through the usual processes of a partisan election. In these selection processes, the party has the opportunity to achieve two goals: the selection of judges who are sensitive to the values for which the party stands, and the appointments of deserving (and qualified) lawyers for service to it.

In some instances, the relationship between judge and party may extend beyond the politics of appointment. In some parts of the country, the local district or county judge sometimes still retains hidden ties to local politics. In a few American counties, he is the *éminence grise* of the party, slating candidates behind the scenes, directing party strategy, arbitrating among the conflicting ambitions of the party's candidates. Moreover, the local administration of justice occasionally opens new reservoirs of patronage for the party. The judge who is a loyal member of a political party may parcel out guardianships, receiverships in bankruptcy, and clerkships to loyal lawyers of the party. Many commentators and journalists, and many party officials, believe that such appointments go chiefly to attorneys active in the party ranks.[25]

How is it that the tie between the judiciary and the parties is so substantial in the United States? The factors are complex and mixed. The phenomenon of the elective judiciary, compounded by the political appointment process, is one factor. Then, too, there is no career vocation, no special training process or examination for the judiciary; any lawyer can be a judge. By contrast, in many continental European countries, the career of judging requires special preparation, study, and apprenticeship, and one enters it by special civil service examination. In the American context, then, the additional factor of the dominance of our politics by the legal profession is free to operate. Lawyers are everywhere in American political and public life, and many of them hope for ultimate reward in appointment to the bench.

CONCLUSION

Surprisingly, the influence of the political party on the executives and judiciaries of the American political system differs in degree but not in kind. The main avenue of party influence is indirect, and in both cases it stems from the kinds

---

[25]On judicial patronage, see Herbert Jacob, *Justice in America* (Boston: Little, Brown, 1965), pp. 87–89; and Martin and Susan Tolchin, *To the Victor . . . : Political Patronage from Clubhouse to White House* (New York: Random House, 1971), pp. 131–86.

of commitments and values that membership in a party—or loyalty to one—represents. Without the means to enforce party discipline through patronage appointment or removal for partisan disloyalty, it primarily depends, in other words, on the ideological impact or presence of the party *within* the men and women who hold administrative or judicial office.

Furthermore, in both the executive and the judiciary, one observes the conflict between the policy purpose—even when pursued within the limits of judicial propriety—and the demands of the party organization. The administrative position and the judgeship are two of the few available positions with which to reward party leaders, and the party is not anxious to have them pass to party "nobodies." In the filling of positions in both branches, however, one sees again the struggle between the party's own important need for organizational incentives and the need to recruit people who can best meet the responsibilities of governing. Set in a political culture and an era that disparages parties and partisanship, it is a struggle the parties have great difficulty winning.

Chapter
16

The Quest for
Party Government

Political parties are everywhere in American legislatures and executives, and even in American judiciaries. Almost all American executives, American legislatures, and most of the American judiciaries are selected in processes that weigh heavily the party affiliation of the office seeker. Moreover, the appearances of party power are plentiful in the party leaders and whips of the legislatures and in the clearly partisan cast of many executive appointments. Even the elemental struggle between government and opposition, between ins and outs, largely follows political party lines in the American system. To a political order designed two hundred years ago to fragment rather than concentrate power, the political parties have brought a vital element of governmental coordination.

Yet, despite the trappings and portents of power, the American major parties do not govern easily. They find it hard to mobilize cohesive groups of officeholders behind programs and ideologies to which their organizations, activists, and candidates have committed themselves. Compared with the tightly disciplined parties that dominate the politics of parliamentary systems, the American parties are weak institutions indeed. Not only do they find it difficult to act cohesively within the various branches of government as we have seen, but they face considerable limitations on their ability to serve as an ongoing force for the entire political system.

This inability of the American parties to govern is an old source of discontent for many political scientists.[1] The dissatisfactions, however, are with more than the American parties. They extend to the entire American political system and its fragmented centers of authority, its tendency to blur political alternatives and differences, and its built-in barriers to strong and vigorous govern-

---

[1]Austin Ranney, *The Doctrine of Responsible Party Government* (Urbana: University of Illinois Press, 1962).

mental initiatives. The critics, many of them admirers of the cohesive parties in the British Parliament, have long hoped that by joining electoral majorities and officeholders to party programs, they could surmount the diffusion of power in the American polity. The 1950 report *Toward a More Responsible Two-Party System*, written by some of the leading specialists on political parties of their day,[2] gave the controversy its major postwar stimulus. The ensuing controversy has slowly simmered down, but it is by no means quiet today in this time of divided, or what James Sundquist has called "coalition," government.[3]

While the controversy over party responsibility and party government has embroiled academic political science for more than a generation, a parallel concern has agitated the world of political parties. From the ideologically oriented activists in both parties have come wails of dissatisfaction with the issuelessness of American politics and the tendency of the major parties to take similar centrist positions. They complain, much as did the distinguished British observer of American politics, Lord Bryce, some seventy years ago[4], that the American parties are as similar as Tweedledum and Tweedledee. In working for the nomination of Barry Goldwater in 1964, Republican conservatives pleaded for "a choice, not an echo." Eight years later, the major ideological pressures were from the left; the New Left and a coalition of the young, the disadvantaged, and the disaffected spearheaded a movement that won the 1972 Democratic presidential nomination for George McGovern and rejected the American status quo and the centrist politics of the established leadership of its party. Some twenty years after the smashing Goldwater defeat, with Goldwater's ideological heir, Ronald Reagan, occupying the White House, the controversy over centrist versus ideological politics came to the highest levels of government, and it continues as the less ideological leadership of George Bush has rekindled the discontent of his party's conservatives.

At first blush, it may seem that the academic controversy over party responsibility does not have a great deal to do with the distinct programs of the parties. The two questions are to a great extent the same, however. The scholars who favor party government (or responsibility) and the ideologues of the left and right in American politics both want the major American parties to present more specific and differentiated programs. Both groups also want the parties to govern by carrying their programs into public policy. To the extent that such goals require some degree of consensus on basic values and long-term philosophies, they both also want greater ideological clarification and commitment within the parties.

---

[2]Committee on Political Parties of the American Political Science Association, *Toward a More Responsible Two-Party System* (New York: Rinehart, 1950).

[3]James L. Sundquist, "Needed: A Political Theory for the New Era of Coalition Government in the United States," *Political Science Quarterly* 103 (1988): 613–35.

[4]James Bryce, *The American Commonwealth* (New York: Macmillan, 1916).

THE LOGIC OF THE RESPONSIBLE PARTY

Despite the nomenclature, the doctrines of party government (or party responsibility) are only secondarily concerned with political parties. They are fundamentally doctrines of democratic government—or, more precisely, doctrines that advocate one particular variety of American democracy. Much of the debate over them has been over the kind of democracy we are to have. The whole movement for party government, in other words, has sprung from discontent over what some have seen as the ills of American democracy.

The Case for Party Government

The proponents of party government begin with a belief in strong, positive government as a necessary force for the solution of problems in the American society and economy. Like so many of the advocates of positive government in the context of the American separation of powers, they see a need for strong executive leadership if the whole complex governmental apparatus is to move forward with vigor and with a semblance of unity. Yet they know all too well that the institutions and traditions of American government diffuse and divide governmental power in ways that prevent the generation of aggressive and responsive governmental programs.

Theirs is the old complaint that American political institutions—suited, perhaps, for the limited, gingerly governing of the eighteenth and nineteenth centuries—are far less adapted to the present century's need for positive government action. Clearly, decentralized political parties, each of them divided by a vast diversity of interests and points of view, only accentuate the problem of diffusion. In a sense, therefore, doctrines of party responsibility are attempts to bind American politics and government into a cohesive and integrated whole of the kind more typical of parliamentary government.

To be sure, the various proponents of party government do not agree on the purposes that a strong, positive government should serve. Once leery of a powerful and unified central government, many modern-day conservatives nonetheless have come to view untrammeled presidential power as necessary for the conduct of foreign policy and also have become impatient with the constraining influence a Democratic Congress has imposed on the Reagan and Bush attempts to reduce domestic spending and eliminate liberal programs. By contrast, liberals, who chafed at the bit because of separation of powers in years past, now look with favor on congressional ability to check presidential initiatives. Both groups, it now seems clear, recognize the value of party government if presidents they support are to change the status quo and, by the same token, the danger of party government to their cherished beliefs when the opposition is in charge.

A second thread of argument runs through the political diagnoses of the proponents of party government: concern for the minuscule influence of individuals in a mass, popular democracy. Contemporary government is complex and remote, and individuals find it hard to have the time, attention, and political knowledge for an active role in it. They find it especially difficult to assess what their elected representatives have been doing in public office. Into the political void resulting from their ineffectiveness and ignorance rush well-organized and well-financed minorities—local elites, interest groups, party bosses, or political action committees. Consequently, so the argument goes, important decisions frequently are made by public officials and organized minorities without the participation or even the retrospective judgment of the great majority of individual citizens. Individuals drift from one meaningless decision to another; they do not know what the candidates stand for when they first elect them, and they have no standards or information for judging their performance in office when they come up for reelection.[5] These tendencies are seen as having been exacerbated in recent years by a candidate-centered electoral politics fostered by television, individualistic campaigns, the general weakening of the political parties in the electorate, and of course the diffusion of governmental responsibility that divided government brings.

This sense of alarm about the American democracy is by no means limited to the proponents of party government. It is a more or less standard critique from those quarters of American life committed to the confidence in the usefulness of a broad governmental role and to the belief in the rationality and desirability of citizen involvement in a popular democracy. What sets the school of party government apart is its reliance on the organizing and consolidating powers of the competitive political party. A reconstructed (and responsible) pair of political parties, it is hoped, would bring together masses of voters behind meaningful party programs and candidates loyal to them, would give one party control of all popular branches of government, and then would hold their elected candidates to the obligation of carrying those programs into public policy. The responsible political party thus would bridge the gulf between the disoriented individual and the complex institutions of government and stimulate greater participation in electoral politics. It would also bind the divided institutions of government into an operating whole.

In essence, these are proposals for the reinvigorating and animating of popular democratic institutions through the prime organizing role of the political party. Why use the political party for so crucial a role? It is because

> . . . the parties have claims on the loyalties of the American people superior to the claims of any other forms of political organization. . . . Moreover, party government is good democratic doctrine because the parties are the special form of political organization adapted to the mobilization of majorities. How else can the majority get organized? If democracy means anything at all it means that the majority has the right to organize for the purpose of taking over the government.[6]

---

[5]See Ranney, *The Doctrine of Responsible Party Government*, Chaps. 1 and 2, for an analysis of what party government presumes about democracy.

[6]E. E. Schattschneider, *Party Government* (New York: Rinehart, 1942), p. 208.

Only the parties, their supporters believe, are stable and visible enough to carry this representational burden. As the only completely political organization and the only one with a public or semipublic character, the political party alone has the capacity for developing the essential qualities of responsibility. Moreover, they are much superior as democratic institutions to the pressure groups, their major rivals as intermediaries between citizens and government.[7]

The call for responsible political parties, therefore, is a call for political parties with new capacities and new goals. Specifically, the responsible political party must:

- Enunciate a reasonably explicit statement of party programs and principles.
- Nominate candidates loyal to the party program and willing to enact it into public policy if elected.
- Conduct its electoral campaigns in such a way that voters will grasp the programmatic differences between the parties and make their voting decisions substantially on that basis.
- Guarantee that public officeholders elected under the party label will carry the party program into public policy and thus enable the party to take responsibility for their actions in office.

The entire argument, therefore, rests on replacing individual or group responsibility for governing with the responsibility of the political party.

Concern for developing and enacting programs must infuse all relationships within the party and all steps in the contesting of elections. As the report of the committee of the American Political Science Association argues in its very first paragraph:

> While in an election the party alternative necessarily takes the form of a choice between candidates, putting a particular candidate into office is not an end in itself. The concern of the parties with candidates, elections and appointments is misunderstood if it is assumed that the parties can afford to bring forth aspirants for office without regard to the views of those so selected. Actually, the party struggle is concerned with the direction of public affairs. Party nominations are no more than a means to this end. In short, party politics inevitably involves public policy in one way or another.[8]

The whole idea of party government is policy- and issue-oriented. It is concerned with capturing and using public office for predetermined goals, not merely for the thrill of winning, the division of patronage and spoils, or the reward of the office itself. The winning of public office becomes no more than a means to policy ends.

---

[7]This point is made in E. E. Schattschneider, *The Semi-Sovereign People* (New York: Holt, Rinehart, and Winston, 1960).

[8]Committee on Political Parties, *Toward a More Responsible Two-Party System*, p. 15.

The Case Against Party Government

Despite the persuasiveness of the advocates of party government, there still remains a sizable platoon of American political scientists and political leaders who are definitely unconvinced. The journals of American political science, in fact, were dotted with rejoinders for several years after the publication of the report of the Committee on Political Parties in 1950. Their collective case against party government and responsibility divides into two related but independent arguments: the *undesirability* of party government and its *impossibility* (or at least its improbability) in the American context. Although the two points are related, both logically and polemically, one does not have to make both in order to venture one.[9]

On the grounds of undesirability, the skeptics raise a number of fundamental issues of political philosophy. They fear that party government would stimulate a more intense politics of dogmatic commitment—one in which the softenings and majority building of compromise would be more difficult. They fear, too, that by making the political party the prime avenue of political representation, the advocates of party government would destroy the richness and multiplicity of representational mechanisms in the American democracy. Interest groups and other nonparty political organizations, they feel, are necessary means of political representation in a large and heterogeneous polity. Channeling the representation of such a diversity of interests into the party system would overload two parties and risk the development of multipartyism, which would further fragment the American system. Moreover, the skeptics are concerned lest party government destroy the deliberative quality of American legislatures, for legislators would cease to be free, independent men and women and would become the mandated representatives of a fixed party position. In short, they fear what European critics often call "partyocracy"—the domination of politics and legislatures by a number of doctrinaire, unyielding political parties, none of them strong enough to govern and none willing to let others govern.

On the related grounds of realism, the critics of responsible parties have argued:

- The American voter remains insufficiently involved in issues to be coaxed easily into viewing politics and electoral choices in programmatic terms.
- The complexity of American society and the diversity of interests it generates are too great to be expressed in the simple set of alternatives a two-party system can frame.
- The parties themselves are too diffuse and decentralized—too lacking in central disciplinary authority—and the nation too large and diverse for

---

[9]The literature critical of the concept of party responsibility is a large one. Pendleton Herring's *The Politics of Democracy* (New York: Rinehart, 1940) presented an early argument against the reformers. Also see Evron Kirkpatrick, "Toward a More Responsible Two-Party System: Political Science, Policy Science, or Pseudo-Science?" *American Political Science Review* 65 (1971): 965–90.

the parties ever to take a single national position and then enforce it on their holders of public office.

- The institutions of American government stand in the way at a number of crucial points. The direct primary, for example, makes it difficult for the parties to choose nominees loyal to their programs, and the near-monopoly it has recently achieved over the nomination process makes it impossible for the parties to enforce party discipline. Moreover, the separation of powers (and bicameralism) often prevents the control of all executive and legislative authority by a single party.
- Americans have distrusted parties too much, as is evidenced by their recurrent attempts to reform politics to reduce rather than increase their influence, to be mobilized in support of institutional changes to increase party power.

In other words, the model of the responsible, governing political party appears to the critics to demand too much of the American voters, of the parties themselves, of the institutions of American government, and of the will of the people in an antipartisan political culture.

Ways of Achieving Cohesion

If the major American parties are to meet the demands and roles of party government, they must find some way to overcome their egregious disunity. The problem is really one of uniting the party organization, the party in the electorate, and the party in office in active and responsible support of a party program—despite their different political goals, different political traditions and interests, and different levels of attention, information, and activity. There are three ways in which the necessary cohesiveness might be achieved: they involve changes in institutional arrangements, organizational discipline, and ideological agreement.

In many systems, party cohesion is promoted by *institutional arrangements* and their imperatives for political activity. The parliamentary system demands that the majority party maintain cohesion in the legislature—and to a lesser extent in the electorate and the party organization—if it is to stay in office. In the United States, federalism and the separation of powers have just the opposite effect of fragmenting constitutional authority by dividing it between levels and branches of government.[10] Indeed, in the current era of divided government, institutional fragmentation probably has never been greater. It is far fetched to imagine that the Constitution would ever be amended to reduce this fragmentation through, for example, creation of a parliamentary system.

---

[10]See Leon D. Epstein, "A Comparative Study of Canadian Parties," *American Political Science Review* 58 (1964): 46–59; and Austin Ranney, "Candidate Selection and Party Cohesion in Britain and the U.S.," in William J. Crotty (ed.), *Approaches to the Study of Party Organization* (Boston: Allyn and Bacon, 1968), pp. 139–68.

Cohesion may also be promoted by *organizational discipline*. A strong party organization may impose its discipline and cohesion on balky partisans in office if it can control renomination to office. The proliferation of the American direct primary, now more dominant than ever before, however, makes that a hard task. Alternatively, powerful party leaders or executives may enforce discipline through the manipulation of the rewards they control (patronage, preference, access to authority, etc.). The value of these rewards is shrinking, however, and political ethics in the United States no longer easily accept an enforced toeing of the line. Although the available rewards and a tolerant political culture permit this kind of discipline in a few American states and localities, it is impossible in most. Still there is a possibility, albeit remote, that the increased resources of the national (and perhaps even state) party organizations might be employed to enforce some degree of ideological discipline.

Finally, the cohesion may be produced "naturally" by an all-pervasive, intraparty *agreement on ideology or program*. All three components of the party may reach some consensus on a basic party ideology or program—or at least on a "silent ideology" of commonly held interest. The activists and identifiers of the party would then achieve a cohesion arising from common philosophy and goals, and their cohesion, to a considerable extent, would be a result of internalized and self-enforced commitment to those goals. Distasteful external constraints and restraints would thus be less necessary.

Because it seems, given the arguments in earlier chapters, that only the third avenue to party government is a likely one for contemporary American parties, the issue of party government for the United States becomes one of ideological—or more ideological—politics and parties. A pervasive ideological commitment appears to be the necessary condition for party cohesion in the American system, which in turn is a necessary condition for responsible governing parties. Organizational discipline may supplement and buttress the ideology, but it does not appear to be a realistic alternative to it.

IDEOLOGICAL PARTIES IN THE UNITED STATES?

Throughout their long histories, the American political parties have been remarkably nonideological. Even the Republican party, born out of the impassioned abolitionist movement of the 1850s, soon moved away from its ideological roots as slavery ended and it attempted to hold together a national constituency as a majority party. The reasons for the pragmatic nature of American parties are several. First and perhaps foremost, there are only two of them to divide up the political world. The parties in a multiparty system, by contrast, can cater to a special ideological niche within the electorate in a way that parties in a two-party system can not if they wish to survive. The very size and diversity of the American nation itself also limit the ideological purity of its parties. With so many different interests and people to represent, it is little wonder that they are wide coalitions of office seekers and organizational activists, the epitome of what Otto Kirchheimer once called "catch-all" parties.[11] Finally, of course, one is led back to the American people themselves, whom scholars agree are unusually free of the kinds of deep-seated animosities that fuel an ideological politics in other democratic systems.[12]

The Nature of Party Differences

This is not to say, however, that there are no important differences of principle between the parties. They clearly diverge on specific policy questions. These differences appear in the platforms they adopt every four years at their national nominating conventions (see box), in the speeches of their candidates for president and other offices, and in the policies they pursue when they occupy governmental office.[13] The roots of such differences are to be found in the nature of the party coalitions, particularly as they were shaped in the realigning periods (see Chapter 6) that have defined the different American party systems.

But the policy stands and even principles that have been identified with the American parties fall short of being ideologies in the conventional sense because they are not sharply articulated or codified as all-encompassing political philosophies, such as those found in the old-style Communist or Socialist parties of Europe or the Moslem fundamentalist parties that have arisen in the Middle East. Nor do the American parties insist upon faithful obedience to these principles from their members. They permit, and the localism inherent in the American system encourages, their leaders and their followers alike to be drawn into the party on their own terms, for their own reasons, rather than having to pass some sort of ideological "litmus test" for involvement.

Some kind or degree of ideology, however, is implicit in every demand for party government. In a heterogeneous society of many conflicting interests, parties cannot take stands on ten or fifteen separate issues if there is no similarity among the coalitions on each issue. There must be some clustering of one group of voters, as well as politicians, on one set of issue positions and of another group on the opposing sides, and issues that crosscut the party coalitions must be relegated to a remote position on the political agenda. That alignment of voters along a single axis presumes, in turn, some kind of ideology, some basic commitments or values that connect separate issues into logical structures

---

[11]Otto Kircheimer, "The Transformation of the Western European Party Systems," in Joseph La-Palombara and Myron Weiner (eds.), *Political Parties and Political Development* (Princeton, N.J.: Princeton University Press, 1966), pp. 184–92.

[12]On the consensus among Americans on the basic principles of politics, see Louis Hartz, *The Liberal Tradition in America* (New York: Harcourt, Brace, 1955).

[13]Ian Budge and Richard I. Hofferbert have demonstrated that, for the 1948–1985 period, a strong relationship existed between the parties' platforms and the policies they enacted, as measured by federal expenditures, when the party controlled the presidency. See their "Mandates and Policy Outputs: U.S. Party Platforms and Federal Expenditures," *American Political Science Review* 84 (1990): 111–32.

and govern stands on a number of them. Thus, call it what one will (the ASPA report refers at several points to general party principles), greater programmatic commitment in the American parties depends on underlying values or philosophies to reduce the vast number of policy issues to one or at least a few dimensions.

At certain points in American political history, the parties seem to have moved in the direction of the kind of programmatic unity necessary for responsible parties. During periods of partisan realignment, the party coalitions achieve their sharpest definition along a single line of political cleavage, and their respective members exhibit their greatest agreement with one another and their greatest differences with the other party.[14]

Yet, even during realignments, partisan cohesion in adherence to common ideological principles has fallen short of what is necessary for truly responsible parties. The realignment of the 1930s, for example, produced a majority Democratic party by joining a liberal northern wing, attracted to the party because it gave voice to the aspirations of disadvantaged groups and championed the developing welfare state, with a conservative southern wing that often opposed both of these policy directions. His congressional majority was large enough for Franklin Roosevelt to achieve many of his policy goals as president, but throughout he was faced with persistent and outspoken opposition within his own party. In short, even at the peak of their unification around a single political agenda, American parties have been broad coalitions. They have never been sufficiently consolidated around common principles to completely overcome the powerful centrifugal effects of constitutionally-imposed federalism or separation of powers.

The Rise of More Ideological Parties

Attention to issues and even ideology within the parties, though, has risen over the past several decades. Both major parties seem to have become more cohesive and, as a consequence, more ideological. As new issues have emerged as important subjects of policy debate, particularly involving civil rights for blacks, white southerners have deserted the Democratic party. While this has eroded that party's electoral strength, it also has reduced the principal barrier to Democratic party cohesiveness along more or less ideological lines.[15] One major effect of this is the greater voting cohesiveness within the congressional Democratic party. With the demise of the liberal northeastern wing of the party (led for many years by people such as Governor Nelson Rockefeller of

---

[14]See Paul Allen Beck, "The Electoral Cycle and Patterns of American Politics," *British Journal of Political Science* 9 (1979): 129–56; and James L. Sundquist, *Dynamics of the Party System* (Washington, D.C.: Brookings, 1983).

[15]On the importance of racial issues in the changing nature of the party coalitions among both voters and political leaders, see Edward G. Carmines and James A. Stimson, *Issue Evolution: Race and the Transformation of American Politics* (Princeton, N.J.: Princeton University Press, 1989).

What the Democrats and Republicans Stand For: Key Elements of the 1988 Party Platforms

Party platforms are not binding upon their candidates or their followers, and they sometimes mask more than they reveal. Nonetheless, they do express the sentiments of the national party conventions about what the parties stand for at a particular time and, in this sense, serve as a valuable encapsulation of party positions on the issues of the day. A good summary of party differences on these issues comes from the *Congressional Quarterly Weekly Report*'s (October 22, 1988, pp. 3042–3) comparison of the Democratic and Republican platforms in 1988 on the key issues in the 1988 campaign.

Issue	Democratic Platform Position	Issue	Republican Platform Position
Defense	Calls for "stable" defense spending and "readiness and mobility" over "dubious new weapons."	Defense	Calls for modernizing land, sea and air nuclear arms (B-1, B-2, Trident, MX) and for "rapid and certain" deployment of strategic defense not subject to negotiation; 600-ship Navy with two new carriers; updated chemical weapons.
Superpower relations	Calls for testing intentions of new Soviet leaders on arms control, emigration, human rights, then reciprocating; allies should pay for more of common defense.	Superpower relations	Avoid "naive inexperience or overly enthusiastic endorsement of current Soviet rhetoric"; Soviets must release political prisoners, open borders.
Central America	Support for Arias plan; no mention of contras.	Central America	Supports military aid to Nicaraguan contras.
Trade	Use all tools "to export more goods and fewer jobs."	Trade	Renews free-trade commitment.
Economics	Advance notice of plant closings, major layoffs; opposition to "unproductive mergers, takeovers."	Economics	Supports enterprise zones, deregulation, free-market principles
Spending cuts	Restrain defense spending, farm subsidies.	Spending Cuts	"With Gramm-Rudman and a flexible freeze," budget can be balanced by 1993.
Taxes	Calls for "the wealthy and the Pentagon" to pay "fair share," "for investing in America" and reducing deficit.	Taxes	"We oppose any attempts to raise taxes" and support new tax incentives for saving; lower taxes on capital gains; taxpayers' Bill of Rights.

Issue	Democratic Platform Position	Issue	Republican Platform Position
Health	"Every family should have the security of basic health insurance."	Health	"Nationalized medicine" is disastrous; competition and choice are only cost-cutters.
Education	Deserves "highest priority"; no one to be denied college for lack of funds; create National Teachers Corps.	Education	Parents have right to control child's education; competition, choice produces quality.
Drugs	Calls for "drug czar" empowered to use every agency necessary, including armed forces.	Drugs	"Strict accountability" for users and traffickers.
Housing	"Steps should be taken to ensure a decent place to live for every American."	Housing	"The best housing policy is sound economic policy; low inflation rates; low interest rates and the availability of a job with a good paycheck. . . ."
Environment	Calls for aggressive enforcement of toxic cleanup, anti-dumping laws, ban on offshore drilling in sensitive areas.	Environment	Takes credit for Superfund Act; but also supports cost-benefit analysis of cleanups; urges new nuclear power plants with uniform design.
Women	Supports Equal Rights Amendment. Supports pay equity. Supports right to abortion regardless of ability to pay	Women	Opposes Equal Rights Amendment; supports rights of fetus that "cannot be infringed" for any reason; opposes funding of abortion.
Minorities	Supports affirmative action goals, timetables, and procurement set-asides.	Minorities	Expanding economy should provide opportunity for all regardless of race or gender; opposes timetables, quotas.
Farm	Mix of supply management and "reasonable" price supports.	Farm	Opposes production controls; upholds price support system of 1985 farm bill.
Crime	Calls for ban of "cop-killer" bullets; abhors greed in economy and in Reagan administration.	Crime	Supports death penalty for capital crimes; would deny prison furloughs for murderers; opposes gun control.

New York), the Republicans too seem to have become more homogeneous on key party principles. Men and women are increasingly being drawn to party work out of their involvement with issues and ideologies. The triumph of political ideas and values thus becomes a major incentive to party activity. To some extent, it replaces the older incentives of patronage and preference, which have been waning on their own accord as discussed in Chapter 5. Another clear symptom of this ideological renaissance in American party politics was the election of Ronald Reagan, a candidate well identified with the conservative wing of his party, to the presidency in 1980 and his landslide reelection in 1984.

Most of these signs of increased ideological concern are visible chiefly among the activists of the party organization. What of the American voters, however, especially the less partisan electorate? It may very well be that the small core of party activists will bring their new involvement to a deaf or hostile public, that their "ideologizing" will only bore or alienate the majority of the electorate. Moreover, the issue of the differences in ideological concern between activists of the party organization and the electorate is not merely a scholarly one. The ideologues of American politics have long claimed that a horde of ideological voters is increasingly alienated by parties unwilling or unable to give them clearly defined ideological alternatives. Are the American parties, then, reflecting a nonideological electorate or suppressing an ideological one?

IDEOLOGY IN THE AMERICAN ELECTORATE

For decades, some have characterized the American electorate in liberal or conservative terms, often depicting decisive ideological mood swings from one period to the next in tandem with changes in the directions of government. But, until the late 1950s, no one had undertaken in a systematic fashion to actually measure the ideological thinking of ordinary citizens.

The Nonideological Electorate of the 1950s

Philip E. Converse directly addressed this matter from surveys of the electorate conducted by the University of Michigan during the 1952 and 1956 presidential elections.[16] He conceived of ideological thinking in two related ways. First, he examined the extent to which voters employed an ideological framework in their evaluations of parties and candidates. Even by the most generous criteria, only

---

[16]Philip E. Converse, "The Nature of Belief Systems in Mass Publics," in David Apter (ed.), *Ideology and Discontent* (New York: Free Press, 1964), pp. 206–61. Also see Angus Campbell, Philip E. Converse, Warren E. Miller, and Donald E. Stokes, *The American Voter* (New York: Wiley, 1960), Chap. 10.

about 12 to 13 percent of all adult Americans made reference to ideology or applied ideological principles in discussing the parties and candidates for president at that time. Beneath this thin stratum of "ideologues" in the hierarchy of ideological thinking lay an electorate much more inclined to evaluations based on the interests of their group, a single issue, or personal characteristics of the candidates.

Converse realized, however, that ideology can influence beliefs without its user necessarily being able to invoke overarching organizing principles or explicitly conceive of politics in ideological terms. In an ideological world, positions on the issues of the day go together in packages. The proper way to assess the extensiveness of this ideological packaging was, he argued, to determine levels of consistency or "constraint" (in the sense that the position taken on one issue constrains options on a second issue) across voters' positions on key issues. Those taking the liberal position on the issue of government guaranteeing jobs and a good standard of living, for example, should be more likely to take a liberal position on aid to minorities or defense spending if they are at all ideological. While considerable consistency in positions on domestic issues was discovered by this method, there were many voters who professed liberal positions on one issue but not on another, and consistency was virtually absent between foreign policy and domestic policy issues. By this measure, too, the American electorate was characterized as remarkably nonideological.

The Controversy Over the Rise in Ideological Thinking

Subsequent studies of the American electorate, using continuing University of Michigan presidential election surveys, challenged Converse's findings. Research conducted in the 1960s and early 1970s found a larger number of so-called ideologues and greater consistency in issue positions. These changes were explained by those who chronicled them as a response to the greater ideological tenor of the campaigns of Barry Goldwater in 1964, George Wallace in 1968, and even George McGovern in 1972—and the strategies adopted by their opponents to position these candidates at the ideological extremes in voters' perceptions.[17]

This research, in turn, was challenged. The increase in ideologues brought their total to no more than 23 percent by 1968, an increase that could be explained by the increased political involvement and greater education of the electorate.[18] More critically, the rise in issue consistency appeared to be mostly an artifact of the improved issue questions in surveys conducted after the

---

[17]See Norman H. Nie, Sidney Verba, and John R. Petrocik, *The Changing American Voter* (Cambridge, Mass.: Harvard University Press, 1976), Chaps. 7–9.

[18]See Philip E. Converse, "Public Opinion and Voting Behavior," in Fred I. Greenstein and Nelson W. Polsby (eds.), *Handbook of Political Science*, Volume 4 (Reading, Mass.: Addison-Wesley, 1975).

1950s.[19] While some increase in ideological thinking may have appeared after the 1950s, it was found to be modest at best and still left the American electorate as quite nonideological even in response to the heightened level of ideological discourse that had characterized the presidential campaigns from 1964 through 1972.

With the domination of American national politics by an unabashedly conservative Ronald Reagan and a conservative policy agenda, the 1980s brought renewed attention to the ideological capabilities of the American electorate. Perhaps the most paradoxical feature of the Reagan years was that his popularity and electoral success were gained in spite of his conservative policy positions. In both 1980 and 1984, the voting public on balance preferred the policy positions of Reagan's electoral opponent.[20]

What benefitted Reagan, instead, was his relative standing in retrospective evaluations of presidential performance—that is, more in how well things had turned out than in exactly what he had done. In 1980, looking back on the four preceding years, many found Carter's performance wanting (e.g., in allowing inflation to soar and American hostages to be held for over a year in the U.S. embassy in Iran) and voted for the GOP alternative. In 1984, Reagan campaigned on his performance, which most voters evaluated favorably. The GOP's performance advantage even carried over into the 1988 election, as George Bush was able to capitalize upon his association with the Reagan administration. These were results-oriented evaluations, not ideological or policy judgements. Thus, even when conditions were more propitious than ever for ideological thinking, the American electorate could hardly be characterized in ideological terms—and certainly not to the degree required for responsible parties to emerge.[21]

This is not to say that the American public thinks about politics in very simple-minded and unsophisticated ways. Scholars have shown that many voters develop elaborate schemes to incorporate parties, candidates, and issues in their conceptual maps of politics.[22] Few voters, however, organize their

---

[19]See George F. Bishop, Alfred J. Tuchfarber, and Robert W. Oldendick, "Change in the Structure of American Political Attitudes: The Nagging Question of Question Wording," *American Journal of Political Science* 23 (1978): 250–69; and John L. Sullivan, James E. Piereson, and George E. Marcus, "Ideological Constraint in the Mass Public: A Methodological Critique and Some New Findings," *American Journal of Political Science* 23 (1978): 233–49.

[20]See Thomas Ferguson and Joel Rogers, *Right Turn: The Decline of the Democrats and the Future of American Politics* (New York: Hill and Wang, 1986), especially Chap. 1; and Paul R. Abramson, John H. Aldrich, and David W. Rohde, *Change and Continuity in the 1988 Elections* (Washington, D.C.: CQ Press, 1989), Chap. 6.

[21]Abramson, Aldrich, and Rohde, *Change and Continuity in the 1988 Elections*, Chap. 6.

[22]Pamela Conover and Stanley Feldman, "How People Organize the Political World: A Schematic Model," *American Journal of Political Science* 28 (1984): 95–126; and Mark A. Peffley and Jon Hurwitz, "A Hierarchical Model of Attitude Constraint," *American Journal of Political Science* 29 (1985): 871–90.

political worlds into a common ideological system of beliefs—even in terms of the wide-ranging liberal, conservative dimension that characterizes elite political discourse. Responsible parties can not emerge from such a foundation of idiosyncratic voter belief systems.

The Meaning of Ideological Self-Identification

Nonetheless, it is true that large numbers of Americans can think of themselves in ideological terms. Based on the 1988 Michigan surveys, some 52 percent of Americans could locate themselves at a liberal or conservative position along a liberal-conservative continuum, and another 22 percent were self-identified moderates or middle-of-the-road. The acceptance of such labels is easy, however, and tells us nothing about how much ideological thinking underlies them. It is difficult, for example, to imagine what the moderate or middle-of-the-road political ideology is; to take that position is probably another way of saying that one has no ideology.

Moreover, as much as the liberal-conservative dichotomy may suggest alternative views on the major political issues of the day to political experts, it is not an unfailing guide to the issue positions of many other people. This can be seen in the absence of a one-to-one correspondence between ideological identification and beliefs about what government should do on three key policy issues of the 1980s—government activity to provide jobs and a high standard of living, government aid to minority groups, and spending on national defense (Table 16.1). In 1988, many people did not take the issue position that was consonant with their ideological identification. The agreement between ideology and issue position was highest among the strongest liberals and strongest conservatives, but these extreme ideological groups comprise only a small share of the American public and even among them may be found a number who fail to line up as expected on a particular issue. Thus, many of those willing to adopt a liberal or conservative label lack the consistent, all-encompassing thinking of the ideologue. Ideological self-identification can not provide the foundation for responsible parties.[23]

The politics of ideology is abstract and remote, and it persists with difficulty in the politics of personal followings, family political traditions, patronage and preference, and candidate-centered campaigns. In the increasing reliance on campaigning in the mass media, furthermore, all advantages are with the campaigns that stress personal appeal and punchy sloganeering. Most voters cannot sustain the interest or provide the intellectual sophistication that ideas demand; theirs is not the ideologue's view of American society. Once the short-term ideological stimulus has disappeared, the concern with issues abates. Thus, although an ideological minority within the parties and the electorate will see American politics largely in ideological terms, the American majority appar-

---

[23]Pamela Conover and Stanley Feldman, "The Origins and Meaning of Liberal/Conservative Self-Identification," *American Journal of Political Science* 25 (1981): 617–45.

Table 16.1   IDEOLOGY AND ISSUE POSITIONS, 1988

	Self-placement on ideological continuum						
	Strong Liberal. . . . . .Moderate. . . . . .Conservative					Strong	
Issue							
Government should guarantee jobs and standard of living							
Liberal side	62%	46%	36%	31%	22%	14%	24%
Middle	22	19	21	24	21	15	16
Conservative side	16	35	43	45	57	71	60
Government should help minorities							
Liberal side	85%	52%	35%	32%	26%	15%	10%
Middle	8	17	28	25	23	24	10
Conservative side	7	29	37	43	51	61	80
Defense spending should be increased							
Liberal side	57%	51%	50%	34%	26%	17%	22%
Middle	17	21	32	34	41	33	27
Conservative side	27	18	18	32	33	50	51
Percent in each category along the ideological continuum	2%	6%	10%	48%	16%	15%	3%

Note: Entries are percentages of people within each of seven categories of ideology who took liberal, middle, or conservative positions on the issue. They total 100% reading down for each issue. Ideological moderates and the large number who do not think of themselves in liberal or conservative terms at all are treated as equivalent and combined in the middle "moderate" category on ideology.

Source: Center for Political Studies, University of Michigan; data made available by the Inter-University Consortium for Political and Social Research.

ently will do so only under special circumstances. What is an easy and natural way to understand American politics for some is an unusual, even unnatural way for most others.

THE DILEMMA OF IDEOLOGY

In general, the uneven and uncertain rise of ideology risks a discontinuity between the ideological minority within the parties and the essentially nonideological majority in the electorate. At best, the full electorate is only sporadically given to ideologies. It responds selectively to issues, to be sure, but it also responds to a personality, a deeply felt personal interest, a campaign, a group loyalty, an ancient tradition, or an incumbent's performance in office. The parties and their candidates may respond to that gulf between the ideological minority and the nonideological majority with appeals on a number of levels—

ideological arguments for some parts of the audience, nonideological arguments for others. Always, however, there is danger of alienating a majority irritated and ultimately repelled by a discourse they find obscure, irrelevant, and sometimes even frightening.

Low Levels of Ideological Thinking

Thus, the establishment of an ideological party is impeded, first of all, by the fact that only some Americans see party politics consistently in issue or ideological terms. Those ideological concerns are spread unevenly across American social classes. Because they are so strongly associated with higher levels of formal education, one finds them disproportionately among higher SES Americans. They are, in a sense, the political preoccupations of an affluent, well-educated, upper-middle-class elite in American politics for whom the abstractions and verbal content of ideology come easily. Thus, they increasingly tend to be the preoccupations and even the political incentives of the middle-class activists within each party's organization.

Differences Between Activists and Voters

That gulf between an ideological elite of activists and a less ideological party electorate would pose problems for the parties in itself. That problem is made even more serious, however, by the fact that the party activists tend to take more extreme ideological positions than the party voters. Careful scholarly studies both of officials in the party organizations and of delegates to the two national parties' nominating conventions have consistently found the electorates of both parties close to the center on the left-right continuum, with the activists of the Democratic party farther to the left and the Republican activists and officials farther to the right. In fact, when measured on a simple left-to-right issue continuum, Republican activists are often located farther away from the average voter at the nonideological center of the scale than are Democratic activists (see Figure 16.1). In some years and on some issues, moreover, the party activists are farther away from their own rank and file supporters on this continuum than are the activists of the opposing party.[24]

---

[24]See Herbert McClosky, Paul J. Hoffman, and Rosemary O'Hara, "Issue Conflict and Consensus among Party Leaders and Followers," *American Political Science Review* 54 (1960): 406–27; Jeane Kirkpatrick, "Representation in the American National Conventions: The Case of 1972," *British Journal of Political Science* 5 (1975): 265–322; Robert S. Montjoy, William R. Shaffer, and Ronald E. Weber, "Policy Preferences of Party Elites and Masses: Conflict or Consensus?" *American Politics Quarterly* 8 (1980): 319–44; John S. Jackson III, Barbara L. Brown, and David Bositis, "Herbert McClosky and Friends Revisited: 1980 Democratic and Republican Party Elites Compared to the Mass Public," *American Politics Quarterly* 10 (1982): 158–80; Warren E. Miller and M. Kent Jennings, *Parties in Transition* (New York: Russell Sage Foundation, 1986), pp. 189–219; and Denise L. Baer and David A. Bositis, *Elite Cadres and Party Coalitions* (New York: Greenwood Press, 1988) pp. 100–107.

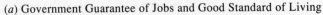

(*a*) Government Guarantee of Jobs and Good Standard of Living

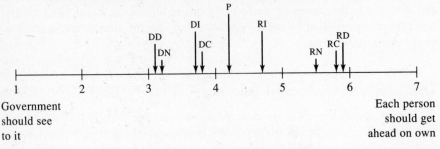

| 1 | 2 | 3 | 4 | 5 | 6 | 7 |

Government
should see
to it

Each person
should get
ahead on own

(*b*) Government Help for Minority Groups

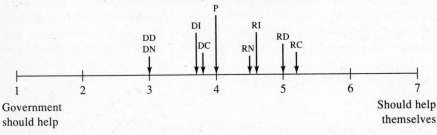

| 1 | 2 | 3 | 4 | 5 | 6 | 7 |

Government
should help

Should help
themselves

(*c*) Defense Spending

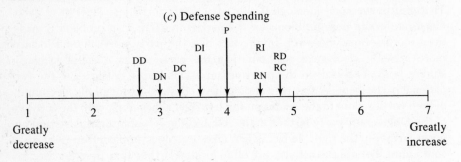

| 1 | 2 | 3 | 4 | 5 | 6 | 7 |

Greatly
decrease

Greatly
increase

Key:

RD = Republican
   delegates

RC = Republican
   county chairs

RN = Republican
   National Commitee

RI = Republican
   party identifiers

P = Public

DI = Democratic
   party identifiers

DN = Democratic
   National Committee

DC = Democratic
   county chairs

DD = Democratic
   delegates

Figure 16.1 Party Elites, Party Identifiers, and the Public on Key Issues, 1984.

Source: Denise L. Baer and David A. Bositis, *Elite Cadres and Party Coalitions* (New York: Greenwood, 1988), pp. 192, 202, 204.

In short, the activists and voters in the two parties differ both in the extent and in the direction of their ideologies. Caught in the middle of these differences are the party candidates and officeholders. The only alternatives open to them—conflict with the party's activists, lack of candor with the electorate, or defeat at the next election—are hardly attractive. It is no wonder that the party in government so strongly resists fixed issue and ideological commitments within the parties and is inclined toward ideological ambiguity in political campaigns.[25]

Differences Between Party Sectors

A major American party, faced with the development of a cadre of ideological activists, may develop an internal, private ideology or issue consensus at odds with the stance necessary to win elections. That divergence aggravates, in yet another way, the tensions and strains among the party organization, the party in government, and the party in the electorate. There are periodic eruptions of dissatisfaction among the ideologues of both parties with the moderation of the party in office. For example, in the 1970s, even so conservative a "moderate" as President Gerald Ford found himself rejected by many of the organization Republicans in favor of the more conservative Ronald Reagan. Reagan himself, as president in the 1980s, found that his brand of Republican conservatism was not conservative enough for the stalwarts of some Republican organizations. His successor, George Bush, in turn felt the wrath of his party's conservative ideologues in agreeing to reduce the budget deficit by raising taxes.[26]

Regional Differences

Beyond these differences in levels of issue involvement and in distances from the political center, ideologies within each party differ from state to state and from region to region. A persistent ideological factionalism in both parties has been evident in the behavior of state delegations to the two national party conventions over recent decades.[27] Those differences obviously reflect the different economies and demographies of the states, as well as different state political cultures.[28] Thus, lacking any unifying structures, the two national parties speak

---

[25]On the use of ambiguity as a political strategy, see Benjamin Page, *Choices and Echoes in Presidential Elections* (Chicago: University of Chicago Press, 1978).

[26]The tendency for candidates seeking office in the general elections and officeholders to converge upon the center in a two-party system is given theoretical expression in Anthony Downs, *An Economic Theory of Democracy* (New York: Harper and Row, 1957).

[27]David Nice, "Ideological Stability and Change at the Presidential Nominating Conventions," *Journal of Politics* 42 (1980): 847–53.

[28]Howard L. Reiter, "Party Factionalism: National Conventions in the New Era," *American Politics Quarterly* 8 (1980): 303–18.

in a babel of ideological voices. They are structurally incapable of articulating, much less monopolizing, the ideological content of American politics.

Containing Ideological Commitment

Ideology thus brings all manner of torments and problems to the American parties. For them, the question is not primarily whether they can become ideological parties, for they cannot. It is, rather, whether they can contain the ideological commitment to their activists without it tearing them apart. The threat to the parties is, in part, one of factionalism, conflict, and splintering—the usual forms of intraparty bickering. Beyond that threat is another: Greater numbers of ideologues threaten the party organizations with an inflexibility of goals that rejects the parties' traditional electoral pragmatism. Many delegates to the Republican conventions of 1964 and 1976 and the Democratic conventions of 1968, 1972, and 1988 were prepared to nominate candidates without greatly considering their electability. Some, indeed, preferred defeat with principle to victory with compromise. If the importance of the ideological goal of the party ever crowds out the electioneering role, then the parties themselves will be greatly altered. So, too, will most of American electoral politics.

PARTY RESPONSIBILITY AMERICAN-STYLE

The model of the responsible political party is an ideal. One does not look for it in reality, for no political system yet has developed the cohesion, discipline, and unity that its pure form demands. Even in Great Britain, home of the hopes of the American reformers, practice falls short of the model. Party cohesion in the British Parliament, though significantly greater than that in the American Congress, is by no means perfect. Recent governments even have been defeated on key votes in Parliament without falling. British cabinets and parliamentary parties, moreover, have long insisted that constitutional traditions forbid them from being bound by party decision or commitment. Even within the Labour party, historically committed to the binding discipline of party decisions, Labour prime ministers have made it clear that although a Labour government will consult with the party's national executive, it cannot be bound by it.[29]

American practice is even further from the model. To be sure, one finds in some state legislatures a high order of party discipline behind or in opposition to a party program. The programs of principles, however, spring not so much from a party organization or from the decision of the electorate as from the ini-

---

[29]For a discussion of the British responsible party model as an ideal and a reality, see Leon D. Epstein, "What Happened to the British Party Model?" *American Political Science Review* 74 (1980): 9–22.

tiative of the governor or the party's legislative leadership. What responsibility there is to the voters for their program is established at later elections, when the voters reward or punish their programmatic stewardship.[30] Even when sophisticated voters may be able to identify a past policy or decision with a party, such a quasi responsibility diverges from the model in one major way: There is little role in it for the party organization, since the legislative party or the executive originates the program and enforces discipline behind it. The responsibility rests not on the overt program of party activists and organizations but on the homogeneous interests of the voters, party leaders, and constituencies that support the legislative and executive parties. It is a cohesion and responsibility that springs essentially from the coalescing of common interests in electoral politics.

Crisis—Stimulated Responsibility

Occasionally, American politics approaches the model of party responsibility even more closely. In the presidential election of 1936, for example, the Democrats and Republicans were identified with sharply differing solutions to the nation's economic woes. If their positions were not truly ideological, they were at least determinedly programmatic. The burdens of the depression may have focused voter attention on the hopes and remedies of policy to an unusual degree. Much of the campaign oratory centered on the Roosevelt program for social and economic change and on his opponent's charges that Roosevelt was proposing radical changes in the American polity and economy. The programmatic rhetoric and identification, combined with high voter attention, may well have produced something close to a mandate election and a mandated congressional contingent of Democrats. That election of 1936 suggests that the kind of ideology or programmatic concern necessary for "pure" party responsibility may be a product of crisis conditions that have prevailed only for short periods in American experience.

Presidential Responsibility

More common than the case of crisis-stimulated responsibility is the type of responsibility that results from presidential government. Strong presidential leadership, especially when aided by majorities of the same party in the Congress, produces a somewhat cohesive program that becomes the program of the president's party. Indeed, some presidents, such as Lyndon Johnson and Ronald

---

[30]This is largely the point V. O. Key makes in *The Responsible Electorate* (Cambridge: Harvard University Press, 1966). Alternatively, retrospective policy voting may be viewed from the Downsian perspective in which the past is the best rational guide to the future. See Downs, *An Economic Theory of Democracy*. For a contrast between these two types of retrospective voting and a powerful application of the Downsian approach, see Morris P. Fiorina, *Retrospective Voting in American National Elections* (New Haven: Yale University Press, 1981).

Reagan, have been able to organize the enactment of large parts of the party platform on which they ran for office. Presidential government, however, produces only the kind of post hoc responsibility that we noted earlier in which presidential performance rather than policy guides voter decision making. It need not produce the kind of clear programmatic alternative the reformers want. Presidential government does stamp some differences on the parties, however, and it does fashion points of reference for the approval or disapproval of voters.

Realignment and Responsibility

As a more general rule, it is during the periods of partisan realignment, when party loyalties most parallel opposite sides on the dominant policy conflicts of the day, that the American system has most closely approached the requirements for party government. Realignments sustain a unified federal government—with the same party controlling both houses of Congress and the presidency and a judiciary that, through the appointment power, subsequently comes to reflect the new majority. On only five occasions in American history has one party enjoyed control of Congress and the presidency continuously for more than a decade, and each time this control was initially established during a realignment. Such party control is certainly no guarantee of cooperation among the policymaking branches of the national government. Nonetheless, it is far easier for a president to deal with a majority of his own party in Congress than with opposition majorities. Moreover, during realignments, party cohesion in the Congress is especially high. Therefore, it should come as little surprise to find that the major bursts of comprehensive policy change typically have followed realignments.[31] It is the wholesale realignments of the party system, as well as the atmosphere of crisis and the strong presidential leadership that have accompanied them, that produce the highest levels of responsible party government in the United States. Even during realignments, when the conditions for responsible parties are most propitious, however, the American version of party government is a pale imitation of its European counterparts.

Barriers to Party Responsibility

Outside of the infrequent periods of crisis, strong presidential leadership, and realignment, the achievement of party responsibility is stymied by any number of barriers, which have seemed especially imposing in recent years.

1. The most formidable, of course, are the classic American institutions that fragment the powers of government—federalism and the separation of powers—and thereby disconnect the parties that would govern in

---

[31]For further development of these points, see Paul Allen Beck, "The Electoral Cycle and Patterns of American Politics," and the works cited therein; and Jerome M. Clubb, William H. Flanagan, and Nancy H. Zingale, *Partisan Realignment* (Beverly Hills, Calif.: Sage, 1980), pp. 155–88.

them. Circumstances that can unite what the Constitution has separated are rare and ephemeral.

2. The frequent insulation of legislative from executive elections, which is accomplished by holding elections for each office on separate schedules, further mitigates against party government. This practice limits the possibility that the governor's and especially the president's coattails might produce the kind of unified government and cohesive party that is the almost automatic result of elections in a parliamentary system.

3. Even when there is a rise of ideological and issue concerns in the electorate, the American parties face severe tests and strains in converting themselves into ideological parties. The proliferation of single-issue groups in recent years, in fact, further divides the parties as different groups and individuals within them attach themselves to the party for different causes.

4. American electoral politics has developed in directions not easily compatible with party government. The parties have lost control of nominations and find it increasingly hard to manage election campaigns and to establish election programs in ways that promote a unified party "team." The new campaigning and its new campaign finance have freed candidates and officeholders even more from the party organization. Even legislators who are at odds with the platforms of their party and the programs of their party's executive do not find it hard to survive.

5. The weakness of American party organization, in spite of the unprecedented strength of the national organizations, is apparent to all observers. It does not involve large numbers of Americans—even the most political Americans—either as members or as officials or volunteer activists. Its eclipse by the party in government leaves it woefully short of the authority necessary to integrate a political party and to police its use of public office.

6. More Americans today than just a few decades ago resist giving loyalty to or taking cues from a party. This weakening of the party as a cognitive symbol matches the weakening of its organization. The contemporary electorate takes its cues from a far broader range of sources than just the political party.

Divided Government

Beyond these factors is another that makes the goal of responsible party government seem especially distant in recent times. Through 1992, control of the national government has been divided between a Republican president and a Democratic Congress (at least in one house) for twenty of the last twenty-four and twenty-eight of the last forty years. Such split control has not been unknown in the past due to occasional midterm election reversals for the president's party. But only nine presidents in 200 years—Taylor, Hayes, Garfield, Cleveland, Wilson, Eisenhower, Nixon, Reagan, and Bush—were elected at the same time that the opposition party won control of at least one house of

Congress. Only Taylor among the pre-1952 presidents faced opposition majorities in both houses. Hayes, Garfield, and Cleveland all took office in an era when the two major parties were so evenly balanced nationwide that split electoral results could occur without any appreciable amount of split-ticket voting.

The divided governments in modern times, by contrast, have been the result of voter behavior, widespread ticket splitting to be precise, rather than electoral rules. Never before has the American national government experienced such a long period of divided control. An unprecedented amount of divided party control also has appeared in many of the states. In 1990, for example, divided government was to be found in twenty-nine of the fifty states, and many of the remainder had experienced divided government at some point during the 1980s.[32]

Concern over the consequences of continued divided government has extended far beyond the small circle of scholars and political activists who have advocated responsible parties. The barriers to government action imposed by separation of powers are made far more formidable when the Congress and the presidency are controlled by different political parties. Government's continuing failure to address pressing domestic problems—from foreign policy stalemates over Vietnam and Nicaragua to the spiraling public debt are all attributed to the constant bickering between Republican presidents and Democratic Congresses that has become a familiar feature of our time.

Some even feel that divided government undermines the democratic process itself. The lack of clarity about which party is responsible for governing, they observe, strips the electorate of its most effective instrument of popular control—the ability to replace the party in charge with the opposition when voters are dissatisfied with governmental performance. It is debatable how much the American national government is malfunctioning due to prolonged divided government, and a few pundits even credit the public with consciously seeking divided government to check and balance parties they equally distrust. What is undeniable, however, is that America's unique brand of "coalition government" has ushered in a kind of governmental politics that is almost the antithesis of the doctrine of responsible party government.[33]

---

[32]On divided government and its causes, see the essays by Gary C. Jacobson, John Petrocik, Martin Wattenberg, Morris Fiorina, and Charles Stewart in Gary Cox and Samuel Kernell (eds.), *The Politics of Divided Government* (Boulder, Co.: Westview, 1991); Morris P. Fiorina, "An Era of Divided Government," in Bruce Cain and Gillian Peele (eds.), *Developments in American Politics* (London: MacMillan, 1990); and Gary Jacobson, *The Electoral Origins of Divided Government: Competition in U.S. House Elections, 1946–1988* (Boulder, Co.: Westview, 1990).

[33]On the consequences of divided government, see the essays by Samuel Kernell, Mathew McCubbins, and Gary Cox and Mathew McCubbins in Cox and Kernell (eds.), *The Politics of Divided Government;* Fiorina, "An Era of Divided Government"; David R. Mayhew, "Does It Make a Difference Whether Party Control of the American National Government is Unified or Divided?" paper delivered at the 1989 Meeting of the American Political Science Association, Atlanta; and Sundquist, "Needed: A Political Theory for the New Era of Coalition Government in the United States."

Toward Responsible Party Government

Ironically, the parties that the responsible party reformers sought to strengthen forty years ago are in important respects even weaker today. Contemporary hopes to strengthen the parties, consequently, focus more on recapturing the parties' former role than on attaining greater party government than ever before. How this might be accomplished is suggested in the following recommendations of the 1950 Committee of Political Parties of the American Political Science Association (APSA).[34] An examination of how these recommendations have fared over the years can provide a valuable perspective on the quest for party government in the United States.

A Massive Shoring Up of the National Parties and Their Organizations
The committee recommended that the national conventions meet at least biennially and exercise greater control over the national committees. Above all, it suggested a national party council that would draft a platform for the national convention, interpret and apply it to issues between conventions, make "recommendations . . . in respect to congressional candidates" and about "conspicuous departures from general party decisions by state or local party organizations," provide a forum for the "discussion of presidential candidacies," and coordinate relations among national, state, and local party organizations.

A Perfecting of the Instruments of Ideology   The committee proposed that the platform bind the party officeholders and organizations. The platform ought to deal at least partially with the party's "permanent or long-range philosophy," and it ought also to be carefully prepared and systematically interpreted.

An Assertion of Party Control Over the Congressional Party   To tackle so protean a task, the committee recommended both a consolidation of the present congressional party organizations into a single party leadership group and the elimination of practices (such as the seniority system and the traditional power of the House Rules Committee) that undermine party discipline.

A Remodeling of the American Parties into Membership, Participatory Parties   The committee called for the creation of a dues-paying party membership at the grass roots, which would participate in developing the party's platform and selecting its candidates free from the "internal dictation by a few in positions of influence."[35]

The committee's report ranged beyond these general points. It dealt with other barriers to party responsibility: the direct primary ("the closed primary deserves preference"), the electoral college (it "fosters the blight of one-party

---

[34]The proposals in the following paragraphs are from the report of the committee, *Toward a More Responsible Two-Party System*. Emphasis in the original has been eliminated.

[35]Committee on Political Parties, *Toward a More Responsible Two-Party System*, p. 70.

monopoly"), political finance, and barriers to full and meaningful adult suffrage (e.g., the long ballot). In short, to achieve the goal of government by responsible parties, it envisioned a wholesale reconstruction not only of the American parties but of the American electorate and political environment as well.

Other proponents of party responsibility, however, have been more modest in their goals. One of the most persistent, James MacGregor Burns, touches on many of the same themes as the APSA Committee.[36] He emphasizes the building of grass-roots, membership parties, the buttressing of the national party (the presidential party), and the reconstructing of a vigorous congressional party. He evinces the same recognition of the need for change in the parties' political environment (e.g., the restrictions on adult suffrage and the status quo in political finance). Yet the reforms Burns suggests are less drastic and more realistic, even though their direction and their pinpointing of the causes of the present lack of responsibility are not greatly different from the APSA committee report. Perhaps Burns's relative moderatism springs, in part, from his recognition of an essentially Madisonian political culture that has not tolerated any one instrument—party or other—of national majoritarian political power. More contemporary proposals for reform, emerging in a time dominated by divided government, however, have sought to overturn this cultural norm, and its accompanying structural institutionalization, by championing a more parliamentary form of government (see box).

Some of these various proposals to strengthen the American parties have been implemented in recent years, but without much effect on party responsibility. For about a decade, the Democrats held midterm conventions, which have been discontinued as at worst divisive and at best irrelevant to the major business of the national parties, electing a president. The party platforms, especially for the Republicans in recent years, also appear more ideological, but the parties have moved no closer to enforcing them upon their officeholders. In the Congress, the decentralized power of seniority has been weakened under pressure of a revived Democratic party caucus, but the consequence is more autonomy for the individual representative rather than greater party control. With direct mail fundraising, important steps have been taken toward a mass membership base for the parties, yet these donors are contributing more to particular candidates than to the party. The national parties have become more enmeshed in enforcing uniform party rules (especially the Democrats) and in coordinating the activities of the national, state, and local parties; but so far they have failed to use their new powers to force more ideological cohesion in the party. In a paroxysm of internal party democracy, rank-and-file party members also have become more involved in the selection of party candidates, yet dissatisfaction with party nominees has hardly abated. Even the resurgence of ideological conflict at the elite level in the 1980s was set upon the base of an

---

[36]See James MacGregor Burns, *The Deadlock of Democracy* (Englewood Cliffs, N.J.: Prentice-Hall, 1963), especially Chap. 14.

The Recurrent Cry for Party Government

Recommendations for stronger party government were presented in early 1987 by the blue-ribbon 300-member Committee on the Constitutional System. Writing in *The New York Times* (January 11, 1987, p. 1), reporter Stuart Taylor, Jr., described their proposals in the following way.

A draft report by the bipartisan group, the Committee on the Constitutional System, asserts that the separation of powers between the executive and legislative branches, while guarding against tyranny and the abuse of high office, has produced chronic "confrontation, indecision, and deadlock" and diffused "accountability for results." It says the decline of political parties, the increase in ticket-splitting and the rise of monied single-interest groups have aggravated those problems. . . .

[T]he committee proposes a number of changes in party rules and Federal law aimed at strengthening political parties, including partial public financing of Congressional campaigns in which party leaders in Congress would control half the funds, . . . constitutional amendments to improve "collaboration between the executive and legislative branches" (by, among other things,) extending the terms of (House and Senate members by two years), scheduling all Congressional elections in Presidential election years . . . , and allowing members of Congress to serve in the Cabinet and other positions in the executive branch. (Other reforms, not requiring constitutional changes, were suggested) . . . to strengthen political parties and foster party loyalty (by giving) congressional nominees a greater voice in choosing Presidential nominees, strengthening party caucuses in Congress, and requiring states to give voters the chance to cast a single straight-line party ballot for all Federal elections.

electorate engaging in retrospective evaluations of presidential performance as much as being motivated by any heightened issue or ideological concerns. Moreover, some of the barriers to party government—e.g., the independence of candidates from party—have been buttressed in recent years (campaign finance reforms have had this effect), and the traditional institutional barriers imposed by separation of powers, with increased voter ticket splitting, have become more formidable than ever.

For the immediate future, barring the special conditions of crisis or realignment, then, it seems likely that the American parties will achieve no more, and sometimes even less, than to continue the modest governing role that has characterized them during most of the twentieth century—a post hoc responsibility for carrying out programs that generally promote the interests of the party's activists and loyal electorate. Neither the American parties nor the voters can at present meet the demands that the classic model of party responsibility would impose on them. Rather, the various sectors of the party are increasingly bound together by a commitment to a set of issue positions that separates the activists, candidates, and voters of one party from those of the other. In a loose sense, each of the two parties is a distinct group of like-minded men and women. That tentative and limited agreement on issues, reinforced by executive leadership of the party in government, may produce enough cohesion for a modest, variable degree of responsibility. Ironically such a degree of party responsibility must be achieved without the central role—drawing up a program and enforcing it on candidates and officeholders—that the reformers planned for party organizations and often in the presence of divided party control of government. Whether this level of party responsibility will be sufficient for democratic accountability or adequate to the tasks of solving pressing national problems are vexing questions indeed for the 1990s and beyond.

THE POLITICAL PARTIES: ROLE AND THEORY

The preceding chapters have reviewed in fine detail the various facets of the American parties and party system. It is now appropriate to step back from this detailed picture to conclude with a broader view of political parties in America.

Political parties are complex institutions, and they operate in an even more complex political setting. They also are live entities that cannot be understood if observed in isolation from their natural habitat in the controlled situations that enable scientists to study other complex phenomena. The study of parties and party systems instead must progress by the slow process of comparison and contrast, by observing how they have changed and what else has changed in their environment over the course of their lives. As the parties develop new activities, depend on new incentives, take new organizational forms, for example, one is naturally led to wonder how and why the changes came about. What changes in the parties' environment accompanied those changes in the parties? Is there a causal relationship between changes in the parties and those outside them? If the decline of patronage accompanies the decline of the old-style urban machine, does it cause or result from the change in party organization? Is the decline of party loyalties in the electorate the result of an eviscerated party organization or one of its causes? We learn much about the parties if we put the changes together into a pattern and adduce explanations for them.

Chapter 17 begins the analytical task by examining the changes presently under way in the American parties. It brings together the trends and changes that have been mentioned throughout the book and concludes with an explanation of those changes and a series of projections of what's ahead for the American parties. The central theme—already more than hinted at in earlier chapters—is that the powerful, predominant role of the major parties in American politics has eroded but that the parties have responded to the new realities by adjusting what they are and what they do. Of necessity, the questions of what produced these changes and how they will alter the landscape of American politics are also addressed.

The last chapter, Chapter 18, carries the analysis beyond the specific changes presently abroad in the American parties to the broader level of parties in general and to the American parties in other periods of time and to parties in other places. In that chapter, too, the theoretical problems and issues suggested by the contemporary changes will be brought together into some more general categories. The chapter will be concerned with changes in the parties' roles and activities within the larger political system. It concludes with the proposal of a developmental approach to the parties, an approach suggesting that parties usually enjoy their heyday when electorates are less educated, less secure, and politically unsophisticated, and that as populations develop political knowledge and sophistication, the parties become less important to the mass electorate.

The goal for the tentative suggestions that follow is a modest one: to raise the understanding of American political parties beyond the level of analysis of specific events to a more general knowledge that provides insights into continuing trends and into groups of events or phenomena. After a journey through a book such as this, one at least ought to be able to explain why the American parties differ at any one time and from one time to another.

Chapter

17

The Future of the
American Parties

The American parties have experienced considerable change in the last several decades. By the late 1960s, they appeared to be in decline on a number of fronts. They also received a good deal of the blame for the general malaise and decay of public confidence in many institutions that beset American society during this period. Because their troubles had started a decade or two earlier in response to long-term changes in American society and politics, it was easy to conclude that the decline was permanent. By the time their decay had become the central theme of chronicles of the parties, however, signs of party resurgence had begun to emerge. Although this resurgence seems to have fallen short so far of restoring parties to the position in American politics they once enjoyed, it may be a harbinger of brighter prospects for them in the coming years. Any assessment of the future of the American parties, therefore, should begin by taking into account both the direction of recent trends and the levels to which these trends have carried the parties in modern times.

THE DECAY OF PARTIES

The American parties have long been characterized by the loose set of relationships that have bound the three party sectors together. That looseness, or lack of integration, is indeed one of their most fundamental features. The party organization has never been able either to bring a substantial part of the party electorate into membership or to assert its leadership or discipline over the campaigns and policymaking of the party in government. It is not surprising, therefore, that the decline of parties that had become apparent by the 1960s hit the three sectors quite differently.

The Party in the Electorate

The American electorate weakened its long-run attachment and loyalty to the American parties through the late 1960s and into the 1970s. More and more

American adults considered themselves independents rather than members of or identifiers with a major party. Even among those who professed a loyalty or attachment to a party, that attachment no longer dominated the decision on how to cast the vote, as it once did. The result, obviously, was a shrinking of the size of party electorates and an eroding of the quality of their loyalty. Even a slight surge in Republican party identifiers in the 1980s, especially among the young, has not returned the party in the electorate to its previous prominence.

If the American electorate in this period was not responding eagerly to its party loyalties, to what did it respond? Some segments were attuned to the appeals of program and ideology. The Goldwater campaign of 1964, the McCarthy and Wallace appeals of 1968, the McGovern candidacy of 1972—along with those of any state and local issue-oriented candidacies—drew on and activated higher levels of issue awareness. The Reagan candidacies of 1980 and 1984 featured a return to frankly ideological appeals. For less sophisticated voters, the appeals that registered most effectively were those of candidate personality and image. The handsome faces, ready smiles, and graceful life-styles that television screens so fully convey attracted some of the support that party symbols once commanded. Since candidates and issues change far more frequently than parties, the consequence was an unstable, less predictable pattern of voting.

The decline of party identification in the American electorate is clearly manifested in recent electoral results. The electorate has been more inclined in recent decades to respond to candidates as individuals than as members of a particular political party. At the presidential level, for example, independent candidates have won unprecedentedly high levels of voter support. The little-advertised independent candidacy of Eugene McCarthy in 1976 drew more than 750,000 votes, and John Anderson attracted almost 6 million in 1980. In 1990, moreover, two governors were elected as independents. Even the strong third-party candidacy of George Wallace in 1968 fits the pattern of diminished party-based voting, since the American Independent (the name says it all!) party was more a vehicle for him as an individual candidate than an effort to build a base of loyalists for a new political party. Such candidate-centered voting also is illustrated in the inordinate number of split electoral results in recent years. In 1964, the congressional districts awarding victories to presidential and congressional candidates of different parties topped 30 percent (at 33 percent) for the first time in history, and only once since then (in 1976 at 28 percent) has it fallen below that figure. In the Republican presidential landslides of 1972 and 1984, a staggering 44 and 43 percent of all congressional districts, respectively, produced such split results.[1]

The Party Organizations

In the party organizations during the same period, the last of the party machines were passing from the scene, and with them their activists and incen-

---

[1] These figures are taken from Harold W. Stanley and Richard G. Niemi, *Vital Statistics on American Politics* (Washington, D.C.: CQ Press, 1990), p. 133.

tives. Even the famous Daley organization in Chicago suffered a series of humiliating defeats, and it is doubtful that even Richard Daley, Jr., can pull it back together. Many organizations of all kinds no longer could depend on the patronage and preferments or the guaranteed election to public office that once recruited their full-time, vocational activists. Instead, they were drawing a better educated, part-time leadership, whose incentives more often inclined to issues or ideology and who brought with them new demands for intraparty participation. Indeed, some among them rejected the politics of compromise, accommodation, and pragmatism that resulted from the assumption that the capture of public office is the highest goal of American politics. If their ideological goals were not satisfied—or even recognized—within the party, they stood ready to leave it for particular candidates or issue organizations.

Increasingly, too, the internal, intraorganizational processes ceased to be under the organization's control. Under the force of growing participatory expectations, these processes became more public; the private sphere of the party organization shrank accordingly. The direct primary began the process of taking decisions from the party organization, and its dominance is now virtually complete. The convention is no longer a device for the organization's deliberation and choice making. Its processes are public, and, more important, its options have been sharply restricted in recent years by the activities of the would-be candidates in the preconvention politicking. Even the preconvention scramble for votes has increasingly been removed from the hands of party organizations, as most convention delegates are now chosen in states with presidential primaries.

At the same time that they were undergoing internal changes, the party organizations were losing their capacity for controlling American electoral politics. No longer could they consistently control either nominations (thanks to the direct primary) or the politics of election compaigning. Candidates increasingly found themselves able to build their own campaign organizations, raise their own campaign funds, and go on their own merry ways in the campaign. The campaign assets they once received from the local party organizations and their workers—skills, information, pulse readings, manpower, exposure—they now were able to get directly from pollsters, the media, public relations people, volunteer workers, or even by "renting a party" in the form of a campaign management firm. Especially because the local party organizations were unwilling or unable to provide the new arts for the candidates, they waned in influence in the contesting of elections. Their fairly primitive campaign skills were superseded by a new campaign technology, and more and more they found themselves among the technologically obsolescent. Even though in recent years the national parties have become important suppliers of campaign expertise and resources and have increasingly shared this wealth with the state and local parties, so far they have been unable to return the party organization to its once central role in electoral campaigns.

Above all, the party organizations remained substantially decentralized in the face of the increasing centralization of life and politics in the United States. The electorate was looking more and more to national political symbols and figures, but the party organizations still tended to be collections of state and local fiefdoms. The national committees and the national conventions have always been loose confederations of local organizations and, despite new signs of life in the national committees and more central authority, seemed destined to remain so.

The Party in Government

The men and women of the party in government, freed from reliance on the party organizations by the direct primary, by access to the media, by independent sources of funds, and by supportive personal followings, came to depend more than ever upon a direct appeal to the voters. No longer able to rely so heavily on abstract party loyalties, they developed more personal appeals and relied on personal style, physical appearance, even what personal magnetism they could generate. They found in many ways, that it is quite a different matter to be advertised by the media than by party canvassers.

The successful candidates are the parties' contingents in American legislative bodies. There, reflecting the decline of party loyalties among voters and the decline of party organizations' power over legislators, they voted during this period of party decay as legislative parties with low levels of party cohesion. The instances in the Congress in which a majority of one party opposed a majority of the other in recorded roll-call votes fell to an all-time low in the late 1960s and early 1970s. Although such party voting increased in the 1980s as a result of the partisan conflict over the Reagan program and a more long-term reshaping of the party system, it remains well below earlier highs in the 1930s and before. Freed from the party demands of both voters and the party organizations, legislators became more exposed to the nonparty pressures—the local interests of the constituency, primarily, but also of interest groups. More important, perhaps, with the decline of competition (especially for incumbents) in congressional elections, they were not often exposed to serious challengers, even though most perceived their hold on office as precarious no matter how wide their previous victory margin.

When the legislative party lacks cohesion and strength, the executive party rushes into the vacuum. Presidents and governors enjoy increased governmental power and leadership of the executive branch at the very time at which they increasingly represent the party and its programs to so many voters. More than anyone else, they came to personify the party and give tangible content to its labels and symbols. In a period when many partisans sought programmatic goals, they alone formulated programs and controled policy initiatives. Therefore, it is no exaggeration to speak of the parties as executive-centered coalitions during the late 1960s and 1970s. Nowhere was the phenomenon clearer than in the ability of presidents to dominate the national party organization of their parties, to give life and meaning to the symbol of their parties, and, with the help of federal subsidies, to mount campaigns free of obligation to the party organization. Nonetheless, the long period of divided government beginning in 1969 and interrupted only from 1977–1980, has prevented this newly-energized presidential party from dominating the national political system.

This much is merely a summary of what has been said in greater detail in earlier chapters. The changes cumulatively amounted to a vast shift of power within the American political party from the decentralized party organization to the executive-led party in government and, more generally, from the parties to other political intermediaries.

At the core of this change was the progressive isolation of the party organization in the American political parties. The organizations had their days of glory in some of the larger cities, but they never succeeded in enrolling any significant measure of the party electorate on a membership basis. Isolated from the electorate and without its broad-based support or participation, they have always been vulnerable to suspicions that they were run by irresponsible oligarchies. The smoke-filled room myths have never died, and the cries of bossism are as alive at today's party conventions as they were at the turn of the century.

What assets the party organizations once had were substantially eroded. In most locales, even many bastions of their former strength, they no longer controlled the chief incentives for political activity, as they did when it was patronage and preference that made the activists active. They no longer monopolized the resources and technology of campaigning and of electoral politics. Also, they no longer invoked strong feelings of party loyalty in their electorate. What kind of party is it, however, in which the party organization loses a preeminent or even equal position? Is not the party organization the only sector of the party that has more at stake than the winning of individual elections, that offers some possibility of life and principle beyond specific elections and even beyond electoral defeat?

In the American parties, in any event, a coalition of an executive-led party in government and a somewhat restive and fickle party electorate resulted, with the legislative party in a divided government often going its own way. The executive rather than the party organization controled and manipulated the party symbols. The alliance of the executive with the party electorate was based on the message of the mass media and political personalism; the organization as a channel of communications no longer mattered so much. That coalition is all the more natural because the party organization has not been able to centralize as much as the other two party sectors. Especially in national politics, that centralization or nationalization of party messages, cues, and personalities unites the president-led party in government and the large numbers of voters who react primarily to national issues and faces.[2]

---

[2]The voluminous literature on the "decline of parties" during the 1960s and 1970s has been cited at the appropriate points in earlier chapters. Representative of these works are David S. Broder, *The Party's Over* (New York: Harper and Row, 1972); Jeane J. Kirkpatrick, *Dismantling the Parties: Reflections on Party Reform and Party Decomposition* (Washington, D.C.: American Enterprise Institute, 1978); James L. Sundquist, "Party Decay and the Capacity to Govern," in Joel Fleishman (ed.), *The Future of American Political Parties* (Englewood Cliffs, N.J.: Prentice Hall, 1982), pp. 42–69; Alan Ware, *The Breakdown of the Democratic Party Organization: 1940–1980* (New York:
(*continued*)

THE NEW POLITICS

These changes in the contemporary American parties took place in the context of broader ferments and upheavals in American politics and even in American society. Because most of them came to a head in the 1960s and 1970s as the political parties seemed to be in decline, it is natural for the changes in the parties to be linked to what was going on within this broader environment.

In an American society that believes change is invariably good and innovation always newsworthy, it was perhaps inevitable that this new politics would be called "the new politics." The term, however, is one of considerable variety and looseness, and one commentator's description of the new doesn't always match that of another.[3] There is some consensus, however, that it included these elements:

- *Concern for issues and principles*. In substance, the new politics connoted a heightened concern for issues and ideology. It often has focused on new issues such as the environment, American intervention in other nations' internal affairs, and abortion. At a more abstract level, it also marked a commitment to values and principles in public policy and a concomitant reluctance to compromise them.
- *Increased citizen participation*. The new politics exalted the mass participatory ethic to broaden the base of American politics. (It was opposed, of course, to elites, bosses, establishments, and all other forms of limited decision making.) It demanded a voice in government down to the local neighborhood level, and it was committed to more representative participation that includes women, minorities, and the disadvantaged. At a less active level, it paid new attention to mass opinion (e.g., the polls) and devices for citizen consultation. With some reason, therefore, it has been said that there is a new populism in the new politics.
- *Personalism and the "new individualism."* In a rejection of institutions and structures, the new politics put new value on the individual, whether as citizen, candidate, or officeholder. Candidates were to run for office on personal magnetism and govern on the basis of personal trust. They were to be judged on their performance as individuals, not as members of a governmental team. It is a political style perfectly adapted to the messages of the mass media, except, perhaps, that the media easily trivialize the messages. The individual too readily becomes merely an image, a smile, a well-clothed appearance, or a celebrity. At the level of the indi-

---

(*continued*)
Oxford University Press, 1985); and Martin P. Wattenberg, *The Rise of Candidate-Centered Politics* (Cambridge: Harvard University Press, 1991).

[3]One well-known vision of the new politics in the United States and Western Europe was that provided by Ronald Inglehart in *The Silent Revolution: Changing Values and Political Styles Among Western Publics* (Princeton, N.J.: Princeton University Press, 1977) and "Post-Materialism in an Environment of Insecurity," *American Political Science Review* 75 (1981): 880–900.

vidual voter, the new individualism translated into a new independence from parties and into a hesitation to make any form of collective action possible by moderating one's views or interests.

- *Reformism and political skepticism.* The new politics was certainly marked by skepticism, even cynicism, about traditional social and political institutions. It questioned traditional processes (the "system") and traditional leadership (the "establishment"), and it fueled a vigorous program of reform for the parties, presidential nominations, and campaign finance, among others.
- *New techniques of campaigning.* From the early 1960s to the 1980s, the ways of campaigning for public office were revolutionized. The use of the media, advances in opinion polling, the development of computer-based information systems and mailing lists, and the rise of a new breed of campaign specialists transformed the search for major office in the United States. To pay for those new techniques, vastly greater sums of cash were required. Candidates who could raise them thus were free to run their own campaigns.

The new has not, to be sure, completely replaced the old. Nor have all of these elements of the new politics endured into the 1980s or 1990s. Instead, significant elements of the new politics joined older political styles and modes in the mainstream of American politics. It is only part of a new amalgam, but it is an important part nonetheless. One need only look at the 1976 and 1980 elections and the candidacies of Jimmy Carter and Ronald Reagan for illustration. Both ran as critics of and outsiders to "Washington," and both traded heavily on personal appeal and trust. Reagan, furthermore, ran as an admitted ideologue, and Carter's campaign was substantially an exercise in the new populism.

The Clash of Old and New Styles

For the parties, the advent of the new politics seems to have introduced a sharp division—in all three sectors—between old-style and new-style politics, and so between old-style and new-style activists. This division pervades both major parties. On the one hand, there are the upper-middle-class ideologues, the so-called amateurs, who demand a politics of differentiation, attention to issues and ideology, and a major participatory role in the party. On the other hand, there are the more traditional, perhaps older, partisans, whose politics are centrist and consensual, whose incentives for activity are less ideologically-based, and who are willing to accept the old modes of authority in the party organization. It was that difference that lay, in good measure, behind the battle in the Democratic party in 1972 between the McGovernites and their opponents, in the Republican party in 1976 between the Reagan and Ford forces, and in the Democratic party between Carter and Kennedy supporters in 1980 and Mondale and Hart forces in 1984. It underlies an increasing number of durable factional divisions in the parties, and it promises to remain with them for the foreseeable future.

The impact of the new politics on the political parties is readily apparent if one looks at one of its chief by-products: single-issue politics. The parties traditionally have been committed to the building of consensus and the fashioning of majorities—with all the compromise and pragmatism that implies in a complex society. They build those majorities to win elections, to organize cohesive legislative parties, and, in their fashion, to govern. Single-issue politics threatens all of that. It is, by definition, a commitment to an issue position that is so deep and principled that compromise is often ruled out. The single issues spawn political organizations in which activity for many of the new activists is more satisfying than involvement in a political party. Loyalty to a single-issue position—and the rewarding or punishing of a candidate or officeholder on that basis alone—is quite different from the pragmatic acceptance of a variety of candidates and issue positions that loyalty to a political party assumes. Perhaps most troubling of all for the parties, the organization of political activity single issue by single issue bespeaks, in the aggregate, a degree of politicization, a sheer quantum and intensity of political feeling, that the major American party cannot easily integrate or contain.

How Meaningful a Change?

Two caveats about the new politics and the changes in the parties that encouraged or responded to it must be entered, however. The first is merely that predictions about American politics are very perishable. In the 1960s, there were many predictions of sweeping and fundamental changes in American politics, and the turmoil on the campuses and in the streets did, indeed, seem to promise major changes in other parts of American society. It also seemed that the dawn of a new age of ideology had arrived—just a few years, ironically, after some scholars with great fanfare had announced the "end of ideology." The issues, causes, and enthusiasms that stir Americans, however, shift with unexpected speed. Thus, the new politics and the attendant decay in the American parties may turn out to have been, contrary to expectations, an interlude of no lasting force in American politics.

Second, it is terribly important to realize that these developments in American politics have not been of a single piece. They constituted no one movement or logical, coherent program. (Nor should we expect logic or consistency in a politics marked by a history of diversity and accommodation.) To some extent, they pulled and tugged against each other as well as against the traditions of the past. The commitments to issue and ideology flowered simultaneously with an increase in personalism, life-style appeals, and media images. Not only is most of the personalism distinctly *not* issue- or policy-oriented, but in its most attenuated form—the concern for the profile, the smile, the hair, the clothes of the candidate—it is supremely nonpolitical. At its worst, it is less political in a broad, programmatic sense than the reliance on party loyalties and identifications that it replaces. The choice made on the basis of party label certainly weighs more political factors than the choice made on the basis of the candidate's cultivated image on TV or negative "spot ads" attacking an opponent.

A RENAISSANCE OF THE PARTIES?

It is one of the comforting beliefs of the conventional wisdom that social systems contain their own self-adjusting mechanisms. The free-market, competitive economic system, which freely adjusts prices and production to changes in supply and demand, offers a ready example. So, too, does the self-correcting system of checks and balances that generations have trusted to keep the American separation of powers in a well-tuned equilibrium.

Because the American party system and the American parties also have shown a remarkable ability to adapt to changing circumstances in the past, it seems reasonable to expect them to rise to these new challenges in their environments in ways that maintain their centrality in American politics. For the ills of unresponsiveness and dissatisfaction in the electorate, the cure was said to be a readjustment of party appeals (spurred by competition) and a consequent realignment of party loyalties in the electorate. For the new realities of campaigning, including the growth of ideological activists and the greater candidate-centered nature of campaign organizations, the solution was thought to be a service-oriented party that can supply candidates with the resources and expertise they need to compete for office. There have been signs in the 1980s and 1990s that such adaptations are taking place and that, with them, has come an end to the decay of parties and perhaps even their renaissance.

A Coming Realignment?

Recent years have produced changes in the party coalitions and have rekindled talk of party realignment. The external symptoms that ordinarily precede a realignment have been evident since the 1960s: low turnout levels, support for "third party" candidates, a widely fluctuating presidential vote from one election to the next, extensive ticket splitting, the diluted effects of party loyalties on the voting of individuals, and divided government.[4] The electoral ascendancy of the Republican party in the 1980s, which reversed the decline of party loyalties and brought the number of GOP loyalists up to the level achieved by their Democratic opponents for the first time in fifty years, has been viewed by some observers as the final realization of the long-awaited realignment. If so, however, it leaves the parties, even the Republican party, with a far weaker base of loyal supporters than previous majority parties have experienced.

This raises the possibility that even realigning the parties will fail to restore them to their previous political preeminence. Realigment is no solution to the erosion of the party's organizational capacity to nominate and elect candidates. Nor is it any guarantee that large numbers of Americans will return to an unswerving partisanship or that they will again mark the straight party ticket. The

---

[4]For a discussion of these characteristics of dealignment and how they might serve as necessary, though not sufficient, conditions for a subsequent realignment, see Paul Allen Beck, "The Electoral Cycle and Patterns of American Politics," *British Journal of Political Science* 9 (1979): 129–56.

truth is that a party realignment is only a readjustment of the parties to new cleavages in the society. It does not strengthen them per se, which leaves the possibility that a new realignment may be hollow or incomplete in terms of the strength of the party in the electorate.[5]

It is quite possible, in fact, that the 1960s and 1970s have produced an irreversible "sea change" in the role of party loyalties within the American electorate. Large numbers of voters now have cues and sources of information outside the parties. Many of them also are less and less inclined to accept the omnibus commitments that party loyalty implies. They want to pick and choose among issues and candidates—and they are encouraged to do so by the low profile of party labels in modern campaigns. Party loyalty demands that they buy a whole collection of commitments; in effect, it asks them to divide the political world into two simple categories, ours and theirs. The simple, dichotomized choice that party loyalty within a two-party system demands may no longer appeal to an educated, issue-oriented electorate. Knowing, confident, even assertive adults may be less and less willing to surrender their selective judgment in favor of an unquestioning loyalty to party.[6]

The Resurgence of Partisanship

Even if the recent changes in party loyalty fall short of realignment proportions, however, there are a number of signs that partisanship has rebounded from its difficulties of the 1960s. For one thing, the actual decline of the parties in the electorate has halted. The growth of independents literally stopped between 1972 and 1980. Voters resorted to their party identifications in 1976, and to a lesser extent in 1980, with an old-time confidence. In the 1980s, in fact, the relative number of partisans even increased with the attractiveness of a Reagan-led Republican party, and the 1988 presidential election produced levels of party fidelity in voting that matched those in the 1960 contest between Kennedy and Nixon.

This return to partisanship appears in other sectors of American political life as well. By the 1980s, party cohesion in the legislatures had halted its long period of decline. In the Congress, in fact, partisanship grew during the 1980s. Especially in the House of Representatives, the parties emerged as more cohesive and party leadership became stronger and more assertive. With the arrival of interparty competition in the South and other historically one-party

---

[5]The concept of the "hollow" realignment is developed in Martin P. Wattenberg, "The Hollow Realignment: Partisan Change in a Candidate-Centered Era," *Public Opinion Quarterly* 51 (1987): 58–74. For the concept of "incomplete" realignment, see Paul Allen Beck, "Incomplete Realignment: The Reagan Legacy for Parties and Election," in Charles O. Jones (ed.), *The Reagan Legacy* (Chatham, N.J.: Chatham House, 1988), pp. 145–71.

[6]For an elaboration of this view, see W. Phillips Shively, "The Development of Party Identification among Adults: Exploration of a Functional Model," *American Political Science Review* 73 (1979): 1039–54.

areas in the last few decades, the party coalitions in both the electorate and the government have become more homogeneous, which makes it easier for them to offer clearly alternative programs and policies. Moreover, the Democrats and Republicans monopolize political competition more today than they probably ever have.[7]

The New "Service" Parties

Nowhere has the renaissance of parties been more apparent than in the party organizations. Out of the ashes of the traditional urban machines have arisen powerful new national "service" parties—financially well-to-do, staffed with skilled professionals applying the latest campaign technologies, dedicated to distributing their resources to candidates and organizations nationwide, and active in recruiting candidates for office. With the assistance of the national parties, as well as the existence of their model to emulate, the state and local parties also seem to have become stronger in recent years—at least in comparison to just a decade or two before. The infusion of soft money into the state party organizations, particularly in 1988, enabled them to step up their role in political campaigns. The spread of two-party competition into formerly one-party strongholds has surely accelerated these trends, as more than a modicum of party organization now is required in many locales just to keep up with the competition.

Thus, the parties remain alive in America—and are involved in political life with a renewed vigor.[8] Their renewal has been achieved through creative, albeit reluctant, *adaptations* to new conditions, however, rather than through a return to previous practices. Moreover, they have come back to a political world in which they must share their position with other intermediaries (e.g., the mass media, interest groups, PACs, candidate organizations, and ideological and single-issue movements) as transmitters of political communications to the public. The number of PACs active in national politics, for example, increased sevenfold from 608 in 1974 to 4,172 by the end of 1990, and whereas PAC funds accounted for only 13 percent of the money that general election candidates for Congress received in 1974, their contributions accounted for 37 percent in 1990. Quite apart from their direct expenditures in campaigns, a growing number of non-party groups are also mounting registration and get-out-the-vote campaigns. Organized labor has been the traditional leader in those activities,

---

[7]Joseph A. Schlesinger, "The New American Political Party," *American Political Science Review* 79 (1985): 1152–69.

[8]The renewed strength of the parties since the late 1970s has triggered a shift in the emphasis of scholarly studies of parties from decay to renewal. Representative of this new approach are Xandra Kayden and Eddie Mahe, Jr., *The Party Goes On* (New York: Basic Books, 1985); Gerald M. Pomper (ed.), *Party Renewal in America* (New York: Praeger, 1981); David E. Price, *Bringing Back the Parties* (Washington, D.C.: CQ Press, 1984); Larry J. Sabato, *The Party's Just Begun* (Glenview, Ill.: Scott Foresman/Little, Brown, 1988); and Schlesinger, "The New American Political Party."

of course, but in recent years it has been joined by religious, ethnic, and single-issue organizations. The value of the mobilization efforts of these various groups in presidential and congressional elections may conservatively be placed in the millions of dollars.[9]

In other words, the political organizations of today appear to have rediscovered the fundamental truth that political influence throughout the American political system flows from the election of public officials. So too have the political party organizations. They appear now to be turning away from the membership organizations, the intraparty participation, and the explicit commitments to ideology that marked them in the 1960s and 1970s. They faced the great choice between ideology and issue on the one hand and pragmatic electoral politics on the other, and, led by the resurgence of the Republican National Committee, they have made their commitment to electoral politics. Even the Democrats now seem willing to move away from some of the reforms of 1968 and after, as they have followed the Republican lead in turning their national party committees into valuable sources of campaign funds and expertise.

The point can easily be overstated, of course. Where voters are politically more sophisticated and more committed to a set of issue positions, ideological activists will continue to exert strong influence over the party organization. Furthermore, in many localities the party organizations still have a long way to go in order to achieve the level of campaign involvement and influence that they enjoyed some decades ago. In today's more candidate-centered political environment, in fact, it is doubtful that they can ever recover the effectiveness of their golden years after the Civil War. Nonetheless, in the aggregate, the thousands of organizations in each party seem to be exhibiting a new-found robustness and pragmatism in electoral politics.

Since the key to the revived electoral role is money, there has been a good deal of comment about the parties becoming "super PACs." In a sense, they are moving in that direction. To recapture or refashion a significant role in campaign politics, they must dispense cash or the new campaign expertise. They may combine that aid—also in the manner of PACs—with attempts to recruit or nominate candidates in the first place. Simply because they *are* political parties, however, they can more easily convert electoral success into some greater degree of cohesion in the party in government. That is not the vision of the advocates of "responsibility," for it generates a capacity for governing out of the fashioning of electoral successes—and the obligation and gratitude that follow them—rather than out of the refining of party principles. Nor is there any evidence that the parties are systematically using their support to influence officeholders. That tension between electoral pragmatism and ideological commitment is an enduring one for the parties, as can be seen in the battles for the

---

[9]The growing strength of competitors to political parties has been found throughout the western world. See Kay Lawson and Peter H. Merkl, *When Parties Fail: Emerging Alternative Organizations* (Princeton: Princeton University Press, 1988).

presidential nominations. By adapting themselves to the new campaigning and trying to find a role in it, pragmatically rather than ideologically, the parties have made their choice.[10]

The Future

What seems likely for the foreseeable future, in other words, is a politics of continued fluidity and instability, carried on by a wide range of political organizations. The parties will exert their influence over nominations, elections, and policymaking, but so will other political organizations. In many instances, the candidate—aided by the media or single-issue groups—will attract the voter loyalties and activist labors that the party organization once did. The erosion of the one, stable, long-run loyalty in American politics has contributed to a politics often dominated by the short-term infuences of the charismatic candidate or the very salient issue. The diversity of goals in the American electorate, multiplied by the intensity of feelings about them, cannot easily be met even by two pragmatic, compromising political parties. Voters now seem to want more specialized cues for political choice and action, and the activists among them want to discriminate among the causes and people for whom they will work. Consequently, the parties must continue to fight to define and protect *a* role, not *the* role, for themselves in American electoral politics.

THE PROBLEM OF A POLITICS WITHOUT PARTIES

With the recent renaissance of American parties, it is much less likely now than it was just a decade or so ago that the foreseeable future will contain a politics without parties. Yet political life in the United States without the guiding dominance of two assertive political parties is not unthinkable. Much of our local politics has been nonpartisan in reality as well as in name for some time. At the national level and in many of the states, moreover, a long period of divided government in which one party controls the executive and the other the legislature has produced a level of *interparty* coalitional politics that is unprecedented on the American scene. A diminished role for the parties throughout much more of electoral politics, however, suggests impacts of a greater magnitude. The consequences, not only for the political processes but for the quality of American democracy, trouble many observers. Walter Dean Burnham has put the concern directly and simply:

> Political parties, with all their well-known human and structural shortcomings, are the only devices thus far invented by the wit of Western man that can, with

---

[10]On the financial role of the parties and on parties as "super PACs," see F. Christopher Arterton, "Political Money and Party Strength," in Joel Fleishman (ed.), *The Future of American Political Parties* (Englewood Cliffs, N.J.: Prentice-Hall, 1982), pp. 101–39.

some effectiveness, generate countervailing collective power on behalf of the many individually powerless against the relatively few who are individually or organizationally powerful. Their disappearance as active intermediaries, if not as preliminary screening devices, would only entail the unchallenged ascendancy of the already powerful, unless new structures of collective power were somehow developed to replace them, and unless conditions in America's social structure and political culture came to be such that they could be effectively used.[11]

The American parties—and all others for that matter—mobilize sheer numbers against organized minorities with other political resources, especially status and money, and they do so in the one forum of political action in which sheer numbers of individuals count most heavily: elections. Thus, the parties traditionally were the mechanisms by which newly enfranchised and powerless electorates rose to power. The old-style urban machine in the United States, for example, was the tool by which the recently arrived, urban masses won control of their cities from older, largely "Wasp" elites. In a more fluid politics of bargaining among a larger number of political organizations and millions more uncommitted voters, the fear is that the advantage will be on the side of the well-organized minorities that have other political resources.

A movement toward ideology and away from electoral pragmatism in weakened parties might have additional elitist consequences. The educated, sophisticated, and involved political minority may impose a new kind of political tyranny on the less involved, lower SES segments of the electorate. Its brand of ideological politics may lack salience and be incomprehensible to the less sophisticated. At the same time, it may contribute to the decline of the most useful cue-giver, the major political party. The removal of the political party as an organizer and a symbol in our present nonpartisan elections helps upper SES elites, both of the right and the left, to dominate those politics.[12] The political party, in other words, is the political organization of the masses who lack the cues and information—as well as the political resources of status, skills, and money—to make a major impact on public decisions via other means. A diminution of the power of the parties makes the game of politics more difficult for these people to play and win. That may be one reason why the turnout declines of the last few decades have come disproportionately from lower status and less-educated Americans, disenfranchised so to speak by a growth of politics less and less linked to parties.[13]

---

[11]Walter Dean Burnham, "The End of American Party Politics," *Transaction* (December 1969): 20.

[12]Willis D. Hawley, *Nonpartisan Elections and the Case of Party Politics* (New York: Wiley, 1973).

[13]Studies of voter participation in other nations, where socioeconomic status differences in turnout are negligible, demonstrate the importance of the political parties for mobilizing the lower status groups into politics. See Sidney Verba, Norman H. Nie, and Jae-On Kim, *Participation and Political Equality* (Cambridge, U.K.: Cambridge University Press, 1978).

Finally, weakened parties would rob the political system of an important vehicle for the building of majorities. Although imperfectly, the major American parties have helped piece together majority coalitions. American presidents have enjoyed the legitimacy of majority coalitions much of the time, and the party majority in legislatures has at least permitted them to organize for action. Without at least moderately strong parties, how are we to create majorities in a fragmented politics? Are we to rely on the personal appeals and promises of national candidates? Or do we face the kind of political immobility that has resulted elsewhere from the splintering of majorities into intransigent groups with deeply felt loyalties and sentiments? Without a strong sense of party in the electorate, additionally, how are we to avoid the continuation of divided government and the policy-making paralysis it often brings? Will American politics increasingly involve coalition-building *across* party lines and the inevitable blurring of governmental responsibility that produces?

To be sure, it is easy to overestimate what the parties traditionally have contributed to our politics, but the contributions, if more modest than many want to believe, are still real and important. Certainly a mature political system can and will work out its adaptations. There are, indeed, workable alternatives to stable, two-party systems that dominate electoral choice, although no democracies have survived without parties. The issue for the United States is whether any of the alternative organizations could pull together the separate pieces of politics and political institutions across a broad and diverse nation as effectively as the parties have. For the new democracies of Eastern Europe, struggling to shape a viable political system amidst great economic and social turmoil, this issue is much more immediate and compelling. The danger for the future of course, in either stable or emerging democracies, is that the disadvantages of a politics without parties would not be appreciated until it is too late for them to play an important role in the political system.[14]

---

[14]With a little imagination, informed by examples from historical experience, one can conceive of a few alternative forms this politics without parties might take. At one extreme, it might take on a plebiscitary form in which a dominant national leader (today a president, a popular monarch in an earlier day) faces an up or down vote at regular intervals. The leader's command of television and how the country was faring under his or her stewardship might figure most prominently in how both other political leaders and voters would respond. At the other extreme, one can imagine a multiplicity of narrow interests vying with one another for political dominance, with no one of them strong enough to hold the reins of government alone or pragmatic enough to be willing to join with other interests in enduring governing coalitions. Under either of these alternatives, it is not difficult to envision how some of the basic functions we take for granted that parties will perform—e.g., selecting candidates for office, organizing the electorate, coordinating the government, simplifying policy alternatives—might be performed in ways that favor a few people at the expense of others and that are, in the end, quite inimical to political democracy.

Political Parties in the American Setting: Some Theoretical Perspectives

The political parties are inevitably the centerpiece of a book on party politics in United States. That they have been colorful and important players in the American political pageant there can be no doubt. That they have contributed vitally to the development of American democracy is undeniable. That something of value would be lost were they to atrophy from their contemporary presence should, by this point, be unquestionable.

Yet to view parties as *the* guiding force to American politics now or in years past, as some studies have been tempted to do, is sheer hyperbole. It has never been the case that all of our politics has been channeled through the political parties. They have never even monopolized our *electoral* politics. Americans always have pursued many routes to political influence—by dealing directly with public officials, by working through interest groups and other nonparty groups, by engaging in various forms of direct representation and demonstration, as well as through the political parties. The American parties have not even easily controlled nominations or elections, nor have they readily governed on behalf of party programs. The foundations of the American polity, in truth, are far more diverse than to be attributable to any single institution.

Moreover, a realistic view of the American parties sees them as effects as well as causes, as being shaped by forces in their environment as well as shaping them. This perspective is sometimes lost by those who have wanted to reform the parties. The Progressives were wont to attribute many of the ills they saw in the American political scene to the parties, just as the responsible party theorists seemed to think that the American system would function more to their liking if only they could alter the nature of the parties. Yet the persistent urges to reform them by their very nature assume that the parties can be transformed by changes in their environment—and the accomplishments of some of these reform efforts are testimony to how malleable, in the end, they are.[1] Parties do, indeed, have an impact on political processes and institutions, but other political and nonpolitical forces, in turn, have effects on the parties.

Before concluding our treatment of party politics in America, then, it is important to view the parties from this broader perspective more fully and explicitly than we have in previous chapters. Why are the political parties—especially the American parties—what they are and why have they developed as they have? What shapes the particular structure of the parties, the relationships among their three sectors, and their various activities and roles in the political system? What accounts for changes in them over time, and for variations in them from place to place? Why do they differ from the parties of the other Western democracies? What follows are four common ways in which these and related questions have been addressed.

THE IMPACT OF THE EXTERNAL ENVIRONMENT

The first chapter briefly discussed the major environmental influences that impinge on the parties (Table 18.1), and subsequent chapters elaborated on these influences, especially on the ways in which they shape and mold the parties.

This treatment visualizes the parties as surrounded by a context, an environment of the most varied sort (Figure 18.1). The parties are always the dependent object or result of external, independent forces, yet they do have some control over their environment. They participate, for example, in the making of public policy on who votes, on the kinds of ballots voters use to mark their choices, and on the kinds of primary elections at which candidates will be nominated. They also shape, by education and by their own performance, public attitudes about the parties themselves and, more generally, about politics.

Figure 18.1 suggests that the parties both give and receive. They receive in the sense that they recruit the inputs or resources that they need to function: money, skills, labor, and loyalty. They give in that they convert these resources into outputs or party activities: the contesting of elections, organizing of public officeholders, and propagandizing on behalf of issues or ideologies. All three sectors of the party, in their various ways, must mobilize resources, and all three generate results in their special ways.

Thus, the political party in such a conception is a conversion mechanism for changing resources and demands into goal-seeking activities. It must mobilize resources to maintain itself and undertake its activities. Obviously, a change in the statutes regulating campaign finance or a further contraction of patronage impinges on those efforts. The vitality of the party organization, an essential element in the conversion mechanism, also depends on the network of state

---

[1]Various efforts to reform American parties are analyzed in Austin Ranney, *Curing the Mischiefs of Faction* (Berkeley: University of California Press, 1975).

Table 18.1   MAJOR CATEGORIES OF INFLUENCES IN THE ENVIRONMENT
OF THE POLITICAL PARTIES

Influences	Examples
1. Political institutions	Federalism, separation of powers, development of presidency
2. Statutory regulation	Legislation on campaign finance, structure of party organization, merit system
3. Electoral processes	Definition of franchise, the direct primary, nonpartisan elections
4. Political culture	Attitudes about politics and the two-party system
5. Nonpolitical forces	State of economy, affluence and education of population, use of TV

legislation and, increasingly, national judicial decisions that set its outlines and powers. The outputs—the activities or functions—of the parties are similarly sensitive to changes in the environment. Any change in electoral law—whether it is the closing of a primary in one state, the enfranchisement of new voter groups, or the abolition of the electoral college—clearly affects their electoral activities. The electorate itself is shaped by birth and mortality rates, patterns of education, and the spread of democratic and participatory expectations. Also, the demands the party activists and electorate bring to politics reflect issues of a war or a depression, for example, or alienation and trust in government.

There is a sense in which all the elements of their environment generate needs or demands on the parties. The concepts of "needs" and "demands" offer a way of viewing that environment. For instance:

- A parliamentary system operates in a specific way, and that operation "requires" or "needs" or "demands" certain kinds of parties and certain kinds of party capabilities and activities.
- As the new campaign experts broke the party's monopoly of the skills and information for contesting elections, candidates no longer "needed" the party organizations as they once did.

The use of *demands* and *needs* in this explanatory sense is simply another way of stating the cause-effect relationship. Some observers find these terms more comfortable intellectually than bald statements of cause; but—and it is a big "but"—we also use the concept of demand in another, more direct way. We refer, for example, to the demand of citizens for government action of one kind or another or the demands of party activists for patronage or for a voice in party affairs. These are demands as *goals* of voters and party workers. Those individ-

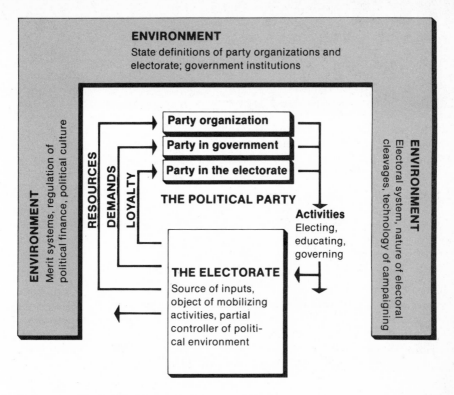

Figure 18.1 The Political Party: Structure and Environment.

uals seek those goals, those demands, through the political party. The goals, too, are shaped by the broader political and social environment, just as the party is.

Obviously, the environment of the parties embraces an enormous range of components—from laws regulating the registration of voters in one state to the social-medical-technical forces affecting the national mortality and birth rates. Is it not possible to group the components into a manageable set of categories, or to establish some hierarchy of importance that will enable us to say that one element of the environment is more important than another? It is possible to do so to some extent, but that attempt should be postponed until we look at the other three theoretical perspectives on what the parties are and what they do.

TWO TYPES OF PARTY STRUCTURES

Nothing characterizes the parties as political organizations quite so clearly as their three-part structure. Much of what they are, what they do, and how they do it is suggested merely by calling to mind that political parties include a party organization, a party in government, and a party in the electorate. It is not surprising that differences among the parties often come down to questions of the activities of the three parts or sectors and the relationship among them.

Organization-Dominated Versus Government-Dominated Parties

When measured by the roles and influence of their sectors, political parties in democratic regimes have tended to fall into two groups: those dominated by the party organization and those dominated by the party in government. The American parties are moving increasingly to the type headed by the party in government—that is, by the party's candidates and officeholders. In their glory days at the turn of the twentieth century, one might have argued that they were organization-dominated, but no longer. The American party in government increasingly determines the party candidates, contests elections, controls the party image and reputation, supplies the campaign resources, and governs in office without important constraints or even contributions from the party organizations.

A party dominated by its organization differs in several very fundamental ways from the party led by its party in government (Table 18.2). The party controlled by the party in government, almost by definition, is a heavily electoral party. The concerns of the party's officeholders are in winning elections, and they establish both the priority of the electoral mission and their control over the resources and choices for it. Once elected, they govern in response to the need for securing reelection and for making a record of accomplishment in governance. The alternative—the party dominated by its organizational sector—is best typified by the early working class parties of the European parliamentary

Table 18.2   CHARACTERISTICS OF TWO TYPES OF POLITICAL PARTY STRUCTURES

Party organization dominates	Party in government dominates
1. Party in electorate assumes (in part) a membership role in the organization	1. Little or no membership component in party organization
2. Party organization controls nomination of candidates and much of election campaign	2. Party in government largely free from organizational control in nomination and election
3. Relatively high degree of cohesion in legislative party	3. Relatively low degree of cohesion in legislative party
4. High degree of integration of three sectors	4. Low degree of integration of three sectors
5. Unified by goals of party organization's activists	5. Unified (if at all) by goals and programs of executive party
6. Activities substantially electoral, but programmatic as well	6. Activities almost exclusively electoral

democracies, although even they have come under more control by their officeholders in recent years. The issue commitments or ideologies of the organization's activists assume a greater importance in the life of the party. They have such an impact within the party precisely because the organization speaks for the party, picks its candidates, and maintains some degree of leverage over its parliamentarians.

One can summarize many of the differences between the party models in terms of their ability to integrate their three sectors. In the organization-centered model, the three sectors are bound closely by ties of loyalty and discipline. A substantial part of the party electorate, in fact, joins the organization as members, and the debts of candidates for nomination and election assistance bind them to the party organization. The key to the organization-centered party lies in the ability of the organization to unite the party in government to it and to the goals of its activists. In the classic urban machine of patronage and preference, both sectors were united in the overarching goal of electoral victory and the electoral pragmatism it demanded. Or as in the now dated "textbook" model of the British parties, the party organization's ability to discipline officeholders by denying them renomination was the glue that held the two sectors together. Alternatively, the two sectors might be united, as the "party responsibilitarians" argue, by loyalty to the same principles or issue positions.

In the party controlled by the party in government, in contrast, everything depends on the pragmatic alliances of convenience at election time. The dominant party in government, indeed, is free to form alliances with nonparty organizations, such as interest groups, rather than working with its own party organization. Indeed, the eviscerated American party organization has had so little to offer to the candidate running for office that it has been virtually ignored at election time, and consequently thereafter. The distance between the congressional parties, which have created their own campaign committees, and the national party committees illustrates this point—as does the tendency of recent presidential candidates to keep their election campaigns independent from the national committee. The party in government establishes contact with the party electorates without relying greatly on the party organization.

Obviously, the differences between these two varieties of political party run to deeper, more basic issues. Should a political party be something more than the sum total of the candidates who choose to run on its label? At the very least, it seems unlikely that the party led by its party in government can provide the continuity and breadth that distinguishes the party from other political organizations. The parties that are strong in their ability to dominate or monopolize certain forms of activity have been those led by the organizational sector. Only the party organization has the range of skills and resources, as well as the commitment to all party goals and even to the party itself, to fill this leadership role within the party. Only such a party can approach the model of the responsible party. Only strong parties that exert policy leadership as well as leadership in the recruitment of public officials—and in providing a stable cue to millions of voters—can augment or support the officeholder's responsibility to his or her electorate.

Roots of Different Party Structures

These two kinds of parties do not occur without reason or explanation. What differences are there in the different environments from which they come that will explain their differences? One can also put the question in more parochial terms. Since the American party is the archetype of parties controlled by the party in government, what accounts for the differences between American parties and parties dominated by their organizations? Some persuasive answers to these questions are:

- Scholar after scholar has noted that the American party is not associated with parliamentary institutions and that the organization-dominated party is. The very nature of a parliamentary system demands discipline and integration of the parties; the American separation of powers does not.
- American electoral law (primaries and the regulation of finance, for example) is all on the side of the party in government, giving it easy access to nomination and great freedom from the party organization in waging campaigns.
- State regulation of and legislation on parties has placed a set of heavy constraints on the party organization; the reformist urge has indeed been heavily antiorganization in its goals. The states have imposed cumbersome forms and a weakening openness and permeability on the organizations, while making it difficult for them to develop large memberships.

Once one part of the party comes to dominate, moreover, it usually has been able to perpetuate its control through the laws and customs that govern party practices. In the United States, for example, the new campaign arts and technologies have provided the party in government with an alternative to party organizations by destroying the organization's monopoly over election campaigning. The new campaigning is available everywhere, however, and one must ask why it has freed the parties in government in the United States but not elsewhere. The answer, of course, is that elsewhere there are parliamentary institutions and election legislation that limit the freedom of candidates and restrict their access to the tools of the new campaigning (e.g., television appearances are controlled by the party and public funding goes to the party in many nations), thus buttressing the central, dominant role of the party organization.

PARTIES AS INTERMEDIARIES BETWEEN VOTERS AND GOVERNMENT

Among political organizations, the parties alone attach their names to candidates for public office. The willingness or need to respond to that label on the part of large numbers of Americans is what makes the party label so valuable. Political parties originated in large part from the need of voters for a guide, a set of symbolic shortcuts, to the confusing and often trackless political terrain. The labels, activities, and personages of the parties ran as a clearly perceptible thread through the jumble of political conflict and the baffling proliferation of American elections. When that cue-giving also produced loyalties and identifications with the parties, when those loyalties were stable and enduring, and when they dominated so many voting decisions, the conclusion was inescapable that this pattern of reliance and loyalty was a primary determinant of the role played by the American political parties.

The parties' symbolic importance, the value of their labels in elections, is greatest in meeting the informational needs and problems of a new mass electorate. Those needs may change as the electorate matures, however. Note, for example, the reduced incidence of and reliance on party loyalties in the American electorate of recent years. One attractive explanation for this phenomenon is that voters are better educated and better informed than they were sixty or eighty years ago. They also are more exposed to nonparty political messages—especially those of the personalities and personal images that the mass media carry so effectively—and, in our highly mobile society, less influenced by the traditional intermediaries that had homogenized their political preferences. The net effects are a reduced need for the simplifying shorthand of the party label and less reinforcement for partisan views of the political world.

This is not to say that American voters no longer need cues or labels. Rather, they may increasingly seek the differentiated cues that the party organization cannot provide. The integrated party dominated by an organization may have been suited to an earlier American electorate seeking a single, consistent cue to a great many political decisions and judgments. As voters become more sophisticated, however, they are better prepared to handle a wider range of political perceptions and loyalties and to sift through a greater variety of political messages. They may form an attachment to an issue or two—or to an entire ideology—and they are not prepared to surrender those loyalties to an overriding loyalty to a political party. Although they may find many of the candidates of "their" party perfectly acceptable, they refuse to accept party loyalty as a reason to favor all of its candidates. In short, voters increasingly want to pick and choose in their political decisions. The American electorates thus find the loose, candidate-centered party better tailored to their preferences than the party dominated, integrated, and unified by a party organization.

In another, more general sense, too, parties reflect the political-psychological needs of voters. The rise of personalism in political campaigning is a case in point. It is easy to attribute this personalism to the new campaign technology and reliance on the mass media. Behind the personalism, however, is the need of many citizens for personal leadership, for flesh-and-blood embodiment of distant government, even for the vicarious ego strength of a confident public figure. It is ironic that the modern electorate, more sophisticated in some senses, nevertheless exhibits signs of the personalism typically associated with the poorly educated electorates of developing democracies. Perhaps, too, this new personalism reflects a dissatisfaction with the parties (and other political organizations) as lifeless and impersonal abstractions.

There is an almost irresistable temptation to view the present as unique, as qualitatively different from the past. Therefore, we must caution against facile acceptance of an explanation for the recent decline of party loyalties based on the different capabilities and needs of today's voter. In fact, a careful examination of the realignment process suggests an alternative explanation in which present-day voters bear a striking resemblance to voters in earlier times. Historically, cyclical ebbs and flows are apparent in the ties of American voters to a political party. During a party realignment and its immediate aftermath, the party in the electorate has seemed particularly strong. But as the prevailing party system has aged and its original rationale has become more remote, particularly to newer voters, the party in the electorate has withered—until the burst of political change we call realignment gives a new definition to the parties. If they had possessed instruments as finely calibrated as ours today, one can almost imagine political analysts in the dealignment periods of the 1850s, the late 1880s and early 1890s, and the 1920s chronicling as we have the decline of parties as organizing devices for the mass electorate. In each of these earlier periods, however, the weakening of parties was only a temporary interlude before a new realignment rejuvenated the party system and solidified the loyalties of the party in the electorate. While there is no reason why this cycle *must* be repeated, and persuasive reasons why it might not be, it is conceivable that a future realignment could produce an electorate fully as dependent upon party cues as in the past.

DEMOCRACY AND THE DEVELOPMENT OF PARTIES

The origin and rise of the political parties has been intimately bound up with the sweep and spread of democracy. The parties grew as the first mobilizers of electoral power while the electorates expanded. The relationship of the parties to democracy, however, extends beyond their origins and initial growth. Democracy presupposes a degree of citizen participation and choice. By definition, it involves a broad distribution of political power and requires organizational intermediaries to mobilize the political power of individuals in order to make it effective. The entire development of the parties reflects these imperatives of democracy, and changes in the parties have paralleled changes in the very nature of democracy and its electorates.

The democracy of the mass political parties, however, is not necessarily democracy's pure or final realization. Democratic expectations, institutions, and processes change, and with them so do the parties. The political parties may have been essential, as many have suggested, during the initial politicization of the uneducated, economically disadvantaged masses. When education and affluence open new channels of political information and activity, however, competitors rise with new organizational forms, new appeals, and new political resources. We see the growth of a politics that is more issue-oriented, more committed to goals and values, and perhaps even less pragmatic and compromising. The argument that only the parties can aggregate or mobilize political influence is no longer so convincing as it once was.

Stages in Party Development

The relationship of the changes in the parties to those in the democratic processes is closer than one might infer from mere assertions that everything changes. In the United States and many of the other Western democracies, the changes in the parties occur in phases related to the development of democratic politics and modern political institutions. Three phases seem evident so far:[2]

1. The first parties in most of the Western democracies were parties of limited access and narrow appeal. Originating in a time of a restricted suffrage, they were limited in personnel, confined largely to electioneering, and closed to mass participation. This formative, premodern period in the American experience came before the 1830s.

2. As the electorates expanded, the parties also expanded their organizational forms to include more activists and members. (Although the American parties resisted more than most the development of mass membership bodies, they were no longer largely legislative caucuses.) The parties dominated the political loyalties and even the political socialization of the new electorates. As the dominant political organizations of a citizenry marked by relatively low levels of political information and sophistication, they became the chief givers of political cues. In the American experience, of course, this stage of their development reached its zenith around the turn of the last century, especially with the urban machines.

3. Finally, as electorates mature along with democratic processes, as political loyalties and interests become more complex, politics becomes more diverse and differentiated. The political party in this phase becomes merely *primus inter pares*. Its sole control of the mobilization of power ends amid growing competition from other political organizations. The party remains both a potent organization and a powerful reference symbol, but its total role in the politics of the nation diminishes.

These stages in party development reflect no organic growth or inherent life cycle. They are direct responses to changes in democratic processes and economic development, and they certainly do not appear to be limited to the United States. Parties in Western Europe, for example, are losing members

---

[2]For another developmental approach to political parties, see Samuel P. Huntington, *Political Order in Changing Societies* (New Haven: Yale University Press, 1968), especially Chap. 7. His four stages seem to coincide with the first two here.

and appear to be entering the third phase, too.[3] When an electorate reaches a certain point of politicization, party loyalties and parties themselves are no longer so useful as they once were.

The Next Stage for American Parties

Does such a developmental sequence foretell the continued decline of the parties? Are they merely the relics of a simpler political age? There is considerable opinion that two modern developments may have undermined the role of the American political parties as intermediaries between citizens and government. First, what many have come to call "postindustrial politics" seems to have produced a more active and participatory middle class, a greater individualism in politics, and a resistance to authority that makes it difficult for the parties to function as they traditionally have.[4] Second, constitutional federalism and a traditional aversion to strong government, combined with the very heterogeneity and continental expanse of the nation, historically have forced the decentralization of American politics. The American party organizations, often strong in their local parts but largely hollow in their national whole, have been the quintessential expression of this decentralization. With the enhanced role of the national government after the 1930s and World War II and the emergence of a truly national mass media, however, American politics has become more centered on Washington and the presidency. For decades, the parties were relegated more and more to the sidelines because they resisted these nationalizing forces. In the greater authority of the national party conventions, the increased activities of the national party committees, and even the erosion of one-party politics in the states, though, one sees signs that the parties are responding to this nationalization of American political life, but their response may be too feeble and too late for them to regain their dominant role.[5]

WHAT SHAPES THE PARTIES?

These considerations return us to the question of how their environments have led the parties to become what they are. Two main influences or sets of influ-

---

[3]Anthony King discusses this and related points in his excellent essay, "Political Parties in Western Democracies," *Polity* 2 (1969): 111–41. See also Russell J. Dalton, Scott C. Flanagan, and Paul Allen Beck, *Electoral Change in Advanced Industrial Democracies: Realignment or Dealignment?* (Princeton, N.J.: Princeton University Press, 1984).

[4]On the subject of postindustrial politics, see, for example, Samuel P. Huntington, "Post-Industrial Politics: How Benign Will It Be?" *Comparative Politics* 6 (1974): 163–91; and Ronald Inglehart, *The Silent Revolution: Changing Values and Political Styles Among Western Publics* (Princeton: Princeton University Press, 1977).

[5]For a more optimistic view than ours that these and other changes have enabled the parties to retain their positions in American politics, see Joseph A. Schlesinger, "The New American Political Party," *American Political Science Review* 79 (1985): 1152–69.

ences from the environments of the American parties meet to shape their outlines and dimensions. They are, first, those that define and mold the electorate and, second, those that set the basic electoral and governmental structures of the political system. These influences set the outlines of the parties in the United States and in all the Western democracies.[6]

The Definition of the Electorate

That first set of influences—the one defining the electorate—is in fact made up of a number of components. It includes the legal statements, both constitutional and legislative, that define which individuals will be in the electorate. It includes the social conditions that determine the numbers, the age distribution, the education, the affluence, and the other social characteristics of the electorate. It also includes the factors that shape the levels of political awareness and information, the attitudes and expectations, and the sheer political understanding of the electorate. Finally, it encompasses the political cleavages that divide the electorate into the various parties and therefore define the party systems.

The nature of the electorate, in all of these facets, changes over time. In particular, the changes from lesser to greater politicization, from fewer to more democratic and participatory expectations, and from a limited to a larger or universal adult suffrage are obviously interrelated, although they happened at different rates and sequences in different political systems. Taken together, they constitute the rise of mass popular democracy, a process that began in the United States at the beginning of the Republic and has expanded virtually to this day—with the enfranchisement of southern blacks, and the consequent reshaping of the party system in that region, coming as recently as the 1960s. Only one trend in the American electorate appears to move in the opposite direction—rates of voter turnout. The downturn of turnout since 1960 may be temporary, or it may signal a fundamental, long-term change in the electorate—perhaps involving the withdrawal of the lower classes from an increasingly middle-class politics.

The nature of the electorate impinges on the parties principally by shaping the distribution of party loyalties and the reliance on the parties for political cues and information. It also affects the nature of campaigns and candidates, the relationship of the officeholders with the parties and with their constituencies once they are elected, and the kinds of activists who are drawn to the parties. Thus, the shape of electoral politics depends to a great extent on the nature of the electorate.

The Governmental and Electoral Institutions

The second cluster of influences on the parties includes the chief governmental institutions and structural constraints within which the parties work and to

---

[6]For a systematic attack on these explanatory problems, see Robert Harmel and Kenneth Janda, *Parties and Their Environments: Limits to Reform* (New York: Longman, 1982).

which they relate. Foremost within this cluster is the basic configuration of political institutions—federalism or unitary government, parliamentary forms or a separation of powers, the nature of the executive, and the extent of governmental authority. Second, it includes the myriad laws and constitutional provisions that define the election processes (and those for nominations, too, where that is a matter of public policy). Finally, there are the regulations of the parties per se and of the activities carried out under their labels. They run the gamut from laws creating party organizational structure to those regulating the spending of money in campaigns. Often, too, they merge almost imperceptibly into the legislation creating election machinery. The impact of all this on the parties is an old subject involving, for example, the effect on the democratic parties and party systems of the separation of powers, the impact on party organizations of the direct primary as a way of choosing party candidates, and the use of single-member districts rather than proportional representation from multimember constituencies.

These segments of the parties' environments change, too. Constitutions and electoral systems are often replaced, though not usually in the United States. If one compares the United States and Great Britain to the nations of continental Europe on this point, the contrast is striking. Although their basic systems change and adapt, there have not been any abrupt breaks with the past in the last 100 years in either Britain or the United States. In that time, however, France has launched five entirely separate republics, each one intended to be a break with, even a repudiation of, its predecessor. Similarly, large numbers of European countries have tinkered with various election systems, whereas Britain and the United States (at least at the national level[7]) have stayed with plurality election from single-member constituencies. On the other hand, the American parties have been subjected to a range of legislation on themselves and their activities quite unknown anywhere else. The direct primary constrains their selection of candidates, for example; and state laws defining the party organizations have no parallel elsewhere. The effect, and in most cases the intention, of such regulation is to restrict the party organization; an unintended consequence is that they boost the party in government. What is more, the reformist zeal behind much of this legislation lives on in, for example, reform of the national party conventions.

These two sets of variables interact in a special way on the American parties to produce their rather different, special qualities. First of all, many of the important institutional-structural influences on the parties are almost uniquely American: the direct primary, the separation of powers, the nationally elected executive, and the network of regulatory legislation on the parties. It is precisely these factors that are instrumental in shaping the American two-party system and in vaulting the parties in government to a dominant place in the

---

[7]Multimember districts have been common at the state level in the United States, although their number has declined considerably in recent decades. See Theodore J. Lowi, "Toward a More Responsible Three-Party System," *PS* 16 (1983): 699–706.

American parties (at the expense of the party organizations). Second, although the first set of influences—those shaping the electorate—have changed over time both in the United States and in the other democracies, the second set has remained fairly constant in the United States. For that reason, changes in the American parties seem more directly related to changes in the electorate.

There is also a third set of environmental variables that ought to be mentioned: variables of the nonpolitical environment. These are the events and trends beyond the political system that nonetheless shape politics (e.g., wars, international crises, recessions, economic prosperity, birth and mortality rates, energy shortages, and new moralities). Their effect on the parties, however, is not really *on* the parties, except insofar as they shape the electoral coalitions that define the parties. They define the policy issues of a time, and thus they shape the demands and goals that individuals try to achieve *through* the parties. They originate outside the parties and the political system, and they are to a great extent beyond their influence. The ultimate impact of these variables is beyond the parties. It is not primarily on the parties as conversion mechanisms but on the goals for which the mechanisms are employed.

Finally, it is important to appreciate how much the parties compete with other organizations and avenues for representing large numbers of individuals. If there are other more effective ways for individuals to seek their political goals than through political parties, they will use them. If a relationship with a particular congressman and his attentive staff secures a social security check or access to federal contracts or if an interest group is more forthright and effective in opposing abortion or gay rights, why work through a party? What the parties are at any given time, therefore, is determined, in part, by the alternatives to them that are available and how they respond to their competitors.

Indeed, the major problem for the American parties today arises from the increased differentiation of American aggregative politics. As the American electorate continues to develop more complex interests and a greater sense of individualism evolves from the breakdown of traditional group ties, it acquires more differentiated loyalties and responds to more complex and differentiated cues. It maintains identifications with parties, but it also responds to candidates and to issues, programs, and ideologies. It responds differentially to different elections and even to the choice between electoral and nonelectoral politics. The ultimate consequence is a more diverse, complex politics that no single set of loyalties, and thus no single set of political organizations, can easily contain.

Therefore, the American parties find it increasingly difficult to be all things to all citizens. There probably will never again be a dominant, all-purpose political organization in our politics. The parties, especially, cannot easily meet the expectations of ideological politics and pragmatic electoral politics at the same time. Their symbols cannot continue to work their old magic on all elements of so diverse a political population. The continuing challenge for the American parties then is how to adapt to this fragmented politics without losing the distinctive character that has sustained them over the long course of democratic politics.

INDEX

Hikes 86, 87, 88, and 89: Sullivan Lake Ranger District, 12641 Sullivan Lake Road, Metaline Falls, WA 99153, (509) 446-7500.

Hike 90: Mount Spokane State Park, North 26107 Mount Spokane Park Drive, Mead, WA 99021.

ABOUT THE AUTHOR

Ron Adkison has been exploring wildlands and studying the natural environment of the West for many years. He has walked each hike in this guide to provide precise, firsthand information about not only the trails but features and processes of ecological interest as well. Adkison, the author of *Hiking California*, lives with his wife and two children near Whitehall, Montana, where they raise llamas and sheep.

American Hiking Society

American Hiking Society is the only national nonprofit organization dedicated to establishing, protecting and maintaining foot trails in America.

Establishing...

American Hiking Society establishes hiking trails with the AHS National Trails Endowment, providing grants for grassroots organizations to purchase trail lands, construct and maintain trails, and preserve hiking trails' scenic values. The AHS affiliate club program, called the Congress of Hiking Organizations, brings trail clubs together to share information, collaborate on public policy, and advocate legislation and policies that protect hiking trails.

Protecting...

American Hiking Society protects hiking trails through highly focused public policy efforts in the nation's capital. AHS affects federal legislation, shapes public lands policy, collaborates with grassroots trail organizations, and partners with federal land managers to protect the hiking experience. Members become active with letter-writing campaigns and by attending the annual AHS Trails Advocacy Week.

Maintaining...

American Hiking Society maintains hiking trails by sending volunteers to national parks, forests and recreation lands; organizing volunteer teams to help affiliated hiking clubs; and publishing national volunteer directories. AHS members get involved, get dirty and get inspired by participating in AHS programs like National Trails Day, America's largest celebration of the outdoors; and Volunteer Vacations—week-long work trips to beautiful, wild places.

Join American Hiking Society...

Be a part of the organization dedicated to protecting and preserving the nation's footpaths, our footpaths, the ones in our backyards and our backcountry. Visit American Hiking Society's website or call to find out more about membership. When you join, Falcon Publishing will send you a FREE guide as a special thank you for contributing to the efforts of American Hiking Society.

American Hiking Society
1422 Fenwick Lane
Silver Spring, MD 20910
OR CALL: (888) 766-HIKE ext. 1
OR VISIT: www.americanhiking.org